Frommer's®

Amalfi Coast
with Naples, Capri & Pompeii
2nd Edition

by Bruce Murphy & Alessandra de Rosa

Here's what the critics say about Frommer's:

"Amazingly easy to use. Very portable, very complete."
—*Booklist*

"Detailed, accurate, and easy-to-read information for all price ranges."
—*Glamour Magazine*

"Hotel information is close to encyclopedic."
—*Des Moines Sunday Register*

"Frommer's Guides have a way of giving you a real feel for a place."
—*Knight Ridder Newspapers*

WILEY

Wiley Publishing, Inc.

Published by:

Wiley Publishing, Inc.

111 River St.
Hoboken, NJ 07030-5774

ISBN: 978-0-470-20954-7

Editor: Alexia Travaglini
Production Editor: Jana M. Stefanciosa
Cartographer: Andrew Murphy
Photo Editor: Richard Fox
Production by Wiley Indianapolis Composition Services

Front cover photo: Ravello: View of Annunziata Church
Back cover photo: Pompeii: Roman sea life mosaic

For information on our other products and services or to obtain technical support, please contact our Customer Care Department within the U.S. at 800/762-2974, outside the U.S. at 317/572-3993 or fax 317/572-4002.

Wiley also publishes its books in a variety of electronic formats. Some content that appears in print may not be available in electronic formats.

Manufactured in the United States of America

5 4 3 2

Contents

List of Maps

An Invitation to the Reader

In researching this book, we discovered many wonderful places—hotels, restaurants, shops, and more. We're sure you'll find others. Please tell us about them, so we can share the information with your fellow travelers in upcoming editions. If you were disappointed with a recommendation, we'd love to know that, too. Please write to:

Frommer's Amalfi Coast with Naples, Capri & Pompeii, 2nd Edition
Wiley Publishing, Inc. • 111 River St. • Hoboken, NJ 07030-5774

An Additional Note

Please be advised that travel information is subject to change at any time—and this is especially true of prices. We therefore suggest that you write or call ahead for confirmation when making your travel plans. The authors, editors, and publisher cannot be held responsible for the experiences of readers while traveling. Your safety is important to us, however, so we encourage you to stay alert and be aware of your surroundings. Keep a close eye on cameras, purses, and wallets, all favorite targets of thieves and pickpockets.

About the Authors

Bruce Murphy has lived and worked in New York City, Boston, Chicago, Dublin, Rome, and Sicily. His work has appeared in magazines ranging from *Cruising World* to *Critical Inquiry*. In addition to guidebooks, he has published fiction, poetry, and criticism, most recently the *Encyclopedia of Murder and Mystery* (St. Martin's Press).

Alessandra de Rosa was born in Rome and has lived and worked in Rome, Paris, and New York City. She did her first cross-Europe trip at age 2, from Rome to London by car. She has continued in that line ever since, exploring three out of five continents so far. Her beloved Italy remains her preferred destination.

Other Great Guides for Your Trip:

Frommer's Italy
Pauline Frommer's Italy
Frommer's Italy's Best-Loved Driving Tours
Suzy Gershman's Born to Shop Italy
MTV Italy
Italy For Dummies

Frommer's Star Ratings, Icons & Abbreviations

Every hotel, restaurant, and attraction listing in this guide has been ranked for quality, value, service, amenities, and special features using a **star-rating system.** In country, state, and regional guides, we also rate towns and regions to help you narrow down your choices and budget your time accordingly. Hotels and restaurants are rated on a scale of zero (recommended) to three stars (exceptional). Attractions, shopping, nightlife, towns, and regions are rated according to the following scale: zero stars (recommended), one star (highly recommended), two stars (very highly recommended), and three stars (must-see).

In addition to the star-rating system, we also use **seven feature icons** that point you to the great deals, in-the-know advice, and unique experiences that separate travelers from tourists. Throughout the book, look for:

Finds	Special finds—those places only insiders know about
Fun Fact	Fun facts—details that make travelers more informed and their trips more fun
Kids	Best bets for kids, and advice for the whole family
Moments	Special moments—those experiences that memories are made of
Overrated	Places or experiences not worth your time or money
Tips	Insider tips—great ways to save time and money
Value	Great values—where to get the best deals

The following **abbreviations** are used for credit cards:

AE	American Express	DISC	Discover	V	Visa
DC	Diners Club	MC	MasterCard		

Frommers.com

Now that you have the guidebook to a great trip, visit our website at **www.frommers.com** for travel information on more than 3,600 destinations. We update features regularly to give you instant access to the most current trip-planning information available. At Frommers.com, you'll find scoops on the best airfares, lodging rates, and car-rental bargains—and you can even book travel online through our travel booking partners. Other popular features include:

- Online updates to our most popular guidebooks
- Vacation sweepstakes and contest giveaways
- Newsletter highlighting the hottest travel trends
- Online travel message boards with featured travel discussions

The Best of Campania & the Amalfi Coast

Campania—the region that encompasses Naples and the Amalfi Coast—is, for many tourists, *terra incognita.* But for Italians, it is a place of myth. In fact, centuries before the rise of Rome, it was coveted by Greek settlers and other immigrants, and the ancient Romans may have valued this region more than all their far-flung possessions. In this chapter, we'll help you discover the best of the region by pointing you toward its major treasures.

1 The Best Travel Experiences

- **Visiting Naples and its *Centro Antico:*** One of Italy's lesser-known art cities, Naples will surprise you with its stunning collection of exquisite frescoes, paintings, and sculptures, which cover its numerous monasteries, palaces, churches, and museums. From the early Greek settlers to modern times, Naples has been the most important harbor in the south of Italy. Kings and noble families have lavished art on the city as nowhere else in Italy except Rome, making Naples a competitor with Florence and Venice. A key stop for art lovers during the "Grand Tour," Naples was later forgotten due to the complete abandonment of its monuments. But thanks to sustained efforts over the past 15 years, Naples is again experiencing a tourism boom. See "Exploring Naples" in chapter 4.

- **Arriving in Naples by Boat:** You don't have to book a transatlantic cruise to have this marvelous experience. While arriving in Naples by car can be nerve-racking, confusing, and hot, with most landmarks annoyingly out of view, gliding into the bay with a sea breeze behind you and the city spread out ahead can be magnificent. The majestic and somewhat ominous presence of Vesuvius looming over the bay makes it that much more dramatic. You can arrive by regular ferry from one of the islands or even from one of the other harbors in Campania, such as Salerno or Sorrento. We highly recommend arriving during the very early morning or in the evening when the sun is sinking below the horizon, bathing the city in gold and orange; this is when the view is most magical. Upon soaking in the sight, you'll instantly understand the motivation behind the old saying, "See Naples and die." See "Getting There" in chapter 4.

- **Hiking the Ancient Paths of the Amalfi Coast:** Taking a stroll on one of the Amalfi Coast's footpaths— once the only means of communication between the region's towns—is the best way to soak in the intensity of this amazing seascape. No matter your level of fitness, you'll find a stretch of path that's right for you. The region's main road—the famed Amalfi Drive—was built in 1840 and made the area more accessible, perhaps too much so. The old trails, on the other hand, are unique, and lead you through the Amalfi Coast missed by so many tourists. Trails come in all levels of difficulty, from flat stretches (such as the footpath from Amalfi to Atrani) to downhill ones (such as the footpath from Ravello to Minori) to more demanding ones (including the Sentiero degli Dei and the Via degli Incanti from Positano). See chapter 7.

- **Exploring Greek Ruins:** The first colony the Greeks established in Italy was Cuma, near Pozzuoli. From there, they expanded south to the rest of the Campanian coast. The heritage they left in Campania is immense—rivaled in Italy only by Sicily—and in a state of conservation seen only in Greece itself. This is *Magna Grecia,* where ancient Greece first spread its influence into Italy, setting the stage for what we call Western culture. In these temples and towns, you literally get the chance to walk in the footsteps of Plato and Aristotle's contemporaries. See chapters 4 and 10.

- **Eating Pizza Neapolitan Style:** For Neapolitans, there is no other "style" of pizza, because they invented it. Whether you prefer a simple pizza joint or an elaborate restaurant, you'll share the pride Neapolitans feel for their invention, now taken over by the whole planet. The decor may be simple and traditional (sometimes nonexistent), and you'll usually have a modest choice of toppings—only two at Da Michele, reputed to make the best pizza in Naples. Yet at whichever place you choose, the outcome will be tasty, satisfying, and distinctive, because in Naples, no two pizzas are alike. See "Where to Dine" in chapter 4.

- **Shopping in Capri and Positano:** The best exclusive shopping in the region can be found at these two famous and trendy resorts, which stock treasure troves of unique, handmade clothes and shoes. You can still find tailors in Positano and cobblers in both towns who will make you sandals or garments on the spot, while you wait—or, even better, while you go for a swim. See chapter 7 for addresses in Positano and chapter 8 for Capri.

- **Wandering through Ancient Roman Lanes:** Walking among ancient ruins is romantic and sad, and even a little creepy at times. Campania affords you many opportunities to live this unique experience. Of all the sites in the region, Pompeii and Herculaneum are justly famous: Walking their streets gives you a particularly eerie feeling. At the center of the lanes' mesmeric attraction is the knowledge that their violent destruction and miraculous preservation both happened on one terrible day nearly two thousand years ago. And somehow it feels as it is *always* that day here. Imagination easily bridges the gap to the time when these rooms resounded with talk and laughter (or, for more morbid minds, screams and cries of terror). Yet the best sites in the region might be some of the lesser known, such as the magnificent Villa di Poppea in Oplontis with its wonderful frescoes, the Villa Arianna and the Villa di San Marco in Castellammare di Stabia, and the Villa Romana of Minori. See chapters 5, 7, and 10.

- **Listening to a Concert in a Medieval Cloister:** The unique blend of cultures operating in Campania gave birth to some of the most

Regions of Italy

splendid medieval cloisters ever built. Intertwined arches of Sicilian-Norman architecture are used here to support the loggias of delightful inner gardens where the sun, more often than not, is shining on fruit-laden citrus trees and ancient stone and tile work. During the summer, music festivals are held in most coastal towns to take advantage of these magical spaces. The best of these medieval marvels are the Chiostro del Paradiso in Amalfi, the Villa Rufolo cloister in Ravello, and the cloister of San Francesco in Sorrento. See chapters 6 and 7.

2 The Best Ruins

- **The Temples of Paestum:** This site's complete set of walls and three temples are simply the best Greek ruins in existence outside Greece. One of the three temples—the grandiose **Temple of Neptune,** whose restoration was finished in 2004, is actually the best-preserved Greek temple in the world, along with the Theseion in Athens. We highly recommend timing your visit in spring or fall, when the roses are in bloom and the ruins are at their most romantic. The site is also stunning at dawn and sunset in any season, when the temples' surfaces glow golden in the sun. See chapter 9.

- **The Acropolis of Cuma:** The first Greek colony in Italy and a beacon of Greek culture, Cuma was built on one of the most picturesque promontories in Campania. In the once enchanting area of the Phlegrean Fields, where so many myths reside (the Cave of the Sybil, Lake Averno and the entrance to the underworld, and so on), Cuma offers a stunning panorama and atmospheric ruins. See "Phlegrean Fields" in chapter 4.

- **The Anfiteatro Campano:** The largest Roman amphitheater after the Colosseum, this splendid ruin offers a glimpse at ancient artistry in spite of the active pillage that occurred here from the 9th century onwards. On-site is the Museo dei Gladiatori, a permanent exhibit reconstructing the life of a gladiator; it is housed in a building located on the probable site of Capua's Gladiator School—whose most famous graduate was Spartacus, the slave made famous by the 1960 Stanley Kubrick film. It is located in Santa Maria Capua Vetere, which occupies the grounds of Roman Capua, the city that Cicero considered second only to Rome in the whole ancient world. The area is rich in other noteworthy ruins, such as the splendid Mitreo (Temple to the Persian god Mithras), and museum collections. See chapter 10.

- **Pompeii and Herculaneum:** Will enough ever be said to describe these incredible sites? Even if you have already visited them in the past, new findings are reason enough for a return visit. The magnificent Villa dei Papiri in Herculaneum was opened to the public for the first time in 2004; the Terme Suburbane in Pompeii was opened in 2002. The riches of the archaeological area are best complemented by a visit to the Museo Archeologico Nazionale in Naples (see below), to view its massive array of frescoes and mosaics from earlier excavations at both sites. See chapter 5.

- **Oplontis:** Also called the Villa of Poppea, these are the ruins of a splendid Roman villa—believed to be that of Nero's wife—with magnificent frescoes and decorations. Less known than other sites and often passed by hurried tourists who stop only in Pompeii or Herculaneum, this villa is unique, not only for its state of conservation, but also because modern archaeology requires materials to be left *in situ*. The frescoes and statuary grant you a fuller experience of the Romans' daily lives. See chapter 5.

- **Trajan's Arch in Benevento:** This little-known and out-of-the-way find is the world's best-preserved example of an ancient Roman triumphal arch. Recently restored—it took 14 years of work before the arch was opened again to the public in 2001—it is a masterpiece of carving that depicts the deeds of the admired (and fairly benevolent) Roman Emperor Trajan. Careful cleaning has eliminated darker areas in the marble, making the reliefs much easier to read. Inside a little Longobard church nearby is a permanent exhibit on the arch, its restoration, and Roman life under Trajan. See chapter 10.

- **Pozzuoli:** The ruins of the ancient Roman town of Puteoli have been difficult to excavate since the busy modern town occupies exactly the same area as the original (much as Rome does). In the splendid frame of Pozzuoli's bay, you'll find an underground Pompeii—buried not by a volcanic explosion, but by sinking under unstable volcanic ground. The main attractions are the Rione Terra, with Roman streets and shops; the 1st-century Greco-Roman market (Serapeo); and the Roman amphitheater (Anfiteatro Flavio), where musical performances are held during summer. See chapter 4.

- **The Underwater Archeological Park of Baia:** Due to subsiding ground, a large part of the ancient Roman town of Baia was submerged by the sea. Excavated and transformed into an archaeological park, it can now be visited with scuba equipment or—if you don't like to get wet—in a glass-bottomed boat. The itinerary leads you through the streets of the ancient town and inside its beautiful villas, now water-filled. This magical experience truly deserves the word *unique*. See "Pozzuoli & the Phlegrean Fields" in chapter 4.

- **Velia:** Overshadowed by Paestum and just a bit too far from Naples for a day trip, Velia was the site of an important Greek settlement started around 540 B.C. It gave birth to one of the most important philosophical schools of antiquity—the Eleatic school of Parmenides and Zeno. Velia is one of the only Greek archaeological sites showing remains not only of an acropolis with its ruined temples, but also of a lower town with some houses. Portions of the walls here date from the 5th and 4th centuries B.C. A stretch of the original Greek pavement climbs towards the town gate, the famous Porta Rosa. A highlight of the Roman period is the thermal baths. See chapter 9.

3 The Best Churches & Cathedrals

- **Casertavecchia Cathedral:** This medieval church is one of the most beautiful extant examples of Norman-Arab architecture, built with two colors of tufa stone and white marble, and dotted with strange human and animal figures. See chapter 10.

- **Naples's Duomo:** The most splendid of Naples's churches, and home of superb artwork, you'll find that the Duomo is three churches in one. The Cappella di San Gennaro is really a church in its own right, with a fantastic treasure on display in the attached museum. Santa Restituta, the original

6th-century church, contains a magnificent 4th-century baptistery. See chapter 4.

- **Complesso Monumentale di Santa Chiara:** Another star on the Neapolitan scene, this splendid church-cum-monastery holds splendid examples of 14th-century sculpture that escaped the tragic bombing of World War II. (Other parts of the massive structure were not so lucky but have been restored.) The spacious majolica cloister holds a plethora of mythological, pastoral, and whimsical scenes enchanting to behold in the open air. See chapter 4.

- **San Lorenzo Maggiore:** Originally built in the 6th century, this lesser-known church in Naples is famous for its literary guests: from Boccaccio, who met his darling Fiammetta here, to Francesco Petrarca and others. It holds splendid Renaissance masterpieces and a multilayered archaeological site, where you can descend like a time traveler through layers of buildings all the way down to a paleochristian basilica and the 1st-century Roman Macellum (Market). See chapter 4.

- **Chiesa della Santissima Annunziata:** This church is located in Minuto, one of the medieval hamlets of the township of Scala, which stretches along the cliffs of the Amalfi Coast. The church offers not only some of the region's best examples of Romanesque architecture and beautiful 12th-century frescoes, but also a superb panorama. See chapter 7.

- **Duomo di Santa Maria Capua Vetere:** Dating originally from the 5th century, this beautiful paleochristian church has been redecorated in later centuries, but it contains artworks reaching back to Roman times (its columns and capitals), as well as examples of Renaissance frescoes and carvings. See chapter 10.

- **Sant'Angelo in Formis:** This is one of the most important Romanesque churches in the whole country. Its entire interior is graced with beautiful frescoes. The church's lovely setting is Mount Tifata, near Capua. See chapter 10.

- **Santa Sofia:** Dating back to the early Longobard kingdom in Benevento, this small medieval church is famous for its unique star-shaped floor plan and the integration of Longobard and Catholic symbols. See chapter 10.

- **Certosa di Padula (Carthusian Monastery of San Lorenzo):** Begun in the 14th century, this magnificent monastery—one of the largest in the world—is a baroque masterpiece, chock-full of art and architectural details. Off the beaten path, but only a short distance from Salerno, it is a destination not to be missed. See chapter 9.

4 The Best Castles & Palaces

- **Castel dell'Ovo:** The symbol of Naples and the most picturesque icon of the Naples waterfront, this castle is the city's oldest fortification—its foundation dates back to the 9th century B.C. Greek settlement. It is said to be built over a magic egg hidden by the poet-magician Virgil for the defense of the city (which will crumble into ruin if the egg is destroyed). See chapter 4.

- **Reggia di Caserta:** The Versailles of Italy, this splendid royal palace was built by the famous architect Vanvitelli for the Bourbon kings in the 18th century. It holds fantastic works of art and the decorations—walls and floors included—are magnificent.

The Reggia is also justly famed for its massive Italian garden, one of the most beautiful in the world. See chapter 10.

- **Castel Nuovo (Maschio Angioino):** This 13th-century castle was the residence of Neapolitan kings until the 17th century. Although a fire in the 16th century destroyed its frescoes by Giotto, there is still enough in this majestic fortress to impress visitors. See chapter 4.
- **Palazzo Reale:** The beautiful Royal Palace of Naples dominates wide Piazza del Plebiscito with its neoclassical facade and statues of kings. Inside, you'll find a rich collection of art and decorations as well as a wonderful library. See chapter 4.

- **Castel Lauritano:** This ruined castle in Agerola, a town on the Amalfi Coast, is incredibly picturesque and offers extensive views over both the coast and the interior. See chapter 7.
- **Villa Rufolo:** This splendid villa in Ravello has been made famous by its terrace and gardens, which inspired Wagner to write some of his *Parsifal,* so moved was he by its vistas. Today, you can listen to concerts of Wagner's work in the same setting. See chapter 7.
- **Villa Cimbrone:** The second most famous villa in Ravello, also with a splendid panoramic terrace, the Villa Cimbrone has another attraction: It houses a small hotel and a restaurant, which was opened to the public in 2005. See chapter 7.

5 The Best Museums

- **Museo Nazionale di Capodimonte:** Created by the Bourbon kings, this picture gallery is one of the best in the world, holding paintings from the 13th century onwards. The catalogue looks like a book on art history, complete with all the famous names of Italian art and many members of the Flemish school. The regular special exhibits draw visitors from all over Italy, Europe, and the world. (The success of these special exhibits is such that you'll need advance reservations to get in, unless you don't mind standing in line for several hours.) See chapter 4.
- **Museo Archeologico Nazionale:** Even if you are only mildly interested in archaeology, you should not miss this unique museum, which holds the largest collection of ancient Roman artifacts in the world. Created in the 17th century—with original Roman mosaics re-used in the floors and statues incorporated in the facade decoration—this is where the best finds from Pompeii and other local sites

were placed on display. The huge quantity of frescoes, statuary, and precious objects has greatly benefited from a reorganization, which was finished in 2005. See chapter 4.
- **Museo Nazionale della Ceramica Duca di Martina:** Housed in the elegant Villa Floridiana up in Naples's Vomero neighborhood, this rich ceramic collection includes the most important assemblage of Capodimonte porcelain in the world. See chapter 4.
- **Museo Campano:** This museum in Capua has a tall order, as the repository of the history and culture of the whole Campania region. It does a great job, though, with its several collections, covering the whole ancient history of the area, from the Oscans (about 6th century B.C.) to the Renaissance. It has a magnificent collection of parchment and illuminated manuscripts. See chapter 10.
- **Museo del Duomo:** This museum in Salerno is not large, but it holds a number of invaluable masterpieces

ranging from Roman times to the Renaissance and baroque periods. It includes a unique collection of ivory carvings, a great picture gallery, and a rich collection of illuminated manuscripts. See chapter 9.

- **Museo del Sannio:** Housed in the atmospheric cloister of Santa Sofia in Benevento, this is a small but well-rounded collection of artifacts from local sites. It includes the largest collection of Egyptian art found at one Italian archaeological site, a local temple. See chapter 10.

- **Museo Irpino:** This modern museum displays a collection of artifacts found in the rich archaeological sites in the outlying region of Avellino. The objects date back into the distant past long before the Romans (or even the Greeks) came to the region—as far back as 4000 B.C. See chapter 10.

- **Museo Archeologico dei Campi Flegrei:** Housed in the picturesque Aragonese Castle of Baia, this is another great treasure trove of Roman and Greek art in the vicinity of Naples. See chapter 4.

6 The Best Swimming & Sunbathing Spots

- **Vico Equense:** This lesser-known resort town on the Sorrentine peninsula is blessed with several beaches—most of them small and hidden away inside picturesque coves—such as **Marina di Equa,** dominated by a powerful 17th-century tower. See chapter 6.

- **Punta del Capo:** This lovely beach near Sorrento under the cliffs has attracted visitors from time immemorial. Nearby, you'll find the ruins of a Roman villa and a small pool of water enclosed by rocks, known as the Bath of Queen Giovanna. See chapter 6.

- **Bay of Ieranto:** Part of the Marine Preserve of Punta Campanella, this unique fjord was almost lost to developers, who would have spoiled its beauty forever. When the light is just right at day's end, the clarity of the waters here creates the illusion of boats floating in mid-air. See chapter 6.

- **Grotta dello Smeraldo:** Although this grotto in the village of Conca dei Marini on the Amalfi Coast is usually visited by boat, it is also the destination of a scuba procession on Christmas night. The pretty beach can be visited anytime, however. See chapter 7.

- **Positano:** The most famous resort on the Amalfi Coast, Positano has several

picturesque beaches—although they are hardly deserted. Besides the central **Spiaggia Grande** by the Marina, you'll find **Fornillo** to the west of town, and **La Porta, Ciumicello, Arienzo,** and **Laurito** to the east. See chapter 7.

- **Spiaggia di Citara:** This is the most scenic beach on the island of Ischia, near the little town of Forio. Besides the lovely scenery, there are several natural thermal springs. See chapter 8.

- **Marina di Paestum:** Greek temples are not the only reason to come to Paestum. The sandy beach here is one of the best in Italy, extending for miles along the clear blue sea. See chapter 9.

- **Baia della Calanca:** In beautiful Marina di Camerota, this is one of the nicest beaches in the Cilento, and is famed for its clear waters. See chapter 9.

- **Bagni di Tiberio:** This is the best of the rare and tiny beaches of Capri. As the name suggests, it lies near the ruins of one of Emperor Tiberius's notorious pleasure palaces. It is accessible by a rocky steep path or by boat. See chapter 8.

7 The Best Spas

- **Parco Termale Giardini Poseidon:** This is our favorite thermal spa. Located on beautiful Ischia, the Poseidon boasts scenic outdoor thermal pools from which you can enjoy great views and a variety of aesthetic and health treatments. See chapter 8.
- **Ischia Thermal Center:** In the small town of Ischia, this is one of the most modern spas on the island, where you can enjoy a variety of state-of-the-art modern services. See chapter 8.
- **Terme della Regina Isabella:** Among the most famous and elegant spas on Ischia, this historical establishment in exclusive Lacco Ameno offers state-of-the-art facilities. See chapter 8.
- **Castellammare di Stabia:** This pleasant seaside resort is blessed with 28 natural thermal springs which you can enjoy at one of the two public spas: the historical one built by the Bourbon kings or the modern establishment on the slopes of Mount Faito. Both offer a wide range of services, from beauty and relaxation treatments to medical ones. See chapter 5.
- **Scrajo Terme:** At the beginning of the Sorrentine peninsula, just outside the pleasant resort town of In Vico Equense, you'll find this historic thermal establishment dating back to the 19th century. Stayovers are offered so that visitors can "take the waters" in style. See chapter 6.

8 The Best Vistas

- **Lungomare di Salerno:** Italy's best-kept secret may be the seaside promenade of laid-back Salerno. A splendid and completely pedestrian walkway lined with palm trees, it offers views encompassing the whole bay from Capri to Punta Licosa in the Cilento. See chapter 9.
- **Deserto:** From the terraces of this Carmelite hermitage near Sant'Agata dei Golfi, you can enjoy the famous, unique circular panorama encompassing both the Gulf of Naples with Sorrento and the islands, and the Gulf of Salerno with the Amalfi Coast. On a good day, you can see almost the whole region, from the Cilento—way off to the south of Paestum—to Capo Miseno, to the islands of Ischia and Procida, and to Capri. See chapter 6.
- **Belvedere dello Schiaccone:** This is the best lookout along the whole Amalfi Drive, located immediately west of Positano and accessible from the road; the views are indeed superb. See chapter 7.
- **Lake Fusaro:** In the once picturesque Phlegrean Fields, not far from Pozzuoli, this beautiful lake was chosen by the Bourbon kings as the site for the Casina Reale, a structural jewel designed by the architect Vanvitelli. Today, as back then, the Casina Reale commands royal views perfect for picture taking. See chapter 4.
- **Monte Cervati:** The highest peak of the Cilento massif, Cervati is famous for its beauty in summer—when it turns purple with lavender fields—and for the magnificent views from its top. See chapter 9.
- **Agropoli:** From the walls of the medieval citadel you can look down on vast stretches of coastline—a view that helped the Saracens hold onto Agropoli as the base for their incursions until they were finally dislodged in the 11th century. See chapter 9.

9 The Best Restaurants

- **Don Alfonso 1890:** This is one of the top Italian gourmet addresses and the best restaurant south of Naples, created and maintained by hosts Lidia and Alfonso Iaccarino. The restaurant, a member of the Relais & Châteaux association, has a luxurious decor and offers superb food made of ingredients mainly from the chefs' own organic farm. See chapter 6.

- **Oasi Olimpia Relais:** Competing for the title of best restaurant on the Sorrento peninsula with Don Alfonso, this is our favorite spot to eat in the area. It might not have the over-the-top elegance of Don Alfonso (though it's not a place to drop by in your bathing attire, either); it has a more down-to-earth atmosphere and an enthusiasm for homegrown food that we find irresistible. The alfresco dining under the arbor is a plus. See chapter 6.

- **Faro di Capo d'Orso:** Owned by a young, emerging chef—Rocco Iannone—the Faro (Lighthouse) is one of the culinary highlights of the Amalfi Coast, supplemented by a unique location that offers stunning views of this stretch of coast. See chapter 7.

- **Il San Pietro di Positano:** The restaurant of the famous hotel in Positano with the same name (see later in this chapter), Il San Pietro offers the fine cuisine of chef Alois Vanlangenacker—all based on ingredients from the hotel's own farm—and a delightfully romantic setting which is worth a visit all by itself. See chapter 7.

- **La Stanza del Gusto:** This small restaurant in Naples is the kingdom of Mario Avallone, chef and perfect host. The "Hall of Tastes," as it might be called in English, is a wonderful world where only the best ingredients and most pleasurable associations—some based on traditional Neapolitan cuisine—are to be found. The decor is intimate and vaguely bohemian, serving as the perfect background for the chef's inventive dishes. The prix-fixe menu is an adventure more than a sampler, and the wine list is a tome. See chapter 4.

- **George's:** Located on the roof terrace of the Grand Hotel Parker's (see below), this is a truly elegant restaurant happily devoid of stuffiness or ostentation. There's no snobbery here, only the best that money can buy. Chef Baciòt brings together the ingredients of tasty and healthy dishes which marry tradition with nutrition. The service and surroundings are impeccable, and the wine list is among the best in Italy. See chapter 4.

- **La Cantinella:** This well-known restaurant proudly serves a classic version of traditional Neapolitan cuisine, with a large share of the menu dedicated to seafood. Make reservations well ahead, as it is very popular with local crowds. See chapter 4.

- **Relais Blu:** This newly opened restaurant-cum-small-hotel is a hot address on the Sorrento peninsula. The delightful manager/host will introduce you to the flavors of his beloved native peninsula, be it for pre-dinner drinks, which are served with creative nibbles based on local ingredients, or for a perfectly romantic dinner. High above the rocky coast overlooking Capri, the open-air terrace is spectacular. See chapter 6.

10 The Best Luxury Stays

- **Grand Hotel Parker's** (© 081-7612474): This is Naples's most romantic luxury hotel, competing with the Vesuvio (see below) for the title of best hotel in town. Housed in a magnificent Liberty-style building, it offers superb service, classy accommodations, and one of the best restaurants in the country (see earlier). See chapter 4.

- **Grand Hotel Vesuvio** (© 081-7640044): This is generally considered the best hotel in Naples, offering palatial accommodations and exquisite service. You will be pampered the moment you step through the doors. The turndown service includes fine small-batch signature chocolates, the linens are royalty class, and the sumptuous breakfast is served in the most panoramic room you can imagine, with views over the picturesque Castel dell'Ovo. The gourmet roof-restaurant is another plus. Every detail here is truly first-class. See chapter 4.

- **Hotel San Pietro Positano** (© 800-7352478): A member of the Relais & Châteaux group, this elegant hotel tops our list of favorite places to stay in the whole of Italy. You'll understand why as soon as you step inside. The kind and attentive service, the tastefully colorful furnishing details, the romantic views from their terraces—we love everything about this place. See chapter 7.

- **Grand Hotel Excelsior Vittoria** (© 081-8071044): This gorgeous hotel is the best in Sorrento, housed in what once was a palatial residence overlooking the sea. The antiques in the guest rooms, the picturesque terraces, and the service make this an ideal hotel, right in the center of town (with its own elevator down to a private beach). See chapter 6.

- **Hotel Santa Caterina** (© 089-871012): Amalfi's most luxurious hotel, on a cliff just out of town, this is where you'll want to come to be pampered away from the crowds—and to enjoy the hotel's beautiful private beach, swimming pool, and lush gardens. See chapter 7.

- **Hotel Le Sirenuse** (© 089-875066): Competing for the title of best hotel in Positano with the San Pietro above, this gorgeous hotel is housed in a beautiful 18th-century villa overlooking the sea. It offers palatial accommodations and fine service. See chapter 7.

- **Grand Hotel Quisisana** (© 081-8370788): The glitziest resort on Capri, this luxury hotel provides its guests with splendid accommodations and exquisite service. The hotel's bar and restaurant are popular spots for visiting socialites, so it's worth stopping by just to enjoy the atmosphere. See chapter 8.

- **Capri Palace** (© 081-9780111): This is the best hotel on Capri, which naturally means elegance, breathtaking views, and deluxe furnishings in rooms decorated with artwork and antiques. The service is impeccable. See chapter 8.

- **Mezzatorre Resort & Spa** (© 081-986111): Taking its name from the 15th-century watchtower that houses part of the hotel, the Mezzatorre is the most splendid accommodation in Ischia. On its own secluded promontory off the exclusive town of Lacco Ameno and not far from Forio, it pampers its guests in perfect elegance and style. The views from the park and the swimming pool are breathtaking. See chapter 8.

2

Planning Your Trip to Campania & the Amalfi Coast

This chapter is devoted to the where, when, and how of your trip. To entice you, we'll start off with a quick rundown of the various areas that make up this large region. To see Campania's highlights, plan on spending at least 5 to 7 days; 10 days will give you the leisure to enjoy things without feeling too pressed for time, and 14 days is about perfect.

1 The Regions in Brief

More than any other Italian region, **Campania** reverberates with the memories of antiquity: from the Greeks, to the Etruscans, to the ancient Romans, all favored its strong sunlight, fertile soil, and bubbling sulfurous springs, and made this region their preferred vacation destination.

Its marvelous spas, beaches, and islands still attract visitors from all around the world, but Campania also has a few surprises for those who take time to go off the beaten path. Norman and Longobard castles, delightful medieval bourgs, huge and rich monasteries, high mountains, and exceptional caves compose only part of what Campania has to offer. Campania boasts one of the lowest population densities in Italy—in the mountains of the Cilento—as well as the highest—in the urban area of Naples, which is what most tourists experience.

THE AMALFI COAST

The most famous destination in the region, the Amalfi Coast will enchant you with its dramatic coastline and picturesque cliff villages. From **Vietri sul Mare**—a town famous for its ceramics

and majolica—to Piano di Sorrento, the Amalfi Drive is home to leading resorts (even though they're not exactly undiscovered) in **Ravello** (not on the sea) and **Positano** (on the sea). In spite of its small and crowded beaches, **Amalfi** is a town we love for its harbor-town feeling and its rich history and art. It is a good starting point for walking tours and offers more moderate hotel choices than any other town on this stretch of coast. Amalfi is also an excellent base for exploring the lesser-known little towns: **Cetara, Atrani, Conca dei Marini, Praiano,** and **Vettica Maggiore** are all delightful villages right by the sea. We also recommend going off the beaten path to explore lesser-known interior towns such as **Scala, Furore, Agerola,** and **Tramonti,** all rich in history and impressive views of the coast below.

NAPLES

You should allow at least 2 full days for this city, with its matchless museums and amazing churches (in addition to the world's worst traffic outside Cairo). Moreover, the city's artistic and historical riches are more easily accessed since the historic

Campania & the Amalfi Coast

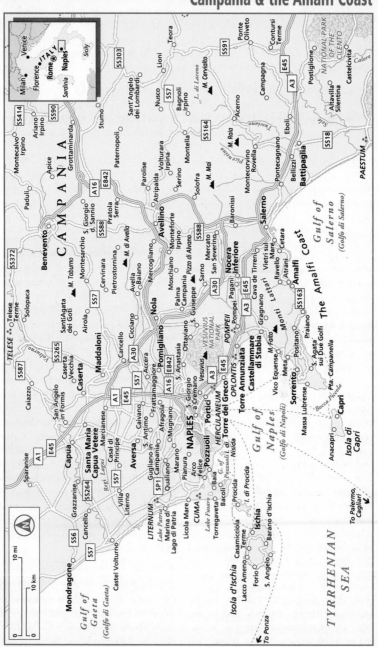

center's thorough refurbishment during the 1990s. Also, police work has been effective in reducing crime and making the tourist areas safer than ever. Yet, Naples *is* a big city, and you should still keep a careful eye on your belongings.

THE PHLEGREAN FIELDS

Campania contains many sites identified in ancient mythology, and most of them can be found in this volcanic area to the northwest of Naples, where bubbling springs and hot mud conjure images of the underworld. Once a paradise on earth, this area is now a suburb of Naples, complete with pockets of squalor. Nonetheless, its standout natural attractions include **Lake Fusaro** (a picturesque view of which can be enjoyed from the Casina Reale); **Solfatara** with its volcanic hot mud and sulfur springs; the promontory of **Capo Miseno,** affording views of the delightful bay; and **Lake Averno,** the mythical entrance to the Kingdom of the Dead. The area's rich archaeological remains are a paramount reason to come, from the fascinating ruins of **Cuma**—the first Greek colony in Italy—to the Rione Terra and the Anfiteatro Flavio of **Pozzuoli,** to the out-of-the-ordinary underwater archaeological park of **Baia** and the **Museo Archeologico** in the local **Aragonese Castle.**

ISCHIA & PROCIDA

The natural continuation of Capo Miseno in the Phlegrean Fields, small and exclusive Procida, and peaceful Ischia, are volcanic islands of great beauty. Procida is where the most fortunate of VIPs have their hideaway villas overlooking one of the most beautiful bays in the world, while other mortals—us, for instance—come to enjoy fantastic meals in remote, romantic restaurants. Ischia is where those in the know come for delicious spa vacations. The volcano of Ischia—Monte Epomeo—was still quite active when the Greeks tried to establish their first colony

on this coast; but today, the inactive volcano serves only to feed the mineral hot springs and therapeutic muds that are used by the over 150 spas on the island. Beaches galore are another attraction.

CAPRI

The most famous of Campania's islands, Capri is the preferred destination for those seeking fun in the sun. The island is indeed spectacular, with postcard-worthy soaring cliffs, surrounded by a deep-blue sea. Besides being a choice resort for VIPs and wannabes, it is also an important gay destination. Positively overcrowded with day visitors during the summer and early fall, Capri gives its best if you stay overnight.

THE VESUVIAN AREA

What would Naples's skyline be like without Mount Vesuvius? You'll discover the love-fear relationship that Neapolitans have with their volcano when you climb its slopes and taste its marvelous *Lacrima Christi* wine. The region is home to some of the world's most renowned ancient ruins, such as **Pompeii** and **Herculaneum,** as well as some lesser-known ones like the Roman villa of **Oplonti** with its magnificent frescoes (a UNESCO World Heritage Site), the rural Roman villas of **Boscoreale,** and the thermal resort of **Stabiae,** by the lively town of **Castellammare di Stabia.** The town is a great place to stay overnight if you'd like a more in-depth visit to this area and, perhaps, an exploratory trip to the seaside town of **Torre del Greco,** home to one of the oldest crafts on this coast, the carving of *cameos.*

SORRENTO & ITS PENINSULA

The beautiful seaside setting of **Sorrento** has long been celebrated, and justly so. We cannot add to the renown of its rocky cliffs, elegant hotels, vivacious nightlife, and blue waters. The rest of the Sorrento peninsula—from elegant **Vico Equense** to out-of-the-way **Massa Lubrense** and **Sant'Agata sui due Golfi** with its incredible views—has much to offer, including off-the-beaten-track destinations where you can get away from the crowds, and yet be only minutes from the action.

SALERNO

This is our favorite less-trafficked destination. A very active town at the eastern edge of the Amalfi Coast, Salerno prides itself on having Italy's most beautiful seafront promenade and a delightful medieval center—rich in small shops and restaurants—with a superb 11th-century Duomo. The Duomo and its museum are reason enough to justify a visit to Campania. Its low hotel and restaurant rates are another plus.

THE CILENTO

Completely unknown to foreign tourists and very little known even to Italians, the Cilento is Italy's second largest natural park, containing some of the most exciting natural attractions—including two huge caves, delightful fishing towns, and seaside resorts with fine sand beaches. Within easy striking distance are the famous Greek ruins of **Paestum,** home to the best conserved Greek temple after the Theseion in Athens.

BENEVENTO

This is Campania's prettiest large town, situated up in the hilltops and way off the beaten track. It hides some wonderful art treasures, including the best-preserved ancient Roman arch in existence and an intriguing Longobard star-shaped church. As the producer of some of Italy's best D.O.C. *(Denominazione di Origine Controllata)* wines, the hilly areas surrounding the town are a perfect destination for wine lovers.

AVELLINO

This small town, with its beautiful cathedral and wonderful archaeological museum, is the capital of Irpinia, an area known for its food and wine. Also worth visiting in the area are the village of **Sant' Angelo dei Lombardi** and the nearby Convento di San Marco, one of the most romantic monasteries around (now being restored).

CASERTA

If the Reggia di Caserta were to compete with Versailles on matters of elegance and beauty, Caserta would emerge the victor. Overlooking Caserta, you'll find the medieval bourg of **Casertavecchia,** one of the best preserved in Italy. Also nearby is the very little-visited **Basilica di Sant'Angelo** in **Formis,** with its magnificent 11th-century frescoes, as well as the ruins of ancient Roman Capua (in the town of **Santa Maria Capua Vetere**). During Roman times, this was the most prosperous city in the empire right after Rome.

2 Visitor Information & Maps

The **Italian National Tourist Board** (www.italiantourism.com) is a good source of information before you go.

In the **United States:** 630 Fifth Ave., Suite 1565, New York, NY 10111 (© 212/245-4822; fax 212/586-9249); 500 N. Michigan Ave., Suite 2240, Chicago, IL 60611 (© 312/644-0996; fax 312/644-3019); and 12400 Wilshire Blvd., Suite 550, Los Angeles, CA 90025 (© 310/820-1898; fax 310/820-6357).

In **Canada:** 175 Bloor St. E., South Tower, Suite 907, Toronto, ON M4W 3R8 (© 416/925-4882; fax 416/925-4799).

In **Australia:** Level 4, 46 Market St., NSW 2000 Sydney; P.O. Box Q802, QVB NSW 1230 (© 02-92-621666; fax: 02-92-621677).

In the **United Kingdom:** 1 Princes St., London W1B 2AY (© 020/7408-1254; fax 020/7399-3567).

We also recommend writing directly (in English or Italian) to the local tourist boards for a variety of brochures as well as maps. The **Campania tourist board** covers the whole region; its address is Centro Direzionale – Isola C/5, Napoli 80143 (℃ **081-7968974;** fax: 081-7958576; www.regione.campania.it).

Campania is administratively divided into five provinces, each with its own **provincial tourist board** (Ente Provinciale per il Turismo, or EPT):

EPT Napoli (covering Naples, Phlegrean Fields, Herculaneum, Pompeii, Ischia, Capri, and the Sorrento peninsula): Piazza dei Martiri 58, 80121 Napoli (℃ **081-405311;** fax: 081-401961; www.eptnapoli.info).

EPT Salerno (covering Salerno, the Amalfi Coast, and the Cilento): Via Velia 15, Cap 84125 Salerno (℃ **089-230411;** fax: 089-251844; www.crmpa.it/ept).

EPT Caserta (covering Caserta, Caserta Vecchia, and Capua): Palazzo Reale, 81100 Caserta (℃ **0823-322233;** fax: 0823-326300; www.casertaturismo.it).

EPT Avellino: Via Due Principati 5, 83100 Avellino (℃ **0825-74695;** fax 0825-74757; www.provincia.avellino.it and www.e-irpinia.it).

EPT Benevento: Via Sala 31, 82100 Benevento (℃ **0824-319911;** fax 0824-312309; www.eptbenevento.it).

In addition to the above, local tourist boards operate in all places of tourist interest; we have listed them in each individual chapter.

These offices are the best place to find user-friendly local **maps,** usually available for free. Should you require more detailed maps, the best are available from **Touring Club of Italy** (www.touring.it); buy directly from their website, at bookstores abroad, or from most bookstores and newsstands in Italy.

3 Entry Requirements & Customs

PASSPORTS

For information on how to get a passport, go to "Passports" in the "Fast Facts" section of this chapter—the websites listed provide downloadable passport applications as well as the current fees for processing passport applications.

VISAS

U.S., Canadian, U.K., Irish, Australian, and New Zealand citizens with a **valid passport** don't need a visa to enter Italy or Campania if they don't expect to stay more than 90 days and don't expect to work or study there. Contact your nearest **Italian Embassy** for further information: in Washington, D.C. for the **United States** (www.ambwashingtondc.esteri.it); in Camberra for **Australia** (www.amb canberra.esteri.it); and in Wellington for **New Zealand** (www.ambwellington. esteri.it).

Tourists planning to stay in Italy more than 8 business days need to file a *permesso di soggiorno* (permit of stay) with the post office; you'll need a photocopy of your passport, two photographs, proof of medical insurance, proof of adequate means of financial support, and a photocopy of your return tickets. See www.portaleimmigrazione.it for more info.

MEDICAL REQUIREMENTS

For information on medical requirements and recommendations, see "Health," p. 33.

CUSTOMS

For information on what you can bring into and take out of Campania, go to the "Fast Facts" section of this chapter.

4 When to Go

From **April to June** and **September to October** are generally the best times to visit Campania; temperatures are usually mild and the crowds aren't quite so intense. Starting in mid-June, the summer rush begins, especially at the seaside resorts, and from **July to August** the coast teems with visitors. **Mid-August** is the worst on the coast in terms of crowds: The entire country goes on vacation around the holiday of **Ferragosto,** on August 15; while the cities tend to be deserted—in Naples, Benevento, Avellino, Caserta, and Salerno many restaurants and shops will be closed—the seaside towns and island resorts buzz with activity. By contrast, the region's interior never gets really crowded. From **November to Easter** most attractions go on shorter winter hours or are closed for renovation, while a number of hotels and restaurants close or take extended vacations. Especially between **November and February,** spa and beach destinations become padlocked ghost towns. Also, it can get much colder than you'd expect (it might even snow).

High season on most airline routes to Naples usually stretches from June to the beginning of September. This is the most expensive and most crowded time to travel. **Shoulder season** is from April to May, early September to October, and December 15 to January 14. **Low season** is from November 1 to December 14 and from January 15 to March 31.

WEATHER

July and August are very hot in Campania, especially in low-lying areas. The high temperatures (measured in Italy in degrees Celsius) begin in Naples in May, often lasting until sometime in October. For the most part, the humidity is lower in Campania than, say, in Washington, D.C., so high temperatures don't seem as oppressive. In Naples, temperatures can stay in the 90°F (30°C) range for days, but nights are often comfortably cooler.

Winters are mild by the sea, with temperatures averaging 50°F (10°C), but it gets much colder in the interior and the mountains, which often are subject to rain and snow.

Campania's Average Daily Temperature & Monthly Rainfall

Naples	Jan	Feb	Mar	Apr	May	June	July	Aug	Sept	Oct	Nov	Dec
Temp. (°F)	50	54	58	63	70	78	83	85	75	66	60	52
Temp. (°C)	9	12	14	17	21	26	28	29	24	19	16	11
Rainfall (in.)	4.7	4	3	3.8	2.4	.8	.8	2.6	3.5	5.8	5.1	3.7

Salerno	Jan	Feb	Mar	Apr	May	June	July	Aug	Sept	Oct	Nov	Dec
Temp. (°F)	50	53	55	60	66	75	78	81	75	66	59	55
Temp. (°C)	10	11	13	16	19	24	26	27	24	19	15	13
Rainfall (in.)	6.2	5.4	4.5	3.7	2.9	1.5	.7	1.1	4.1	6.5	7.5	7.1

Benevento	Jan	Feb	Mar	Apr	May	June	July	Aug	Sept	Oct	Nov	Dec
Temp. (°F)	45	46	52	57	64	71	77	77	71	63	54	50
Temp. (°C)	7	8	11	14	18	22	25	25	22	17	12	10
Rainfall (in.)	2.8	2.8	2.1	2	2.1	1.4	.6	1.2	2.1	3	3.7	3.5

HOLIDAYS

Offices and shops in Campania are closed on the following **national holidays:** January 1 (New Year's Day), Easter Monday, April 25 (Liberation Day), May 1 (Labor Day), August 15 (Ferragosto/Assumption of the Virgin), November 1 (All Saints' Day), December 8 (Feast of the Immaculate Conception), December 25 (Christmas Day), and December 26 (Santo Stefano).

Closings are also sometimes observed on **feast days** honoring the patron saint of each town and village. In Naples, September 19 is the Feast of St. Gennaro; in Avellino, February 14 is the Feast of St. Modestino.

CAMPANIA CALENDAR OF EVENTS

For an exhaustive list of events beyond those listed here, check http://events.frommers.com, where you'll find a searchable, up-to-the-minute roster of what's happening in cities all over the world.

For major events in which tickets should be procured well before your arrival, we prefer using Italy-based services; they are often cheaper and have more comprehensive events offerings (see box p. 23). You can also check with **Global Edwards & Edwards** in the United States at ℂ **800/223-6108.**

January

Il Presepe nel Presepe (Manger in a Manger), Morcone. This suggestive little town near Benevento is a natural background for the reenactment of Jesus's birth. Each January, the villagers here transform their town into a version of Bethlehem, and open their homes to visitors. January 3.

Epiphany celebrations, regionwide. All Roman Catholic holidays are deeply felt in Campania, and festive celebrations for the Epiphany include numerous fairs and processions celebrating the arrival of the Three Kings at Christ's manger. January 6.

Festival Internazionale della Canzone Napoletana ed Italiana (International Festival of Italian and Neapolitan Song), Capua. Gathering performers and lovers of Italian and Neapolitan music for more than 3 decades (the festival reached its 30th anniversary in 2007), this 3-day event is a celebration of Italian folk music both new and the traditional. End of January.

February

Carnival, regionwide. During the period before Lent, float parades, and histrionic traditional shows take place in most towns, big and small, throughout the region. Some of the best are in **Capua,** which puts on a grand parade and cabaret and theater performances (call the tourist office at ℂ **0823-321137**); and in **Montemarano,** where celebrations start on January 17 (call the tourist office at ℂ **082-524013** for a schedule of events). **Paestum** schedules great parade and dance shows (call the tourist office at ℂ **0828-811016**). Dates vary, but it's generally held the week before Ash Wednesday.

SorrentoCarnevale, Sorrento. Celebrating its seventh year in 2008, this 3-day festival focuses on the circus, staging events by local and international performers (www.carnevale sorrento.it). Three days preceding Ash Wednesday.

Carnevale Irpino, Avellino. This festival includes traditional representations such as the famous *Zeza*—a musical farce, parades, and the **Concorso della Zeza,** a large competition for group mummers (masked performers). Contact the **EPT** (ℂ **0825-74732** or 0825-74695) for a schedule of the events. The 2 weeks before Ash Wednesday.

March

Nauticsud, Mostra d'Oltremare, Napoli. Spanning both land and water, this boat show boasts displays of the latest motor and sailing boats and equipment. Check their website for information at www.nauticsud.info. Mid-March.

Comicon, Napoli. This international event at Castel Sant'Elmo, in its eighth year in 2006, is a must-see for fans of comic books and animation. Each year the fair picks a country as its main theme, but includes a large number of previews and presentations of new productions. Contact the organization for a schedule of events (© **081-4238127;** www.comicon.it). First weekend in March.

Primavera Sorrentina, Sorrento. The town celebrates the spring and then the summer with an array of events, including various flower fairs, food fairs, and a few musical venues. March through July.

April

Easter (Pasqua), regionwide. Celebrations for the resurrection of Christ include several events: Processions for the benediction of the symbolic palm—usually olive tree branches—take place on the Sunday before Easter Sunday; Stations of the Cross processions (reenacting Jesus's ascent to Golgotha) are staged in almost every church on Holy Friday; finally, Easter Sunday is marked by special religious celebrations. Various dates between end of March and April.

Pasqua a Sorrento (Easter in Sorrento), Sorrento. These Easter celebrations last a whole week; religious processions and concerts are scheduled in the town's cathedral and in the delightful cloister of San Francesco. Other processions take place on the night of Holy Thursday through Holy Friday in the towns surrounding Sorrento: Meta, Piano di Sorrento, and Sant'Agnello. Week before Easter.

Processione dei Misteri (Procession of the Mysteries), Procida. This is one of the most famous traditional religious events in Campania, a procession of plastic scenes from the Passion of Christ sculpted by local craftspeople. Evolving from its original procession in 1627, it is now a glorious show of entire scenes depicting the betrayal of Judas, the Last Supper, and so on, as well as large statues of the Christ and the Madonna. Holy Thursday night into Holy Friday morning.

Salerno Film Festival (Linea d'ombra), Salerno. This major international event, in its 13th year in 2008, is dedicated to new talent in Europe and focuses on the passage from adolescence to adulthood—the "shadow line" written about by Joseph Conrad. Contact the festival office (© **089-2753673;** fax 089-2571125; www.shadowline.it). Varying weeks in April.

May

Feast of San Costanzo, Marina Grande, Capri. Honors St. Costanzo, whose remains preserved in the local basilica protected the island from the Saracens' attacks during the Middle Ages. Bishop Costanzo died on the island during his apostolic mission in Capri on his way to Constantinople around A.D. 677. Call the local tourist office for a program at © **081-8370424.** Third week of May.

Maggio dei Monumenti (Monuments in May), Napoli. The *centro storico* (city center) of Naples comes alive with cultural events and extraordinary openings of private collections and monuments for a whole week. 2008 marks the 14th anniversary of this successful special event. Contact the tourist office for a schedule of events. Last week of May.

June

Historic Regatta of the Maritime Republics, Amalfi. Each of Italy's four historical towns—Genova, Pisa, Venice, and Amalfi—alternate turns hosting this annual regatta. Amalfi's turn was in 2005 and will occur again in 2009. Contact the tourist office (✆ **089-871107**). First Sunday in June.

Il Trionfo del Tempo e del Disinganno (The Triumph of Time and Enlightenment; trionfo.altervista.org), provinces of Caserta and Benevento. Reaching its 15th year in 2008, this festival of medieval, renaissance, and baroque music is beloved by connoisseurs, who delight not only in the high quality of the performances, but also in the venues: All concerts are held in little-known historical buildings, some of which are not usually open to the general public. Second half of June through end of July.

Concerti al Tramonto, Anacapri. Each summer, the Foundation Axel Munthe organizes a series of sunset classical concerts in the Villa San Michele, in a spectacular setting overlooking the island and the sea. Contact the tourist office for details (✆ **081-8371401;** www.sanmichele.org). June through August.

Leuciana Festival, Caserta (✆ **0823-444234;** www.leuciana.org). With a rich program of musical, theatrical, and dance performances held in Caserta's Reggia and in the scenic Belvedere di San Leucio, this festival celebrates its 10-year anniversary in 2008. June through August.

Estate Amalfitana, Amalfi. Starting in June, the town of Amalfi organizes this series of musical and artistic events. At the end of July and into August, the

splendid Chiostro del Paradiso near Amalfi's cathedral becomes the setting for concerts, usually of classical music, including piano soloists and vocal performances. Contact the tourist office (✆ **089-871107**) for a program. Friday evenings, June through September.

Summer Music Festival, Minori. Classical and jazz music concerts are scheduled throughout the summer along the Amalfi Coast, but the setting in Minori is particularly pleasant. Contact the tourist office (✆ **089-877087** or 089-877607) for a program. June through September.

Summer Fest, Conca dei Marini. This little town's special take on the Amalfi Coast Summer Festival is the performing arts, including theater, ballet, and art shows. Contact the tourist office (✆ **089-831301**) for a program. June through September.

July

Sagra del Limone (Lemon Fair), Massa Lubrense. Celebrating the fruit that characterizes so much of the local culture and cuisine, this 4-day festival (celebrating 34 years in 2008) includes walks in the countryside, farm visits, and culinary events. First weekend in July.

Opera and Drama Season at the Roman Theater, Benevento. The ancient Roman theater of Benevento is the venue for a full-fledged summer season of opera and drama. Contact the tourist office (✆ **0824-319911**). July through August.

Sagra del Tonno (Tuna Festival), Cetara. At this traditional celebration of tuna fishing, the town's main activity, you can partake in tuna tastings and musical events. Contact the tourist office (✆ **089-261474**) for more information.

Festival di Ravello, Ravello. This international music festival includes jazz, dance, and visual arts; you must make reservations well in advance for the most important performances. Contact the festival office (© **089-857096** or 199-109910; fax 089-858422; www.ravellofestival.com) for reservations. July through September.

Summer Program, Atrani. This rich program of music and art events is part of the Amalfi Coast Summer Festival. The events vary each summer but usually include classical music sunset concerts and exhibits by local and international artists. Contact the tourist office (© **089-871185**) for a schedule of events. July and August.

Summer Theater Festival, Scala. Each summer, Casa Romano becomes the setting of drama and concert performances. Contact the tourist office (© **089-858977** or 089-857325) for a schedule of events. July and August.

Jazz on the Coast, Minori. This international festival heralds jazz singers and musicians from around the world who come to perform with the Amalfi Coast as their backdrop. Concerts are usually scheduled over a period of 2 weeks starting at the end of July. Contact the local tourist office (©/fax **089-877087**; www.proloco.minori.sa.it). Last week in July and first week of August.

Caserta Summer Festival, Caserta (© **0823-353336;** www.casertasummerfestival.it). Going strong since 2005, this new music festival offers a rich program of events including musical performances and cabaret. July through September.

Festa del Mare, town of Ischia. These spectacular celebrations mark the occasion of the Festival of Sant'Anna. A procession of boats and floats crosses the harbor under the town's illuminated castle. July 26.

August

Sagra della Sfogliatella di Santa Rosa, Conca dei Marini. This delicious event celebrates the local version of *sfogliatella,* the most famous of Neapolitan pastries, filled with pastry cream and a sour cherry confection. August.

Summer Festival, Furore Marina. Art and music events take place in the *monazzeri.* Call © **089-830525** for a schedule. July and August.

Festival of the Assunta, Positano. In the 9th and 10th centuries A.D., when the Saracens had established themselves in nearby Agropoli (see chapter 9), the whole coast was endangered by their repeated incursions and bloody robberies. This festival reenacts the Saracens' attack on Positano and the miraculous intervention of the Madonna who, legend has it, saved the town. August 14 and August 15.

September

Festa di Piedigrotta, Naples (www.festadipiedigrotta.it). This centuries-old religious and musical festival has been revived after years of neglect. Coupled with a musical event celebrating 19th-century Neapolitan music (such as *O Sole Mio,* which was presented in 1898), it progressively lost its followers during the 1980s. Featuring religious and musical events, as well as a children's program and a parade of floats, the successful 2007 event was the first to be held in over 2 decades. First 2 weeks in September.

Festival Musica d'Estate (Summer Festival of Music), Positano. Celebrating its 39th year in 2006, this series of concerts focuses on chamber music. In addition to the concerts—which include everything from classical to jazz—you can sign up for classes taught by internationally renowned musicians. Call ✆ **089-875067** for a schedule of events. End of August to beginning of September.

Settembre al Borgo (September in the Village), Casertavecchia (www.casertamusica.com). In the romantic setting of the medieval town, this festival celebrates its 37th year in 2008. The ancient burg comes alive with performances focusing on a different theme each year; in 2007 it was the tradition of the open-air theater. Two weeks at the beginning of September.

Incontri Musicali Sorrentini (Sorrentine Musical Encounters), Sorrento. In 2007, the famous festival that has enlivened 35 summers in this delightful town resumed its original title and moved to September. It was as appealing as ever, with a rich program of musical events both in the traditional venue of the cloister of the church of St. Francis, and in other churches and gardens throughout the town. Ask the tourist office (✆ **081-8074033**) for a schedule of events. September through October.

Salerno Etnica, Salerno. This music festival is part of the celebrations for Salerno's patron saint, San Matteo. The focus is on music as an expression of culture and tradition. Contact the tourist office for a schedule of events (✆ **089-224744**). Week of September 21.

Santa Maria della Libera, Capri. Starting from the St. Costanzo in Marina Grande church and crossing the town of Capri, grand processions are staged at this festival, which includes music, fireworks, and market stalls. Contact the tourist office (✆ **081-8375308**) for more information. The Sunday closest to September 12.

Ischia Jazz Weekend, Ischia. This event is organized by the famous Umbria Jazz group, with important international performers. Call ✆ **081-4972777** for information. Usually second weekend of September.

October

Annali delle Arti (Arts Yearbook), regionwide. At this annual event exploring contemporary art around the world, museums, historical palaces, and archaeological areas throughout Campania become the seat for exhibits by important artists from the international art scene. Contact the regional tourist office at ✆ **081-6174239** for information. October through January.

November

Bread and Olive Oil, Vico Equense. At the heart of the production area of one of the best olive oils in Italy, this little town celebrates the pressing of the new olive harvest with extra-virgin olive-oil tastings, and an open house of one of the facilities. Contact the local tourist office for more information, at ✆ **081-8015752.** Last Sunday of November.

Feast of St. Andrew, Amalfi. St. Andrew, the patron of Amalfi and the protector of fishermen, is honored annually by local fishermen who run with his heavy statue on their shoulders from the beach up the hundreds of steps of the cathedral, and then present him with offerings of fish—both fresh and carved. The town also celebrates with games, folk shows, and magnificent fireworks. The feast is repeated in a mellower form on June 27, the anniversary of the day the saint miraculously saved the town from an attack by the Saracen pirates. November 30.

December

Sagra della Salsiccia e Ceppone (Sausage and Bonfire Fair), Sorrento. In this celebration of Saint Lucia, locals and visitors cook—and eat—about 200 pounds of delicious local

---

> *Tips* **Before You Leave Home: Tickets & Seats in Advance**
>
> You absolutely need advance reservations for the Capodimonte Museum in Naples (the one museum in Campania where lines are always several hours long in occasion of the many special exhibits) and for special guided tours of Pompeii, but you might want to make reservations for a number of other attractions and events as well. The best place to make reservations is **Pierreci** (© 063-9967050; www.pierreci.it), the official advance reservation service for a number of museums and events in Campania and in Italy. To get tickets for all kinds of events, the best Italy-based operators are **TicketOne** (© 023-92261 for an English-speaking operator; www.ticketone.it); **Charta** (www.charta.it); and **Viva Ticket** (www.vivaticket.it). They all have English-language websites where you can make reservations and purchase tickets. U.S.-based companies offering advance tickets for a variety of museums and events in Italy are convenient, but they are usually more expensive and cover only a small selection of monuments and events. The best of these is **Culturalitaly.com** (© 800/380-0014; fax 928/639-0388; www.culturalitaly.com), a Los Angeles–based company which offers seats and reservations for operatic performances in Naples, special guided tours in Pompeii, and even tickets to the famed Festival of Ravello. Most reservations carry a $10/£5 fee, plus the cost of the event.

---

sausages barbecued over a huge fire (prepared in the heart of the Santa Lucia neighborhood). The food is accompanied by bottles of the excellent local wine. December 13.

Avellino Christmas Concerts, Avellino. For 5 days, the town is alive with music as local choirs give concerts inside the town's beautiful cathedral. Contact the tourist office (© **0825-74695**) for a program. Usually December 13 through December 18.

Feast of the *Torrone*, San Marco dei Cavoti. The typical Christmas candy, the *torrone,* becomes an occasion for celebrations in the little town that has been famous for making its special version—the *croccantino*—since the Middle Ages. You can taste all the variations of the treat along Via del Torrone (Via Roma), and then watch the building of a giant *croccantino* by local masters in the town's main square. Call the tourist office at © **0824-984009.** December 8 and the following weekends until Christmas.

Divers' Procession to Grotta dello Smeraldo, Conca dei Marini. Each December and January, a special pilgrimage embarks to this town's greatest attraction, Grotta dello Smeraldo. Local and guest scuba divers swim from the beach to an underwater manger inside the grotto (see chapter 7). Call the visitor center in Amalfi at © **089-871107** for more information. December 24 and January 6.

Live Manger, Belvedere di San Leucio, Caserta. Come to see this hamlet turn the clock back to the 18th century with historical reenactments, music, and performances during the Christmas period. Contact © **333-8283690** or e-mail info@presepevaccheria.it for information. December 25 to January 6.

Live Manger, Pietrelcina. This picturesque little town near Benevento hosts another reenactment of Christmas, involving the whole town, with events spread over several days. December 27 through December 29.

Sagra della Zeppola (Feast of the Zeppola), Positano. Celebrants at this feast ring in the New Year by feasting on *zeppolas,* delicious fried sweet pastries, and by enjoying the Kermesse of dances, music, and fireworks on the beach of Marina Grande. December 31 through January 1.

5 Getting There

BY PLANE

Campania is served by Naples's **Capodichino Airport** (© **081-7896259;** www.gesac.it); its international airport code is **NAP.**

Fares are constantly changing, but you can expect to pay somewhere in the range of $460 to $1,460 (£230–£730) for a direct round-trip ticket from New York to Naples in coach class.

Flying time to Rome from New York, Newark, and Boston is 8 hours; from Chicago, 10 hours; and from Los Angeles, 12½ hours. Flying time to Milan from New York, Newark, and Boston is 8 hours; from Chicago, 9¼ hours; and from Los Angeles, 11½ hours.

Only Alitalia's vacation company **Eurofly** (© **091-5007704;** www.eurofly. it) offers transatlantic nonstop flights to Naples from New York. From elsewhere in North America and from Australia and New Zealand, you will have to fly first into Rome or Milan and take a connecting flight (Rome is only 50 min. away, and Milan about 90 min.). You can also fly nonstop into Naples from most European airports and from all Italian ones.

Alitalia (© **800/223-5730;** www. alitalia.com), the Italian national airline, offers the most nonstop flights to Rome and Milan from different North American cities, including Atlanta, Boston, Chicago, Miami, New York (JFK), Newark, Toronto, and Washington, D.C. From Milan or Rome, Alitalia can easily book connecting domestic flights if your final destination is Naples. Alitalia participates in the frequent-flier programs of other airlines, including Continental and US Airways.

American Airlines (© **800/433-7300;** www.aa.com) offers daily nonstop flights to Rome from Chicago's O'Hare airport, with flights from all parts of American's vast network making connections into Chicago. **Delta** (© **800/241-4141;** www.delta.com) flies from New York's JFK airport to Milan, Venice, and Rome; separate flights depart every evening for both destinations. **US Airways** (© **800/428-4322;** www.usairways. com) offers one flight daily to Rome out of Philadelphia (you can connect through Philly from most major U.S. cities). **Continental** (© **800/525-0280;** www. continental.com) flies five times a week to Rome and Milan from its hub in Newark. **United** (© **800/538-2929;** www.united.com) and **Northwest/KLM Airlines** (© **800/447-4747;** www.nwa. com) offer nonstop flights to Rome or Milan from their hub in the United States, at least during peak season.

Tips Don't Stow It—Ship It

Though pricey, it is worthwhile to travel luggage free, particularly if you're toting heavy or cumbersome items such as sports equipment, meetings materials, or baby equipment. Specialists in door-to-door luggage delivery include **Virtual Bellhop, SkyCap International** (www.skycapinternational.com), **Luggage Express,** and **Sports Express** (www.sportsexpress.com).

Flying with Film & Video

Never pack film—exposed or unexposed—in checked bags, because the new, more powerful scanners in U.S. airports can fog film. The film you carry with you can be damaged by scanners as well. X-ray damage is cumulative; the faster the film, and the more times you put it through a scanner, the more likely the damage. Film under 800 ASA is usually safe for up to five scans. If you're taking your film through additional scans, U.S. regulations permit you to demand hand inspections. In international airports, you're at the mercy of airport officials. On international flights, store your film in transparent baggies, so you can remove it easily before you go through scanners. Keep in mind that airports are not the only places where your camera may be scanned: Highly trafficked attractions are X-raying visitors' bags with increasing frequency.

Most photo supply stores sell protective pouches designed to block damaging X-rays. The pouches fit both film and loaded cameras. They should protect your film in checked baggage, but they also may raise alarms and result in a hand inspection.

You'll have little to worry about if you are traveling with **digital cameras**. Unlike film, which is sensitive to light, the digital camera and storage cards are not affected by airport X-rays, according to Nikon. Carry-on scanners will not damage **videotape** in video cameras, but the magnetic fields emitted by the walk-through security gateways and handheld inspection wands will. Always place your loaded camcorder on the screening conveyor belt or have it hand-inspected. Be sure your batteries are charged, as you may be required to turn the device on to ensure that it's what it appears to be.

Air Canada (② 888/247-2262; www.aircanada.ca) has flights daily from Toronto to Rome. Two of the flights are nonstop; the others touch down en route in Montreal, depending on the schedule.

From Australia, **Qantas** (② 13-13-13; www.qantas.com) offers nonstop flights to Rome, daily from Melbourne and several days a week from Sydney.

Major European carriers such as **British Airways** (② 800/AIRWAYS; www.britishairways.com); **Virgin Atlantic Airways** (② 800/862-8621; www.virgin-atlantic.com); **Air France** (② 800/237-2747; www.airfrance.com); **Northwest/KLM** (② 800/374-7747; www.klm.com); **Lufthansa** (② 800/399-LUFT; www.lufthansa-usa.com); **Iberia** (② 800/772-4642; www.iberia.com); **Air Lingus** (② 866/886-8844; www.airlingus.com); **Austrian Airlines** (② 800/843-0002; www.aua.com); and **Finnair** (② 800/950-5000; www.finnair.com) offer nonstop flights to Naples—and a number of other Italian airports—from their hubs in Europe, as well as attractive transatlantic deals with a stopover in their European hub. Of the smaller European companies, **EasyJet** (② 0871-244-2366 from the U.K.; www.easyjet.com), **BMI** (② 0870-6070-555 from the U.K.; ② 44 (0)1332 64 8181 from outside the U.K.; www.flybmi.com), **Air One** (② 199-207080 within Italy or 06-4888069; www.flyairone.it), and **Meridiana** (② 0789-52682; www.meridiana.it) all fly nonstop to Naples from various destinations within Europe.

ARRIVING AT THE AIRPORT

Capodichino is a small but well-run airport that is easy to get around. The arrival concourse has a bank with ATM, currency exchange booth, and tourist information desk; public transportation is just outside (see below). If your flight to Naples originates from a Schengen country within the European Union (Austria, Belgium, Denmark, Finland, France, Germany, Greece, Iceland, Italy, Luxembourg, the Netherlands, Norway, Portugal, Spain, or Sweden), you'll have already cleared customs and be able to exit the airport without further ado (except for possible random security checks). If Naples is your port of entry to the Schengen area, you'll need to pass passport control and, after retrieving your luggage, go through customs, where random luggage checks are performed.

GETTING INTO TOWN FROM THE AIRPORT

About 7km (4 miles) from the city center, the airport is only 15 minutes away. The easiest way to get into town is by taking a **taxi** directly to your hotel: The flat rate for Naples is 20€ ($27/£14) plus gratuities. For a limousine booked through your hotel, you'll pay about 35€ ($49/£25). If you don't have much luggage, consider riding the **shuttle bus** (© 800-639525; www.anm.it): At 3€ ($4.20/£2.10), it is a cheaper alternative. With departures every 30 minutes, it stops on Corso Garibaldi near Napoli Centrale train station, and in Piazza Municipio at the heart of the historic district. Shuttle bus service to other nearby towns (Sorrento and Castellammare di Stabia, for instance) is also available; see "Getting There" under each destination. Of course, you can hire a limousine service to these destinations as well.

BY BOAT & FERRY

The region is served by two major ports, Naples and Salerno. Naples is the main port of central Italy, receiving daily ships and ferries from international destinations. Salerno is somewhat smaller but has a good share of traffic as well.

A number of cruise-ship companies sail to Naples, especially in the good season, from spring well into fall. Arriving in Naples by ship is a magnificent experience and the best approach to Campania. You'll land at **Stazione Marittima,** only steps from the Maschio Angioino in the heart of the historical district, the *città antica.* Most hydrofoil regular service operates from nearby **Mergellina's Terminal Aliscafi.**

The major companies offering regular service are **Tirrenia** (© **199-123199** or 081-2514711; www.tirrenia.it), with boats to Cagliari and Palermo; **Siremar** (© **081-5800340;** www.siremar.it), with ships to the Aeolian Islands and Milazzo; **TTTLines** (© **800-915365**), with ships to Catania and Palermo; **Medmar** (© **081-5513352**), with boats to Tunis (© **081-3334411**); **SNAV** (© **081-4285555** or 081-4285111; www.snav.it), with boats to Palermo, Sardinia, and the Aeolian and Pontine islands.

Salerno is a major harbor, with regular international service from Valencia in Spain, Malta (La Valletta), and Tunis via **Grimaldi Ferries** (© **081-496444;** www.grimaldi-ferries.com), which also offers regular service to Palermo. **Caronte & Tourist** (© **800-627414** toll-free within Italy, or 089-2582528; www.carontetourist.it) travels from Salerno to Catania and Messina.

BY CAR

If you're already on the continent, particularly in a neighboring country such as Austria, you may want to drive to Naples. It's possible to drive from London to Naples, a distance of 1,951km (1,210 miles), via Calais/Boulogne/Dunkirk, or 1,888km (1,170 miles) via Oostende/Zeebrugge, not counting channel crossings by hovercraft, ferry, or the Chunnel. If you cross over from England and arrive at one of the continental ports, you still face a 24-hour drive. Most drivers play it safe and budget 3 days for the journey.

Most of the roads from Western Europe leading into Italy are toll free, with some notable exceptions. If you use the Swiss superhighway network, you'll have to buy a special tax sticker at the frontier. You'll also pay to go through the St. Gotthard Tunnel into Italy. Crossings from France can be through the Mont Blanc Tunnel, for which you'll pay; or you can leave the French Riviera at Menton and drive directly into Italy along the Italian Riviera toward San Remo.

If you don't want to drive such distances, ask a travel agent to book you on a Motorail arrangement whereby the train carries your car. This service, however, is good only to Milan, as there are no car-and-sleeper expresses running the 785km (487 miles) south to Naples.

If you are driving to save money, think again. All highways in Italy are toll roads, and fuel prices are quite high, with gasoline in Europe rating among the highest prices around. Also, we recommend using a car only to explore the most remote areas of Campania; if these areas are not on your travel itinerary, you'll be much happier—and safer—using public transportation (see "Getting Around by Car," later in this chapter).

If you decide to drive, you will need an **International Driver's License** in Italy only if you are driving a private car. Apply for your license in the United States at any **American Automobile Association (AAA)** branch; contact **AAA's national headquarters** (© 800/222-4357 or 407/444-4300; www.aaa.com). Remember that an International Driver's License is valid only if physically accompanied by your original driver's license and only if signed on the back. Canadians can get the address of the nearest **Canadian Automobile Association** by calling © 613/247-0117; or go to www.caa.ca.

To rent a car in Italy, a driver must have a valid driver's license obtained at least a year before the trip, and a valid passport. Most companies require a minimum age of 23 or 25, but a few will accept a minimum age of 21 for their cheaper models. Most rental companies will not rent a car to drivers older than 75. Insurance on all vehicles is compulsory and can be purchased at any reputable rental firm. You will also need a valid credit card (not a prepaid or debit card) for a regular car and two credit cards for a deluxe model; cash payments will not be accepted.

Cars in Italy have manual shift, but you can request a car with automatic shift; they usually rent at a premium.

Besides the major international rental companies—**Avis** (© 800/331-1212; www.avis.com), **Budget** (© 800/472-3325; www.budget.com), and **Hertz** (© 800/654-3131; www.hertz.com)—other companies specializing in European car rentals are **Auto Europe** (© 800/223-5555; www.autoeurope.com), **Europe by Car** (© 800/223-1516 or 212/581-3040 in New York; www.europebycar.com), and **Kemwel Holiday Auto** (© 800/678-0678; www.kemwel.com). The primary rental company in Campania and Italy is **Maggiore** (© 1478-67067 toll-free in Italy; www.maggiore.it), associated with **National** in the U.S. (© 800/CAR-RENT; www.nationalcar.com). Another reputable and sometimes cheaper company is **Sixt** (© 888/749-8227 in the United States; © 199-100666 in Italy; www.e-sixt.it or www.sixtusa.com for U.S. citizens).

In some cases, slight discounts are offered to members of the American Automobile Association (AAA) or AARP (formerly called American Association of Retired Persons). Be sure to ask when you book. Renting online usually will get you the best prices, but it is worth checking with the local rental office for a better deal. Package discounts are sometimes available when you book your car together with your flight.

For the best routes between various destinations within the region, refer to the map on p. 13.

BY TRAIN

The region's railways are often the most convenient way to get from one destination to another. Electric high-velocity trains have made travel within Europe and Italy faster and more comfortable than ever. Italy's **ETR** (ElettroTreno-Rapido) trains travel at speeds of up to 233kmph (145 mph). A new high-velocity line recently added to Naples (see below) is being extended south.

Naples lies on Italy's main southern corridor, making it an easily accessible from other Italian and European towns. The new Alta Velocità (high-speed) train takes only 87 minutes between Rome and Naples, making it by far the best way to move between the two cities; regular trains take about 2½ hours for the same connection. With easy connections to Sorrento, Salerno, Caserta, Benevento, and the Vesuvian attractions of Herculaneum and Pompeii, the train is also a good way to move between towns within Campania, the added advantage being that the rail station is usually in the center of town, well connected by public transportation and taxis. For fares and information, contact the Italian railroad company **Trenitalia** (© **892021** from anywhere in Italy; www.trenitalia.it).

If you plan to travel extensively in Europe by train, you might want to take advantage of one of the greatest travel bargains: The **Eurailpass,** which permits unlimited first-class rail travel in any country in western Europe (except the British Isles), and in Hungary in eastern Europe. Oddly, it doesn't include travel on the rail lines of Sardinia, which are organized independently of the rail lines of the rest of Italy.

The advantages are tempting: in addition to your train pass, you'll get a free timetable for service within Europe as well as a traveler's guide including useful information and a map of Europe. The system is ticketless; simply show the pass to the ticket collector and then settle back to enjoy the scenery. Seat reservations are required on some trains. Many of the trains have couchettes (sleeping cars), for which an extra fee is charged. Obviously, the 2- or 3-month traveler gets the greatest economic advantages. To obtain full advantage of a 15-day or 1-month pass, you'd have to spend a great deal of time on the train.

Eurailpass holders are entitled to considerable reductions on certain buses and ferries as well. You'll get a 20% reduction on second-class accommodations from certain companies operating ferries between Naples and Palermo or for crossings to Sardinia and Malta.

At presstime, a **Eurailpass** was $675 (£338) for 15 days, $1,089 (£545) for 1 month, and $1,899 (£950) for 3 months. Children age 3 and younger travel free, provided that they don't occupy a seat; children age 4 to 11 are charged half-fare. If you're younger than age 26, you can buy a **Eurail Youthpass,** entitling you to unlimited second-class travel for $439 (£220) for 15 days, $709 (£355) for 1 month, and $1,235 (£618) for 3 months. Other options exist, including selected-countries passes, regional passes, and national passes. The **Eurail Italy pass** is available for 3 to 10 travel days within a 2-month period; it comes in both first- and second-class options. The cheaper pass is $195 (£98) and the most expensive is $449 (£225).

Get all the details and purchase the pass directly online at **www.eurail.com**. If you prefer to discuss your options with a travel agent, contact **Rail Europe**

(© 877/272-RAIL; www.raileurope.com) or your own travel agent, but they'll charge a commission. You can also buy your Eurailpass at any major train station in Europe, but it might be more expensive than purchasing online.

For details on rail travel from the **United Kingdom,** stop at or contact the **International Rail Centre,** Victoria Station, London SW1V 1JZ (© 087-05848848). The staff can help you find the best option for the trip you're planning. Some of the most popular are the **Inter-Rail** and **Under 26** passes, entitling you to unlimited second-class travel in 26 European countries.

6 Money & Costs

It's always advisable to bring money in a variety of forms on a vacation: a mix of cash, credit cards, and traveler's checks. You should also exchange enough petty cash to cover airport incidentals, tipping, and transportation to your hotel before you leave home, or withdraw money upon arrival at an airport ATM.

In many international destinations—Italy included—ATMs offer the best exchange rates. Avoid exchanging money at commercial exchange bureaus and hotels, which often have the highest transaction fees.

CURRENCY

The **euro** (EUR), the single European currency, became the official currency of Italy and 11 other participating countries on January 1, 1999. You will still occasionally run into prices quoted in both euros and lire, but for all other purposes, the old currency, the Italian lira, was completely replaced by the euro on January 1, 2002. Exchange rates of participating countries are locked into a common currency that fluctuates against the dollar. For more details on the euro, check out **www.europa.eu.int/euro**.

Conversion ratios between the U.S. dollar and other currencies fluctuate, and their differences could affect the costs of your holiday. The figures reflected in the currency chart below were valid at the time of writing, but they might not be valid by the time of your departure. Check for more updated rates prior to making any serious commitments. For up-to-the minute exchange rates between the euro and the dollar, check the currency converter website **www.xe.com/ucc**.

Exchange rates are more favorable at the point of arrival. Nevertheless, it's often helpful to exchange at least some money before going abroad. (Standing in line at the *cambio,* or exchange bureau, in the Milan or Rome airport could make you miss the next bus leaving for downtown.) Inquire at any local American Express or Thomas Cook office or major bank. Or order euros in advance from **American Express** (© 800/221-7282; www.americanexpress.com) or **Thomas Cook** (© 800/223-7373; www.thomascook.com). Note the rates and ask about commission fees; it can sometimes pay to shop around.

ATMS

The easiest and best way to get cash away from home is from an ATM (automated teller machine), sometimes referred to as a "cash machine," or a "cashpoint." The **Cirrus** (© 800/424-7787; www.mastercard.com) and **PLUS** (© 800/843-7587; www.visa.com) networks span the globe. Go to your bank card's website to find ATM locations at your destination. Be sure you know your daily withdrawal limit before you depart. *Note:* Many banks impose a fee every time you use a card at another bank's ATM, and that fee can be higher for international transactions (up to $5/£2.50 or more) than for domestic ones (where they're rarely more than $2/£1). In addition, the bank from which you withdraw cash may charge its own fee. For international withdrawal fees, ask your bank.

Note: Banks that are members of the **Global ATM Alliance** charge no transaction fees for cash withdrawals at other Alliance member ATMs; these include Bank of America, Scotiabank (Canada, Caribbean & Mexico), Barclays (U.K. and parts of Africa), and Deutsche Bank (Germany, Poland, Spain, and Italy), and BNP Paribus (France).

Make sure that the PINs on your bank cards and credit cards will work in Italy. You'll likely need a **four-digit code** (six digits may not work), so if you have a six-digit code you'll want to go into your

bank and get a new PIN for your trip. If you're unsure about this, contact Cirrus or PLUS (see above). Be sure to check the daily withdrawal limit at the same time.

CREDIT CARDS

Credit cards are another safe way to carry money. They also provide a convenient record of all your expenses, and they generally offer relatively good exchange rates. You can withdraw cash advances from your credit cards at banks or ATMs but high fees make credit card cash advances a pricey way to get cash. Keep in mind that you'll pay interest from the moment of your withdrawal, even if you pay your monthly bills on time. Also, note that many banks now assess a 1% to 3%

The Euro, the U.S. Dollar & the British Pound

For American Readers After inception of the euro, the U.S. dollar and the euro traded on par for a bit (in other words, $1 approximately equaled 1€). But as this book went to press, the euro had gained strength over the years against the dollar. In converting prices to U.S. dollars, we used a conversion rate of 1€ = $1.40.

For British Readers At this writing, £1 = approximately $2, and approximately €1.44. These were the rates of exchange used to calculate the values in the table below.

Euro €	US$	UK£	Euro €	US$	UK£
1.00	1.40	.70	75.00	105.00	52.50
2.00	2.80	1.40	100.00	140.00	70.00
3.00	4.20	2.10	125.00	175.00	87.50
4.00	5.60	2.80	150.00	210.00	105.00
5.00	7.00	3.50	175.00	245.00	122.50
6.00	8.40	4.20	200.00	280.00	140.00
7.00	9.80	4.90	225.00	315.00	157.50
8.00	11.20	5.60	250.00	350.00	175.00
9.00	12.60	6.30	275.00	385.00	192.50
10.00	14.00	7.00	300.00	420.00	210.00
15.00	21.00	10.50	350.00	490.00	245.00
20.00	28.00	14.00	400.00	560.00	280.00
25.00	35.00	17.50	500.00	700.00	350.00
50.00	70.00	35.00	1000.00	1400.00	700.00

What Things Cost in Naples

Item	Euro €	US$	UK£
A metro or city bus ride	1.00	1.40	.70
Can of soda	2.00	2.80	1.40
Pay-phone call	.20	.28	.14
Movie ticket	8.00	11.20	5.60
Caffè lungo (American-style espresso)	1.00	1.40	.70
Ticket to the Museo Nazionale Capodimonte (including reservation)	9.00	12.60	6.30
Gasoline (per gallon)	6.00	8.40	4.20
Taxi from the airport	20.00	28.00	14.00
Moderate 3-course dinner for one w/out alcohol	30.00	42.00	21.00
Moderate hotel room (double)	225.00	315.00	157.50
Liter of house wine in a restaurant	10.00	14.00	7.00
First-class letter to United States (or any overseas country)	.85	1.20	.60

"transaction fee" on *all* charges you incur abroad (whether you're using the local currency or your native currency). Visa and MasterCard are almost universally accepted in Italy, followed by American Express. Diners Club and Discover are less widely accepted.

TRAVELER'S CHECKS

You can buy traveler's checks at most banks. They are offered in denominations of $20, $50, $100, $500, and sometimes $1,000. Generally, you'll pay a service charge ranging from 1% to 4%.

The most popular traveler's checks are offered by **American Express** (© 800/807-6233 or © 800/221-7282 for cardholders—this number accepts collect calls, offers service in several foreign languages, and exempts Amex gold and platinum cardholders from the 1% fee); **Visa** (© 800/732-1322)—AAA members can obtain Visa checks for a $9.95 fee (for checks up to $1,500) at most AAA offices or by calling © 866/339-3378; and **MasterCard** (© 800/223-9920).

Be sure to keep a record of the traveler's checks serial numbers separate from your checks in the event that they are stolen or lost. You'll get a refund faster if you know the numbers.

American Express, Thomas Cook, Visa, and **MasterCard** offer **foreign currency traveler's checks,** useful if you're traveling to one country or to the Euro zone; they're accepted at locations where dollar checks may not be.

Another option is the prepaid traveler's check card, a reloadable card that works much like a debit card but isn't linked to your checking account. The now defunct **American Express Travelers Cheque Card,** for example, requires a minimum deposit, sets a maximum balance, and has an issuance fee of $14.95. You can withdraw money from an ATM (for a fee of $2.50 per transaction, not including bank fees), and the funds can be purchased in dollars, euros, or pounds. If you lose the card, your available funds will be refunded within 24 hours.

7 Travel Insurance

The cost of travel insurance varies widely, depending on the destination, the cost and length of your trip, your age and health, and the type of trip you're taking, but expect to pay between 5% and 8% of the vacation itself. You can get estimates from various providers through **InsureMyTrip.com**. Enter your trip cost and dates, your age, and other information, for prices from more than a dozen companies.

U.K. citizens and their families who make more than one trip abroad per year may find an annual travel insurance policy works out cheaper. Check **www.money supermarket.com**, which compares prices across a wide range of providers for single- and multi-trip policies.

Most big travel agents offer their own insurance and will probably try to sell you their package when you book a holiday. Think before you sign. **Britain's Consumers' Association** recommends that you insist on seeing the policy and reading the fine print before buying travel insurance. **The Association of British Insurers** (© 020/7600-3333; www.abi. org.uk) gives advice by phone and publishes *Holiday Insurance,* a free guide to policy provisions and prices. You might also shop around for better deals: Try **Columbus Direct** (© 0870/033-9988; www.columbusdirect.net).

TRIP-CANCELLATION INSURANCE

Trip-cancellation insurance will help retrieve your money if you have to back out of a trip or depart early, or if your travel supplier goes bankrupt. Trip cancellation traditionally covers such events as sickness, natural disasters, and State Department advisories. The latest news in trip-cancellation insurance is the availability of **expanded hurricane coverage** and the **"any-reason"** cancellation coverage—which costs more but covers cancellations made for any reason. You won't get back 100% of your prepaid trip cost, but you'll be refunded a substantial portion. **TravelSafe** (© 888/885-7233; www.travelsafe.com) offers both types of coverage. Expedia also offers any-reason cancellation coverage for its air-hotel packages.

For details, contact one of the following recommended insurers: **Access America** (© 866/807-3982; www.access america.com); **Travel Guard International** (© 800/826-4919; www.travel guard.com); **Travel Insured International** (© 800/243-3174; www.travel insured.com); and **Travelex Insurance Services** (© 888/457-4602; www.travelex-insurance.com).

MEDICAL INSURANCE

For travel overseas, most U.S. health plans (including Medicare and Medicaid) do not provide coverage, and the ones that do often require you to pay for services upfront and reimburse you only after you return home.

As a safety net, you may want to buy travel medical insurance, particularly if you're traveling to a remote or high-risk area where emergency evacuation might be necessary. If you require additional medical insurance, try **MEDEX Assistance** (© 410/453-6300; www.medex assist.com) or **Travel Assistance International** (© 800/821-2828; www.travel assistance.com; for general information on services, call the company's **Worldwide Assistance Services, Inc.,** at © 800/777-8710).

Canadians should check with their provincial health plan offices or call **Health Canada** (© 866/225-0709; www.hc-sc.gc.ca) to find out the extent of their coverage and what documentation and receipts they must take home in case they are treated overseas.

LOST-LUGGAGE INSURANCE

On international flights (including U.S. portions of international trips), baggage coverage is limited to approximately $9.07 per pound, up to approximately $635 per checked bag. If you plan to check items more valuable than what's covered by the standard liability, see if your homeowner's policy covers your valuables, get baggage insurance as part of your comprehensive travel-insurance package, or buy Travel Guard's "BagTrak" product.

If your luggage is lost, immediately file a lost-luggage claim at the airport, detailing the luggage contents. Most airlines require that you report delayed, damaged, or lost baggage within 4 hours of arrival. The airlines are required to deliver luggage, once found, directly to your house or destination free of charge.

8 Health

STAYING HEALTHY

There are no particular health concerns in Campania. A recent small outbreak of Chikungunya Fever (a tropical disease) was limited to northeastern Italy and has had no consequences in Campania. It is always, however, a good idea to protect yourself from mosquito bites even in the most developed countries, as an increasing number of diseases previously contained within the tropical areas of the world have started spreading.

During the past couple of years Naples and its suburbs—and occasionally other areas of the region—have been enmired in a political **sanitation crisis.** Garbage collectors have been on strike in response to the lack of sufficient dump facilities, and refuse has subsequently accumulated in many areas. As a form of protest, residents resorted to burning the piles of garbage, creating toxic fumes, which were particularly dangerous this summer. The authorities have largely tackled the problem, but, should it reoccur during your visit, avoid the fumes as they can aggravate respiratory problems, particularly in warmer months.

GENERAL AVAILABILITY OF HEALTH CARE

There are no special health requirements for travel to Campania and Italy.

Over-the-counter medicines are widely available, and **prescriptions** are easily filled in any pharmacy. **Pharmacies** are abundant: even small towns will have one. Names of products will be different, so make sure you know the active ingredient of your brand and that your doctor writes the prescription clearly, mentioning both the generic name and its dosage. Most likely you will find an English-speaking doctor in the pharmacy who will be able to assist you.

Contact the International Association for Medical Assistance to Travelers (IAMAT; © 716/754-4883 or, in Canada, 416/652-0137; www.iamat.org) for tips on travel and health concerns in the countries you're visiting, and for lists of local, English-speaking doctors. The United States Centers for Disease Control and Prevention (© 800/311-3435; www.cdc.gov) provides up-to-date information on health hazards by region or country and offers tips on food safety. Travel Health Online (www.tripprep. com), sponsored by a consortium of travel medicine practitioners, may also offer helpful advice on traveling abroad. You can find listings of reliable medical clinics overseas at the International Society of Travel Medicine (www.istm.org).

COMMON AILMENTS

DIETARY RED FLAGS You should always exercise caution when eating seafood, especially in summer when improperly refrigerated seafood spoils faster. Also, be cautious of street food, only buying from vendors whose facilities look neat and clean. Water in Campania's cities and towns is potable. The quality varies in some areas of Naples, but hotels, restaurants, and bars all have their own water-purification systems. If you're still concerned, order bottled water.

Vegetarians can go into any restaurant in Campania, even those specializing in meat and fish, and find a variety of vegetarian dishes on the menu—from antipasti to pasta dishes. Most restaurants will try their best to accommodate your dietary restrictions.

SUN/ELEMENTS/EXTREME WEATHER EXPOSURE Do not underestimate the sun when you visit archeological areas such as Pompeii and Herculaneum in the summer, as heat stroke is not unheard of. Always use sunscreen and a hat, and carry adequate water supply.

WHAT TO DO IF YOU GET SICK AWAY FROM HOME

You'll find English-speaking doctors at hospitals with well-trained medical staff nearly everywhere in Italy. All major cities and towns in Campania have reputable hospitals and excellent private clinics, and smaller facilities exist in more remote places. We have listed the best hospital or local medical facility under "Fast Facts" for each destination.

For travel abroad, you may have to pay all medical costs upfront and be reimbursed later. Medicare and Medicaid do not provide coverage for medical costs outside the U.S. Before leaving home, find out what medical services your health insurance covers. To protect yourself, consider buying medical travel insurance (see "Medical Insurance," under "Travel Insurance," above).

Very few health insurance plans pay for medical evacuation back to the U.S. (which can cost $10,000 and up). A number of companies offer medical evacuation services anywhere in the world. If you're ever hospitalized more than 150 miles from home, **MedjetAssist** (© **800/527-7478;** www.medjetassistance.com) will pick you up and fly you to the hospital of your choice virtually anywhere in the world in a medically equipped and staffed aircraft 24 hours a day, 7 days a week. Annual memberships are $225 individual, $350 family; you can also purchase short-term memberships.

U.K. nationals will need a **European Health Insurance Card (EHIC)** to receive free or reduced-costs health benefits during a visit to a European Economic Area (EEA) country (European Union countries plus Iceland, Liechtenstein, and

---

Avoiding "Economy-Class Syndrome"

Deep vein thrombosis, or as it's known in the world of flying, "economy-class syndrome," is a blood clot that develops in a deep vein. It's a potentially deadly condition that can be caused by sitting in cramped conditions—such as an airplane cabin—for too long. During a flight (especially a long-haul flight), get up, walk around, and stretch your legs every 60 to 90 minutes to keep your blood flowing. Other preventative measures include frequent flexing of the legs while sitting, drinking lots of water, and avoiding alcohol and sleeping pills. If you have a history of deep vein thrombosis, heart disease, or another condition that puts you at high risk, some experts recommend wearing compression stockings or taking anticoagulants when you fly; always ask your physician about the best course for you. Symptoms of deep vein thrombosis include leg pain or swelling, or even shortness of breath.

Healthy Travels to You

The following government websites offer up-to-date health-related travel advice.
- **Australia:** www.dfat.gov.au/travel
- **Canada:** www.hc-sc.gc.ca/index_e.html
- **U.K.:** www.dh.gov.uk/PolicyAndGuidance/HealthAdviceForTravellers
- **U.S.:** www.cdc.gov/travel

Norway) or Switzerland. The European Health Insurance Card replaces the E111 form, which is no longer valid. For advice, ask at your local post office or see www.dh.gov.uk/travellers.

We list **hospitals** and **emergency numbers** under "Fast Facts," p. 55.

If you suffer from a chronic illness, consult your doctor before your departure.

Pack **prescription medications** in your carry-on luggage, and carry them in their original containers, with pharmacy labels—otherwise they won't make it through security. Carry generic names of prescription medicines, in case a local pharmacist is unfamiliar with the brand.

9 Safety

STAYING SAFE

Pedestrians are at increasing risk in large cities, and Naples is one of them. Your biggest risk is being run over by a car or a motor scooter. Always be vigilant, particularly when crossing the street or walking in narrow streets with no sidewalks. Look very carefully before crossing, even if you have a green light and are using a pedestrian crossing.

The crime rate in Italy and Campania is generally low, with most crimes occurring only in Naples. Even there, crime is concentrated only in certain parts of the city, such as near the Stazione Centrale and in the poverty-stricken neighborhoods of the city's suburbs. The countryside is quite tranquil.

The most common menace, especially in Naples, is the plague of pickpockets and car robbers. Pickpockets are active in all crowded places, particularly tourist areas. Note that they are sometimes dressed in elegant attire, and often work in pairs or groups, using various techniques, from distraction routines to razor blades to cut the bottom of your bag. Always be vigilant.

The city is also where most car thefts occur, although vehicles are always at risk, except in the most remote and quiet rural areas. Never leave valuables inside your car, never travel with your doors unlocked, and always park in a garage with an attendant. Be careful when traveling on highways at night as robbery scams have been reported; see "Getting Around by Car," later in this chapter.

We have heard a few reports of robberies performed by individuals befriending travelers at stations, airports, and bars, and taking advantage of their lower level of vigilance caused by alcohol ingestion, or even induced by drinks laced with sleeping drugs. Choose your friends carefully.

One further concern is the ATM skimming device: Attached to legitimate bank ATMs usually located in tourist areas, these electronic devices can capture your credit card information and record your PIN through a pin-hole camera. Always make sure the ATM you are planning to use does not look as if it has been tampered with, and cover the keypad with one hand as you enter your PIN.

Italian law is generally fair; but if you commit a crime, the law will be enforced. Do not drink and drive, do not traffic or carry illegal drugs, and do not engage in illicit sexual activities. While there is no prohibition on alcohol consumption except when driving, loud and drunken behavior is severely punishable.

DEALING WITH DISCRIMINATION

Naples and its environs are remarkably open-minded. For the most part, Naples is a safe haven for all kinds of religious, sexual, and cultural minorities. Even solo woman travelers, who used to face harassment in the once seedy areas of the historical centre, can now visit in relative peace (See "Women Travelers" in "Specialized Travel Resources," below).

10 Specialized Travel Resources

TRAVELERS WITH DISABILITIES

Laws in Campania and in Italy have compelled train stations, airports, hotels, and most restaurants to follow a stricter set of regulations for **wheelchair accessibility** to restrooms, ticket counters, and the like. Museums and other attractions have conformed to the regulations, which mimic many of those presently in effect in the United States. Always call ahead to check on accessibility in hotels, restaurants, and sights you want to visit.

Organizations that offer a vast range of resources and assistance to travelers with disabilities include **MossRehab** (© 800/ CALL-MOSS; www.mossresourcenet. org); the **American Foundation for the Blind** (AFB; © 800/232-5463; www. afb.org); and **SATH** (Society for Accessible Travel & Hospitality; © 212/447-7284; www.sath.org). **AirAmbulance Card.com** is now partnered with SATH and allows you to preselect top-notch hospitals in case of an emergency.

Access-Able Travel Source (© 303/ 232-2979; www.access-able.com) offers a comprehensive database on travel agents from around the world with experience in accessible travel; destination-specific access information; and links to such resources as service animals, equipment rentals, and access guides.

Many travel agencies offer customized tours and itineraries for travelers with disabilities. Among them are **Flying Wheels Travel** (© 507/451-5005; www.flying

wheelstravel.com); and **Accessible Journeys** (© 800/846-4537 or 610/521-0339; www.disabilitytravel.com).

Flying with Disability (www.flying-with-disability.org) is a comprehensive information source on airplane travel. **Avis Rent a Car** (© 888/879-4273) has an "Avis Access" program that offers services for customers with special travel needs. These include specially outfitted vehicles with swivel seats, spinner knobs, and hand controls; mobility scooter rentals; and accessible bus service. Be sure to reserve well in advance.

Also check out the quarterly magazine *Emerging Horizons* (www.emerging horizons.com), available by subscription ($16.95 per year U.S.; $21.95 outside U.S.). The "Accessible Travel" link at **Mobility-Advisor.com** (www.mobility-advisor.com) offers a variety of travel resources to persons with disabilities.

British travelers should contact **Holiday Care** (© 0845-124-9971 in the U.K. only; www.holidaycare.org.uk) to access a wide range of travel information and resources for elderly people and those with disabilities.

GAY & LESBIAN TRAVELERS

Since 1861, Campania and Italy have had liberal legislation regarding homosexuality. Ischia and Capri have long been gay meccas, and you'll find a somewhat active gay life in Naples. Still, open displays of same-sex affection are sometimes frowned upon in the highly Catholic country (despite the fact that people in Campania are very physical, and men and women alike embrace when saying hello and goodbye).

ARCI Gay (www.arcigay.it) is the country's leading gay organization, with branches throughout Campania and Italy.

The International Gay and Lesbian Travel Association (IGLTA; ✆ 800/448-8550 or 954/776-2626; www.iglta.org) is the trade association for the gay and lesbian travel industry, and offers an online directory of gay- and lesbian-friendly travel businesses and tour operators.

Many agencies offer tours and travel itineraries specifically for gay and lesbian travelers. **Above and Beyond Tours** (✆ 800/397-2681; www.abovebeyond tours.com) are gay Australia tour specialists. San Francisco–based **Now, Voyager** (✆ 800/255-6951; www.nowvoyager. com) offers worldwide trips and cruises, and **Olivia** (✆ 800/631-6277; www. olivia.com) offers lesbian cruises and resort vacations.

Gay.com Travel (✆ 800/929-2268 or 415/644-8044; www.gay.com/travel or www.outandabout.com) is an excellent online successor to the popular *Out & About* print magazine. It provides regularly updated information about gay-owned, gay-oriented, and gay-friendly lodging, dining, sightseeing, nightlife, and shopping establishments in every important destination worldwide. British travelers should click on the "Travel" link at **www.uk.gay.com** for advice and gay-friendly trip ideas. The Canadian website **GayTraveler** (gaytraveler.ca) offers ideas and advice for gay travel all over the world.

The following travel guides are available at many bookstores, or you can order them from any online bookseller: *Spartacus International Gay Guide, 35th Edition* (Bruno Gmünder Verlag; www.

spartacusworld.com/gayguide) and *Odysseus: The International Gay Travel Planner, 17th Edition* (www.odyusa. com); and the *Damron* guides (www. damron.com), with separate, annual books for gay men and lesbians.

SENIOR TRAVEL

Mention the fact that you're a senior when you first make your travel reservations. Most major airlines and many international chain hotels offer discounts for seniors.

Members of **AARP,** 601 E St. NW, Washington, DC 20049 (✆ 888/687-2277; www.aarp.org), get discounts on hotels, airfares, and car rentals. AARP offers members a wide range of benefits, including *AARP: The Magazine* and a monthly newsletter. Anyone over 50 can join.

Many reliable agencies and organizations target the 50-plus market. **Grand Circle Travel** (✆ 800/221-2610 or 617/350-7500; www.gct.com) offers package deals for the 50-plus market, mostly of the tour-bus variety, with free trips thrown in for those who organize groups of 10 or more. **Elderhostel** (✆ 877/426-8056; www.elderhostel.org) arranges study programs for those age 55 and over (and a spouse or companion of any age) in the U.S. and in more than 80 countries around the world, including Italy.

Recommended publications offering travel resources and discounts for seniors include: the quarterly magazine *Travel 50 & Beyond* (www.travel50andbeyond. com) and the bestselling paperback *Unbelievably Good Deals and Great Adventures That You Absolutely Can't Get Unless You're Over 50, 2007–2008, 17th Edition* (McGraw-Hill), by Joann Rattner Heilman.

Many discounts on admission to museums and attractions in Italy are available only to citizens of the European

Community because of the lack of reciprocity with the United States and other countries.

FAMILY TRAVEL

The whole culture of traveling with children, especially in Southern Italy, is completely foreign to travelers coming from Anglo-Saxon countries. Italians love kids and take them with them wherever they go. Hotels, restaurants, and attraction managers will always be most accommodating of your children's special needs, but don't expect special amenities: There will be no playroom, no babysitting program, and no kiddy-area with small tables and crayons. Children in Italy partake in their parents' lives: They eat at the same table and from the same menu, though you can obtain half portions *(mezza porzione)* in most restaurants and ask for specially prepared dishes not on the menu. Kids sleep in the same room or suite—though most hoteliers will add a cot to your room for your child, and most have special rooms or suites designed for families with children, but you need to book in advance. Even the largest hotels will offer babysitting only on request.

Luckily, the region is particularly suited for a vacation with children: the ancient sites stimulate children's imagination while the many beaches and resorts are a perfect place for them to vent their energy. If you have younger children, you might want to avoid the rocky Sorrento peninsula, Amalfi Coast, and Capri, while favoring the beautiful beaches of Ischia and the Cilento.

Throughout the region, private attractions offer discounts to all children, while in state-run museums only E.U. citizens younger than age 18 are admitted free. To locate accommodations, restaurants, and attractions that are particularly kid friendly, refer to the "Kids" icon throughout this guide.

Recommended family travel websites include **Family Travel Forum** (www.

familytravelforum.com), a comprehensive site that offers customized trip planning; **Family Travel Network** (www.familytravelnetwork.com), an online magazine providing travel tips; **Travel WithYourKids.com** (www.travelwithyourkids.com), a comprehensive site written by parents for parents offering sound advice for long-distance and international travel with children.

WOMEN TRAVELERS

Naples used to be on the black list for women travelers, but conditions have improved enormously after years of refurbishment in the city's historical district. Southern Italians are also much more accustomed to seeing blond visitors. However, women will attract men's attention and often have to fend off their proffered "friendship." Most often, ignoring remarks, avoiding eye contact, and proceeding on your way as if you hadn't noticed anything is the best approach. Should you perceive a real threat, though, immediately ask assistance from a policeman, a store-keeper, or even a passerby (elderly women are usually perceived as particularly forbidding by young Italian males). In general, avoid seedy neighborhoods where you don't see many women strolling around, and use your common sense.

Always dress appropriately. Especially in summer, remember that Italian women dress more conservatively in urban surroundings than their counterparts in the United States: Reserve your halter tops and short-shorts for the beach.

If you are a solo-traveler, see "Single Travelers," later in this chapter.

Check out the award-winning website **Journeywoman** (www.journeywoman.com), a "real life" women's travel-information network where you can sign up for a free e-mail newsletter and get advice on everything from etiquette and dress to safety. The travel guide *Safety and Security for Women Who Travel,* by Sheila

Swan and Peter Laufer (Travelers' Tales Guides), offering common-sense tips on safe travel, was updated in 2004.

AFRICAN-AMERICAN TRAVELERS

Black Travel Online (www.blacktravel online.com) posts news on upcoming events and includes links to articles and travel-booking sites. **Soul of America** (www.soulofamerica.com) is a comprehensive website, with travel tips, event and family-reunion postings, and sections on historically black beach resorts and active vacations.

Agencies and organizations that provide resources for black travelers include: **Rodgers Travel** (© 800/825-1775; www.rodgerstravel.com); the **African American Association of Innkeepers International** (© 877/422-5777; www. africanamericaninns.com); and **Henderson Travel & Tours** (© 800/327-2309 or 301/650-5700; www.hendersontravel. com), which has specialized in trips to Africa since 1957.

Go Girl: The Black Woman's Guide to Travel & Adventure (Eighth Mountain Press) is a compilation of travel essays by writers including Jill Nelson and Audre Lorde. *The African-American Travel Guide* by Wayne C. Robinson (Hunter Publishing; www.hunterpublishing.com) was published in 1997, so it may be somewhat dated. *Travel and Enjoy Magazine* (© 866/266-6211; www.traveland enjoy.com) is a travel magazine and guide. The well-done *Pathfinders Magazine* (© 877/977-PATH; www.pathfinders travel.com) includes articles on a wide range of topics, often related to travel in Italy.

STUDENT TRAVEL

Naples and Campania are heaven for students, especially those who are into art, antiquity, or music.

The **International Student Travel Confederation** (ISTC; www.istc.org) was formed in 1949 to make travel around the world more affordable for students. Check out its website for comprehensive travel services information and details on how to get an **International Student Identity Card (ISIC),** which qualifies students for substantial savings on rail passes, plane tickets, entrance fees, and more. It also provides students with basic health and life insurance and a 24-hour helpline. The card is valid for a maximum of 18 months. You can apply for the card online or in person at **STA Travel** (© 800/781-4040 in North America; www.statravel.com), the biggest student travel agency in the world; check out the website to locate STA Travel offices worldwide. If you're no longer a student but are still under 26, you can get an **International Youth Travel Card (IYTC)** from the same people that entitles you to some discounts. **Travel CUTS** (© 800/592-2887; www.travelcuts.com) offers similar services for both Canadians and U.S. residents. Irish students may prefer to turn to **USIT** (© 01/602-1904; www.usit.ie), an Ireland-based specialist in student, youth, and independent travel.

SINGLE TRAVELERS

Solo travelers do not usually have a problem in Campania, as many hotels have single rooms for business travelers. On package vacations, however, single travelers are often hit with a "single supplement" to the base price. To avoid it, you can agree to room with other single travelers or find a compatible roommate before you go, from one of the many roommate-locator agencies.

Solo women travelers may face some risks in Naples, where they should avoid deserted areas and be particularly careful at night. Elsewhere in the region, and particularly in seaside resorts during the summer, they may face some unpleasantness caused by excessive male attention, but this is usually easily brushed off by avoiding eye contact and ignoring the offender. Dressing conservatively is also a good idea: You'll notice that Italian women show a lot of flesh only when they are in a group, and cover up when they travel alone.

Whether you are male or female, it is imperative you remain vigilant for shady characters, as solo travelers are easy prey for crooks, who will try to befriend (and then rob) you. If you feel uncomfortable, ask for help; speaking up will often diffuse a potentially dangerous situation.

TravelChums (© 212/787-2621; www.travelchums.com) is an Internet-only travel-companion matching service with elements of an online personals-type site, hosted by the respected New York–based Shaw Guides travel service.

Many reputable tour companies offer singles-only trips. **Singles Travel International** (© 877/765-6874; www. singlestravelintl.com) offers singles-only escorted tours to Southern Italy. **Backroads** (© 800/462-2848; www.backroads. com) offers "Singles + Solos" active-travel trips to destinations worldwide, including Italy.

For more information, check out Eleanor Berman's classic *Traveling Solo: Advice and Ideas for More Than 250 Great Vacations, 5th Edition* (Globe Pequot), updated in 2005.

11 Sustainable Tourism/Ecotourism

Each time you take a flight or drive a car, CO_2 is released into the atmosphere. You can help neutralize this danger to our planet through "carbon offsetting"—paying someone to reduce your CO_2 emissions by the same amount you've added. Carbon offsets can be purchased in the U.S. from companies such as **Carbonfund.org** (www.carbonfund.org) and **TerraPass** (www.terrapass.org), and from **Climate Care** (www.climatecare.org) in the U.K.

Although one could argue that any vacation that includes an airplane flight can't be truly "green," you can go on holiday and still contribute positively to the environment. You can offset carbon emissions from your flight in other ways. Choose forward-looking companies that embrace responsible development practices, helping preserve destinations for the future by working alongside local people. An increasing number of sustainable tourism initiatives can help you plan a family trip and leave as small a "footprint" as possible on the places you visit.

Responsible Travel (www.responsible travel.com) contains a great source of sustainable travel ideas run by a spokesperson for responsible tourism in the travel industry. **Sustainable Travel International** (www.sustainabletravel international.org) promotes responsible tourism practices and issues an annual Green Gear & Gift Guide.

You can find eco-friendly travel tips, statistics, and touring companies and associations—listed by destination under "Travel Choice"—at the TIES website, www.ecotourism.org. Also check out **Conservation International** (www. conservation.org)—which, with *National Geographic Traveler,* annually presents **World Legacy Awards** (www.wlaward. org) to those travel tour operators, businesses, organizations, and places that have made a significant contribution to sustainable tourism. **Ecotravel.com** is part online magazine and part ecodirectory that lets you search for touring companies in several categories (water-based, land-based, spiritually oriented, and so on).

In the U.K., **Tourism Concern** (www. tourismconcern.org.uk) works to reduce social and environmental problems

> ## *Tips* It's Easy Being Green
>
> We can all help conserve fuel and energy when we travel. Here are a few simple ways you can help preserve your favorite destinations:
>
> - Whenever possible, choose nonstop flights; they generally require less fuel than those that must stop and take-off again.
> - If renting a car is necessary on your vacation, ask the rental agent for the most fuel efficient one available. Not only will you burn less gas, you'll save money at the tank.
> - At hotels, request that your sheets and towels not be changed daily. You'll save water and energy by not washing them as often, and you'll prolong the life of the towels, too. (Many hotels already have programs like this in place.)
> - Turn off the lights and air-conditioner (or heater) when you leave your hotel room.

connected to tourism and find ways of improving tourism so that local benefits are increased.

The **Association of British Travel Agents** (ABTA; www.abtamembers.org/responsibletourism) acts as a focal point for the U.K. travel industry and is one of the leading groups spearheading responsible tourism.

The **Association of Independent Tour Operators** (AITO; www.aito.co.uk) is a group of interesting specialist operators leading the field in making holidays sustainable.

Naples might hardly be what you picture as an eco-friendly destination, but the rest of the region is actually one of the prime destinations for ecotourism in Italy.

Campania is home to Italy's second largest National Park—the Cilento—and to a large number of parks and nature preserves, including the National Park of Mount Vesuvius, the Amalfi Coast, the Monti Lattari on the Sorrento peninsula, and a number of marine bioparks along the coast: Baia (near Pozzuoli), Procida, Ischia, Massa Lubrense, parts of Capri, and, of course, the coast of the Cilento.

Moreover, a few decades ago, faced with fast acquisition of abandoned farms by developers, and growing areas of endangered nature, the Italian government came up with a great way to promote sustainable tourism: Allow farms to increase their income by turning them into small resorts (similarly to some ranches in the United States). The idea took root and *agriturismo* is now a hugely widespread movement in Italy. *Agriturismo* has found a perfect home in Campania, where the countryside often offers dramatic natural attractions and close proximity to the seaside. Also, most of the *agriturismi* have embraced the organic movement, adding increased environmental benefit. Operations are controlled through methods such as surprise inspections, and *agriturismi* are strictly regulated by law to prevent exploitation by corporations and developers: In order to obtain the right to call itself *"agriturismo,"* the farm must: (a) offer fewer than 30 beds total; and (b) make most of its profits from the agricultural component of the property—in

Frommers.com: The Complete Travel Resource

It should go without saying, but we highly recommend **Frommers.com**, voted Best Travel Site by *PC Magazine*. We think you'll find our expert advice and tips; independent reviews of hotels, restaurants, attractions, and preferred shopping and nightlife venues; vacation giveaways; and an online booking tool indispensable before, during, and after your travels. We publish the complete contents of over 128 travel guides in our **Destinations** section covering nearly 3,600 places worldwide to help you plan your trip. Each weekday, we publish original articles reporting on **Deals and News** via our free **Frommers.com Newsletter** to help you save time and money and travel smarter. We're betting you'll find our new **Events** listings (http://events.frommers.com) an invaluable resource; it's an up-to-the-minute roster of what's happening in cities everywhere—including concerts, festivals, lectures, and more. We've also added weekly **Podcasts, interactive maps,** and hundreds of new images across the site. Check out our **Travel Talk** area featuring **Message Boards** where you can join in conversations with thousands of fellow Frommer's travelers and post your trip report once you return.

other words, the property has to remain a farm and not become a glorified hotel.

Staying in an *agriturismo* is a great way to contribute to green tourism in Italy; it can also be quite attractive for the special amenities it offers. For more information, see "Tips on Accommodations," on p. 49.

12 Staying Connected

TELEPHONES

To call Italy:

1. Dial the international access code: 011 from the U.S.; 00 from the U.K., Ireland, and New Zealand; or 0011 from Australia
2. Dial the country code for Italy: 39.
3. Dial the local area code and then the number. Telephone numbers in Italy can have any number of digits depending on the location and the type of telephone line, which can be very confusing to foreigners. The amount of numbers can range from 5 (for special switchboards of hospitals and other public services, such as the railroad info line of Trenitalia, ℭ 892021 for example) to a maximum of 10 (for some land lines and all cellular lines). Telephone numbers always include the area code, which can have two or three digits. Area codes begin with 0 for land lines and with 3 for cellular lines, and you always need to dial the 0.

To make international calls: To make international calls from Italy, first dial 00 and then the country code (U.S. or Canada 1, U.K. 44, Ireland 353, Australia 61, New Zealand 64). Next, dial the area code and number. For example, if you wanted to call the British Embassy in Washington, D.C., you would dial 00-1-202-588-7800.

For directory assistance: Dial ℭ 1240.

For operator assistance: Dial ℭ 170; the service is available only from 7am to midnight.

Toll-free numbers: Numbers beginning with 800 or 888 within Italy are toll-free, but calling a 1-800 number in the States from Italy is not toll-free: It costs the same as an overseas call.

Local pay phones in Italy require pre-paid telephone cards *(carta telefonica)*, which you can buy at a tobacconist *(tabacchi,* marked by a sign with a white *T* on a black background), bar, or newsstand. The local Telecom card costs 5€ ($7/£3.50) and gives you unlimited call time within Italy for 1 month. The card has a perforated corner that you need to tear off before inserting it into the phone slot. If you are using coins, a local call in Italy costs .10€ (14¢/7p).

To make international calls you need to purchase an international prepaid card, which varies depending on which country you will be calling the most. The cards are sold at tobacconists and some bars and newsstands. They usually allow from 200 to 700 minutes call time for 5€ ($7/£3.50). You need to scratch the back to reveal the secret code and dial it after the access code indicated on the card; then dial the number you want to call.

More convenient but not necessarily cheaper, your own calling card linked to your home phone or a prepaid calling card you pay monthly by credit card are also good options. Some calling cards offer a toll-free access number in Italy, while others do not; the first kind is obviously more convenient. When calling from a public phone booth, you sometimes need to put in money or a *carta telefonica* just to obtain the dial tone, even if you are using a prepaid card; you may be charged only for a local call or not at all. Check with your calling-card provider before leaving on your trip.

You can also make collect calls directly by calling the operator (see above) or through a telephone provider in your country. For **AT&T,** dial ✆ **800-1724444;** for **MCI,** dial ✆ **800-905825;** and for

Sprint, dial ✆ **800-172405** or 800-172406. Remember that calling from a hotel is convenient but usually very expensive.

CELLPHONES

The three letters that define much of the world's wireless capabilities are **GSM** (Global System for Mobile Communications), a big, seamless network that makes for easy cross-border cellphone use throughout Europe and dozens of other countries worldwide. In the U.S., T-Mobile, AT&T Wireless, and Cingular use this quasi-universal system; in Canada, Microcell and some Rogers customers are GSM, and all Europeans and most Australians use GSM. GSM phones function with a removable plastic SIM card, encoded with your phone number and account information. If your cellphone is on a GSM system, and you have a world-capable multiband phone such as many Sony Ericsson, Motorola, or Samsung models, you can make and receive calls across civilized areas around much of the globe. Just call your wireless operator and ask for "international roaming" to be activated on your account. Unfortunately, charges can be high—anywhere from $1 to $5 (50p £2.50) per minute.

For many, **renting** a phone is a good idea. While you can rent a phone from any number of overseas sites, including kiosks at airports and at car-rental agencies, we suggest renting the phone before you leave home. North Americans can rent one before leaving home from **InTouch USA** (✆ **800/872-7626;** www.intouchglobal.com) or **RoadPost** (✆ **888/ 290-1606** or 905/272-5665; www.roadpost.com). InTouch will also, for free, advise you on whether your existing phone will work overseas; simply call ✆ **703/222-7161** between 9am and 4pm EST, or go to **http://intouchglobal. com/travel.htm.**

Rentacell (© **877/736-8355** in the U.S.; 028-86337799 in Italy; www.renta cell.com) will deliver a phone to you anywhere for free. You can pick it up in the U.S. before you leave or directly in Italy. Incoming calls are free. **Easyline** (© **800-010600** toll-free within Italy) also delivers phones for free in Italy. Both companies will issue you your phone number upon reservation, before you leave for your trip.

Buying a phone can be economically attractive, as many nations have cheap prepaid phone systems. Once you arrive at your destination, stop by a local cellphone shop and get the cheapest package; you'll probably pay less than $100 (£50) for a phone and a starter calling card. Local calls may be as low as 10¢ (5p) per minute, and in many countries incoming calls are free.

VOICE-OVER INTERNET PROTOCOL (VOIP)

If you have Web access while traveling, you might consider a broadband-based telephone service (in technical terms, **Voice over Internet Protocol,** or **VoIP**) such as Skype (www.skype.com) or Vonage (www.vonage.com), which allows you to make free international calls if you use their services from your laptop or in a cybercafe. Check the sites for details.

INTERNET/E-MAIL
WITHOUT YOUR OWN COMPUTER

To find cybercafes in Campania check **www.cybercaptive.com** and **www.cyber cafe.com**. You'll find a number of cybercafes in Naples and in Salerno in the historic district, and at least one Internet access point in most smaller towns throughout the region. Only in the most remote countryside areas might you not be able to find a connection. However, most hotels throughout the region, even

in rural areas, provide free Internet access to their guests either via an Internet point in a common area or by letting you (briefly) check your mail through the computer at the front desk (if you need to browse for hours, ask for the nearest Internet point).

Most major airports have **Internet kiosks** that provide basic Web access for a per-minute fee that's usually higher than cybercafe prices. Check out copy shops like **Kinko's** (FedEx Kinko's), which offers computer stations with fully loaded software (as well as Wi-Fi).

WITH YOUR OWN COMPUTER

More and more hotels, resorts, airports, cafes, and retailers are going **Wi-Fi** (wireless fidelity), becoming "hotspots" that offer free high-speed Wi-Fi access or charge a small fee for usage. Most laptops sold today have built-in wireless capability. To find public Wi-Fi hotspots at your destination, go to **www.jiwire.com**; its Hotspot Finder holds the world's largest directory of public wireless hotspots.

For dial-up access, most business-class hotels throughout the world offer dataports for laptop modems, and a few thousand hotels in Europe now offer free high-speed Internet access.

Note: Italy uses 220V electricity and round-pronged plugs: See "Electricity" in "Fast Facts," p. 56. Always bring a **connection kit** of the right power and phone adapters, a spare phone cord, and a spare Ethernet network cable—or find out whether your hotel supplies them to guests. Most phone plugs in hotels and private homes throughout Italy have been upgraded to the standard phone jack used on computers, but some of the old ones with three round prongs are still in use. You can easily buy an adaptor at any local hardware store if your hotel doesn't have one for you.

> *Tips* **Ask Before You Go**
>
> Before you invest in a package deal or an escorted tour:
> - Always ask about the **cancellation policy.** Can you get your money back? Is there a deposit required?
> - Ask about the **accommodations choices and prices** for each. Then look up the hotels' reviews in a Frommer's guide and check their rates online for your specific dates of travel. Also find out what types of rooms are offered.
> - Request a complete **schedule.** (Escorted tours only)
> - Ask about the **size** and demographics of the group. (Escorted tours only)
> - Discuss what is included in the **price** (transportation, meals, tips, airport transfers, and so on). (Escorted tours only)
> - Finally, look for **hidden expenses.** Ask whether airport departure fees and taxes, for example, are included in the total cost—they rarely are.

13 Packages for the Independent Traveler

Package tours are simply a way to buy the airfare, accommodations, and other elements of your trip (such as car rentals, airport transfers, and sometimes even activities) at the same time and often at discounted prices.

One good source of package deals is the airlines themselves. Most major airlines offer air/land packages, including **American Airlines Vacations** (© 800/321-2121; www.aavacations.com), **Delta Vacations** (© 800/654-6559; www.deltavacations.com), **Continental Airlines Vacations** (© 800/301-3800; www.covacations.com), and **United Vacations**

(© 888/854-3899; www.unitedvacations.com). Several big **online travel agencies**—Expedia, Travelocity, Orbitz, and Lastminute.com—also do a brisk business in packages.

The best deals for Italy are usually offered by **Italiatour** (www.italiatour.com), part of the **Alitalia** group.

Travel packages are also listed in the travel section of your local Sunday newspaper. Or check ads in national travel magazines such as *Arthur Frommer's Budget Travel Magazine, Travel & Leisure, National Geographic Traveler,* and *Condé Nast Traveler.*

14 Escorted General-Interest Tours

Escorted tours are structured group tours with a group leader. The price usually includes everything from airfare to hotels, meals, tours, admission costs, and local transportation. Among major companies, we recommend **Italiatour** (© 800/845-3365; fax 212/765-2183; www.italiatour.com); their prices and quality are very competitive, and they are the only company that offers exclusive tours of Campania.

Other tours merely pause in the region as part of Italy-wide itineraries. Among them, we recommend **Perillo Tours** (© 800/431-1515; www.perillotours.com), family operated for three generations—perhaps you've seen the TV commercials that used to feature the "King of Italy," Mario Perillo, and the current ones that feature his son, Steve—and **Trafalgar Tours** (© 800/854-0103; www.trafalgartours.com), one of Europe's largest tour operators, offering affordable guided tours with lodgings in unpretentious hotels. Leading competitors to the previous two companies are **Globus + Cosmos Tours** (℀ 800/338-7092; www.globusandcosmos.com), offering first-class escorted coach tours as well as budget tours, and **Insight Vacations** (℀ 800/582-8380; www.insightvacations.com), which books superior, first-class, fully escorted motorcoach tours. Among smaller companies, Connecticut-based **Tour Italy Now** (℀ 800/955-4418; www.touritalynow.com) offers a variety of tours to the Amalfi Coast and Campania.

Abercrombie & Kent (℀ 800/323-7308 in the U.S. or 020/7730-9600 in the U.K.; www.abercrombiekent.com) offers luxurious premium packages. Your overnight stays will be in meticulously restored castles and exquisite villas. The oldest travel agency in Britain, **Cox & Kings** (℀ 020/7873-5000; www.coxandkings.co.uk), specializes in unusual, if pricey, holidays, focusing on special interests, such as gardens or religion. The company is noted for its focus on tours of an ecological and environmental interest.

15 Special-Interest Trips

HIKING & BIKING

The Sorrento peninsula and Amalfi Coast are hikers' heavens, while the Cilento offers the best to hikers as well as bicycle enthusiasts. A great number of agencies, both local and international, offer hiking and biking trips, but you can also hire local guides to organize your own individual trip (see our suggestions in the destination chapters that follow).

Our favorite locally based organization is **Cycling Cilento Adventure** (℀ 328-3652736; www.cyclingcilentoadventure.com), based in Cilento National Park. They offer a great—both in number and quality—choice of road bike, mountain bike, and hiking tours, all of which allow you to sample the local cuisine and see the best sights.

Another excellent agency is the U.K.–based **Sherpa Expeditions** (℀ 20-8577-2717; www.sherpa-walking-holidays.co.uk), offering several guided and self-guided walking tours in Campania, both on the Amalfi Coast and in Cilento National Park.

La Dolce Vita Wine Tours (℀ 888/746-0022; www.dolcetours.com) organizes easier walking tours, including one that covers Capri, Mount Vesuvius, and Pompeii, as well as some of the best vineyards in the region.

Breakaway Adventures (℀ 800/567-6286; www.breakaway-adventures.com) organizes cycling and walking tours in the Sorrento peninsula and Amalfi Coast as well as in the Cilento.

FOOD & WINE TOURS & COOKING SCHOOLS

As home to some of the best culinary traditions in Italy, Campania offers a number of food-oriented tours. The best are offered by the **Sorrento Cooking School** (℀ 081-8783255; www.sorrentocookingschool.com), whose program includes a large variety of choices both in length (from daily excursions to longer tours lasting up to 8 days) and content (from cooking classes and wine tours to gastronomic and cultural explorations).

Specializing in culinary vacations, **Epiculinary** (℀ 888/380-9010; www.epiculinary.com) hosts a large variety of Italian classes and tours, several of which are in the Sorrento and Amalfi Coast areas.

Chicago-based **International Kitchen** (℀ 800/945-8606; www.theinternationalkitchen.com) is one of the best companies devoted to culinary tours, and their program includes several destinations on the Amalfi Coast, such as the delightful Oasi Olympia Relais in Sant'Agata sui due Golfi, between Sorrento and Positano.

With their "taste your travel" slogan, Italy-based **Pagine di Gusto** (℮ 0461-829964; www.paginedigusto.com) organizes several discovery tours of Campania, highlighting its art, food, and wines.

OTHER SPECIAL INTEREST CLASSES & TOURS

The best special-interest tour group in the region is the lively Napoli-based

Rising Incoming Organizer, or **RIO,** Via Monte di Dio 9, 80132 Napoli (℮ 081-7644934; www.riorimontitours. com), a family business now in its third generation. They offer a variety of unique, off-the-beaten-path tours that cover all kinds of special interests, from classic art and ceramics—a 12-day course and tour in Naples, Vietri, the Amalfi Coast, and Cerreto Sannita (near Benevento) that we particularly recommend—to golf, sailing, and culinary adventures, including one featuring Neapolitan pastries.

16 Getting Around Campania

BY TRAIN

Trains, which connect most of the best attractions and destinations in the region, provide a convenient, moderately priced means of transport. The national railway system **FFSS** (℮ 892021 from anywhere in Italy; www.trenitalia.it) serves the area together with **Alifana** (℮ 800-127157 or 081-5993254; www.alifana.it), covering Benevento and surrounding areas; **Circumvesuviana** (℮ 800-053939; www. vesuviana.it), connecting Naples with the Vesuvian area and Sorrento; and **Metronapoli** (℮ 800-568866; www.metro. na.it), connecting Naples with Pozzuoli and the Phlegrean Fields.

FFSS offers local trains as well as the faster, more expensive EuroStar and InterCity trains (designated ES and IC on train schedules, respectively), which make limited stops. Children ages 4 to 11 receive a discount of 50%, and children ages 3 and younger travel free with their parents. Seniors and youths under age 26 can purchase discount cards. Advance seat reservations, which are obligatory on all ES trains, are highly recommended for other trains during peak season and on weekends or holidays.

One of the best deals for Campania is the **Italy Rail 'n Drive Pass:** Good for 2 months, it includes 4 days of unlimited

train travel within Italy and 2 days of car rental with unlimited mileage.

See "Getting There, By Train" on p. 28, for information on the Eurailpass.

BY BUS

Local bus companies operate throughout Campania, particularly in hilly and mountainous areas where rail service isn't available. The leading bus operators are **SITA** (℮ 081-5522176; www.sita-on-line.it), serving the Sorrento peninsula and the Amalfi Coast; **SEPSA** (℮ 800-001616; www.sepsa.it), serving Pozzuoli, Baia, Cuma, and Miseno, as well as Procida and Ischia; **CTP** (℮ 800-482644; www.ctpn.it), serving Naples and linking it with neighboring towns; **AIR** (℮ 0825-204250; www.air-spa.it), connecting the Avellino area with Naples; and **CSTP** (℮ 800-016659 or 089-487001; www. cstp.it), with trains in Salerno, Paestum, and the Cilento.

For more information, see "Getting There" in the destination chapters throughout this book.

BY FERRY

Some of the most charming destinations in Campania are right on the water, making the sea a very important means of transportation, and one of the most pleasant because of its unique views. Naples is the region's major harbor, followed by Salerno, Amalfi, and Sorrento.

Hydrofoil service (suspended in winter) operates chiefly from Naples's **Terminal Aliscafi** in Mergellina, with frequent and fast runs to Capri, Ischia, Procida, Sorrento, Positano, Amalfi, Salerno, and Sicily (Milazzo and the Aeolian Islands). The major operators are **Tirrenia** (© **199-123199** or 081-2514711; www.tirrenia.it), with ships to Cagliari and Palermo; **Siremar** (© **081-5800340;** www.siremar.it), with ships to the Aeolian Islands and Milazzo; **TTTLines** (© **800-915365**), with service to Catania and Palermo; **Medmar** (© **081-5513352**), with ships to Tunis and with ferries (© 081-3334411) to Ischia; **Caremar** (© **081-5513882;** www.caremar.it), with ferries and hydrofoils to Ischia, Capri, and Procida; **Alilauro** (© **081-7611004;** www.alilauro.it), with hydrofoils to Ischia and Positano; **SNAV** (© **081-4285555** or 081-4285111; www.snav.it), with hydrofoil service to Ischia, Capri, and Procida, and ships to Palermo, Sardinia, and the Aeolian and Pontine islands; **LMP** (© **081-5513236**), with hydrofoils to Sorrento; and **NLG** (© **081-5527209**), with hydrofoils to Capri.

BY CAR

Neapolitans have truly earned their reputation for aggressive and daring driving. You need to be a skilled and alert driver if you want to move at ease on Italian roads, with super-high speeds on the *autostrade* (national express highways) and supernarrow streets in the cities and towns. You will literally be taking your life into your hands, as Italy has one of the highest fatal road accident rates in Europe.

However, driving will allow you to see much more of the countryside at your own pace, and it makes sense if you have the time to go exploring off the beaten path. If you are planning to visit only major destinations in the region, you'll be better off using public transportation, or hiring a car with a driver.

For information on car rental, see "Getting There" on p. 27.

RULES OF THE ROAD   In Italy, driving is on the right-hand side. Unless otherwise marked, **speed limits** are 50km/hour within urban areas 90km/hour outside cities, and 130km/hour on toll highways. Roads in the region are much narrower than in the U.S., are often congested with all kinds of vehicular and non-vehicular traffic, and have guardrails only when the road is on a cliff. Motor scooters are extremely prevalent and often do not obey traffic laws, so be mindful of them as they zoom and swerve in between cars. Right of way is from the right at the intersection of regular roads, but don't expect traffic to move to the left lane to let you in on a highway or main road: The left lane is exclusively for passing, so you'll have to wait for a break in the flow. It is mandatory to have your headlights on at all times outside urban areas, and to use seat belts and age-appropriate car seats for children.

High beams are used to signal to fellow drivers: If you are in the left passing lane and a driver flashes you from behind, you need to move out of the way. If an oncoming car signals you from the other lane, it means that some danger is ahead—so slow down. If cars ahead of you put on their hazard lights, slow down: The traffic is completely stopped ahead.

FINDING YOUR WAY   Road signs are posted with one sign about 1 mile before an exit, and then another right at the exit. Destination signs are blue for local roads and green for the toll highway. Destinations of cultural interest (such as monuments and archaeological areas) are posted on brown signs. Often, only the major town on a local road is marked, while smaller towns and villages on the way will not be posted. See p. 15 for information on buying some reliable maps.

GASOLINE Gas stations are disseminated along local roads at sensible intervals, however, large stretches of countryside are without stations. Pumps are generally open Monday to Saturday from 7 or 8am to 1pm and 3 or 4pm to 7 or 8pm (some will have a self-service pump accessible during closing hours). On toll highways gas stations are positioned every 32km or 48km (20 or 30 miles) and are open 24 hours daily. Most cars take *benzina senza piombo* (unleaded fuel), but regular fuel is still sold for older cars and motorcycles. A number of cars have diesel engines, but only the newest models take the ecological variety labeled "blue diesel." Be prepared for sticker shock every time you fill up even a medium-sized car, as fuel is priced throughout the country at around 6€

($8.40/£4.20) per gallon. Do make sure the pump registers zero before an attendant starts refilling your tank: The old scam of filling your tank before resetting the meter (so that you also pay the charges run up by the previous motorist) is still performed by some dishonest attendants.

BREAKDOWNS & ASSISTANCE Roadside aid in Italy is excellent. For 24-hour **emergency assistance,** contact the national department of motor vehicles, **Automobile Club d'Italia** (© **803-116** toll-free within Italy, or © **800/116-800** for visitors with a foreign cellphone service; www.aci.it).

For multilingual information on road and weather conditions, travel itineraries, mileages, ferries, and procedures, call © **06-491716.** Also, check with the Italian tourist office at www.italiantourism.com.

17 Tips on Accommodations

On the Amalfi Coast, the climate is mild, so hotels are structured to maximize outdoor enjoyment with guest rooms opening onto patios, balconies, terraces, and gardens. Carpeting is the exception, while a tiled floor—often with hand-decorated tiles from the local industry—is the rule. Some of the local cultural idiosyncrasies (such as lack of amenities and small bathrooms) can be less charming; they become more and more apparent as you go down in the level and price of accommodations.

In general, hotels tend to have fewer amenities, particularly in urban areas, than their same-level counterparts in the U.S. and Britain. Swimming pools are a rare luxury in town, though outdoor summer-only pools are more common in seaside and some mountain resort destinations. Fitness clubs and gyms are becoming more widespread, but only in top-tier hotels. Spas are routinely offered only in luxury hotels; you'll find some in more moderate

hotels, but only in thermal destinations. In-room dining is offered only in the most expensive hotels and rarely on a 24-hour basis. Moderate hotels may not have a restaurant at all, just a breakfast service which they may even cater from the nearby bar. Only the cheapest accommodations don't have TVs, but more expensive hotels may offer satellite TV (necessary for programs in English). Air-conditioning instead is far from standard, but the climate is so nearly perfect—warm and breezy—that you will rarely need it.

Also, since buildings are old—sometimes centuries old—elevators tend to be small and rarely fully accessible: Steps tend to be ubiquitous. Rooms also tend to be smaller than in the U.S. or Britain, but the biggest difference can be found in the bathrooms, which tend to be tiny, rarely featuring a bathtub, with fixtures that look old-fashioned even if they are in perfect working order.

Hence, if you are planning to spend a lot of time in your room—having drinks with friends and romantic dinners—and in the hotel, lounging in the public areas, the spa, the swimming pool, and the hotel's restaurants and bars, you should consider only the most luxurious hotels. Only there will you find the level of amenities you are seeking. If instead you want to spend most of your time exploring your destination, using your hotel as a sleeping base, then you should definitely consider moderate hotels because, while their extra amenities are basic, you'll get spacious—sometimes even luxurious—rooms with modern bathrooms.

If all you really want is a good bed, then you can consider inexpensive hotels, where the room's decor will be simpler but always including all the basic amenities (comfortable and scrupulously clean bed and bathroom, telephone, and local TV).

Hotels with restaurants often offer a meal plan to go with the room. You can usually choose among B&B service (breakfast only), half-board (breakfast and either lunch or dinner), and full board (breakfast, lunch, and dinner). Some smaller establishments make a meal plan mandatory during the month of August, when many of these same hotels may enforce a minimum-stay requirement of 3 or 7 days.

Most hotels in the region are private—often family-run—properties, yet you will also find a few hotels run by some major chains: In addition to **Best Western** (www.bestwestern.com), **Hilton** (www. hilton.com), **Holiday Inn** (www.holiday-inn.com), and **Starwood Hotels**—including Sheraton, Four Points, Le Meridien, Westin, St. Regis, and Luxury Collection—(www.starwoodhotels.com), you'll find the Italian chain **Jolly Hotels** (www.jollyhotels.it), catering to business as well as family travelers. You'll also find the French chain **Sofitel** (www.sofitel. com), which offers somewhat simpler accommodations and caters mostly to families, and the European **Accor Hotels** (www.accorhotels.com) with its moderately priced Novotel and its more elegant Mercure hotels.

SURFING FOR HOTELS

In addition to the online travel booking sites **Travelocity, Expedia, Orbitz, Priceline,** and **Hotwire,** you can book hotels through **Hotels.com, Quikbook** (www.quikbook.com), **hoteldiscounts. com,** and **Travelaxe** (www.travelaxe.net).

HotelChatter.com is a daily webzine offering smart coverage and critiques of hotels worldwide. Go to **TripAdvisor. com** or **HotelShark.com** for helpful independent consumer reviews of hotels and resort properties.

Since most hotels in the area are private, often family-run businesses—including some of the most famous luxury hotels such as the San Pietro in Positano—you'll do much better checking an Italy-based search engine such as **Venere Net** (www.venere.com). Other sites to check out are **Italyhotels** (www. italyhotelink.com), **ITWG.com** (www. italyhotels.com), **Welcome to Italy** (www.wel.it), **Europa Hotels** (www. europa-hotels.com), and **Italy Hotels** (www.hotels-in-italy.com).

Also, always check the hotel's website directly, since these often list the same rates as some supposed discount agencies, but without the extra fee, or even better unique online deals.

Remember: It's a good idea to **get a confirmation number** and **make a printout** of any online booking transaction.

AGRITURISMO (STAYING ON A FARM)

Another option—a favorite with Italians—is *agriturismo:* staying on a working farm or former farm somewhere in the countryside (see "Sustainable Tourism," p. 40). Your lodging usually includes

A Home Away from Home: Renting Your Own Apartment or Villa

If you're looking to rent a villa or an apartment, **The Right Vacation Rental** (www.therightvacationrental.com) offers apartment, farmhouse, or cottage stays of 2 weeks or more. Best of all, it is a subsidiary of **Idyll Untours** (**888/868-6871**; www.untours.com)—named the "Most Generous Company in America" by Newman's Own—and donates most profits to provide low-interest loans to underprivileged entrepreneurs around the world.

Among the more traditional agencies, one of the best to call is **Rent Villas** (© **800/726-6702** or 805/641-1650; fax 805/641-1630; www.rentvillas. com). It represents the Cuendet properties, some of the best in Campania and in Italy, and its agents are very helpful in tracking down the perfect place to suit your needs. Cuendet's representative in the United Kingdom, and one of the best all-around agents in London, is **International Chapters** (© **08450/700-618**; www.villa-rentals.com). Also in the U.K., contact **Cottages to Castles** (© **1622/775-217**; www.cottagestocastles.com). For some of the top properties, call **The Parker Company, Ltd.** in the U.S. (© **800/ 280-2811** or 781/596-8282; fax 781/596-3125; www.theparkercompany.com). This agency rents apartments, villas, restored farmhouses, and even castles throughout Campania. One of the most reasonably priced agencies is **Villas and Apartments Abroad, Ltd.** (© **800/433-3020** or 212/213-6435; fax 212/ 213-8252; www.ideal-villas.com). A popular but very pricey agency is **Villas International** (© **800/221-2260** or 415/499-9490; www.villasintl.com).

breakfast and at least one other meal (your choice of dinner or lunch), prepared with ingredients produced on the farm or by nearby local farms. Among the multiplying online agencies, the best are **Agriturist.it** (www.agriturist.it) and **Agriturismo.it** (www.agriturismo.it). Accommodations are usually pretty posh, and range from palatial (for example, on famous wine-producing estates) to country-inn style. They all usually offer such amenities as swimming pools and outdoor activities. However, some *agriturismi* offer only basic accommodations: you'll be satisfied only if you were really after the barn experience. Rates are usually proportional to what is provided.

18 Tips on Dining

Dining hours tend to be later than in the United States. Locals eat their lunch around 1:30pm and their dinner around 8:30pm. Restaurants will rarely open before 12:30pm or 7:30pm, and often they'll only be setting up at that time.

Italians usually start a meal with a first course of pasta or rice *(primo)*, or with an appetizer *(antipasto)*—sometimes both— which they follow by a second course of meat or fish *(secondo)*, and/or a vegetable side dish or a salad *(contorno)*. Italians will finish a meal with cheese *(formaggio)*, or a piece of fruit *(frutta)*, and, of course, *caffè* (coffee). They'll have dessert *(dolce)* only occasionally, often opting, instead, for a gelato at a nearby ice-cream parlor.

Impressions

In Italy, the pleasure of eating is central to the pleasure of living. When you sit down to dinner with Italians, when you share their food, you are sharing their lives.

—Fred Plotkin, *Italy for the Gourmet Traveler* (1996)

Note: Ordering a cappuccino after lunch or dinner is a social blunder: Cappuccino is a breakfast or mid-morning drink. Also, don't ask for a latte if what you want is the American version: What you'll get in Italy is a glass of milk, which is what *latte* means in Italian.

If pasta is all you want, some restaurants that specialize in first courses—called *spaghetterie*—serve a large variety of pasta dishes; they are usually youth-oriented hangouts. *Pizzerie* are restaurants specializing in individual pizzas, usually cooked in wood-burning ovens. They will also sometimes serve pasta dishes, and, typically, the menu includes an array of appetizers as well. *Pizza a metro* and *pizza a taglio* are both casual pizza parlors where pizza is sold by weight, with limited or nonexistent seating. A *tavola calda* (literally "hot table") serves ready-made hot foods you can take away or eat at one of the few small tables. The food is usually very good. A *rosticceria* is the same type of place; you'll see chickens roasting on a spit in the window. *Friggitoria* usually sell pizza and deep-fried *calzone*.

For a quick bite, you can also go to a **bar.** Although bars in Italy do serve alcohol, they function mainly as cafes. Prices have a split personality: *Al banco* is the price you pay standing at the bar, while *al tavolo* means you are charged two to four times as much for sitting at a table where you'll be waited on. In bars, you can find local pastries, panino sandwiches on various kinds of rolls, and *tramezzini* (white-bread sandwich triangles with the crusts cut off). The sandwiches run 1€ to 3€

($1.25–$3.75/75p–£1.90) and are traditionally put in a kind of tiny press to flatten and toast them so the crust is crispy and the filling is hot and gooey.

A full-fledged restaurant will go by the name *osteria, trattoria,* or *ristorante.* Once upon a time, these terms meant something—*osterie* were basic places where you could get a plate of spaghetti and a glass of wine; *trattorie* were casual places serving full meals of filling peasant fare; and *ristoranti* were fancier places, with waiters in bow ties, printed menus, wine lists, and hefty prices. Nowadays, fancy restaurants often go by the name of *trattoria* to cash in on the associated charm factor; trendy spots use *osteria* to show they're hip; and simple, inexpensive places sometimes tack on *ristorante* to ennoble themselves. Many restaurants double as *pizzerias,* with a regular menu and a separate selection for pizza, sometimes offering a separate casual dining area as well.

The *enoteca* is a popular marriage of a wine bar and an *osteria;* you can sit and order from a host of good local and regional wines by the glass while snacking on appetizers or eating from a full menu featuring local specialties. Relaxed and full of ambience, these are great spots for light inexpensive lunches—or simply recharging your batteries.

The *pane e coperto* (bread and cover) is a 1€ to 3€ ($1.40–$4.20/70p–£2.10) cover charge that you must pay at most restaurants for the mere privilege of sitting at a table. To request the bill, say, *"Il conto, per favore"* (eel *con*-toh, pore fah-*vohr*-ay). A tip of 15% is usually included

Campanian Nightlife

By American and British standards, nightlife in Campania's provincial towns tends to be dull. There isn't a bar culture in southern Italy, and often what's called a pub here is a rather pale imitation. Cultural and social life, though, are always lively, from strolling to and fro along the main street, to going out for dinner, to having an aperitivo, to eating handmade gelato ice cream, to going to the theater or to a movie.

Clubs can be found, but you may not want to go out of your way to be seen there. While there are some great clubs in Naples, the situation is quite different in the rest of the region. You'll find some good ones along the Amalfi Coast in summer, but in the interior you are in a very different atmosphere—it isn't at all unusual for young people to drive all the way to Naples for a good evening out. Your best option will often be a concert. Musical events (both classical and pop, though the pop is in Italian) are sometimes staged in even the most remote little towns and villages.

in the bill these days but, if you're unsure, ask, "*È incluso il servizio?*" (ay een-*cloo*-soh eel sair-*vee*-tsoh?).

At many restaurants, especially larger ones and in cities, you'll find a *menu turistico* (tourist's menu), sometimes called *menu del giorno* (menu of the day) or *menu à prezzo fisso* (fixed-price menu). This set-price menu usually covers all meal incidentals—cover charge and 15% service charge—along with a first course *(primo)* and second course *(secondo)*, and sometimes even a drink, but it almost always offers an abbreviated selection of pretty commonplace dishes. The above

menu should not be confused with the *menu degustazione* (tasting menu) offered by more elegant gourmet restaurants: That's usually the way to go for the best selection of food at the best price. Except in those special restaurants, ordering a la carte will offer you the best chance of a memorable meal. Even better, forego the menu entirely and put yourself in the capable hands of your waiter.

Note: Refer to Appendix A for an extended description of Campania's culinary specialties and a lowdown on its best wines and drinks.

19 Recommended Books & Films

BOOKS

GENERAL

Besides his more famous *Italian Neighbors* (Grove Press, 2003), Tim Parks wrote a delightful account of his encounters with Italian culture (his wife is Italian) full of humor and insight, in *Italian Education* (Harper Perennials, 1996).

TRUE STORIES

If you want to bone up on the ancient Romans, Edward Gibbon's *History of the Decline and Fall of the Roman Empire* (begun in 1776) is still unrivaled today, but it will take you a minimum of 3 months to get through the several volumes (Penguin Classics, 1983).

Among the many travel writers who wrote on this region, one of the first is also one of the best and most charming: Johann Wolfgang von Goethe's *Italian Journey* (1816; reprinted by Penguin Books, 1992). Goethe much preferred Naples to Rome and writes vividly about a wide range of social and natural phenomena, from his mingling with the aristocracy to a trip up Mount Vesuvius during an eruption. The 19th century saw an explosion of travel writing by eminent authors on the "Grand Tour"; William Dean Howells recorded his impressions in *Roman Holidays and Others* (Kessinger Publishing, 2004). The impoverished English "slum novelist" George Gissing was finally able to travel to Italy toward the end of his life and wrote with great enthusiasm about his experiences in *By the Ionian Sea* (Marlboro Press, 1996). Henry James's *Italian Hours* (Penguin Classics, 1995) is a collection of essays, one of which describes the novelist's visit to the bay of Naples and its islands. Barbara Grizzuti Harrison describes her time in Italy, including a stay Naples, in *Italian Days* (Atlantic Monthly Press, 1998).

ART HISTORY

For a modern history of art, the touchstone is the massive *History of Italian Renaissance Art* (H. N. Abrams, 1994) by Frederick Hartt. Naples was not central to the art of that great period—Rome, Florence, and Venice were the major focal points—but you will find an interesting treatment of Naples's renaissance legacy in Laurie Scheider Adams's *Italian Renaissance Art* (Westview Press, 2001). To home in on Naples's baroque heritage, try John Varriano's *Italian Baroque and Rococo Architecture* (Oxford, 1986). Giorgio Vasari's *Lives of the Artists Vols. I and II* (Penguin Classics, 1987) is a collection of biographies of the great artists from Cimabue up to Vasari's own 16th-century contemporaries.

FICTION

The English writer Norman Douglas came to the bay of Naples early in the 20th century and was gripped by a lifelong fascination with the region. His most famous novel, *South Wind* (Indy-Publishing, 2002), is set on a fictional version of Capri, and reproduces the glamorous and eccentric expatriate community. Susan Sontag's historical novel, *The Volcano Lover* (Anchor, 1997), is set in the Napoleonic era, and is based on the true story of the love triangle between Sir William Hamilton (British ambassador to the Kingdom of the Two Sicilies), his wife, and her lover, Lord Horatio Nelson. *The Uncle from Rome* (Viking, 1992), by American author Joseph Caldwell, is the story of an opera singer from Indiana who comes to Naples to play a role. He befriends a family of Neapolitans, and becomes involved in family dynamics at least as theatrical as his stage performance. For a look at Naples's dark side, there is the tragicomic *Così fan Tutti* (Vintage/Black Lizard, 1998), a mystery by English novelist Michael Dibdin in his detective Aurelio Zen series.

Several Italian authors have written movingly of the harsh and beautiful rural life of southern Italy. Most famous perhaps is Carlo Levi's *Christ Stopped at Eboli* (English translation Farrar, Straus & Giroux, 2000), about the author's sojourn in a small village where he was exiled during the Fascist period.

FAST FACTS: Campania & the Amalfi Coast

American Express Travel agencies representing American Express are found in major cities. In Naples, check out **Dusila Travel,** also at Capodichino Airport (Viale Fulco Ruffo di Calabria; ℂ **081-2311281**).

Area Codes **081** for the province of Naples (including Sorrento, Pozzuoli, Ischia, and Capri); **082** for the provinces of Caserta, Benevento, and Avellino; **089** for the province of Salerno (including the Amalfi Coast); and **097** for the Cilento. To call to and from this region, see "Staying Connected," p. 42, and "Telephone Tips" on the inside front cover of this book.

Business Hours General business hours are Monday through Friday 8:30am to 1pm and 2:30 to 5:30pm. Banks are generally open Monday through Friday 8:30am to 1:30pm and 2:30 to 4pm. Some banks and businesses will also open on Saturday mornings. Shops are usually open Monday through Saturday from 8 or 9am to 1pm and 4:30 to 7:30 or 8pm, with one extra half-day closing per week at the shop's discretion. *Note:* A growing number of shops in tourist areas stay open during the lunch break and on Sundays.

Customs **What You Can Bring Into Italy** Rules governing what tourists can bring in duty-free are detailed at www.agenziadogane.it (click on "Traveler's custom card"). Foreign visitors from outside the European Union can bring up to 175€ ($210/£105) worth of goods for personal use (visitors below 15 years of age only up to 90€/$108/£54). Visitors over 17 years of age can also bring up to 200 cigarettes or 100 cigarillos (up to 3g each) or 50 cigars or loose tobacco not exceeding 250 grams; and up to 2 liters of alcoholic beverages under 22 percent by vol. or 1 liter under. Visitors over 15 years of age can also bring up to 500 grams of coffee; and all visitors can bring up to 100gr of tea, 50 grams of perfume, and 25cl of eau de toilette.

What You Can Take Home Returning **U.S. citizens** who have been away for at least 48 hours are allowed to bring back, once every 30 days, $800 (£400) worth of merchandise duty-free. You'll pay a flat rate of duty on the next $1,000 (£500) worth of purchases. Any dollar amount beyond that is subject to duties at whatever rates apply. On mailed gifts, the duty-free limit is $200 (£100). Be sure to keep your receipts for purchases accessible to expedite the declaration process. *Note:* If you owe duty, you are required to pay on your arrival in the United States—either by cash, personal check, government or traveler's check, money order, or, sometimes, a Visa or MasterCard. With some exceptions, you cannot bring fresh fruits and vegetables into the United States. For specifics on what you can bring back, download the invaluable free pamphlet *Know Before You Go* online at **www.cbp.gov**. (Click on "Travel," and then click on "Know Before You Go! Online Brochure.") Or request the pamphlet from the **U.S. Customs & Border Protection (CBP),** 1300 Pennsylvania Ave. NW, Washington, DC 20229 (ℂ **877/287-8667**).

For a clear summary of **Canadian** rules, write for the booklet *I Declare,* issued by the **Canada Border Services Agency** (ℂ **800/461-9999** in Canada, or 204/983-3500; www.cbsa-asfc.gc.ca). Canada allows its citizens a C$750 exemption, and you're allowed to bring back duty-free 1 carton of cigarettes, 1 can of tobacco, 40 imperial ounces of liquor, and 50 cigars. In addition, you're allowed to mail gifts to Canada valued at less than C$60 a day, provided they're unsolicited and don't contain alcohol or tobacco. (Write on the package: "Unsolicited gift, under $60 value.") *Note:* The $750 exemption can only be used once a year and only after an absence of 7 days.

Citizens of the U.K. who are **returning from a European Union (E.U.) country** will go through a separate Customs Exit (called the "Blue Exit") especially for E.U. travelers. No limits are placed on what you can bring back from an E.U. country, provided the items are for personal use (this includes gifts), and you have already paid the duty and tax. You may be asked to prove that the goods are for your own use if you exceed the set *guidance levels:* 3,200 cigarettes, or 200 cigars, or 400 cigarillos, or 3 kilograms of smoking tobacco, 10 liters of spirits, 90 liters of wine, 20 liters of fortified wine (such as port or sherry), and 110 liters of beer. For more detailed information, contact **HM Customs & Excise** (© **0845/010-9000;** from outside the U.K. 020/8929-0152; www.hmce.gov.uk).

The duty-free allowance in **Australia** is A$400 or, for those under 18, A$200. Citizens can bring in 250 cigarettes or 250 grams of loose tobacco, and 1.125 liters of alcohol. A helpful brochure available from Australian consulates or Customs offices is *Know Before You Go.* For more information, contact the **Australian Customs Service** (© 1300/363-263; www.customs.gov.au).

The duty-free allowance for **New Zealand** is NZ$700. Citizens over 17 can bring in 200 cigarettes, 50 cigars, or 250 grams of tobacco (or a mixture of all three if their combined weight doesn't exceed 250g); plus 4.5 liters of wine and beer, or 1.125 liters of liquor. New Zealand currency does not carry import or export restrictions. A free pamphlet is available at New Zealand consulates and Customs offices: *New Zealand Customs Guide for Travellers, Notice no. 4.* For more information, contact **New Zealand Customs,** The Customhouse, 17–21 Whitmore St., Box 2218, Wellington (© **04/473-6099** or 0800/428-786; www.customs.govt.nz).

Electricity The electricity in Campania is an alternating current (AC), varying from 42 to 50 cycles. The voltage is 220. It's recommended that any visitor carrying electrical appliances obtain a transformer (laptop computers usually have one built in their cord; check on the back for allowed voltages). Italian plugs have prongs that are round, not flat; therefore, an adapter plug is also needed. You can purchase both transformer and adaptor in any local hardware store.

Embassies & Consulates All embassies are located in Rome, but you'll find most consulates in Naples: The **U.S. Consulate** is at Piazza della Repubblica 2 (© **081-5838111;** fax 081-7611869; www.usis.it); the **Canadian Consulate** is at Via Carducci 29 (© **081-401338;** fax 081-406161; www.canada.it); the **U.K. Consulate** is at Via Crispi 122 (© **081-663511** or 081-663589; fax 081-7613720; www.britain.it).

Emergencies Dial © **113** or **112** for the police; © **118** for an ambulance; and © **115** for a fire. For road emergencies dial © **803-116.**

Etiquette & Social Customs Volumes have been written on Italian etiquette, as there are rules on everything. Yet, Italians are pretty forgiving of foreigners;

and, if you are observant and mold your behavior to theirs, you'll stay away from most blunders.

Appropriate Attire: Italians tend to dress more formally, particularly in urban settings. Shorts and tank tops are reserved for the beach. Women tend to dress more conservatively, particularly if they are alone. The Catholic Church has strict dress codes for both women and men: No showing of shoulders or legs above the knee in a church or on sacred ground.

Courtesy: Get up for everybody who's hampered by packages or children, for the elderly, and for women; and open doors for them especially if you are a man. Offer your seat to elderly and pregnant women, or anybody carrying a small child. Don't cut in line: Italians might not queue in an orderly manner like the English, but they respect the order of arrival at an establishment, from the ice-cream counter to the post office. Always acknowledge people when entering and exiting a place, such as a shop, with *Buongiorno* and *Grazie*.

Gestures & Contact: Italians do gesticulate a lot, but pointing at someone with your index is considered rude. Shaking hands should be with your right, and hugging and kissing on the cheek among friends is common.

Eating & Drinking: It is customary for two parties to "fight" over the dinner bill, and you are expected to offer to pay, even if you won't be allowed. If you have been taken out for a meal, it is then good manners to return the invitation. If that is impossible, a small gift (flowers, for example) sent to their home (if it was a private party) or a thank-you note (if it was a business meal) will do the trick. If you are invited to someone's home, never come empty handed: Flowers, pastries, chocolates, or a small gift for the children are the right way to go.

Photography: It is forbidden to take photographs of military, police, and transport (including subway and airport) facilities.

Language Italian is the local language, but English is generally understood at most attractions, hotels, and restaurants that cater to visitors, as well as in many pharmacies. Even if not all the staff at a restaurant or other business speak English, almost always one person does and can be summoned. The glossary in Appendix B will prove helpful as you travel in remote towns and villages, and a Berlitz Italian phrase book is a handy accompaniment.

Laundromats Public laundromats *(lavanderia a gettoni)* are extremely rare, but you can drop your laundry at most *tintoria* (dry cleaners) to have it washed and folded.

Legal Aid The consulate of your country is the place to turn for legal aid, although offices can't interfere in the Italian legal process. They can, however, inform you of your rights and provide you with a list of professional attorneys. If you're arrested for a drug offense, the consulate will notify a lawyer about your case and perhaps inform your family.

Liquor Laws There's no legal drinking age in Italy. Alcohol is sold day and night throughout the year, and the only limitations are the operating hours of bars and shops (see "Business Hours," above). The law is extremely tough though on drunken behavior, and disturbance of the *quiete pubblica* (public quiet) will be punished with stiff fines and jail time. Littering (including potential littering such as drinking from your beer bottle while sitting on an ancient wall) is also severely penalized. Drinking and driving can result in jail time as well as loss of your driving permit.

Mail Mail delivery in Italy had a remarkably bad record, but things have improved enormously in recent years. Postcards (not in regular letter envelopes) pay a reduced rate, but are also the slowest. Your family and friends back home might receive your postcards in 1 week, or it might take 2 weeks (sometimes longer). Letters mailed to locations outside Europe with *Posta Prioritaria* take 4 to 8 days depending on the destinations; letters to Europe and Mediterranean countries take 3 days. Postcards and letters weighing up to 20 grams sent to the United States, Canada, Australia, and New Zealand cost .80€ ($1/50p); to the United Kingdom and Ireland, .62€ (90¢/ 45p). You can buy stamps at all post offices and at *tabacchi* (tobacconist) stores.

Passports Allow plenty of time before your trip to apply for a passport; processing normally takes 4 to 6 weeks but can take longer during busy periods (especially spring). If you need a passport in a hurry, you'll pay a higher processing fee.

For Residents of the United States: Whether you're applying in person or by mail, you can download passport applications from the U.S. State Department website at **http://travel.state.gov**. For general information, call the **National Passport Agency** (© 202/647-0518). To find your regional passport office, either check the U.S. State Department website or call the **National Passport Information Center** (© 900/225-5674); the fee is 55¢ per minute for automated information and $1.50 per minute for operator-assisted calls.

For Residents of Canada: Passport applications are available at travel agencies throughout Canada or from the central **Passport Office,** Department of Foreign Affairs and International Trade, Ottawa, ON K1A 0G3 (© **800/567-6868;** www.ppt.gc.ca).

For Residents of the United Kingdom: To pick up an application for a standard 10-year passport (5-year passport for children younger than age 16), visit your nearest passport office, major post office, or travel agency. You can also contact the **United Kingdom Passport Service** at © 0870/521-0410, or search its website at www.ukpa.gov.uk.

For Residents of Ireland: You can apply for a 10-year passport at the **Passport Office,** Setanta Centre, Molesworth Street, Dublin 2 (© **01/671-1633;** www.irlgov.ie/iveagh). Those younger than age 18 and older than 65 must apply for a 12€ ($17/£8.40), 3-year passport. You can also apply at 1A South Mall, Cork (© **021/272-525)** or at most main post offices.

For Residents of Australia: You can pick up an application from your local post office or any branch of Passports Australia, but you must schedule an interview at the passport office to present your application materials. Call the **Australian Passport Information Service** at © 131-232, or visit the government website at www.passports.gov.au.

For Residents of New Zealand: You can pick up a passport application at any New Zealand Passports Office or download it from their website. Contact the **Passports Office** at © 0800/225-050 in New Zealand or 04/474-8100, or log on to www.passports.govt.nz.

Restrooms Airports, train stations, museums, and major archaeological areas and attractions all have restrooms, often with attendants who expect to be tipped. Bars, nightclubs, restaurants, cafes, gas stations, and hotels should have facilities as well, but they are open only to customers. Public toilets are found near many of the major sights. Usually they're designated WC (water closet) and bear international symbols or the signs DONNE (women) and UOMINI (men). The most confusing designation is SIGNORI (gentlemen) and SIGNORE (ladies), so watch that final i and e! Many public toilets charge a small fee or employ an attendant who expects a tip. It's a good idea to carry some tissues in your pocket or purse—they often come in handy.

Smoking Smoking is very common but is forbidden in enclosed public spaces, except those with separate ventilated smoking areas. If smoking is important to you, call the venue of your choice to find out if it's allowed.

Taxes As a member of the European Union, Italy imposes a value-added tax (called IVA in Italy) on most goods and services. The tax that most affects visitors is the one imposed on hotel rates, which ranges from 9% in first- and second-class hotels to 19% in deluxe hotels.

Non-E.U. (European Union) citizens are entitled to a refund of the IVA if you spend more than 155€ ($194/£109) at any one store, before tax. To claim your refund, request an invoice from the cashier at the store and take it to the Customs office *(dogana)* at the airport to have it stamped before you leave. **Note:** If you're going to another E.U. country before flying home, have it stamped at the airport Customs office of the last E.U. country you'll be in (for example, if you're flying home via Britain, have your Italian invoices stamped in London). Once you're back home, mail the stamped invoice (keep a photocopy for your records) back to the original vendor within 90 days of the purchase. The vendor will, sooner or later, send you a refund of the tax that you paid at the time of your original purchase. Reputable stores view this as a matter of ordinary paperwork and are businesslike about it. Less-honorable stores might lose your file. It pays to deal with established vendors on large purchases. You can also request that the refund be credited to the card with which you made the purchase; this is usually a faster procedure.

Many shops are now part of the "Tax Free for Tourists" network (look for the sticker in the window). Stores participating in this network issue a check along with your invoice at the time of purchase. After you have the invoice stamped at Customs, you can redeem the check for cash directly at the Tax Free booth in the airport (in Rome, it's past Customs; in Milan's airports, the booth is inside the duty-free shop) or mail it back in the envelope provided within 60 days.

Time Zone Campania is 6 hours ahead of Eastern Standard Time in the United States and 1 hour ahead of Greenwich Mean Time in the U.K. Daylight saving time goes into effect in Italy each year from the last Sunday in March to the last Sunday in October.

Tipping In **hotels,** a service charge of 15% to 19% will be added to your bill. In addition, it's customary to tip the maid .50€ to 2€ (70¢–$2.80/35p–£1.40) per day, the doorman (for calling a cab) .50€ (70¢/ 35p), and the bellhop or porter 1€ to 5€ ($1.40–$7/70p–£3.50) for carrying your bags to your room. A concierge expects up to 15% of his or her bill, as well as tips for extra services performed, which could include help with long-distance calls.

In **restaurants and cafes,** 15% is usually added to your bill to cover most charges. If you're not sure whether this has been done, ask, *"È incluso il servizio?"* (ay een-*cloo*-soh eel sair-*vee*-tsoh). An additional tip isn't required, but it's customary to leave the equivalent of an extra couple of euros if you've been pleased with the service. Checkroom attendants expect .50€ to 1€ (70¢–$1.40/35p–70p), and washroom attendants should get at least .50€ (70¢/35p). Restaurants are required by law to give customers official receipts.

Taxi drivers can be tipped 10% to 15% of the fare.

Water In restaurants, most locals drink mineral water with their meals; however, tap water is safe everywhere, as are public drinking fountains. Some areas of Naples have had long-term problems with the water supply, and this is why all public establishments in the city—hotels, bars, cafes, restaurants, and so on—have their own filtering devices. If you are staying in a private home, though, make sure you ask about the water supply. Unsafe sources and fountains will be marked ACQUA NON POTABILE.

3

Suggested Campania & the Amalfi Coast Itineraries

There are any number of ways to go about exploring all that Campania has to offer. Public transportation in the region is good, so you can easily move about from one destination to the other by train or bus. Exploring the countryside, though, will require a car, which you can rent in any city or large town for just the time you need it—with the rocketing car theft rates in Campania (and the parking woes in the coastal towns), having a car is more a liability than a commodity. Another possibility is renting a car with a driver, an increasingly popular option, particularly for exploring the Sorrento peninsula and the famous Amalfi Drive.

While Naples is usually your port of entry to the region—it is the largest city, and is served by an international airport and harbor—we recommend you keep your exploration of this bustling city for last: Naples can be overwhelming, literally bursting with life and noise, and you'll appreciate it a lot more if you ease yourself slowly into this special cultural universe by starting your visit in smaller towns. Plus, with so much to see in Naples, you might never get to explore the rest of the region. The itineraries below take in all our favorite destinations; you can mix and match them depending on your particular interests and the amount of time you have.

1 Campania & the Amalfi Coast in 1 Week

One week is not long to visit the whole Amalfi Coast region, but you'll certainly be able to get a good idea of its key attractions. Since your time is short, you'll have to pare your exploration to the essentials. You'll miss a lot of the pleasurable lingering, which is so suitable to this region, but you'll have enough time to plunge right into the most phenomenal sights.

You can do a lot of this itinerary by public transportation (including ferries), but you might want to have a car for days 2 and 3, while exploring the region's southern area.

Days ❶ & ❷: Sorrento & the Amalfi Coast

Fly into Naples's Capodichino Airport and get yourself directly to **Sorrento** (there's bus as well as limo service from the airport, or you can rent a car if you feel more daring). Once there, allow yourself a day of relaxation to recover from jet lag. Stroll the **Lungomare,** do some swimming and, if you are more ambitious, catch a concert in the evening. The best—if you have planned in advance to get tickets—are those offered in the cloister of San Francesco (see "Campania Calendar of Events," in chapter 2). On day 2, get an early start and explore the **Sorrento peninsula** and **Amalfi Coast.** (Hiring a limo is the best option, as your driver will double as guide.) Hike, swim, visit the splendid **Amalfi cathedral** (don't miss the interior). You might even have time for some of the smaller towns off the beaten track. Have dinner at one of our favorite restaurants in the area: **Relais Blu, San Pietro, Faro di Capo d'Orso, Taverna del Capitano, Olimpia Relais,** or **Don Alfonso 1890**—on this stretch of coast you'll find the region's best gourmet haunts, as well as those with the best views. See chapters 6 and 7.

Day ❸: Padula, Paestum & Salerno

In the morning, go to **Certosa di Padula** (you can use public transportation, but you'll have to keep a strict timetable; it is best to rent or hire a car) and devote a few hours to this architectural marvel. In the afternoon, drive or take a bus to **Paestum** to visit the stunning temples at sunset—on the way, you'll cross through Cilento National Park. Spend the night in **Salerno** (where you can relinquish your car if you rented one), and have dinner in the **medieval town.** See chapter 9.

Day ❹: Salerno & Capri

After an early stroll through **Salerno,** enjoying its splendid **Lungomare,** take a ferry to **Capri,** where you can spend the rest of the day shopping and seeing the sights. Stay overnight—this is especially important in summer—to get the full flavor of this mythical island after most of the crowds have gone back to the mainland). See chapter 8.

Days ❺ & ❻: Naples

The next morning, catch one of the frequent ferry or hydrofoil services to **Naples.** At this point you'll be ready for the big city and its vast artistic riches. Start your visit with the **Maschio Angioino,** not far from the harbor. You might have time for a short visit to both **Palazzo Reale** and the **Museo Nazionale di Capodimonte** before you call it a day. Proceed to the **Lungomare** to enjoy the panoramic views of **Borgo Marinari** over a well-deserved dinner.

On day 6, take the **walking tour of SpaccaNapoli** (p. 114) and have a pizza lunch in one of the nearby historical *pizzerie* to round out your Old Naples experience. Spend the afternoon at the **Museo Archeologico Nazionale** in preparation for your last day. See chapter 4.

Day ❼: Herculaneum, Pompeii & Mount Vesuvius

For a relaxing, quiet excursion, catch a train on the Circum Vesuviana railroad to **Herculaneum;** or go to **Pompeii** if you like grandiose stretches of excavations. Both sites offer enormous amounts to see—covering both in 1 day is impossible, and we don't recommend trying. Use the other half of your day to climb **Mount Vesuvius,** the burning heart of Campania, and visit one of the ancient Roman villas there. See chapter 5.

2 Campania & the Amalfi Coast in 2 Weeks

Two weeks is an ideal amount of time to explore this culturally and naturally rich region. You'll be able to see some of the best artistic treasures in Italy, but you can also relax and enjoy the sea, coastline, and mountains. We have organized this itinerary so that you can choose whether to rent a car or to use public transportation. If you decide not to rent a car, you can skip the countryside and concentrate on the main destinations, which are all well connected by public transportation. Should you change your mind, you can always hire a car with a driver for a day or two, or rent a car in any big town.

Campania & the Amalfi Coast in 1 Week & 2 Weeks

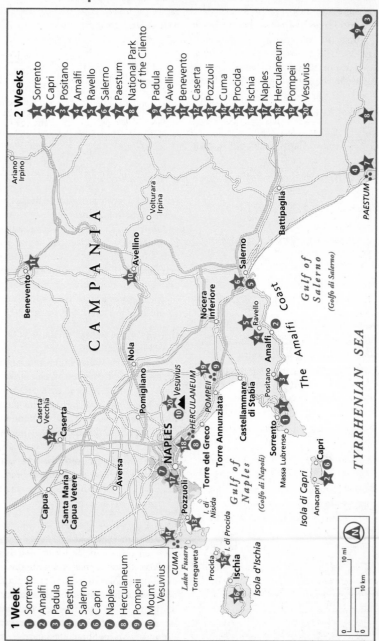

1 Week
1. Sorrento
2. Amalfi
3. Padula
4. Paestum
5. Salerno
6. Capri
7. Naples
8. Herculaneum
9. Pompeii
10. Mount Vesuvius

2 Weeks
1. Sorrento
2. Capri
3. Positano
4. Amalfi
5. Ravello
6. Salerno
7. Paestum
8. National Park of the Cilento
9. Padula
10. Avellino
11. Benevento
12. Caserta
13. Pozzuoli
14. Cuma
15. Procida
16. Ischia
17. Naples
18. Herculaneum
19. Pompeii
20. Vesuvius

Day ❶: Sorrento

Fly into Naples and take either the bus or a limo service to **Sorrento** (you could rent a car at the airport, but you won't need one until day 3). Recover from jet lag while relaxing in this splendid resort town: Take in the sights, do some shopping, have a swim (see chapter 6).

Day ❷: Capri

Take a ferry to **Capri,** where you'll spend the night: You'll have a full day to explore this unique island, hike, swim, sunbathe, and shop. See chapter 8.

Days ❸ & ❹: The Sorrento Peninsula & the Amalfi Coast

Take a morning ferry to **Positano,** where you'll visit the town and pick up your car (you can also use public transportation for your exploration, but you'll have to keep a stricter schedule). Spend days 3 and 4 taking in **Amalfi, Ravello,** and the lesser-known towns both along the coast and the interior. See chapter 7.

Day ❺: Salerno & Paestum

Arrive in **Salerno** in the morning. This town makes a good base for your explorations: Plan to spend 2 nights here.

After a stroll along the **Lungomare,** head for the **medieval town** to visit the splendid **cathedral** and have lunch. In the afternoon, arrive in **Paestum,** with its unique temples: Be sure to stay until sunset to enjoy the views. See chapter 9.

Day ❻: Padula & the Cilento

Hire a car to explore the **Park of the Cilento** and its memorable coast in the morning. Then make your way to the **Certosa di Padula** for an afternoon visit, crossing through the imposing Cilento Massif, with its eerie caves and soaring peaks. You could rely solely on public transportation here, but you'll have to keep to a strict timetable. See chapter 9.

Day ❼ & ❽: Avellino & Benevento

Dedicate days 7 and 8 to **Avellino** and **Benevento.** These two towns are each the capital of a sub-region rich in cultural, natural, and artistic heritage. You could easily dedicate a few days to each; but if you're on a strict schedule, you'll have to satisfy yourself with the highlights. Having a car will allow you to make the most of it, and you can add a quick tour of the countryside. We recommend that you make time for a visit to the little town of **Sant'Angelo dei Lombardi,** with its castle and famous abbey. Spend day 8 in **Benevento,** taking in the town's attractions. See chapter 10.

Day ❾: Caserta & Surroundings

Leave early in the morning for **Caserta** and start with a visit to the awesome **Reggia** and its gardens. We suggest you also visit the **Cathedral of Casertavecchia** and the **Belvedere di San Leucio,** maybe taking in a concert there if you are visiting during the season and have planned in advance for tickets. See chapter 10.

Day ❿: Pozzuoli, Cuma & the Phlegrean Fields

Arrive in the morning in the splendid Bay of **Pozzuoli,** home to treasures from antiquity and views beloved by Neapolitans. Spend the day visiting the **Parco Archeologico Subacqueo di Baia** and the **Acropolis of Cuma.** (See chapter 4.) In the evening, catch a ferry from Pozzuoli to have dinner on the island of **Procida,** where you can spend the night. See chapter 8.

Day ⓫: Ischia

From Pozzuoli (or Procida), catch a ferry to **Ischia.** On the island, hire a local taxi to take you on a tour, or use the excellent public bus system. Then spend a few hours in **Giardini Poseidon**—our favorite outdoor spa on the island—or pick one of the indoor ones we recommend. Then head for the beach: **Spiaggia di Citara** and **Lido dei Maronti** are the best on the island. For dinner, sample the local cuisine and wines. See chapter 8.

Days ⑫ & ⑬: Naples

In the early morning, catch a ferry to **Naples;** arrive in its famous harbor under the towering shadow of Vesuvius before the sun rises too high and enjoy the scene in its best light. To see the city, follow days 5 and 6 of our "Campania & the Amalfi Coast in 1 Week" itinerary, above.

Day ⑭: Herculaneum, Pompeii & Mount Vesuvius

Follow day 7 of our itinerary for "Campania & the Amalfi Coast in 1 Week."

---

3 Campania & the Amalfi Coast for Families

If you had any concerns before starting out on this vacation with your kids, they'll melt away as soon as you arrive in this warm and welcoming region. Depending on the attention span and specific interests of your family members, you might have to cut out some artistic attractions, but you'll be more than rewarded with outdoor activities. This itinerary minimizes boring car trips and, instead, relies on ferries—usually more fun for children—to explore the seaside offerings of this region.

Day ① & ②: Ischia

From Naples's Capodichino Airport, take a taxi to Mergellina Harbor where you can catch the ferry to **Ischia.** With lots of water activities and beautiful sandy beaches (instead of the rocky ones on Capri and the Sorrento peninsula), this lesser-known island is more geared to families than its more famous sibling. You'll have your choice of hotels that are beautiful but less expensive and stuffy than the ones in the region's more glamorous destinations. Pack a picnic lunch and enjoy the views before descending to the beach—**Spiaggia di Citara** and **Lido dei Maronti** are the best on the island. Treat yourself and the kids to some ice cream while strolling along the seaside promenades. See chapter 8.

Day ②: Capri

Make an early start and catch a ferry to Capri. Spend the rest of the day and night on this mythical island, enjoying its rocky beaches and hiking trails. Climb the **Fenician Staircase** and take a boat tour of the island (much better than waiting in line for the Blue Grotto if you're there in high season). See chapter 8.

Day ③: Salerno & Paestum

Catch a ferry to **Salerno** early enough for a leisurely morning: Stroll along the

splendid **Lungomare** and pay a visit to the noteworthy **cathedral** before having lunch in the **medieval district.** Then, catch one of the frequent buses to **Paestum,** where you'll spend the night in one of its seaside hotels. The afternoon is beach time: You can go swimming if the weather's nice, and then pay a sunset visit to the ancient Greek temples (or save your visit for early the next morning). See chapter 9.

Day ④: The Amalfi Coast

Hire a car with a driver for a tour of the **Amalfi Coast:** You'll eliminate parking headaches and make the most of your day. You'll want to allot more time to swimming, ice-cream sampling, and hiking than to visiting churches and driving; still, don't miss the splendid **Amalfi cathedral** (see chapter 7). Have the car drop you in Naples for the night.

Days ⑤ & ⑥: Naples

Follow days 5 and 6 of our itinerary for "Campania & the Amalfi Coast in 1 Week," but don't try too hard to pack everything in. Concentrate on the many mighty castles—**Castel Nuovo, Castel dell'Ovo, Castello di Sant'Elmo**—and the church of **San Lorenzo Maggiore,** where you can explore several layers of excavations: Most kids should find this

Campania & the Amalfi Coast for Families

1. Ischia
2. Capri
3. Salerno
4. Paestum
5. Amalfi
6. Naples
7. Herculaneum
8. Pompeii
9. Vesuvius

exciting. Also, do not miss a pizza lunch at the historical **Pizzeria Di Matteo.** (These are individual pizzas; order one each plus a deep-fried one for the table, to share as appetizer.) Make sure you take your children on a funicular ride as well, and have dinner in the Vomero area. If you have little ones along, visit the playground in the Villa Comunale on the Lungomare. (This was greatly appreciated by our own little guy—so much so that we now have to squeeze in an hour there every day we are in Naples.) See chapter 4.

Day ❼: Herculaneum, Pompeii & Mount Vesuvius

Follow day 7 of our itinerary for "Campania & the Amalfi Coast in 1 Week." The casts of dead bodies in the museum in **Herculaneum** might be just the thing if your teenagers and pre-teens are like some we know, but they may disturb younger children. **Pompeii** is a larger and more comprehensive site, yet might be more tiring for younger children. Definitely hire a guide to explore **Mount Vesuvius:** Descending into the crater will thrill older kids, while the nature trails on the north slope of the volcano are fun for all ages. See chapter 5.

4 The Natural Wonders of Campania & the Amalfi Coast

If you think Campania is museums, churches, and archaeological areas, you'll miss out on its great attractions not made by human hands. This region offers manifold opportunities to combine culture with outdoor activities and superb natural sights. The itinerary below is designed for a week, but you can shorten or lengthen it at your leisure to accommodate your other plans. Having a car will allow for the greatest freedom.

Days ❶ to ❷: Vico Equense & the Sorrento Peninsula

Start with one of the lesser-known resorts on the Sorrento peninsula, **Vico Equense,** where you can spend the night and have your first encounter with the sea at **Marina di Equa**—the best beach in town—which is dominated by a powerful 17th-century tower. (If you don't have a car, take the Sorrento-bound bus from Capodichino Airport to Vico Equense).

Reserve the afternoon for a beautiful hike through the peninsula, taking the moderately challenging footpath from Sorrento toward **Punta Sant'Elia;** this scenic point overlooks the islets of Li Galli in the Bay of Salerno, which have made Positano famous. See chapter 6.

On day 2, continue on to the tip of the peninsula and the beach of **Punta del Capo.** Beloved by the locals, it is located near the ruins of a Roman villa. Nearby, a small pool of water enclosed by rocks is known as the Bath of Queen Giovanna.

In the afternoon, hire a boat from Marina del Cantone to reach the Bay of Ieranto and its marine preserve. You will be rewarded with magical surroundings—when the light is just right toward the end of the day, the boats appear to float in mid-air. Overnight in Marina del Cantone. See chapter 6.

Day ❸: The Amalfi Coast

Get an early start for your ride along the historic **Amalfi Drive.** Stop for a swim (or have a rowboat take you) into the Grotta dello Smeraldo in the village of **Conca dei Marini.** Continue with a hike from

Furore down to **Furore Marina,** the deep fjord graced by a small beach, over the ancient footpath. You can then hike the Sentiero degli Dei or the Via degli Incanti, and finish your day visiting the natural preserve of Capo d'Orso. From here, walk to the 11th-century monastery and have dinner at the lighthouse. Overnight in Salerno. See chapter 7.

Day ❹: Capri

Take an early-morning ferry or hydrofoil to **Capri,** where you'll spend the night. Use the day to explore the island, taking the chairlift up to the top of **Monte Solaro** and descending the famous **Scala Fenicia** into town. End your day with a swim at the **Bagni di Tiberio,** near the ruins of one of Emperor Tiberius's notorious pleasure palaces. See chapter 8.

Days ❺ to ❻: Paestum & the Cilento

Hop on a ferry early in the morning and rejoin your car in **Salerno.** Head for the **National Park of the Cilento,** starting with the beautiful coast where you can enjoy a variety of water sports, including diving and water-skiing. The best beach is **Baia della Calanca,** in Marina di Camerota. Don't forget the interior, though. Schedule a visit to the **Grottoes of Castelcivita** or **Grottoes of Pertosa** for fantastic spelunking (nothing demanding athleticism or ropes), as well as a hike on **Monte Cervati,** the highest peak of the Cilento massif; another excellent hike is **Monte Alburno.**

Make sure you reserve the afternoon of day 6 for **Paestum,** to visit its temples,

The Natural Wonders of Campania & the Amalfi Coast

① Vico Equense   ④ Furore   ⑦ Paestum
② Punta del Capo   ⑤ Capri   ⑧ Mount Vesuvius
③ Conca dei   ⑥ National Park of   ⑨ Oplontis
　 Marini   　 the Cilento   ⑩ Boscoreale

Benevento

Mondragone   Capua   Caserta Vecchia

Santa Maria   Caserta
Capua Vetere

CAMPANIA

Aversa

LITERNUM   Nola   Avellino
Lake Patria

Pomigliano

Volturara
Irpina

Licola Mare   NAPLES   ⑧ Vesuvius
CUMA
Lake Fusaro   Pozzuoli   ⑩ ▲ BOSCOREALE
Torregaveta   Baia   HERCULANEUM   OPLONTIS   Nocera
Procida   I. di   Torre del Greco   ⑨   POMPEII   Inferiore
Nisida   Torre Annunziata
Ischia   I. di Procida   Gulf of   Castellammare   Salerno
    Naples   di Stabia
Isola d'Ischia   (Golfo di Napoli)   Vico
    Equense   Conca dei   Ravello
    Sorrento   Positano   Marina   Amalfi
    Massa Lubrense   ④③   Coast   Battipaglia
    Furore   The Amalfi   Gulf of
Isola di Capri   ②   Salerno
Anacapri ⑤ Capri   Punta del   (Golfo di Salerno)
    Capo

0   10 mi
0   10 km   TYRRHENIAN SEA   ⑥
    PAESTUM ⑦

---

walk its walls, and swim from one of the best beaches in Italy. See chapter 9.

Day ⑦: Mount Vesuvius & Ancient Roman Villas

For your last day, head toward Naples's **Mount Vesuvius** area. Start your visit with **Oplontis** and **Boscoreale**—two excellent sites for exploring ancient Roman ruins—and then take your leave of the region with a hike to the crater of Naples's volcano. What could be more appropriate than ending your trip with a blast? See chapter 5.

Naplcs

Much has been written on Naples ("Napule," in local parlance), but nothing can render the multifaced reality of this city better than a visit—or actually several visits. Once you get past the initial grit, you'll find art treasures galore, equaling and often surpassing many more popular destinations in Italy, and you'll discover the city's unique soul.

The first adjective that comes to mind to define it is "ebullient." You'll feel this energy in the traffic, the noise, but also in the cultural life: in the music, in the performing arts, in the people's deep love for and pride in their city, and in their fervent religiosity. Above all, you'll pick up on a sense of enthusiasm for what the city has to offer, from romantic evening walks along the shore; to magnificent views over the bay with Mount Vesuvius in the background; to the beauty of Piazza del Plebiscito, Castel Nuovo, and Castel dell'Ovo. And, of course, this being Italy, Neapolitans are proud of all the good things to eat here, especially the fresh seafood; local tomatoes, which make the best fresh sauces; and the pizza they invented.

The second adjective that describes Naples is "welcoming." If you take the time to notice, you will see that Neapolitans really reach out to visitors and relish in others' enjoyment of their beloved city. Maybe that is the most truly fascinating thing about Naples: It has incredible architectural and artistic attractions, natural beauty, and fantastic food and wines, but ultimately, when you fall in love with the city—as you will if you let it get to you—you'll do so because of its humanity. When you walk the streets of Naples, you'll understand that its underlying character hasn't changed much in 2 millennia. It takes a certain kind of people, surely, to live in the shadow of a very dangerous volcano, century after century, and to find it beautiful.

This appreciation should not make you less careful: Naples is legendary for its pickpockets and other petty criminals. Also, a large part of Naples is unbelievably poor, and it's as plagued as anywhere in the modern world by drugs and thievery. Though depressed areas of Naples are well in the outskirts, pickpockets and thieves from those areas come regularly into the city to conduct their "business." This sort of thing gave Naples a bad name for many years, but police have recently been doing an excellent job at curbing crime.

The other unsavory thing about Naples is the traffic; the resulting confusion and dirt have put off many visitors. If you get past—or literally, away from—the noise, you can relax and discover a city that many visitors over the centuries have described in justly heavenly terms.

1 Essentials

GETTING THERE

BY PLANE   Naples's airport, **Aeroporto Capodichino** (© 081-7896259; www.gesac.it), is only about 7km (4 miles) from the city center. It is a small but well-organized airport, receiving flights from many Italian and European cities, as well as a few intercontinental flights. See "Getting There" in chapter 2 for more information on airlines that service Capodichino. From the airport you can easily take a taxi into town; the flat rate for the 15-minute trip is 19.50€ ($27/£14) including all extras such as luggage and evening and Sunday supplements (but not gratuities). Many hotels offer a limousine service, but it is more costly, hovering around 35€ ($44/£25). If you don't have much luggage, for 3€ ($3.75/£2.10) one-way, a convenient ANM bus (© 800-639525; www.anm.it) runs to Piazza Municipio in the town center (it stops across from the Teatro Mercadante), with an intermediary stop in Piazza Garibaldi (by the post office at Corso Novara). Buses run every 30 minutes from the airport (Mon–Fri 6:30am–11:39pm; Sat–Sun 6:30am–11:50pm) and from Piazza Municipio (Mon–Fri 6am–12:12am; Sat–Sun 6am–midnight).

BY TRAIN   Naples lies on the main southern rail corridor and is served by frequent and fast service from most Italian and European cities and towns. *EuroStar* trains (marked ES) make very limited stops, *intercity* trains (IC) make limited stops, and *AltaVelocità* (AV) trains are high-speed. Regular trains take between 2 and 2½ hours between Rome and Naples, while the AV train takes only 87 minutes, making it by far the best method of transport between the two cities and to destinations farther north. The fare is about 23€ ($32/£16). Contact **Trenitalia** (© 892021 from anywhere in Italy; www.trenitalia.it) for fares and information.

Trains arrive at the **Stazione Centrale** (© 081-5543188) on Piazza Garibaldi, northeast of the city's historical center. You will find **taxis** just outside the station. *Note:* You will be approached by "taxi" drivers—actually Gypsy taxis—inside the station. Ignore them: They ask for outrageous rates and are a source of Naples's bad rap for dishonesty. See "Getting Around by Taxi," later in this chapter. Under the station is the **subway** *(Metropolitana)* as well as the urban rail *(Cumana)*. Across from the station on Piazza Garibaldi is the **bus station,** with both city and suburban buses and trams. City bus no. R2 and tram no. 1 both go to the city center.

Slower trains also stop at the **Stazione Mergellina** (© 081-7612102), on Piazza Piedigrotta, to the west of Naples's historical center. This station is convenient for transfers to the **ferry** (Terminal Aliscafi). Taxis, subways, and buses connect this station with the town center and other destinations nearby.

BY BOAT   Arriving into the bay of Naples by boat is an unforgettable experience and the best introduction to the city. The major port of central Italy, Naples's **Stazione Marittima** (just off Via Cristoforo Colombo, steps from the Castel Nuovo) receives both cruise ships and regular ferry service from many destinations in Italy, including Ischia, Capri, Sicily (Messina, Siracusa Catania, Palermo, and the Aeolian Islands), and Sardinia (Cagliari). Hydrofoil service (suspended in winter) operates mostly from Mergellina's nearby **Terminal Aliscafi,** with frequent and fast runs to Capri, Ischia, Procida, Sorrento, Positano, Amalfi, Salerno, and Sicily (Milazzo and the Aeolian Islands). The major operating companies—all offering similar levels of service and fares but varying hours of operation—are **Tirrenia** (© 199-123199 or 081-2514711; www.tirrenia.it), with ships to Cagliari and Palermo; **Siremar** (© 081-5800340;

www.siremar.it), which serves the Aeolian Islands and Milazzo; **TTTLines** (*©* **800-915365**), with service to Catania and Palermo; **Medmar,** with ships (*©* **081-5513352**) to Tunis as well as ferries (*©* **081-3334411**) to Ischia; **Caremar** (*©* **081-5513882;** www.caremar.it), with ferries and hydrofoils to Ischia, Capri, and Procida; **Alilauro** (*©* **081-7611004;** www.alilauro.it), with hydrofoils to Ischia and Positano; **SNAV** (*©* **081-4285555** or 081-4285111; www.snav.it), with hydrofoils to Ischia, Capri, and Procida, as well as ships to Palermo, Sardinia, and the Aeolian and Pontine islands; **LMP** (*©* **081-5513236**), with hydrofoils to Sorrento; and **NLG** (*©* **081-5527209**), with hydrofoils to Capri. The **Metrò del Mare** (*©* **199-446644;** www.metrodelmare.com) operates commuter service between Bacoli and Salerno with intermediary stops in Pozzuoli, Naples, Vico Equense, Sorrento, Positano, and Amalfi; during the summer they make additional trips to the islands, with limited service. **Taxi del Mare** (*©* **081-8773600;** www.taxidelmare.it) is a water taxi available to take passengers to and from Naples and to any destination within the Naples and Salerno bays. Prices vary depending on the distance: The most expensive ride at presstime was Naples to Amalfi for 905€ ($1,267/£634), while the cheapest was Capri to Nerano for 356€ ($498/£249).

BY CAR   Car theft—even from guarded parking lots—fierce traffic, and the local passion for speed make driving in Naples a real hassle. Still, arriving or leaving the city by car is not horribly difficult: Major highways connect the city to most other destinations in Italy. From the north, take the *autostrada* A1 MILANO ROMA NAPOLI, whereas from the south take the *autostrada* A3 REGGIO CALABRIA SALERNO NAPOLI. If you are not returning your rental car, you can leave it at your own risk in one of the large and well-posted public parking lots at the city's entrance. The most convenient is the **Parcheggio Brin** at the Via Brin corner of Via Volta (*©* **081-7632855;** .30€/40¢/20p per hour). Although most hotels offer (expensive) parking, driving to your hotel is a challenge best left to those who know the city, with its narrow and labyrinthine streets, pedestrian areas, and one-way streets (which sometimes suddenly turn into one-way streets going *against* your direction of travel). Unless you have very precise and up-to-date driving directions or an excellent and recent driving map of Naples (one that marks every street and its driving direction), do not attempt it.

VISITOR INFORMATION

Naples's Provincial Tourist Office, **EPT,** Piazza dei Martiri 58, by Riviera di Chiaia (*©* **081-4107211;** www.eptnapoli.info; bus no. 152; Mon–Fri 9am–2pm) maintains tourist booths in the Stazione Centrale (*©* **081-268799;** Metro: Piazza Garibaldi; Mon–Sat 9am–7pm) and at the Stazione Mergellina (Piazza Piedigrotta 1; *©* **081-761-2102;** Metro: Mergellina; Mon–Sat 9am–7pm). The city's office, **AASCT** (*©* **081-2525711;** www.inaples.it), has two excellent tourist information points, one in Via San Carlo 9, off Piazza del Plebiscito (*©* **081-402394;** Mon–Sat 9am–1:30pm and 2:30–7pm), and one in Piazza del Gesù (*©* **081-5512701;** Mon–Sat 9am–1:30pm and 2:30–7pm). **Museo Aperto Napoli** (*©* **081-5636062;** www.museoapertonapoli.com) maintains a cultural center offering free information and guided tours (with a live guide or an audioguide in six languages) of the historical center. It's at Via Pietro Colletta 85 and is open daily 10am to 6pm; the center also houses a cafe, bookshop, and small exhibit space selling crafts.

CITY LAYOUT

A crescent-shaped city resting along the shores of a bay, Naples extends vertically up the steep hills that surround it. Proceeding from west to east, you will find **Posillipo,** then **Mergellina, Chiaia, Santa Lucia,** the **historical center** with the **Quartieri Spagnoli** along its western side and the **Stazione Marittima** on its southern side, then **Piazza Garibaldi** with the **Stazione Centrale** and **Stazione Circumvesuviana,** and finally a number of industrial and poorer neighborhoods.

Above Chiaia and the historical center lies the **Vomero;** farther east is **Capodimonte.** The historical center is the fat part of the crescent, crossed north-south by three major avenues: **Via Toledo, Via Medina,** and **Via Agostino Depretis.** These are crossed west-east by the continuous **Via Armando Diaz–Via G.Sanfelice–Corso Umberto I** and by the continuous Via Benedetto Croce–Via San Biagio dei Librai, also known as **Spaccanapoli,** both leading to **Piazza Garibaldi** and the **Stazione Centrale.**

THE NEIGHBORHOODS IN BRIEF

In this section, we give you a short description of each of Naples's central neighborhoods—including its major monuments—to give you some idea of what each is like and where you might want to stay.

Posillipo This residential neighborhood is graced by a number of dramatic villas perched on rocky cliffs over the sea, as well as a few restaurants offering great food and fantastic views.

Mergellina Situated well to the west of the historical center, this residential neighborhood is served by its own train and hydrofoil stations. It lies near Naples's pleasant marina: The small harbor is lined with restaurants and cafes, where Neapolitans come for dinner by the sea and a romantic promenade.

Chiaia Charming and elegant, this neighborhood is graced by the public park **Villa Comunale.** The hillside area has elegant villas and a couple of hotels and restaurants, which enjoy dramatic views over the bay. The shore area along Riviera di Chiaia is famous for its upscale shopping and restaurants, where Neapolitan nightlife congregates. The historical center and its monuments are a short ride away on public transportation, but it is also possible to walk.

Santa Lucia Once a village by the sea and retaining some of that character,

this neighborhood is separated from the historical center by steep Monte Echia. It is probably Naples's most famous neighborhood, and a favorite with visitors for its unique charm and splendid views. **Via Partenope**—the promenade created in the 19th century by filling in part of the harbor—overlooks the bay and **Castel dell'Ovo** and is lined with elegant hotels and restaurants. **Borgo Marinari** under Castel dell'Ovo, is another popular nighttime spot. Behind the major hotels, you'll find a less-explored neighborhood with grocery shops and cafes frequented by locals.

Quartieri Spagnoli North of **Piazza del Plebiscito**—the monumental heart of the city—this neighborhood of closely knit narrow streets lies on the western side of **Via Toledo** (called "Via Roma" by Neapolitans). Prior to the 1990s, this area was considered quite dangerous, but the blocks around Via Toledo have experienced an urban renewal, with small hotels and quite a few nice restaurants sprouting up. This budget-friendly area is a perfect base for cost-conscious visitors as it is walking distance from most of Naples's major attractions. The streets farther out, however, still show the original grunginess and are not the best place for your romantic evening stroll.

Historical Center This is Naples's heart, extending from the **Castel Nuovo** and the **Stazione Marittima** by the sea to the **Museo Archeologico Nazionale** to the north, the **Quartieri Spagnoli** to the west, and **Castel Capuano** to the east. Many of the city's political and administrative offices as well as the University of Naples are here—along with the cascade of small restaurants, bars, and clubs fostered by such institutions. You'll find all of Naples represented here, from the most elegant palaces to pockets of unbelievable grittiness. Many of Naples's major historical and religious attractions are located here, making it a perfect location for visitors. Most of the hotels here are small, and housed in historical buildings, but larger and more modern hotels line Via Medina and the parallel Via Agostino Depretis, at the southern edge of this area.

Piazza Garibaldi Across from Naples's main rail station, Stazione Centrale, this location is definitely less-than-glamorous (some of the area, behind the station and away from the main avenues, is positively grungy, with decaying buildings and cheap street vendors lining the narrow lanes). Yet, it has some distinct advantages: The top-notch hotels here charge a fraction of the price you would pay in

Santa Lucia or Chiaia (usually way below their official rack rates), and you'll be very well connected through public transportation to all major tourist destinations both within the city and without (the Circumvesuviana rail station, with service to Herculaneum, Pompeii, and Sorrento, is only steps away). The historical center's eastern edge along **Castel Capuano** is within walking distance, past a somewhat unsavory belt around the train station (factor in a taxi ride after dark). You'll also be near a full range of convenience shopping, from groceries to clothing stores, and you'll find a number of good restaurants in the area.

Vomero This is the dwelling place of the *Napoli bene* (the city's middle and upper classes), where residents enjoy fresher air and some spectacular views. A quiet and residential neighborhood, Vomero is mostly composed of elegant 19th- and early-20th-century buildings, with a few local restaurants and good shopping. Three famous attractions are located up here: the **Castel Sant'Elmo, Certosa SanMartino,** and **Villa Floridiana.**

Capodimonte A middle-class and blue-collar residential neighborhood, this is a good choice in summer, when the air is cooler up in the hills. This is also a good base if you plan to spend a lot of your time in the giant **Museo di Capodimonte** and the wonderful public park that surrounds it. There are plenty of local grocery shops and bars to be had, but only a couple of hotels and restaurants.

GETTING AROUND

Walking is the best way to explore the historical heart of Naples. Public transportation works well when you need to travel greater distances and if you want to take in some local color, although at rush hours there might be too much of the latter on the major subway and bus lines. Time your movements so that you can avoid rush hours. If you have to travel during those hours, take the diminutive electric buses which service the city center and are rarely crowded, or take a taxi.

Heads Up

Always beware of pickpockets and purse grabbers in Naples; they favor crowded places such as public transportation and busy streets like Via Toledo. At night, avoid badly lit and solitary places because mugging is not completely unknown in these parts.

On Foot   Naples is a beautiful city to discover on foot; its attractions are close together and the sea is always present in the background. Walking is also an excellent way to notice the thousands of details that make this city so special, including small shops and craft *laboratori* (workshops).

While the free city map given by the tourist office is perfectly sufficient for your general orientation, we recommend you purchase a more detailed map with a *stradario* (alphabetical list of streets) if you are planning more extensive explorations (see "Fast Facts," below).

By Public Transportation   When you're tired of walking, the best ways to get around Naples are the bus and subway. The small electric buses serving the historical center are particularly good for reaching points tucked away on narrow streets, while buses, trams, subway, and funiculars provide faster transportation to major hubs. Naples's **Transportation Authority** (© **800-482644** toll-free in Italy; www.ctpn.it) provides information on all the above and keeps an information booth on Piazza Garibaldi where, if you are in luck, you can get an excellent public transportation map. Public transportation tickets are sold at tobacconists and at some bars and newsstands. You can get a regular *biglietto* (ticket) valid 90 minutes for 1€ ($1.40/70p); or a *giornaliero* (day pass) valid until midnight for 3€ ($4.20/£2.10). Both cover the whole metropolitan area of Naples, including funicular, tram, bus, Metro, and urban railway service. The **Artecard** (p. 100) also includes a public transportation pass.

The **Metropolitana** has two lines, line 1 from Piazza Dante to the Vomero and beyond (daily 6am–11pm); and line 2 from Pozzuoli to Piazza Garibaldi and beyond (daily 5:30am–11pm). The **Cumana** (urban railroad) runs from Montesanto to Pozzuoli and beyond (daily 5am–11pm). Among the **buses,** the *linee rosse* (red lines marked by the letter **R**) are special fast lines serving tourist destinations with frequent service; they run daily from 5:30am to midnight. Regular buses tend to be slower and many stop running by 8:30pm. A few lines are actually **tramways** with dedicated tracks, but because of traffic invading their lines, these can be as slow as the regular buses. At nighttime, the few *linee notturne* (night lines) start around midnight and run every hour.

Dear to the hearts of Neapolitans is the **Funicolare,** a cable railway tunneled through rock to reach the cliffs surrounding the bay. Three funiculars reach the Vomero: **Montesanto** (at Metro station Montesanto; daily 7am–10pm), **Chiaia** (from Piazza Amedeo; daily 7am–10pm), and **Centrale** (from Via Toledo, off Piazza Trieste e Trento; Mon–Tues 6:30am–10pm and Wed–Sun 6:30am–12:30am). **Mergellina** also has a funicular, from Via Mergellina by the harbor up to Via Manzoni (daily 7am–10pm).

One more important element of Naples's public transportation, a public *ascensore* (elevator) is tucked away in Via Acton at the corner of Palazzo Reale, to climb up to Piazza Plebiscito. On the Vomero, several escalators ascend the steepest slopes.

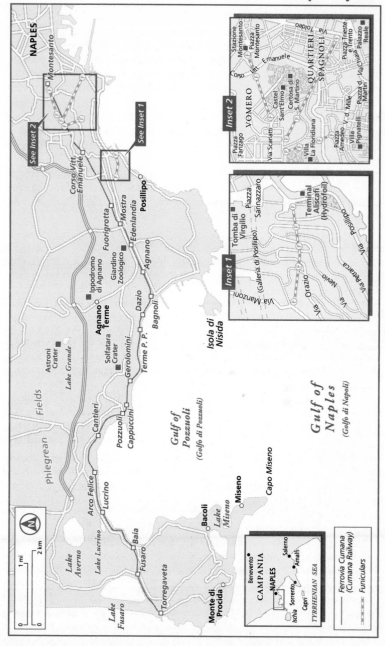

Taxi Rates in Naples

Because the municipality has not raised official taxi rates since 2002, most drivers will ask a certain percentage increase, and it is common practice to grant it, provided it is reasonable. The minimum cost of a ride is 4.50€ ($6.30/£3.15). The meter starts at 3€ ($4.20/£2.10) on Monday to Saturday from 7am to 10pm; otherwise, the meter starts at 5.50€. It adds .05€ every 65 meters or every 10 seconds when waiting or stopped in traffic. Each piece of luggage adds another .50€ (70¢/35p). The most recent flat rates from the airport are as follows:

Piazza Municipio to Museo Capodimonte	9.50€ ($13/£6.65)
to Stazione Centrale	12.50€ ($18/£8.75)
to destinations by Piazza Municipio	16€ ($22/£11)
to and Molo Beverello	16€ ($22/£11)
to destinations in Santa Lucia, Chiaia, and Mergellina	19€ ($27/£13)
to destinations on Corso Vittorio Emanuele	20€ ($28/£14)

By Taxi   Taxis are an excellent, relatively inexpensive way to get around the city. If you've heard that they're dishonest, these stories originate with people who have not visited Naples in the past decade or two or who have fallen prey to gypsy cabs. Today, taxis are very reliable and strictly regulated. Official taxis are painted white and marked by the *Comune di Napoli* (Naples municipality). Inside, on the back of the front seat, you'll find a sign listing official flat rates to the seaports, central hotels, and major attractions—although it might be an old sign; refer to the box above for current established rates. Also, don't fret if your driver doesn't use the meter—*not* using the meter is legal for all rides that have established flat rates. As elsewhere in Italy, taxis do not cruise but can be found waiting at the many taxi stands around town, or, for an extra 1€ surcharge, can be called by phone (restaurants and hotels will do this for you): **Consorzio Taxi** (© 081-444444); **Consortaxi** (© 081-5525252); **Radio Taxi Napoli** (© 081-5564444); **RadioTaxi Free** (© 081-5515151); **Radio Taxi Co.Ta.Na** (© 081-5707070); and **Radio Taxi Partenope** (© 081-5560202; www.taxivagando.it).

Naples also has a water taxi that offers private and public service, **Taxi del Mare** (© **081-8773600;** www.taxidelmare.it).

FAST FACTS: Naples

American Express   **Every Tours** travel agency on Piazza del Municipio 5 (© **081-5518564;** bus: no. R2 or R3 to Piazza del Municipio) handles American Express business. It is open Monday through Friday from 9:30am to 1pm and 3:30 to 7pm, Saturday 9:30am to 1pm.

Banks   Most banks are located in the city center and near the major hotels, and have **ATMs** outside their doors. **BNL (Banca Nazionale del Lavoro;** © **081-7991111)** offers the PLUS network you'll likely need for your ATM card. Its several locations in Naples include Via Toledo 126 and Piazza dei Martiri 23.

Currency Exchange   Among the numerous choices in town, the most convenient exchange places are the ones at the airport and around the Stazione

Centrale on Piazza Garibaldi (Metro: Piazza Garibaldi). There are four *cambios* on Corso Umberto at nos. 44, 92, 212, and 292 (bus: no. R2 to Corso Umberto). Thomas Cook is on Piazza del Municipio (bus: no. R2 or R3 to Piazza del Municipio).

Doctors **Guardia Medica Specialistica** (℡ 081-431111) is on call 24 hours a day. Consulates maintain a list of English-speaking doctors.

Embassies & Consulates See "Fast Facts: Campania & the Amalfi Coast," (p. 55) in chapter 2.

Emergencies Call ℡ **113** or **112** for the **police.** For an **ambulance,** call ℡ **118;** for the **fire department** call ℡ **115;** for **first aid** *(pronto soccorso),* call ℡ **081-7520696.**

Hospital **Ospedale Fatebenefratelli,** the central hospital, is at Via Manzoni 220 (℡ **081-7697220).**

Internet Access The three locations of **Internet Point** (℡ **081-4976090** or 081-19568227) are conveniently located and offer ADSL connection at 1€ ($1.40/70p) for 30 minutes: They are Vico Tre Re a Toledo 59/a (off Via Toledo to the left coming from Piazza Trieste e Trento, across from the Banco di Napoli); Via Montecalvario 9 (also off Via Toledo to the left, a few streets farther up); and Via Francesco Sav Correra 245 (3 blocks north and then left from Piazza Dante).

Laundry/Dry Cleaning Self-service laundromats are rare in Naples; your best bet is a *tintoria* (dry cleaner's) or a *lavanderia* (dry cleaner's and laundry service). A few good and central addresses are **Lavanderia Tintoria** at Via San Tommaso d'Aquino 43 (℡ **081-5511895), Lavanderia Helvetia** (Via San Mattia 1; ℡ **081-415635),** and the *lavanderia* at Salita Sant'Anna di Palazzo 4 (℡ **081-407222).**

Mail The **Central Post Office (Ufficio Postale)** is at Piazza Matteotti (℡ **081-5511456;** bus: no. R3 to Piazza Matteotti).

Maps You can buy a good map with a *stradario* (street directory) of Naples at any newspaper stand in town (most carry the reliable **Pianta Generale** by N. Vincitorio); if you prefer something smaller, buy the excellent, foldable, credit card–size **Mini-City** sold at museum shops in town (try the shop at Palazzo Reale).

Newspapers & Magazines Foreign newspapers and magazines are sold at train station kiosks and near the American Consulate. Do not miss *QuiNapoli,* the dashing free monthly (bilingual Italian/English) prepared by the city tourist office, which lists all the latest events as well as opening hours of monuments and museums. (It's also online at www.inaples.it.)

Pharmacies There are several pharmacies open weekday nights and taking turns on weekend nights. A good one is located in the Stazione Centrale (Piazza Garibaldi 11; ℡ **081-5548894;** Metro: Piazza Garibaldi).

Police Call ℡ **113** for emergencies or ℡ **112.**

Safety Pickpocketing and car thefts are fairly common throughout Naples. In dark alleys and outside the city center, getting mugged is possible, particularly at night. Steer clear of the area behind the Stazione Centrale at dark, when it gets particularly seedy. The poorest suburbs in the outskirts of Naples to the east and southeast are where crime rates tend to be highest, but these are removed from the major tourist areas.

Smoking Thanks to a 2005 law, smoking is not allowed in public areas, including cafes and restaurants. It remains very common, however, and you will find that separate smoking areas are often available.

Taxis See "Getting Around," earlier in this chapter.

Toilets Public bathrooms are basically nonexistent outside museums and major attractions. Your best bet is to use those in bars and cafes; they are reserved for clients, though, so you'll have to buy at least a coffee or a glass of mineral water.

Weather Watch the news or check out http://meteo.tiscali.it.

2 Where to Stay

SANTA LUCIA
VERY EXPENSIVE

Grand Hotel Santa Lucia ✿ At this historic hotel, you'll find old-fashioned atmosphere mixed with elegant decor. The professional service is impeccable, and the public spaces are grand—if a bit dusty and worn in places—graced by curving staircases, marble floors, and Murano chandeliers. Guest rooms are good size but not enormous, with wood or carpet floors, period or reproduction furniture, marble bathrooms, and great views over the Castel dell'Ovo and the bay. Most rooms have balconies to take in the view—they're too small for a table and chairs, though. The buffet breakfast is excellent and the hotel's restaurant elegant. One drawback is the lack of a fitness center if you are keen on exercising.

Via Partenope 46, 80121 Napoli. ℂ 081-7640666. Fax 081-7648580. www.santalucia.it. 96 units. 295€–396€ ($413–$554/£207–£277) double, from 485€ ($679/£340) suite. Extra bed 60€ ($84/£42). Children 2 and under stay free in parent's room. Rates include buffet breakfast. Internet specials available. AE, DC, MC, V. Parking 25€ ($35/£18). Bus: 152, 140, or C25. **Amenities:** Restaurant; bar; business center; room service; same-day laundry service. *In room:* A/C, TV/VCR/DVD, minibar.

Grand Hotel Vesuvio ✿✿ This elegant hotel claims to be the best in Naples, and indeed, it is, when it comes to exquisite service and room quality. It compensates for a less romantic atmosphere with the most comfortable accommodations in town. Even the standard doubles are very roomy (with large marble bathrooms and Jacuzzi tubs), and come furnished with special details such as linen sheets and extra-firm mattresses. Superior rooms and suites have large balconies from which you can enjoy views over Borgo Marinari or Mount Vesuvius. The breakfast buffet—served in a delightful bright room with a view—is superb, including several kinds of juice, fresh fruit, bacon, and eggs, along with Neapolitan pastries, local cheeses and cold cuts, and several breads. The **Caruso Roof Garden** restaurant is very good and affords splendid views.

Via Partenope 45, 80121 Napoli. ℂ 081-7640044. Fax 081-7644483. www.vesuvio.it. 161 units. 420€–430€ ($588–$602/£294–£301) double; from 700€ ($980/£490) suite. Extra bed 60€ ($84/£42). Children 2 and under stay free in parent's room. Internet specials available. Rates include buffet breakfast. AE, DC, MC, V. Parking 25€ ($35/£18). Bus: 152, 140, or C25. **Amenities:** Rooftop restaurant; bar; business center; fitness center and spa; room service; same-day laundry service. *In room:* A/C, TV/VCR/DVD, hair dryer, minibar, safe.

Hotel Excelsior ✻ *Kids*   The third of three biggie hotels fronting the bay on Via Partenope, the Excelsior is owned by Starwood and has more moderate prices than its neighbors listed above. It has the same gorgeous views, of course, and five-star service, plus a splendid roof garden-terrace. The rooms are good size and tastefully decorated, with marble bathrooms and linen sheets, as well as all the amenities you expect at this level (and price); however, everything comes in a slightly smaller scale than at the Grand Hotel Vesuvio and the Santa Lucia.

Via Partenope 48, 80121 Napoli. ✆ **081-7640111.** Fax 081-7649743. www.excelsior.it. 121 units. 360€ ($504/£252) double, from 650€ ($910/£455) suite. Rates include buffet breakfast. Extra bed 55€ ($77/£39). Children 2 and under stay free in parent's room. AE, DC, MC, V. Parking 23€ ($32/£16). Bus: 152, 140, or C25. **Amenities:** Restaurant; bar; babysitting; business center; concierge; health club; roof garden; room service; same-day laundry service. *In room:* A/C, TV/VCR/DVD, hair dryer, minibar, safe.

MODERATE
Hotel Miramare *Value*   On the waterfront overlooking Castel dell'Ovo, this small, elegant hotel offers excellent value and warm service. Originally a private villa built in 1914, it briefly housed the American Consulate before opening as a hotel in 1944. The public areas are still decorated in Liberty style, but guest rooms have been renovated, each with its own whimsical assortment of furniture. The attentive family management is reflected in little touches like cool linen sheets in the summer. The rooms overlooking the sea have splendid views, and all those above the mezzanine level are graced by private balconies. We recommend the deluxe rooms, which are oversized, with large balconies, and have baths with tub and shower—others are shower-only. In clement weather, breakfast is served on the roof terrace overlooking the bay. You'll get special treatment at the restaurants run by the owner's brothers: **La Cantinella** (p. 92), **La Piazzetta, Il Posto Accanto, Rosolino,** and **Putipù.** They all feature Neapolitan cuisine and pizza, and some double as nightclubs.

Via Nazario Sauro 24, 80132 Napoli. ✆ **081-7647589.** Fax 081-7640775. www.hotelmiramare.com. 18 units. 269€–340€ ($377–$476/£188–£238) double. Extra bed 70€ ($98/£49). Children 5 and under stay free in parent's room. Weekend and Internet rates available. Rates include buffet breakfast. AE, DC, MC, V. Bus: 152, C25, or 140. Parking 25€ ($35/£18) in nearby garage. **Amenities:** Bar; babysitting; concierge; free Internet access; laundry service; lounge; room service. *In room:* A/C, satellite TV/VCR (free videos in lobby), hair dryer, kettle w/tea, minibar, safe.

INEXPENSIVE
Hotel Rex *Value*   This hotel is a steal: Housed in a 19th-century palace by the most famous harbor-side area of Naples, only steps from top-notch hotels of Via Partenope (see above), it offers spacious accommodations at moderate prices. Word has gotten out about this family-run spot, and it's very popular, especially with groups; so you must reserve well in advance. Guest rooms are simply but carefully decorated; some come with views over the harbor or Mount Vesuvio, and some come with private balconies. Bathrooms are modern and roomy. A simple continental breakfast, served in your room, is included in the rates.

Via Palepoli 12, 80132 Napoli. ✆ **081-7649389.** Fax 081-7649227. www.hotel-rex.it. 34 units. 150€ ($210/£105). Rates include continental breakfast. Extra bed 25€ ($35/£18). Children 3 and under stay free in parent's room. AE, DC, MC, V. Parking 25€ ($35/£18) in nearby garage. Bus: 152, C25, or 140. **Amenities:** Babysitting; concierge; small lounge. *In room:* A/C, satellite TV, minibar, safe.

CHIAIA
EXPENSIVE
Grand Hotel Parker's ✻   A landmark building of the Liberty (Italian Art Nouveau) style, this glorious villa served as Allied headquarters in World War II and still

Where to Stay in Naples

Costantinopoli 104 **7**
Grand Hotel Oriente **9**
Grand Hotel Parker's **22**
Grand Hotel
  Santa Lucia **17**
Grand Hotel Vesuvio **18**
Hotel Art Resort **13**
Hotel Britannique **23**
Hotel Europeo **6**
Hotel Excelsior **16**
Hotel Executive **8**
Hotel Il Convento **12**
Hotel Majestic **21**

Hotel Miramare **14**
Hotel Palazzo
  Alabardieri **20**
Hotel Palazzo Turchini **10**
Hotel Rex **15**
Hotel Toledo **11**
Nuovo Rebecchino **2**
San Francesco
  al Monte **19**
Starhotel Terminus **3**
Suite Esedra **5**
Una Hotel Napoli **4**
Villa Capodimonte **1**

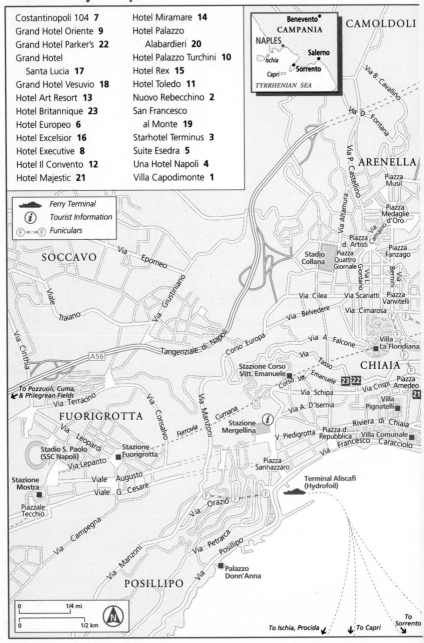

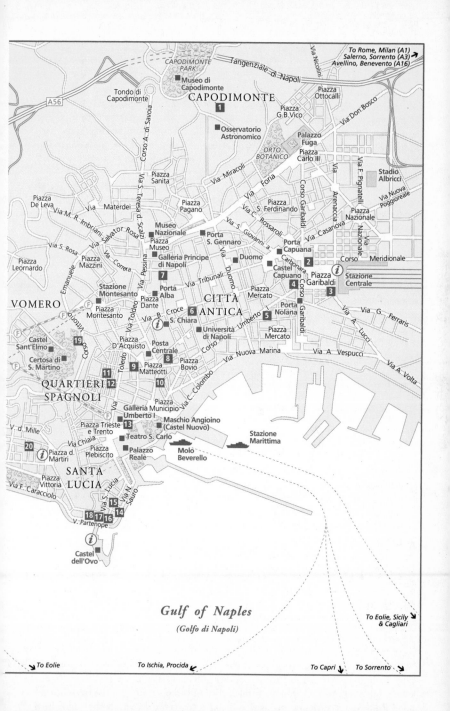

CAPODIMONTE PARK

Museo di
Capodimonte

CAPODIMONTE

1

Tondo di
Capodimonte

A56

Corso A. di Savoia

Tangenziale di Napoli

Via Nicolini

To Rome, Milan (A1)
Salerno, Sorrento (A3)
Avellino, Benevento (A16)

Piazza
Ottocalli

Via Don Bosco

Osservatorio
Astronomico

Piazza
G.B.Vico

ORTO
BOTANICO

Palazzo
Fuga

Piazza
Carlo III

Stadio
Albricci

Via F. Pignatelli

Via Nuova
Poggioreale

Piazza Sanita

Via Miracoli

Via Foria

Via S. Teresa d. Scalzi

Piazza
De Leva

Via M. R. Imbriani

Via Materdei

Via S. Ferdinando

Via C. Rossaroli

Corso Garibaldi

Arenaccia

Via Casanova

Piazza
Nazionale

Via Nazionale

Piazza
Pagano

Piazza
Leonardo

Via S. Rosa

Via Salvator Rosa

Via Correra

Piazza
Mazzini

Piazza
Museo

Museo
Nazionale

Galleria Principe
di Napoli

7

Porta
S. Gennaro

Via S. Giovanni

Duomo

Via Duomo

Porta
Capuana

Carbonara

Porta
Capuana

Castel
Capuano

Corso Meridionale

Via Nazionale

VOMERO

Via M. Emanuele

Via Pessina

Via Toledo

Stazione
Montesanto

Piazza
Montesanto

Porta
Alba

Piazza
Dante

S. Chiara

CITTÀ
ANTICA

Via Tribunali

Piazza
Mercato

4

Piazza
Garibaldi

2

3

Stazione
Centrale

Corso Umberto

S. Croce

6

Università
di Napoli

Porta
Nolana

5

Piazza
Mercato

Corso Garibaldi

Via G. Ferraris

Castel
Sant'Elmo

Certosa di
S. Martino

19

Corso Vittorio

F

F

F

F

Piazza
D'Acquisto

Posta
Centrale

8

Piazza
Bovio

Corso

Via Nuova Marina

Via A. Lucci

Via A. Vespucci

Via A. Volta

QUARTIERI
SPAGNOLI

11

12

Toledo

9

Piazza
Matteotti

10

Via C. Colombo

Piazza
Municipio

Galleria
Umberto I

13

Maschio Angioino
(Castel Nuovo)

Stazione
Marittima

V. d. Mille

20

Via Chiaia

Piazza Trieste
e Trento

Teatro S. Carlo

Piazza d.
Martiri

Piazza
Plebiscito

Palazzo
Reale

Molo
Beverello

SANTA
LUCIA

Piazza
Vittoria

Via F. Caracciolo

Via S. Lucia

Via N. Sauro

15

14

18

17

16

V. Partenope

Castel
dell'Ovo

To Eolie, Sicily
& Cagliari

Gulf of Naples

(Golfo di Napoli)

To Eolie

To Ischia, Procida

To Capri

To Sorrento

features most of its original architectural details and statuary. The public spaces are splendid and definitely worth a visit even if you are not staying in the hotel. The commodious guest rooms fronting the bay share the same spectacular views as the public spaces and are decorated with elegant period furniture (different floors are decorated in various styles—Louis XIV, Empire, and so on). Suites are truly elegant duplex apartments on two levels. The back rooms, however, are unremarkable, overlooking some greenery and the garage. The spa is world class, with treatments like hydrotherapy, inhalation therapy, and Turkish baths. **George's,** on the roof garden, is one of the best restaurants in Naples (see later in this chapter), and the bar features a separate cigar room.

Corso Vittorio Emanuele 135, 80121 Napoli. ⓒ 081-7612474. Fax 081-663527. www.grandhotelparkers.com. 83 units. 255€–360€ ($357–$504/£179–£252) double; from 450€ ($630/£315) suite. Extra bed 60€ ($84/£42). Children 1 and under stay free in parent's room. Internet specials available. Rates include buffet breakfast. AE, DC, MC, V. Parking 21€–23€ ($29–$32/£15–£16). Bus: C24 or C27 to Via Tasso-Corso Vittorio Emanuele II. Metro: Piazza Amedeo. **Amenities:** Restaurant; bar; babysitting; business center; concierge; health club; same-day laundry service; nonsmoking floor; room service; spa. *In room:* A/C, TV/VCR/DVD, fax, hair dryer, minibar, safe.

MODERATE

Hotel Majestic   Popular with Italian businesspeople and well-to-do travelers, this hotel is located at the end of the elegant shopping strip in the lower part of Chiaia and offers upscale accommodations. The large guest rooms are decorated with low-key elegance, sporting hardwood floors, streamlined modern furniture, and marble bathrooms. Many of the rooms afford great views of the bay. **La Giara,** the hotel's restaurant, is quite good.

Largo Vasto a Chiaia 68. ⓒ 081-416500. Fax 081-410145. www.majestic.it. 230€–260€ ($322–$364/£161–£182) double; from 390€ ($546/£273) suite. Rates include buffet breakfast. Extra bed 40€ ($56/£28). Children 2 and under stay free in parent's room. Internet specials available. AE, DC, MC, V. Parking 23€ ($32/£16). Metro: Piazza Amedeo. **Amenities:** Restaurant; piano bar; babysitting; concierge; laundry service; lounge; room service. *In room:* A/C, satellite TV/VCR, hair dryer, minibar, safe, tea kettle w/tea.

Hotel Palazzo Alabardieri 🌟🌟   This is one of our favorite hotels in Naples for location and style. Housed in an elegant palace created in 1870 in the ancient cloister of the convent of Santa Caterina a Chiaia, it opened in 2004, after a careful restoration that respected the building's history. Sleek marble floors in the public areas contrast the warm hardwood floors in the guest rooms, which are furnished with period furniture and color-coordinated in earth and pastel colors. The junior suites are especially pleasant, with stylish furnishings and designer accents. All units come with good-size marble bathrooms.

Via Alabardieri 38, 80121 Napoli. ⓒ 081-415278. Fax 081-19722010. www.palazzoalabardieri.it. 33 units. 190€–220€ ($266–$308/£133–£154) double; 320€ ($448/£224) junior suite. Rates include buffet breakfast. Internet specials available. Extra bed 40€ ($56/£28). Children 2 and under stay free in parent's room. Children 3 to 11 stay in parent's room for 20€ ($28/£14). AE, DC, MC, V. Parking 23€ ($32/£16). Metro: Piazza Amedeo. **Amenities:** Bar; babysitting; business center; concierge; fitness center; same-day laundry service; room service. *In room:* A/C, satellite TV w/pay movies, hair dryer, Internet, minibar, safe.

San Francesco al Monte   You cannot beat the atmosphere of this elegant hotel inside an ex-Franciscan convent on the slope of the hill overlooking Riviera di Chiaia. The views are quite spectacular, particularly from the terrace (often booked for wedding receptions, which can be one drawback) with its restaurant and heart-shaped swimming pool. All the tastefully furnished guest rooms open onto the bay; they are good size, with tiled floors, lots of wood, and pastel-colored walls. Some highlighted with original architectural details such as an arched doorway or a rounded window. The hotel's restaurant, **Terrazza dei Barbanti,** is excellent and affords matchless views over the bay.

Corso Vittorio Emanuele 328, 80135 Napoli. ℂ 081-4239111. Fax 081-2512485. www.sanfrancescoalmonte.it. 44 units. 295€ ($413/£207) double; 350€ ($490/£245) suite. Rates include buffet breakfast. AE, DC, MC, V. Parking 25€ ($35/£18). Metro: Piazza Amedeo. **Amenities:** Restaurant; bar; babysitting; dry cleaning; laundry service; nonsmoking rooms; outdoor pool; room service. *In room:* A/C, satellite TV/DVD, hair dryer, minibar, safe.

INEXPENSIVE

Hotel Britannique *Kids*   Next door to Grand Hotel Parker's, the Britannnique is a good solution for those who don't want to shell out money for the luxury of staying at that landmark hotel, but who would like to enjoy its perfect location. Housed in a less grand building than its neighbor Parker's (above), it offers a beautiful garden and the same spectacular views. The rest of the hotel, though, is a bit dusty and in need of a face-lift, which justifies the lower prices. Guest rooms are large and decorated in Louis XVI or Empire style; most of them offer beautiful views over the Gulf. Bathrooms are old-fashioned but functional. Some rooms have cooking facilities, an added value for families with young children.

Corso Vittorio Emanuele 133, 80121 Napoli. ℂ 081-7614145. Fax 081-660457. www.hotelbritannique.it. 86 units. 170€–190€ ($238–$266/£119–£133) double; 220€ ($308/£154) junior suite. Internet specials available. Rates include buffet breakfast. Extra bed 28€ ($39/£20). Children 5 and under stay free in parent's room. AE, DC, MC, V. Free parking. Bus: C24 or C27 to Via Tasso-Corso Vittorio Emanuele II.Metro: Piazza Amedeo. **Amenities:** Restaurant; bar; babysitting; concierge; laundry service; room service. *In room:* A/C, TV, hair dryer, minibar.

PIAZZA DEL PLEBISCITO
EXPENSIVE

Hotel Art Resort Galleria Umberto ✿   You cannot beat the location of this newly opened hotel, smack in the heart of the city and only steps from most Naples attractions. It occupies the upper floors of one of the city's landmarks, the Galleria Umberto I (p. 113), which explains its hidden entrance inside the gallery and up an early-20th-century elevator. The hotel is lavishly decorated in an eclectic style, mixing baroque and Liberty elements, and each of its rooms is dedicated to an artist, from Klee to van Gogh. Rooms with interior windows that open onto the gallery can be a bit dark, while those facing the street are a bit noisy; but the quality of the furnishings and decor—with four-poster beds, elegant marble floors, and state-of-the-art bathrooms—more than compensate for it.

Galleria Umberto I 83, 80132 Napoli. ℂ 081-4976224. Fax 081-4104114. www.artresortgalleriaumberto.it. 16 units. 240€–300€ ($336–$420/£168–£210) double; 280€–400€ ($392–$560/£196–£280) junior suite. Rates include buffet breakfast. Children 2 and under stay free in parent's room. Internet specials available. AE, DC, MC, V. Parking 25€ ($35/£18) in nearby garage. Bus: R2 to Piazza Municipio. **Amenities:** Babysitting; concierge; laundry service. *In room:* A/C, TV/VCR, hair dryer, minibar, safe, Wi-Fi.

QUARTIERI SPAGNOLI
MODERATE

Hotel Il Convento ✿   Family-run, this hotel offers very pleasant accommodations at moderate prices in the heart of Naples. Housed in a 17th-century *palazzo,* it has been carefully restored. Guest rooms are decorated with pastel-colored plaster walls that highlight varying architectural details, such as wooden beams in some rooms and arches in others; the two junior suites on the top floor enjoy delightful private roof gardens, while each of the two very nicely appointed family rooms has a loft bedroom. All have modern bathrooms and are furnished with quality modern furniture in dark wood. Breakfast is served in two small breakfast rooms; the buffet includes breads and jams, fruit, cold cuts, and cheese. Guests have access to the sauna facility at the Hotel Executive (see below) and can check their e-mail in the reception area.

Via Speranzella 137/a, 80134 Napoli. ℂ **081-403977.** Fax 081-400332. www.hotelilconvento.com. 14 units. 180€ ($252/£126) double; 210€ ($294/£147) junior suite; 240€ ($336/£168) 4-person family room. Rates include buffet breakfast. Extra bed 60€ ($75/£42). Children 2 and under stay free in parent's room. Internet specials available. AE, DC, MC, V. Parking 22€ ($31/£15) in garage nearby. Bus: R2 to Piazza Municipio. **Amenities:** Bar; concierge, fitness room w/sauna. *In room:* A/C, TV/VCR, hair dryer, minibar, safe.

Hotel Toledo   This picturesque small hotel is on a narrow side street off Via Toledo. Less charming than the Convento above, it is equally convenient. Guest rooms are good size, with simple but adequate furnishings, and modern, tiled bathrooms. The hotel also offers a free Internet point, Wi-Fi, and a small fitness room, as well as a bar and a restaurant on the roof garden, where breakfast is served.

Via Montecalvario 15, 80134 Napoli. ℂ **081-406800.** Fax 081-406871. www.hoteltoledo.net. 35 units. 140€ ($196/£98) double. Rates include buffet breakfast. Extra bed 40€ ($56/£28). Children 2 and under stay free in parent's room. AE, MC, V. Parking 22€ ($31/£15) in nearby garage. Bus: R2 to Piazza Municipio. **Amenities:** Restaurant; bar; fitness room. *In room:* A/C, satellite TV, hair dryer, minibar, safe.

CITTA ANTICA
EXPENSIVE
Grand Hotel Oriente   Located at the southern edge of the historical district, this modern hotel belongs to the same group as the Grand Hotel Santa Lucia (p. 78), and offers a less pricey but convenient location in the heart of Naples. Popular with businessmen, its guest rooms are spacious and pleasantly furnished, all with carpeting and good-size, modern bathrooms. Those on the higher floors have balconies affording good views of Mount Vesuvius and the Gulf. The excellent **restaurant** is popular for its Neapolitan cuisine.

Via Armando Diaz 44, 80134 Napoli. ℂ **081-5512133.** Fax 081-5514915. www.naples-hotel-oriente-turinhotels. com. 131 units. 280€–310€ ($392–$434/£196–£217). 390€ ($546/£273) suite. Rates include buffet breakfast. Extra bed 55€ ($77/£39). Internet specials available. Children 2 and under stay free in parent's room. AE, DC, MC, V. Parking 22€ ($31/£15). Bus: C25, E2, or R2 to Via Toledo; C57, E3, or R3 to Via Medina. **Amenities:** Restaurant; bar; business center; concierge; room service; same-day laundry service. *In room:* A/C, satellite TV/VCR, minibar.

Hotel Palazzo Turchini   This centrally located hotel offers modern accommodations inside the shell of a 17th-century palace, once part of an orphanage specializing in musical studies. Guest rooms have been redone using state-of-the-art technology to completely soundproof them; all have hardwood floors and are furnished with a stylish mix of modern and period furniture. The marble bathrooms are good sized. Their "executive" doubles are larger and brighter than the "classics," which mostly open onto light shafts and the narrow street. Some executive doubles come with small private terraces, and others come with lounge areas. Some units are accessible for travelers with disabilities. Breakfast is served on the roof terrace in clement weather.

Via Medina 21, 80132 Napoli. ℂ **081-5510606.** Fax 081-5521473. www.palazzoturchini.it. 27 units. 320€–420€ ($448–$588/£224–£294) double, 650€ ($910/£455) suite. Rates include buffet breakfast. Extra bed 50€ ($70/£35). Internet specials available. Children 2 and under stay free in parent's room. AE, DC, MC, V. Parking 22€ ($31/£15) in nearby garage. Bus: C57, E3, or R3 to Via Medina. **Amenities:** Bar; babysitting; concierge; laundry service. *In room:* A/C, satellite TV, hair dryer, minibar, safe.

MODERATE
Costantinopoli 104 ✿ *Finds*   Located in the heart of the historical center, this small hotel is housed in a19th-century Italian Art Nouveau palace that belonged to a marquis.

Behind the gates you'll discover a harbor of peace and luxury from the city's noise and grit. Public spaces have kept the charm of a private palatial home, from the living room with fireplace to the private courtyard with palm trees, chaise longues, and a bean-shaped swimming pool (delightfully refreshing in the summer months). Some guest rooms open onto the terrace where breakfast is served in fair weather, and others have private balconies. All are medium size and individually decorated with modern furnishings and hardwood floors or hand-painted tiles. Suites have Jacuzzi tubs. Room service shows excellent attention to detail, with homemade liquors and ice cream and a fabulous breakfast.

Via Santa Maria di Costantinopoli 104, 80134 Napoli. ✆ 081-5571035. Fax 081-5571051. www.costantinopoli 104.com. 19 units. 210€ ($294/£147) double; 245€ ($343/£172) suite. Rates include buffet breakfast. AE, DC, MC, V. Parking 22€ ($31/£15). Metro: Piazza Cavour. **Amenities:** Bar; babysitting; dry cleaning; laundry service; nonsmoking rooms; outdoor pool; room service. *In room:* A/C, satellite TV/DVD, hair dryer, minibar, safe.

Hotel Executive *Value*   This comfortable hotel enjoys an excellent location in central Naples and offers a lot for its price, making it a good address for both moderately oriented business travelers and tourists. Guest rooms are nicely appointed, with tiled floors, tasteful modern furniture, and good-size, modern bathrooms. The one available suite is definitely "executive" level, with two balconies as well as a Jacuzzi in the bathroom. The hotel also offers a sizeable sauna and a delightful roof garden, where breakfast is served in good weather.

Via del Cerriglio 10, 80134 Napoli. ✆ 081-5520611. Fax 081-5520611. info@sea-hotels.com. 19 units. 165€–180€ ($231–$252/£116–£126) double; 238€ ($333/£167) suite. Rates include buffet breakfast. Extra bed 30€ ($42/£21). Internet specials available. Children 2 and under stay free in parent's room. AE, DC, MC, V. Parking 22€ ($31/£15). Bus: CS, CD, or C25 to Via San Felice. Pets accepted. **Amenities:** Bar; concierge; roof garden; sauna. *In room:* A/C, satellite TV, hair dryer, minibar, safe.

Suite Esedra *Value*   This pleasant small hotel offers moderately priced rooms in the heart of Naples. Housed in an aristocratic palace that has been completely restored, bedrooms are tastefully furnished with excellent care to details; some have sweet little balconies. Of the two suites, one of them offers a fantastic private terrace equipped with a small pool. Breakfast is served in a pleasant common room.

Via Arnaldo Cantani 12, 80134 Napoli. ✆ 081-5537087. Fax 081-5537087. esedra.hotelsinnapoli.com. 17 units. 165€–180€ ($231–$252/£115–£125) double; 310€ ($434/£216) suite. Rates include buffet breakfast. Extra bed 40€ ($50/£25). Internet specials available. Children 5 and under stay free in parent's room. AE, DC, MC, V. Parking 22€ ($31/£15) in nearby garage. Metro: Piazza Garibaldi. **Amenities:** Bar; concierge; small health club. *In room:* A/C, satellite TV, hair dryer, minibar, safe.

INEXPENSIVE

Hotel Europeo *Value*   It is difficult to find nicer budget-friendly accommodations in Naples. Located right in the heart of the historical center, this modest hotel offers good-size rooms (it is worth the money to upgrade to a larger one) that are functional and tastefully appointed. The secret? It doesn't have public spaces, and it is located on the upper floors (4th and 5th) of a residential building. Yet, if you can do without a breakfast room and a lounge, the only drawback is that you'll need a small reserve of .10€ (15¢/7p) in coins to operate the elevator.

Via Mezzocannone 109/c, 80134 Napoli. ✆ 081-5517254. Fax 081-5518787. www.sea-hotels.com. 17 units. 105€–130€ ($147–$182/£74–£91) double. Extra bed 40€ ($56/£28). Internet specials available. Children 5 and under stay free in parent's room. AE, DC, MC, V. Parking 22€ ($31/£15) in nearby garage. Metro: Piazza Garibaldi. **Amenities:** Concierge. *In room:* A/C, satellite TV, hair dryer, minibar (in some rooms), safe.

PIAZZA GARIBALDI
EXPENSIVE
Una Hotel Napoli *✦* A welcome addition to Naples's accommodations roster, this recently opened hotel is housed in an elegant 19th-century *palazzo*, conveniently located in front of Naples Stazione Centrale and near the Transvesuviana rail station. The hotel's pleasant public spaces include a trendy panoramic roof terrace featuring both bar and restaurant. The spacious guest rooms are stylish, with a streamlined modern design, and neutral colored decor. The good-size bathrooms are ultra modern.

Piazza Garibaldi 9, 80142 Napoli. (€ 081-5636901. Fax 081-5636972. www.unahotels.it. 89 units. 323€ ($453/£226) double; 478€ ($669/£335) suite. Rates include buffet breakfast. Internet specials available. AE, DC, MC, V. Free parking in garage. Metro: Piazza Garibaldi. **Amenities:** Restaurant; bar; concierge; laundry service; room service. *In room:* A/C, satellite TV w/pay movies, hair dryer, minibar, safe, Wi-Fi.

MODERATE
Starhotel Terminus *✦* Member of the Italian Starhotel group, this hotel offers elegant accommodations with full amenities and excellent service. The commodious guest rooms are stylishly furnished, with warm wood, modern furniture, tasteful carpeting and fabrics, and elegant bathrooms. The "executive" doubles have extras such as trouser presses, a second TV in the bathroom, a cutting-edge CD/cassette system, and a complimentary tea/coffee/hot chocolate tray. The panoramic restaurant and bar on the roof garden have become quite a hit with Neapolitan socialites (see "Naples After Dark," later in this chapter).

Piazza Garibaldi 91, 80142 Napoli. (€ 081-7793111. Fax 081-206689. terminus.na@starhotels.it. 171 units. 230€ ($322/£161) double; 290€ ($406/£203) suite. Rates include buffet breakfast. Extra bed 20€ ($28/£14). Internet specials available. Children 11 and under stay free in parent's room. AE, DC, MC, V. Free parking in garage. Metro: Piazza Garibaldi. Pets accepted. **Amenities:** Restaurant; bar; babysitting; business center; concierge; gym; roof garden; room service; same-day laundry service. *In room:* A/C, satellite TV w/pay movies and Internet, hair dryer, minibar, safe, Wi-Fi.

INEXPENSIVE
Nuovo Rebecchino *Value* Not far from the Stazione Centrale and within walking distance of the ancient city, this hotel offers pleasant accommodations at reasonable rates. One of the oldest hotels in Naples, it was redone in 2004, and its pleasant public spaces have been completely restored. Guest rooms are ample and elegantly furnished in classic style, with carpeting. Bathrooms are good sized.

Corso Garibaldi 356, 80142 Napoli. (€ 081-5535327. Fax 081-268026. www.nuovorebecchino.it. 58 units. 160€ ($224/£112) double. Rates include buffet breakfast. Extra bed 35€ ($49/£25). Children 2 and under stay free in parent's room. AE, DC, MC, V. Parking 22€ ($31/£15) in nearby garage. Metro: Piazza Garibaldi. **Amenities:** Restaurant; bar; babysitting; business center; concierge; laundry service; room service. *In room:* A/C, TV, hair dryer, minibar.

CAPODIMONTE
MODERATE
Villa Capodimonte *✦* This 1995 hotel is just steps from the Royal Park of Capodimonte and is surrounded by its own park with splendid views. Family-run, it offers a variety of public rooms, including several terraces, a solarium, a pleasant garden, and even a chapel and an auditorium. Guest rooms are large and nicely appointed, with classic furniture and wooden floors; each is basically a junior suite opening onto either the garden or a terrace. Many enjoy vistas of Mount Vesuvius and the Gulf.

Via Moiariello 66, 80131 Napoli. (€ 081-459000. Fax 081-299344. www.villacapodimonte.it. 57 units. 220€ ($308/£154). Rates include buffet breakfast. Extra bed 40€ ($56/£28). Internet specials available. Children 5 and under stay free in parent's room. AE, DC, MC, V. Free parking. Bus: C66 or 24 to Via Ponti Rossi. Pets accepted. **Amenities:** Restaurant; bar; babysitting; concierge; garden; laundry service; room service. *In room:* A/C, satellite TV w/pay movies, hair dryer, minibar, safe.

3 Where to Dine

Neapolitans love to eat and love their traditions: While new, fashionable restaurants are opening, the old ones are getting face-lifts, and you will find a number of good restaurants respectful of the local culinary traditions as well as many innovative ones. Seafood and pizza dominate the scene (see appendix A for an introduction to local cuisine and wines, and see appendix B for a glossary of menu terms), yet many traditional local dishes are vegetarian or meat-based (just don't expect a big, juicy steak). In addition to our suggestions below, consider also some of the **hotel dining** recommended above, and look under nightlife on p. 120 for several highly recommended *enoteche* (winebars doubling as restaurants).

POSILLIPO
EXPENSIVE

Giuseppone a Mare ✦ NEAPOLITAN/SEAFOOD   Going on 200 years of service, this restaurant is right on the seashore and commands a beautiful view of the bay looking back toward Napoli. The menu is large—two pages are devoted solely to pasta—but the specialties are fish and seafood, which can be cooked to order (priced by the kilo). We recommend the delicious *polpi Giuseppone* (squid in a tomato and black olive sauce) and the exceptional *fusilli della Baia* (pasta with swordfish and pumpkin served in a crunchy cheese crust). The space is bright and airy, with an antique majolica floor in lemon hues. Towards the back wall, you can see how the building was literally hewn out of the looming cliff above it. During warm months, you can dine on the terrace outside.

Via Ferdinando Russo 13. ✆ 081-5756002 or 081-7691384. Reservations recommended. Secondi 8€–15€ ($11–$21/£5.60–£11). AE, DC, MC, V. Tues–Sat 10:30am–3:30pm and 8–11:30pm; Sun 10:30am–5:30pm. Closed 2 weeks in Aug. Bus: C3 to Mergellina (end of line); switch to 140.

Rosiello *Finds* NEAPOLITAN/SEAFOOD   This restaurant is beloved not only for the quality of its cuisine, but also for the exceptional sea views from its terrace. Locals will line up for an outdoor table from spring to fall in order to delight in the excellent dishes that emerge from the kitchen. We highly recommend the *risotto alla pescatora* (seafood risotto) and the rare *scialatielli con melanzane e provola* (fresh pasta with local cheese and eggplants), as well as the perfectly fried calamari and the *pezzogna all'acquapazza* (local fish in light tomato herbed broth).

Via Santo Strato 10. ✆ 081-7691288. Reservations required. Secondi 10€–18€ ($14–$25/£7–£13). AE, DC, MC, V. Thurs–Tues 12:30–3pm and 8–11:30pm. Closed 2 weeks each in Jan and Aug. Bus: C3 to Mergellina (end of line); switch to 140.

MODERATE

Ristorante La Fazenda NEAPOLITAN/SEAFOOD   With a beautiful view over the bay and an informal atmosphere, La Fazenda pleases both locals and visitors. La Fazenda is famous for its fish specialties, and we loved their *pasta alle vongole* (pasta with clams) and fresh grilled seafood. The terrace here is popular in summer (don't try to go then without a reservation).

Via Mare Chiaro 58/a. ✆ 081-5757420. Reservations required. Secondi 12€–20€ ($17–$28/£8.40–£14). AE, DC, MC, V. Tues–Sun 12:30–4pm; Mon–Sat 7:30–11:30pm; closed 1 week in Aug. Bus: C3 to Mergellina (end of line); switch to 140.

Where to Dine in Naples

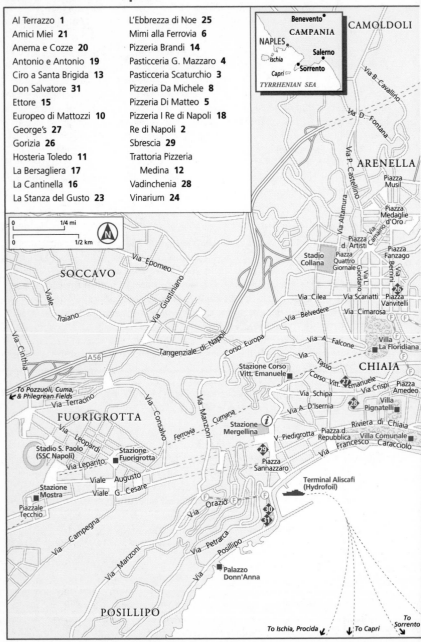

Al Terrazzo **1**
Amici Miei **21**
Anema e Cozze **20**
Antonio e Antonio **19**
Ciro a Santa Brigida **13**
Don Salvatore **31**
Ettore **15**
Europeo di Mattozzi **10**
George's **27**
Gorizia **26**
Hosteria Toledo **11**
La Bersagliera **17**
La Cantinella **16**
La Stanza del Gusto **23**

L'Ebbrezza di Noe **25**
Mimi alla Ferrovia **6**
Pizzeria Brandi **14**
Pasticceria G. Mazzaro **4**
Pasticceria Scaturchio **3**
Pizzeria Da Michele **8**
Pizzeria Di Matteo **5**
Pizzeria I Re di Napoli **18**
Re di Napoli **2**
Sbrescia **29**
Trattoria Pizzeria
    Medina **12**
Vadinchenia **28**
Vinarium **24**

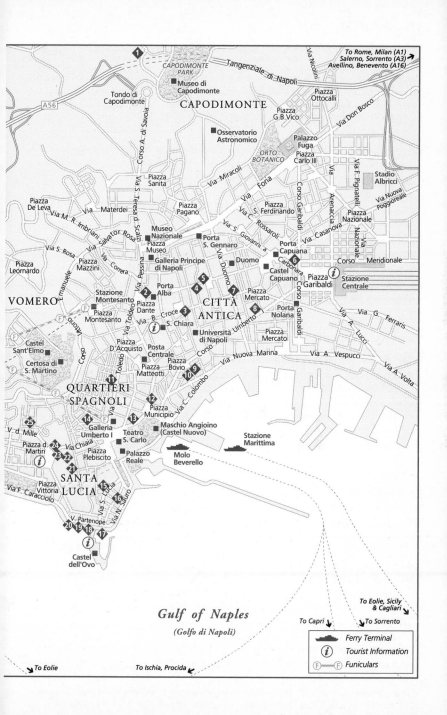

To Rome, Milan (A1)
Salerno, Sorrento (A3)
Avellino, Benevento (A16)

Via Nicolini

Tangenziale di Napoli

CAPODIMONTE PARK

❶

Tondo di Capodimonte

■ Museo di Capodimonte

A56

Corso A. di Savoia

CAPODIMONTE

Piazza Ottocalli

Via Don Bosco

Piazza G.B.Vico

■ Osservatorio Astronomico

Palazzo Fuga

ORTO BOTANICO

Piazza Carlo III

Stadio Albricci

Via S. Teresa d. Scalzi

Piazza Sanita

Via Miracoli

Via Foria

Via F. Pignatelli

Via Nuova Poggioreale

Piazza De Leva

Via M. R. Imbriani

Via Materdei

Piazza Pagano

Via C. Rossaroli

Piazza S. Ferdinando

Corso Garibaldi

Arenaccia

Piazza Nazionale

Via Salvator Rosa

Via S. Rosa

Via Correra

Piazza Mazzini

Museo Nazionale ■

Piazza Museo

Galleria Principe di Napoli

■ Porta S. Gennaro

Via S. Giovanni a Carbonara

Via Duomo

Duomo ■

Via C. Casanova

Porta Capuana

❻

Via Nazionale

Corso Meridionale

Piazza Leonardo

Emanuele

Via Pessina

Porta Alba

❷

Piazza Dante

B. Croce

❸

S. Chiara

CITTÀ ANTICA

❺

❹

❼

Castel Capuano ■

Piazza Garibaldi

🛈

Stazione Centrale

VOMERO

Stazione Montesanto

Piazza Montesanto

🛈

Piazza Mercato

❽

Porta Nolana

Via G. Ferraris

Via Toledo

Via Vittorio

F

Castel Sant'Elmo ■

Università di Napoli ■

Piazza Mercato

Via A. Lucci

Certosa di S. Martino ■

F

Piazza D'Acquisto

Posta Centrale

Piazza Bovio

Corso Umberto I

Via Nuova Marina

Via A. Vespucci

Via A. Volta

Corso

Piazza Matteotti

❾

❿

F

QUARTIERI SPAGNOLI

⓫

Via C. Colombo

⓬

Piazza Municipio

⓭

❶④

Galleria Umberto I

Teatro S. Carlo

Maschio Angioino (Castel Nuovo)

Stazione Marittima

Via Chiaia

Piazza Plebiscito

Palazzo Reale

Molo Beverello

V. d. Mille

㉕

Piazza d. Martiri

㉔ ㉓ ㉒ ㉑

🛈

SANTA LUCIA

Piazza Vittoria

⓯

Via S. Lucia

Via N. Sauro

Via F. Caracciolo

⓰

V. Partenope

⓴ ⓳ ⓲ ⓱

🛈

Castel dell'Ovo

To Eolie, Sicily & Cagliari

To Capri

To Sorrento

Gulf of Naples

(Golfo di Napoli)

	Ferry Terminal
🛈	Tourist Information
F━F	Funiculars

To Eolie

To Ischia, Procida

Sbrescia *(Finds* NEAPOLITAN/PIZZA   This is a real local hangout where Neapolitans of all ages come to enjoy the view of the nearby bay and the classic cuisine. The menu varies, but when you're in luck, this is a great place to taste Naples's traditional specialty, *sartù* (a baked rice dish filled with baby meatballs, cheese, and other ingredients). You'll find many other classics of Neapolitan cuisine, among them the well-prepared *fritto misto* (deep-fried seafood). They also have a wood-fired oven and prepare excellent pizza here.

Rampe Sant'Antonio 109. © 081-669140. Reservations recommended. Secondi 6€–14€ ($8.40–$20/£4.20–£9.80). AE, MC, V. Tues–Sun noon–3:30pm and 7:30–11pm. Bus: C3 to Mergellina (end of line); switch to 140.

MERGELLINA
MODERATE

Ciro a Mergellina *(* NEAPOLITAN/PIZZA/SEAFOOD   This historic restaurant is a favorite destination for tourists and locals alike, who come for the fish prepared many ways, from sautés of mussels and small clams to pasta dishes and entrees, but also for the excellent pizza, still made with *mozzarella di bufala* (buffalo mozzarella), and for the excellent service. We also love their *spaghetti alle vongole* (spaghetti with baby clams), and *pasta all'aragosta* (pasta with local lobster), or *spigola fritta* (deep-fried sea bass). Among the appetizers, the seafood salad is a particular favorite of ours. Their wonderful, homemade ice cream comes in a variety of flavors.

Via Mergellina 18. © 081-681780. Reservations recommended. Secondi 6€–18€ ($8.40–$25/£4.20–£13). Tues–Sun 11:30am–11:30pm. AE, DC, MC, V. Bus: 140. Metro: Mergellina. Tram: 1.

Don Salvatore NEAPOLITAN/SEAFOOD   On the Mergellina waterfront, near the dock where the ferries leave for Capri, Don Salvatore is a perfect example of a Neapolitan seaside trattoria. In this atmospheric restaurant, housed in what was once a boat shed, you can enjoy nicely grilled fresh fish, accompanied by local vegetables, or opt for a risotto or seafood pasta, like the winning *linguine incaciate* (linguine with cheese). The restaurant features an excellent wine list.

Strada Mergellina 4/a. © 081-681817. Reservations recommended. Secondi 10€–21€ ($14–$29/£7–£15). AE, DC, MC, V. Thurs–Tues 12:30–3:30pm and 8–11:30pm (daily in summer). Bus: 140. Metro: Mergellina. Tram: 1.

CHIAIA
EXPENSIVE

George's ** NEAPOLITAN   A temple of good taste, located on the top floor of Grand Hotel Parker's, this place has a view second to none. You can watch the sun set on the Gulf as your taste buds are pampered by chef Baciòt's preparations. He likes to revisit the ancient dishes of Neapolitan tradition, removing a bit of fat and adding a lot of imagination. The menu is seasonal and might include *pizzelle foglia* (eggless homemade leaves of pasta with sautéed garden vegetables), *pezzogna arrosto in guazzetto di tartufi* (local fish in a light sauce with truffles), and *costolette d'agnello con le melanzane* (lamb with eggplants). In addition to its regular menu, George's serves a "de light" menu, in line with the therapies proposed in the hotel's spa and based on the principles of Marc Messegué, the herbal specialist; it's detoxifying yet extremely satisfying. The wine list is extensive, including a large variety of Campanian and Italian wines (no foreign wines, not even French, which apparently is why this restaurant has no Michelin rating).

Corso Vittorio Emanuele 135. © 081-7612474. www.grandhotelparkers.com. Reservations required. Secondi 22€–25€ ($31–$35/£15–£18). AE, DC, MC, V. Daily 12:30–2:30pm and 8–10:30pm. Bus: C24 or C27 to Via Tasso-Corso Vittorio Emanuele II. Metro: Piazza Amedeo.

MODERATE

Amici Miei ⭐ *Finds* NEAPOLITAN/ITALIAN   If you are tired of seafood, this restaurant located on the hill between Chiaia and the Quartieri Spagnoli is for you. The menu focuses on meat—as in goose, lamb, pork—as well as on vegetarian choices. We recommend the homemade *fusilli alle melanzane* (fresh pasta with eggplant), the *pappardelle al sugo di agnello* (fresh large noodles with a lamb sauce), and the *costine e salsicce alla brace* (chargrilled lamb ribs and sausages), but anything on the seasonal menu is good. Just try not to fill up on the tasty homemade bread before your meal.

Via Monte di Dio 77. ℂ 081-7646063. www.ristoranteamicimiei.com. Reservations required. Secondi 11€–13€ ($15–$18/£7.70–£9.10). AE, DC, MC, V. Tues–Sun 12:30–3:30pm; Tues–Sat 7:30–11:30pm; closed 2 weeks in July and Sept. Tram: 1 to Piazza dei Martiri.

Jap-One *Finds* SUSHI   This trendy sushi bar, hidden away at the end of a winding narrow alley under the cliff of Monte di Dio (taking a cab is the best way to find it), feels more New York than Napoli with its uber-stylish decor. But thanks to the care and warm personality of owner Roberto Goretti, the atmosphere is friendly and relaxed, with cool jazz in the background and chefs preparing food at the sushi bar in view of the diners. Although the restaurant is Japanese, it has that irrepressible Neapolitan flair, seen in the use of local fish—for example the *maki di astice* (local lobster maki), or the coccio sashimi (sashimi of coccio, a local fish), depending on the day's catch.

Via Santa Maria Cappella Vecchia 30/i, off Piazza dei Martiri. ℂ 081-7646667. Reservations required. Secondi 14€–36€ ($20–$50/£9.80–£25). AE, DC, MC, V. Tues–Sat 8:30–11pm. Tram: 1 to Piazza dei Martiri.

La Stanza del Gusto ⭐⭐ MODERN NEAPOLITAN   Self-taught chef Mario Avallone has attracted a loyal following to this one-of-a-kind restaurant, which caters to gourmet tastes and wine aficionados. With its dark wood paneling, warm yellow walls, coffered ceiling, and array of curios, it can be best described as old-world funky. The extensive wine list has lots of local vintages that you would be hard-pressed to find elsewhere in Italy, let alone abroad, and includes many half bottles and by-the-glass offerings. The meal is built around a series of *assaggi:* small portions of skillfully prepared, beautifully presented dishes, taken from the local tradition and reinterpreted by the chef, such as his *sartù di riso* (a baked rice dish). The dishes are presented as a prix-fixe menu (definitely the way to go), but you can order a la carte; just remember that portions are not exactly hearty, so this isn't a great place for young children or the famished.

Vicoletto Sant'Arpino 21, a ramp of steps off Via di Chiaia to the right, coming from Piazza dei Martiri. ℂ 081-401578. Reservations required. Vegetarian menu 48€ ($67/£34); tasting menu 66€ ($92/£46); secondi 8€–25€ ($11–$35/£5.60–£18). AE, DC, MC, V. Mon–Sat 7:30–10:30pm. Tram: 1 to Piazza dei Martiri.

INEXPENSIVE

Vadinchenia ⭐ *Finds* MODERN CAMPANIAN   This restaurant, beloved by local connoisseurs, offers excellent food and professional service in a welcoming setting. The menu is large, including many unusual and surprisingly delicious offerings, such as the *ricotta farcita* (stuffed ricotta cheese) appetizer, the *paccheri alici e pecorino* (fresh large pasta with sardines and pecorino cheese), and the *calamaro ripieno di verdure e salsiccia* (squid stuffed with greens and sausage). The menu is well complemented by the moderately priced wine list.

Via Pontano 21, off Corso Vittorio Emanuele. ℂ 081-660265. www.vadinchenia.it. Reservations required. Secondi 8€–14€ ($11–$20/£5.60–£9.80). AE, DC, MC, V. Mon–Sun 12:30–3pm; Mon–Sat 7:30–11:30pm. Closed Aug and Dec 25. Bus: C24 or C27 to Via Tasso-Corso Vittorio Emanuele II. Metro: Piazza Amedeo.

SANTA LUCIA
EXPENSIVE

La Cantinella ✪ NEAPOLITAN/SEAFOOD   A well-established address in Naples, this local favorite is always bursting with chic clientele. The stylish old-fashioned nightclub atmosphere doubles with top-quality—and mostly strictly traditional—Neapolitan food. The choice of *antipasti* is good and savory. You can follow it with *pappardelle "sotto il cielo di Napoli"* (homemade pasta with zucchini, prawns, and green tomatoes) or *tubetti con le cozze* (short pasta with mussels). For your *secondi,* the *frittura* (deep-fried seafood) is a winner. Do not skip dessert—all are deliciously homemade (such as the superb soufflé, if you have the patience to wait). The attached club features live music and a similar menu. The wine list is huge at both spots.

Via Cuma 42. ✆ **081-7648684.** www.lacantinella.it. Reservations required. Secondi 19€–30€ ($27–$42/£13–£21). AE, DC, MC, V. Mon–Sat 12:30–3:30pm and 7:30pm–midnight. Closed 1 week in Jan and 3 weeks in Aug. Bus: 152, C25, or 140.

MODERATE

Antonio e Antonio PIZZA/NEAPOLITAN   Located on the beautiful *lungomare* (oceanfront), this restaurant is popular with locals, many of whom come for its youthful atmosphere. The two Antonios who created this restaurant grew up and were trained in two of Naples's most famous, historic restaurants, Zi Teresa and Giuseppone a Mare. The open kitchen zips out 40 types of pizza and all the great Neapolitan classics, including *fusilli di pasta fresca ai pomodorini del Vesuvio* (fresh pasta with cherry tomatoes from Mount Vesuvius, an especially tasty variety) and *polipetti affogati in cassuola* (squid cooked in an earthware pot with tomatoes and herbs). Appetizers and side dishes are served buffet style. A second location in Chiaia is located on the slopes of the Vomero, at Via Francesco Crispi 89 (✆ **081-682528** or 081-682438).

Via Partenope 24. ✆ **081-2451987.** Reservations recommended. Secondi 6€–17€ ($8.40–$24/£4.20–£12). AE, DC, MC, V. Daily 12:30–3:30pm and 7:30–11:30pm. Bus: 152, C25, or 140.

La Bersagliera *Kids* NEAPOLITAN/SEAFOOD   One of Naples's most historic restaurants, La Bersagliera has been managed by the same family for generations. Signora Elvira Chiosi, the current owner/manager, is the granddaughter of the original, 19th-century founder. Overlooking the yachts and fishing boats of the harbor at the Castel del' Ovo, the restaurant has kept much of its original decor and offers terrace dining in the summer. On the walls you'll see signed pictures of famous guests—Sophia Loren, Tyrone Power, Omar Sharif, and Pavarotti (who even indulged in a little *bel canto*). The food is excellent, and the menu is centered on seafood: We recommend the *tagliatelle Santa Lucia* (fresh pasta with swordfish and artichokes) and the *grigliata mista* (grilled medley of prawns, shrimp, red mullet, and calamari). The highly professional, courteous staff is very kind to children, who can get highchairs and half-portions. There's a good selection of local wines, and a more extensive and expensive list of offerings from farther afield.

Borgo Marinari 10, Santa Lucia. ✆ **081-7646016.** www.labersagliera.it. Secondi 8€–15€ ($11–$21/£5.60–£11). AE, MC, V. Wed–Mon 11:30am–3:30pm and 7:30–11pm. Closed 1 week after Epiphany (Jan 6). Bus: 152, C25, or 140.

INEXPENSIVE

Anema e Cozze PIZZA/SEAFOOD   A busy restaurant with a youthful, casual atmosphere, this is mostly a pizza place but, as its name suggests (it translates as "Soul and Mussels"), it also features mussels and seafood. Popular with locals who come here to enjoy the *lungomare,* it is a good place to eat typical Neapolitan *impepata di cozze* (steamed mussels with white pepper) and *cozze in padella* (sauté of mussels and toma-toes), and of course to enjoy great pizza. You can take Metro to Garibaldi stop for their second location at Via Caracciolo 13 (© **081-2482158**).

Via Partenope 15. © 081-2400001. Reservations not necessary. Secondi 6€–12€ ($8.40–$17/£4.20–£8.40). AE, MC, V. Daily noon–3:30pm and 7:30–11:30pm. Bus: 152, C25, or 140.

Ettore *(Finds)* NEAPOLITAN/PIZZA   This unpretentious and untrendy restaurant is a real neighborhood place. It's so popular with locals, in fact, that you might want to come early to get a seat. The menu is simple but varies often according to the season. They make excellent pizza, and their specialty is *pagnottiello*—calzone filled with moz-zarella, ricotta, and prosciutto.

Via Santa Lucia 56. © 081-7640498. Reservations recommended. Secondi 6€–15€ ($8.40–$21/£4.20–£11). AE, DC, MC, V. Tues–Sun 12:30–3:30pm and 7:30–11:30pm. Bus: 152, C25, or 140.

Pizzeria I Re di Napoli PIZZA/NEAPOLITAN   Not to be confused with the restaurant I Re di Napoli (p. 94), this is run by the same folks as nearby Anima e Cozze but is a bit more upscale. The menu is also more rounded, featuring not only pizza and appetizers, but also a choice of *primi, secondi* (mostly meat, depending on the market offerings), and *contorni*. The dining rooms—a second one is up a spiral stair-case—are warm and welcoming, and there are tables outside under umbrellas.

Via Partenope 29. © 081-7647775. Secondi 8€–15€ ($11–$21/£5.60–£11). AE, MC, V. Daily noon–1am. Closed Dec 25. Bus: 152, C25, or 140.

QUARTIERI SPAGNOLI
INEXPENSIVE

Hosteria Toledo NEAPOLITAN   A picturesque restaurant, Hosteria Toledo serves tasty but not too expensive meals in a lively atmosphere. It's been serving traditional Neapolitan food to locals and visitors since 1951, and people keep coming, for the great pasta—*alle cozze e vongole* (mussels and clams)—and main courses—*polipo in guazzetto* (squid in a tomato sauce), *arrosto di maiale* (pork roast), and *salsicce* (sausages) are highly recommended. If you have room left after those entrees, try one of the lus-cious desserts, which often include such great classics as *babà* (a sort of brioche with rum) and *pastiera* (a creamy sort of thick pie).

Vico Giardinetto 78/a. © 081-421257. Secondi 6.50€–14€ ($9.10–$20/£4.55–£9.80). AE, DC, MC, V. Mon–Sat 12:30–3pm and 7:30–11pm. Bus: R2 or R3 to Piazza Trieste e Trento. Coming from Piazza Trieste e Trento, it's off Via Toledo to the left, across from the Banco di Napoli.

Pizzeria Brandi *(Kids)* PIZZA   Opened in 1780, Brandi was so renowned for the quality of its pizza that in 1889, the *pizzaiolo* (pizza chef) was invited to prepare pizza for the royal family who had never tasted it. He created a pizza with mozzarella, basil, and tomatoes—the colors of the newly unified country's flag—and named his creation *pizza alla margherita* in honor of the first queen of Italy, Margherita di Savoia. The queen accepted the offering, and the pizza became an instant favorite throughout the country. The tradition has been maintained, and the restaurant succeeds in being good and authentic in spite of the streams of tourists now mixed in along the locals. Among the many pizzas on the menu, try the *alla Totò*, a deep-fried pizza somewhat like a cal-zone. Children are welcomed with highchairs, child-size pizzas, and infinite patience from the staff.

Salita Sant'Anna di Palazzo 1, at the corner with Via Chiaja. © 081-416928. Reservations recommended. Secondi 7€–18€ ($9.80–$25/£4.90–£133). No credit cards. Tues–Sun 12:30–3:30pm and 7:30pm–midnight. Bus: R2 or R3 to Piazza Trieste e Trento.

CITTA ANTICA
EXPENSIVE
Europeo di Mattozzi ⭐ NEAPOLITAN/PIZZA/SEAFOOD   This landmark of Neapolitan dining is consistently very rewarding. The chef/owner has created a welcoming atmosphere and offers a winning interpretation of traditional dishes. Among the *primi* you can have a very tasty *zuppa di cannellini e cozze* (bean and mussel soup) or *pasta e patate con provola* (pasta and potatoes with melted local cheese); for a *secondi* you could try *ricciola all' acquapazza* (a local fish in a light tomato and herb broth) or *stoccafisso alla pizzaiola* (dried codfish in a tomato, garlic, and oregano sauce). Pizza is also on the menu and is very well prepared, as are the desserts, including hometown favorites such as *babà* and *pastiera*.

Via Marchese Campodisola 4. ℭ 081-5521323. Reservations required. Secondi 11€–16€ ($15–$22/£7.70–£11). AE, DC, MC, V. Mon–Sat noon–3:30pm and Thurs–Sat 7:30–11pm. Closed 2 weeks in Aug. Bus: R2 or R3 to Piazza Trieste e Trento.

MODERATE
Ciro a Santa Brigida ⭐ NEAPOLITAN   A traditional restaurant with a formal—but absolutely not stuffy—atmosphere and very professional service, Ciro a Santa Brigida is one of the most famous, and most typical, Neapolitan restaurants around. The restaurant was opened in 1932 by the father of the current owner/managers at Via Foria, and transferred here by his children. Since then, Santa Brigida has become a gastronomical institution, serving cuisine in a warm atmosphere laden with traditional decor. Popular with locals for its *fritto* (deep-fried dishes including meat cutlets and seafood), and for side dishes like hard-to-find traditional vegetables, it also serves good pizza and excellent desserts. Of the traditional Neapolitan specialties on hand, try *rigatoni ricotta e polpettine* (pasta with ricotta and baby meatballs) and *polpi alla Luciana* (squid cooked in a pocket with tomato and herbs). Counted among the restaurant's famous and faithful customers were the writers Pirandello, the artist De Filippo, and the actors Gassman and Totò.

Via Santa Brigida 71, off Via Toledo. ℭ 081-5524072. Reservations required. Secondi 8€–16€ ($11–$22/£5.60–£11). AE, DC, MC, V. Mon–Sat noon–3:30pm and 7–11:30pm. Bus: R2 or R3 to Piazza Trieste e Trento.

Napoli Mia NEAPOLITAN   Tucked away on a small street, this local favorite serves traditional dishes with an innovative twist. We warmly recommend the appetizers, so delicious and varied that you'll have trouble pacing yourself and doing justice to the rest of the meal, which would be a big mistake. The menu varies seasonally, but look for their superb bean and clam soup, as well as a unique rabbit stuffed with *friarelli e provola* (broccoli and local cheese).

Via M. Schilizzi 18. ℭ 081-5522266. Reservations recommended. Secondi 8€–18€ ($11–$25/£5.60–£13). AE, DC, MC, V. Mon–Sat 12:30–2pm and Fri–Sat 7:30–10pm. Closed Christmas to New Year's, Easter, and Aug. Bus: R2 or R3 to Piazza Trieste e Trento.

INEXPENSIVE
I Re di Napoli NEAPOLITAN/PIZZA   This is a simple restaurant offering good food at inexpensive prices in two convenient locations. Their specialty is pizza—which they prepare in their brick oven. All of the many pizza options here are tasty, but if you decide you don't want pizza, they have a small menu of other dishes and a substantial buffet of appetizers/side dishes, including wonderful *involtini di melanzane* (rolled-up fried eggplant filled with mozzarella and basil in a tomato sauce) and *peperonata* (sauté

The Best Neapolitan Pizza in the Historic District

Forget all you have ever known about this cheesy treat and open your mind to the experience of pizza in Naples, so different from what we call pizza in the rest of the world. Here is the lowdown on the absolute best Naples pizzerie, where the decor is minimal or nonexistent, and an individual pizza costs between 3€ and 8€ ($4.20–$11/£2.10–£5.60):

- **Acunzo,** Via D. Cimarosa 60 (📞 081-5785362; closed Sun), is a historical address where you'll find pizza with unusual toppings along with typical Neapolitan dishes, like *friarelli* (sautéed broccoli), eggplant parmigiana, and bean soup.

- **Mattozzi,** Piazza Carità 2 (📞 081-5524322; closed Fri) is one of the oldest pizzerie in Naples, using strictly local ingredients, from the regional flour and the tomatoes of Mount Vesuvio to the *fiordilatte* from the Lattari Mountains on the Sorrento peninsula and the *mozzarella di bufala*.

- **Pizzeria Da Michele,** Via Sersale 1, off Via Forcella (📞 081-5539204; www. damichele.net; closed Sun), is where you'll find the best pizza in Naples, according to many locals. In business since 1888, it serves only two varieties: *margherita* or *marinara,* basically with or without cheese. Come early; it is usually quite crowded.

- **Pizzeria Di Matteo,** Via dei Tribunali 94, at Vico Giganti (📞 081-455262; closed Sun), is another historical establishment serving excellent classic pizza and specializing in the to-die-for *pizza fritta,* a delicacy of fluffy thin dough filled with a mix of ham, tomatoes, and local cheese—provola, ricotta, and mozzarella—that you can split as an appetizer or eat on your own. President Clinton ate here during the G7 summit in 1994.

- **Pizzaiolo del Presidente,** Via Tribunali 120 (📞 081-210903; closed Sun), was opened in 2000 by Ernesto Cacialli, the former *pizzaiolo* (pizza chef) of Di Matteo, above. He is the one who personally served Bill Clinton in 1994—apparently convincing the president to try his special margherita pizza—and has named his pizzeria after that event. Do not miss the *margherita* or the *pizza fritta.*

- **Sorbillo,** Via Tribunali 32 (📞 081-446643; closed Sun), provides a somewhat more formal setting and an equally—if not superior—quality of pizza. Open since 1935, it specializes in pizza made exclusively with local high-quality ingredients: the fiordilatte from Agerola on the Sorrento peninsula, the extra-virgin olive oil, the oregano from Frattamaggiore, which is best savored on the simple marinara. The other house specialty is the pizza with olives, capers, Vesuvian tomatoes, and *provola* (local cheese).

- **Starita,** Via Materdei 27 (📞 081-5441485; closed Mon), is a pleasant small pizzeria run by one of the best pizzaioli in the city. It is popular for the unique quality of its dough and famous for its *pizza fritta* as well as its *pizza coi fiori di zucca* (with zucchini flowers) that is available only in summer.

- **Trianon da Ciro,** Via P. Colletta 42 (📞 081-5539426; open daily), is an extremely popular pizzeria where you'll have to compete for a table with the students of the nearby university and the many local aficionados who come to savor the exceptional *pizza con salsiccia e friarelli* (with sausages and broccoli) and *pizza con pomodorini e mozzarella di bufala* (with Vesuvian tomatoes and buffalo mozzarella).

For Your Sweet Tooth

Naples is famous for its desserts, which include such world-famous specialties as *babà, sfogliatelle,* and *pastiera* (see appendix B, "Molto Italiano"). To taste those and many others, head to the **Pasticceria Scaturchio** 🐾🐾 (Piazza San Domenico Maggiore 19; ☎ 081-5516944). This historical pastry and coffee shop opened in 1903 and has been a favorite with locals ever since. Locals come here for a pick-me-up (there's nothing better than a *sfogliatella* as a mid-morning or mid-afternoon snack), or to buy dessert to bring to their hosts and family for dinner. Beside the excellent typical pastries, a chocolate candy developed here made them famous: the *Ministeriale,* a medallion of dark chocolate with a special liqueur cream filling.

Another excellent dessert stop is **Caffetteria Pasticceria Gelateria G. Mazzaro** 🐾 (Palazzo Spinelli, Via Tribunali 359; ☎ 081-459248; www.pasticceriamazzaro.it; Wed–Tues 7am–midnight), which makes scrumptious pastries and excellent gelato in many flavors.

---

of sweet peppers). You can take bus R2 or R3 to their second location at Piazza Trieste e Trento 7

Piazza Dante 16. ☎ 081-423013. Reservations recommended on weekends. Secondi 5€–9€ ($7–$13/£3.50–£6.30). AE, DC, MC, V. Daily 11:30am–1am. Bus: R4, 24, CS, or 201. Metro: Piazza Dante.

Pisano (Value) (Finds) NEAPOLITAN/SEAFOOD   Hidden behind the Duomo, this pleasant family-run restaurant serves well-prepared dishes from the local culinary tradition. The menu is large and includes both surf and turf. We recommend the *scialatielli ai frutti di mare* (fresh pasta with seafood) and the *linguine al coccio* (pasta with local fish), as well as the *spigola all'acquapazza* (sea bass in a light tomato herbed broth) and the roasted sausages.

Piazzetta Crocelle ai Mannesi 1. ☎ 081-5548325. Reservations recommended on weekends. Secondi 6€–12€ ($8.40–$17/£4.20–£8.40). AE, DC, MC, V. Mon–Sat noon–3pm and 7:30–10:30pm. Bus: R2.

Trattoria Pizzeria Medina NEAPOLITAN/PIZZA   It is easy to mistake this large, glitzy, and centrally located restaurant for a tourist trap when you see it from the outside. Inside, you'll find an informal setting where only pizza is served—popular with the younger crowds. In the more elegant upstairs restaurant, which will surprise you with its spacious dining rooms with 6m (20-ft.) beamed ceilings and walls decorated with painted scenes of Napoli, you'll find a healthy mix of locals and visitors. The full menu includes excellent pizza with a large variety of toppings, and a number of traditional dishes. We recommend the *tortelli al sugo* (filled homemade pasta in a tomato sauce), *trancio di cefalo in guazzetto* (steak of gray mullet in a light tomato sauce), and *costolette in padella* (sautéed cutlets). The *secondi* come—unusual in Italy—garnished with vegetables. We also recommend the self-serve buffet of *antipasti* and *contorni,* with an ample choice of vegetarian and fish dishes.

Via Medina 32. ☎ 081-5515233. Reservations recommended on weekends. Secondi 7€–14€ ($9.80–$20/£4.90–£9.80). AE, DC, MC, V. Daily noon–3pm and 7pm–midnight. Bus: R2.

PIAZZA GARIBALDI
MODERATE

Mimì alla Ferrovia ★ *(Finds* NEAPOLITAN   This is another of Naples's historical landmark restaurants. Its recent face-lift has not diminished its popularity with locals, nor changed its cuisine, which remains true to Neapolitan tradition. The chef prepares excellent renditions of local favorites, varying according to the season. Depending on the time of year, you'll probably find *scialatielli ai frutti di mare* (eggless homemade pasta with seafood), *polipo alla Luciana* (squid cooked in a pocket with tomato and herbs), *in guazzetto* (squid in a light tomato sauce), and *sartù* (rice with baby meatballs and cheese). Not surprisingly, the desserts are those of the Neapolitan tradition—*babà* and *pastiera*.

Via Alfonso d'Aragona 21. © 081-5538525. Reservations recommended on weekends. Secondi 8€–15€ ($11–$21/£5.60–£11). AE, DC, MC, V. Mon–Sat noon–3pm and 7:30–10:30pm. Metro: Piazza Garibaldi.

VOMERO
INEXPENSIVE

Gorizia ★ *(Finds* NEAPOLITAN/PIZZA   This excellent pizzeria was started in 1916 by the grandfather of the current owners (brothers Salvatore and Antonio). True to local tradition, the two brothers are convinced the secret is in the crust and don't believe pizza needs to be dressed up with fancy toppings to be good. According to them, the crust has to be puffy but not gummy, with a slightly crunchy edge. Once you taste the result, you can only agree. Pizza's not the only thing on the menu, however: They offer a small daily menu which always includes one soup and a few choices of antipasto, primo, secondo, and contorno. We recommend the pasta with artichokes, olives, and tomatoes, as well as *pasta e ceci* (a thick soup made of garbanzo beans). The delicious escarole is stuffed with bread crumbs, olives, pinoli nuts, and raisins. This is a popular place for business lunches, and it helps to have a reservation in the evening.

Via Bernini 31, off Piazza Vanvitelli. © 081-5782248. Reservations recommended for dinner. 6€–18€ ($8–$25/£4.20–£13). AE, DC, MC, V. Tues–Sun 12:30–4pm and 6pm–1am. Bus: V1. Funicolare to Vomero.

CAPODIMONTE
INEXPENSIVE

Al Terrazzo NEAPOLITAN/PIZZA   This large, simple neighborhood restaurant has been around since 1945 and is a convenient stop before or after visiting the Museo Capodimonte. It makes excellent pizza—try the *Antica Capri* (with smoked provola and fresh tomatoes)—and has a large menu including specialties such as *scialatielli ai frutti di mare* (eggless fresh pasta with seafood). The restaurant prides itself on its large buffet of antipasti and side dishes, offering 50 choices daily. During clement weather, you can dine on the terrace, which is on the second floor and above the traffic and street noise.

Viale Colli Aminei 99, off Via Capodimonte. © 081-7414400 or 081-7414680. Secondi 4€–10€ ($5.60–$14/£2.80–£7). AE, DC, MC, V. Daily 11am–3:30pm and 6:30–11pm, later on Fri and Sat. Bus: R4.

4 Exploring Naples

For those who accept the challenge and look beyond the curtain of noise and urban grit, Naples reveals itself full of fun, surprise, and wonder. Naples is particularly loved by art lovers and history buffs. To brush up on local history and art, see appendix A for help understanding this complex and multilayered city.

What to See & Do in Naples

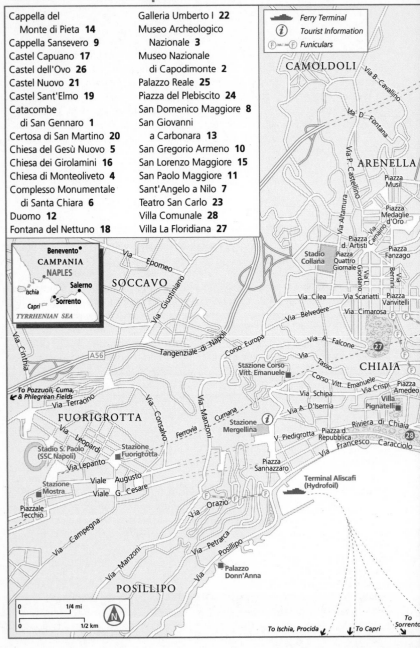

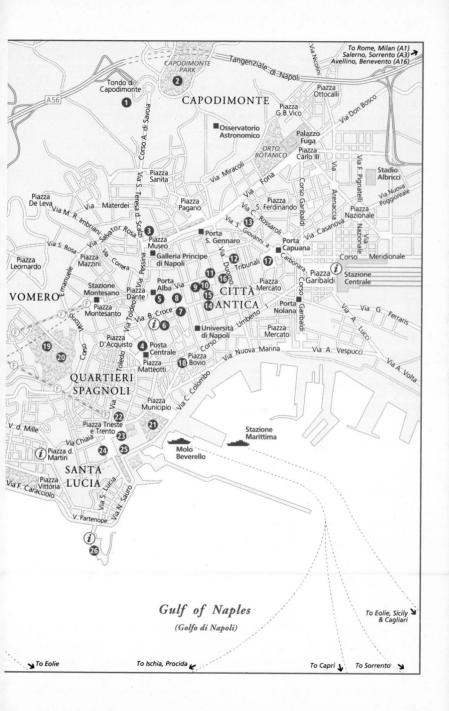

To Rome, Milan (A1)
Salerno, Sorrento (A3) ➤
Avellino, Benevento (A16)

Via Nicolini

CAPODIMONTE
PARK

Tangenziale di Napoli

Piazza
Ottocalli

A56

Tondo di
Capodimonte

❶

❷

CAPODIMONTE

Corso A. di Savoia

Piazza
G.B. Vico

Via Don Bosco

■ Osservatorio
Astronomico

Palazzo
Fuga

Via F. Pignatelli

ORTO
BOTANICO

Piazza
Carlo III

Stadio
Albricci

Piazza
De Leva

Via S. Teresa d. Scalzi

Piazza
Sanita

Via Miracoli

Via Foria

Corso Garibaldi

Via Nuova
Poggioreale

Via M. R. Imbriani

Via   Materdei

Piazza
Pagano

Piazza
S. Ferdinando

Arenaccia

Piazza
Nazionale

Via Salvator Rosa

Via Pessina

Via S. Rosa

Piazza
Mazzini

Via Correra

Piazza
Museo

❸

Porta
S. Gennaro

Via S. C. Rossaroli

❶❸

Via S. Giovanni a...

Porta
Capuana

Via Casanova

Via Nazionale

Corso   Meridionale

Piazza
Leonardo

Galleria Principe
di Napoli

Via Duomo

❶❷

Carbonara

Piazza
Garibaldi

ⓘ

Stazione
Centrale

VOMERO

Via E. Emanuele

Stazione
Montesano

Porta
Alba

❶❶ ❶❶

Tribunali

❶❼

Via Toledo

Piazza
Dante

❺ ❽

❾ ❶❶

❶❻

CITTÀ
ANTICA

Piazza
Mercato

Corso Garibaldi

Piazza
Montesanto

Via B. Croce

❶❺

Porta
Nolana

Via A. Lucci

Via G. Ferraris

ⓘ ❻

❶❹

❼

Piazza
D'Acquisto

❹

Posta
Centrale

Università
di Napoli

Corso   Umberto

Piazza
Mercato

Via A. Vespucci

QUARTIERI
SPAGNOLI

Piazza
Matteotti

❶❽

Piazza
Bovio

Via Nuova Marina

Via A. Volta

Via C. Colombo

Via Toledo

Piazza
Municipio

V. d. Mille

❷❷

Piazza Trieste
e Trento

❷❶

Stazione
Marittima

❷❸

Via Chiaia

ⓘ Piazza d.
Martiri

❷❹

❷❺

Molo
Beverello

SANTA
LUCIA

Via S. Lucia

Via N. Sauro

Piazza
Vittoria

Via F. Caracciolo

V. Partenope

ⓘ

❷❻

Gulf of Naples

(*Golfo di Napoli*)

To Eolie, Sicily ↘
& Cagliari

↘ To Eolie   To Ischia, Procida ↙   To Capri ↓   To Sorrento ↘

Value   Campania Artecard

The **Artecard** (© **800-600601** or 063-9967650; www.campaniartecard.it) gives you discounted admission to a great number of attractions, free access to public transportation, and discounts to a number of participating businesses. The pass comes in several "region" and "city" versions:

- The **"3 days all sites"** pass (25€/$35/£18 adult; 18€/$25/£13 youth under 25) grants free admission to the first two attractions you visit from the list below (to all attractions for youth under 25); 50% discount on all the others, between 10% and 25% discount on several other museums and attractions; and free access to all public transportation—including regional trains and special buses—for 3 days. Note that the youth card is offered only to citizens of the European Union and other countries with reciprocity rights.
- The **"3 days Naples and Campi Flegrei"** (13€/$18/£9.10 adults; 8€/$11/£5.60 youth under 25) grants you the same advantages as above but only within Naples and the Campi Flegrei area. (Even if you are not going to the Campi Flegrei, this works out as a great deal for Naples.)
- The **"7 days all sites"** (28€/$39/£20 adult; 21€/$29/£15 youth under 25) grants you the same advantages as above, excluding public transportation, for 7 days instead of 3.

The sites that qualify for free or 50% admission are:

- Within Naples: Museo Archeologico Nazionale, Museo di Capodimonte, Certosa and Museo Di San Martino, Complesso Museale Santa Chiara, Castel Sant'Elmo, Museo Civico di Castelnuovo, Palazzo Reale, Città Della Scienza, and the Campi Flegrei's five sites (Flavian Amphitheatre, Serapeum, archaeological areas of Baia, Cuma, and Rione Terra), counted as one admission only.
- Outside Naples: Anfiteatro Campano, archaeological areas of Pompeii, Herculaneum, Paestum, Stabia, Velia, Oplontis, and Boscoreale, Certosa di Padula, Grotte dell'Angelo di Pertosa, Capua's Mitreo, Museo Archeologico dell'Antica Capua, Museo dei Gladiatori, and Museo del Santuario di Hera Argiva.

The list of sites and businesses offering discounts between 10% and 25% is too long to report here; please refer to our listings throughout the book. The card is for sale at all participating sites listed above as well as at Capodichino Airport; the Molo Beverello (harbor); the train stations of Napoli Cantrale and Mergellina; major hotels; and newspaper kiosks.

We highly recommend you purchase the **Artecard** (see box above) before starting your exploration of the region. The **City Sightseeing** hop-on-and-off tour is another good idea, particularly if your time is limited (see "Guided Tours," later in this chapter); it will give you a great introduction to the city and provide convenient transportation between major attractions without forcing you to worry about bus numbers, tickets, and taxis.

ROYAL NAPLES: PALACES & CASTLES

Castel Capuano   A fortress built by Guglielmo I d'Altavilla in the 12th century and restored in the 13th century by Carlo d'Angió, this castle was transformed into a royal residence by the Aragona dynasty in 1484. In 1540, Don Pedro di Toledo, the viceroy of Naples, decided to change the residence to the seat of tribunals, a function it has maintained to this day. Castel Capuano takes its name from the nearby gate, Porta Capuana, once at the head of the main road leading to Capua. Inside the courtyard, the medieval structure is visible. You can visit some of the decorated halls and the Cappella Sommaria, with its 16th-century frescoes.

Via Concezio Muzy, off Via dei Tribunali. Free admission. Daily 9am–6pm. Metro: Piazza Garibaldi.

Castel dell'Ovo 🏰   Built over the small island where the first Greek colony was created in the 9th century B.C., this castle is one of Naples's most famous sites; its profile graces most pictures of the bay. According to legend, its name, "Castle of the Egg," refers to the magic egg that the classic poet Virgil—the author of the *Aeneid* and a reputed magician—placed under the foundations to protect it. The fortress evolved from the villa of the Roman Lucullus (a celebrated gourmand), which was fortified in the Middle Ages and transformed into a castle by Frederick II. Enlarged and strengthened between the 16th and the 18th centuries, it remained a royal residence until the 20th century. Part of the castle now houses the Museum of Ethno-Prehistory, which is open only for special exhibits. The rest of the castle can be visited: You will be able to admire the **Sala delle Colonne (Hall of the Columns)** 🏰, and the **Loggiato** 🏰— both architectural masterpieces, and great views from two towers, **Torre Maestra** and **Torre Normanna.** The castle occupies only part of the island, which is connected to the shore in front of the Santa Lucia neighborhood. Around it are the picturesque alleys and fishermen's houses of the **Borgo dei Marinari** 🏰—many of which have been transformed into restaurants.

Borgo Marinari. © 081-2400055. Admission depends on exhibit; 10% discount with Artecard. Mon–Sat 8am–6pm; Sun 8am–2pm. Bus: 152, C25, or 140.

Castel Nuovo, aka Maschio Angioino & Museo Civico 🏰   An imposing fortress dominating the bay only steps from the shore, this castle was created by the French architect Pierre d'Angicourt in the 13th century for the new king, Carlo I d'Angió. The first king of the Angevin dynasty, he wanted a more suitable residence than the castles—Castel dell'Ovo and Castel Capuano—that had been used by previous sovereigns. Started in 1279 and finished in 1282, Castel Nuovo was enlarged in the 15th century by Alfonso I d'Aragona, first king of the Aragonese dynasty. The castle has five towers—del Beverello (overlooking the harbor), di San Giorgio, di Mezzo, di Guardia, and dell'Oro (showing its tufa stone structure)—and a facade (facing inland) graced by the grandiose **Triumphal Arch of Alfonso I of Aragona** 🏰. This is a splendid example of early Renaissance architecture by Francesco Laurana and Pietro de Martino, commemorating Alfonso I's ascent to power after his victory over the Angevins in 1443.

Across from the entrance in the courtyard and up a 15th-century staircase, you can access the magnificent **Sala dei Baroni** 🏰🏰, an architectural masterpiece. The monumental room is an enormous cube, 27m (89 ft.) wide and 28m (92 ft.) high, with a star-shaped vaulted ceiling originally decorated by Giotto in the 14th century. (His frescoes and most of the sculptures that decorated the room were unfortunately lost in a fire in 1919.)

Today, the castle houses the **Museo Civico (Civic Museum)** 𝓕, holding a rich collection of artworks from the castle itself and other important monuments in Naples. Part of the museum's exhibit is inside the **Cappella Palatina** 𝓕, the only surviving part of the Angevin castle. The Chapel's facade opens onto the courtyard and is graced with a beautiful 15th-century carved **portal** and a **rose window** 𝓕. Built in 1307, the chapel was completely decorated by Giotto, but only a few fragments remain. Inside you'll see a fine selection of 14th- and 15th-century sculptures, including a **Tabernacle** 𝓕𝓕 by Domenico Gagini (a pupil of Donatello and Brunelleschi) depicting a Madonna with Child, and two **Madonnas with Child** 𝓕 by Francesco Laurana—one from the portal of this chapel and the second from a nearby church. In the vestibule on the second floor, you'll find a **bronze door** 𝓕 with a cannonball hole: It is the original 15th-century door of the castle, which was taken as war booty by the French in 1496 and later returned. In the other rooms, you'll find a collection of 16th- and 17th-century paintings, including works by Luca Giordano and Francesco Solimena. On the third floor is an interesting collection of paintings dating from the 18th to the 20th centuries.

Piazza Municipio. ✆ **081-7955877** or 081-4201241. Admission 5€ ($7/£3.50). Mon–Sat 9am–7pm. Ticket booth closes 1 hr. earlier. Bus: R1 or R4.

Castel Sant'Elmo   Located up the hill of the Vomero, near the Certosa di San Martino (see later in this chapter), this majestic star-shaped construction, with its six points and several moats, is visible from everywhere in the city. It was originally built by the Angevins in 1329 and called Belforte, then was remade into the present fortress by Viceroy Pedro Toledo in the 16th century. Used as a prison during the Masaniello revolution in 1799, it has been recently restored and now houses special exhibits. You can visit the prisons and the terraces, which offer great views over Naples and the bay.

Via Tito Angelini 20. ✆ **081-5784030.** www.musis.it. Admission 1€ ($1.40/70p); free with admission to the Certosa di San Martino; additional fee for special exhibits. Thurs–Tues 8:30am–7:30pm. Ticket booth closes 1 hr. earlier. Closed Jan 1 and Dec 25. Metro: Vanvitelli. Bus: V1 from Piazza Vanvitelli. Funicolare to Vomero.

Palazzo Reale 𝓕   This imposing palace was designed by Domenico Fontana and built in 2 years, from 1600 to 1602, for the Spanish king Filippo III. Ironically, he never made it to Naples, and the castle was used by later kings who enlarged it in the 18th century. Luigi Vanvitelli worked on the **facade** 𝓕, closing some of the arches to strengthen the walls and creating niches that were filled in 1888 by Umberto I, king of Italy, with eight statues of Neapolitan kings. Badly damaged during World War II, the building has been completely restored. Today, you can admire much of the interior, and we recommend doing so by guided tour to get a full appreciation of the sprawling place. The **Royal Apartment** 𝓕 occupies one half of the palace, and is still furnished with the original furniture plus a number of masterpieces taken from Neapolitan churches that have closed. From the elegant **Cortile d'Onore (Court of Honor)** the double ramp of the main staircase leads to the first floor and the **Teatrino di Corte,** the private "home theater" of the royal family. Continuing through, you enter the semi-public rooms, including the **Throne Room.** Beyond the corner begins the **Private Appartment,** where the kings lived until 1837, when a fire obliged them to move upstairs. Its rooms open onto the manicured elevated gardens, affording beautiful views over the Gulf. Decorated with colored marble, tapestries, frescoes, and 19th-century furniture, the rooms are quite splendid, especially the beautifully furnished **Studio del Re (King's Study),** where you can admire a **desk** and two *secretaires* 𝓕 made for Napoleon Bonaparte by Adam Weisweiler. The following room contains two paintings—*San Gennaro* and a *Crucifixion*—by Luca Giordano, and two paintings by Andrea Vaccaro. From here on, colorfully stenciled doors lead through a seemingly endless array of rooms, most with 18th-century white and gilt original ceilings, marble floors, and dozens of paintings. The magnificent **Hall of Hercules** ⚔, the ballroom, is hung with Neapolitan tapestries and decorated with some beautiful Sèvres vases. The chapel, **Cappella Palatina,** is worth a visit for its carved wooden **doors** ⚔ dating from the 16th century, its beautiful baroque **marble altar** ⚔ by Dionisio Lazzari, with inlays of lapis lazuli, agate, amethyst, and gilt, and the splendid 18th-century **Presepio del Banco di Napoli (Manger Scene)** ⚔⚔. One of the best examples of this art, the altar includes many figures carved by great Neapolitan sculptors of the time.

The other half of the palace contains the reception wing: the **Appartamento delle Feste** ⚔, with elegant rooms dedicated to public celebrations and festivities. It is now, together with the second floor, occupied by the **Biblioteca Nazionale di Vittorio Emanuele III,** the library which was originally established by Charles de Bourbon. Accessible from a separate entrance on the ground floor, the library is one of the greatest in the south, with about two million volumes (including 32,950 manuscripts, 4,563 incunabula, and 1,752 papyrus manuscripts from Herculaneum).

Piazza del Plebiscito 1. ✆ 081-5808111. Admission 4€ ($5.60/£2.80); courtyard and gardens free. Guided tour by reservation 3€ ($4.20/£2.10). Thurs–Tues 9am–8pm. Ticket booth closes 1 hr. earlier. Bus: R2 or R3 to Piazza Trieste e Trento.

Villa La Floridiana & Museo Nazionale della Ceramica Duca di Martina ⚔⚔

Surrounded by a magnificent park, this museum was once the 18th-century *casale* (country house) of Lucia Migliaccio, duchess of Floridia and second wife of Ferdinand II di Borbone. It now houses the **Museo Nazionale della Ceramica Duca di Martina** ⚔, a rich collection of ceramics. The core of the museum is the private collection of Duc Placido De Sangro di Martina who, through his travels in Europe, collected precious objects not only in majolica and porcelain, but also glass, ivory, and coral. The collection was then expanded with objects from other museums in Naples. The star of the show is the collection of **porcellane di Capodimonte (Capodimonte porcelain)** ⚔, the most important collection in the world of this kind, with works from 1743 to 1759 by important artists such as Giuseppe Gricci; and the collection of **Japanese and Chinese porcelain** ⚔, including precious Ming and Edo dynasty pieces. Decorating the walls are **sketches** by great Neapolitan artists of the 18th century, including Francesco Solimena, Domenico Antonio Vaccaro, and Corrado Giaquinto.

Note: Visits to the museum are only possible during fixed hours with an official guide. Even if you are not interested in ceramics, the villa is well worth a stop both for its architecture and for the splendid views over the whole bay.

Via Aniello Falcone 171. ✆ 081-407881 or 081-5788418. www.musis.it. Admission 2.50€ ($3.50/£1.75); 10% discount with Artecard. Wed–Mon 8:30am–2pm; ticket booth closes 1 hr. earlier. Closed Jan 1 and Dec 25. Museum visit only by guided tour starting at 9:30am, 11am, and 12:30pm. Funicolare to Piazza Fuga.

GREAT MUSEUMS

MADRE (Museo d'Arte Contemporanea Donnaregina)
This modern museum has recently opened after a major renovation of the historical **Palazzo Regina,** in the heart of the historical district. The rich collection of the museum comes both from the city's endowment, bestowed in recent decades, and from permanent loans from private collectors. Some of the world's best contemporary artists are represented, including Horn, Kapoor, and Lewitt, as well as a number of Italian artists such as Fabro,

Clemente, and Serra. In addition to the permanent collection, the MADRE houses noteworthy temporary exhibits (check with the tourist office for current events).

Via Settembrini 79. (©) **081-19313016.** www.museomadre.it. Admission: Mon free; other days 7€ ($9.80/£4.90); 50% discount with Artecard. Sun–Mon and Wed–Thurs 10am–9pm; Fri–Sat 10am–midnight. Metro: Cavour.

Museo Archeologico Nazionale 𝕶𝕶𝕶 *(Kids)* This 16th-century palace was remodeled in the 17th century to house the National Archaeological Museum. According to the fashion of the time, precious antiquities were embedded in the building as decoration: The marble statues on the **facade** were found during early excavations of Pompeii; the mosaics embedded in many of the **floors** are originals from the ancient Roman villas excavated in the 17th century. The whole collection is jaw-dropping and very extensive; even children will love the Egyptian section, and teens will be fascinated by the amazing precious Gemme collection (see below).

The original core of the museum is the Farnese Collection, which was moved here in 1777 and enriched with treasures found during the archaeological excavations of Pompeii, Herculaneum, Stabia, and the rest of the region. The first-floor galleries here hold a superb collection of Roman sculptures, illustrating the integration of Hellenic principles into Roman art, and including such masterpieces as the **Doriforo (Spear Bearer)** 𝕶𝕶 from Pompeii, a unique, complete copy of the famous 5th-century-B.C. bronze statue by the Greek sculptor Policleto (in the Galleria dei Grandi Maestri, section 2). Other great masterpieces on display in the Farnese Collection include the superb *Ercole Farnese* 𝕶𝕶, a Hercules copied from a 4th-century-B.C. bronze by Greek sculptor Lisippo (found in the Terme di Caracalla in Rome, this sculpture had enormous influence on Renaissance artists); and the exceptional *Toro Romano* or *Toro Farnese* 𝕶𝕶, one of the largest existing sculpture groups from antiquity. Standing over 4m (13 ft.) high, the Toro Farnese is a copy of a Greek original from the 2nd century B.C., representing the torment of the queen of Beotia as she is tied to a bull. Also part of the Farnese Collection are the three rooms of the **Gemme della Collezione Farnese** 𝕶𝕶, a matchless collection of precious objects (over 2,000 pieces), including the unique *tazza farnese* 𝕶𝕶 created in Alexandria in the 2nd century B.C.: Carved from a single piece of agate into the shape of a drinking cup, it is one of the largest cameos ever created.

From the first floor, you can also access the **Epigraphic Collection** (inscriptions) 𝕶— the most important epigraphic collection in the world that pertains to ancient Roman and Greek civilizations—and the **Egyptian Collection** 𝕶, holding artifacts from 2700 B.C. up to the Ptolemaic-Roman period of the 2nd and 1st centuries B.C.

On the mezzanine level, besides the reorganized **Numismatic Collection** 𝕶, with over 200,000 coins and medals from antiquity, you'll find the richest **mosaic collection** 𝕶𝕶𝕶 in the world, with pieces spanning from the 2nd century B.C. to the 1st century A.D. Among the many works of art here is the magnificent **Alexander the Great defeating Darius of Persia** 𝕶𝕶𝕶, a huge mosaic covering 20 sq. m (216 sq. ft.), which was found in the Casa del Fauno in Pompei.

More Ancient Roman mosaics line the floors of the second level, where you'll find the beautiful **Meridiana Hall** 𝕶 and the complete findings from the several Roman towns and villas destroyed by the eruption of Mount Vesuvius in A.D. 79. The collection of Ancient Roman **paintings** 𝕶𝕶𝕶 covers the period from the 1st century B.C. to the 1st century A.D. *Note:* If you have time for only one section of the museum, make it this one: Entire rooms have been reconstructed from villas in Pompeii, Herculaneum, Boscoreale, Boscotrecase, and other locations. Our single favorite room is

#77, with its **landscapes** and a portrait of the girl **Saffo.** (At presstime, the frescoes of this room were under restoration and only visible on selected days, so call ahead.) Don't miss the room dedicated to the Herculaneum's **Villa dei Papiri** ✿✿. Further collections here include precious objects—silver, ivory, pottery, and glass—as well as weaponry and a scale reconstruction of Pompeii. Also on this floor, are unique findings from the Naples area's prehistoric through Etruscan and Greek periods.

We recommend the helpful audioguides. You may also make a reservation for a guided tour of the Roman erotica (famous since Goethe's day) in the **Gabinetto Segreto (Secret Room)** ✿✿. The collection documents the acceptance of sexuality in everyday Roman life until Christians demonized it as the embodiment of paganism.

Piazza Museo 19. ✆ 081-4422149. www.musis.it. Admission 6.50€ ($9.10/£4.55). Audioguide 4€ ($5.60/£2.80) in Italian or English. Guided tours (90 min.) 4€ ($5.60/£2.80). Wed–Mon 9am–7:30pm. Ticket booth closes 1 hr. earlier. Closed Jan 1 and Dec 25. Metro: Museo or Piazza Cavour.

Museo Nazionale di Capodimonte ✿✿✿   Sitting in the middle of a magnificent park that once was a hunting preserve for the Bourbon kings, this museum was created by Carlo III di Borbone in 1743 to house his mother's art collection (she was Elisabetta Farnese and had her own share of the family's art endowment). Also on the grounds, the king founded the Capodimonte workshops in 1739 in his endeavor to develop a local high-end industry. The workshops produced artistic ceramics following a unique technique and style that made them famous around the world. The laboratories slowed down considerably in 1759, when the king left Naples to become king of Spain, but his son Ferdinando kept it going until 1805.

While the wooded park—still called *bosco reale* (royal woods) by locals—is a pleasant destination for a stroll (locals love to come here for family outings, especially on weekends), the museum is a prime destination for art lovers. In addition to its own huge collection, the museum hosts stellar annual exhibits. *Note:* You'll have to book your tickets well in advance if you are planning your visit during this yearly event.

While the **19th-century Gallery** on the mezzanine level includes a number of interesting paintings, if this is your first visit, we recommend you head for the **Farnese Gallery** ✿✿ on the second floor, which features the stars of the collection, with several paintings by some of the best Italian artists—**Tiziano, Raffaello, Masaccio, Botticelli, Perugino, Luca Signorelli, Sandro Botticelli, Correggio, Giovanni Bellini, Mantegna, Parmigianino, Guido Reni, Caravaggio**—and by a number of the best artists from the Flemish school, such as **Pieter Bruegel the Elder** and **Van Dyck.** Besides paintings, the gallery holds sculptures and precious tapestries. Smaller but also worth a visit is the **Borgia Collection** ✿, also on the second floor. It contains many precious Renaissance **ivory** and **enamel** pieces.

The **Royal Apartments** ✿ take up much of the second floor. In the **Porcelain Gallery** ✿, you'll find a number of unique pieces, with objects and dinner plates from all the royal palaces of Naples, including *bisquits* (a firing process) of **Sèvres** and **Vienna,** and porcelains of **Meissen** and, of course, the famous **Capodimonte** ceramics created in the local workshops. Nearby is the **De Ciccio Collection** with more porcelain, but also paintings and precious objects. **The Armory** has interesting pieces, but is overshadowed by the famous **Salottino di Porcellana** ✿✿, a small room completely inlaid with porcelain, made for Maria Amalia in the 18th century for the royal palace of Portici.

A **gallery** ✿ dedicated to "Painting in Naples from the 13th to the 19th Centuries" occupies the third floor, and provides a unique overview of artists who worked in

Naples. It includes works by **Sodoma, Vasari, Tiziano, Caravaggio,** and **Luca Giordano;** here you can also admire the seven beautiful 16th-century **tapestries** ⚓ from the **d'Avalos Collection,** and also their picture collection including work by **Ribera** and **Luca Giordano.** The contemporary art collection extends from the third to the fourth floor, with works by Alberto Burri, Jannis Kounellis, Andy Warhol, and Enzo Cucchi, among others. On the fourth floor you can also find a **Photography Collection** and the **Galleria dell'Ottocento** focusing on painters of the 19th century (Neapolitans, but also other Italians and foreigners).

Palazzo Capodimonte, Via Miano 1; also through the park from Via Capodimonte. ⓒ 081-7499111. www.musis.it. Admission 7.50€ ($11/£5.25); 6.50€ ($9.10/£4.55) after 2pm. Audioguide 4€ ($5.60/£2.80). Thurs–Tues 8:30am–7:30pm. Ticket booth closes 1 hr. earlier. Closed Jan 1 and Dec 25. Bus: R4 or 24.

RELIGIOUS NAPLES: CHURCHES & MONASTERIES

Perhaps the most religious city in Italy, Naples rivals Rome when it comes to the number and beauty of its churches. It is impossible to list them all, although we wanted to; we cover only the best.

Cappella del Monte di Pietà *(Finds)* The sober 16th-century *palazzo* of the Monte di Pietà hides one of Naples's art treasures: a perfectly preserved and richly decorated 16th-century chapel. Opening onto the palazzo's courtyard, the chapel is decorated by important artists of the 16th and 17th centuries. On the facade are two **sculptures** by Pietro Bernini, father of the famous Lorenzo. Inside the church, the **ceiling** bears a beautiful **fresco** depicting scenes from the life of Jesus by Belisario Corenzio. Farther on, you can visit the adjoining rooms, in particular the **sacristy** ⚓ at the beginning, and the **Sala delle Cantoniere** ⚓ at the end, perfectly preserved in 17th-century style, down to the furnishings and floors.

Via Biagio dei Librai 114. ⓒ 081-5807111. Free admission. Sat 9am–7pm; Sun 9am–2pm. Bus: R1, R2, or R3. Metro: Dante.

Cappella di Sansevero ⚓ In the 18th century, Prince Raimondo di Sangro of Sansevero remodeled this funerary chapel—built in the 16th century for his family—and lavishly decorated it with sculptures. Among those are some particularly renowned works, starting with Giuseppe Sanmartino's ***Cristo Velato*** **(Veiled Christ)** ⚓, created by the Neapolitan sculptor in 1753, and still with the original patina. The challenge of depicting veiled figures in stone seems to have obsessed the prince: Other sculptures here are the ***Disinganno,*** a technical virtuoso by Queirolo showing a standing figure of a man disentangling himself from a net; and ***Pudicizia,*** a masterpiece by Corradini showing a veiled naked woman. The prince—a student of science, an inventor, and an alchemist—achieved fame as a master of the occult, and the decoration of the chapel has contributed to this reputation. The most striking (and weird) objects here are two actual human bodies conserved in the crypt, whose circulatory systems are perfectly preserved after 2 centuries. The chapel is also used for art exhibits and concerts—call for schedules.

Via Francesco De Sanctis 19. ⓒ 081-5518470. www.museosansevero.it. Admission 6€ ($8.40/£4.20); 2€ ($2.80/£1.40) discount with Artecard. Mon and Wed–Sat 10am–6pm; Sun 10am–1:30pm. Last admission 20 min. before closing. Bus: R1, R2, or R3. Metro: Dante.

Catacombe di San Gennaro (Catacombs of St. Gennaro) ⚓ These catacombs attached to the church of San Gennaro extra Moenia are the most important in southern Italy, prized for both the length of the period they were in continued use—from the emergence of Christianity until the 10th century—and the well-preserved **fresco**

cycles ✱ that decorate their corridors and chapels—spanning from the 2nd to the 10th centuries. Organized on two levels, its broad corridors and halls distinguish it from the narrower Roman catacombs. Among the most interesting things here is the **Cripta dei Vescovi** ✱, a bishop burial chamber magnificently decorated with mosaics dating from the 5th century. The lower level holds the **Basilica di Sant'Agrippino** *ipogea* ("ipogean," or subterranean) where St. Agrippino, the 3rd-century bishop of Naples, is buried. Also nearby is the **Cubicolo di San Gennaro,** with the tomb of the patron saint of Naples, whose remains were moved here in the 5th century.

Via Capodimonte 13. ✆ **081-7411071.** Admission 3€ ($4.20/£2.10). By guided tour only: Tues–Sun 9, 10, 11am, and noon. Bus: 24 or R4 to Via Capodimonte, and then down an alley alongside the church Madre del Buon Consiglio.

Certosa e Museo Nazionale di San Martino (Carthusian Monastery and National Museum of St. Martin) ✱

Originally built in 1325 and redone in the 17th century, this great monastery has been restored to all its original beauty. Entering from the courtyard, you first come to the **church** ✱, a masterpiece of baroque decoration, from the marble **floor** to the various works of art by artists such as Jusepe de Ribera (various paintings), Giuseppe Sanmartino (sculptures), and Battistello Caracciolo (frescoes). Do not overlook the marble **transenna** of the presbytery, decorated with precious stones (lapis lazuli and agate), and the **Cappella del Tesoro** ✱, with a rich altar made of the same materials; beautiful **frescoes** by Luca Giordano—including the *Trionfo di Giuditta*—decorate the ceiling. You can also view the *Deposizione* by Jusepe de Ribera. You can then continue to the **Chiostro Grande** ✱✱. The **Quarto del Priore** ✱✱—the elegant apartment used for the reception of important personalities—contains a number of masterpieces, including a *Madonna col Bambino e San Giovannino* by Pietro Bernini. The monastery also houses the **Museo Nazionale di San Martino,** which has several sections. One of our favorites is the ***presepi*** section (or **manger scenes**) ✱, off the Chiostro dei Procuratori. Some of the scenes are unbelievably complex, such as the *presepio* **Cuciniello,** created in 1879 with a collection of 18th-century figures and accessories. Other sections include the **Images and Memories of Naples exhibit** ✱✱ on the first and second floors, displaying paintings, sculpture, porcelain, and precious objects, and the **Collezione Rotondo** ✱, with paintings and bronze sculpures by Neapolitan artists of the 19th century. In the Gothic **cellars** of the monastery you will find sections dedicated to sculpture and epigraphy. On the second floor is the library that houses the **Prints and Drawings Collection,** with over 8,000 pieces.

Largo San Martino 8. ✆ **081-5781769.** www.musis.it. Admission 6€ ($8.40/£4.20). Thurs–Tues 8:30am–7:30pm; ticket booth closes 1 hr. earlier. Closed Jan 1 and Dec 25. Bus: V1 from Piazza Vanvitelli. Any one of the Funicolare to Vomero. Metro: Vanvitelli.

Chiesa del Gesù Nuovo ✱

Built by Jesuits in 1470, this church transformed Palazzo Sanseverino, the palace of the Prince of Salerno. Its striking facade in the rare technique *bugnato a punta di diamante* (ashlar work) was preserved from the palazzo's original facade, while a baroque portal was created to englobe the original Renaissance portal. The church's interior is majestic, featuring stucco, frescoes, and marble decorations by some of Naples's best artists from the 16th century to the beginning of the 19th. Among the masterpieces are the impressive **fresco** ✱ by Francesco Solimena depicting the *Expulsion of Eliodorus from the Temple,* and the rich decorations in the left transept, including a beautiful **altar** ✱ and **statues** ✱ of Jeremiah and David by Cosimo Fanzago.

On the piazza outside the church, you'll find one of Naples's several baroque spires, the **Guglia dell'Immacolata,** a tall pile of statues and reliefs. Typically Neapolitan, this kind of religious monument is modeled after processional objects—part float, part conglomeration of statues and figures—built for religious celebrations from baroque times until the 1950s. This particular spire was created in 1750 by Matteo Bottighero and Francesco Pagano to celebrate one of the major points of the Jesuits' teachings; it depicts Jesuit saints and the story of Mary.

Piazza del Gesù. (℃) 081-5518613. Free admission. Daily 7am–12:30pm and 4–7:30pm. Bus R1, R2, R3, or R4. Metro: Dante.

Chiesa dei Girolamini 🏛 *(Finds)*   Rarely visited, this church and its attached convent hide a great collection of artwork by some prominent Italian Renaissance artists. The church was built between the end of the 16th century and the beginning of the 17th. Among the masterpieces you'll find inside are: in the counter-facade, a **fresco** by Luca Giordano; in the first chapel to the right, *Sant'Alessandro Moribondo* by Pietro da Cortona; in the transept, **frescoes** by Francesco Solimena and **statues** by Pietro Bernini; and over the altar in the sacristy, the painting *San Giovanni Battista* by Guido Reni.

In the annexed **Casa dei Padri dell'Oratorio** (entrance on Via Duomo 142), you can visit the beautiful **Chiostro Maggiore** 🏛 and the **Quadreria dei Girolamini** 🏛🏛, a rich collection of paintings donated to the convent and including notable artists such as Cavalier d'Arpino, Sermoneta, Guido Reni, and Jusepe de Ribera. You can also visit the splendid **library** 🏛, with its beautiful halls, especially the **Sala Grande.**

Chiesa: Via dei Tribunali. (℃) 081-292316. Free admission. Mon–Sat 9am–1pm and 4–7pm; Sun 9am–1pm. **Quadreria:** Via Duomo 142. (℃) 081-449139. www.girolamini.it. Admission 3€ ($4.20/£2.10). Tues–Sun 9am–3pm. Bus R1, R2, R3, or R4. Metro: Dante.

Chiesa di Monteoliveto (aka Sant'Anna dei Lombardi, aka Santa Maria di Monteoliveto) 🏛🏛   Built in 1411, the Chiesa di Monteoliveto is not large but is chock-full of art works, as this was one of the favorite churches of the Aragonese royal family. The church opens onto a pretty square graced by the **Fontana di Monteoliveto,** considered to be the most beautiful baroque fountain in Naples. This fountain was built for Don Pedro de Aragona in 1699, based on a design by Cosimo Fanzago: It is a grandiose celebration of royal authority, with white marble eagles and lions crowned by the bronze statue of Carlo II d'Asburgo.

In the atrium, behind the church's elegant facade in *piperno* (a unique colorful stone which was carved in underground quarries in the Naples area), is the tomb of the architect Domenico Fontana. Inside the church are three superb Renaissance chapels: **Cappella Correale** 🏛 to the right of the entrance, with an altar by Benedetto da Maiano and the *San Cristoforo* over the altar by Francesco Solimena; **Cappella Piccolomini** 🏛 to the left of the entrance—an almost perfect replica of the more well-known Chapel of the Cardinal of Portugal in the Florentine San Miniato al Monte church, graced by the tomb of Maria d'Aragona by Antonio Rossellino and Benedetto da Maiano; and **Cappella Tolosa** 🏛, also to the left, attributed to Giuliano da Maiano and decorated in the styles of Brunelleschi and della Robbia. This last chapel is a triumph of sculpture, and gives a good overview of 15th- and 16th-century Neapolitan sculpture. From the right of the presbytery you can access the old **sacristy** 🏛 with its vaulted ceilings frescoed by Giorgio Vasari. Its walls, decorated with wood inlays depicting classical panoramas, musical instruments, and other scenes, were created by Giovanni da Verona between 1506 and 1510.

Piazza Monteoliveto 44. © 081-5513333. Free admission. Mon–Fri 9am–noon; Sat 9am–noon and 5:30–6:30pm. Bus R1, R2, R3, or R4. Metro: Dante.

Complesso Monumentale di Santa Chiara (Monumental Complex of St. Clare) ✶✶

The most famous basilica in Naples, this church was built in 1310 by king Roberto I d'Angió as the burial church for the Angevin dynasty. In the 18th century, it was lavishly decorated by the best artists of the time, but bombings in 1943 destroyed much of the art. A subsequent restoration in 1953 brought it back to its original Gothic structure. A large rose window decorates the facade, flanked by a majestic bell tower that dominates the neighborhood (its lower part is 14th century).

The interior is simple but monumental in size, with 10 chapels opening onto the central nave. It contains many royal tombs, including the grandiose **tomb of Roberto d'Angió** ✶, a magnificent example of Tuscan-style Renaissance sculpture. From the sacristy you can access the **Coro delle Clarisse (Choir of the Clares)** ✶, with its beautiful 14th-century marble portal. The nuns sat in the coro during Mass, protected from the public; only fragments remain, sadly, of Giotto's frescoes that decorated its walls. After your visit to the basilica, walk behind the church and enter the door to the right: It leads to the unique **Chiostro delle Clarisse** ✶✶, the monastery's main cloister. Strikingly decorated with bright majolica tiles in the mid-18th century, it is considered a masterpiece of Neapolitan art. The spaces adjacent to the cloister house a museum, the **Museo dell'Opera di Santa Chiara,** dedicated to the history of the monastery and attached basilica. It exhibits sculptures and reliefs by local artists, including a beautiful *Crucifiction* and a *Visitation,* both by Tino di Camaino; it also gives access to the excavations of thermal baths from the 1st or 2nd century A.D.

Basilica: Via Santa Chiara 49. © 081-5526280. Free admission. Thurs–Tues 9:30am–1pm and 4–6pm; Sun 9am– 1pm. **Cloister & Museum:** Via Benedetto Croce 16. © 081-7971256. www.santachiara.info. Admission 3€ ($4.20/£2.10). Mon–Sat 9:30am–1pm and 2:30–5:30pm; Sun 9:30am–1pm. Bus R1, R2, R3, or R4. Metro: Dante.

Duomo (aka Cattedrale di Santa Maria Assunta) ✶✶✶

A monumental construction, graced inside by 110 ancient granite columns which support its Latin Cross structure, the Duomo was begun by King Carlo I d'Angió in the 13th century and finished by his successor Roberto d'Angió in 1313. The grandiose interior of the cathedral is lavishly decorated. Among the most precious artwork is the painting of the *Assunta* by **Perugino,** located on the right side of the transept. Several chapels open from both naves and the transept; the most splendid is the Gothic **Cappella Capece Minutolo** ✶✶, with its beautiful 13th-century frescoes and mosaic floor. To the right of the presbytery is another Gothic chapel of great beauty, the **Cappella Tocco** ✶. You'll also want to descend downstairs to access the **Succorpo** or **Cappella Carafa** ✶, one of the most elegant Renaissance architectural structures ever created, in the style of **Bramante.**

From the right nave, the third chapel to the right is the monumental **Cappella di San Gennaro** ✶✶, dedicated to the patron saint of Naples. Richly decorated with precious marbles, gold leaf, frescoes, and artworks, it is considered by art historians as the highest achievement of Neapolitan baroque. The fresco cycle around the dome, illustrating the life of San Gennaro, is by **Domenichino,** while the oil painting over copper, depicting San Genarro, is by Jusepe de Ribera—the rich frame of gilded bronze and lapis lazuli is by Onofrio D'Alessio. The famous reliquaries containing the skull and the blood of San Gennaro—which is said to miraculously liquefy each September 19 (Feast Day of San Gennaro) as well as the first Sunday in May and December 16—are inside a safe over the main altar; they are exposed to the public only on the dates of the miraculous event: for 1 week in May, 1 in September, and on the 16th of December.

From the left nave, the third chapel entrance to the left gives access to **Santa Restituta** 𝕲𝕲, the oldest basilica in Naples and the city's Duomo until the new one was finished in the 14th century. Built in the 4th century by the Emperor Constantine, it is a very atmospheric church in spite of the many changes it underwent—its facade and atrium were demolished when it was annexed to the Duomo, while its apse was redecorated in baroque style in the 17th century; also, to strengthen its structure, the two outermost of its original five naves were closed into chapels. We love the sixth chapel on the left, with its luminous 14th-century **mosaic** by Lello da Orvieto and two beautiful 13th-century reliefs. Also, make sure not to miss the **Baptistery of San Giovanni in Fonte** 𝕲𝕲, which you can access from an entrance at the end of the right nave. Founded in the 4th century, it is the world's oldest Western baptistery. Its cupola is decorated with beautiful **mosaics** from the 5th century (unfortunately, some of them are damaged). From the end of the left nave you can access the archaeological excavations under the Duomo, which date back to Greek times.

Adjacent to the Duomo is the entrance to the **Museum of the Treasure of San Gennaro** 𝕲. The holdings here are exceptional in quality and quantity: The amount of the treasure is so great that the museum rotates its exhibits annually over a multiple-year cycle. An additional reason to visit is that the museum gives access to the Duomo's **Sacristy** 𝕲𝕲, beautifully decorated with **frescoes** by Luca Giordano and paintings by **Domenichino.** In the sacristy, you can also arrange an appointment to visit Santa Restituta and the Cappella Minutolo if you find them closed.

Cathedral: Via Duomo 147. ✆ 081-449097. Free admission. Mon–Sat 8am–12:30pm and 4:30–7pm; Sun and holidays 8:30am–1pm and 5–7pm. **Excavations:** Mon–Fri 9am–noon and 4:30–7pm; Sat–Sun and holidays 9am–12:30pm. **Museum:** Via Duomo 149. ✆ 081-421609. www.museosangennaro.com. Admission 5.50€ ($7.70/£3.85); 25% discount with Artecard. Tues–Sat 9:30am–7pm; Sun and holidays 9:30am–2:30pm. Metro: Piazza Cavour.

San Domenico Maggiore 𝕲𝕲   Opening onto one of Naples's most beautiful squares—graced by the **Guglia San Domenico,** a marble spire erected between 1658 and 1737 in gratitude for the end of that century's plague—this church actually offers its back to the public: Its facade, following an Angevin tradition, is only visible from the inner courtyard. Built by Carlo II d'Angiò between 1283 and 1324, San Domenico Maggiore encloses the older church of **San Michele Arcangelo a Morfisa,** which is still accessible from the transept. Inside both are innumerable works of art, including many **Renaissance monumental tombs** graced by sculptures and carvings, as well as 14th-century **frescoes** and 15th- and 16th-century **paintings.** The main **altar** is a beautiful work of marble inlay from the 16th century.

Piazza San Domenico Maggiore. © 081-449097 or 081-459298. Free admission. Daily 9am–noon and 5–7pm. Metro: Piazza Cavour.

San Giovanni a Carbonara ✿ *Finds*   Built in 1343 with the annex convent, this church was used by the Angevin dynasty to bury their last members. It is one of Naples's undiscovered jewels, which is not surprising, considering that it's rather difficult to find. First, you'll need to climb a scenic staircase leading to the baroque Consolazione a Carbonara church, and continue farther up until you reach three portals. Admire the central one—the Gothic entrance to the Cappella Santa Monica—and take the portal to the left. This will lead you into a terraced courtyard, and there you will finally find the entrance to San Giovanni, which you can access from its 15th-century lateral portal. Inside the church are several important works of art, including, in the apse—flat, not rounded as is usual—the **Monumental Tomb of King Ladislao,** a 15th-century masterpiece by several Tuscan artists. Behind the monument is the circular **Cappella Caracciolo del Sole,** with a majolica floor and beautiful **frescoes** from the 15th century, very handsome but less harmonious than the other circular chapel in this church—**Cappella Caracciolo di Vico.** This chapel, located to the left of the presbytery, is an architectural tour-de-force from the beginning of the 16th century, graced by a beautifully carved 16th-century altar. At the end of the courtyard, an entrance gives access to yet another chapel: the **Cappella Seripando** with a *Crucifiction* by Vasari.

Via San Giovanni a Carbonara 5. © 081-295873. Free admission. Mon–Sat 8am–noon and 4:30–8:30pm; Sun 8am–2pm. Metro: Piazza Cavour.

San Gregorio Armeno   Giving its name to the street famous for its manger artists and vendors (see "Shopping," later in this chapter), this church and its adjoining monastery are little visited. Yet they are well worth a visit to admire the bell tower and the richly decorated interior. Dating from the 8th century, the church's interior was redone in 1580, with lavish use of gold leaf and artwork by famous masters of the time: The exceptional **wooden ceiling** ✿ was carved and painted by Teodoro d'Errico, while the **frescoes** ✿ in the counter-facade are by Luca Giordano. You should also visit the pretty **cloister** ✿ of the attached monastery (through the entrance outside the church, beyond the bell tower), beautifully preserved and graced by a marble **fountain** depicting Jesus meeting the Good Samaritan.

Via San Gregorio Armeno 44. Free admission. Daily 9:30am–noon. Metro: Piazza Cavour.

San Lorenzo Maggiore ✿✿   The most beautiful of Naples's medieval churches, San Lorenzo is famous for its literary past—here Giovanni Boccaccio met his Fiammetta in 1334, and the attached convent hosted Francesco Petrarca for a period. Originally a basilica from the 6th century A.D., the church was rebuilt in 1270 by Carlo I d'Angiò and his successor in Gothic style; its facade is baroque as the original was partially destroyed by an earthquake. The interior is airy and holds innumerable works of art, including 13th- and 14th- century **frescoes,** as well as beautiful **altars** and monumental tombs. From the baroque cloister you can visit the Chapter Hall and the refectory of the monastery, built in the 13th century. From the 14th-century cloister, enter the **Greek and Roman excavations** ✿ where you'll see a slice of the city's layers of construction, from the Roman Macellum—the city market dating from the 1st century A.D.—complete with merchant stalls, to a paleochristian basilica, to a medieval building to, finally, the existing buildings. The best pieces from the excavations are displayed in the **museum,** which also features a collection of historical ceremonial religious attire and a collection of 18th-century *presepio* (manger scene) figures. *Note:* At presstime, the museum is still being organized and is only partially accessible.

Church: Piazza San Gaetano. ℂ 081-290580. www.sanlorenzomaggiorenapoli.it. Free admission. Mon–Sat 8am–noon and 5–7pm. Excavations: ℂ 081-2110860. Admission 4€ ($5.60/£2.80). Mon–Sat 9am–5:30pm; Sun and holidays 9am–1:30pm. Metro: Piazza Cavour.

San Paolo Maggiore ℛ   Founded between the 8th and 9th centuries A.D. over a pre-existing Roman Temple of the Dioscuri—two of its columns remain on the facade—San Paolo Maggiore was completely redone in the 16th century. The interior was decorated by many important artists of the 17th and 18th century, but the standouts here are the statue of *Angelo Custode* by Domenico Antonio Vaccaro to the left of the central nave; the **frescoes** in the sacristy—considered the best work of Francesco Solimena; and the **Cappella Firrao** to the left of the presbytery, one of the most beautiful baroque chapels in Naples.

Piazza San Gaetano. ℂ 081-454048. Free admission. Daily 8am–noon and 5–7pm. Metro: Piazza Cavour.

Sant'Angelo a Nilo   Built in 1385 for the Brancaccio family and redone in the 18th century, this church merits a visit for its **Funerary Monument of Cardinal Rinaldo Brancaccio** ℛℛ. This monument to the church's founder was created in Pisa by **Donatello** and **Michelozzo** between 1426 and 1427, and shipped by sea to Naples. Very modern for its time, the work merges Gothic and Renaissance elements. The two portals to the right of the presbytery, one from the 14th and the other from the 16th century, are also noteworthy.

The Church of Sant'Angelo a Nilo gets its name from the Greek-Roman **Statue of the Egyptian god Nile** in the small square near the church. Originally carved for merchants from Alexandria who worked in the area, the statue was lost for centuries and was found again in the 15th century. In typical Neapolitan spirit, the statue of the river god, with his babies representing the river tributaries, was interpreted as a representation of motherly Naples, nourishing its children; hence the nickname still in use today among the locals—*cuorp'e Napule* or "body of Naples." The statue's head was a 17th-century addition.

Piazzetta Nilo, off Via Benedetto Croce. Free admission. Mon–Sat 8:30am–1pm and 4:45–7pm; Sun 8:30am–1pm. Bus: E1 or R2. Metro: Piazza Cavour.

PUBLIC NAPLES

Fontana del Nettuno   Naples's most beautiful fountain has had a unique history of mobility. Originally built for Viceroy Enrico Guzman, Count of Olivares, it was located in front of the Arsenal for 30 years. In 1622, the Duca d'Alba had it moved to the Piazza del Palazzo Reale. In 1637, it was moved again in front of the Castel dell'Ovo. A few years later, worried that it was dangerously positioned (open to attacks from the sea), city authorities moved it "temporarily" to Piazza delle Corregge. It stayed there until the beginning of the 20th century, when it was moved again to its present—and maybe permanent—position.

Piazza G.Bovio off Via Medina. Bus: C57, E3, or R3.

Galleria Umberto I   This gallery is an elegant glass-and-iron covered passage following a Greek cross shape, with each of its four arms opening onto a street on one end and meeting at a rotunda, covered with a cupola, on the other. Built at the end of the 19th century—20 years after its larger Milanese counterpart—this is a splendid Liberty-style (Italian Art Nouveau) construction with obvious Parisian inspiration. Inside, the galleria is lined with elegant shops and cafes.

You'll find a second Liberty-era gallery in town, **Galleria del Principe di Napoli** (off Piazza Cavour to the right; Metro Piazza Cavour), which is virtually unknown, probably because of its location outside the most touristy area of Via Toledo.

4 entrances: To the right off Via Toledo as you come from Piazza del Plebiscito, Via Giuseppe Verdi, Via Santa Brigida, and Via San Carlo. Bus: R2 or R3 to Piazza Trieste e Trento.

Piazza del Plebiscito 🅐🅐   This is the most beautiful piazza in Naples, defined by the majestic colonnade of **San Francesco di Paola**—an 1817 church built in full neoclassical style and inspired by the Roman Pantheon—and the elegant neoclassical facade of the Royal Palace. In the square are two equestrian statues, one of **Carlo III** by Antonio Canova and one of **Ferdinando I** (only the horse is by Canova). The square is fittingly called the "salotto" (living room) by Neapolitans, since it has been completely closed to traffic and locals use it as a gathering place. Nearby is Piazza Trieste e Trento, with the Fontana del Carciofo, and the start of Via Toledo (Neapolitans call this Via Roma), an extremely popular promenade and shopping street.

Off Piazza Trieste e Trento, between Via Chiaia and Via C. Console. Bus: R2 or R3 to Piazza Trieste e Trento.

Teatro San Carlo 🅐   Built for Carlo Borbone by Antonio Medrano, the Teatro San Carlo is among Europe's most beautiful opera houses and one of the most famous. A neoclassical jewel with an ornate gilded interior, the San Carlo was the first opera theater in the world; it was inaugurated on November 4, 1737. The facade was added in 1812 by Antonio Piccolini, who rebuilt the interior after a fire destroyed it in 1816. The theater hall, which holds 1,470 seats, is considered to have even better acoustics than Milan's famous La Scala, and such artists as Donizetti, Rossin, and Verdi produced and directed masterpieces here. You can appreciate its architecture and decoration by taking the free guided tour (by reservation), or come for a performance (see "Naples After Dark," later in this chapter) and see the building in its full glory.

Via San Carlo 93. ✆ 081-400300 or 081-7972111 for reservations. Bus: R2 or R3 to Via San Carlo.

Villa Comunale 🅐   Created in 1780 according to a design by Luigi Vanvitelli, as the private Royal Promenade for King Ferdinando IV Bourbon, this park was later transformed by the king into a public garden. The park is a baroque creation graced by statues, fountains—including the beloved **Fontana delle Paperelle** ("fountain of the ducks")—and several elegant buildings such as **Casina Pompeiana, Chiosco della Musica,** and **Stazione Zoologica** with Europe's oldest **Aquarium,** specializing in the study of local marine life. On the first Saturday of each month, the Villa Comunale hosts an antiques market, which is open 8:30am to 1pm.

Park: Piazza Vittoria. ✆ 081-7611131. Daily 7am–midnight. Aquarium: ✆ 081-5833111 or 081-2452099. Tues–Sun 9am–5pm. Bus: C82 or R2.

GUIDED TOURS

If you are only planning a short stay, the best introduction to the city is the double-decker bus tours offered by **CitySightseeing** (✆ **081-5517279;** www.napoli.city-sightseeing.it). All their tours start from Piazza Municipio/Parco Castello. Line A is a hop-on-and-off loop to the Museo di Capodimonte, with buses operating daily May 1 to September 30 every 45 minutes from 9:45am to 5:45pm. Line B is a hop-on-and-off loop winding along the seashore to Posillipo; buses operate April 1 to September 30 daily from 9:30am to 5:45pm, every 45 minutes. Line C is a hop-on-and-off circuit to the Certosa di San Martino; buses operate on Saturday, Sunday, and holidays with departures at 10am, noon, and 2, 4, and 6pm. Line D is a tour to Mount Vesuvius with stops at Herculaneum and the Vesuvian Villas (see chapter 5) with departure June 1 to October 31 on Sundays at 10am. Tickets are valid for 24 hours on all lines and can be purchased on board for 22€ ($31/£15) adults, 11€ ($15/£7.70) children ages 6 to 15; and 66€ ($92/£46) family (2 adults and 3 children). You'll get a 10% discount with your Artecard (p. 100).

Museo Aperto Napoli (© **081-5636062;** www.museoapertonapoli.com) is the cultural organization serving Naples's historic district. They are based in a large cultural and information center (Via Pietro Colletta 85, to the right of Castel Capuano, at the eastern edge of the historic district; daily 10am to 6pm) where you'll find a knowledgeable and kind multi-lingual staff, a multi-media center with information on the historic district, exhibits on the area, as well as a cafe offering typical local products, a bookshop, a small space with crafts for sale, and, luckily, bathrooms. The center offers all kinds of services useful to the tourist, from maps and information on the historic district, to umbrellas on loan and excellent guided tours: Choose among four self-guided audio tours or walking tours with a live guide; all tours are offered in six languages.

For more classic city tours, the agency **Every Tours** (Piazza del Municipio 5; © **081-5518564**) works for American Express in Naples; it organizes tours of the city as well as day excursions to Vesuvio and other sights. It's open Monday through Friday from 9am to 1:30pm and 3:30 to 7pm and Saturday from 9am to 1pm. Another good agency is **NapoliVision** (© **081-5595130;** www.napolivision.it), offering guided tours of Naples, Pompei, and Capri starting at 30€ ($42/£21) per person.

5 SpaccaNapoli: A Walking Tour in the Very Heart of Naples

SpaccaNapoli refers to the succession of streets that divides Naples's historic district into two equal halves (*spacca* means "cracks"). The oldest part of town, it dates back to Greek and Roman times and has been the city's heart ever since. If you have only one afternoon in Naples, you should definitely dedicate it to this area: Along Spacca-Napoli and its cross streets, you will find Naples's most interesting artistic and cultural highlights, including the city's best churches, as well as notable small shops and traditional craftsmakers.

Start:	Piazza del Gesù.
Finish:	Duomo.
Time:	2 hours for the walk, but you could turn it into a day-long tour with all the interior visits.
Best Times:	Tuesday to Saturday 9am to 1pm and 4 to 7pm, when most of the churches and museums are open.
Worst Times:	Evening, when everything is closed. Sunday morning, because many churches cannot be visited during Mass. Monday, when some of the museums are closed. Lunchtime is also tricky, because only some of the attractions are open then.

① Piazza del Gesù
② Complesso Monumentale
 di Santa Chiara
③ Palazzo Filomarino
④ Piazza San Domenico
 Maggiore
☕ Pasticceria Scaturchio
⑤ Cappella Sansevero
⑥ Piazzetta Nilo
⑦ Cappella del
 Monte di Pietà
⑧ Chiesa di San Severino
 e San Sossio
⑨ Via San Gregorio Armeno
⑩ Piazza San Gaetano
☕ Pasticceria G. Mazzaro &
 Pizzeria Di Matteo
⑪ Chiesa and Quadreria
 dei Girolamini
⑫ Duomo

① Piazza del Gesù

This pleasant piazza is defined by the **Guglia dell'Addolorata** at its center. One of Naples's typical baroque spires, this particular one was created by the Jesuits to commemorate their principles and was placed in front of their church, the **Chiesa del Gesù.** Its striking facade was once that of Palazzo Sanseverino, sold to the Jesuits in the 15th century and preserved when the church was built. Inside, you'll find several noteworthy works of art, including a **fresco** by Solimena.

Cross the *piazza* to the beginning of Via Benedetto Croce. A few steps farther up to the right is the:

② Complesso Monumentale di Santa Chiara

This huge religious complex includes a church, a monastery, and a museum. The church itself contains some beautiful **monumental tombs** and the **Choir of the Clares,** but if your time is tight, walk along the church's outer wall and take the entrance to the right, leading to **the Clares' Cloister,** a majolica masterpiece that shouldn't be missed.

Return to Via Benedetto Croce and continue on to no. 12 at your left. It is:

③ Palazzo Filomarino

This palazzo is one of the oldest in Naples, built in the 14th century and redone in the 16th. You can go through its portal and peek at its monumental **internal court,** dating from the 16th century. Here lived and died the Italian 20th-century historian and philosopher Benedetto Croce, after whom the street is named.

Return to Via Benedetto Croce and continue on, passing a number of other elegant palazzi, until you reach:

❹ Piazza San Domenico Maggiore

This is one of the most beautiful squares in Naples, graced in the center by the **Guglia di San Domenico,** another of Naples's spires. This one was built between 1658 and 1737, in thanks for the end of a plague that struck in 1656. It is lined by beautiful *palazzi;* we recommend you peek into no. 17, the 18th-century **Palazzo di Sangro di Casacalenda,** finished by Vanvitelli and with a beautiful inner court; and no. 3, the 15th-century **Palazzo Petrucci,** with its striking original portal and loggias. Also in the square is **San Domenico Maggiore:** The artwork in this church is exceptional, including 14th-century **frescoes** and spectacular 16th-century **sculptures.**

PASTICCERIA SCATURCHIO
Whether you need a break or not, you should stop at **Pasticceria Scaturchio** (Piazza San Domenico Maggiore 19; ✆ 081-5516944), a historical pastry and coffee shop right on the square across from the church. Here you can enjoy excellent coffee and sample wonderful pastries or try their *Ministeriale,* a medallion of dark chocolate with a liqueur cream filling.

Go back toward the church and walk along its side on Vicolo San Domenico. Take the first right, to Via Francesco de Sanctis. At no. 19 you will find the:

❺ Cappella di San Severo

This private chapel is decorated with some of the best Neapolitan sculptures from the 17th and 18th centuries. It is imbued with the spirit of its decorator, the mysterious alchemist and scientist Prince Raimondo de Sangro (see earlier in this chapter).

Walk back to Piazza San Domenico Maggiore and continuing east on Via Benedetto Croce you'll find yourself in the:

❻ Piazzetta Nilo

This piazza was named after the Hellenistic Egyptian statue of the Nile that graces one of its corners. Believed in medieval times to depict a mother with her children, the statue was adopted as an image of the city of Naples, hence its name in local parlance—*cuorp'e Napule,* or body of Naples. You'll also find the **Sant'Angelo a Nilo** church here, with its monumental tomb of Cardinal Brancaccio, designed and partly sculpted by **Donatello.**

Continue on Via Benedetto Croce, which turns into Via San Biagio dei Librai, named after the bookstores which traditionally have lined this street. At no. 114, to your right, is the:

❼ Cappella del Monte di Pietà

This small chapel is a beautiful example of 16th-century art, perfect in style and richly decorated. Its sacristy and adjoining rooms are in perfectly preserved 18th-century style, down to the floors and furnishings.

Take the alley on the right before the Cappella, Vicolo Santi Severino e Sossio, and follow it to the entrance, to your left, of the:

❽ Chiesa dei Santi Severino e Sossio (with Adjoining Monastery and State Archives)

This church is part of a large religious complex, the monastery of Saints Severino and Sossio, which is one of the oldest and richest monasteries of Naples. Both the church and the monastery are beautifully decorated with 16th-, 17th-, and 18th-century art. The monastery today houses the **State Archives** (entrance on Piazzetta Grande Archivio; ✆ **081-563811**), but it is open to the public, who can visit its 16th-century cloisters and beautifully frescoed rooms.

Return to Via San Biagio dei Librai and continue on to:

⑨ Via San Gregorio Armeno

This is one of Naples's most famous streets, known for the many artist's workshops and merchants, specializing in *presepio* works (manger scenes; p. 118). On this lively street (hold on to your wallet and other precious belongings in the crowds), you'll find the **Church and Convent of San Gregorio Armeno** with its beautifully preserved cloister and stunning artwork.

Continue on to the end of Via San Gregorio Armeno and turn right onto Via dei Tribunali to arrive at:

⑩ Piazza San Gaetano

This piazza is home to two of Naples's major churches, **San Lorenzo Maggiore** (to your right) and **San Paolo Maggiore** (to your left). Both are rich in art and history and well worth a visit (see earlier in this chapter). In San Lorenzo Maggiore, you can descend into an archaeological excavation going back to the Greek layer of town, ancient Neapolis.

CAFFETTERIA PASTICCERIA GELATERIA G. MAZZARO
Caffetteria Pasticceria Gelateria G. Mazzaro (Palazzo Spinelli, Via Tribunali 359; ℂ 081-459248; www. pasticceriamazzaro.it) is a valiant competitor of Pasticceria Scaturchio, above. In addition to excellent coffee and pastries, this shop makes some of the best *gelato* in town, in a variety of flavors.

Continue on Via dei Tribunali to Piazza dei Girolamini, opening to your left. Here is the:

⑪ Chiesa and Quadreria dei Girolamini

This church and attached monastery hold a treasure trove of artwork by great artists, including Luca Giordano, Pietro da Cortona, Francesco Solimena, Guido Reni, and Cavalier d'Arpino.

Return to Via dei Tribunali and continue on it until you reach Via del Duomo, where you'll make a left. To your right is the entrance to the:

⑫ Duomo

Monumental in scope, this church actually houses two other churches, the paleochristian **Santa Restituta**—known as Naples Duomo until the 14th century—and the 17th-century **Real Cappella del Tesoro di San Gennaro,** considered the most richly decorated chapel in Naples. The museum attached to the church is also well worth a visit.

PIZZA BREAK
Via dei Tribunali is home to some of the best pizzerie in Naples: If you're hankering for something substantial, head back along this street to **Pizzaiolo del Presidente** (Via Tribunali 120; ℂ 081-210903; closed Sun), **Pizzeria Di Matteo** (Via dei Tribunali 94; ℂ 081-455262), or, farther along, **Sorbillo** (Via Tribunali 32; ℂ 081-446643; closed Sun). They all prepare excellent pizza (see the best Neapolitan pizza in the historic district, p. 95).

6 Shopping for Local Crafts

Naples is a great source of Italian designer clothes and accessories, as well as for antiques and crafts. You have to know your stuff, though, and be careful, since Naples is where fakes were invented back in the 17th or 18th century—and the industry is still very much alive. It is a good idea to stay away from counterfeit goods altogether, even if you know that what you are buying is a fake and the price is right, as you risk heavy fines at customs on your way home: Most countries are cracking down on such purchases as a way to protect brand identity.

The *Presepio*

Although the tradition of nativity scenes—called *presepio* in Italy—dates back to the 13th century, the art form really reached its peak in the 18th and 19th centuries when the aristocracy competed to acquire figurines for their mangers, modeled by the famous sculptors of the time. All the great names of sculpture participated in this game, creating the terra-cotta parts of the figurines (usually the head and limbs). These were then mounted on a mannequin of wire and *stoppa* (fiber) by craftsmen, and richly dressed with precious silk clothes embroidered with gold. Only the wealthier aristocrats could purchase such works of art, and all others had to make do with copies produced by nativity craftsmen. These skilled artists-artisans were sculptors, goldsmiths, tailors, and scenographers, who created everything from the figures to the complicated settings—grottoes, buildings, rivers, and ponds—combining their crafts into the first examples of multimedia art. These figures, which depicted popular characters and scenes, created somewhat faithful renditions of society at the time.

The *presepio* tradition is still alive today, and Neapolitan mangers continue to go beyond typical nativity representations to depict current historical and political happenings. Among the figures you'll find on sale are such recognizable characters as Lady Diana, Mother Teresa of Calcutta, and even Versace. **Via San Gregorio Armeno** near the Duomo is where most of the historic workshops, along with several merchants, are located. The artisans who have carried on their crafts from father to son have organized into a guild that protects their traditions, but only a few of them have survived the times. In the shops along this street, you'll find everything from characters and rocks, to grottoes and miniature street lamps. At the back of the few authentic laboratories, you'll also find figurines carefully crafted in different sizes, from amazingly precise half-inch miniatures, to life-size figures, to realistic sceneries. While commercial mangers come in a variety of prices, the real thing is rather expensive, and few customers can afford the real thing: A medium-size hand-painted and -crafted terra-cotta shepherd can cost as much as 300€ ($420/£210).

You'll be perfectly safe in the reputable shops we list below. Opening hours for stores are generally Monday to Saturday from 10:30am to 1pm and from 4 to 7:30pm.

Chiaia is where to go for the big names of **Italian fashion,** such as Valentino, Versace, Ferragamo, Prada, and local designer **Marinella** (Via Riviera di Chiaia 287; *©* **081-7644214**), famous for classic and colorful ties. You'll also find a number of interesting boutiques. Nearby, you'll find some of the most reputable **antiques** dealers, such as **Regency House** (Via D. Morelli 36; *©* **081-7643640**) and **Navarra** (Piazza dei Martiri; *©* **081-7643595**). Every third Saturday and Sunday of each month from 8am to 2pm (except in Aug), a **Fiera Antiquaria,** or Antique Fair, (*©* **081-621951**) is held in the Villa Comunale di Napoli on Viale Dohrn.

For more casual shopping and some specialty stores, try strolling popular **Via Toledo.** Here you will find the historical chocolate factory **Gay-Odin** (Via Toledo 214 and Via Toledo 427). You'll also find the elegant shops of the **Galleria Umberto I,** such as **Ascione 1855** (✆ **081-421111**) and its **cameo** workshop, where you can witness the delicate carving of agate and coral and purchase unique jewelry.

The best place to shop for crafts is the historic district. Head for **Via San Gregorio Armeno** ★★ if you are looking for presepio: The most reputable workshops are **Gambardella Pastori** (Via San Gregorio Armeno 40; ✆ **081-5517107**) and **Giuseppe Ferrigno** (Via San Gregorio Armeno 8; ✆ **081-5523148**). Via San Biagio dei Librai is lined with interesting shops selling paper goods and jewelry. A good address for antique prints and books is **Libreria Colonnese** (Via San Pietro a Majella 32; ✆ **081-459858**), nearby.

7 Naples After Dark

A warm southern city, Naples is best experienced outdoors. Neapolitans know this, and they enjoy spending their evenings on the terraces of the city's many popular cafes. One of the best is **Gran Caffè Gambrinus** (Via Chiaia 1, in Piazza Trento e Trieste; ✆ **081-417582** or 081-414133). The oldest cafe in Naples, its original Liberty-style interior was decorated by Antonio Curri in the 1860s. Another very popular spot is **La Caffetteria** (Piazza dei Martiri 25; ✆ **081-7644243**), frequented by local elegant crowds who come here for evening aperitifs.

OPERA If you have the time, book yourself for a performance at **Teatro San Carlo** (Via San Carlo 98/f; ✆ **081-7972412** or 081-7972331; fax 081-400902; www.teatrosancarlo.it), a world-class venue with a consistently high-level program. Performances take place Tuesday through Sunday, December through June. Tickets run between 45€ and 100€ ($63–$140/£32–£70); you'll get a 20% discount with an Artecard (p. 100).

Another historic theater we recommend is **Teatro Mercadante** (Piazza Municipio 1; ✆ **081-5513396**), which always has a prestigious program. Tickets are around 50€ ($70/£35), depending on the performance; you'll get a 10% discount with an Artecard (p. 100).

MUSIC If you love music, Naples is the place to be. At any given time the city is alive with concerts spanning from the classics to the most avant-garde. If classical music is your preference, besides the concerts at **Teatro San Carlo** (see above), the **Centro di Musica Antica Pietà dei Turchini** (Via Santa Caterina da Siena 38; ✆ **081-402395;** www.turchini.it) is one of the best venues in town; ticket prices depend on the performance, and you'll get a 25% discount with your Artecard (p. 100). Another excellent venue is the **Associazione Alessandro Scarlatti** (Piazza dei Martiri 58; ✆ **081-406011;** www.associazionescarlatti.it), which also organizes a successful concert series at Castel Sant'Elmo; tickets prices range from 15€ to 25€ ($21–$35/£11–£18), with a 20% discount given to those with an Artecard (p. 100). For immersion in Neapolitan traditional music, the best address in town is the **Trianon, Teatro della Canzone Napoletana** (Piazza Vincenzo Calenda 9; ✆ **081-2440411;** www.teatrotrianon.it); the concert season usually starts in April, with performances Thursdays through Sundays, but check the theater for changes in their programs. Ticket prices depend on seat and performance, but you'll get a 10% discount with the Artecard (p. 100).

ENOTECHE   The taste for good wine has been increasing, and Naples counts a growing number of excellent *enoteche*. This unique Italian venue merges the wine store and wine bar, often doubling as a restaurant. Following the popular Italian adage, never drink on an empty stomach, enoteche offer a small menu of high-quality local specialties. We recommend the quiet **Berevino,** Via Sebastiano 62 (© **081-290313**), as well as **Barrique,** Piazzetta Ascensione 9 (© **081-662721;** closed Mon), where you can sample the best local wines and a large choice of *grappe* and *rhums* while delighting in scrumptious small dishes from the weekly menu. The elegant and trendy **L'Ebrezza di Noè,** Vico Vetriera 9 (© **081-400104;** daily 7:30pm–12:30am), serves a simple menu of cured meats, cheeses, and appetizers to accompany the wide selection of wines from its excellent cellar. Their specialty is the discovery of unusual and lesser-known wines and vintages of great quality; don't be afraid to ask for guidance from the experienced staff. **Vinarium,** Vico Cappella Vecchia 7 (© **081-7644114;** Mon–Fri 10:30am–4:30pm; Mon–Sat 7pm–2:30am), is also popular but less upscale. It serves a more rounded menu to accompany the large choice of Campania's best D.O.C. wines (see appendix A) as well as other wines from farther afield. A specially priced selection of wines is introduced each day. **Cantina di Triunfo,** Via Riviera di Chiaia 64 (© **081-668101;** Tues–Sat 10am–7:30pm as wine store and Mon–Sat 7:30pm–midnight as wine bar cum restaurant), offers a limited but excellent menu to accompany its large choice of wines.

BARS, DISCOS & CLUBS   Naples is a port, a cosmopolitan city, and a university town all in one, so its lively nighttime scene is not surprisingly eclectic and has something that will appeal to all tastes. Trendy bars and cafes stay open until the wee hours (at least until 2am) every day of the week, while clubs stay open even later—usually until 4 or 5am—but often only from Thursday to Saturday. While bars and cafes usually don't charge covers, club entrance costs around 14€ ($20/£9.80).

The **roof bar** of the **Starhotel Terminus** (Piazza Garibaldi 91; © **081-7793111**) is a popular scene for Neapolitan socialites. Other good places to grab a drink range from **Conoco Club** (Via Nilo 33; © **081-5517784**), a pub with a good beer selection and a relaxed atmosphere, to the sleek and exotic recently re-opened **Miami Bar Club** (Via Morghen 68C; © **081-2298332**).

For jazz, head to **Riot** (Via San Biagio 38; © **081-5523231**), which has a young ambience; for live Neapolitan bands, check out **Vibes Cafè** (Via San Giovanni Maggiore Pignatelli 10; © **081-5513984**), where you can dance inside or outside on the terrace in summer. Another good place for live music is **Il Re Nudo** (Via Manzoni 126; © **081-7146272**), where you can hear anything from jazz to South American groups.

An elegant nightclub worth checking out is **Chez Moi** (Via del Parco Margherita 13; © **081-407526**) in the Riviera di Chiaia. Nearby **La Mela** (Via dei Mille; © **081-4010270**) is not bad either; neither is **Tongue** (Via Manzoni 202; © **081-7690888**) in Posillipo, a club with a good mix of gays and lesbians as well as a straight clientele.

For a more specifically gay spot, head for **Bar B** (Via Giovanni Manna, off Via Duomo; © **081-287681**), a famous gay sauna—with Turkish and Finnish spas on three levels and with two bars and five dark rooms—that turns into a disco on Thursday and Saturday nights; music ranges from Latin to techno.

8 Vesuvius, an Easy Excursion from Naples

This dangerous volcano—it has demonstrated its destructive capacity more than once—is the sort of volcano that blows its top when erupting, Mount St. Helens style, instead of quietly oozing out lava, like the volcano on the Big Island of Hawaii.

Dangerous as Vesuvius might be, though, people continue to live on its fertile slopes, as they have since antiquity (and since the last eruption in 1944). The most recent signs of activity were in 1999—some puffs of smoke, just to keep everybody on their toes.

Named Vesvinum or Vesuvinum after its vineyards, which were famous for their excellent wine even centuries ago, Vesuvius surprised everybody when it erupted in A.D. 79, since apparently nobody at that time knew it was an active volcano. Eruptions followed in 202, 472, 512, 1139, and 1306, but then a long period of quiet tricked everybody—until a 1631 eruption caused great destruction again. Other eruptions were in 1794 (nicely timed for Goethe's visit; a guide hauled him up through the poisonous smoke to look into the crater), 1871, 1906, and 1944.

GETTING THERE

You can easily get to Vesuvius by public transportation through **Circumvesuviana Railway** (© 800-053939; www.vesuviana.it), which leaves from Stazione Circumvesuviana (Corso Garibaldi, off Piazza Garibaldi; Metro: Garibaldi). Take any train to Sorrento or to Poggiomarino via Pompeii and get off at the station **Ercolano Scavi,** a 15-minute trip from Naples; the fare is 1.50€ ($2.10/£1.05). Taxi and a bus shuttle service departs from outside the station for the Mount Vesuvius park entrance. Ercolano Station is also where you'll meet your group if you have signed up for one of the specialty tours organized by **La Porta del Vesuvio** (© 081-274200; www.laporta delvesuvio.it; 9am–1:30pm), offering walks along nature trails on the slopes, to scenic night tours of the crater.

You can also arrange for a guided tour starting in Naples (see earlier in this chapter), or a limousine service directly from your hotel. Good providers are **ANA Limousine Service** (Piazza Garibaldi 73; ©/fax **081-282000**) and **Italy Limousine** (© 081-8016184, 335-6732245, or 338-9681866; www.italylimousine.it). *Note:* All transportation gets you only as far as the park entrance at 1,017m (3,106 ft.) in altitude; the trails are not wheelchair accessible.

WHAT TO SEE & DO

The only Continental volcano still active in Europe, Mount Vesuvius is enclosed within **Parco Nazionale del Vesuvio** (Vesuvius National Park, © **081-7710911;** www.parconazionaledelvesuvio.it).

The entrance to the park is at an altitude of 1,000m (3,280 ft.) above sea level. The **Centro Visite (Visitor Center;** © **081-7775720,** 081-7391123, or 033-7942249), is where you can sign up for tours, check on the meteorological situation and whether the trails—including the one to the crater—are open, and buy a map of the trails. At the historical *osteria* you can have a bite to eat or a drink—including the famous local wine, Lacrima Christi, made from the vineyards on Mount Vesuvius. You can buy local products at a small shop. The park is open daily (Nov 1–Mar 31 9am–3pm; Apr 1–May 31 9am–5:30pm; June 1–Aug 31 9am–6:30pm; Sept 1–Oct 31 9am–5pm) and admission is free. Of the several trails inside the park, the most popular is the one ascending to the **crater** ♠. Follow the dirt trail up to 1,118m (3,667 ft.), where the ticket booth is located. Admission (6.50€/$9.10/£4.55 adults, 4.50€/$6.30/£3.15 youth 8 to 17, free for children 7 and under) includes a guided tour by a volcanologist (no reservation necessary). The climb traverses hardened lava to the rim, 170m (558 ft.) above the park entrance, and 1,170m (3,838 ft.) above sea level. The trail affords great views of the crater itself and the whole Gulf of Naples.

Below the park entrance, at 608m (1,994 ft.) is the **Observatory** (© 081-5832111; www.ov.ingv.it): Established in 1841 to monitor Mount Vesuvius's activity, it is the oldest and one of the best volcanology research centers in the world. You can visit its rich scientific library and **Geological Museum** ⊀, Via Osservatorio 14 (© 081-6108483), which holds a vast collection of minerals and scientific instruments from the 18th century onward.

9 Pozzuoli & the Phlegrean Fields ⊀

18km (11 miles) W of Naples

The peninsula that flanks the Gulf of Naples to the west is a land of hills, craters, lagoons, and tarns. Sprawling urban development fostered by the proximity of Naples has tarnished the original charm of the area, but it is still possible to catch a glimmer of what it must have looked like less than a century ago. The area was officially established as a national park in 1993 to protect it from further development, but most of the damage had already occurred. On the positive side, urban sprawl could not take away the magnificent sea views: Overlooking the Gulf of Naples and the islands of Ischia and Procida, this peninsula still affords a unique vantage point over one of the most scenic spots on earth.

Named the "burning fields" during antiquity because of its active sulfur springs and boiling mud craters, this area was highly populated during Greek and Roman times, for its warm and hot springs, its fertile soil, and good harbors. Excavations have brought to light many ruins and archaeological remains of great interest. Indeed, because of the region's geological instability—eruptions as well as cyclical surging and subsiding of the land level—entire ancient Roman neighborhoods have been preserved where the coastline receded, causing the abandonment of inhabited areas. Highlights here are Pozzuoli, with its amphitheater and temples; Baia with its submerged Roman city; and Cuma, with its Sybilla Cave and Greek ruins (see below).

POZZUOLI ⊀⊀

This lively small town was once the Greek colony of Dicearchia, founded in 530 B.C.; it then became the Roman Puteoli in 194 B.C., an important Roman harbor favored by the Roman emperors over Partenope (Naples), which had maintained closer allegiance to Greece. The town was destroyed by the barbarian Alaric in A.D. 410, but the acropolis, on a tufa stone promontory protruding over the sea, continued to be inhabited, and Pozzuoli slowly developed around it. Since the town is just a few kilometers from Naples, you'd expect it to be downright suburban, but it has kept a life of its own—even though many of its residents commute to Naples for work every day. The town boasts unique monuments from its antique past as well as sweeping views over the sea and the islands of Ischia and Procida on one side, and the island of Nisita (today linked to land by a causeway) on the other.

VISITOR INFORMATION The **tourist office,** Via Campi Flegrei 3, 80078 Napoli (© 081-5262419; www.infocampiflegrei.it), dispenses information on Pozzuoli, the Phlegrean Fields region, and the province of Naples, including the islands.

GETTING THERE As Pozzuoli is logistically a neighborhood of Naples, it is extremely well connected by public transportation. It is also the harbor from which a number of ferry lines serve the nearby islands, including Ischia and Procida (see chapter 8). From Naples, city bus no. 152, which starts in Piazza Garibaldi near the

Pozzuoli

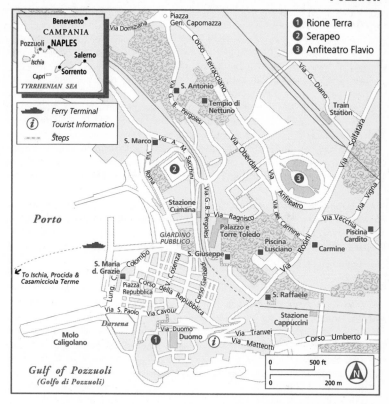

Stazione Centrale, passes through the neighborhoods of Santa Lucia and Chiaia following the shoreline and ends its run in the center of Pozzuoli. It's slow, but very scenic. The Metro (line 2) also makes stops in Pozzuoli; it is faster but less scenic. From Piazza Montesanto, off Riviera di Chiaia, you can catch the **Cumana Railroad** (© **800-001616**); trains leave every 10 minutes for the Phlegrean Fields, from dawn till 9:20pm, with stops in Pozzuoli.

GETTING AROUND   The easiest way to move about is by taxi. Taxis (© **081-5265800**) operate from a stand in Piazza della Repubblica. You can also use the local bus system operated by **SEPSA** (© **800-001616;** www.sepsa.it), with several lines connecting the train and Metro stations with the harbor and other parts of the Phlegrean Fields. Friday through Sunday you can also use the **ArcheoBus** (see box below).

WHAT TO SEE & DO   The modern town closes tightly around Pozzuoli's monuments of antiquity. The original Greek Acropolis, **Rione Terra** (★), Largo Sedile di Porta (© **848-800288** or 081-7410067 for advance reservation), was the first inhabited area of Pozzuoli. Located near the harbor, it has been progressively subsiding under the sea, so much so that it had to be abandoned in the 1970s. A large, ongoing excavation and restoration campaign begun in 1993 has uncovered a virtually untouched Roman town—sort of an underground Pompeii. The site is open to the public by guided tour

The ArcheoBus Flegreo

Piazza della Repubblica in Pozzuoli is the departure point for the **ArcheoBus**. This hop-on-and-off tourist bus is dedicated to the archaeological areas and natural park of Phlegrean Fields. It operates Friday to Sunday from 9am to 7pm. The bus makes 16 stops along a loop between Piazza della Repubblica in Pozzuoli and the archaeological area of Cuma, convenient to all points of interest of the park. Departures are every hour between 9am and 7pm from Pozzuoli, and the whole loop takes 80 minutes. The fare (8€/$11/£5.60) is included in the Artecard (p. 100). At presstime, service is offered only Friday to Sunday, but be sure to contact **SEPSA** (© **800-001616**; www.sepsa.it) for the most current information.

only (admission 3.50€/$4.90/£2.45; children 5 and under free; guided visits Sat–Sun at 11am, noon, 4pm, and 5pm); along the main *Decumano* (the central avenue running east-west) and some minor streets, you'll discover shops, *osterie* (taverns), a *pistrinum* (mill), and the *ergastula* (slaves' cells) with some drawings by prisoners still visible on the walls. Sculptures and other important objects from this site are on display in the Museo Archeologico dei Campi Felgrei in Baia (p. 127).

Not far from the harbor, you'll find the **Serapeo** ⚑, Via Roma 10 (© **081-5266007**), the ruins of the ancient Roman town market. The large porticoed structure, of which you can still see the perimeter—lined with ancient Roman shops and taverns—was built in the 1st century A.D. At its center are the remains of a temple, much spoiled during the centuries (its alabaster columns, for instance, were used to decorate the Royal Palace in Caserta; see chapter 9). Named after the Egyptian god Serapis because of the statue found here during its excavation, this ruin has been used to study the volcanic phenomenon called *bradisism* (alternated periods of subsiding and surging of the ground's level), which is typical of this area—you can still see little holes in the marble of the columns where they were submerged in water. Admission (4€/$5.60/£2.80; daily 9am to 1 hr. before sunset; last entrance 1 hr. earlier; closed Jan 1, May 1, Dec 25) includes access to Anfiteatro Flavio, Museo Archeologico dei Campi Flegrei, Zona Archeologica di Baia, and Scavi di Cuma.

Another interesting archaeological ruin is the **Anfiteatro Flavio** ⚑, Via Terracciano 75 (© **081-5266007**), located in the upper part of town, where the roads to Cuma, Pozzuoli, and Naples converged in Roman times. This was the third largest amphitheater after the Colosseo and the Anfiteatro Campani in Capua (see chapter 10). Built by Vespasian, it is a grandiose sight, especially because of the perfect conservation of the walls and the vaulted ceilings under the arena. Admission (4€/$5.60/£2.80) includes access to Anfiteatro Flavio, Museo Archeologico dei Campi Flegrei, Zona Archeologica di Baia, and Scavi di Cuma. Hours are daily from 9am to 1 hour before sunset, with last admission 1 hour earlier (closed Jan 1, May 1, Dec 25). The theater, which could accommodate more than 20,000 spectators, is still used today for special musical events; check with the local tourist office for information.

SOLFATARA ⚑

This active volcano is the largest within the Phlegrean Fields and is protected as a designated nature preserve. A favorite stop during 19th-century Grand Tours (aristocratic children's educative trips through Europe), it is one of the best preserved attractions

Phlegrean Fields

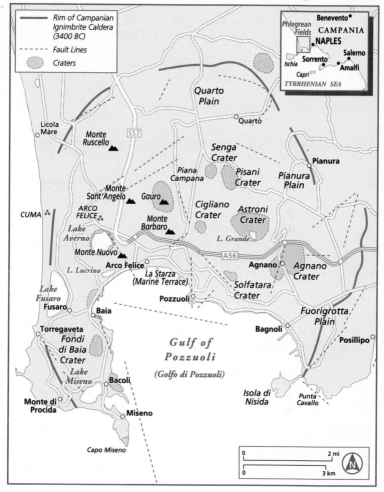

Legend:
- Rim of Campanian Ignimbrite Caldera (3400 BC)
- Fault Lines
- Craters

Inset map: Phlegrean Fields, Benevento, CAMPANIA, NAPLES, Ischia, Sorrento, Salerno, Capri, Amalfi, TYRRHENIAN SEA

Quarto Plain, Quarto, Licola Mare, Monte Ruscello, SS7, Senga Crater, Pianura, Piana Campana, Pisani Crater, Pianura Plain, Monte Sant'Angelo, ARCO FELICE, Gauro, Cigliano Crater, Astroni Crater, CUMA, Monte Barbaro, Lake Averno, L. Grande, Monte Nuovo, A56, Arco Felice, L. Lucrino, La Starza (Marine Terrace), Agnano, Agnano Crater, Lake Fusaro, Fusaro, Baia, Pozzuoli, Solfatara Crater, Fuorigrotta Plain, Torregaveta, Fondi di Baia Crater, Bagnoli, Posillipo, Lake Miseno, Bacoli, Gulf of Pozzuoli (Golfo di Pozzuoli), Monte di Procida, Miseno, Isola di Nisida, Punta Cavallo, Capo Miseno

0 / 2 mi / 0 / 3 km

in the area, thanks to its very nature. Today as 2 centuries ago, you can marvel at the impressive **volcanic phenomena:** bubbling hot mud, sulfurous hot water, and steam issuing from fissures in the soil.

GETTING THERE   The park is 10km (6¼ miles) from Naples. The easiest means of travel is the Metro (line 2) to **Pozzuoli-Solfatara** station, which is only about 800 yards from the entrance to the park. You can walk the distance or catch the local P9 bus from outside the Metro station. City bus 152 from Naples also stops at Solfatara, after a scenic but long trip. You can also walk the 1.6km (1 mile)—a 20-minute trek uphill from Pozzuoli.

WHAT TO SEE & DO   The preserve covers an expanse of 33 hectares (81 acres), with large wooded areas where a number of rare birds, plants, and small animals have found refuge. The **entrance** is at Via Solfatara 161 (© **081-5262341;** www.solfatara.it). From there, follow the trail to the points of major interest (consider about 45 min. for the walk). The best spots are the **Fangaia,** with its huge bubbling mud holes, and the **Bocca Grande,** or main crater, which is the epicenter of the Phlegrean Fields' volcanic area—the ancients believed it was the residence of the god Vulcanus. The **Stufe** are also quite interesting: These small caves filled with hot steam were used during antiquity as natural saunas. Entry fees are 5.50€ ($7.70/£3.85) adults, 4€ ($5.60/£2.80) children 4 to 9, and children 3 and under enter free; Artecard holders receive a 20% discount. The preserve is open daily from 8:30am to 1 hour before sunset.

BAIA 𝄞𝄞

Resting on the coastal stretch that bounds the Gulf of Pozzuoli to the west, the fishing town of **Baia** maintains something of its picturesque past, with pastel-colored buildings opening onto a small harbor. Ancient Roman Baia was a flourishing harbor and seaside resort, and much of it has been preserved through the geological phenomenon of *bradisism,* in which large tracts of land slowly subside beneath sea level, while others rise up.

GETTING THERE   Baia is well connected to Pozzuoli (p. 122). If you are visiting the area from Friday to Sunday and are planning to visit other attractions, the best mode of transport is the **ArcheoBus,** which leaves from Piazza della Repubblica, making four stops in Baia. You can also take a taxi (same rates as in Naples; see "Getting Around," p. 73) from Pozzuoli. Local buses are run by **SEPSA** (✆ **800-001616** or 081-7354311; www.sepsa.it), but they are more cumbersome to use, as you need to follow their timetable.

WHAT TO SEE & DO   The most unique attraction here is obviously the **Parco Archeologico Subacqueo** 𝄞, Harbor of Baia (✆ **081-5248169;** www.baiasommersa. it), a submerged archaeological area that has been excavated and in places roped off and labeled for visitors. The ruins are submerged only a few feet below the surface, and the visit is an eerie and magical experience, however you choose to go about viewing it. Admission (Mid-Mar to mid-Nov Tues–Sun 9:30am–1:30pm and 3:30–7:30pm) is 10€ ($14/£7). **Guided scuba tours** are offered by the park during summer and fall; the 35€ ($49/£25) fee covers admission, insurance, boat transport, basic equipment, and use of the changing room onshore. Artecard entitles you to 20% off admission and 10% off scuba gear rentals.

For the same cost, you can enjoy the ruins from one of the park's **glass-bottomed boats;** you can book lunch for an additional 15€ ($19/£11). If you prefer to make your own arrangements, contact one of the local diving centers, **Blue Point** (✆ **081-8704444)** or **Cardone Sub** (✆ **081-8706886)**, that is authorized to guide scuba divers through the park (they also rent equipment).

The unsubmerged part of the ancient Roman ruins is divided between two archaeological parks connected by a scenic **footpath** 𝄞. Begin with the **Parco Monumentale** 𝄞, Via Bellavista (✆ **081-5233797;** free admission; daily 9am to 1 hr. before sunset; last entrance 1 hr. before closing time; closed Jan 1, May 1, Dec 25), a huge archaeological area covering 14 hectares (34 acres) of "historical landscape" on which excavations are ongoing. Walk among the ruins of **imperial residences** and **elegant villas,** and then, if you already have tickets to the second park, take the path starting from the **Esedra,** the park's main square. The path descends along the hill, affording beautiful views over the craters and the bay, and leads to a side entrance of the **Parco Archeologico Terme di Baia** 𝄞𝄞, whose main entrance is at Via Sella di Baia 22

(© **081-8687592;** admission, 4€/$5.60/£2.80, includes Anfiteatro Flavio and Ser-apeo in Pozzuoli, Museo Archeologico in Baia, and Scavi di Cuma; Tues–Sun 9am to 1 hr. before sunset; last entrance 1 hr. before closing time; closed Jan 1, May 1, Dec 25). Terme di Baia features the ruins of the most celebrated of ancient Roman baths, beloved by the VIPs of ancient Rome both for the therapeutic properties of their waters and for the matchless scenery. Built by Emperor Ottaviano between 27 B.C. and A.D. 14, the baths took advantage of local, natural hot springs and were hydraulically engineered to be fed by gravity only. The subsiding of the ground, though, altered the original construction, and little water reaches the baths today.

Baia is also a good base for exploring the bay; you can rent a boat from the **Asso-ciazione Barcaioli di Baia** (© **081-8701222**), or join an organized boat excursion with **Peppe Navigazione del Golfo** (© **333-8877883**) or with the ferry company **Alilauro** (© **081-7611004** or 081-4972293; www.alilauro.it). All the above compa-nies are located along the dock in the harbor.

Overlooking the harbor from a small promontory is the scenic **Castello Aragonese,** built in 1442 by Alfonso d'Aragona. Worth a visit in itself, the castle houses the **Museo Archeologico dei Campi Flegrei** ⭐, Via Castello 39 (© **081-5233797** or 848-8002884), whose rich endowment is second only to the archaeological museum in Naples. Of the three sections of the museum, one holds artifacts from the excava-tions of Baia and Miseno, such as the **Sacello degli Augustali** and the famous **Com-plex of the Ninfeo di Punta Epitaffio** (a *ninfeo* being an ancient Roman porch enclosed with columns). Another section displays a collection of ancient Roman **plas-ter casts** of some of the most celebrated Greek masterpieces. The final section on the upper floor holds the reconstruction of the **Ninfeo of the Emperor Claudius.** Admis-sion is 4€ ($5.60/£2.80) and includes admission to Anfiteatro Flavio and Serapeo in Pozzuoli, Zona Archeologica in Baia, and Scavi di Cuma. Hours are Tuesday to Sun-day from 9am to 8pm, with the ticket booth closing 1 hour earlier (museum closed Jan 1, May 1, Dec 25).

CUMA ⭐⭐

This is the site of the first colony the ancient Greeks founded in the western Mediter-ranean, giving birth to what would become Magna Grecia. After having moved from nearby Ischia because of the overactive volcano (see appendix A), in the 8th century B.C., they chose this extremely scenic position: high up on a promontory and dominating the Phlegrean Fields peninsula, with a green expanse of land interspersed with volcanic lakes, and the sea on both sides. The city of Cuma proved to be the most important Greek colony on this coast, keeping the Etruscans and later the Romans at bay.

GETTING THERE   If you are visiting Friday through Sunday and planning to visit other area attractions, your best choice is the **ArcheoBus** (p. 124), making stops at all the tourist destinations highlighted below. Another excellent option is to take a taxi from Pozzuoli (same rates as in Naples; p. 76). The **Cumana Railroad** (see "Getting There," p. 70) makes a stop at **Fusaro,** where you can connect to transport run by **SEPSA** (© **800-001616** or 081-7354311; www.sepsa.it): the Miseno-Cuma bus stops at the entrance to the archaeological area.

WHAT TO SEE AND DO   Today, only ruins remain of this once great city. Inside the archaeological area, **Scavi di Cuma,** Via Monte di Cuma 3, Pozzuoli (© **081-8543060**), you'll find the **Acropolis** with its impressive **temples,** one dedicated to **Apollo** and the other to **Jupiter.** Preserved only because they were used as churches in the Middle Ages, these temples reflect the city's succession of cultures: They bear decorative details added through the centuries by the city's inhabitants, from the Sannites and the Romans to the early Christians. Admission (4€/$5.60/£2.80) includes entry to Anfiteatro Flavio and Serapeo in Pozzuoli, and Museo Archeologico and Zona Archeologica in Baia (daily 9am to 1 hr. before sunset; last admission 1 hr. before closing time; closed Jan 1, May 1, and Dec 25).

Outside the remains of the **fortified walls,** you'll find the **North Necropolis** and an **amphitheatre** dating from the late 2nd century B.C. Nearby is the mysterious **Antro della Sibilla (Sibylla's cave)** ❀, where the famous priestess to the god Apollo allegedly received her supplicants. This tunnel of majestic proportions was excavated through the mountain down to the nearby lake, probably for defensive purposes. Some of the internal halls are decorated, a fact that gave birth to the legend of Sybilla, and gave the tunnel its name. The terrace outside the cave provides a splendid **view** ❀❀ over the harbor of Cuma, which is itself worth the visit.

Nearby is the **Arco Felice,** a huge ancient Roman arch under which the local road passes. This immense engineering feat was realized under Emperor Domitian in the 1st century A.D., when the mountain was cut and a viaduct was built for the passage of the Domitian Road. Also nearby is **Lake Averno:** Described by Virgil in the *Aeneid* as the entrance to the underworld, this volcanic lake is strangely dark and quiet. Its name is ancient Greek for "no birds," and it is believed that volcanic vapors might have kept the animals away. In spite of its dark fame, in 37 B.C. Marco Agrippa had it connected via channel to the nearby lagoon Lucrino for use as a Roman shipyard. On the eastern shore you'll find the remains of a large **thermal bath complex,** known locally as Tempio di Apollo.

The largest of the volcanic lakes is **Lake Fusaro** ❀, a short distance farther to the south. It was known to the ancients as *Acherusia Palus,* or the infernal swamp. In 1782, quite indifferent to the ancients beliefs, Ferdinando IV Bourbon had the architect Carlo Vanvitelli (son of the famous Luigi) build a hunting and fishing lodge on a little island in the lake, the **Casina Reale** ❀, Via Fusaro, Bacoli (✆ **081-8687080;** Sat–Sun 9am–1pm). The elegant construction (today connected by a footbridge to the shore) is well worth a visit, and you can enjoy unique lakeside views, far away from the surrounding noise and urban sprawl.

WHERE TO STAY IN THE AREA

Staying locally is a good alternative to booking a more expensive hotel in Naples, particularly if you are planning a full day of sightseeing followed by a visit to Ischia or Procida (see chapter 8).

Moderate

Cala Moresca ❀ Picturesquely situated on the cliffs of Capo Miseno, this pleasant and welcoming hotel offers comfortable accommodations and lots of extras, such as an outdoor swimming pool, a playground for small children, a country trail, and outdoor activities like tennis and squash. A path descends to a large shelf of rock from which swimmers plunge into the blue sea. Guest rooms are large and bright, furnished with simple modern furnishings, tiled floors, and good-size bathrooms. Most rooms have private balconies overlooking the sea.

Via Faro, 44 80070 Bacoli. ✆ 081-5235595. Fax 081-5235557. www.calamoresca.it. 27 units. 145€ ($203/£102). Rates include buffet breakfast. Children 2 and under stay free in parent's room. AE, DC, MC, V. Free parking. Closed Dec 24–26. **Amenities:** Restaurant; bar; babysitting; basketball and squash courts; business center; laundry service; outdoor pool; outdoor tennis courts; playground; room service. *In room:* A/C, satellite TV, minibar, hair dryer, safe.

Villa Giulia The delightful host of this abode has restored the ancient farmhouse with good taste, creating a haven of beauty in the mist of unsightly new construction (happily invisible from the premises). This B&B offers only five units, ranging in size from studios to huge one-bedrooms, each complete with kitchen and its own patio or garden. The welcoming furnishings give the illusion of walking into a private home. The large garden is full of flowers in fair weather, and the good-size pool is another plus. The week-long cooking classes that focus on pizza and other Neapolitan specialties are fun and well organized.

Via Cuma Licola 178, 80072 Pozzuoli. ⓒ 081-8540163. Fax 081-8044356. www.villagiulia.info. 5 units. 130€–160€ ($182–$224/£91–£112) double. Rates include buffet breakfast. Children 2 and under stay free in parent's room. AE, DC, MC, V. Free parking. **Amenities:** Restaurant (reservations necessary and available to guests only); laundry service; outdoor pool. *In room:* Satellite TV.

Inexpensive
Santa Marta Located near Arco Felice, this moderately priced hotel offers excellent management and an ideal location not far from the sea and convenient to area attractions. Bedrooms are spacious and pleasant, with basic contemporary furnishings and tiled floors. The bathrooms are good-size and modern, and the whole establishment is cleaned scrupulously. The restaurant offers well-prepared local food.

Via Licola Patria 28, 80072 Arco Felice–Pozzuoli. ⓒ 081-8042404. Fax 081-8042406. www.santamartahotel.com. 34 units. 84€ ($118/£118) double; 114€ ($160/£80) triple; 140€ ($196/£98) quad. Rates include buffet breakfast. Children 2 and under stay free in parent's room. AE, DC, MC, V. Free parking. **Amenities:** Restaurant; bar; business center; solarium. *In room:* Satellite TV.

WHERE TO DINE
Expensive
La Misenetta ★★ NEAPOLITAN With upscale decor, superb food, and a lakeside location, this restaurant is perfect for a memorable dinner. The menu includes an ample choice of seafood dishes (but you can also find some meat and vegetarian choices), all prepared with great skill and creativity. We love their rendition of traditional dishes like the *polpi in cassuola* (casserole of squid in a tomato-based sauce) and the fish fillet *all'acquapazza;* the more elaborate *ravioli di astice* (lobster ravioli) is also excellent. Superior desserts and a good wine list round out the meal.

Via Lungolago 2, Bacoli. ⓒ 081-5234169. Reservations recommended on evenings and weekends. Secondi 18€–35€ ($25–$49/£13–£25). AE, DC, MC, V. Tues–Sun noon–3pm and 7–11pm.

Moderate
Bobò ★ NEAPOLITAN Located along the harbor in Pozzuoli, this is an excellent choice for a seafood dinner by the shore. The cuisine is traditional but prepared with high-quality, fresh ingredients and infused with a spark of creativity. We recommend the homemade fresh fusilli with zucchini, baby clams, and *pecorino di fossa* (aged sheep cheese) or the excellent grilled fish. The tasting menu for 50€ ($70/£35) is the way to go if you have a hearty appetite.

Lungomare Cristoforo Colombo 20, Pozzuoli. ⓒ 081-5262034. www.ristorantebobo.it. Reservations recommended. Secondi 12€–24€ ($17–$34/£8.40–£17). AE, DC, MC, V. Wed–Mon 12:30–2pm, Wed–Sat and Mon 7:30–11pm.

Cagi Da Ludovico NEAPOLITAN This is a good address in Pozzuoli for meat as well as seafood. All dishes are prepared traditionally, with good local ingredients. We are partial to *spaghetti alle vongole* (spaghetti with clams), but the fusilli *al ragù* (with Neapolitan meat sauce) are also excellent; for *secondo* we recommend the *fettina alla pizzaiola* (beef in a tomato and oregano sauce).

Via Nicola Fasano 6, Pozzuoli. ⓒ 081-5268255. Reservations recommended on weekends. Secondi 9€–15€ ($13–$21/£6.30–£11). AE, DC, MC, V. Tues–Sun noon–3pm and Tues–Sat 7:30–11pm.

Garibaldi NEAPOLITAN   This seaside place makes for an excellent stop after a visit to the museum or the archaeological area of Baia. It takes advantage of its prime location by specializing in fish—simply prepared, but using fresh ingredients and traditional recipes. *Fusilli ai frutti di mare* (short pasta with seafood) is a perfect way to begin the meal, but you shouldn't miss out on the secondo: excellent *polpi in guazzetto* (squid in a tomato sauce), as well as some of the most flavorful grilled fish in the area.

Via Spiaggia di Bacoli 36, Bacoli. ⓒ 081-5234368. Reservations recommended on weekends. Secondi 8€–16€ ($11–$22/£5.60–£11). AE, DC, MC, V. Tues–Sun noon–3pm and 7–11pm.

Inexpensive

Arturo al Fusaro ⭐ *(Finds)* NEAPOLITAN   This excellent restaurant offers traditional local cuisine in a pleasant decor, and at reasonable prices. The specialty is seafood, which is extremely fresh and served in a variety of ways, from appetizers, to pasta and rice dishes, to main courses. You might want to sample flawless *risotto ai frutti di mare* (seafood risotto); *vermicelli cozze e vongole* (thin spaghetti with mussels and clams); or one of the catches of the day prepared *all'acqua pazza* (in light herbed broth), grilled with herbs, or baked over a bed of potatoes.

Via Cuma 322, Bacoli. ⓒ 081-8543130. Reservations recommended on weekends. Secondi 7€–14€ ($9.80–$20/£4.90–£9.80). AE, DC, MC, V. Daily noon–3pm and 7–10:30pm.

Il Tucano PIZZA   It's a bit touristy, yes, but excellent pizza and traditional specialties make this restaurant worth a visit. The heir of the historical Trattoria Miramare, which existed in this same spot since 1929, Il Tucano serves up a large variety of pizzas—including the exceptional *quattro formaggi e gamberetti* (four cheeses and shrimp). The pizza here is served "by the foot"—you ask for a length, and they cut it and charge you accordingly. The owner has made a real effort to honor the old trattoria's menu of local specialties and to offer a wide selection of local wines.

Via Molo di Baia, Baia. ⓒ 081-8545046. Reservations not necessary. Pizza 3€–8€ ($4.20–$11/£2.10–£5.60; charged by length). MC, V. Tues–Sun noon–midnight.

Vineria del Mare ⭐ *(Finds)* ITALIAN/ENOTECA   This welcoming restaurant started out as an enoteca, serving only tidbits alongside the ample choice of wines and vintages; but the menu has multiplied over the years and the faithful now come for the food as well as the wine. We loved the pasta dishes, the carpaccio, and the scrumptious homemade desserts.

Vico Torrione 14, Pozzuoli. ⓒ 081-5266656. Reservations recommended on weekends. Secondi 8€–16€ ($11–$22/£5.60–£11). AE, DC, MC, V. Tues–Sun 7pm–midnight.

Pompeii & Herculaneum: the Vesuvian Archaeological Area

Mount Vesuvius had been dormant for centuries when the great explosion of A.D. 79 occurred. At the time of the eruption, it seems that nobody knew it was a volcano, and its slopes—much sought after for the fertile soil and for the vineyards which produced an excellent wine—were heavily inhabited. Towns, villages, and estates were covered by lava or ash during the eruption, causing thousands of deaths and immense economic loss. Pompeii was the first of the lost towns to be excavated—the discovery dates from the 16th century—and more towns were uncovered in later centuries. Recently, modern archaeologists have unveiled many other sites that were not spoiled by illegal digs over the years.

While Pompeii is rightly the most famous of the Vesuvian archeological sites, we also highly recommend the newer digs,

particularly to second-time visitors. Herculaneum, for example, is more striking than Pompeii, because of how well the houses have been preserved. Rarely visited by foreign tourists, the grandiose Roman villa of Oplontis is still decorated with magnificent frescoes, and is a perfect choice for those who don't have the taste or the time for a lengthier visit to Roman ruins. We also recommend the villas of Boscoreale and Boscotrecase, smaller but each very interesting.

All of the destinations we describe in this chapter make an easy day trip from Naples, but if you are not planning to visit the city itself, it is a good idea to stay in the area, which offers less pricey accommodations. The best options are Pompeii and nearby Torre del Greco, or, a bit farther down the coast, Castellammare di Stabia (see chapter 6).

1 Herculaneum ★ ★

9.5km (6 miles) SE of Naples

The volcanic mud that covered Herculaneum during the A.D. 79 Mount Vesuvius eruption, killing most of the town estimated 5,000 inhabitants, quickly hardened to a semi-rock material, protecting the structures underneath but also making archaeological excavations much slower than at other sites. Herculaneum was discovered in 1709, and although excavations started shortly after and proceeded alongside those in Pompeii, the uncovered area here is much smaller than that of the more famous sibling site. Also, unlike at Pompeii, much of the ancient town lies under the modern one, making excavation even more difficult. The findings, though, are stunning.

Although many questions about Herculaneum remain to be answered, researchers tell us that this town was about a third of the size of Pompeii and had a different urban makeup. A glitzy seaside resort for wealthy Romans, Herculaneum had little commercial and industrial activity. Most of the town was composed of elegant villas—many even more richly decorated than those of Pompeii—and some apartment blocks for poor laborers, while the middle-class of merchants and artisans, which was so largely represented in Pompeii, was almost completely absent here. The town was also a harbor, with moderate activity.

ESSENTIALS

GETTING THERE   You can easily get to Herculaneum by public transportation using the **Circumvesuviana** railway (© **800-053939** toll-free within Italy; www. vesuviana.it); trains leave from the Stazione Circumvesuviana (Corso Garibaldi, off Piazza Garibaldi; Metro: Garibaldi). Both the Sorrento and the Poggiomarino lines make a stop at **Ercolano Scavi,** and the 20-minute ride costs 1.70€ ($2.40/£1.20). Outside the station, you can then get a shuttle bus to the archaeological site or grab a taxi.

A good alternative is using a limo service from Naples or any other town. Recommended providers are **ANA Limousine Service,** Piazza Garibaldi 73 (© **081-282000**) and **Italy Limousine** (© **081-8016184,** 335-6732245, or 338-9681866; www.italylimousine.it). Another excellent option is to sign up for a guided tour from Naples (see chapter 4, p. 113).

We do not recommend driving, as modern Ercolano lies in the poorer outskirts of Naples, with terrible traffic, difficult parking, and questionable safety (your car is at certain risk, and you don't want to leave it unattended). If you really need to use your car, Ercolano lies along busy coastal route SS18, which links Naples to Torre del Greco and Pompeii. From autostrada A3, take the ERCOLANO-PORTICI exit and follow the brown signs for the archaeological area, or *scavi.*

EXPLORING HERCULANEUM

The archeological area lies in the heart of the modern town of Ercolano, a relatively depressed and not exactly tourist-friendly suburb of Naples. The town is perfectly safe during the day, particularly by the archaeological area, but rather ugly. If you are up for a little exploring, though, you might also want to visit the showroom of a local talented artist, a maker of **cameos,** named **Biagio Piscopo** (Corso Resina 318; © **081-7322736**), conveniently located near the archaeological site. The difficult art of cameo making was first developed in nearby Torre del Greco (see later in this chapter), and the beautiful jewels produced here are exported all over the globe.

The archeological area of Herculaneum is one of the **Artecard** sites (see box in chapter 4, p. 100); you can also save on the admission price by purchasing the **3-day cumulative ticket,** which grants access to all the archaeological sites of the Vesuvian area—Herculaneum, Pompeii, Oplontis, Stabiae, and Boscoreale—for 20€ ($28/£14).

Herculaneum Archeological Area ⟨⟨⟨   Smaller and easier to visit than Pompeii, Herculaneum may appear at first to be also less impressive. You'll be quickly pervaded by the eerie sensation that, far from being a place of dusty ruins, the town was abandoned only a short time ago, instead of nearly 2,000 years in the past. Part of this feeling of entering a ghost town stems from the fact that many of the houses still have their upper floors. The volcanic mud that enveloped the site has allowed for the unusual preservation of wood, from housing structures to room furnishings, allowing archeologists to learn an incredible deal about daily life and building techniques in Roman times.

The excavated area stretches from Herculaneum's **Decumanus Maximus** (the town's main street) to the shore; the rest of the Roman town away from the water

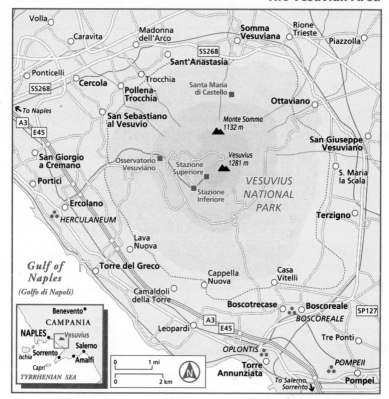

remains inaccessible beneath the buildings of modern Ercolano. The archaeological area is in continuous evolution as ongoing excavations lead to new discoveries. For instance, a boat was found near the shore in the 1990s: It was still filled with the corpses of victims caught in frantic postures of escape.

The highlights of a visit should definitely include the **Collegio degli Augustali (College of the Augustali)** ⭐⭐, with its marble floor and wall paintings; the custodian's room has also been preserved, together with the bed—on view here—where the man's corpse was found, presumably killed in his sleep. We also recommend a tour of the elegantly decorated **Thermal Baths,** and the **Palestra,** a monumental sports arena for competition and training. Among the private homes, the most interesting are the **Casa del Tramezzo di Legno (House of the Wooden Partition),** with its perfectly preserved facade, and the **Casa dei Cervi (House of the Stags),** the most elegant ruin in the excavated area, with terraces overlooking the sea and top-quality decorations. The **Casa a Graticcio (House of the Latticework)** is particularly fascinating because it's one of the very few examples of lower-class housing that has emerged from antiquity (usually only grand public buildings and the solidly constructed villas of the wealthy have survived); notice the partitions, cheaply made of interwoven cane and plaster. Another interesting house is the **Casa del Mosaico di Nettuno e Anfitrite**

(House of the Neptune and Anfitritis Mosaic) and the annexed shop, still with merchandise on the counter and goods in the cabinets.

Corso Resina, Ercolano. (✆ 081-8575347. www.pompeiisites.org. Guided tours reservations daily 10am–1:30pm. Admission 11€ ($15/£7.70). Daily Nov 1–Mar 31 8:30am–5pm; Apr 1–Oct 31 8:30am–7:30pm. Last admission 90 min. earlier. Closed Jan 1, May 1, and Dec 25.

Villa dei Papiri 👁👁 Opened to the public in 2004 after a lengthy restoration, this villa was first discovered in 1750 and later excavated as was then customary: by removing everything of value and then reburying the site. The most striking find of the original excavation was the villa's library, chock-full of **papyrus rolls** (there were about 1,000) that gave the name to the villa and are now preserved in the Biblioteca Nazionale Vittorio Emanuele III inside Palazzo Reale (see chapter 4). The villa also yielded a treasure trove of elegant sculptures which increased the collection of the Museo Archeologico Nazionale in Naples (see chapter 4). After years of work, modern archeologists have revealed the actual structure of the grandiose mansion itself. Built in A.D. 60, the villa stretched over 250m (820 ft.) along the coast: Its magnificent position on a cliff overlooking the sea will make your mouth water. Open to visitors are both floors of the villa—with over 16 rooms decorated with rich mosaic tiles and frescoes—as well as the interior garden with pool, and the panoramic terrace. Visits are by guided tour only, and you need to pick up your tickets at the entrance 20 minutes before the scheduled time of your visit. *Note:* At presstime the Villa was closed for extraordinary restorations, and no date for its reopening was provided; so check with the excavation office before your visit.

Corso Resina, to the west of the archaeological area of Herculaneum. (✆ 081-8575347. www.pompeiisites.org. Advance reservations at (✆ 081-7390963 or www.arethusa.net. Admission included with ticket to the Herculaneum site; advance reservation 2€ ($2.80/£1.40). Sat–Sun 9am–noon.

WHERE TO STAY

You really don't want to spend more time in Ercolano than is necessary. If you want to sleep in the area, we recommend heading for nearby **Torre del Greco.** This modern seaside resort located 9.5km (6 miles) SE of Naples, is a perfect base for an exploration of Herculaneum and the whole Vesuvian area. Its several hotels and restaurants cater both to tourists and business travelers, attracted here by the seaside and the flourishing craft of cameo making. By public transportation the town is two stops beyond the Ercolano Scavi station on the **Circumvesuviana** railway (✆ **800-053939;** www.vesuviana.it); take either the Sorrento or the Poggiomarino line (see "Getting There," earlier). **Taxis** also wait outside the train station. By **car,** take the very busy SS18 toward Torre del Greco and Pompeii, or, from the autostrada A3, take the exit marked TORRE DEL GRECO NORD or TORRE DEL GRECO SUD.

MODERATE

Hotel Marad 👁 Located in a quiet area outside town, and enjoying a great panoramic position, this is a relaxing place to take a break from visiting the ruins. Public spaces include pleasant gardens and a swimming pool, and guests have access to a spa and gym nearby. Rooms are quiet and well appointed, with quality furniture, tiled or carpeted floors, and modern bathrooms. All rooms have a private balcony.

Via San Sebastiano 24, 80059 Torre del Greco. (✆ 081-8492168. Fax 081-8828716. www.marad.it. 74 units. High season 140€ ($196/£98) double. Rates include buffet breakfast. Children 2 and under stay free in parent's room. AE, DC, MC, V. Free parking. **Amenities:** 2 restaurants; bar; babysitting; business center; concierge; gym; laundry service; outdoor pool; spa; room service. *In room:* A/C, satellite TV, minibar, Wi-Fi.

Herculaneum

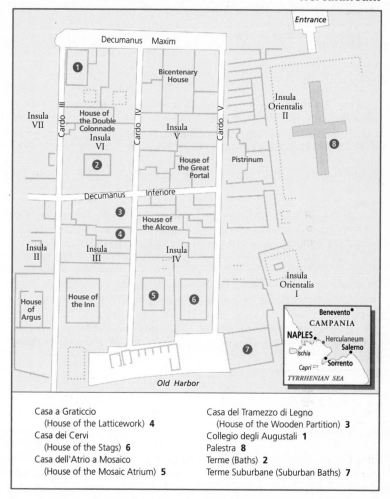

Entrance

Decumanus Maxim

Bicentenary House

Insula VII

Cardo III

House of the Double Colonnade

Cardo IV

Insula V

Cardo V

Insula Orientalis II

Insula VI

Palestra 8

House of the Great Portal

Pistrinum

Decumanus Inferiore

House of the Alcove

Insula II

Insula III

Insula IV

Insula Orientalis I

House of Argus

House of the Inn

Old Harbor

Benevento
CAMPANIA
NAPLES · Herculaneum
Ischia · Salerno
Capri · Sorrento
TYRRHENIAN SEA

Casa a Graticcio
(House of the Latticework) 4
Casa dei Cervi
(House of the Stags) 6
Casa dell'Atrio a Mosaico
(House of the Mosaic Atrium) 5

Casa del Tramezzo di Legno
(House of the Wooden Partition) 3
Collegio degli Augustali 1
Palestra 8
Terme (Baths) 2
Terme Suburbane (Suburban Baths) 7

Sakura ★ (Kids) This hotel is more stylish than the Marad (see above), although both offer quality accommodations. The Sakura is surrounded by a large private park, and is located on the slopes of the Vesuvio, affording cooler air during the summer. Public spaces are large and welcoming, and the swimming pool, *calcetto* field (calcetto is an Italian form of soccer, with five players on each side), and pine forest are great outlets for children and grown-ups alike. The spacious guest rooms are individually decorated with a mix of classic and contemporary furniture, hardwood floors, and state-of-the-art bathrooms with Jacuzzi tubs.

Via Ettore De Nicola 26, 80059 Torre del Greco. ✆ **081-8493144.** Fax 081-8491122. www.hotelsakura.it. 80 units. 145€ ($203/£102) double; 195€ ($273/£137) junior suite. Rates include buffet breakfast. Extra bed 45€ ($63/£32). Children 5 and under stay free in parent's room. AE, DC, MC, V. Free parking. **Amenities:** Restaurant; 2 bars; babysitting; business

Cameo Making

Coral jewelry and cameos have a long history in Torre del Greco. Fishing for coral has been a traditional activity since antiquity, when the art of the cameo was first invented. Lost during the Middle Ages, the craft boomed in the 19th century when local artisans took inspiration from the jewelry of the excavations of Pompeii and Herculaneum. In 1879 the Scuola di Incisione del Corallo (School of Coral Carving) opened, giving further impulse to the development of the industry. Today, the school is called the **Istituto Statale per l'Arte del Corallo e l'Oreficeria,** and maintains its own museum, the **Museo del Corallo** ★★, Piazza Palomba (✆ 081-8811360), where you can admire a fairly large collection from the 18th century onward. Also in town is the privately held—it belongs to one of the historical cameo factories—**Museo Liverino del Corallo e dei Cammei** ★★, Via Montedoro 61 (✆ 081-8811225), which displays over 3,000 pieces from the 16th century on.

Although the local coral beds are practically exhausted, cameo making still flourishes today, thanks to the use of corals and shells from the Pacific Ocean. About 90 percent of all coral fished around the world makes its way to this little town on the Italian coast, and the jewelry produced here is exported all over the world. Among the many cameo workshops in the area, some of the most reputable congregate around Via Ettore de Nicola. At no. 1 is **Giovanni Apa** (✆ 081-8811155); no. 25 is **Antonino del Gatto** (✆ 081-8814191); **Baldo Liguoro** (✆ 081-8812600) inhabits no. 35; and **Vincenzo Ricevuto** (✆ 081-8814976) occupies no. 38. Other noteworthy workshops are **Fratelli De Simone,** Via Roma 4 (✆ 081-8829368), **B. & E. Mazza,** Via Tironi 14 (✆ 081-8812665), and **Giuseppe Pepere,** Via Friuli 11 (✆ 081-8834888).

center; concierge; outdoor pool; room service; same-day laundry service. *In room:* A/C, satellite TV, hair dryer, minibar, safe, trouser press.

INEXPENSIVE

Hotel Holidays   This modern family-run hotel caters mostly to Italian tourists and offers welcoming accommodations at a moderate price in a seaside location, only steps from the beach. Guest rooms are spacious and nicely appointed, with tiled floors, comfortable furnishings, and updated bathrooms. Only the best rooms—with sea views or private terraces—have air-conditioning and a minibar.

Via Litoranea 154, Santa Maria La Bruna, 80059 Torre del Greco. ✆ 081-8832170. Fax 081-8836591. www.holidays hotel.it. 38 units. 75€–110€ ($105–$154/£53–£77) double. Rates include breakfast. Extra bed 25€ ($35/£18). Children 1 and under stay free in parent's room. AE, DC, MC, V. Free parking. **Amenities:** Restaurant; bar; babysitting; business center; concierge; laundry service; room service. *In room:* A/C (some rooms), satellite TV, minibar (some rooms).

WHERE TO DINE

Ercolano itself does not offer recommendable dining, although just outside the entrance to the site, you'll find snack bars and grocery shops on the main road. If you have the time for a detour, you can get a real meal—and an excellent one—in nearby Torre del Greco (see "Where to Stay," above). A major dining destination, Torre del Greco is popular with Italians who come here to sample the excellent local cuisine, famous for its fresh seafood dishes, and partake of the local D.O.C. wines. The whole stretch of the main seashore road is lined with restaurants large and small, some more upscale and others simple shacks. Lots of others are hidden away on the inner streets. The town also has an array of excellent pizzerias; we recommend **Pizzeria la Bruna** (G) *(Kids)*, Via Nazionale 678 ((C) **081-8832431;** daily), which makes delicious Neapolitan pizza and has a private garden.

MODERATE
Ristorante Pernice Salvatore (G) NEAPOLITAN/SEAFOOD   A bit more upscale than Gaetano a Mare or Chiarina A'Mmare (below), this restaurant offers dining both indoors and outdoors on its terrace. The menu is seasonal and depends on the offerings of the day's market, but you'll usually find their delicious version of *acqua pazza* (light herbed broth) and the *pesce al sale* (daily catch baked in a bed of salt that seals in the natural flavor of the fish). Two of the most outstanding first courses are *risotto alla pescatora* (risotto with seafood) and *scialatielli ai frutti di mare* (fresh pasta with shellfish).

Via Ruggiero 45, Torre del Greco. (C) **081-8832297.** Reservations recommended on weekends. Secondi 16€–28€ ($22–$39/£11–£20). AE, DC, MC, V. Daily noon–3pm and 7:30–11pm.

INEXPENSIVE
Chiarina A'Mmare (G) NEAPOLITAN/SEAFOOD   Another local favorite, this restaurant gets very crowded on weekends with locals craving seafood. The seasonal menu always includes traditional local favorites, of which we'd recommend *spaghetti zucchine e cozze* (spaghetti with mussels and zucchini), *frittelle di alghe* (seaweed fritters), *impepata di cozze* (mussels steamed with white pepper), and *pesce all'acquapazza* (fish cooked in a light tomato broth).

Via Calastro, Torre del Greco. (C) **081-8812067.** Reservations recommended on weekends. Secondi 12€–18€ ($17–$25/£8.40–£13). AE, DC, MC, V. Daily 12:30–3:30pm and 7:30–10:30pm.

Gaetano a Mare *(Kids)* NEAPOLITAN/SEAFOOD   This is one of the town's best-established restaurants, favored by locals who love to come here on weekends for traditional cuisine and good wine (while the children play in the restaurant's playground). The menu is seasonal and based on market selection, but you'll usually find an excellent *frittura* (medley of deep-fried seafood) and delicious *pasta alle cozze* (pasta with sautéed mussels). Catches of the day are prepared according to your choice, *all'acquapazza* (poached with an herb broth), baked, or grilled.

Via Litoranea 5, Torre del Greco. (C) **081-8831558.** Reservations recommended on weekends. Secondi 12€–22€ ($17–$31/£8.40–£15). No credit cards. Sat–Thurs noon–3pm and 7:30–11pm.

2 Oplontis (G)

20km (12 miles) SE of Naples

Near the harbor town of **Torre Annunziata**—famous for its flour mills and its pasta industry—this is one of the more recently excavated archaeological areas on the slopes of Mount Vesuvius. Much remains to be done here, but what has already been uncovered is quite spectacular. The size of the site is much more manageable than Pompeii or even Herculaneum, making it a good choice for those desiring a brief archaeological visit.

ESSENTIALS
GETTING THERE   You can easily get to Oplontis by public transportation using the **Circumvesuviana** railway ((C) **800-053939** toll-free within Italy; www.vesuviana.it),

Impressions
Live in danger. Build your cities on the slopes of Vesuvius.
—Friedrich Nietzsche (1844–1900)

which leaves from the Stazione Circumvesuviana in Naples (Corso Garibaldi, off Piazza Garibaldi; Metro: Garibaldi). Take a train bound for Torre Annunziata, Sorrento, or Poggiomarino, and get off at **Torre Annunziata-Oplonti Villa di Poppea** (a few stops after Ercolano Scavi). Trains leave every half-hour; the 30-minute ride costs 2€ ($2.80/£1.40).

By car, take the autostrada A3 Napoli-Salerno and exit at TORRE ANNUNZIATA SUD. Then follow the brown signs for SCAVI DI OPLONTI.

EXPLORING OPLONTIS

As of the 1st century B.C., Oplontis was already an elegant residential suburb of nearby Pompeii The very rich had their countryside villas here, and the very name might come from the Latin *opulentia,* or opulence. Discovered in the 18th century, the site was not excavated until the 1960s. Only the ruin of one extraordinary villa is currently open to the public, yet it is well worth the visit.

The archaeological area of Oplontis is a participating **Artecard** site (see box in chapter 4, p. 100); you can also save on admission prices by purchasing the **3-day cumulative ticket,** which includes Herculaneum, Pompeii, Oplontis, Stabiae, and Boscoreale, for 20€ ($28/£14).

Villa di Poppea 👁👁   This is the largest ancient Roman suburban villa ever discovered. It was declared a UNESCO World Heritage Site because of the unique quality of its frescoes. It was certainly a villa belonging to the imperial family, and scientists believe it was the property of the famous Poppea Sabina, the second wife of the Emperor Nero: An amphora bearing the name of her freedman and a vase bearing her mark were found on the villa's grounds, thus giving evidence justifying the claim. The villa is enormous, with a large portico opening onto a garden with a huge pool surrounded by statues, and innumerable rooms, passages and cubicles, including a still-recognizable kitchen.

The greatest feature is the villa's absolutely superb decorations: Frescoes, stucco work, and mosaics have been left *in situ,* unlike in Pompeii or Herculaneum where, except in the latest excavations, they were removed to museums. Most of the interior was lavishly painted and many of the frescoes are still in very good repair, closely recalling the more well-known frescoes in the Villa dei Misteri of Pompeii and in the Museo Archeologico Nazionale of Naples.

The villa also yielded a treasure trove of high-quality statuary—a very rich collection, second only to what was found in the Villa dei Papiri in Herculaneum (see earlier in this chapter)—but, oddly, it was found tucked away in a storeroom. Actually, the whole villa was devoid of signs of daily life, leading the experts to believe that it was being restored at the moment of the eruption—maybe as a consequence of the preceding earthquake of A.D. 62.

Via Sepolcri 12, Torre Annunziata. ✆ 081-8621755. www.pompeiisites.org. Admission 5.50€ ($7.70/£3.85) includes same-day entry to Boscoreale and Stabiae. Daily Nov 1–Mar 31 8:30am–5pm; Apr 1–Oct 31 8:30am–7:30pm. Last admission 90 min. earlier. Closed Jan 1, May 1, and Dec 25.

3 Boscoreale

31km (19 miles) SE of Naples

In ancient Roman times, this agricultural center for wine, wheat, and olive oil on the slopes of Mount Vesuvius was part of the northern suburbs of Pompeii. Boscoreale today is still comprised of farms and vineyards (the adjacent Boscotrecase is famous for the production of *Lacrimae Cristi,* the amber-colored D.O.C. Vesuvian wine). Over 30 Roman villas have been found in Boscoreale to date, but only one has been completely excavated.

ESSENTIALS

GETTING THERE   Circumvesuviana trains (© 800-053939; www.vesuviana.it) leave from Stazione Circumvesuviana, Corso Garibaldi, off Piazza Garibaldi (Metro: Garibaldi). Board a train bound for Poggiomarino and get off at the **Boscoreale** stop; trains leave every hour, and the 25-minute ride costs 2.10€ ($2.95/£1.50). From the station, take a taxi or switch to the local bus to Villa Regina. By **car,** take the autostrada A3 and exit at TORRE ANNUNZIATA; follow the brown signs for COMUNI VESUVIANI and BOSCOREALE.

EXPLORING THE ARCHAEOLOGICAL AREA OF BOSCOREALE

Excavations in this area started at the end of the 19th century and were mostly performed by local landowners for the sole purpose of gathering valuable art. Once the objects were extracted and the frescoes detached, the villas were buried again. Most of the finds from these early excavations are on display in various museums around the world, including Paris's Louvre and the Metropolitan Museum in New York. Of some 30 villas discovered in the area, one, the **Villa della Pisanella,** yielded a real treasure: over 1,000 gold coins, some jewelry, and a complete set of silverware, including richly decorated cups and pitchers. Most of this treasure is now in the Louvre.

Modern excavations are ongoing, and archeologists have learned a great deal about ancient Roman life. Farms were typically organized around a rural villa, with richly decorated apartments for the rare visits of the landlord, and larger quarters for the workmen and slaves.

Adjacent to the antiquarium (below), **Villa Regina** is the only local villa that was completely excavated, and with the aid of modern technology. Discovered in the 1970s, the villa is modest in size, but reflects the typical structure of Roman rural villas, with an elegant residential space for the owner and a farm producing wine and grains. The villa is now a sort of living museum: Vineyards have been replanted with historical accuracy, and the ancient *torcularium* (the room for pressing grapes) and the cellar, which had a capacity of 10,000 liters (over 2,600 gal.), have been replicated.

Sweet Stop

If you have a sweet tooth like us, you'll love the local specialty, the *zandraglia.* Sold at pastry shops in the area, this traditional treat is a large sweet cookie shaped like a butterfly. Dedicated to the pastry, the *Sagra della Zandraglia* is a fair that's held on the second Sunday of July. For the best *zandraglia,* head for **Vaiano,** with one shop near the excavations at Via Cirillo Emanuele 163 (© 081-5374372), and the other at Via Marra (© 081-8593732).

The sites of Boscoreale are part of the **Artecard** sites (see box in chapter 4, p. 100); you can also save on admission prices with the **3-day cumulative ticket,** which includes all the archaeological sites of the Vesuvian area: Herculaneum, Pompeii, Oplontis, Stabiae, and Boscoreale, for 20€ ($28/£14).

Antiquarium Nazionale Uomo e Ambiente nel Territorio Vesuviano *(Kids)*
Most of the recent finds from the local sites have been collected in this museum and divided into two sections. The first is dedicated to the running of a Roman farm, with exhibits on the techniques and objects related to agriculture and husbandry; the second focuses on architecture and, specifically, how these farming villas were structured differently than other Roman villas on the coast, which were solely dedicated to leisure.

Via Settetermini 15, Località Villaregina, Boscoreale. ⓒ 081-5368796. www.pompeiisites.org. Admission 5.50€ ($7.70/£3.85); includes same-day admission to excavations of Villa Regina, Oplonti, and Stabiae. Daily Nov 1–Mar 31 8:30am–6:30pm; Apr 1–Oct 31 8:30am–7:30pm. Last admission 90 min. earlier. Closed Jan 1, May 1, and Dec. 25.

4 Pompeii ★★★

27km (17 miles) SE of Naples

Pompeii is Italy's most famous archaeological site and with good reason: With an excavated area of 44 hectares (almost 109 acres), Pompeii is unique in the world. No other ancient town has been brought to light so completely. Discovered by chance during excavations for a canal in the 16th century, the ruins of Pompeii were not recognized for what they were until further explorations in the 18th century. Scientific excavations started only at the end of the 19th century, but continued steadily until most of the ancient town was uncovered and are still ongoing today. Based on calculation of the city walls—only partly excavated—Pompeii covered an area of 66 hectares (163 acres). Originally an Etruscan and then a Sannite town, it was colonized by the Romans in 80 B.C. At the time of the eruption, experts estimate the town counted about 35,000 inhabitants.

GETTING THERE   You can easily get to Pompeii by public transportation using the **Circumvesuviana railway** (ⓒ **800-053939;** www.vesuviana.it), which leaves from Naples's Stazione Circumvesuviana, Corso Garibaldi, off Piazza Garibaldi (Metro: Garibaldi). On the Sorrento line, get off at **Pompeii Villa dei Misteri,** only a few yards from the Porta Marina entrance to the archaeological area. If you take the Poggiomarino line, get off at **Pompeii Santuario,** in the center of Pompeii, only steps from the sanctuary and a couple hundred yards from the Piazza Anfiteatro entrance to the archaeological area. Trains leave every half-hour, and the 45-minute ride costs 2.50€ ($3.50/£1.75).

By **car,** take the autostrada A3 and exit at POMPEI OVEST or POMPEI EST. Follow the brown signs for POMPEI SCAVI.

EXPLORING POMPEII

In recent decades, the city of Pompeii was very depressed—run-down by cheap sprawl, slums, and the resultant petty crime. The town has experienced successful urban renewal, however, and visitors now can enjoy its other attractions. The **Santuario della Madonna del Rosario,** Piazza Bartolo Longo 1 (ⓒ **081-8577111;** www. santuario.it; Mon–Sat 6:15am–7:30pm; Sun and holidays 5:45am–8:30pm), is one of Italy's major religious centers dedicated to the Madonna, and a pilgrimage destination

Pompeii

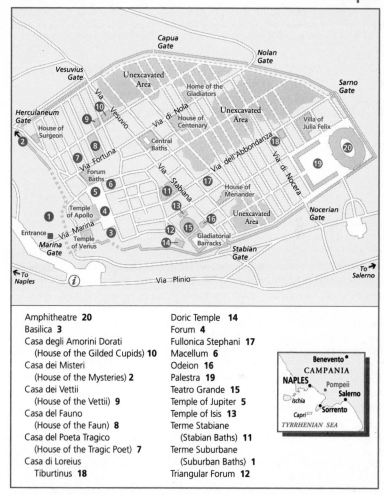

Amphitheatre **20**
Basilica **3**
Casa degli Amorini Dorati
   (House of the Gilded Cupids) **10**
Casa dei Misteri
   (House of the Mysteries) **2**
Casa dei Vettii
   (House of the Vettii) **9**
Casa del Fauno
   (House of the Faun) **8**
Casa del Poeta Tragico
   (House of the Tragic Poet) **7**
Casa di Loreius
   Tiburtinus **18**

Doric Temple **14**
Forum **4**
Fullonica Stephani **17**
Macellum **6**
Odeion **16**
Palestra **19**
Teatro Grande **15**
Temple of Jupiter **5**
Temple of Isis **13**
Terme Stabiane
   (Stabian Baths) **11**
Terme Suburbane
   (Suburban Baths) **1**
Triangular Forum **12**

for Catholics worldwide. Built in the 19th century, the richly decorated sanctuary is well worth a visit. The attached buildings house a school and the offices of a number of important charities.

The archaeological area is, of course, the main attraction in Pompeii. Come prepared as the site is huge and a visit here is quite demanding in both time and energy. Bring comfortable shoes, a hat, sunscreen, and plenty of water. We also recommend taking a guided tour or, at least, purchasing the official guidebook, complete with itineraries and photographs, for sale at the bookstore located just beyond the ticket booth. Guidebooks are available in various languages, including English. The **Ufficio Scavi** (✆ **081-8575347;** www.pompeiisites.org) offers thematic guided tours that are fascinating; they each focus on one aspect of the town's life, and some of them are seasonal—such as the **Vendemmia (Grape Harvest),** where you can visit the vineyards

Treading Lightly on Mt. Vesuvius

Stand at the bottom of the great market-place of Pompeii, and look up at the silent streets . . . over the broken houses with their inmost sanctuaries open to the day, away to Mount Vesuvius, bright and snowy in the peaceful distance; and lose all count of time, and heed of other things, in the strange and melancholy sensation of seeing the Destroyed and the Destroyer making this quiet picture in the sun.

—Charles Dickens, *Pictures from Italy*

A volcano that has struck terror in Campania, the towering, pitch-black **Mt. Vesuvius** looms menacingly over the Bay of Naples. August 24, A.D. 79, is the infamous date when Vesuvius burst forth and buried Pompeii, Herculaneum, and Stabiae under ash and volcanic mud. Vesuvius has erupted periodically ever since (thousands were killed in 1631): The last major spouting of lava occurred in the 20th century (it blew off the ring of its crater in 1906). The last spectacular eruption was on March 31, 1944. The approach to Vesuvius is dramatic, with the terrain growing foreboding as you near the top. Along the way you'll see villas rising on its slopes, and vineyards—the grapes produce an amber-colored wine known as Lacrimae Christi (Tears of Christ); the citizens of ancient Pompeii enjoyed wine from here, as excavations have revealed. Closer to the summit, the soil becomes puce-colored and an occasional wildflower appears.

It might sound like a dubious invitation (Vesuvius, after all, is an active volcano), but it's possible to visit the rim of the crater's mouth. As you look down into its smoldering core, you might recall that Spartacus, a century before the eruption that buried Pompeii, hid in the hollow of the crater, which was then covered with vines.

The **Parco Nazionale del Vusuvio** contains an **Observatory** (© 081-6108483) at 608m (1,994 ft.). It's the oldest in the world, dating from 1841. Charging 4.50€ ($5.85/£3) for admission, the park is open daily from 9am until sunset.

To reach Vesuvius from Naples, take the Circumvesuviana Railway or (summer only) bus service from Piazza Vittoria, which hooks up with bus connections at Pugliano. You get off the train at the Ercolano station, the 10th stop. Some bus or van will generally be on hand to take you from Herculaneum to the top. Negotiate the price before getting in, however. Once at the top, you must be accompanied by a guide, which will cost 6€ ($7.80/£4). Assorted willing tour guides are found in the bus parking lot; they are available from 9am to about 4pm. For details, contact **Guide Vulcanologiche** (© 081-7775720).

that produce an excellent red wine (the *Villa dei Misteri* label), using the techniques of 2,000 years ago. You can reserve these and other guided tours at © **081-8616405,** or online at www.arethusa.net.

The archaeological area of Pompeii is a participant in the **Artecard** program (see box in chapter 4, p. 100).

The Excavations (Scavi) ✹✹✹   In Roman times, Pompeii was an important industrial and commercial town, with a complex layered society, which is reflected in the urban structures on view today. Besides elegant villas belonging to the richer citizens, there were blocks of more modest housing, as well as many shops, restaurants, hotels, and public buildings. The eruption covered Pompeii with volcanic ash and pumice stone, a much lighter material than in Herculaneum; therefore, the survivors of the disaster were able to retrieve some of their possessions, leaving less behind than in other locations. This also made it easier for the site to be excavated—and, unfortunately looted—in more recent centuries. You will recognize the different excavation styles: In the 19th and early 20th century, precious mosaics and frescoes were carefully detached and placed on display in museums; the contemporary approach is to leave everything *in situ* to depict the town as it must have been.

Surrounded by walls, the city was much closer to the sea than it is now, as the water has receded substantially since the days of the eruption. Pompeii had three centers of civic life: the **Forum;** the **Triangular Forum** with the **Theater District;** and the complex with the **Amphitheatre** and the **Palestra.** The rest of town was residential and commercial. Streets were lined with small shops and taverns, and the walls were covered with red writing advertising the candidates to the local elections. You'll also see black charcoal graffiti, and painted signs for bars and shops. All these are still visible in the area of the so-called **Nuovi Scavi** (considered to be new excavations, although they started around 1911!) to the southeast of town.

The **Forum** is a large rectangular open space covering over 17,400 sq. m. (58,000 sq. ft.) and surrounded by a portico on three sides. On the fourth is the **Temple of Jupiter,** from the 2nd century B.C., built over a high foundation. The Forum was decorated with bronze and marble statues of important citizens, but the niches stand empty because their objects were taken away shortly after the tragedy in A.D. 79. On the Forum opened the **Macellum,** the covered food market. At the opposite side, opening onto the street, was the **Basilica,** the largest building in town, which housed the meeting hall and tribunal.

The **Triangular Forum**—so called because of its shape—is another large area that was once surrounded by a portico. In the middle are the ruins of the **Doric Temple** from the 6th century B.C. This was the heart of the **Theater District,** with the beautiful **Teatro Grande** ✹ from the 2nd century B.C. to the east, which could hold an audience of 5,000 for the most important theatrical representations. Farther on is the **Odeion,** or Small Theater, from the 1st century B.C., for music and mime shows, which could hold 1,000 spectators. Nearby is the **Temple of Isis** ✹, one of the best-conserved temples to this goddess to survive from antiquity. Also nearby are the **Terme Stabiane (Stabian Baths)** ✹, one of the town's three **public bath** establishments and among the finest conserved ancient baths in the world, with well-preserved decorations in mosaic, painting, and marble.

From the Forum, you can take **Via dell'Abbondanza,** the town's main commercial street, lined with shops of all kinds and leading to the southeast of town, the most recently excavated area. One of the most curious shops is the **Fullonica Stephani ("Stephen's Dry-Cleaning");** the shop is on the ground floor and the owner's apartment on the second. Farther on is the **Casa di Loreius Tiburtinus,** with an elegant internal **loggia** ✹ bordering a long pool and decorated with small marble statues; at the end is the **Triclinium** with two beautiful **paintings** ✹✹. At the end of the road to the right is the complex with the **Palestra,** where sports events were held, with a grandiose swimming pool and surrounded by plane trees (you can see the plaster casts of the stumps). Farther on is the **Amphitheatre,** the oldest Roman amphitheater in the world, built in 80 B.C., with seating for 1,000 people.

Among the other famous private houses here is the elegant **Casa dei Vettii (House of the Vettii),** with its magnificent paintings belonging to two rich merchants; they had just redecorated after the damages caused by the earthquake in A.D. 62, so all of the paintings were in excellent shape. Besides several small paintings in a number of rooms in the house, you'll find the magnificent **frescoed Triclinium (Dining Room)** 🎭🎭, where you'll see figures and *amorini* (cupids) on Pompeiian red-and-black backgrounds. Nearby is the **Casa del Fauno (House of the Faun),** the largest of private homes—it takes up an entire city block. This was an exquisite mansion, whose finest decorative pieces are now in the Museo Nazionale Archeologico in Naples. Also renowned (though again, most of its paintings have been moved to Naples's museums), is the **Casa del Poeta Tragico (House of the Tragic Poet),** with its famous CAVE CANEM (Beware of Dog) mosaic by the entrance; the mosaic is oft replicated, and the warning has been adopted by homeowners the world over.

Some of the houses, such as the **Casa dell'Ara Massima,** or the **Casa degli Amorini Dorati (House of the Gilded Cupids)** 🎭 are accessible only by guided tour with advance reservations. You must sign up at ✆ 081-8616405, or online at www.arethusa.net. If you are signing up for more than one tour, keep in mind that it might take more than 30 minutes to walk between the various sites.

Two entrances: Porta Marina, Via Villa dei Misteri; or Piazza Anfiteatro, Pompeii. ✆ 081-8575347. www.pompeii sites.org. Guided tours reservations ✆ 081-8616405 or online at www.arethusa.net. Admission 11€ ($15/£7.70). Daily Nov 1–Mar 31 8:30am–5pm; Apr 1–Oct 31 8:30am–7:30pm. Last admission 90 min. earlier. Guided tours daily Nov 1–Mar 31 9am–4pm; Apr 1–Oct 31 9am–7pm. Closed Jan 1, May 1, and Dec 25.

Casa dei Misteri (House of the Mysteries) 🎭🎭🎭

From the Forum you can take the Via Consolare to the Via dei Sepolcri—a road lined with funerary monuments that leads outside the city walls toward the Porto Ercolano, Pompeii's harbor (about a 1km/½-mile walk). There you'll find the most noteworthy suburban villa of Pompeii, famous both for its architecture—a dramatic terrace built over steeply sloping ground—and its paintings. Built in the 2nd century B.C. and restored around 60 B.C. and then again before the eruption, the villa was decorated with all three styles of Pompeiian paintings. Its most famous is the large **fresco** on the wall of what was probably a *triclynium* (dining room), depicting several figures on a red background participating in a ceremony thought to be related to the cult of Dionysus (Bacchus).

Via dei Sepolcri, off Via Consolare, outside Pompeii's walls, Pompeii. ✆ 081-8575347. www.pompeiisites.org. Guided tours reservations ✆ 081-8616405 or online at www.arethusa.net. Admission included in purchase of ticket to Pompeii's Scavi. Daily Nov 1–Mar 31 8:30am–5pm; Apr 1–Oct 31 8:30am–7:30pm. Last admission 90 min. earlier. Closed Jan 1, May 1, and Dec 25.

Terme Suburbane (Suburban Baths) 🎭🎭

Located outside the walls of Pompeii, off Porta Marina to the north, these privately owned thermal baths were opened to the public in 2002 after lengthy restoration. Much looted over the centuries, they were the newest of the bath establishments in Pompeii and the most unusual. Contrary to the traditional Roman custom, the baths are "mixed," for both men and women. The interior holds beautiful **frescoes** and **mosaic** decorations, including some that are curiously erotic: One shows a homosexual scene between women, unique in Roman iconography.

Via Villa dei Misteri, Pompeii. ✆ 081-8575347. www.pompeiisites.org. Guided tours reservations ✆ 081-8616405 or online at www.arethusa.net. Admission included in entrance to Pompeii's Scavi. Visits by guided tour daily 10am–1:30pm (advance reservation required). Closed Jan 1, May 1, and Dec 25.

Virtual Pompei *(Kids)*   An interesting thing to do before or after visiting the archaeological area is to check out a reconstruction of the ancient town to see how it must have looked before the eruption. The 3-D films are quite well made and seemingly bring the place back to life. In addition, demonstrations of ancient Roman craft making are given by live artists.

Via Plinio 105, 100 yards from the entrance to the archaeological area of Porta Marina, Pompeii. ✆/fax 081-8610500. www.virtualpompeii.it. 7€ ($9.80/£4.90) for 1 show, 12€ ($17/£8.40) for 2. 10% discount with Artecard. Daily 11:30am–5pm.

WHERE TO STAY

We used to recommend that visitors not stay in Pompeii overnight. The town has notably improved, though, and quite a few nice hotels are convenient to the ruins. You should still be careful, though, and avoid night strolls along deserted streets, as in any urban area.

MODERATE

Hotel Forum *(★) (Kids)*   More elegant than the Bristol, this family-run hotel is quite close to the excavations and convenient to the Santuario as well. Guest rooms are individually decorated, some with tiled floors, others with wooden floors; all have modern quality furnishings and good-size bathrooms. Some rooms open onto the garden, while the suites afford panoramic views over the excavations or Vesuvius, and have Jacuzzi tubs in their bathrooms. The largest rooms, which can accommodate up to five guests, are a good choices for families.

Via Roma 99, 80045 Pompeii. ✆ 081-8501170. Fax 081-8506132. www.hotelforum.it. 36 units. 120€ ($168/£84) double; 170€ ($238/£119) suite. Rates include buffet breakfast. Children 2 and under stay free in parent's room. AE, DC, MC, V. Free parking. **Amenities:** Bar; babysitting; concierge; free Internet point in lobby; lounge. *In room:* A/C, satellite TV, hair dryer, minibar, safe.

Hotel Maiuri *(★★)*   Although farther from the ruins and from the center of modern Pompeii than the other hotels we recommend, this is the best hotel in town, providing excellent and quiet accommodations at a moderate price. The hotel is modern, with completely soundproofed guest rooms opening onto the hotel's pleasant garden. All rooms are good-size, with quality modern furniture and small balconies; most have tiled floors. A number of rooms are dedicated nonsmoking rooms. The hotel provides free parking near the archaeological area for its guests as well as a shuttle bus to and from Naples's airport (for a fee).

Via Acquasalsa 20, 80045 Pompeii. ✆ 081-8562716. Fax 081-8562716. www.maiuri.it. 30 units. 110€ ($154/£77) double. Rates include buffet breakfast. Extra bed 30€ ($42/£21). Children 2 and under stay free in parent's room. AE, DC, MC, V. Free parking. **Amenities:** Restaurant; bar; babysitting; business center; concierge; laundry service; room service; Wi-Fi. *In room:* A/C, satellite TV, hair dryer, minibar, safe.

INEXPENSIVE

Hotel Bristol *(Kids)*   This modern hotel is not far from the town center and the archaeological area, and it's quite close to the Santuario. Family-run, it offers both courteous and personalized service in a relaxed and welcoming ambience. Guest rooms are large and simply appointed, with large modern bathrooms—both bed- and bathrooms are tiled. They also have a few double rooms, which are suitable for families.

Piazza Vittorio Veneto 1, 80045 Pompeii. ⓒ 081-8503005. Fax 081-8631625. www.hotelbristolpompei.com. 50 units. 90€ ($126/£63) double; 130€ ($182/£91) suite. Rates include buffet breakfast. Children 2 and under stay free in parent's room. AE, DC, MC, V. Free parking. **Amenities:** Restaurant; bar; babysitting; business center; concierge; room service. *In room:* A/C, TV, hair dryer, minibar, safe.

Hotel Villa dei Misteri   This old-fashioned family-run hotel has the advantage of being right at the excavations. Built in the 1930s, it has a certain charm and is an excellent choice if you don't mind lacking some in-room amenities. Guest rooms are spacious and well-appointed, with modern quality furnishings and tiled floors; some have private balconies. Some of the rooms overlook the amphora-shaped pool, while others overlook the street. If you want one of the few rooms that has A/C (for which there is an additional charge), you must book well in advance; and the hotel's phone service does not allow any external calls (in or out). The staff, though, is extremely kind. Amenities include an outdoor swimming pool and a good restaurant.

Via Villa dei Misteri 11, 80045 Pompeii. ⓒ **081-8613593.** Fax 081-8622983. www.villadeimisteri.it. 40 units. 70€ ($98/£49) double. Children 2 and under stay free in parent's room. DC, MC, V. Free parking. **Amenities:** Restaurant (closed Nov 1–Feb 28); lounge; outdoor pool. *In room:* A/C (10€/$14/£7) in some rooms.

WHERE TO DINE

Most establishments in Pompeii are tourist joints catering to large groups of visitors from around the world. The following restaurants have their share of tourist groups but are also favored by locals for their high-quality food.

EXPENSIVE

Il Principe ✹✹ NEAPOLITAN/ANCIENT ROMAN   With a dining room that attempts to create a modern version of Pompeii's luxury, this is the best restaurant in the area. Right in the center of town, it provides excellent food, a lively atmosphere, and also offers outdoor dining. The owner is a real epicurean; besides many creative and traditional dishes, the seasonal menu includes a choice of tasty ancient Roman recipes, such as the *lagane al garum* (homemade egg-free pasta with an anchovy-paste sauce). More modern choices include excellent spaghetti *alle vongole* (with baby clams) and delicious *maccheroni* with zucchini and prawns.

Piazza Bartolo Longo. ⓒ **081-8505566.** www.ilprincipe.com. Reservations recommended. Secondi 15€–24€ ($21–$34/£11–£17). AE, DC, MC, V. Tues–Sun 12:30–3pm and Tues–Sat 8–11pm.

Ristorante President ✹ NEAPOLITAN   This is the most upscale place to eat in the area, offering gourmet food and great service. In addition to the wine list you'll be offered a water list, a beer list, a cheese list, and a honey and dried fruit list, as well as the more traditional dessert menu. The food is seasonal and focuses on seafood, with appetizers like smoked swordfish or tuna and, delicious pasta dishes such as the *paccheri allo scorfano, zucchine e vongole* (fresh homemade flat pasta with scorpion-fish, zucchini, and clams). The *secondi,* which come with a vegetable side dish—unusual for Italy, but most welcome—include a large choice of fish masterfully prepared either au gratin, or baked in a salt crust. Desserts are excellent and strictly homemade.

Piazza Schettino 12. ⓒ **081-8507245.** www.ristorantepresident.it. Reservations recommended on weekends. Secondi 12€–25€ ($17–$35/£8.40–£18). AE, DC, MC, V. Tues–Sun noon–3pm and Tues–Sat 7:30–11:30pm. Closed 2 weeks in Aug and 3 days for Christmas.

MODERATE

Lucullus Attempting to recreate the kind of atmosphere its namesake would have approved of—Lucullus was famous for his love of luxury and good food—this restaurant is decorated with palm trees and copies of Roman statues. The large outdoor dining area is a plus during the summer season. We love their large buffet of *antipasti*, ranging from seafood to vegetable dishes, the excellent fresh fettuccine *ai funghi* (with mushrooms), and the scrumptious grilled meats.

Via Plinio 129. ℂ 081-8613055. www.ristorantelucullus.it. Reservations recommended on weekends. Secondi 7€– 15€ ($9.80–$21/£4.90–£11). AE, DC, MC, V. Wed–Mon noon–3pm and 7–11pm.

INEXPENSIVE

Zi Caterina ⭐ *(Kids* NEAPOLITAN/PIZZA A cheaper choice than those reviewed above, this restaurant is conveniently located between the Scavi and the center of town. It offers well-prepared, traditional food and welcoming service, which appeals to locals. Try the vegetable appetizers, as well as the excellent *spaghetti alle vongole* (with clams), or the very good pizza, which is prepared for lunch as well as for dinner.

Via Roma 20. ℂ 081-8507447. www.zicaterinapompei.it. Reservations recommended on weekends. Secondi 6€– 15€ ($8.40–$21/£4.20–£11). AE, DC, MC, V. Daily noon–10:30pm.

6

The Land of Sirens:
Sorrento & its Peninsula

The unique beauty of Sorrento's coast has inspired many myths: This, for instance, is where the Sirens are said to have waylaid travelers with their irresistible song, as happened to Ulysses in Homer's *Odyssey*. Today, the pull of the sea and imposing rock-bound coast remain as strong as in Homer's day, attracting legions of visitors. Indeed, it is unlikely that you will feel alone here, especially if you come during the summer months. Sorrento's charms are not tarnished by the crowds, though, as the town is only made merrier by the bustle. You will also always find many off-the-beaten-path attractions along this peninsula, which is simply one of the most beautiful in the Mediterranean. A rocky point of land jutting into the sea and dominated by the high mountains of Monti Lattari, the Sorrentine peninsula stretches for about 20km (13 miles). It is a finger of land pointing to Capri—which is only 5km (3 miles) away at Punta Campanella, the closest point—and dividing the Gulf of Naples from the Gulf of Salerno. Visitors come here to hike rugged paths, discover towers and rural villages, explore ancient ruins, and

sample a cuisine rich with locally produced ingredients, including cheeses and cured meats so good they don't make it to the rest of the mainland.

The gateway to the Sorrento peninsula is **Castellammare di Stabia,** a modern town and thermal resort built over the ancient Roman settlement of Stabiae. **Sorrento** is the main town of the peninsula, located about midway to the tip on the northern shore, opening onto the Gulf of Naples. On the mountains above Sorrento and on the cliffs beyond are many villages connected by winding—and often bumpy—narrow local roads, which remain undiscovered precisely because of their inaccessibility. On the other side of the mountains is a very authentic and little-explored stretch of coast. Harsh and rocky, it is the continuation of the famous Amalfi Coast—which starts at Positano (see chapter 7)—and of the Sorrentine peninsula's southern shore. As happens so often in Italy, even in the midst of celebrated attractions and hordes of tourists, you'll find yourself only a stone's throw from quieter byways and hidden pleasures.

1 Castellammare di Stabia ★

33km (20 miles) SE of Naples

If you have a taste for restful and leisurely sightseeing, then the town of Castellammare di Stabia is the place for you. Opening like a fan onto the Bay of Naples, the town enjoys a beautiful location between beaches and hills. It is blessed with several natural springs—28 of them, each with its own therapeutic characteristics—that have

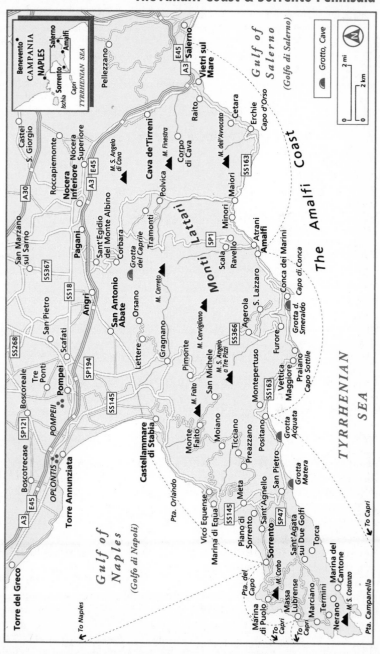

The Amalfi Coast & Sorrento Peninsula

made Castellammare a popular resort since antiquity. It was then called Stabiae, and Cicero, among other prominent Romans, used to spend his vacations here until the eruption of A.D. 79 obliterated the town. The settlement was reborn after the disaster, but its inhabitants were forced to take refuge in the mountains to escape from the incursions of Goths and Longobards. In the 9th century, the citizens build Castrum a Mare, the castle that lent the town its modern name. The Angevin dynasty later surrounded the town with walls, enlarged its harbor, and built the Royal Palace for the king's vacations. The Bourbons subsequently created a prosperous shipyard that fueled the development of the town. Today, it remains one of the most important shipyards in Italy.

ESSENTIALS

GETTING THERE & AROUND   The most scenic method of travel to Castellammare is the ferry: **Metro del Mare** (© 199-600700; www.metrodelmare.com) offers regular sailings from Pozzuoli, Naples, and Sorrento (service is suspended in winter). You can arrive via **Circumvesuviana** (© 800-053939; www.vesuviana.it) railroad from Naples and nearby towns. Trains leave from Stazione Circumvesuviana (Corso Garibaldi, off Piazza Garibaldi; Metro: Garibaldi). Take the Sorrento line and get off at Castellammare; departures are every half-hour and the 35-minute ride costs 2.40€ ($3.35/£1.70). You can also use the national rail service of **FFSS** (© 892021 from anywhere in Italy; www.trenitalia.it), but you'll need to switch to the local train in Torre Annunziata.

You can also take a **SITA** (© 081-5522176; www.sitabus.it) bus toward Sorrento from Naples or the Capodichino Airport; it stops in Castellammare di Stabia. By **car,** take autostrada A3, exiting the highway at CASTELLAMMARE DI STABIA; once on SS 145, follow the CASTELLAMMARE DI STABIA signs directly into town.

The best way to get around town is by taxi. As elsewhere in Italy, drivers don't cruise for customers but can be called at one of the taxi stands, at Piazza Matteotti (© 081-8706251) and Piazza Unità d'Italia (© 081-8710577).

VISITOR INFORMATION   The **tourist office,** Piazza Matteotti 34; 80053 Castellammare di Stabia (© 081-8711334; www.stabiatourism.it), provides information on all things Castellammare, from spas to archaeology. You'll find a **pharmacy** at Via Plinio il Vecchio 62 (© 081-8701077). The **hospital,** Ospedale San Leonardo, is on Viale Europa (© 081-8729111). Dial © **118** for an **ambulance** and © **113** or © **112** for the **police.** The **post office,** Piazza Giovanni XXIII 4 (© 081-8711449), is open Monday to Saturday from 8am to 2pm. For your banking needs, **Banco San Paolo** is at Corso Vittorio Emanuele 76 (© 081-8713501).

EXPLORING THE TOWN

Modern in appearance, Castellammare prides itself on a number of worthy attractions. We highly recommend an excursion up **Monte Faito** ✦, the tall mountain (1,100m/3,608 ft. high) looming over Castellammare and the sea: You'll enjoy unrivaled views over the Gulf of Naples. Although you can drive, we'd much rather take the **funicular (funivia)** from the center of town (Piazza Stazione Circumvesuviana). It runs every half-hour, and the round-trip fare is 7€ ($9.80/£4.90). You can return via funivia, but it is also quite pleasant to hike down (consider about an hour for the descent). We also encourage a visit to the thermal spas. If you have only 1 day to dedicate to a spa, make it **Nuove Terme Stabiane** ✦, Viale delle Terme 3 (© 081-391311; www.termedistabia.com). This state-of-the-art establishment is located on the slopes

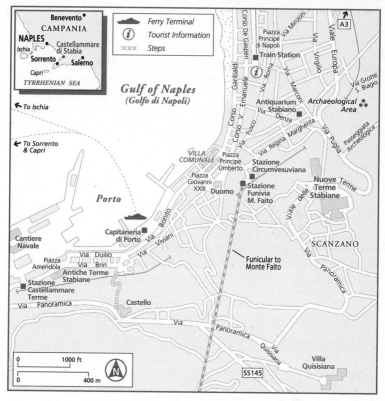

Benevento
CAMPANIA
NAPLES
Castellammare
di Stabia
Ischia
Sorrento
Salerno
Capri
TYRRHENIAN SEA

Ferry Terminal
Tourist Information
Steps

Gulf of Naples
(Golfo di Napoli)

← To Ischia

← To Sorrento
& Capri

Porto

Corso De Gaspari
Garibaldi
Corso Vittorio Emanuele
Corso G. Fusco
Via Minzoni
Via Roma
Via Marconi
Piazza
Principe
di Napoli
Train Station

Antiquarium
Via Stabiano
Denza

Via Virgilio
Via Grotte
S. Biagio

Archaeological
Area

Via Regina Margherita
Via Puglia
Passeggiata Archeologica

VILLA
COMUNALE
Piazza
Principe
Umberto
Piazza
Giovanni
XXIII   Duomo

Stazione
Circumvesuviana

Stazione
Funivia
M. Faito

Nuove Terme
Stabiane

Capitaneria
di Porto

Cantiere
Navale

Piazza
Amendola

Via Duilio
Via Brin
Antiche Terme
Stabiane

Stazione
Castellammare
Terme

Via Panoramica

Castello

Via Bonito
Via Viviani

Funicular to
Monte Faito

SCANZANO

Via Panoramica

Viale delle Terme

Via Panoramica
Via Quisisana

Villa
Quisisana

SS145

0   1000 ft
0   400 m

of Monte Faito, below **Villa Quisisana,** the royal palace originally built by King Carlo II d'Angiò for his vacations and later restored by Ferdinando I di Borbone in 1820. At an altitude of 173m (567 ft.), it was immediately dubbed the *Casa Sana,* or "Healthy House," for the renowned healing qualities of the region; the name later evolved into "Qui Si Sana" (meaning "Here One Heals"). The idea is that the spa benefits from the same advantages. Its waters are recommended for digestive ailments and skin problems, but you'll find beauty and relaxation treatments as well.

Antiche Terme Stabiane, Piazza Amendola 18, off Via Brin (© **081/391336;** Mon–Sat 7am–1pm)—built in 1827 for King Ferdinando IV—is noteworthy as the oldest spa in town and for its location on the seashore near the harbor. Its waters herald from 17 different natural sulfur springs that descend from Monte Faito, with temperatures between 14°C and 17°C (57°F–67°F). The original building was torn down and replaced with the current building in 1956.

Downtown, **Villa Comunale,** off Piazza Giovanni XXIII, near the Stazione Circumvesuviana (free admission; open from sunrise to sunset) is a public garden that opens onto the Gulf of Naples. Not to be missed is the elegant **Cassa Armonica** (bandstand)—a Liberty masterpiece created by Eugenio Cosenza in 1901.

Scavi di Stabia ⚔ This archaeological area contains the remains of Stabiae, the ancient Roman resort town destroyed in the same eruption as the more famous

Pompeii and Herculaneum. While 18th-century excavations removed much of the art that was found—most of it is now on display in the Archaeological Museum of Naples—modern digs have uncovered additional artifacts since the 1950s. We recommend a visit to the **Villa di Arianna** ⚘, Via Piana di Varano (from town, take Viale Europa and turn left onto the SS 366 toward Gragnano, and then immediately left again onto Via Piana di Varano), a typical example of an ancient Roman patrician villa that takes its name from a painting found inside: a beautiful **fresco** depicting the mythological Ariadne as she is discovered sleeping by Dyonisius. In a dramatic location, the villa was designed to take maximum advantage of the views over the sea and Mount Faito. Though partly ransacked in the 18th century after its discovery, the villa retains much of its decorative elements: Of particular beauty are the frescos in the summer *triclinium* **(dining room)**—the one of Ariadne described above and another depicting Ganimede taken by an eagle up to Jupiter—and the room decorated with diagonal stripes of delicately **painted tiles**—only a few remain as many have been removed (some can be seen at the archaeological museum in Naples). You should also visit **Villa di San Marco** ⚘, Via Passeggiata Archeologica, a very impressive patrician villa (in spite of the damages it suffered in the earthquake of 1980), with a great number of rooms and splendid views. The villa takes its name from the small 18th-century church that was built inside its walls. Built in the 1st century B.C. as the residence of a rich family, it was later enlarged in the 1st century A.D. and became quite palatial, with porticos, halls, and private thermal baths (in three temperatures: *calidarium, tepidarium,* and *frigidarium*), all decorated with stucco, paintings, and frescoes.

Within walking distance, you'll find the **Grotta di San Biagio** (St. Biagio's Grotto), a tufa-stone quarry—used in Roman times for the construction of the villas in Stabiae—that was transformed into a paleochristian oratory in the 5th to 6th centuries A.D. The first bishops of Stabiae are buried here, making it one of the oldest known Christian burial sites. It is decorated with well-preserved frescoes and paintings that date from the 5th to 6th centuries and from the 9th to 10th centuries A.D., except for three frescoes by the entrance which are from the 14th century.

The **Antiquarium Stabiano,** Via Marco Mario 2 (closed for restoration) holds the findings from those excavations which were not left *in situ. Note:* At presstime, **Villa Quisisana** (see above) had been chosen as the new location for the museum, but efforts for the restoration of the historical palace are advancing very slowly. Check with the local tourist office before your visit.

Via Passeggiata Archeologica (follow directions for Grand Hotel La Medusa). ℰ 081-8575347. www.pompeiisites. org. Admission 5.50€ ($7.70/£3.85); includes same-day admission to Boscoreale and Oplonti. **Artecard** discount available (see chapter 4, p. 100); you can also save on admission price by purchasing the **3-day cumulative ticket** that includes Herculaneum, Pompeii, Oplontis, Stabiae, and Boscoreale for 20€ ($28/£14). Daily Nov 1–Mar 31, 8:30am–6:30pm; Apr 1–Oct 31 8:30am–7:30pm. Last admission 90 min. earlier. Closed Jan 1, May 1, and Dec. 25.

WHERE TO STAY

In addition to the suggestions below, a new **Crowne Plaza** (ℰ **081-3946700;** fax 081-3946770; www.crowneplaza.com) just opened in a former cement factory by the sea in Pozzano, with an amazing location beneath a cliff.

EXPENSIVE

Grand Hotel La Medusa ⚘   This luxury hotel has the best setting in town: In a beautifully restored 19th-century villa surrounded by a splendid park and terraced garden, it is simply picture perfect and oh so romantic. It is convenient to the archaeological area, albeit farther from the center of town and the shore. The hotel features plush public spaces and salons, and elegantly appointed guest rooms, which are decorated with a sophisticated mix of classic and modern furnishings, beautiful tiled floors, and Oriental carpets, as well as fine linens and fabrics. Bathrooms are good-sized and the best rooms have Jacuzzi tubs and views over the Gulf of Naples. We recommend upgrading to a superior or a deluxe room as the "traditional" ones are a bit dark.

Via Passeggiata Archeologica 5, 80053 Castellammare di Stabia. © **081-8723383.** Fax 081-8717009. www.lamedusa hotel.com. 52 units. High season 190€–210€ ($266–$294/£133–£147) double; 280€ ($392/£196) suite. Rates include buffet breakfast. Extra bed 45€ ($63/£32). AE, DC, MC, V. Free parking. **Amenities:** Restaurant; 2 bars; babysitting; business center; concierge; laundry service; outdoor pool; outdoor tennis courts; room service. *In room:* A/C, satellite TV, hair dryer, minibar, safe.

MODERATE

Hotel dei Congressi 🟊 *(Kids*   This highly service-oriented establishment is conveniently across from the Nuove Terme Stabiane and a short distance from the archaeological area. In a more modern building than La Medusa above, the hotel offers spacious public spaces, including a large swimming pool and a pleasant terrace garden. Guest rooms are large and bright, each with a private balcony large enough for a table and chairs. The furnishings are tasteful, and rooms have tiled floors and ample modern bathrooms. The best rooms share superb panoramic views with the terraced swimming pool. The triple and quad rooms are a plus for those traveling with families.

Viale Puglia 45, 80053 Castellammare di Stabia. ©/fax **081-8722277.** www.hoteldeicongressi.it. 84 units. 120€–150€ ($168–$210/£84–£105) double; 220€ ($308/£154) suite. Rates include buffet breakfast. Children 2 and under stay free in parent's room. AE, DC, MC, V. Free parking. **Amenities:** Restaurant; bar; babysitting; business center; concierge; same-day laundry service; outdoor pool; room service. *In room:* A/C, satellite TV, hair dryer, minibar, safe.

Hotel Stabia 🟊   Serving guests since 1876 and offering professional service and fine accommodations, this fetchingly pink hotel is the best of Castellammare's historic establishments. Built in the 19th century along the downtown seaside promenade, the hotel was carefully restored to preserve its neoclassical style. Both common spaces and guest rooms have been redecorated, but much of the original furnishings has been incorporated into the design, inspiring a sense of peaceful elegance. Guest rooms are spacious with black-and-white tiled floors and neoclassical furnishings; many rooms have their own small balconies or terraces sharing views of Monte Faito or—the best rooms—of the Gulf of Naples and Ischia.

Corso Vittorio Emanuele 101, 80053 Castellammare di Stabia. © **081-8722577.** Fax 081-8722105. www.hotel stabia.com. 97 units. 120€ ($168/£84) double. Rates include buffet breakfast. AE, DC, MC, V. Free parking. **Amenities:** Restaurant; bar; babysitting; piano bar. *In room:* A/C, satellite TV, hair dryer, minibar, safe.

WHERE TO DINE
MODERATE

Giovanni di Pozzano 🟊 *(Finds* SORRENTINE/SEAFOOD   Adored by locals, this traditional restaurant offers dining rooms and outdoor terraces invigorated by live music on weekend evenings. The menu changes with the season, but fresh homemade pasta and seafood are particularly well-prepared year-round. We highly recommend the cavatelli *alle vongole* (with clams) and the *pezzogna al sale* (local fish baked in a salt crust).

Via Vecchia Pozzano 40. © **081-8026101.** Reservations recommended on weekend evenings. Secondi 12€–18€ ($17–$25/£8.40–£25). AE, DC, MC, V. Wed–Mon noon–3pm and 7:30–11pm.

Tolino dal 1816 🟊🟊 SORRENTINE/PIZZA   This historic restaurant has not lost its touch over the ages. Locals and visitors alike come to enjoy the indoor and outdoor dining as well as the pleasant piano bar. The cuisine is traditional with a focus on seafood, but you'll also find vegetarian and meat choices on the menu. We recommend their linguine *con le zucchine* (with zucchini) and the great *impepata di cozze* (steamed mussels with white pepper). The pizza is also very good.

Corso Vittorio Emanuele 13. © **081-8711607.** Reservations recommended. Secondi 12€–21€ ($17–$29/£8.40–£15). AE, DC, MC, V. Wed–Mon 12:30–3:30pm and 8–11:30pm.

INEXPENSIVE

Osteria da Mena (Finds) SORRENTINE   This little osteria offers well-prepared local specialties in a relaxed atmosphere. The homemade pasta is very good—when in luck, you'll find excellent *scialatielli ai frutti di mare* (thick spaghetti with basil and shellfish)—and the *frittura* (deep-fried medley of seafood) is crisp and juicy. Meat often graces the seasonal menu, including excellent *pollo arrosto* (roasted chicken) and tender *arrosto di maiale* (pork roast).

Via Pietro Carrese 32. © **081-8713048.** Reservations recommended. Secondi 10€–18€ ($14–$25/£7–£13). No credit cards. Daily noon–3pm and 7:30–11pm.

Pignatiello (Finds) SORRENTINE/SEAFOOD   This authentic local hangout is a really excellent address for simple and traditional food. Family run, it always offers some turf dishes, but the surf is its main focus. We recommend the *insalata di polipo* (octopus salad) as an appetizer and the oven-roasted daily catch, with a homemade dessert to finish.

Via Alcide De Gasperi 207 © **081-8715100.** Reservations recommended. Secondi 8€–15€ ($11–$21/£5.60–£11). No credit cards. Daily noon–3pm and 7:30–11pm.

2 Vico Equense ★

42 km (26 miles) SE of Naples

Far less visited than larger and more famous Sorrento, Vico Equense is a pleasant seaside resort. Built on a tufa-stone platform overlooking the sea, the town has a strong personality and a charm that are not lost on Italian tourists, who seek it out especially in August. Foreign tourists are comparatively rare, which will make your stay feel even more special.

ESSENTIALS

GETTING THERE   You can easily reach Vico Equense by public transportation via the **Circumvesuviana Railway,** Stazione Circumvesuviana on Corso Garibaldi in Naples, off Piazza Garibaldi (© **800-053939;** www.vesuviana.it). Take the Sorrento line and get off at the Vico Equense station. Trains leave every 30 minutes for the 40-minute trip from Naples, and the ride costs about 3€ ($4.20/£2.10).

You can also board a **SITA bus** (© **081-5522176;** www.sitabus.it), with daily frequent service between Naples and Sorrento. The ride to Vico Equense takes about 45 minutes and costs 3.20€ ($4.50/£2.25). From Naples's airport, Capodichino, you can take one of the seven daily runs made by the **Curreri Viaggi** (© **081-8015420**) shuttle bus; the ride takes about 40 minutes and costs 6€ ($8.40/£4.20).

If you are coming by **car,** from the autostrada A1, switch to the A3, and take the exit CASTELLAMMARE DI STABIA. Follow the signs for VICO EQUENSE and SORRENTO to SS 145, the coastal road that leads to Vico Equense.

GETTING AROUND Vico is not a large town and everything is pretty much within **walking** distance, including the beaches and mountain trails. You can also call a **taxi** at ✆ 081-8015405, or go to the taxi stand on Piazza Umberto I.

VISITOR INFORMATION The **tourist office** is at Piazza Umberto I 119 (✆ 081-8015752; fax 081-8799351; www.vicoturismo.it). The **hospital** (✆ 081-8015465) is on Via D. Caccioppoli. You'll find a **pharmacy** on Via Roma 18 (✆ 081-8015525), and another on Corso Filangieri, as well as several **banks,** including a Banco di Napoli (✆ 081-8015915). For first aid, the hospital, or an ambulance, dial ✆ 081-8729103. You can call the **police** at ✆ 113 and the **fire department** at ✆ 115. The **post office** (✆ 081-8016811) is at Via San Ciro 57.

EXPLORING THE TOWN

Vico Equense is a very ancient town: Excavations have found remains going back to the 6th century B.C., proving the existence of Oscan, Etruscan, and Greek occupants (evidenced by the **Necropolis** of Via Nicotera). Named *Aequa* during Roman times, the town survived the eruption of A.D. 79 and flourished until it was destroyed by the Goths in 553. It was then reestablished as "Vico Equense" by the Angevins in the 12th century.

To discover the delightful medieval buildings of Vico Equense, take Via Filangieri off the main square, Piazza Umberto I, and turn right onto **Via Monsignor Natale,** the heart of the medieval town. Along this street, enter the splendid medieval court-yard at no. 3. Continuing on, you can enjoy the great view from **Largo dei Tigli,** and, retracing your steps to Vescovado, visit the **Chiesa dell'Annunziata,** Via Cattedrale (daily 8am–12:30pm and 3:30–7pm), a 14th-century church partially redone in the 17th century after the earthquake of 1688. In the upper part of town is a 13th-century castle, renovated and enlarged in later centuries. The town also enjoys some thermal springs, and we highly recommend a visit to the local spas (see below).

Scrajo Terme ✦ A thermal spa created in the 19th century, this is the best place in town to "take the waters." The old-fashioned jewel is a short distance from town, off SS 145 on a cliff overlooking the beach, and offers a wide range of treatments and therapies (fees starting at 24€/$34/£17). The public spaces overlook the shore in a cascade of terraces, and the spa has a delightful ambience. Swim from the private beach where the sulfur spring flows into the sea, creating a mineral mix with unique healing properties. The charming restaurant on the premises is housed in a Liberty-style (Italian Art Nouveau) hall, with a bar and attached terrace affording beautiful views over the sea. The spa also offers seven bright and well furnished guest rooms (150€–220€/$180–$264/£90–£132 double, including breakfast and access to the spa).

Via Luigi Serio 10 (SS 145), Località Scrajo, 80069 Vico Equense. ✆ 081-8015731. www.scrajoterme.it. AE, DC, MC, V. Daily 8am–8pm. Restaurant till 10pm.

STAYING ACTIVE

Vico offers many opportunities to explore the area's natural attractions, and enjoying the sea and the mountains is one of the best things to do in town. Across from the Municipio in the center of town, you can take **Via Castello Marina,** the steep old footpath that, descending through olive groves, will lead you to **Vico Marina.** There you will find small **beaches** hidden inside picturesque coves. One of the nicest is **Marina di Equa,** west of a defensive tower built in the 17th century.

Another great hike—but one that requires you to be moderately fit and is best accomplished with a good trail map (available from the tourist office in town)—is the old footpath to **Positano.** Although the area has been inhabited for thousands of years, the SS 163, the Amalfi Drive, dates only from 1840; before then, the footpaths were the only means of travel and communication on the peninsula. For centuries, residents trekked over mountain paths and commuted by boat to points along the coast. Walking the succession of trails to Positano will require about 3½ hours. Follow the directions for Ticciano until you reach the **bridge over the Milo;** there, on your left, you'll find a dirt road to the pass of **Santa Maria al Castello** (altitude 685m/2,247 ft.). Just before the church, to your left, is the connection to **Sentiero degli Dei (Trail of Gods)** toward Nocelle (see later in this chapter). Instead, turn left at the dirt track directly across from the church; this is the trail that leads to Positano. When you reach the fork, the western spur climbs to Monte Comune (altitude 877m/2,877 ft.), with its sweeping views; the eastern branch begins the descent to Positano. Along this trail are several tricky passages around points of rock, so look carefully at your map.

If you're feeling less adventurous, you may instead choose to visit one of the many *agriturismi* (farmhouses) in the area. These are great places to have lunch and to experience daily agricultural activities; or you can arrange an overnight stay. This area is also famous for its **beekeeping** farms: One our favorite places for a visit to the hives and a taste of the products is **Coop-Agrituristica La Ginestra,** Via Tessa 2, Santa Maria di Castello (🕾 **081-8023211**).

WHERE TO STAY

In addition to the hotels below, consider the agriturismo **Coop-Agrituristica La Ginestra,** mentioned above. They have a few nicely appointed rooms, and the food is delicious. The nightly rates are 130€ ($182/£91) for full board and 98€ ($137/£69) for breakfast only.

EXPENSIVE

Grand Hotel Angiolieri 🏵   Located outside Vico Equense in the village of Seiano, this grand villa was built in the 18th century on the ruins of an ancient Roman villa said to have belonged to Cicero. The restoration added a few questionable details (such as the frenetic harlequin paving), but, on the whole, the place is elegant and the views superb. Guest rooms are not large, but are attractive, with a complementary mix of contemporary furniture and classic details. Bathrooms are good size and very nicely styled with bright mosaic tiles. Their three best rooms and the suites have private terraces. The swimming pool in the park is a plus.

Via Santa Maria Vecchia 2, 80066 Seiano di Vico Equense. 🕾 **081-8029161.** Fax 081-8028558. www.grandhotel angiolieri.it. 40 units. 248€–487€ ($347–$682/£174–£341); suites 552€ ($773/£386) and up. Rates include buffet breakfast. Children 2 and under stay free in parent's room. AE, DC, MC, V. Parking 15€ ($21/£11). **Amenities:** Restaurant; outdoor pool. *In room:* A/C, TV, hair dryer; Internet; minibar; safe.

Hotel Capo La Gala 🏵   This 1950s hotel has reopened in April 2007 after a yearlong restoration. Built hugging the cliffs among olive groves and lemon-tree terraces overlooking the sea, it is our favorite place to stay in Vico. Thanks to the hotel's location by the seaside on a rocky cape that is a short distance from town, guest rooms enjoy a rare quiet. They are bright and tastefully decorated with streamlined modern furniture and local handpainted tiles; each has its own private balcony and great views. The outdoor swimming pool is filled from a natural spring of sulfur thermal water (the smell takes some getting used to but it is oh so good for your skin), and the rocky beach opens onto the clean water of the Tyrrenian Sea. Management might require a minimum stay of 3 nights during the months of July and August.

Via Luigi Serio 8, 1km before Vico coming from Castellammare. Scrajo Terme, 80069 Vico Equense. © 081-8015758. Fax 081-8798747. www.capolagala.com. 18 units. 300€ ($420/£210). Rates include buffet breakfast. AE, DC, MC, V. Free parking. **Amenities:** Restaurant; beach; laundry service; outdoor pool; room service; solarium. *In room:* A/C, satellite TV, hair dryer, minibar, safe, Wi-Fi. Closed 2 weeks in Nov.

MODERATE

Hotel Aequa *Finds* This hotel has been serving its guests in the heart of town by the medieval area since the 1940s, and its old-fashioned charm has only been enhanced by the renovations. The property is perched on the cliffs overlooking the sea and affords excellent views: We love gazing at Mount Vesuvius from under the glorious wisteria on the terrace. Guest rooms are spacious and well appointed with hardwood floors and classic furnishings; bathrooms are modern and good-sized.

Via Filangeri 46, 80069 Vico Equense. © 081-8015331. Fax 081-8015071. www.aequahotel.com. 70 units. 145€ ($203/£102). Rates include buffet breakfast. Children 2 and under stay free in parent's room. AE, DC, MC, V. Parking 12€ ($17/£8.40). **Amenities:** Restaurant; bar; outdoor pool; solarium. *In room:* A/C, TV, minibar.

INEXPENSIVE

Eden Bleu *Kids* This small moderately priced hotel has the great advantage of a beachside location, in Marina di Aequa, a short distance out of Vico. The old-fashioned charm is enhanced by the management's attention to detail and its fastidious cleanliness. Guest rooms are bright, with simple furnishings and good-sized bathrooms. Many rooms have private balconies and the best enjoy pretty sea views. The hotel also has a few mini-apartments with cooking facilities that are great for families.

Via Murrano 17, 80069 Marina d'Aequa, 80069 Vico Equense. © 081-8028550. Fax 081-8028574. www.eden bleuhotel.com. 25 units. 124€ ($174/£87) double; apartment 220€ ($308/£154) and up. Rates include buffet breakfast. Children 2 and under stay free in parent's room. AE, DC, MC, V. Parking 12€ ($17/£8.40). **Amenities:** Restaurant; bar; beach; solarium. *In room:* TV, ceiling fan. Closed Nov 2–Mar 31.

WHERE TO DINE

You can eat very well throughout Vico Equense—the local restaurants are visited by Italians and foreigners hailing from far away—but if you only have time for a quick bite, head to **Da Gabriele,** Corso Umberto I 5 (no phone) **Gigino,** for the makings of a memorable picnic full of wonderful local specialties: You will find a great variety of local cheeses, including fresh mozzarella (which can be braided and studded with olives and prosciutto), as well as fresh cheese with *rucola* (arugula) and red pepper.

EXPENSIVE

Ristorante Torre del Saracino *★★★* MODERN SORRENTINE This is a special and justly renowned restaurant, where the food is truly extraordinary and the service just perfect. Hitting the right note between elegance and country, the warm hospitality of Gennaro Esposito remains unmatched. The recent renovations have not affected the quality and, if anything, have made the restaurant even more welcoming. The menu includes popular traditional mainstays as well as the imaginative creations of this talented chef. We highly recommend the delectable ravioli *di pesce ripieni di verdure* (with fish and vegetables), the dish that made this restaurant famous. We also recommend the two tasting menus (60€/$84/£42 and 75€/$105/£53), which are the best way to experience the culinary spirit of the chef. Whatever you do, leave room for the unique homemade desserts, like the *babà al rhum con crema pasticcera e fragoline di bosco,* rum cake with cream and local wild strawberries.

Via Torretta 9, Marina di Seiano, Vico Equense. 🕐 **081-8028555.** Secondi 15€–35€ ($21–$49/£11–£25). AE, DC, MC, V. Tues–Sun 12:30–3:30pm and Tues–Sat 7:30–11:30pm.

MODERATE

Nonna Rosa *Finds* MODERN SORRENTINE   Tucked away on the road climbing up Monte Faito from the center of town, this restaurant is a well-kept local secret. The countryside elegance of the small dining room provides a comfortable background for the excellent food that includes a few interesting seafood dishes—we recommend the *pasta e ceci con le seppioline* (chickpea and pasta soup with baby squid) if it is on the menu—and many very nice meat dishes. Among the latter, do not miss the lamb roast or the filet mignon with walnuts and local provolone.

Via Privata Bonea 4, Pietrapiano, Vico Equense. 🕐 **081-8799055.** Reservations recommended. Secondi 12€–18€ ($17–$25/£8.40–£13). AE, DC, MC, V. Tues–Sun 7:30–11pm.

INEXPENSIVE

Da Gigino Pizza a Metro, L'Università della Pizza 🏆🏆🏆 PIZZA   At the opposite end of the spectrum from the Torre (above), this eatery is a virtual temple to pizza. In the 1950s, Gigino Dell'Amura baked a pizza that was so long a visiting journalist termed it *"pizza a metro,"* or pizza by the yard. The specialty pizza—perfectly seasoned and made with a uniquely crispy dough—quickly began to attract admirers; today, Dell'Amura's five sons maintain the tradition in their cavernous restaurant. A foot (about 30cm) of pizza is a good serving for one person, and the price depends on the toppings. Not only do they serve the best Italian pizza in the world—really!—but they also offer delightful appetizers such as *frittelle di alghe* (seaweed fritters), a local specialty.

Via Nicotera 15, Vico Equense. 🕐 **081-8798426** or 081-8798309. www.pizzametro.it. Reservations not accepted. Pizza 7€ ($9.80/£4.9) and up. No credit cards. Daily 12:30–3:30pm and 7pm–midnight.

Saracino 🏆 PIZZA   This simple pizzeria is located on the beach of Seiano, a few doors down from Vico's most elegant restaurant, Torre del Saracino (see above). A strong competitor of Da Gino (above), they also prepare excellent pizza a metro here. Only about 10 toppings are available, the best being the traditional *marinara* (tomato sauce with no cheese), *margherita* (cheese and basil), and fresh seasonal veggies.

Via Torretta 12, Marina di Seiano, Vico Equense. 🕐 **081-8028559.** Reservations not accepted. Pizza 7€ ($9.80/ £4.90) and up. No credit cards. Oct 1–May 31 Tues–Sun noon–3:30pm and 7–11pm; Jun 1–Sept 30 daily, same hours.

3 Sorrento

39km (20 miles) SE of Naples

Emperor Augustus and his successor, Tiberius, were two of Sorrento's early devotees. In later years the town became a favorite destination for artists and writers, as well as tourists. Although the presence of crowds may dull some of its magic at times, Sorrento's charming cobblestone streets, alluring *lungomare* (seafront promenade), colorful and fragrant flowers, matchless vistas, and lively cultural scene keep getting our high votes.

ESSENTIALS

GETTING THERE   Sorrento is well connected through the **Circumvesuviana Railway** (Stazione Circumvesuviana on Corso Garibaldi in Naples, off Piazza

Garibaldi; ℂ **800-053939;** www.vesuviana.it), which will take you all the way to Sorrento in about 50 minutes for about 3€ ($4.20/£2.10).

Water travel is our favorite mode of transportation along this coast, and you can easily reach Sorrento by ferry and hydrofoil (though only in the summer season). **Linee Marittime Partenopee** (ℂ **081-55513236**), **Navigazione Libera del Golfo** (ℂ **081-5527209**), and **Linee Lauro** (ℂ **081-5522838;** www.alilauro.it) make daily runs to and from Naples as well as to and from Ischia and Capri; **Caremar** (ℂ **081-5513882;** www.caremar.it) offers daily service to and from Capri. Ferries arrive and depart at the Marina Piccola in downtown Sorrento.

SITA (ℂ **081-5522176;** www.sita-on-line.it) maintains regular bus service between Naples and Sorrento, as well as between Sorrento and Amalfi and Salerno. **Curreri Viaggi** (ℂ **081-8015420**) makes seven daily bus runs to Sorrento directly from Naples airport (Capodichino), with stops in Castellammare di Stabia, Vico Equense, Meta, Piano di Sorrento, and Sant'Agnello. The ride to Sorrento takes about 1 hour and costs 6€ ($8.40/£4.20). *Note:* During the summer, traffic on the coastal road is absolutely abominable and can more than double the regular time.

If Sorrento is your only destination, forget the car—traffic is chronically bad and, in summer, becomes downright horrible; you can always rent one here should you decide you need one (see "Getting Around" later on). If you must use a car, take the exit CASTELLAMMARE DI STABIA off autostrada A3, then follow signs for VICO EQUENSE, META DI SORRENTO, and SORRENTO; these will lead you to route SS 145, the Sorrento peninsula's coastal road.

GETTING AROUND Yellow shuttle **buses** (tickets 1€/$1.40/70p for 90 min. from tobacconists and newsstands) connect the harbor with Piazza Tasso in the center of town and with the Circumvesuviana Railroad station. **Taxi stands** can be found at the harbor (ℂ **081-8783527**), on Piazza Tasso (ℂ **081-8782204**), and in the adjacent village of Sant'Agnello (ℂ **081-8781428**).

VISITOR INFORMATION The **AASCT tourist office** is at Via Luigi De Maio 35, off Piazza Tasso (ℂ **081-8074033;** fax 081-8773397; www.sorrentotourism. com). It's open Monday to Saturday from 9am to 6pm; in July and August it's also open Sunday from 9am to 12:30pm. Besides a good city map, it carries copies of the excellent free magazine *Sorrentum.*

FAST FACTS You'll find a **pharmacy** on Corso Italia 131 (ℂ **081-8781226**). The **hospital** is on Corso Italia 1 (ℂ **081-5331111**). For an **ambulance,** dial ℂ **118.** You can call the **police** at ℂ **112,** 113, or 081-8075311; and you can reach the **fire department** at ℂ **115.** You will find several **ATMs** in town; one is at the **Deutsche Bank** (Piazza Angelina Lauro 22). The **post office** is at Corso Italia 210 (ℂ **081-8781495**); it's open Monday to Friday from 8am to 6pm and Saturday from 8am to 12:30pm. For **Internet access,** go to **Sorrento info** (Via Tasso 19; ℂ **081-8074000**).

EXPLORING THE TOWN

Sorrento has ancient Greek, Etruscan, and Oscan beginnings, and was colonized by the Romans in the 1st century B.C., when it became a valued resort for the affluent. But the town's history has been checkered, to say the least; this jewel by the sea has been fought over many times. After the fall of the empire it was taken by the Goths, and then re-conquered by the Byzantines in A.D. 552. It remained part of the Byzantine Duchy of Naples until the 10th century. Having been conquered by the Prince of Salerno at the beginning of the 11th century, it succeeded in gaining its independence as a Duchy in 1067, and remained so until conquest by the Normans in 1133; it then passed into the hands of the Angevins. Saracen incursions and rivalry between the nearby towns of Vico Equense and Massa Lubrense made life difficult in Sorrento—and there was worse to come. The town was completely destroyed by Barbary pirates on the nights of June 12 and 13, 1558. Still, the town was immediately rebuilt, this time with numerous defensive towers along the surrounding coast and a new set of walls.

We love strolling through the heart of Sorrento, where some medieval buildings are still intact. From the west side of **Piazza Tasso,** start off on **Via Pietà;** at number 14 you'll find **Palazzo Veniero,** with its facade of typical 13th-century decorations, similar to wood marquetry. At number 24 is ex-**Palazzo Correale** with its original 14th-century portal and two windows. A few steps away, we recommend a visit to the beautiful 15th-century **Duomo,** the Cathedral of San Filippo and San Giacomo (Corso Italia 1; ✆ **081-8782248;** daily 8am–noon and 4–8pm), with its striking Romanesque facade graced by a fresco over the portal. The stubby bell tower to the right is particularly interesting, graced by a majolica clock, and four antique columns at its base; only three of its five levels are original (the two top ones were later additions). Inside the Duomo, you can admire 14th- and 15th-century bas-reliefs and a wooden choir decorated with superb intarsia.

Sorrento is famous for the historical craft of marquetry and wood inlay. We suggest a stop at the **Museo Bottega della Tarsia Lignea**⋆, Via San Nicola 28, 2 blocks from Corso Italia (✆ **081-8771942** or 081-8782177; 8€/$11/£5.60; Mon–Sat 10am–1pm; closed holidays), where you can admire an intriguing collection of 19th-century marquetry furniture in addition to the beautiful frescoes that decorate the 18th-century **Palazzo Pomaranci Santomasi,** which houses the museum.

Continuing on our stroll through Medieval Sorrento, you'll come to Piazzetta Padre Reginaldo Giuliani, off Via San Cesareo, where you can take in the elegant and very well-preserved 15th-century palazzo **Sedile Dominova.** Nearby is Sorrento's second-most important church, **Basilica di Sant'Antonino,** Piazza Sant'Antonino, off Via Luigi de Maio. Built in the 11th century over a preexisting oratory dedicated to Saint Anthony, it was later redone in the present baroque style, but the interior retains some 15th-century decorations.

Walking back toward the seafront promenade, you will come upon the 18th-century church of **San Francesco,** Piazza Francesco Saverio Gargiulo (daily 8am–1pm and 2–7pm); hidden inside is the splendid 14th-century **cloister** ⋆⋆, famous for its concert series. Contact the tourist center (p. 159) for details. Across from the church is the entrance to **Villa Comunale,** which has a panoramic terrace and is a perfect spot for a quiet rest. From here, you can take the steep ramps descending to **Marina Piccola,** one of Sorrento's harbors. The town's other harbor is **Marina Grande,** which is lined with restaurants and seaside establishments.

Another interesting attraction is the **Museo Correale,** Via Correale (✆ **081-8781846;** www.museocorreale.com; 8€/$11/£5.60; Wed–Mon 9am–2pm), once the home of the brothers Alfredo and Pompeo Correale, counts of Terranova—an old aristocratic family of Sorrento—who donated their villa and private collections to the public. The place gives a unique overview of decorative art from the 16th to the 19th centuries: Stocked with its original furnishings, it houses some excellent Flemish paintings, a collection of Italian and foreign porcelain from the reputedly best 17th- and 18th-century manufacturers, and a number of unusual clocks. The streets leading

Sorrento

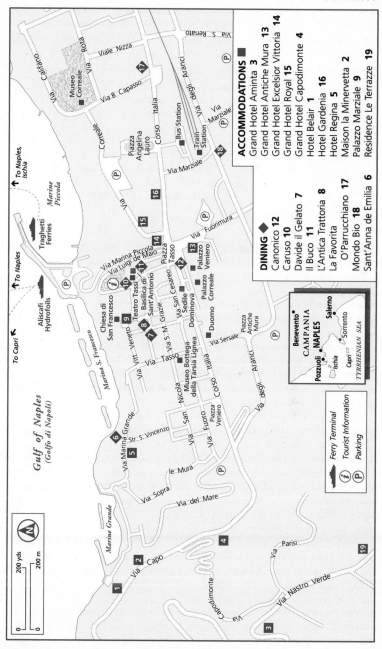

ACCOMMODATIONS ■
Grand Hotel Aminta **3**
Grand Hotel Antiche Mura **13**
Grand Hotel Excelsior Vittoria **14**
Grand Hotel Royal **15**
Grand Hotel Capodimonte **4**
Hotel Belair **1**
Hotel Gardenia **16**
Hotel Regina **5**
Maison la Minervetta **2**
Palazzo Marziale **9**
Residence Le Terrazze **19**

DINING ◆
Canonico **12**
Caruso **10**
Davide il Gelato **7**
Il Buco **11**
L'Antica Trattoria **8**
La Favorita
O'Parrucchiano **17**
Mondo Bio **18**
Sant'Anna de Emilia **6**

Gulf of Naples
(Golfo di Napoli)

To Capri
To Naples
To Naples, Ischia

Marine Piccola

Aliscafi Hydrofoils
Traghetti Ferries

Marina S. Francesco

Marine Grande

Via Marina Grande

Via Capo

Via Capodimonte

Via Nastro Verde

Parisi

le. Mura
Via Sopra
Via del Mare

Str. S. Vincenzo
Via San Nicola
Museo Bottega della Tarsia Lignea
Via Fuoro
Via Tasso
Via Vitt. Veneto
Chiesa di San Francesco
Basilica di Sant'Antonio
Teatro Tassi
Sedile Dominova
Piazza Tasso
Palazzo Veniero
Via S.-M. Grazie
Via San Cesareo
Corso Italia
Duomo
Via Sersale
Palazzo Correale
Piazza Antiche Mura
Via degli Aranci
Via Fuorimura

Via Marina Piccola
Via Luigi de Maio

Via Marziale
Piazza Angelina Lauro
Corso Italia
Bus Station
Train Station
Via Marziale
Via degli Aranci
Via S. Renato

Viale Nizza
Via Rota
Museo Correale
Via B. Capasso
Via Correale
Via Califano

Ferry Terminal
i **Tourist Information**
P **Parking**

CAMPANIA
Benevento
NAPLES
Pozzuoli
Ischia
Capri
Salerno
Sorrento
TYRRHENIAN SEA

0 | 200 yds
0 | 200 m

N

to this museum are part of the package: **Via Correale** 🕸🕸, starting off Piazza Tasso, is one of the few streets that preserves the flavor of 19th-century Sorrento. We encourage you to continue beyond the museum until you reach the little town of **Sant'Agnello,** with its stately villas built in the past century or two, and many elegant hotels.

A GUIDED TOUR 🔑 If you have only 1 day to visit Sorrento, we highly recommend timing it to include a trip on the **Sorrento Express** (ⓒ **081-8780862;** www. sorrentoexpress.it), a special train offered by the **Circumvesuviana** Railroad (see "Getting There," earlier). You will travel on a restored carriage pulled by an original engine, all of which date from 1942 (the only new addition is air-conditioning). The trip is offered only on weekends (departing Naples at 9:06am on Sat and 10:06am on Sun) and includes refreshments on the train, a guided tour of Sorrento, and lunch in a local restaurant that offers traditional 18th-century dishes; the Saturday outing also includes a guided tour of Pompeii. The price for the round-trip is 57€ ($80/£40) on Saturday and 52€ ($73/£36) on Sunday for adults and 26€ ($36/£18) for children 9 and under. Reservations are required.

STAYING ACTIVE

Most visitors come to Sorrento for the cultural activities, but those in the know also take advantage of its many opportunities to enjoy the great outdoors.

You'll soon realize that the ruggedness that makes this stretch of coast so beautiful is a serious obstacle to your physical enjoyment of the shimmering sea: While rocky points and cliffs are, of course, part of the visual charm, swimming from them isn't easy. Most of the major hotels in town have worked this out by building their own private structures—floating docks that are anchored to the rocky shore and equipped with umbrellas and lounge chairs—usually connected by elevator to the top of the cliff and the hotel. The only small stretch of pebbly beach is at **Marina Grande,** but a busy harbor is not our idea of the perfect swimming spot. For real sand, you need to venture east out of town to the small **Marinella Beach,** or farther away to **Vico Equense** (p. 154).

Hiring a **boat** (with or without a driver who can double as a guide) is high up on our list, as it allows for exploration of this rugged coast and its secluded beaches. **Nautica Sic Sic,** Marina Piccola (ⓒ **081-8072283** or 081-8785606; www.nauticasic sic.com; closed Nov–Apr), is a good place to rent boats; they go for 20€ ($28/£14) and up, depending on the size and type. The shop also organizes cruises. Another reputable company is **Tony's Beach,** Marina Grande (ⓒ **081-8785606**). A nice half-hour boat excursion goes to the so-called **Bagno della Regina Giovanna (Queen Giovanna's Bath)** at **Punta del Capo** 🕸 (although you can also reach the spot on foot, from a trail starting from the Calata Capo di Sorrento, off Via Capo). This is our favorite local swimming spot: A small pool of water enclosed by rocks, it was once the private harbor of an ancient Roman villa—**Villa of Pollio Felice**—the ruins of which you can visit at the top of the cliff. Another pleasant boat ride is the one to the **Grotta delle Sirene (Grotto of the Sirens),** which lies east of Marina Piccola and past Sant'Agnello. In the grotto, the water takes on surprising hues—as if by the charm of magical sea creatures—but it's really based on the ever-changing light.

Hiking is also high on our list, and the great number of trails, most of which are well maintained and marked, offer treks for people of all skill levels. We recommend using a good trail map; the best is *Carta dei Sentieri* published by CAI, the Club Alpino Italiano and for sale at libraries and some newsstands in town. It covers the

Monti Lattari, Penisola Sorrentina, and **Costiera Amalfitana,** and costs 8€ ($11/£5.60). One of the most beautiful hikes is the one to **Punta Sant'Elia** ★★★, starting from Piazza Sant'Agnello in Sant'Agnello; the trail ends at a rocky point across the peninsula overlooking the little islands of LiGalli, along the Amalfi Coast in the Gulf of Salerno. To reach the trail, take Via Bonaventura Gargiulo up to **Trasaella,** at an altitude of 196m (643 ft.), and then continue toward **Colli di Fontanelle** at an altitude of 343m (1,125 ft.). From the center of this village and across Via Belvedere begins the trail to Punta Sant'Elia. It is also possible to hire a professional guide; we recommend **Giovanni Visetti** (© **081-8089613;** www.giovis.com), an expert on this coast and its hinterlands, who organizes guided hikes of varying difficulty and cost.

WHERE TO STAY

This mecca of international tourism offers endless choices, but be prepared to shell out if you want to be in Sorrento proper, as the cheaper accommodations are often substandard and can be cramped or noisy. Sant'Agnello, adjacent to Sorrento to the east, is slightly cheaper, but you'll find better hotels for your money outside town, either toward Vico Equense (p. 154) or Massa Lubrense (p. 170).

EXPENSIVE

Albergo Cocumella ★   This luxurious hotel is located in Sant'Agnello, within walking distance of Sorrento's center. The building—originally a 16th-century Jesuit monastery—was turned into a hotel in 1822 and has since been restored and updated to maintain its 19th-century elegance and style. While here, you'll tread in the steps of such famous guests as Goethe and the Duke of Wellington, who enjoyed the magnificent park surrounding the hotel and the terrace—actually a private promenade—overlooking the sea. Public spaces are palatial and even the simpler rooms—furnished with a mix of antiques, quality reproductions, and fine fabrics—partake in the general elegance; some even have frescoed ceilings. Of course, the ones opening over the terrace and the sea are the most beautiful, but all rooms have spacious marble bathrooms. The park offers a multitude of diversions, including outdoor tennis and a delightful pool where, during good weather, barbecue lunches are offered under the orange trees. The seasonal concerts held here are also a popular attraction (see "Sorrento After Dark," later in this chapter).

Via Cocumella 7, 80065 Sant'Agnello. © 081-8782933. Fax 081-8783712. www.cocumella.com. 50 units. 390€ ($546/£273) double; from 490€ ($686/£343) suite. Rates include buffet breakfast. AE, DC, MC, V. Free parking. Closed Nov–Mar. **Amenities:** 2 restaurants; bar; babysitting; concierge; health club; laundry service; outdoor pool; room service; spa; tennis court. *In room:* A/C, satellite TV, hair dryer, minibar, safe.

Grand Hotel Excelsior Vittoria ★★★   Housed on the estate of an impressive villa and surrounded by a park right in the heart of town, this is the best hotel in Sorrento, and one of the best hotels in the world. Welcoming guests since 1834, this exclusive hotel has counted among its guests Lord Byron, Wagner, Oscar Wilde, and a long list of royalty. Still run by the same family (the Fiorentinos) since its opening, it offers exquisite and individualized service. The elegant public spaces and terraces—still with the original 19th-century furnishings—are perfect places to enjoy a drink. The huge guest rooms are elegant abodes that are finely decorated and furnished with many antiques—and all the modern comforts. The refined bathrooms are marble-clad. Most of the rooms open onto a private balcony or terrace, and the best have views over the Gulf of Naples (the others over the delightful orange-tree garden). From the hotel, elevators take guests to the private beach-pier off Marina Piccola. In a splendid setting overlooking the gulf, **Terrazza Bosquet** offers the most romantic gourmet dining in Sorrento. A good way to sample its creative cuisine is the tasting menu, which starts at 53€ ($74/£37).

Piazza Tasso 34, 80067 Sorrento. © 081-8777111. Fax 081-8771206. www.exvitt.it. 105 units. 407€–605€ ($570–$847/£296–£424) double, from 715€ ($1,001/£501) suite. Rates include buffet breakfast. Children 2 and under stay free in parent's room. Internet specials available. AE, DC, MC, V. Free parking. **Amenities:** 2 restaurants; bar; babysitting; concierge; gardens/park; laundry service; outdoor pool; outdoor kiddy pool; private pier/beach; room service; solarium; spa. *In room:* A/C, satellite TV, hair dryer, minibar, safe.

Grand Hotel Royal 🏵

This panoramic hotel offers elegance and refinement just steps from the heart of town. One of the oldest hotels in Sorrento, it was completely renovated in 2003 and now offers modern rooms, a pleasant swimming pool, relaxing public spaces (including a solarium), and private sea access via elevator. Guest rooms are large and bright, decorated with high-quality classic furnishings, fine fabrics, handpainted ceramic floors, and stucco molding. All are equipped with modern bathrooms and open onto private balconies. The best rooms are indeed superb, with marquetry furniture, marbled bathrooms, and breathtaking sea views; the others open onto the garden or the town and feature tiled bathrooms.

Via Correale 42, 80067 Sorrento. © 081-8073434. Fax 081-8772905. www.manniellohotels.it. 100 units. 285€–375€ ($399–$525/£200–£263) double; from 595€ ($833/£417) suite. Rates include buffet breakfast. Extra bed 40€ ($56/£28). Internet specials available. Children 1 and under stay free in parent's room. AE, DC, MC, V. Free parking. Closed Nov 1–Feb 28. **Amenities:** Restaurant; 2 bars; babysitting; business center; concierge; laundry service; outdoor pool; room service; sea access by platform; solarium. *In room:* A/C, satellite TV, hair dryer, minibar, safe.

Grand Hotel Aminta 🏵🏵 (Kids)

Located in a dominant position above the town (3km/2 miles away by free shuttle service), this modern hotel more than compensates for the distance with breathtaking views, kind and attentive professional service, and the quality of its accommodations and amenities. We love the atmosphere here and the management's care for details. Public spaces are welcoming, with plenty of arches and pleasant curving lines, including in the swimming pools. The hotel's annex—Villa Aminta—is a completely renovated 18th-century structure housing a few additional rooms a hundred yards away from the main building via a garden path. Guest rooms are all equally bright and tastefully decorated with modern furniture. Some are more spacious than others, but all have modern and scrupulously clean bathrooms; many have balconies affording great views. The restaurant is very good, with a magnificent terrace where live music and dancing are often scheduled on summer evenings.

Via Nastro Verde 23, 80067 Sorrento. © 081-8781821. Fax 081-8781822. www.aminta.it. 81 units. 320€–350€ ($448–$490/£224–£245) double; 590€ ($825/£413) suite. Rates include buffet breakfast. Internet specials available. Children 2 and under stay free in parent's room. AE, DC, MC, V. Free parking. **Amenities:** Restaurant; 24-hr. bar; babysitting; concierge; garden; laundry service; outdoor pool; solarium. *In room:* A/C, satellite TV, hair dryer, high-speed Internet connection, minibar, safe.

MODERATE
Grand Hotel Capodimonte ✿
This modern family-run hotel located a short way from town in a panoramic setting offers excellent amenities and beautiful views, together with friendly attentive service. It is surrounded by a private garden highlighted by a spectacular cascade of five large swimming pools—a wonderful place to enjoy the sun and the views. The guest rooms are bright, spacious, and elegantly appointed, with high-quality furniture, stuccoed walls, and handpainted Vietri floors. The bathrooms are nicely tiled and good-sized; most of the rooms open onto private balconies with views over the sea or the garden.

Via Capo 16, 80065 Sorrento. © 081 8784555. Fax 081 8071193. www.manniellohotels.it. 90 units. 230€–305€ ($322–$427/£161–£214) double. Rates include buffet breakfast. Internet specials available. Children 1 and under free in parent's room. AE, DC, MC, V. Free parking. **Amenities:** 2 restaurants; 2 bars; babysitting on request; business center; concierge; garden; laundry service; panoramic terraces; 5 pools; room service. *In room:* A/C, satellite TV, hair dryer, minibar, safe.

Hotel Antiche Mura ✿
In the heart of town—one of its entrances is on Piazza Tasso—this hotel is housed in an elegant Italian art nouveau–style palazzo built on top of the town's defensive walls, hence, its name. Restoration in keeping with the Belle Epoque spirit of the historic hotel has brought the sophisticated public spaces back to splendor. Guest rooms are bright, decorated with Vietri-tile floors and Sorrentine marquetry furniture. "Comfort" rooms are spacious, and all rooms are equipped with state-of-the-art bathrooms with tub and special hydro-massage showers.

Via Fuorimura 7 (entrance on Piazza Tasso), 80067 Sorrento. © 081-8073523. Fax 081-8071323. www.hotelantiche mura.com. 46 units. 230€–260€ ($322–$364/£161–£182) double; from 340€ ($476/£238) suite. Rates include buffet breakfast. Internet specials available. Children 2 and under stay free in parent's room. AE, DC, MC, V. Free parking. **Amenities:** Bar; concierge; garden; outdoor pool; solarium. *In room:* A/C, satellite TV, hair dryer, minibar, safe.

Hotel Belair ✿
Suspended between sky and sea, this little hotel has great charm, completely compensating for its location outside the center of town with its matchless views. Built on the cliff overlooking Marina Grande, the hotel is connected to the shore by a picturesque set of stairs carved into the rock. Each of the guest rooms is different in shape and individually decorated, with a small sea-view balcony or terrace. Most rooms are spacious and all are bright and pleasantly decorated with ceramic floors and quality classic furniture. Bathrooms are good size and very clean.

Via Capo 29, 80067 Sorrento. © 081-8071622. Fax 081-8071467. www.belair.it. 49 units. 280€ ($392/£196) double; from 320€ ($448/£224) suite. Rates include buffet breakfast. Internet specials available. Children 2 and under stay free in parent's room. AE, DC, MC, V. Free parking. Closed Nov 1–Mar 31. **Amenities:** Bar; concierge; garden; outdoor pool; solarium. *In room:* A/C, satellite TV, hair dryer, minibar, safe.

Maison La Minervetta ✿
Born as a restaurant in the 1950s, this hotel enjoys a peerless position on the cliff overlooking Marina Grande. Ownership was recently restored to the original hoteliers, who have transformed it into a boutique hotel. Stepping inside is a breath of fresh air from the more typical accommodations of this stretch of coast. The alluring interior design successfully marries hypermodern style—almost Scandinavian in flavor—with bold Mediterranean colors and details. Guest rooms are very different from each other, but all are blessed with huge picture windows; the best enjoy private sun terraces with Jacuzzi pools. Artwork from around the world highlights public spaces, while the pine floors in the guest rooms add warmth. We love the modern bathrooms decorated with hand-painted tiles.

Via Capo 25, 80067 Sorrento. © 081-8774455. Fax 081-8784601. www.laminervetta.com. 12 units. 300€–350€ ($420–$490/£210–£245) double; 400€ ($560/£280) junior suite. Rates include buffet breakfast. Internet specials available. Children 2 and under stay free in parent's room. AE, DC, MC, V. Free parking. Closed 1 week in Jan. **Amenities:** Breakfast room; concierge; solarium; terrace. *In room:* A/C, satellite TV, hair dryer, minibar, safe.

INEXPENSIVE

Hotel Gardenia *Kids*   Located at the edge of town toward Sant'Agnello and away from the sea, this family-run hotel offers moderately priced accommodations. Guest rooms are large and simply but comfortably appointed with modern furniture and tiled floors; all rooms have private balconies. The hotel also prides itself on its Olympic-size swimming pool and a fitness club. The pool and the possibility of triples and quads make it a good choice for budget-oriented families. Since the Gardenia is on the main street in town, it can get a bit noisy, particularly if you like keeping your windows open; although Corso Italia is closed to automobile traffic in summer from 7pm to 7am and again from 10am to 1pm.

Corso Italia 258, 80067 Sant'Agnello. © 081-8772365. Fax 081-8074486. www.hotelgardenia.com. 30 units. 150€–170€ ($210–$238/£105–£119) double; 188€ ($263/£132) triple; 225€ ($315/£158) quad. Rates include buffet breakfast. Children 2 and under stay free in parent's room. AE, DC, MC, V. Free parking. Closed Jan to mid-Feb. **Amenities:** Restaurant; bar; babysitting; concierge; garden w/piano bar in summer; outdoor pool; outdoor tennis court; same-day laundry service. *In room:* A/C, satellite TV, hair dryer, minibar, safe.

Hotel Regina *★*   Just steps from the sea and Marina Grande, and a short walk from the center of town, this hotel offers simple and quiet accommodations at excellent prices. Guest rooms are functional, with tiled floors and simple furnishings; bathrooms are good-sized and immaculate. Most of the rooms open onto private balconies or terraces, which are delightful in good weather, especially if you get one of the rooms that enjoys excellent views over the sea and Vesuvius. The other rooms overlook the hotel's pleasant garden. Book early as this is one of the most sought-after hotels in town. *Note:* Look out for Wi-Fi service, which is coming soon.

Via Marina Grande 10, 80067 Sorrento. © 081-8782722. Fax 081-8782721. www.hotelreginasorrento.com. 38 units. 130€–155€ ($182–$217/£91–£109) double. Rates include buffet breakfast. Internet specials available. Children 5 and under stay free in parent's room. AE, DC, MC, V. Parking 15€ ($21/£11). Closed Nov 15–Jan 31. **Amenities:** Restaurant; bar; babysitting; concierge; garden; laundry service; lounge; room service; solarium. *In room:* A/C, satellite TV, hair dryer, Internet connection, safe.

Palazzo Marziale *Finds*   This B&B is a real find, offering fine accommodations inside a historical palazzo in the heart of town. The delightful hostess, Paola, will warmly welcome you, making you feel both pampered and at home. She has only five rooms, each large and nicely appointed, with attention to detail and enough luxury to satisfy even the most difficult to please. The marble bathrooms are ample, modern, and scrupulously clean. The only possible hitch is the 3-night minimum stay requirement.

Largo San Francesco 2, 80067 Sorrento. © 081-8074406. Fax 081-8774187. www.palazzomarziale.com. 160€ ($224/£112) double; 195€ ($273/£137) junior suite. **Amenities:** Concierge; laundry service. *In room:* A/C, satellite TV, hair dryer, Internet access, minibar, safe.

Residence Le Terrazze *Kids*   This pleasant hotel located in a panoramic position high above Sorrento is convenient to the center of town as well as to the best beaches and attractions in the area. Family-run and immaculately kept, it offers moderately priced mini-apartments in various sizes, all with kitchenette—a good solution for families. The white-washed rooms are plain but bright, with no-frill tiled floors, rattan or pine furniture, and good-sized bathrooms with all the essentials. The new swimming pool is a great addition.

Via Nastro Verde 98, 80067 Sorrento. ⓒ **081-8780906.** Fax 081-8085204. www.residenceleterrazze.it. 16 units. 130€ ($182/£91) double. Rates include buffet breakfast. Internet specials available. Children 2 and under stay free in parent's room. AE, DC, MC, V. Free parking. Closed Jan 8–Feb 28. **Amenities:** Concierge; outdoor pool. *In room:* A/C, satellite TV, fridge, kitchenette.

WHERE TO DINE

Some of the best dining in town is offered by the most exclusive hotels (see above). While those have unique romantic settings on terraces overlooking the sea—sure to inspire future memories—the other restaurants in Sorrento are all usually good and occasionally excellent. The town's waterside and main streets are lined with restaurants big and small, traditional and modern, and you will do well with their fresh fish and savory pastas. Here are a few of our favorites.

EXPENSIVE

Caruso SORRENTINE   This elegant restaurant doubles as a museum dedicated to the famous Italian tenor who so loved Sorrento. The cuisine is excellent, although we find the touch of nouvelle—particularly in the portion sizes—a little passé. The menu is seasonal, and you'll likely find such delicious meals as *ravioli all'aragosta* (lobster ravioli), *ravioli con salsa di melanzane* (ravioli with an eggplant sauce), *lasagne ai frutti di mare* (seafood lasagna), tasty *riso con zucchine e gamberi* (rice with shrimp and zucchini). For *secondo*, we highly recommend the grilled fish. For dessert, *torta di arance e noci* (orange and walnut cake) is not to be missed if it's available.

Via Sant'Antonino 12. ⓒ **081-8073156.** www.ristorantemuseocaruso.com. Reservations recommended. Secondi 16€–32€ ($22–$45/£11–£22). AE, DC, MC, V. Daily noon–3:30pm and 7:30–11:30pm.

MODERATE

Il Buco ✯ CREATIVE SORRENTINE   With an atmospheric setting in the wine cellar of an ancient convent by the ancient city gate, and a delightful outdoor terrace in the summer season, this restaurant never stops improving. The menu of fine, imaginative cuisine changes according to the daily market, and they now offer four highly recommended tasting menus: surf, turf, vegetarian, or a fourth one focusing on traditional local dishes. Only the best of local ingredients make their way to the kitchen, and you won't be disappointed. We loved the *fusilli alla zucca e gamberi* (homemade pasta with shrimp and pumpkin) and the *ravioli di pesce ai peperoni* (seafood ravioli with sweet peppers). Do order the house red—it's a standout.

2d Rampa Marina Piccola 5, off Piazza Sant'Antonino. ⓒ **081-8782354.** www.ilbucoristorante.it. Reservations recommended. Prix-fixe menu 45€–65€ ($63–$91/£32–£46). Secondi 16€–22€ ($22–$31/£11–£15). AE, DC, MC, V. Thurs–Tues 12:30–3:30pm and 7:30–11:30pm. Closed Jan.

L'Antica Trattoria ✯ SORRENTINE   This picturesque restaurant—complete with master mandolin player—has served excellent food, mainly local specialties, for over 200 years. We love everything, but especially adore the menu's ample offerings of both surf and turf. Their antipasti buffet is laden with a large array of seafood and vegetable dishes that we find it difficult to move beyond, but you should definitely allow yourself to be tempted by the house specialty: spaghetti *alla ferrolese* (a complicated seasoning of fish roe, shrimp, red cabbage, and cream) if it is on offer. Otherwise, the homemade lasagna and ravioli are both delicious. We are also partial to the savory and moist daily catch cooked in a salt crust and the creative desserts based on local traditions.

Via Padre Reginaldo Giuliani 33. ⓒ **081-8071082.** Reservations recommended. Secondi 18€–25€ ($25–$35/£13–£18). AE, MC, V. Nov 1–Feb 28 Tues–Sun noon–3:30pm and 7–11:30pm; Mar 1–Oct 31 daily, same hours. Closed Jan 15–Feb 15.

A Gelato to Remember

The absolute best gelato parlor in the whole area—and maybe in the whole country—is **Davide Il gelato** ★★, Via Padre R. Giuliani 39 (✆ **081-8072092**), producing divine homemade gelato made with typical regional fruits and specialties. Among the 60 flavors (more or less, depending on the day), we favor the sweet and deliciously creamy *noci di Sorrento* (Sorrento walnuts), the rich *cioccolato con canditi* (dark chocolate cream studded with candied oranges), the sinful *rhum babà* (rum-flavored cream with bits of soft cake), and the heavenly *delizia al limone* (a delectable lemon cream). You'll definitely have to return, at least once (or twice, or three times . . .) to sample them all.

La Favorita O'Parrucchiano SORRENTINE   Located right in the center of town, this venerable restaurant—in operation since 1868—boasts picturesque dining spaces, including outdoor seating in a beautiful garden. They claim to have invented *cannelloni* (tubes of fresh pasta filled with meat and baked with tomato sauce and cheese). Whether that claim is true or not, the dish is just one of the excellent local specialties on hand. Try *ravioli alla Caprese* (ravioli filled with fresh cheese and seasoned with a sauce of fresh tomatoes and basil) or *frittura* (seafood medley, including calamari, shrimp, and small fish).

Corso Italia 71. ✆ **081-8781321.** Reservations recommended in the evening. Secondi 8.50€–14€ ($12–$20/ £5.95–£9.80). MC, V. Nov 15–Mar 15 Thurs–Tues noon–3:30pm and 7–11:30pm; Mar 16–Nov 14 daily noon–3:30pm and 7–11:30pm.

O'Canonico ★ (Value) SORRENTINE   This traditional restaurant right on Sorrento's main square is both handily located and a good value. Canonico offers professional service and well-prepared traditional cuisine. If you find it on the menu, try their beautifully made local specialty, *gnocchi alla sorrentina* (potato dumplings with fresh tomatoes and *mozzarella di bufala*). Another dish you aren't likely to see elsewhere is *paccheri di Gragnano* (local large pasta, a bit lasagna-like).

Piazza Tasso 5. ✆ **081-8783277.** Reservations recommended on weekends. Secondi 8€–18€ ($11–$25/£5.60– £13). AE, DC, MC, V. Tues–Sun noon–3:30pm and 7–11:30pm.

INEXPENSIVE

Mondo Bio VEGETARIAN   If you are approaching a cholesterol overload or you like to eat vegetarian food, head for this tiny eatery, which doubles as a health food store. The food is strictly organic and the varying menu includes such typical fare as seitan and tofu, along with many other vegetable-based dishes (also vegan).

Via degli Aranci 146. ✆ **081-8075694.** Reservations not accepted. Secondi 5€–9€ ($7–$13/£3.50–£6.30). No credit cards. Mon–Sat 10am–3pm.

Sant'anna da Emilia   This moderately priced restaurant is a local favorite, housed in an ancient boatshed in Marina Grande and complete with an outdoor terrace on a wooden pier. It is mobbed in summer, so be prepared to wait if you want to taste the great homestyle cuisine, with a daily menu that varies with the market offerings. Simplicity is the key to success here, and we promise you won't taste a better *Caprese* (mozzarella and fresh tomato salad) or spaghetti *alle cozze* (with mussels). We also recommend the *gnocchi alla Sorrentina* (Sorrento-style potato dumplings). The house wine is also excellent.

Via Marina Grande 62. ℂ 081-8072720. Reservations not accepted. Secondi 8.50€–14€ ($12–$20/£5.95–£9.80). No credit cards. Sept 1–Feb 28 Wed–Mon noon–3:30pm and 7:30–11:30pm; Mar 1–Aug 31 daily same hours. Closed Nov.

SHOPPING

Sorrento is famous for the bounty of its inland farms and groves: Lemons, walnuts, olive oil, and wine are staples. The local olive oil is special enough to have deserved a D.O.P. label: Penisola Sorrentina D.O.P.; it has an intense and fruity flavor with a sharp, almost peppery aftertaste. The wine has also earned a D.O.C. label, the Penisola Sorrentina, both red and white, called by some experts "the Beaujolais of Campania." And, of course, the cheese, a specialty of these mountains, is top-notch; nowhere more so than at **Apreda,** which has two locations: Via Tasso 6 (ℂ **081-8782351**) and Via del Mare 20 (ℂ **081-8074059**), where you can still get fresh ricotta made in traditional handmade baskets.

Until recent times, craft-making was a popular art form here; sadly, though, it is slowly disappearing. Still, Sorrento has a strong tradition in lace and embroideries, and visitors can continue to buy lovely, intricate examples at **Luigia Gargiulo** (Corso Italia 48; ℂ **081-8781081**). Another of the town's traditional crafts is wood intarsia and marquetry furniture. **Gargiulo & Jannuzzi** (Piazza Tasso 1; ℂ **081-8781041**) has excelled in these crafts since the 19th century; today, you can visit the workshops to see demonstrations of this ancient technique following century-old patterns.

SORRENTO AFTER DARK

The narrow streets of Sorrento's *centro storico* are alive with cafes, clubs, and restaurants, which become positively crowded during the sweet nights of summer. Locals as well as newcomers love sitting on the terrace of the **Fauno Bar,** Piazza Tasso 13 (ℂ **081-8781135;** www.faunobar.it; closed Nov) for an *aperitivo* (aperitif) and people watching till late into the evening. Other popular venues for pre- and post-dinner drinks are, of course, the romantic terraces of the many historic hotels (above) as well as the **Circolo dei Forestieri** (below).

Spring and summer are a special time in Sorrento, as music festivals and other musical programs are staged in venues throughout town. Some of the most popular—and which we highly recommend—are the concerts at the **Albergo Cocumella** (p. 163), and those at the **cloister of San Francesco,** Piazza Francesco Saverio Gargiulo. Contact the tourist center (p. 159) for details. Also, many restaurants and taverns in town offer live music during dinner. It definitely pays to keep abreast of the latest offerings through the tourist office (p. 159), whose agents will be happy to give you a schedule of events.

For more modern entertainment, head to Piazza Tasso and its two nightclubs: **Fauno Notte Club** (ℂ **081-8781021;** www.faunonotte.it; cover 23€/$32/£16); and **Matilda Club** (ℂ **081-8773236;** cover 10€/$14/£7). Both clubs have dancing—usually disco—but the first one has a more mature clientele and offers a colorful **Tarantella Show** (traditional folk dance) between stretches of DJ music; shows are only held March through October (daily 9–11pm). Another good choice is the **Circolo dei Forestieri,** Via Luigi de Maio 35 (ℂ **081-8773012;** closed Nov–Feb), a live music bar with a beautiful terrace and shows every night.

If you like folk music, you might also enjoy *Sorrento Musical,* a revue of Neapolitan songs hosted by **Teatro Tasso,** Piazza Sant'Antonino (ℂ **081-8075525;** www. teatrotasso.com; tickets about 21€/$29/£15 depending on show; Mar–Oct Mon–Sat 9:30pm).

For more leisurely entertainment, among the numerous pubs to choose from here, **Chaplin's Video Pub,** Corso Italia 18 (© 081-8072551) and the **English Inn,** Corso Italia 55 (© 081-8074357), located across from each other, both stock a good selection of beers and maintain a lively atmosphere—sometimes even too lively on summer weekends. Farther along is the **Merry Monk,** Via Capo 6 (© 081-8772409), another good pub with a good choice of beer.

4 Beyond Sorrento: Massa Lubrense & Sant'Agata sui due Golfi

60km (38 miles) S of Naples

Much less traveled, the tip of the Sorrentine peninsula is also the most authentic. Villages—sometimes little more than handfuls of houses—dot the rocky coast and cliffs, and you'll find peace and quiet even in the middle of the summer season. Such a surprising feat has been accomplished via mundane means: terrible transportation. The train stops in Sorrento, and the main road (SS 145) bypasses Massa Lubrense completely, looping back toward the coast on the other side of the peninsula to join SS 163, the famous Amalfi Drive. The result is a little-visited, though ruggedly beautiful corner that feels more remote than it is. You can easily visit the whole area in 1 day; yet, once you have arrived, you'll hardly want to leave.

ESSENTIALS
GETTING THERE & AROUND   **Sorrento** is the gateway to the rest of the peninsula (see "Getting There," p. 158). Although **SITA**'s (© 081-5522176; www.sita bus.it) **bus** service from Sorrento is frequent and efficient, we feel that, unless you have unlimited time, renting a **scooter** or a **car**—or even better, a **taxi** or **limousine** with a driver—is a lot more functional: You'll be able to see more, have a flexible schedule, and your driver will double as a guide. Distances are short, hence charges remain quite reasonable (consider about 45€/$63/£32 per hour for two people, with special discounts for longer periods).

You can rent a car from the major operators listed in chapter 2 (p. 27) or from a number of local vendors, of whom we recommend **De Martino,** Corso Italia 253, Sorrento (© 081 8071013); **Sorrento Car Service,** Corso Italia 210, Sorrento (© 081-8781386; www.sorrento.it); and **Penisola Rent,** Corso Italia 257, Sorrento (© 081-8774664). The last two also rent scooters, and Sorrento Car Service also offers limousine service. Another reliable company is **2golfi car service,** Via Deserto 30/e, 80064 Sant'Agata sui due Golfi (© 339-8307748 or 338-5628649; www.duegolfi carservice). **Bellantonio Limousine Service,** Sorrento (© 081-5342293 or 338-2484301; www.bellantoniolimoservice.com) is another small operation we recommend. Many other companies in the area offer similar service, but make sure they use cars and minivans with air-conditioning (very important in summer), as well as trained, English-speaking drivers.

VISITOR INFORMATION   Your best source of information is the **tourist office** in Sorrento (p. 159). You'll find a **pharmacy** at Via Palma 16, Massa Lubrense (© 081-8789081). The **hospital** is in Sorrento (earlier in this chapter). For an **ambulance,** dial © 118. You can call the **police** at © 113 or 112, and you can reach the **fire department** at © 115. You'll find a **post office** in Massa Lubrense at Via Massa Turro 13 (© 081-8789045) and another in Sant'Agata Sui due Golfi at Corso Sant'Agata 32 (© 081-8780162). There is a **Banco di Napoli** (© 081-8089687) at number 15 on Viale Filangeri in Massa Lubrense, and a **Deutsche Bank** (📞 **081-8089530**) at number 26.

EXPLORING THE AREA

Massa Lubrense was once an important town and a powerful rival to Sorrento for dominance over this coast. Situations have changed, and Massa is now just one of the small villages that dot this rocky point. The diminished political importance of this area has not deprived it of its unique beauty, though, and Italian tourists in the know come to enjoy the cliffs and the increased sense of solitude the environment affords.

Among the villages, **Massa Lubrense** prides itself on its church, **Santa Maria delle Grazie** (Piazza Vescovado), which was built in 1512 and redone in the 18th century. In the transept and presbytery you'll find nice examples of the original **majolica floor** 🏛, but the real attraction here is the fantastic **view** 🏛🏛 over Capri you can enjoy from the terrace to the right of the church. Below the church is **Marina della Lobra** 🏛, a picturesque fishing hamlet with a little harbor—and also one of the peninsula's rare stretches of sand. The sanctuary here—**Santa Maria della Lobra**—was built in the 16th century over a Roman temple, probably dedicated to Minerva. Inside you can see the original 17th-century wood-carved **ceiling** and the 18th-century **majolica floor.**

From Santa Maria delle Grazie, follow the sign toward **Annunziata;** the road leads to the old Massa Lubrense, established in the 10th century and destroyed by the Angevins in the 1300s. Here you'll find the church of the **Santissima Annunziata,** the original cathedral of Massa, redone in the 17th century. Nearby are the ruins of the castle—only one tower is standing—which was built in 1389. From the **Belvedere,** weather permitting, you can enjoy an extraordinary **panorama** 🏛🏛 that encompasses the whole Gulf of Naples.

Farther on toward the tip of the Sorrentine peninsula is the village of **Nerano,** perched atop a cliff at 166m (544 ft.). Below the village is the fishing hamlet of **Marina del Cantone** 🏛 with its lovely beach where locals keep their boats. Nearby **Termini** is another small town built on a natural terrace overlooking Capri. From Termini, drive down the local road to **Punta Campanella,** on the tip of the Sorrento peninsula, with its famous lighthouse (see "Staying Active," later in this chapter).

Finally, you will reach **Sant'Agata Sui Due Golfi** 🏛🏛: One of the region's largest, the village benefits from its matchless position overlooking the two Gulfs—of Naples and of Salerno—hence its name. The village is focused around **Santa Maria delle Grazie,** a 17th-century church that boasts a beautiful **altar** of colored marble and semi-precious stones. Follow the signs toward **Deserto** 🏛, once a Carmelite hermitage and now a Benedictine monastery. At an altitude of 456m (1,496 ft.), it affords a spectacular **circular panorama** 🏛🏛🏛 over the Campanian coast, stretching all the way from Ischia to Punta Licosa, south of Paestum. The monastery is open to visitors October to March (8:30am–12:30pm and 2:30–4:30pm) and April to September (8:30am–12:30pm and 4–8pm).

From Sant'Agata, you can also head toward **Torca,** a village only a few minutes away, perched at 352m (1,155 ft.) above sea level. From the village, take in the beautiful view over LiGalli, Positano's small archipelago.

STAYING ACTIVE

You can do some swimming from the **beach** at **Marina del Cantone,** but to really enjoy the sea, **renting a boat** (with or without driver) is a must: It allows you to discover small beaches, inlets, and hidden bays otherwise inaccessible from the high cliffs. The seashore here is a marine park, **Area Marina Protetta di Punta Campanella** (✆ **081-8089877;** www.puntacampanella.org), extending all the way from Punta del Capo, near Sorrento, to Punta Germano, near Positano. You can rent a small launch from one of the many boatyards in the area, or hire one of their captains to take you where you want. You can also sign up for one of their organized excursions. Reliable companies are **Coop Marina della Lobra,** Marina della Lobra (✆ **081-8089380;** www.marinalobra.com); **Cooperativa S. Antonio,** Marina del Cantone (✆ **081-8081638;** cooperativasantonio@libero.it); and **Nautica 'O Masticiello,** Marina del Cantone (✆ **081-8081443,** 081-8082006, or 339-3142791; www.masticiello.com).

Our favorite excursion is the one to the **Bay of Ieranto** 𝕏𝕏𝕏, a lovely cove with a magical atmosphere. Well-known to the ancient Greeks who named it *Hyeros Anthos,* meaning "Sacred Flower," this bay was declared a protected area in 1984 and, as a result, it remains a completely untouched haven. Cut into the cliff, the cove of clear water ends in a beach, Marina del Cantone, where a few boats are usually moored. In the afternoon, oblique sunlight creates the odd illusion that the water has disappeared and the boats are suspended in thin air, a phenomenon we love to watch. Arriving by boat to this lovely cove is a striking and marvelous experience. Rent a boat—with or without driver—and dedicate about a half-day for the excursion. From the beach, hug the coast heading southwest till you see the large Y-shaped promontory called *Sedia del Diavolo* ("Devil's Chair," a particularly appropriate name when you see it during a flaming sunset). As you pass the first arm of the Y, with the medieval watchtower **Torre di Montalto,** is a pretty little cove, which is an introduction to the more spectacular bay that awaits you farther along. Once you pass the second arm of the Y, the Bay of Ieranto opens like a fan in front of your bow and is closed to the west by Punta Campanella (below). Beyond, starts the Gulf of Naples.

If you are moderately fit, we highly recommend hiking the local **footpaths** for breathtaking views. The area offers 22 marked and maintained hiking trails, for a total length of 110km (66 miles). One of the best hikes is the one to **Punta Campanella** 𝕏, much more impressive than the drive there (mentioned earlier in this section). From the village of Termini, take the small sloping street to the right of the central square: This road slowly descends to the hamlet of Cercito, and then continues down the **Vallone della Cala di Mitigliano.** This beautiful valley is filled with olive groves and typical vegetation (called *macchia mediterranea*), including scented *mirto,* a plant that is quite rare nowadays. The trail then crosses a plateau with large boulders and the ruins of **Torre di Namonte,** a medieval watchtower. Past the tower, the trail begins a steep descent toward the sea as the beautiful profile of Capri looms into view. You'll get clear views of Capri, with Monte Tiberio, Monte Solaro, and the Faraglioni, only 5km (3 miles) away. A modern lighthouse guards this dangerous cape and its waters, made treacherous by the many rocks in the Capri Narrows.

On the last part of the trail, you'll actually be treading the ancient **Via Minerva,** the original road that led to the Greek temple dedicated to Athena (called Minerva by the Romans). To be visible to all passing ships, the temple was positioned near the lighthouse. The olive groves in this area go back thousands of years and were originally planted by the Greeks: Believing that olive oil was a gift from Athena, the goddess of wisdom—we tend to agree with that—they brought gifts of olive oil to her temple.

Punta Campanella takes its name from the bell on **Torre Minerva,** the watchtower—built in 1335 and redone in 1566—that warned of pirate incursions (*campanella* means

Impressions

And lo! the Siren shores like mists arise.
Sunk were at once the winds; the air above,
And waves below, at once forgot to move;
Some demon calm'd the air and smooth'd the deep,
Hush'd the loud winds, and charm'd the waves to sleep.
Now every sail we furl, each oar we ply;
Lash'd by the stroke, the frothy waters fly . . .

—Homer, *The Odyssey*, book XII, lines 97–101,
translation Alexander Pope (1616)

"small bell"). Near the tower are the remains of a Roman villa. From a cliff to the east of the tower, you can look down into the wild, but sheltered, Bay of Ieranto (below). The trail goes from 300m (984 ft.) down almost to sea level; count on spending about 45 minutes for the descent and a bit more for the ascent. If you like a challenge, you could take the alternate trail to Punta Campanella: Starting from Termini, you first climb up **Mount San Costanzo,** at 497m (1,630 ft.) above sea level, before descending to the point. It is even more picturesque, but quite a bit longer and a lot more strenuous (allow about 3 hr. for this trail).

Another of our favorite hikes is the trail to the **Bay of Ieranto** (above). The terrain is quite steep at times and can be moderately challenging. The best time to go is early afternoon to have a chance to experience the water phenomenon described earlier. From Nerano, take the street at the right-hand side of the village, past the last cluster of houses. This street connects to a trail on the slopes of **Monte San Costanzo,** the westernmost peak of the **Monti Lattari.** The trail descends through macchia mediterranea and eventually descends the cliffs overlooking the sea, affording spectacular views. Budget a little over an hour each way.

One last hike we greatly recommend is the one down to **Fiordo di Crapolla** and its beach. From the village of Torca (see earlier), take Via Pedara, which will eventually turn into a dirt path. The trail descends a steep slope among olive groves and old farmhouses, and then among the rocks of a narrow crack in the cliff. As you descend on the western side of the cliff, you will see the ruins of the 12th-century abbey of San Pietro. Once at the bottom, you'll find a small beach; the blue water beyond the cove is broken by many rocks—the very ones, it is said, where the Sirens wrecked the ships of innocent mariners. By the beach you can also see the ruins of a patrician Roman villa, where the ancient town of Capreolae (today Crappolla) was built. Figure on spending about 30 minutes on the descent.

WHERE TO STAY

We review **Don Alfonso, Oasi Olimpia Relais, Quattro Passi, Relai Blu,** and **Taverna del Capitano** in "Where to Dine," below, because they are all outstanding restaurants. Yet we also highly recommend staying in the few delightful rooms they rent, as they also happen to offer some of the best accommodations in the area. Below are a few additional choices.

MODERATE

Hotel Bellavista Francischiello ⋐   This family-run hotel enjoys a wonderfully scenic position on the cliffs. Guest units are bright and comfortable, with tiled floors, spacious bathrooms, and private terraces (the sunset views, with Capri in the foreground, are amazing). Amenities include a swimming pool set on a garden terrace overlooking the sea, and a new spa with attached gym. The attached restaurant, **Riccardo di Francischiello** (see "Where to Dine," later in this section), claims to be the heir of the historic **Antico Francischiello** next door; to settle the score you'll have to give each a fair trial.

Via Partenope 26, 80061 Massa Lubrense. ⟂ **081-8789181.** Fax 081-8089341. www.francischiello.it. 32 units. 140€ ($196/£98) double; 266€ ($372/£186) junior suite. Rates include buffet breakfast. Children 2 and under stay free in parent's room. AE, DC, MC, V. Free parking. **Amenities:** Restaurant; bar; boat and mountain bike rental; concierge; outdoor pool; solarium; spa. *In room:* A/C, satellite TV, minibar, hair dryer, safe.

Hotel Sant'Agata *(Finds)*   Close to the center of town and housed in a modern building, this hotel is a welcome addition to Sant'Agata. Guest rooms vary in size, with corner rooms being the most spacious. They are pleasantly furnished with a mix of rattan and modern furniture, classic details, and ceramic-tiled floors. All the rooms open onto private balconies or terraces and are equipped with modern and well-kept bathrooms. The newly added swimming pool is beautiful, with an adjacent Jacuzzi area.

Via dei Campi 8/a, 80064 Sant'Agata sui due Golfi. ⟂ **081-8080800.** Fax 081-5330749. www.hotelsantagata.com. 28 units. 150€ ($210/£105) double. Rates include breakfast. AE, MC, V. Free parking. **Amenities:** Dining room; bar; concierge; garden; Internet point; outdoor pool; solarium. *In room:* A/C, satellite TV, minibar, safe.

INEXPENSIVE

Hotel La Primavera *(Finds)*   Small and welcoming, this family-run hotel offers comfortable quiet accommodations and a relaxing atmosphere, all at moderate prices. The large guest rooms are simply but pleasantly decorated, with modern wooden furniture, white-washed walls, and ceramic-tiled floors. The nicely tiled bathrooms are spacious and a number of rooms open onto private terraces with sea views. The hotel's restaurant is very good and offers local fare.

Via IV Novembre 3/G, 80061 Massa Lubrense. ⟂ **081-8789125.** Fax 081-8089556. 16 units. 100€ ($140/£70). Rates include buffet breakfast. Children 1 and under stay free in parent's room. AE, DC, MC, V. Free parking. Closed mid-Jan to mid-Feb. **Amenities:** Restaurant; bar; room service; terrace. *In room:* A/C, satellite TV, hair dryer, minibar/fridge; safe.

WHERE TO DINE

After the beauty we have described in the previous pages, you might think that's what attracts most visitors to this area; but the Massa Lubrense region is also one of the most sought-after dining destinations in all of Italy. A number of inspired local personalities have given birth to some of the best dining in the whole country—and possibly in the world. The stiff competition, far from cooling down the entrepreneurial spirit, fosters the creation of great new restaurants and amping up of the old ones. *"Pancia fatti capanna,"* as an old Italian saying goes: "Tummy, become as large as a hut." You would need days to sample just the best offerings of this area, having three full meals a day! Even then, you would still miss out on the snacks, such as the delicious local bread—studded with your choice of salami, local walnuts, olives, or sweet peppers—such as the one made by **Antico Panificio Gargiulo,** Via Rivo a Casa 8, off Via Roma in Massa Lubrense. Excellent local cheeses include multiple varieties of mozzarella—try the *treccia, scamorza,* or the delicious *triavulilli*—and the small *caci-cavalli farciti* (pear-shaped cheese studded or filled with sun-dried tomatoes, butter, olives, or ham). Some of the best purveyors are **Caseificio Cordiale,** Via Campi 30, off Corso Sant'Agata in Sant'Agata sui Due Golfi (⟂ **081-8080888**); **Caseificio**

Savarese, Via IV Novembre 19/a, in Massa Lubrense (© **081-8789825**); and **Caseificio Valestra,** Via Bozzaotra 13, in Monticchio, before Sant'Agata sui Due Golfi (© **081-8780119**). Finally, don't miss the other local farm products, including olive oil, cured meats, dried fruits, and spirits, which you can find at **Da Ferdinando,** Corso Sant'Agata 53, in Sant'Agata sui Due Golfi (© **081-8780196**), or at **Don Alfonso** (below).

EXPENSIVE

Don Alfonso 1890 ✸✸✸ SORRENTINE/CREATIVE   Reputed to be the best restaurant in southern Italy, and a member of the Relais & Châteaux association, Don Alfonso does indeed offer superb everything: food, location, and service. The elegant dining rooms inside this historical pink residence in the heart of town overlook the delightful garden, and the ambience is welcoming and never stuffy. The owners Livia and Alfonso Iaccarino, also started an organic farm—**Azienda Agricola Le Peracciole** on Punta Campanella—in order to have their own source of perfect ingredients. All the food on the menu is prepared with produce and meats from this farm, while fish and cheese come from the best local producers. The way to go is to choose one of the two tasting menus, one with more creative dishes, and the other featuring revisited local classics; but you can also choose a la carte. The menus are seasonal, but we hope you'll find the *pesce spada ai ceci e al timo* (swordfish with thyme and chickpeas) or the *salame di cinghiale affumicato all'alloro* (smoked boar salami with bay leaves). We also highly recommend their roasted chicken (free-range, organically fed, and seasoned with fresh herbs—exquisite). Do ask to visit the century-old cellar, excavated in tufa stone, which spans three levels.

Above the restaurant is the **Don Alfonso 1890 Relais,** with garden, library, bar, private parking, and nine delightfully appointed suites (one is actually an apartment). These are decorated with hardwood floors and elegant classic furnishings, including many antiques (280€/$392/£196 junior suite; 380€/$532/£266 suite, including top-notch breakfast).

Corso Sant'Agata 11. © **081-8780026.** Fax 081-5330226. www.donalfonso.com. Reservations required (also online); children 5 and under not allowed at dinner. Secondi 25€–32€ ($35–$45/£18–£22). Tasting menu 90€–120€ ($126–$168/£63–£84). AE, DC, MC, V. Oct 1–May 31 Wed–Sun 12:30–2:30pm and 8–10:30pm; June 1–Sept 30 Wed–Sun 12:30–2:30pm and Tues–Sun 8–10:30pm.

Quattro Passi SORRENTINE/CREATIVE   From the charming garden-terrace among lemon trees and bougainvillea to the somewhat more formal dining room with arched doorways and hand-painted ceramic floors, what you experience here is the soul of the Mediterranean: Its colors and touches of exuberance are all matched by professional service and excellent food. The sophisticated appetizers might include the likes of *totano ripieno di provola con cozza gratinata e tortino di patate* (stuffed squid and mussel au gratin with potato torte). Among the primi are *pappardelle fave piselli e formaggio* (large fresh pasta with peas, fresh fava beans, and cheese shavings); and the secondi include intriguing choices like *rose di sogliola con capperi pomodorini e patate* (rosettes of sole with capers, cherry tomatoes, and potatoes). The homemade bread is served with citrus- or herb-flavored butter. For dessert, try the local specialty, *delizie al limone* (puff pastry filled with lemon cream), or one of the more creative choices, such as the superb chocolate torte with coffee-flavored ice-cream cake and orange sauce. Under the restaurant is the **Quattro Passi Relais,** with five large guest rooms opening on the garden. Appointed with sober country elegance, rooms include all the usual comforts, like A/C and spacious tiled bathrooms (180€/$252/£126 double, including breakfast).

Via Vespucci 13, Marina del Cantone. © 081-8082800. Fax 081-8081271. www.ristorantequattropassi.com. Reservations recommended on weekends. Secondi 21€–42€ ($29–$59/£15–£29). AE, MC, V. Thurs–Tues 12:30–3:30pm and Thurs–Mon 7:30–11pm; daily in summer. Closed Nov–Dec 25.

Relais Blu ★★ *Finds* Seemingly suspended in thin air, between sea and sky, this recently opened restaurant-cum-hotel is located on the road to Massa Lubrense, a short distance from Sorrento (the bus stops nearby). What was once a private villa has been transformed into a strikingly stylish hotel. The views from the terrace opening onto the sea are absolutely breathtaking—Capri feels so close you could touch it—and we highly recommend a visit, if only for drinks at sunset. The warm welcome of Antonino Acampora will make your visit even more special. The chef has worked with some of the greatest—Heinz Beck and Alain Ducasse for instance—and offers a seasonal menu based on the best ingredients this stretch of coast has to offer. The tasting menus (one for 68€/$95/£48, the other for 80€/$112/£56) are the way to go, but you can also choose a la carte: The updated *pezzogna all'acqua pazza* (local fish in a tomato and herb broth) is a delight as is the lamb with local herbs. The 11 **guest rooms** are in keeping with the decor: elegant contemporary furnishings, picture windows, fine linens, state-of-the-art bathrooms, and private gardens and terraces (300€/$420/£210 double; suite 350€–400€/$490–$560/£245–£280).

Via Roncato 60, Termini, 80061 Massa Lubrense. © 081-8789552. Fax 081-8789304. www.relaisblu.com. Reservations recommended on weekends. Secondi 20€–30€ ($28–$42/£14–£21). AE, DC, MC, V. Daily noon–3:30pm and 7–11:30pm. Closed Jan 1–Feb 28.

MODERATE
Antico Francischiello da Peppino ★ SORRENTINE One of the region's historical restaurants, its fame has not abated in recent years, and it remains a great local favorite. The food is very good—they stick to their traditional guns: No attempts at nouvelle cuisine with skimpy portions here—and you'll find all the local specialties prepared with practiced skill. We like the seafood tasting menu because it allows you to try a large variety of dishes: Our favorites are *cozze gratinate* (mussels au gratin), *gnocchetti verdi all'astice* (green potato dumplings with lobster), and *zuppa di pesce* (fish stew). For smaller appetites, the rich buffet of antipasti is enough to suffice as a light meal. If you are here by sunset, an *aperitivo* on the terrace is an absolute must.

Via Partenope 27, Massa Lubrense. © 081-5339780. www.francischiello.com. Reservations recommended on weekends. Secondi 12€–25€ ($17–$35/£8.40–£18). AE, MC, V. Thurs–Tues noon–3:30pm and 7–11:30pm; daily in summer (June–Sept, though dates vary).

Conca del Sogno ★ *Finds* SORRENTINE SEAFOOD This restaurant is a standout not only for the good food but also for its unique setting perched atop rocks by the beach: The little cove is known locally as "dream cove," which, by the way, is the name of the restaurant. From Marina del Cantone, a few-minutes ride in a motor dinghy will get you to the restaurant, which caters mostly to the owners of the private sailboats and motoryachts anchored in the little bay. Meals as served throughout the day, with a menu based—you guessed—on seafood, as well as on local cheeses and produce. We highly recommend the tasty *gamberetti di Crapolla saltati con sale e pepe* (local shrimp sautéed with salt and pepper) and the perfect grilled catch of the day. Everything is simple and delicious, including the homemade desserts.

Baia di Recommone, Nerano. ℂ 081-8081036. Reservations recommended on weekends. Secondi 12€–21€ ($17–$29/£8.40–£15). AE, MC, V. Daily noon–11pm. Closed Nov 1–Mar 31.

Oasi Olimpia Relais ⍟ SORRENTINE   This excellent restaurant is housed in a former aristocratic villa a short distance away from the center of Sant'Agata. The sur-roundings are splendid and you can take full advantage of the grounds in the summer season when meals are also served in the delightful outdoor arbor terrace covered with wisteria. Otherwise, the elegant dining room provides the perfect background for a romantic dinner. The cuisine is traditional and—while not attempting to rival Don Alfonso's haute cuisine (above)—definitely deserves a mention of honor. The seasonal menu is based on local produce and fish, and we highly recommend the delicate *risotto agli agrumi di Sorrento* (risotto with local citrus fruits) and the tasteful *calamarata* (medley of pasta and squid with fresh tomatoes). The wine list is small but top-notch.

They also offer 11 elegantly appointed rooms, which we like even more than Don Alfonso's (above); they are more airy and bright, with beautiful sea views. Guests can enjoy the outdoor swimming pool and the courtesy van to the beach (320€/$448/£224 double, including buffet breakfast). The cooking classes are very well-organized.

Via Deserto 26. ℂ 081-8080560. Reservations recommended. Secondi 11€–38€ ($15–$53/£7.70–£27). AE, DC, MC, V. Sat–Thurs noon–3pm and 7:30–10:30pm.

Lo Scoglio ⍟ *Finds*   Opened in 1958 by the De Simone family, this restaurant is still run by Signora Antonietta with her children and nephews, all of whom will surely give you a warm welcome. Everything on the menu is made from local ingredients pro-duced by family-run farms in the area. All the fish here are not only caught by local fishermen but also, whenever possible, kept alive in the restaurant's seawater fish tank. We recommend the delectable and simple spaghetti *con le zucchine* (with zucchini), the fancy linguine *all'aragosta* (with local lobster) and, if it is on the menu—and if you don't mind a bit of work—the excellent *zuppa di pesce* (soupy stew with whole fish). We also recommend the homemade desserts.

Piazze delle Sirene 15, Località Marina del Cantone. ℂ 081-8081026. Reservations recommended on weekends. Secondi 12€–28€ ($17–$39/£8.40–£20). AE, DC, MC, V. Daily noon–3pm and 7:30–10:30pm.

Taverna del Capitano ⍟⍟⍟   This is our favorite restaurant on the peninsula. Located right on the best beach in the area, it is a refuge of Mediterranean simplicity. The kitchen offers wonderful local homemade cuisine born from careful research and a great love for the produce of this land. The chef's free interpretation marries the tastes of the sea with those of the vegetable garden he personally supervises. There are three tasting menus at different prices and a menu a la carte, all seasonal; you might find *insalata di aragosta con verdure* (lobster and fresh vegetable salad), *zuppa di gam-beri e cicorie selvatiche* (shrimp and dandelion soup), or *pesce alla salsa di agrumi* (fish in citrus sauce). Desserts, like everything else, are homemade. The wine list has a small but excellent selection of wines, both regional and national. The Caputo family also offers hospitality in the 15 **guest rooms** (150€/$196/£98 double, including break-fast) located above the restaurant; all are nicely appointed with a nautical feeling—the best overlook the sea—and all have private terraces.

Piazza delle Sirene 10, Marina del Cantone, 80061 Massa Lubrense. ℂ 081-8081028. Fax 081-8081892. www.tavernadelcapitano.it. Reservations recommended on weekends. Tasting menus 50€–80€ ($70–$112/£35–£56). Sec-ondi 14€–28€ ($20–$38/£9.80–£20). AE, DC, MC, V. Wed–Sun 12:30–3:30pm and Tues–Sun 7:30–10:30pm; daily in summer. Closed 3 weeks in Jan.

INEXPENSIVE

Beitempi ✦ SORRENTINE/CREATIVE This recently renovated restaurant serves simple but delicious local cuisine in pleasantly rustic small dining rooms (or on the terrace in clement weather). The menu offers such delicious specialties as the unusual *pasta e ceci coi gamberi* (thick soup of garbanzo beans, short pasta, and shrimp) or homemade fettuccine *al peperoncino* (with red pepper)—everything is simple, hearty, and satisfying. You can also take a break from seafood: They prepare a great *misti di carne alla griglia,* a platter of several kinds of perfectly grilled meats. Homemade breads and desserts round out your meal—don't pass up the *delizia al limone* (small puff pastries filled with lemon-flavored cream), a traditional local dessert masterfully prepared here. You'll find several local wines among the fine selections.

Via Termine 3. ⓒ 081-5330240. Reservations recommended on weekends. Secondi 8€–15€ ($11–$21/£5.60–£11). No credit cards. Thurs–Tues noon–3:30pm and 7–11:30pm; summer daily.

Il Grottino SORRENTINE Under the shade of citrus plants and grapevines, this rustic trattoria serves local fare, nicely prepared. The menu is seasonal, but you might find *pennette con le zucchine* (short penne pasta with zucchini) or the scrumptious *manicaretti ripieni di mozzarella e ricotta* (pasta filled with mozzarella and ricotta, all baked and served in a terra-cotta casserole). The winter menu includes platters of grilled meat, which you can enjoy in the small dining rooms containing fireplaces and arched ceilings. The local wine here is excellent.

Via Villaggio Caso 23. ⓒ 081-8081012. Reservations recommended on weekends. Secondi 8€–16€ ($11–$22/£5.60–£11). No credit cards. Thurs–Tues noon–3:30pm and 7–11:30pm; daily in summer.

Lo Stuzzichino SORRENTINE This promising addition to the local dining scene offers an excellent seasonal menu based on the best locally produced ingredients and a down-to-earth welcoming atmosphere. The outdoor terrace is very pleasant. We loved the *antipasto della casa,* and the delicious *ravioli di Sorrento* (mozzarella-filled ravioli), as well as the masterfully prepared *scialatielli ai frutti di mare* (traditional fresh pasta with seafood) and the perfect *frittura di calamari e gamberi* (deep-fried medley of squid and shrimp). If it is on the menu, do taste the delicious *torta di ricotta e pere* (torte with sweet ricotta and pears).

Via Deserto 1, Sant'Agata sui Due Golfi. ⓒ 081-5330010. Reservations recommended on weekends. Secondi 9€–14€ ($13–$20/£6.30–£9.80). AE, MC, V. Thurs–Tues noon–3:30pm and 7:30–11pm; daily Jul–Aug. Closed Jan 25–Feb 20.

7

The Amalfi Coast

Celebrated by 19th-century tourists as the most beautiful stretch of coast in the world, the fame of the Amalfi Coast has not abated in modern days. The Costiera Amalfitana was already well-known for its beauty during antiquity and the Middle Ages. Its unique views and plunging cliffs have inspired the works of many famous artists, from Giovanni Boccaccio to Richard Wagner. The small towns and hamlets along the Costiera have been the preferred refuges of many others, including Henrik Ibsen, Pablo Picasso, Rudolf Nureyev and, more recently, Gore Vidal.

The Amalfi Coast is a magical landscape of cultivated cliffs hanging over a beautiful sea, interspersed with villages that literally appear to have grown from the underlying rocks. Here and there, the mouth of a small river has created a natural harbor and a favorable nook for a larger town. Such is the case in Amalfi, the queen of the Costiera. The valley of its river allowed for the development of paper mills that produced paper for much of Europe during the Middle Ages and well into the Renaissance, while its harbor became the shipyard that fueled Amalfi's political and commercial power.

Amalfi and Positano are not alone by the sea: They share the company of a number of smaller and lesser-known but delightful villages, such as Cetara, Minori, and Praiano. In between these towns and hamlets, small beaches are scattered at the bottoms of the cliffs—which make for beautiful, but sometimes forbidding, landscapes.

Here the sea is never far: Even the mountain villages, of which Ravello is the most famous, afford breathtaking views of the Mediterranean. Hiking this region's many trails is one of the best ways to enjoy its incomparable natural beauty as well as its historical and artistic monuments.

The Amalfi Coast is one of the most visited seaside destinations in the world, particularly during spring and summer, when innumerable art and cultural events take place and the sweet evening air is pervaded by the scent of citrus flowers. In winter, everything is much quieter, as many places close down and the sea gets too chilly to swim in. You may have the place all to yourself in these colder months, but you'll miss much of the spirit it shows when in full bloom.

1 Getting to Know the Amalfi Coast

GETTING THERE

BY FERRY When possible, we prefer to travel to this coast by ferry because we love approaching its destinations from the sea; indeed, you would sell yourself short if you didn't have a look at this stretch of coast from the water. **Alicost** (© **081-7611004** or 081-811986 in Naples; © **089-873301** or 089-871483 in Amalfi; and © **089-875032** or 089-811164 in Positano; www.lauroweb.com/alicost.htm or www.alilauro.it) maintains regular *aliscafo* (hydrofoil) and *motonave* (regular ferry) service

Myth or Reality? The Truth about the Amalfi Coast Drive

Myth or reality? Is the Amalfi Coast Drive as hair-raising as they say? Much depends on whom you ask. One of the world's most famous scenic drives, the whole stretch of road between Vietri sul Mare and Positano is only 36km (22 miles); and while the technical difficulty of the drive is moderate (easier than the road to Hana in Maui, let's say, but more difficult than the Pacific Coast Highway), traffic and the Neapolitan aggressive driving style can turn it into a headache for even the most experienced driver—and into a complete nightmare if you generally drive on spacious freeways in flat or gentle terrain. Alternative forms of transportation are well developed (below), so you might do yourself a favor if you take advantage of one of those. On the other hand, if you want to explore this area in depth within a limited time period, having your own car with driver will provide you with more flexibility.

from Naples, Sorrento, Salerno, and the islands of Capri and Ischia, to Positano, Amalfi, and Minori. Fares run between 2€ ($2.80/£1.40) and 18€ ($25/£13) depending on the distance and the boat. *Note:* You must make reservations at least 24 hours in advance. The **Metrò del Mare** (✆ **199-446644;** www.metrodelmare.com) operates between Naples and Salerno April through September, with stops in Amalfi and Positano. The ferry ride from **Molo Beverello** in Naples to Positano takes 75 minutes with the express line MM2, and about 2 hours with the local line MM3; count on 25 additional minutes to Amalfi on either ferry line. The special ticket **Terra&Mare** includes the ferry plus ground transportation for 45 minutes before and 45 minutes after the ferry link and costs 8.50€ ($12/£5.95). **Cooperativa Sant'Andrea** (✆ **089-873190;** www.coopsantandrea.it) offers regular frequent service between Salerno, Vietri, Maiori, Minori, Cetara, Amalfi, Positano, and Sorrento, as well as special cruises and excursions, including to Capri; tickets are about 5€ to 9€ ($7–$14/£3.50–£6.30) depending on the distance.

BY BUS   SITA (✆ **081-5522176** in Naples and ✆ 089-871016 in Amalfi; www.sitabus.it) maintains regular bus service from Naples, Sorrento, and Salerno to Amalfi and Positano; for most other villages and hamlets you need to switch in Amalfi (bus terminal on Piazza Flavio Gioia, ✆ **089-871009**) to the local lines serving the area.

BY HIRED CAR It may sound extravagant, but hiring a car with a chauffeur makes sense, especially if you plan to stay here only a day or two. This option is gaining popularity because its cost is relatively moderate and it has so many advantages. It removes the stress of driving and parking, it affords you complete comfort and your own pace, and your experienced local driver can double as a guide. You'll spend about 35€ ($49/£98) per hour for two people in a sedan for a half-day trip; less for longer periods. We recommend **ANA Limousine Service** (Piazza Garibaldi 73, 80100 Napoli; ✆/fax **081-282000**); **2golfi car service** (Via Deserto 30/e, 80064 Sant'Agata sui due Golfi; ✆ **339-8307748** or 338-5628649; fax 081-5330882; www.duegolficarservice. com); and **Italy Limousine** (✆ **081-8016184,** 335-6732245, or 338-9681866; www. italylimousine.it). All of these use new cars with air-conditioning (very important in summer) and trained English-speaking drivers.

BY RENTAL CAR If you decide to drive, from the exit VIETRI SUL MARE on the *autostrada* A3 NAPOLI-SALERNO, follow the signs for VIETRI, MAIORI, AMALFI, and

POSITANO; they will lead you to the famed SS 163, the coastal road which meanders all the way from Salerno to Positano and a bit beyond. Many of the villages and hamlets of the Amalfi Coast are right on SS 163—which is why the traffic is unbearable—and those that aren't on SS 163 are on well-indicated side roads off SS 163.

You can also reach SS 163 from Vico Equense and Sorrento heading east. You'll save about 20 minutes, but you'll be driving right at the edge of the cliff; for your peace of mind, choose the inner lane. In any case, you'll enjoy the best views only when you stop and park along this route. *Note:* Because of the solid traffic here in summer, local authorities enforce a system of "alternate plate number" permits, under which only cars with license plates ending in even numbers can circulate one day, and only those with uneven plate numbers on the other. Keep this in mind when making your plans.

GETTING ORIENTED

The Amalfi Coast opens onto the northern half of the Gulf of Salerno, and stretches from the town of Salerno westward to Positano. Farther west, the Sorrento peninsula begins, with Punta Campanella—the narrow point of land that divides the Gulf of Salerno from the Gulf of Naples (see chapter 6). There the SS 163 turns into SS 145, the coastal road of the Sorrento Coast, in the Bay of Naples. The other half of the Gulf of Salerno, from Salerno south, is the plain of Paestum, which we cover in chapter 9.

Starting from the Costiera's easternmost point, you will first find **Vietri sul Mare** and then **Cetara,** both mostly visited by local tourists. Proceeding west and passing Capo (Cape) d'Orso, you will enter the Bay of Amalfi. You'll then come, successively, to the villages of **Maiori, Minori, Atrani,** and, finally, **Amalfi,** the queen of the Costiera. Between Maiori and Atrani are two local roads that proceed upward and inland following the beds of two streams: the road to **Tramonti** (turnoff in Maiori), and the one for **Scala** and **Ravello** (turnoff just after Minori).

The heart of the Amalfi Coast—and its busiest section—is its westernmost stretch between the Costiera's two most famous places, Amalfi and Positano. Past the cape that defines the Bay of Amalfi—Capo di Conca with **Conca dei Marini**—you will find another cape, Capo Sottile, with **Praiano** to the east and **Vettica Maggiore** to the west; this marks the entrance to the deep cove wherein lies **Positano.** At Conca dei Marini you will find the two turnoffs for the terribly steep but immensely rewarding mountain road for **Agerola** and **Furore** (one appears before you enter the village to the east, and the other turns up in Conca itself).

See p. 199 for a map of the Amalfi Coast.

GETTING AROUND

Ferries are really convenient and a lot of locals use them instead of slogging along the local road, often completely clogged with traffic in summer. Vietri, Maiori, Minori, Cetara, Amalfi, and Positano are all connected by ferries (above). Service is really frequent in the good season, when road traffic is at its worst, and with the hydrofoil, you can cut the travel time in half—views, though, tend to be less nice. To reach the other towns and hamlets not on the ferry routes, taking a **bus** (above) is often the most convenient, and certainly the cheapest, way to get from one village to another. For example, the ride from Positano to Amalfi will take you about 20 minutes and cost you about 1.30€ ($1.80/90p); the ride from Amalfi to Ravello takes only 12 minutes and costs 1.20€ ($1.68/ 84p).

Other options are **taxi** (telephone numbers listed for each destination) or **car service** (above). Distances are short and therefore fares remain very reasonable. Make sure drivers use the meter or agree on a price before going. You can also hire a **boat,** with or without a driver, to take you to secluded beaches (or simply to the next town) from the harbors and marinas of Amalfi, Maiori, and Positano.

Renting a **car** is a possibility we don't recommend, especially in summer, though you can do it; if you love to drive but hate the idea of getting stuck in traffic, you might like to try your hand at using an Italian **scooter** and play the locals' dangerous swerving game. You can rent both cars and scooters in Sorrento (see chapter 6); and scooters only in Positano at **Positano Rent a Scooter,** Viale Pasitea 99 (© **089-8122077**). You'll spend about 40€ ($56/£28) per day for a scooter at the height of summer.

As unlikely as it might seem, there is also much that you can do here **on foot** ★★. SS 163 has only been around since 1840; before then, trails and footpaths were the only ways to go (other than by sea). These paths are still used for bringing animals to pasture and are well kept and well marked. We suggest the best ones for each destination in the following sections, but if you are into serious **hiking,** you should contact the local tourist offices. You should also get the very good map published by the C.A.I. Club Alpino Italiano *Monti Lattari Penisola Sorrentina, Costiera Amalfitana: Carta dei sentieri* sold for 8€ ($10/£5) at the best newsstands and bookstores in Ravello, Amalfi, and Tramonti. You might also want to get in touch with **Comunità Montana Penisola Amalfitana** in Via Municipio, 84010 Tramonti (© **089-876354** or 089-876547), for info on guides and trails.

2 Positano ★★

17km (10 miles) W of Amalfi, 51km (101 miles) W of Salerno, 56km (35 miles) SE of Naples

Hugging a semi-vertical rock formation, Positano is the quintessence of picturesque. Once one of the most exclusive retreats in Italy, this seaside resort has been thoroughly "discovered" but retains its character. Its unique mix of seascapes, colors, art, and cultural life has fascinated many famous artists, from Pablo Picasso and Paul Klee to Toscanini, Bernstein, and Steinbeck. Today, it is a favorite destination of tourists and fashionistas, coming to buy what has become known as "Positano Fashion" from the local designer showrooms and elegant boutiques, and partaking of the cultural life.

ESSENTIALS

GETTING AROUND   Orange shuttle **buses** make the loop of Viale Pasitea, Via Cristoforo Colombo, and Via G. Marconi (SS 163), stopping several times along the way. They run every half-hour, saving your tired knees from some of the town's endless steps. You can purchase the 1€ ($1.40/70p) ticket on board.

A **boat service** links Marina Grande to Fornillo during the summer, with boats every half-hour.

Taxis can be called at © **089-875230.**

VISITOR INFORMATION   The **AAST tourist office** is at Via del Saracino 4, 84017 Positano (© **089-875067;** www.aziendaturismopositano.it). It is open Monday to Saturday 8:30am to 2pm, with additional hours (3:30 to 8pm) between July and August.

FAST FACTS   You'll find a **pharmacy** on Viale Pasitea (© **089-875863**). For an **ambulance,** dial © **118.** You can call the **police** at © **113** or at © **112.** The **post office** (© **089-875142**) is at Via G. Marconi 320 (SS 163), at the corner with Viale Pasitea; it is open Monday to Saturday 8am to 2pm. You will find several banks with

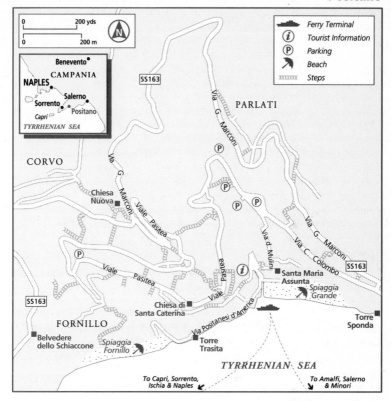

ATMs, including a **Banco di Napoli** at Piazza dei Mulini 18 (© **089-8122367**). The **exchange office** is in Piazza dei Mulini (© **089-875864**).

SPECIAL EVENTS   **Summer Music** is an international chamber music festival that takes place from the end of August to the beginning of September every year (2007 marked its 40th anniversary). The **Festival of the Assunta** is a lively event held August 14 and 15, when the violent attack of the Saracens and the Madonna's miraculous intervention are reenacted, accompanied by much noise and fanfare by Positanese of all ages. The histrionics include a fake fire and colorful historic costumes.

EXPLORING THE TOWN

Luckily, crowds haven't affected Positano's unique location, and the town remains as picturesque as ever. Steep ramps of stairs replace streets. The typical pastel-colored houses—cubes with domed roofs and porticoes or loggias overlooking the sea—poke from the overflowing green of gardens and citrus groves. *Tip:* Wearing comfortable shoes without heels is a must here; otherwise, climbing the steep alleys and many steps will be an ordeal.

The heart of town is **Marina Grande,** the beach where fishermen used to haul up their boats. At its western end is the pier where ferries arrive and depart. From Marina Grande starts **Via Positanesi d'America** ✸✸—a cliffside pedestrian promenade, and the only flat street in Positano—which stretches along the shore past the cape of **Torre Trasita** to the smaller beach of **Fornillo.** Not far from Marina Grande is the **Collegiata di Santa Maria Assunta** ★★ (Piazza Flavio Gioia; © **089-875480;** daily 8am–noon and 4–7pm), founded in the 13th century and later decorated with a gorgeous majolica dome. Inside, you will find the famous *tavola* of the *Madonna Nera* (Black Madonna), an icon in 13th-century Byzantine style. The church is at the center of the **Festival of the Assunta** (see "Special Events," earlier in this section).

In our opinion, though, the best churches of Positano are the lesser-known ones. The small **Chiesa di Nuova** (on Via Chiesa Nuova), restored in the 18th century, which has a striking colored **tile floor** ★★, one of the most beautiful in an area known for its colorful tile work. The **Chiesa di Santa Caterina** ★★ (Via Pasitea), built for the local Porcelli family, is another small architectural masterpiece in neo-Gothic style, with an elegant bell tower. Just west of Positano on SS 163 is the renowned **Belvedere dello Schiaccone** ★★★, the best lookout on Amalfi Drive. At 200m (656 ft.) above sea level, it overlooks the archipelago of LiGalli and Capo Sottile over a palm and citrus grove, with the splendid Monte Sant'Angelo a Tre Pizzi in the background.

STAYING ACTIVE

Positano is blessed with four delightful **beaches** besides the central **Spiaggia Grande** by the marina: **Fornillo** (linked by boat service from the Marina) to the west of town; and **La Porta, Ciumicello,** and **Arienzo** to the east. The sand is rather gray and pebbly, but the views are idyllic and the sea is clear and refreshing. You can rent a chair and umbrella at the reserved areas for about 15€ ($21/£11) per day, or use the free but crowded public beach. Another beach, **Laurito,** is also a bit out of town, but you can easily reach it with the boat service offered by the restaurant Le Sirene (see "Where to Dine," later in this chapter), which also rents chairs and umbrellas.

For a quieter swim, locals like to take a boat to one of the small coves accessible only by sea. You can **rent a boat** at Spiaggia Grande for between 10€ and 25€ ($14–$35/£7–£18) per hour, depending on kind of boat and length of rental. One popular destination is the archipelago of **Li Galli (The Roosters),** the four small islands visible to the west of Marina Grande. Named Gallo Lungo, Castelluccio, Gallo dei Briganti, and La Rotonda, these are the islands where—according to Homer—the Sirens lived. Indeed, the other name of the archipelago is Sirenuse, from the Latin *Sirenusae,* meaning Sirens. According to legend, these creatures attracted mariners with their enchanted songs and caused their ships to crash into the rocks. In Greek mythology, sirens were represented as birds with human faces and the bodies of fish (hence the name Li Galli, "The Roosters"). Once you skirt past the Sirens and arrive safely on Gallo Lungo, you'll spot a watchtower and the remains of a Roman villa; the archipelago is the site of the house where Rudolf Nureyev spent the last years of his life.

Positano offers many **hiking** opportunities on the town's outskirts, in addition to the town's own steep streets. The most famous trail is **Sentiero degli Dei (Trail of the Gods)** ★★★ linking Positano to Praiano. This is a trail of moderate difficulty, requiring some preparation, but it is—as its name suggests—a divine trail. Sections of it are a ridge trail, running high over the sea and affording magnificent views of the entire coast. Starting from Via Chiesa Nuova at the upper end of Positano (north of SS 163), walk around to the right of the church and continue up the steps at the end of the lane. Cross the road there and take the steps to the left; you'll see red and white markers. Allow yourself 5½ hours; you can then catch a bus back to Positano.

Another scenic trail is the climb to **Monte Tre Pizzi** 🐦🐦, the highest mountain of the Costiera at 1440m (4,723 ft.) in altitude. (If you are planning to reach the top, make sure you bring a warm windbreaker jacket.) Birdwatchers should love this trek, because you'll have many occasions to spot the raptors that nest in the area. The trail starts from the Guardia Forestale (Italian Rangers) station in Positano at an altitude of 700m (2,296 ft.). This magnificent trail wends among patches of pine trees and brooks. Eventually, you will reach the ancient village of **Santa Maria di Castello** with its spectacular natural terrace overlooking Positano (just up from the village). You can also cheat and drive yourself to Santa Maria di Castello (the road approaches from Vico Equense, on the Sorrento side of the peninsula, see chapter 6); the top of the mountain is only a short hike up from the village.

An easier hike is the ascent to **Nocelle** 🐦🐦, at an altitude of 443m (1,453 ft.). In this little paradise where cars are not allowed, you can have an excellent lunch (or dinner) at **Ristorante Santa Croce** (make reservations in advance by calling ✆ **089-875319**). The trail starts at the end of Via Monsignor Clinque, in the upper part of town. Count on spending about 1 hour for the ascent; afterwards, you can return to Positano by bus.

The most popular of the trails is **Via degli Incanti (Trail of Charmes)** 🐦🐦, winding between Positano and Amalfi among terraces of citrus groves. The going is easy in this direction but more demanding from Amalfi. You don't need to hike the whole thing (25km/16 miles), because the trail crosses SS 163 at several points (Praiano, or Conca dei Marini, for instance); choose only a section of the trail, if you wish, using the bus to return.

WHERE TO STAY

As you would expect for such a world-renowned resort, hotels here are rather expensive. In downtown Positano, we recommend **Casa Maresca,** Via Lepanto 17 (✆ **089-875679**), **Casa Soriano,** Via Pasitea (✆ **089-875494**), and **La Fenice,** Via Marconi 4, Chetrara, Positano (✆ **089-875513**); and **La Tavolozza** (Via Cristoforo Colombo; ✆ **089-875040**). In the upper part of town, you'll find the pleasant B&B **Villa Rosa,** Via C. Colombo 127 (✆ **089-811955;** www.villarosapositano.com). A few rooms are offered at **Restaurant Le Sirene** (see later in this chapter).

VERY EXPENSIVE

Hotel Le Sirenuse 🐦🐦   This huge red-and-white 18th-century villa with terraced floors overlooking the bay is a picturesque sight—you may have seen it featured in the film *Only You* with Marisa Tomei and Robert Downey, Jr. Just above the harbor, it was the residence of the Marchesi Sersale family until 1951, and the public spaces are palatial. Guest rooms are large and bright, with vaulted ceilings, antiques, handpainted tile floors, and fine fabrics; all have private terraces and luxurious bathrooms. Most rooms have priceless views of the bay. The hotel's swimming pool is perched on a terrace, and a state-of-the-art health club with an attached Aveda spa offers further relaxation. The buffet breakfast here is lavish, and **La Sponda** (closed 3 weeks in Mar and 3 weeks in Nov; reservations are required) is highly recommended for meals. Children 8 and under are not accepted in the hotel from May 1 through September 30, or at the restaurant for dinner.

Via Cristoforo Colombo 30, 84017 Positano. ✆ 089-875066. Fax 089-811798. www.sirenuse.it. 63 units. 500€–850€ ($700–$1,190/£350–£595) double, from 1,200€ ($1,680/£840) suite. Rates include buffet breakfast. AE, DC, MC, V. Parking 35€ ($49/£25). **Amenities:** Restaurant; 2 bars; concierge; health club; laundry service; lounges; outdoor pool; room service; spa. *In room:* A/C, satellite TV/DVD, hair dryer, minibar, safe.

Il San Pietro di Positano ✫✫✫ This family-run member of the Relais & Châteaux group is *the* place to stay on the Amalfi Coast: One of the best hotels in the country, it affords luxurious accommodations and exceptionally professional service in a wonderful location just outside Positano by Laurito Beach. Elegant public areas have French windows opening onto the garden and the sea; spacious guest rooms are decorated with antiques, tiled floors, and pink-marble bathrooms. All have private terrace and some have huge picture windows. The hotel's private beach is accessible by elevator whenever you get tired of the splendid panoramic swimming pool or the tennis court, and the state-of-the-art fitness center has a wonderful spa. *Note:* The hotel welcomes children only age 10 and above.

The Michelin-rated **Il San Pietro** is our favorite restaurant on this coast for the postcard views, cozy terrace, garden, and exceptional food: Chef Alois Vanlangenacker uses local ingredients—mostly from the hotel's own farm—to create sophisticated yet simple concoctions: We need to mention at least the unique *pollo ruspante in crosta di agrumi* (free-range chicken in a citrus crust). The restaurant is closed November through March and reservations are required.

Via Laurito 2, 84017 Positano. ✆ **800-7352478** Relais & Châteaux toll-free in the U.S., or 089-875455. Fax 089-811449. www.ilsanpietro.it. 60 units. 530€–600€ ($742–$840/£371–£420) double; from 730€ ($1,022/£511) suite. Rates include breakfast. AE, DC, MC, V. Free parking. Closed Nov–Mar. **Amenities:** Restaurant; bar; concierge; health club; laundry service; outdoor pool; room service; sauna; spa; tennis court; water activities. *In room:* A/C, TV, hair dryer, iron, minibar, safe.

EXPENSIVE

Covo dei Saraceni ✫ Named after the fisherman's house that was used as the Saracens's hideout (see "Festival of the Assunta" in "Special Events," earlier in this chapter), this establishment offers peaceful and alluring accommodations right on the marina, away from the hubbub. Guest rooms are large and bright, with comfortable furnishings, terra-cotta floors, and lovely private balconies or terraces with great views. The seawater swimming pool on the fifth-floor terrace and the restaurant, **Savino,** are added incentives.

Via Regina Giovanna 5, 84017 Positano. ✆ 089-875400. Fax 089-875878. www.covodeisaraceni.it. 58 units. 296€ ($414/£207) double, from 400€ ($560/£280) junior suite. Rates include buffet breakfast. Children 2 and under stay free in parent's room. AE, DC, MC, V. Parking 25€ ($35/£18). Closed Nov to mid-Mar. **Amenities:** Restaurant; 2 bars; babysitting; concierge; laundry service; outdoor pool; room service. *In room:* A/C, TV, hair dryer, minibar, safe.

Palazzo Murat ✫ This 18th-century baroque palace near the marina is said to have been built for Gioacchino Murat, Napoleon's brother-in-law and later king of Naples. The five more expensive guest rooms in the historical part of the palace are decorated with antiques and original furnishings; the ones in the new wings are also very nicely appointed. All units have good-size bathrooms, and most rooms have ocean views. The rich buffet breakfast is served in the delightful garden court when weather permits; in August and September this is the site of chamber music concerts (see chapter 3). The hotel's restaurant **Al Palazzo** offers alfresco dining.

Via dei Mulini 23, 84017 Positano. ✆ 089-875177. Fax 089-811419. www.palazzomurat.it. 30 units. 255€–475€ ($357–$665/£179–£333) double. Rates include buffet breakfast. Children 2 and under stay free in parent's room. AE, DC, MC, V. Parking 25€ ($35/£18) nearby. Closed Jan to week before Easter. **Amenities:** Restaurant; babysitting; concierge; garden; laundry service; lounge; room service. *In room:* A/C, satellite TV, hair dryer, minibar, safe.

Villa Franca *(Finds* ✫ This delightful family-run hotel overlooking the sea is one of Positano's lesser-known, distinctive hotels. The common areas are decorated with reproduction artwork and fine tiles to evoke a neoclassical feeling. The motif continues in the elegant, comfortable guest rooms, all of which are decorated in Mediterranean style with bright artistic tiled floors and bathrooms; private balconies overlook the sea. The roof terrace has a 360-degree view over the town and a swimming pool with a solarium. An additional 10 rooms are in the less-inspired annex (the cheaper "standard" rooms are likely to be here; inquire when you book). The hotel's restaurant serves good food in a very romantic setting. Another nice feature is the free shuttle bus to the center of Positano.

Via Pasitea 318, 84017 Positano. © 089-875655. Fax 089-875735. www.villafrancahotel.it. 38 units. 235€–430€ ($329–$602/£165–£301) double. Rates include buffet breakfast. Children 2 and under stay free in parent's room. AE, DC, MC, V. Parking 18€ ($23/£13). Closed Nov–Mar. **Amenities:** Restaurant; bar; concierge; health club; laundry service; lounge; outdoor pool; room service; spa. *In room:* A/C, satellite TV w/pay movies, hair dryer, minibar, safe.

MODERATE

Casa Albertina 🎯🎯 *(Kids)*   This small, family-run hotel offers attentive service and great views. The famous Sicilian writer Luigi Pirandello had his usual abode in one of the beautiful guest rooms, and the rooms here do make you want to settle in. Each is individually decorated, with carefully chosen furniture and a simple, monochromatic theme; French doors open onto private balconies (with water views). When the weather's nice, breakfast is served on the terra-cotta tiled terrace. In the high season, rates include half-board (breakfast and dinner).

Via della Tavolozza 3, 84017 Positano. © 089-875143. Fax 089-811540. www.casalbertina.it. 20 units. 180€–250€ ($252–$350/£126–£175) double. Rates include breakfast. Children 2 and under stay free in parent's room. AE, DC, MC, V. Parking 20€–40€ ($28–$56/£14–£28) nearby. **Amenities:** Restaurant; bar; babysitting on request; concierge; room service; solarium. *In room:* A/C, TV, hair dryer, minibar.

Hotel Buca di Bacco   Centrally positioned on the Marina Grande—a great choice if you don't mind a bit of noise—the excellent hotel boasts beautiful rooms that are all large and well furnished. Most have balconies facing the sea, and six superior rooms have full seafront terraces. The less expensive guest rooms in the annexed buildings enjoy similar levels of comfort. The hotel's restaurant, **La Pergola,** is extremely popular, as is the less pricey snack bar.

Via Rampa Teglia 4, 84017 Positano. © 089-875699. Fax 089-875731. www.bucadibacco.it. 54 units. 190€–335€ ($266–$469/£133–£235) double. Rates include buffet breakfast. AE, DC, MC, V. No parking. Closed 2 weeks in winter. **Amenities:** Restaurant; bar; babysitting; concierge; laundry service; room service. *In room:* A/C, satellite TV, hair dryer (in most rooms), minibar, safe.

Hotel Pupetto   Right on the beach of Fornillo, only a short walk from Marina Grande along the seaside promenade, this family-run hotel was created in the 1950s above the popular restaurant of the same name (below). Guest rooms are large, with simple furniture, whitewashed walls, and tiled floors, each with a private small terrace overlooking the sea. The hotel is accessible by elevator from the road above.

Via Fornillo 37, Spiaggia di Fornillo, 84017 Positano. © 089-875087. Fax 089-811517. www.hotelpupetto.it. 34 units. 185€–225€ ($259–$315/£130–£158) double. Rates include buffet breakfast. AE, DC, MC, V. Parking 15€ ($21/£11). Closed mid-Nov to mid-Mar. **Amenities:** Restaurant; bar; beach; concierge. *In room:* A/C, satellite TV, hair dryer, safe.

INEXPENSIVE

Hotel Bougainville *(Finds)*   This family-run hotel is quite small, having only 14 units, but it's a good choice if you don't mind sacrificing amenities for location—it sits in the heart of Positano only steps from the beach. Rates are very reasonable. Some of the rear-facing guest rooms open onto flowery private terraces, where you can have breakfast in good weather; other rooms overlook the village, and few of the standard doubles have only a miniscule window (make sure you don't get one of those). All are decorated with simple but quality modern furniture and pastel-colored tiled floors, and have good-size bathrooms.

Via Cristoforo Colombo 25, 84017 Positano. © **089-875047.** Fax 089-811150. www.bougainville.it. 14 units. 120€–170€ ($168–$238/£84–£119) double. AE, V. Closed Nov to mid-Mar. **Amenities:** Breakfast lounge; concierge. *In room:* A/C, satellite TV, hair dryer, safe.

Hotel Savoia 🏶🏶 Nestled in the heart of Positano, this quiet, well-run hotel is just steps away from shops and the beach. Guest units are spacious, bright, and comfortably furnished (think good beds and roomy cabinets), with tiled floors and good-size modern bathrooms. Some of the rooms have sea views, while others overlook the village; the best have sauna showers or Jacuzzi tubs. This place has been run by the D'Aiello family since 1936, and prides itself on courteous service.

Via Cristoforo Colombo 73, 84017 Positano. © **089-875003.** Fax 089-811844. www.savoiapositano.it. 42 units. 140€–250€ ($196–$350/£98–£175) double; 290€ ($406/£203) suite. Rates include buffet breakfast. AE, DC, MC, V. Parking 25€ ($35/£18). **Amenities:** Bar; babysitting; concierge; same-day laundry service; room service; terrace. *In room:* A/C, satellite TV, hair dryer, minibar, safe.

RENTALS

Renting a room or a mini-apartment with small cooking facilities might be a cheaper alternative when vacationing in Positano, especially for families. We recommend **Casa Maresca** (Via Lepanto 17; © **089-875679**); **Casa Soriano** (Via Pasitea; © **089-875494**); **La Fenice** (Località Chetrara, © **089-875513**); and **La Tavolozza** (Via Cristoforo Colombo; © **089-875040**).

WHERE TO DINE

Some of the best and most elegant dining in Positano is at the town's top hotels, **Il San Pietro** and **Le Sirenuse,** above.

EXPENSIVE

La Cambusa 🏶 AMALFITAN/SEAFOOD Baldo and Luigi created this restaurant in the 1960s vowing to serve traditionally prepared fish of the highest quality, and they have kept their promise. Only the freshest fish—brought in every morning by local fishermen—is prepared with techniques designed to bring out the natural flavors. Try *penne con gamberetti e rughetta* (penne pasta with shrimp and arugula); or our favorite, *spaghetti con le cozze di scoglio* (spaghetti with sautéed mussels and local cherry tomatoes). For the secondi, pick your fish from the display and have it prepared grilled or *all'acqua pazza* (with an herb broth).

Piazza Amerigo Vespucci 4, near Spiaggia Grande. © **089-875432.** Reservations recommended. Secondi 15€–28€ ($21–$39/£11–£20). AE, DC, MC, V. Daily noon–3pm and 7:30–11pm.

MODERATE

Da Adolfo 🏶 AMALFITAN/SEAFOOD You might like the challenge of reaching this picturesque beach restaurant from SS 163 via the flight of 450 rugged steps. If not, a free shuttle service leaves Marina Grande every 30 minutes—you'll recognize the boat by the red fish on its side (daily 10am–1pm and 4–7pm; later on Sat nights in July and Aug). The restaurant has a great laid-back atmosphere, and the menu includes many simple local dishes. The varied antipasti include zesty vegetables and seafood—such as excellent *polpette di melanzane* (eggplant fritters), *spaghetti con le cozze* (spaghetti with sautéed mussels and tomatoes), and *grigliata di pesce* (medley of fresh grilled seafood). Da Adolfo also offers **beach facilities** with changing rooms, showers, and chair-and-umbrella rentals (8€/$11/£5.60 for both per day).

Spiaggetta di Laurito. ⓒ **089-875022.** Reservations recommended. Secondi 12€–18€ ($17–$25/£8.40–£18). No credit cards. Daily noon–3pm; July–Aug also Sat 8pm–midnight. Closed Oct–May.

Da Vincenzo 🍴🍴 AMALFITAN   In the small stone dining rooms of this family-run restaurant, you'll find great down-home local dishes. The menu changes regularly but you will always find *antipasti di mare* (a variety of tasty seafood appetizers) and scrumptious *panzerotti* (deep-fried square ravioli filled with ham and cheese). Other specialties are *panzerottini Margaret* (small square ricotta ravioli in a fresh basil and local cherry-tomato sauce), and *peperoni ripieni* (sweet peppers stuffed with olives, herbs, and cheese).

Viale Pasitea 172. ⓒ **089-875128.** Reservations recommended. Secondi 14€–18€ ($20–$25/£9.80–£13). No credit cards. Wed–Mon 12:30–3pm and daily 7:30–10pm. Closed Nov–Feb.

Donna Rosa 🍴🍴 AMALFITAN   In the green outskirts of Positano, this is where locals come to eat homemade pasta and excellent seafood prepared by two sisters and served—in the good season—on a charming terrace overlooking the sea. The menu surprises with a choice of turf and surf: Our favorites were the *salsicce alla griglia* (grilled local sausages), the *agnello arrosto* (roasted lamb), and the excellent *scialatielli zucchine e vongole* (eggless pasta with clams and zucchini).

Via Montepertuso 97. ⓒ **089-811806.** Reservations recommended. Secondi 12€–21€ ($17–$29/£8.40–£15). AE, DC, MC, V. Wed–Mon 12:30–2:30pm and 7:30–10:30pm; June–July and Sept Wed–Sun 12:30–2:30pm; June–Sept daily 7:30–10:30pm. Closed 11 weeks Jan and Mar.

Hotel Ristorante Le Sirene 🍴 AMALFITAN/SEAFOOD   This popular restaurant is right on the beach of Laurito, about 2km (1¼ miles) from the center of Positano, and makes for a perfect excursion. The restaurant's boat service will pick you up from Marina Grande. The menu focuses on seafood, such as the *scialatielli allo scoglio* (local fresh pasta with seafood), but also offers well-prepared local dishes like *mozzarella alla brace* (grilled on fresh lemon leaves). Above the restaurant are 8 simply but nicely appointed **guest rooms,** which were just renovated in 2007 (140€/$100/£50 double including breakfast).

Via Spiaggia di Laurito 24, 84017 Positano. ⓒ **089-875490.** Fax 089-875353. www.lesirenepositano.com. Secondi 10€–18€ ($14–$25/£7–£13). No credit cards. Daily 12:30–3pm and 7:30–10pm. Closed Oct 1–May 20.

INEXPENSIVE

Il Grottino Azzurro AMALFITAN/WINERY   This historic wine cellar has been a favorite with visitors and locals for decades. They offer a simple menu of well-prepared traditional dishes, centered—for a welcome change—on meat, fresh homemade pasta, and wine. Locals come for delicious *cannelloni* (tubes of fresh pasta filled with meat and baked with cheese and tomato sauce), *parmigiana* (eggplant Parmesan), and succulent roasted chicken. Given the cellar location, you'll find a good number of local and regional vintages to quaff.

Via Guglielmo Marconi 158 (SS 163). ⓒ **089-875466.** Reservations recommended. Secondi 10€–16€ ($14–$22/£7–£11). No credit cards. Thurs–Tues 12:30–3pm and 7:30–10pm; daily in summer.

Il Ritrovo 🍴 AMALFITAN/PIZZA   Off the beaten track high above Positano, this pleasant restaurant offers a great escape from the crowds, high prices, and summer heat below. The menu is seasonal and focuses on meat and vegetables produced on the family farm. Both the *grigliata mista* (medley of grilled meat) and the free-range

chicken baked with herbs are excellent. The restaurant has a cool arbor-covered terrace that makes it a perfect setting in the summer. The SITA bus stop from Positano
is nearby or you can call the restaurant for free pickup.

Piazza Cappella 77, Località Montepertuso. ℂ 089-811336 or 089-875453. Reservations recommended. Secondi
10€–14€ ($14–$20/£7–£9.80). AE, DC, MC, V. Thurs–Tues 12:30–3pm and 7:30–10pm; daily in summer. Closed Jan.

La Chitarrina AMALFITAN/PIZZA   Next door to Il Ritrovo, this simple, family-
run trattoria offers good food at moderate prices. The menu—which includes both
seafood and local meat choices—varies with the day's market offerings; in the evening
they also make good pizza. Signora Giuseppina Marrone makes the bread and pasta
in the open kitchen, while her children help with the service; she takes well-deserved
pride in her *ravioli* and *gnocchi di patate* (potato dumplings). Don't leave without trying the homemade desserts and the family's own *rosolio,* including *limoncello* and the
less usual *mirto* (flavored with myrtle).

Piazza Cappella 75, Località Montepertuso. ℂ 089-811806. Reservations not accepted. Secondi 11€–15€
($15–$21/£7.70–£11). AE, DC, MC, V. Thurs–Tues noon–3pm and 7:30–10pm; daily in summer. Closed 2 weeks in Nov
and Feb. Bus: SITA to Montepertuso.

SHOPPING 🌟🌟

All kinds of small shops and boutiques line the steep streets of Positano, many of them
offering the colorful style that has become known as "Positano Fashion" around the
world. The small tailoring boutiques of the 1960s, where you could have a dress or
trousers made ready for fitting, have evolved into a widely appreciated, specialized
craft. Local fashion designers have developed a unique style of colorful garments that
are the embodiment of Positano's Mediterranean light and outlook. Wonderful summer clothes and beachwear—swimsuits are a specialty—await you in the elegant boutiques, as well as more dressy items. Most of the boutiques line Viale Pasitea. **Sartoria
Maria Lampo** (Viale Pasitea 12; ℂ **089-875021**) is one of the remaining original
1960s boutiques, and is keeping to its reputation. Other favorites are **Pepito's** (Viale
Pasitea 15; ℂ **089-875446**); **La Sirenetta** (Viale Pasitea, 29; and also Via del Saracino 35; ℂ **089-811490** or 089-875383); **Nadir** (Viale Pasitea 44; ℂ **089-875975**);
La Bottega di Brunella (Viale Pasitea 76; ℂ **089-875228**); and **La Tartana** (Via della
Tartana; ℂ **089-875645**).

Positano is also famous for its great handmade sandals. Some of the artisan shops will
make them for you while you wait. Try **La Botteguccia** (Via Trara Genoino 13; ℂ **089-
811824**); **Costanzo Avitabile** (Piazza Amerigo Vespucci 15; ℂ **089-875366**); **Dattilo**
(Via Rampa Teglia 19; ℂ **089-811440**); or **Todisco** (Via del Saracino; ℂ **089-
875656**).

Among the town's many other boutiques, we really like the showroom-workshop of
Obrador (Via Cristoforo Colombo 91; ℂ **089-811049**), an Argentine artist who produces exquisite gold jewelry inspired by antiquity. He will work by commission only.

Positano also has a number of high-quality antiques shops, such as **Cose Antiche**
(Via Cristoforo Colombo 21; ℂ **089-811811**); **Le Myricae** (Via Cristoforo Colombo
27; ℂ **089-875882**), with its splendid collection of Art Deco jewelry; **Objets
Trouvés** (Viale Pasitea 230; ℂ **089-811577**); and **Oggetti di Ieri** (Via Cristoforo
Colombo 171).

POSITANO AFTER DARK

During the sweet summer nights, Positano's bars are packed with locals and visitors
having *aperitivo* and indulging in people watching. A perfect spot is **L'Incanto** (Via

Marina 4; © **089-811177**), not far from the sea at Spiaggia Grande, and so is popular **Chez Black** (Via del Brigantino 19; © **089-875036**) nearby. Right on the beach of Spiaggia Grande is the historical **La Buca di Bacco,** Via del Brigantino35 (© **089-811461;** www.bucapositano.it), which started as a tavern and a nightclub that was the meeting place for the local *dolce vita* back when Positano was an exclusive resort for VIPs; it is poised for a new era of glory. The bar in front is a perfect place for a coffee or a *granite,* while the tavern below has evolved into a pleasant late-night wine bar-cum-art-gallery and Internet cafe. Good food and pizza are available at **La Pergola,** above. Another hot spot is **De Martino,** Viale Pasitea 182 (© **089-875082**), a bar with live music on the terrace over the marina (they also make excellent coffee). The popular **Internazionale,** Via Marconi 306, by Chiesa Nuova (© **089-875434**) has a good wine selection and yummy pastries. If you have a sweet tooth, you will definitely like **La Zagara,** Via dei Mulini 8 (© **089-875964**), where locals love to come after dinner to enjoy excellent homemade ice cream and *granite* in various flavors—try the melon—in a marvelous garden of orange and lemon trees. Their famous pastry shop serves *torta positanese* (a local cake made with almonds), *delizie al limone* (lemon cream puffs), and *Babarese,* a *babà* pastry filled with wild strawberries and whipped cream.

Another wine bar we like is the *enoteca* **I sapori di Positano,** Via dei Mulini 6; © **089-811116**), where you can taste the best wines of the region, including the little-known local spumante, as well as a good selection of national wines. They also produce small batches of quality *rosolio* (sweet liqueur) and excellent citrus marmalades. Another good wine bar is **Con Vinum** (Via Rampa Teglia 12; © **089-811461**), where a trendy local crowd comes to listen to live jazz on summer weekends and to sip at the good vintages.

If your thing is dancing, you should head for **Music on the Rocks** (Via Grotto dell'Incanto 51; © **089-875874;** www.musicontherocks.it), the two-level club owned by the same owners as Chez Black, with a disco and a quieter piano bar. The club is open Friday and Saturday nights in May and September, and daily June through August; it is closed October through April.

3 Praiano

6.5km (4 miles) E of Positano and 9km (5 miles) W of Amalfi

The busiest stretch of the Costiera, the area between Amalfi and Positano, is studded with little towns both by the water and up the cliffs. These are often bypassed by tourists who make a beeline for more famous destinations—a boon for the traveler who chooses to tarry here. Praiano is the abbreviated name for the twin villages (Vettica Maggiore to the west, and Praiano to the east) that are the two faces of Capo Sottile, the promontory east of Positano.

ESSENTIALS

GETTING THERE & AROUND   In addition to the methods of arrival on p. 179, **La Sibilla** (© **089-874365;** www.lasibilla.org) offers boat service to Praiano from Positano (about 55€/$77/£39 round-trip) and from Amalfi (65€/$91/£46).

SS 163 crosses the town and is called Via G. Capriglione to the west of Capo Sottile, and Via Roma to the east. Besides the **SITA bus** mentioned above, your only other way around is **on foot,** unless you came with your own **car** or hired driver. **Benvenuto Limos,** Via Roma 54, Praiano (© **334-3078342;** www.benvenutolimos.com), is the locally based limousine service.

VISITOR INFORMATION   Praiano's **tourist office** is at Via Capriglione (© **089-874557;** www.praiano.org).

FAST FACTS   You'll find a **pharmacy** on Via Capriglione 142 (SS 163) (© **089-874846**). For an **ambulance,** dial © **118.** You can call the **police** at © **113** or at © **112.** The **post office** (© 089-874086) is on Via Capriglione 80 (SS 163). You'll find an **ATM** by the tourist office (see above); the nearest banks are in Agerola and Positano.

EXPLORING THE TOWN AND ITS BEACHES

The favorite residence of the Amalfi doges—who loved the beautiful views over Positano, Amalfi, and the Faraglioni of Capri—Praiano specialized in silk spinning and weaving, as well as coral fishing, traditional crafts that are still alive there today. The medieval village sits 120m (394 ft.) above sea level on the slopes of Monte Sant'Angelo. Away from the tourist crowd, the town is nestled harmoniously into its surroundings, with a graceful profusion of porticos and domes complementing the astounding natural beauty. Allot some time to walk through the streets (well, flights of steps, really) and admire the architecture. **San Gennaro** church, in Vettica Maggiore, is crowned by a beautiful oval dome tiled with colored majolica. Inside, the 18th-century majolica floor was recreated in 1966 according to the original design. The **view** from the church square is superb. A few trails start from this church: Turn left from Piazza San Gennaro onto Via Masa and take the right-hand path, which descends all the way to **Spiaggia della Gavitella** ✦, the beach of Vettica Maggiore, to the west of town (you can also reach it by car from SS 163, down across from the tourist office); or stay on the trail a bit longer and take the public staircase down to the medieval tower **Torre di Grado,** a walk that is particularly romantic at sunset or in the moonlight.

To the east of town, off SS 163 and down the incline, lies the picturesque **Marina di Praia** ✦✦, with its small but nice pebbly beach and wonderful clear waters. Here you can rent a boat to take you to the more secluded **Spiaggia della Gavitella** (above) or to one of the other little rocky coves only accessible by boat. **La Sibilla** (© **089-874365;** www.lasibilla.org) rents boats, organizes excursions farther along the coast, and offers water-taxi service (about 40€/$56/£28 for 1-hr. boat rental and 25€/$35/£18 for a ride to a beach). From Marina di Praia, you can walk **Via Torremare,** the walkway carved along the cliff, to the natural grotto housing the nightclub L'Africana (later in this chapter) or up to the medieval watchtower **Torre Asciola** (aka Torre a Mare, or tower by the sea). This is the studio of local artist **Sandulli,** a painter and sculptor, whom you can visit if he is in.

WHERE TO STAY

We also recommend the rooms offered by **Il Pino** and **Alfonso a Mare** (p. 194). The same family who runs the latter also has a guesthouse in town, **Casa Alfonso,** Via Umberto I 115 (© **089-874048;** fax 0890874489; www.casaalfonso.it). With a delightful terraced Mediterranean garden, it offers similarly appointed guest rooms at a lower rate (70€/$98/£49 double including breakfast).

EXPENSIVE

Grand Hotel Tritone   Off SS 163 a short distance west of Praiano, this elegant hotel offers gorgeous views and quiet accommodations. Completely surrounded by gardens and pines, it is built over a high cliff, with an elevator to the private beach below (some swim here from Marina di Praia nearby). Public spaces are airy and bright; they include a seawater pool, a lemon garden, and a picturesque chapel built inside a grotto. Guest rooms are well appointed and pleasantly furnished, many with private balconies and sea views. The 12 suites are gorgeous, each with its own private terrace overlooking the water.

Via Campo 5 (SS 163), 2km (1¼ miles) west of Praiano, 84010 Praiano. © **089-874333.** Fax 089-813024. www. hoteltritone.com. 62 units. 270€–320€ ($378–$448/£189–£224) double; from 380€ ($532/£266) suite. Rates include buffet breakfast. Children 1 and under stay free in parent's room. AE, DC, MC, V. Free parking. **Amenities:** Restaurant; bar; rocky beach; outdoor pool. *In room:* A/C, satellite TV, hair dryer, minibar, safe.

MODERATE
Hotel Onda Verde   Perched on a cliff, this hotel hangs between sea and sky. It's actually made up of several separate villas, with differences in style but uniform amenities and service. Guest rooms are tasteful and well-appointed, with good-size bathrooms; each unit has its own panoramic small terrace. The modern furniture has been keyed to the colors of the patterned tile floor and to the drapes and linens. The effect is restrained, comfortable, and easy on the eyes. Likewise, the hotel exudes a personal atmosphere and friendly service.

Via Terramare 3, Marina di Praia, 84010 Praiano. © **089-874143.** Fax 089-8131049. www.ondaverde.it. 25 units. 240€–260€ ($336–$364/£168–£182). Rates include buffet breakfast. Children 2 and under stay free in parent's room. AE, DC, MC, V. Free parking. Closed Nov–Mar. **Amenities:** Restaurant; bar; concierge; solarium; Wi-Fi. *In room:* A/C, satellite TV, hair dryer, minibar, safe.

Hotel Tramonto d'oro ★ *Kids*   The name of this elegant hotel means "golden sunset," and indeed, you can enjoy wonderful sunsets over the sea from the guest room windows. On the hotel grounds, you'll find a large swimming pool and a gym; the beach is only a short distance away by the hotel's free shuttle. Guest rooms are spacious and filled with light, individually decorated in modern, contemporary styles with light woods and tiled floors. The warm welcome of the Esposito family is another plus, and the hotel's **restaurant,** with a panoramic terrace affording spectacular views, is very good.

Via Gennaro Capriglione 119 (SS163), 84010 Praiano. © **089-874955.** Fax 089-874670. www.tramontodoro.it. 40 units. 195€–280€ ($273–$392/£137–£196); triple 260€–370€ ($364–$518/£182–£259); quad 300€–440€ ($420–$616/£210–£308). Rates include buffet breakfast. Children 3 and under stay free in parent's room. AE, DC, MC, V. Free parking. Restaurant closed Nov–Feb. **Amenities:** Restaurant; bar; access to beach; babysitting; complimentary shuttle to Praia; concierge; gym; outdoor pool; sauna; solarium. *In room:* A/C, satellite TV, hair dryer, minibar, safe.

INEXPENSIVE
Hotel Margherita ★ *Kids* *Finds*   This family-run hotel offers high-standard accommodations at moderate prices. The swimming pool and panoramic terraces are nice places to lounge, and the beach is only a few minutes away. Guest units are comfortable and well appointed, with tiled floors, modern furniture, and spacious bathrooms. The hotel's **restaurant** is excellent.

Via Umberto I 70, off Via Roma (SS 163), 84010 Praiano. © **089-874628.** www.hotelmargherita.info. 28 units. 110€–120€ ($154–$168/£77–£84) double; 140€ ($196/£98) triple; 180€ ($252/£126) quad. Rates include breakfast. Children 2 and under stay free in parent's room. AE, DC, MC, V. Free parking. **Amenities:** Restaurant; bar; concierge; outdoor pool. *In room:* A/C, satellite TV.

WHERE TO DINE
We also recommend dining at the restaurants of the **Tramonto d'Oro** and the **Margherita,** above.

MODERATE

Alfonso a Mare ★★ AMALFITAN/SEAFOOD   Locals flock to this excellent restaurant to dine on traditional seafood while enjoying views of the nearby sea. Located right in Marina di Praia by the beach, it offers a rich menu of local favorites that varies with the market's offerings. Among the *primi,* we highly recommend the *canneroni ai totani* (pasta with squid) and the *risotto alla pescatora* (risotto with seafood), while among the *secondi* we are partial to the *impepata di cozze* (mussels cooked in a peppered broth) and the *grigliata* (medley of grilled seafood). Go for the house wine, which comes from the family vineyards. Above the restaurant, the Fusco family offers accommodations in 16 spacious and pleasant **guest rooms,** decorated with simple furniture and ceramic floors (140€–175€/$196–$245/£98–£123 double including breakfast). They also rent umbrellas and chairs for the beach in front of the restaurant.

Via Marina di Praia, off Via Roma (SS 163). ℂ 089-874091. Fax 089-874161. www.alfonsoamare.it. Reservations recommended on weekends. Secondi 18€–28€ ($25–$39/£13–£20). MC, V. Daily 12:30–3pm and 7:30–10pm.

INEXPENSIVE

Da Gennarino a Mare ★ AMALFITAN/SEAFOOD   Another of the area's traditional restaurants by the sea, this is located on the beautiful beach of Vettica Maggiore and is perfect for a meal after a swim. The menu changes daily, offering a small variety of simple down-home dishes based on seafood and fresh vegetables. You might be able to sample the *pezzogna,* a fish native to these waters, or *zuppa di pesce* (fish stew).

Spiaggia della Gavitella, Via Gavitella, 1.5km (1 mile) west of Praiano, off Via Capriglione (SS 163). ℂ **089-874068.** Reservations recommended on weekends. Secondi 11€–16€ ($15–$22/£7.70–£11). No credit cards. Daily 12:30–3pm and 7:30–11pm.

Il Pino ★ AMALFITAN/SEAFOOD   This family-run restaurant is popular with locals for its good food and sea views from its pleasant terraces. We found it especially hard to pass up the *scialatelli ai frutti di mare* (fresh pasta with shellfish) and *grigliata di pesce* (grilled fish), but the menu is full of enticing local favorites. Above the restaurant is the small **hotel** where you'll find 16 large and bright guest rooms, each with a private terrace and a view of the Mediterranean (148€/$207/£104 double including breakfast).

Via G. Capriglione 13 (SS163). ℂ 089-874389. www.hotelilpino.it. Reservations recommended on weekends. Secondi 12€–18€ ($17–$25/£8.40–£13). AE, DC, MC, V. Daily 12:30–3pm and 7:30–10pm.

La Brace ★★ AMALFITAN   With a beautiful location, this is a moderately priced place to enjoy both good food and scenery. The seasonal menu includes many simple home-cooked dishes, based on the market offering of local seafood, meat, and veggies, such as tasty *totani e patate* (squid and potatoes stew), and in winter *pappardelle al sugo di coniglio* (homemade pasta with rabbit ragout).

Via G. Capriglione 146 (SS 163). ℂ 089-874226. Reservations recommended. Secondi 9€–14€ ($13–$20/£6.30–£9.80). AE, DC, MC, V. Oct–Mar Thurs–Tues 12:30–3pm and 7:30–11pm; daily in summer.

SHOPPING

Do you have a musician in the family? You might not have thought of purchasing a musical instrument while on your vacation, but once you've visited this artisan's workshop you might change your mind. At **Bottega Scala,** Via Roma 57 (ℂ **089-874894**), the *liutaio* (stringed instruments maker) Pasquale Scala creates instruments using ancient techniques. Many of his clients are famous Italian musicians—one is Pino Daniele. He specializes in classic guitars and ancient instruments, from medieval to baroque.

PRAIANO AFTER DARK

The popular nightclub **L'Africana** (© 089-874042) in Vettica Maggiore was a mythical hangout of the *Anni Ruggenti* (Roaring Years) of the 1960s, when it was the destination of choice of VIPs and their trendy friends. In a grotto right above the lapping sea, it has experienced a second coming and is again a lively scene. Don't be surprised when at one point in the evening, you see a bunch of local fishermen pull their nets from the edges of the dance floor; they are off for the fresh catches for local restaurants. The club is open Friday and Saturday nights May and September, and daily June through August; it is closed October through April.

4 Off the Beaten Track: Conca dei Marini, Furore & Agerola

Conca dei Marini is 5km (3 miles) W of Amalfi. Furore 10.6km (6½ miles) W of Amalfi. Agerola is 14.5km (9 miles) W of Amalfi

The small seaside resort of Conca dei Marini, with its famous Emerald Grotto, is the gateway to the vertical hinterland that lies between Positano and Amalfi. Along the road that winds up the cliff you'll find Furore and, farther in, Agerola.

ESSENTIALS

GETTING AROUND   You can take the SITA **buses** mentioned earlier, or tackle the local **footpaths** if you are feeling fit. For most, a **car** (p. 180) is best for exploration of this area.

VISITOR INFORMATION   You can find **tourist information** at the municipal offices of Conca dei Marini, in the Casa Comunale (© 089-831301), and of Furore, Via Mola 39, Furore (© 089-874100), or at the **Proloco tourist office,** Viale della Vittoria (© 089-8791064) in Agerola.

FAST FACTS   **Pharmacies** are on Via Mola 35, in Furore (© 089-831109), and Via Armando Diaz 14 and 18 in Agerola (© 081-8791085). For an **ambulance,** dial © 118. You can call the **police** at © 113 or at © 112. You'll find **post offices** in Conca dei Marini, on Piazza Olmo 3, off SS 163 (© 089-831286); in Furore, at Via Mola 33 (© 089-874129); and in Agerola, at Via Roma 1 (© 081-8731573) and at Via Ponte 1 (© 081-8731266). You'll find two **banks** in Agerola: Banco di Napoli, Piazza Capasso 3 (© 081-8740323) and Banca Intesa, Via Roma 16 (© 081-8740511).

EXPLORING THE AREA

A delightful hamlet in a picturesque cove by the sea, **Conca dei Marini** is only a few miles west of Amalfi. Unbelievable as it might seem, this was once a powerful commercial center, whose ships crisscrossed the Mediterranean Sea. The quiet little town is famous today for its special *sfogliatella* (a pastry filled with cream and *amarene*—candied sour cherries in syrup—instead of the standard ricotta), which were invented in the 14th-century **Convento di Santa Rosa.** This delicious creation is celebrated with a special festival in August, **Sagra della Sfogliatella di Santa Rosa.** Summer is also the time for the **Summer Fest,** with a series of events including theater, ballet, and art shows. A delightful hamlet in a picturesque cove by the sea, Conca dei Marini is only a few miles west of Amalfi. Unbelievable as it might seem, this was once a powerful commercial center, whose ships crisscrossed the Mediterranean Sea. The quiet little town is famous today for its special *sfogliatella* (a pastry filled with cream and *amarene*—candied sour cherries in syrup—instead of the standard ricotta), which were invented in the 14th-century **Convento di Santa Rosa.** This delicious creation is celebrated with a special festival in August, **Sagra della Sfogliatella di Santa Rosa.** Summer is also the time for the **Summer Fest,** with a series of events including theater, ballet, and art shows. Contact the tourist office (above) for a schedule of what's on.

Here on the outskirts of Conca dei Marini is **Grotta dello Smeraldo** ★★; admission is 6€ ($8.40/£4.20), including the elevator down to sea level and the boat ride from the beach. The grotto is open daily, weather permitting, November to February from 9am to 4pm, and March to October from 9am to 7pm. This beautiful underwater grotto with karst formations of stalactites and stalagmites takes on a unique blue-green color in certain lights. Less famous than the Blue Grotto in Capri, the grotto is still impressive, measuring 30m (98 ft.) in length by 60m (197 ft.) wide, with a maximum depth of 24m (79 ft.). It was discovered in 1932 and is accessible only by boat or by swimming; inside, at a depth of 4m (13 ft.), you'll see the ceramic crèche that was submerged in the grotto in 1956. Admission includes the rowboat ride from the beach and the elevator from the SS 163, which runs high above the cliff. You can also take the hair-rising staircase, should you want more excitement. The grotto's entrance can be reached either by SITA bus (Positano-Amalfi line) or by launch service from Amalfi; launches operate between 9:30am and 4pm and cost 10€ ($13/£6.50) round-trip.

Up the cliff from Conca dei Marini is **Furore,** famous for its D.O.C. wine, and its **fjord,** which was cut into the high limestone cliff by the Schiato brook (the name *Furore* means rage, and refers to the way the sea rises in the fjord during storms). A scenic yet hair-rising hike along **Sentiero della Volpe Pescatrice (Fishing Fox Trail)** ★★ leads down to the fishing hamlet of **Furore Marina** (the trail is marked number 17 on the CAI map, p. 182). The trail is a descent down the rocky walls of the fjord, along the path that was used by local peasant-fishermen to reach their *monazzeni* (the boathouses built on the diminutive beach). Incidentally, you can see the dwellings, built pueblo-style, from the viaduct off SS 163, about midway between Praiano and Conca dei Marini; this is also where you could take the steep stairway—200 steps—that starts from SS 163 and descends to the bottom of the fjord. But perhaps the most romantic way to approach the bottom is via boat, from one of the harbors nearby.

Farther up the cliff from Furore, the high plateau of **Agerola** is famous for its beauty and for its cattle and sheep, which produce the milk for which the Monti Lattari were named for (*latte* means milk). The region's best cheese comes from Agerola's farms—indeed, some of the best cheese in the country can be had here. A collection of farming hamlets, Agerola has its administrative center in **Pianillo.** The most scenic of Agerola's bourgs is **San Lazzaro** where, past the church to the left, you will find the **Punta,** a natural terrace offering dramatic **views** ★★. Taking the road to the right of the church, you will find more awesome panoramas opening from the terrace by the ex-Castle Avitabile, and from the ruins of **Castel Lauritano** ★★★. The whole area offers unending **hiking** opportunities, including the demanding but extremely scenic 5-hour hike to the **Vallone delle Ferriere** waterfall, starting from San Lazzaro.

WHERE TO STAY IN THE AREA
EXPENSIVE
Furore Inn Resort ★★   This luxury spa-hotel (the spa is open to the public) is a striking whitewashed structure merged into the supporting cliff. Its dramatic sea views are pleasantly matched by the elegant interior. The panoramic rooms all feature Vietri

tiled floors and classic furnishings. Each opens onto its own private terrace and is equipped with a spacious and elegantly tiled bathroom. The spa offers a wide range of beauty treatments and massages. Of the hotel's two restaurants, **La Volpe Pescatrice** offers creative Amalfitan fare on the beautiful terrace, while the **Italian Touch** offers modern Italian cuisine in a more formal atmosphere.

Via dell'Amore 1, Contrada Sant'Elia, 84010 Furore. 🕐 089-8304711. Fax 089-8304777. www.furoreinn.it. 22 units. 360€–460€ ($504–$644/£252–£322) double; from 550€ ($770/£385) suite. AE, DC, MC, V. Free parking. Closed 2 weeks Nov–Dec and 2 weeks Jan–Feb. **Amenities:** 2 restaurants; bar; babysitting; concierge; outdoor pool; park; room service; spa. *In room:* A/C, satellite TV, hair dryer, minibar, safe.

MODERATE

Albergo di Bacco ✦   Surrounded by vineyards, this hotel is set in a panoramic position, and offers comfortable accommodations and kind service. Founded in 1930, it is expertly run by the third generation of the family Ferraioli. Guest rooms are bright, and are simply but tastefully furnished. Each has a solarium and a small terrace. The hotel's restaurant is the wonderful **Antica Hostaria di Bacco** (🕐 089-874583), which offers a superb rendition of local traditional cuisine and very nice views.

Via G.B. Lama 9, 84010 Furore. 🕐 089-830360. Fax 089-830352. www.baccofurore.it. 18 units. 115€ ($161/£81) double. AE, DC, MC, V. Free parking. **Amenities:** Restaurant; bar; garden; outdoor tennis court and outdoor pool 5-min. walk away; solarium. *In room:* A/C, TV, hair dryer, minibar, safe.

Hotel Il Belvedere   This beautiful hotel is housed in a 19th-century villa built in a choice position on the cliffs, only minutes from the Emerald Grotto. The public spaces include a great seawater swimming pool overlooking the rocky private beach. The bright, large guest rooms are comfortably furnished with period furniture or reproductions, and have patterned tiled floors. Bathrooms are also nicely tiled, with modern fixtures. Each room has a small terrace (large enough for a table and chairs) with an ocean view.

Via Smeraldo, off SS 163, 84010 Conca dei Marini. 🕐 089-831282. Fax 089-831439. www.belvederehotel.it. 40 units. 220€–240€ ($308–$336/£154–£168) double. Rates include buffet breakfast. Children 1 and under stay free in parent's room. AE, DC, MC, V. Free parking. Closed Nov–Mar. **Amenities:** Restaurant; bar; concierge; outdoor pool; rocky beach access; solarium. *In room:* A/C, TV.

INEXPENSIVE

Albergo Ristorante Risorgimento   Last renovated in 2003, this welcoming hotel has been around since 1878. Your first clue that the owners are seriously interested in cuisine is the fact that the albergo side of the operation is smaller than the restaurant— there are 20 guest rooms, but the large restaurant-pizzeria seats 150. The restaurant serves a good pizza, as well as seafood, homemade pasta, and meat dishes such as rabbit and lamb. Guest rooms are comfortable and functional, with good-size modern bathrooms. The simple rooms (moderate in size, but not small) have been tastefully decorated, with walls done in yellows and light ochres, color-coordinated furnishings, and wrought-iron beds. The hotel's **restaurant** is popular with locals, and serves a good pizza, in addition to a full menu.

Via Antonio Coppola 32, Località San Lazzaro, 84051 Agerola. 🕐/fax 081-8025072. www.hotelrisorgimento.it. 20 units. 90€ ($126/£62) double. Rates include breakfast. Children 1 and under stay free in parent's room. AE, DC, MC, V. Free parking. **Amenities:** Restaurant; bar. *In room:* TV.

WHERE TO DINE

In addition to the below, many of the hotels above feature fine restaurants. For a snack or the makings of a picnic, visit **Cantine Gran Furor,** Via Lama 14; Furore

(📞 089-874489), to sample (or take away) the local D.O.C. wine, and the cheese makers of Agerola, where you can sample and purchase the famous *fiordilatte,* as well as excellent *caciocavallo* and *scamorze.* Among the best are **Caseificio Agerolina,** Via Tutti I Santi 6 (📞 089-8731022); **Caseificio Belfiore,** Via Belvedere 35 (📞 **089-8791338); Caseificio Fior di Agerola,** Via Galli 74 (📞 **089-8791339); and La Montanina,** Via Carlo Poerio 30bis (📞 **089-8731022).**

La Taverna 🍴 AGEROLA   This modern restaurant with a panoramic terrace offers excellent local cuisine, delicious in its simplicity. The *antipasti* can be meals on their own, with a great choice of local cheeses, cured meats, and vegetable preparations. Of the homemade pastas, *pappardelle con funghi e tartufo* (large fresh pasta with mushrooms and truffles) and *spaghetti con i peperoni dolci* (spaghetti with sweet peppers) are truly special. For your secondo, do not miss the flavorful *grigliate* (artfully grilled local meats). All desserts are strictly homemade, too.

Via Radicosa 53, Località San Lazzaro. 📞 **089-8025041.** Secondi 9€–18€ ($13–$25/£6.30–£13). No credit cards. Wed–Mon 12:30–3pm and 7:30–10pm. Closed Sept–Nov.

La Tonnarella 🍴🍴 AMALFITAN   This picturesque restaurant is best reached from the sea—call to be picked up by boat at the nearest harbor. It is also accessible from the road via a steep stairway descending from SS 163 to beach level. A historical address on this coast—it has served VIPs and movie stars of the past, from Jackie Kennedy to Giovanni Agnelli—it was almost wiped out by the landslide that covered the marina in 1996, but reopened in 2002. Of course, the menu's focus is fish, which is always extremely fresh and well prepared. You'll also find *risotto di mare* (with seafood and tomatoes), *pasta al forno* (lasagna), and *zuppa di pesce* (fish stew). Other strong suits are the *grigliate* (grilled seafood) and *fritto misto* (deep-fried medley of seafood).

Via Marina 1, Borgo Marinaro, Conca dei Marini. 📞 **089-831939.** www.ristorantelatonnarella.it. Reservations required. Secondi 12€–25€ ($17–$35/£8.40–£18). No credit cards. Daily 12:30–3pm and 7:30–11pm. Closed Nov–Mar.

5 Amalfi

34km (21 miles) W of Salerno, 61km (38 miles) SE of Naples

The origins of Amalfi go back to ancient Roman times and even to the Byzantine Empire. Visitors often marvel that a town so small and picturesque was once a "maritime republic," but geography and the nature of those times help explain Amalfi's moment of global (or at least Western) prominence. The town declared its independence in A.D. 839, and its perfect strategic location—opening onto a natural harbor at the mouth of a valley rich in water, yet protected by the forbidding Monti Lattari from the incursions of both Turks and Normans—allowed Amalfi to develop into Italy's *first* maritime republic, before either Pisa or Venice. For 2 centuries, Amalfi was a maritime power to be reckoned with: Its navy kept the Turks at bay, and its maritime code—the Tabula Amalphitana—was recognized as law in the Mediterranean. The small republic was rich and cosmopolitan, and its coins were widely used across the Mediterranean, from the Greek empire to Africa to the Longobard territories. Amalfi also dominated the markets in spices, perfumes, silk, and valuable carpets.

Amalfi's toehold among the cliffs eventually became a liability, however; the limited size of its land area and comparable lack of military power obliged Amalfi to accept Norman rule in 1073. Pisa—which had developed into a powerful maritime republic itself in the meantime—then sacked Amalfi in 1135, and in 1143 a terrible seaquake destroyed large parts of the harbor, including the fortifications and the shipyards. The

Amalfi

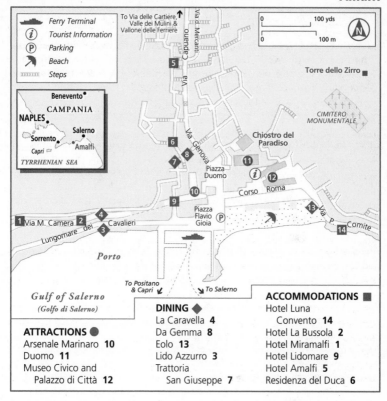

Amalfi of old was completely annihilated 5 years later, when the plague struck in 1348. Afterwards, Amalfi became a pretty fishing village, until it was rediscovered as a tourist destination by 19th-century travelers.

ESSENTIALS

GETTING AROUND　You can accomplish much **on foot** in Amalfi, but **taxis** are a sometimes necessary alternative. You can find them at the stand on Piazza Flavio Gioia in the center of town, or call ℂ **089-872239.**

VISITOR INFORMATION　The **tourist office** is located inside Palazzo di Città (Corso delle Repubbliche Marinare 19, 84011 Amalfi; ℂ **089-871107;** www.amalfi touristoffice.it). In winter, it is open Monday to Friday 8am to 1:30pm and Saturday 8am to noon; in summer, it's open Monday to Friday 3 to 5pm.

FAST FACTS　You'll find a **pharmacy** at Piazza dei Dogi (ℂ **089-871063**) and another at Via L. d'Amalfi (ℂ 089-871045). The **medical center** is at Via Casamare ℂ **089-871449**); for an **ambulance,** dial ℂ **118.** The **police** can be reached at ℂ **113** or ℂ **112.** The **post office** is at Via delle Repubbliche Marinare, next to the tourist office (ℂ **089-872996**), and is open Monday to Saturday 8am to 2pm. Next door you will find a Deutsche Bank **ATM.**

> **Fun Fact Amalfi by the Book**
>
> Amalfi is best known to English readers from John Webster's masterpiece, **The Duchess of Malfi** (1623). This bloody tale of love, lust, and murder captures the scandalous side of Renaissance court life; what's more, it may actually be true. The original source is the **Novelle** of the Dominican priest Matteo Bandello (1485–1561), who served several courts and no doubt knew whereof he spoke.

SPECIAL EVENTS   On the first Sunday of June, the **Historic Regatta of the Maritime Republics** is run, with turns being taken by each of the four historical towns—Genova, Pisa, Venice, and Amalfi. Amalfi's turn was in 2005, and will come again in 2009. Civic pride and thousand-year-old rivalries are at stake, and the boat races are run with pomp, athleticism, and great seriousness. The spectacular, colorful event is accompanied by parades and musical performances.

EXPLORING THE TOWN

Full of mementos of its glorious past and decorated with gardens—olive trees, oranges, and lemons, the groves sloping all the way to the sea—Amalfi is a jewel of a small town. Its central square, **Piazza Flavio Gioia,** commemorates the inventor of the compass (or, at least, the man who perfected it for marine use), according to local legend. Indeed, Amalfi's mariners were the first in Europe to use the properties of magnetism for navigation, starting back in the 12th century; they provided material for the first nautical charts of the Middle Ages.

The medieval heart of Amalfi stretches from **Piazza Duomo** along **Via Genova** and **Via Capuano,** with typical covered porticos and narrow streets. To get its flavor, stroll under the Supportico Sant'Andrea Apostolo till you reach Largo Filippo Augustariccio. There, through a characteristic Arab-style trilobate arch, you can enter another covered passage, Campo de Cinnamellis—the seat, in medieval times, of Amalfi's spice market.

Be sure to visit the **Convento di San Francesco**—now Hotel Luna Convento (later in this chapter). Its 16th-century watchtower over the cape to the east of town is an annex of the hotel. Here you can visit the well-conserved 13th-century cloister and the attached church.

Duomo ✿✿   This superb example of Arab-Norman architecture goes back to the 9th century, when the Republic of Amalfi was just gaining success. The majestic facade is decorated with a mosaic of gold leaf and majolica, with a magnificent 11th-century **bronze door** ✿ made in Constantinople closing the main portal. The lovely Romanesque bell tower was finished in 1276. The Duomo was enlarged between the 16th and 18th centuries, when it was also given a baroque interior together with the majestic, imposing staircase leading to a beautiful atrium in black-and-white marble. It was renovated in 1891 and further restored in 1929, with respect for the 13th-century structures.

To the left of the Duomo is the breathtakingly beautiful cloister, the **Chiostro del Paradiso** ✿✿✿, dating from 1266. The cloister, in Arab-Sicilian style, is decorated with interlaced arches over double columns, and was originally built as the cemetery for the city's religious and political elite. The site now holds a small museum with ancient Roman and medieval artifacts. Among the best pieces are the **Roman sarcophagus of Ottavio Rufo** ✿, richly carved, and two other sarcophagi, also decorated with bas-reliefs. From the cloister you can gain access to the **Chiesa del Crocifisso,** the original cathedral of Amalfi dating from the 10th century, where other artworks are conserved. July through September, concerts are held in the cloister on Friday nights (later in this chapter).

From the right nave of this church you can descend to the **Crypt,** the repository for the remains of the apostle St. Andrew, the protector saint of Amalfi. The crypt was built in the 13th century, when the remains of the saint were brought back from the 4th Crusade; it was redecorated in 1719. An interesting detail is that Andrew's face is missing—it was donated to the church of St. Andrew's in Patras, Greece. Over the main altar is the beautiful bronze **Statue of Sant'Andrea** by Michelangelo Naccherino.

Piazza del Duomo, 84011 Amalfi. Duomo: ✆ **089-871059.** Free admission. Daily Nov–Feb 10am–1pm and 2:30–4:30pm; Mar and Oct 9:30am–5:15pm; Apr–June 9am–7pm; July–Sept 9am–9pm. Museum and cloister: ✆ **089-871324.** 3€ ($4.20/£2.10). Daily June–Oct 9:30am–7pm; Nov–May 9:30am–5:15pm.

Museo Civico & Palazzo di Città

The Palazzo di Città is Amalfi's Town Hall. On its southern wall hangs a famous **Pannello in ceramica** ✷, a majolica panel relating key moments in Amalfi's history. Created in the 1970s by artist Diodoro Cossa, it is made of two series of large colored tiles, which you can read from left to right. It starts with the founding of Amalfi by a group of ancient Roman refugees and proceeds to the town's growth into an important commercial and political power in the Mediterranean, the building of the cloisters, and the arrival of the body of Saint Andrew. Then comes Amalfi's decline and its slow recovery—and along the way, the invention of the compass, and the production of paper. Inside the Town Hall, the **Museum** is interesting mostly for history buffs and concerns local events. It contains, however, at least one very important piece: the *Tabula Amalphitana,* the original Maritime Code written around the 11th century to regulate maritime traffic in the Mediterranean (this was enforced till at least the 16th century). The artifact was redeemed from Austria in 1929 and brought back to Amalfi. Also interesting are the original pastel drawings for the Duomo's mosaics by Domenico Morelli.

Piazza Municipio. ✆ **089-8736211.** www.comune.amalfi.sa.it. Free admission. Mon–Fri 8am–1pm.

Arsenale Marinaro

Here at the Republic of Amalfi's shipyard, citizens built the vessels that maintained power over the Mediterranean back in the Middle Ages. Established in the 11th century, the shipyard was restored in the 13th century, and at its height, it could build galleys up to 40m (131 ft.) long, which were driven by both sails and oars. These were defined by their number of oars, which could number 108, 112, or 120 for the largest ships. Only half of the building remains today—the other half, which reached into the sea, was destroyed by a series of great storms in the 14th century. However, you can still admire the building's beautiful architecture, such as its pointed arches and cross vaults resting over stone pillars. Between the Arsenale and the Porta della Marina you will find a tile panel depicting Amalfi's commercial empire in the Middle Ages; it was created by the artist Renato Rossi in the 1950s.

Via Matteo Camera, off Piazza Flavio Gioia. Free admission. Easter–Sept 9am–8pm.

Museo della Carta (Museum of Paper)

This museum is the perfect place to learn more about the historical aspects of the local paper industry. Created inside one of the abandoned paper mills, it has a great collection of original tools and machines. It also maintains a library with over 3,000 texts on the origins of paper. If you are

Amalfi & the Industry of Papermaking

Amalfi is believed to be the first European location where paper as we know it today was made. The process was discovered by the Arabs and perfected in the Arab town of El-Marubig, where the original name *bambagina* referred to the special kind of paper that became known as *paper of Amalfi*, made from recycled cotton, linen, and hemp cloths. The process was then exported to Amalfi through the close commercial relationship the republic had with the Arab world. Considered less durable than parchment, paper was still forbidden in 1250 for public use, but the industry developed rapidly and Amalfi sold its paper far and wide throughout the Middle Ages and the Renaissance. Paper continued to be made by hand till the 18th century, when machines were finally introduced; at that time there were 16 paper mills in the area, 10 of which are still active today. The cloths (or rags) were reduced to a poultice in large vats and then strained in forms marked with the symbol of the paper mill. The paper was then pressed between layers of woolen felt to extract excess water, air dried, and finally "ironed." Even if it was considered inferior to parchment or vellum, this paper was of high quality: The oldest sheets still in existence date from the 13th and 14th centuries. The *bambagina* of Amalfi is still highly appreciated by many—for example, the Vatican uses Amalfi paper for its correspondence.

If you wish to visit one of the working mills, **Cartiera Amatruda** (Via Marino del Giudice; ✆ **089-871315**) is still run by the original family, who welcomes visitors and will give you a tour of their facilities. **Antonio Cavaliere** (Via Fiume; ✆ **089-871954**), one of the descendants of the ancient master papermakers, is another, smaller option. Antonio's specialty is paper with real dried flowers as filigree, ideal for very special letters.

Both shops produce paper of an almost forgotten quality, made completely by hand, which is sold to the most exclusive paper shops in Italy, Europe, and the U.S. The water for this craft still comes from the covered river that crosses town and was the key resource in the development of Amalfi's paper industry. Both workshops are open regular business hours.

interested in the subject, you can visit two workshops in town (see "Amalfi & the Industry of Papermaking" box above).

Palazzo Pagliara, Via delle Cartiere 23. ✆ 089-8304561. www.museodellacarta.it. Admission 3.40€ ($4.75/£2.40). Tues–Sun 9am–1pm; daily in summer 10am–6pm.

STAYING ACTIVE

Amalfi used to have large **beaches,** but sea erosion and landslides have reduced the beach to two narrow strips on either side of the harbor. Most hotels on the waterfront have small private beaches carved out of the cliffs. You can also take the footpath to Atrani, an easy 15-minute stroll eastward, to the pretty beach there (see earlier in this chapter).

From the harbor at **Marina Grande** you can rent **boats**—with or without driver— to explore the nooks and crannies of this beautiful coast. Or you can sign up for an excursion. The most popular is the one to **Grotta dello Smeraldo** ✸✸ (see "Conca dei Marini," later in this chapter). **Cooperativa Sant'Andrea** (© **089-873190;** www. coopsantandrea.it) offers a regular beach service to Duoglio and Santa Croce, only a few minutes away from Molo Pennello; boats leave every 30 minutes between 9am and 5pm. They also have a regular service to Grotta dello Smeraldo leaving every hour between 9:30am and 3:30pm.

Amalfi is also a great starting point for a number of beautiful **hikes.** The most famous and popular is the pleasant and easy walk along **Valle dei Mulini (Valley of the Mills),** which is the valley of the Torrente Canneto, Amalfi's stream. Head up Via Genova from Piazza del Duomo and continue on as the street turns into a trail up the narrow valley of the river. The picturesque walk will lead you to the area known locally as the **Mulino Rovinato (Ruined Mill),** about 1 hour away. The area is so named because a great number of paper and flour mills used to reside in the valley. The flour mills were put out of business by the development of the pasta industry farther north in Torre del Greco, Torre Annunziata, and Gragnano, where the conditions were more favorable. In contrast, the paper mills continued to prosper until recently, and some are still active today.

The more demanding hike to the **Vallone delle Ferriere** 🌟🌟 was a favorite with 19th-century visitors doing the Grand Tour, who considered this valley one of the most beautiful areas in the whole of southern Italy. In fact, the valley has been declared a World Heritage Site by UNESCO, precisely because of its unique environment. The local limestone mountains were once at the bottom of the sea and have a dolomitic geology. The peculiarities of the area's geophysical configuration have made it into a sort of Mediterranean "lost valley," where plants and animals survive that have disappeared elsewhere on the European continent. Keep your eyes open for the special local fern *Woodwardia radicans,* a species alive since the quaternary or even the tertiary period, before glaciation. It shouldn't be too hard to spot: Its leaves grow up to 2m (8 ft.) in length. However, only a few plants remain. Other rare plants are *pinguicola hirtiflora,* a small carnivorous plant; and saffron, the most expensive spice in the world. Among the rare animals are several species of salamander, such as *salamandrina dagli occhiali* and *tritone italiano,* as well as a variety of birds. To reach the Vallone delle Ferriere, take the trail to the Valle dei Mulini (above) and continue upwards as the rocky trail traverses through citrus groves and by picturesque waterfalls. The going is good but quite steep as you finally reach the ancient Ferriere (Iron Mills), with their imposing walls partly hidden by growth. Already extant in the Middle Ages, they were active until the 19th century. If you are in good shape, you can climb even farther up to the waterfalls; the climb is short but steep. Allow 6 hours for the round-trip on the 12km (7.5-mile) trail.

A less demanding hike is the famous **Via degli Incanti (Trail of Charms),** which connects Amalfi to Positano. The trail is indeed bewitching, wending through the cultivated terraces and citrus groves of the Amalfi countryside. The hike is easy, with some moderately taxing passages, but due to its length—about 25km (16 miles)—most people choose to do only a section of it, or plan on doing the whole trip over several days. In either case, going from Amalfi to Positano is more demanding than going from Positano to Amalfi, so plan your hike accordingly. From Amalfi, follow the Via Maestra, the road that climbs through the outskirts of town; the trail is well marked.

WHERE TO STAY
VERY EXPENSIVE
Hotel Santa Caterina 🌟🌟🌟   This is the most luxurious hotel in Amalfi, offering great, family-run service and a superb location hanging onto a cliff surrounded by

terraces and gardens. The public spaces include a private beach (which you can reach by elevator or a winding garden path), a seawater swimming pool with a sun deck, a gym, a bar, an open-air restaurant serving very good food, luscious gardens, and citrus groves. Guest rooms are large and decorated in a refined manner, each with an antique piece among the furnishings, and luxurious bathrooms. Some of the suites are absolutely fantastic—Follia Amalfitana and Casa dell'Arancio, in particular. They are actually luxurious bungalows immersed in a citrus grove, with a private garden and a small pool.

Via Nazionale 9, 84011 Amalfi. ℂ 089-871012. Fax 089-871351. www.hotelsantacaterina.it. 70 units. 445€–780€ ($623–$1,092/£312–£546) double; from 930€ ($1,302/£651) suite. Rates include buffet breakfast. AE, DC, MC, V. Parking 15€ ($21/£11). Internet specials available. **Amenities:** 2 restaurants; bar; babysitting; beach access; concierge; health center; laundry service; lounge; outdoor pool; room service; solarium. *In room:* A/C, satellite TV, hair dryer, iron, high-speed Internet connection, minibar, safe.

EXPENSIVE
Hotel Luna Convento ★★   Transformed into a hotel in 1822, the Hotel Luna Convento occupies Amalfi's watchtower dating from 1564, and the ancient Franciscan monastery founded by Saint Francis in 1222, complete with its beautiful original cloister and church. Just 273m (896 ft.) from the town's center, on the promontory protecting Amalfi's harbor, this family-run place counts Henrik Ibsen (who wrote *A Doll's House* here in 1879) among its famous guests. The space remains as artistically inspiring as ever: The hotel is surrounded by a garden, with sun terraces and a large seawater swimming pool carved out of the cliff. There is also a private, rather rocky beach and a highly praised gourmet restaurant where you have to make reservations long in advance. The watchtower houses a disco and piano bar, as well as another restaurant with fantastic views (below). Guest rooms vary in size and decor, but all are bright and spacious, with sweeping vistas, commodious tiled bathrooms, and sometimes private terraces.

Via Pantaleone Comite 33, 84011 Amalfi. ℂ 089-871002. Fax 089-871333. www.lunahotel.it. 48 units. 280€– 310€ ($392–$434/£196–£217) double; from 400€ ($560/£280) suite. Rates include buffet breakfast. Children 2 and under stay free in parent's room. AE, DC, MC, V. Parking 18€ ($25/£13). **Amenities:** 2 restaurants; bar; babysitting; concierge; laundry service; outdoor pool; room service. *In room:* A/C, TV, hair dryer, minibar, safe.

Hotel Miramalfi *(Kids)*   Just outside the center of town to the west, this family-run hotel offers attractive rooms and a panoramic position. Perched on a rocky cliff on a point sticking out into the sea, the hotel has a view in every direction. It has its own private beach, as well as a pool at the foot of the cliff, which is accessible by elevator. It is therefore completely self-contained—kids can go back and forth to the beach, room, and pool without leaving the grounds. Guest rooms are modern in style with good-size bathrooms; all have balconies and views overlooking the sea.

Via S. Quasimodo 3, 84011 Amalfi. ℂ 089-871588. Fax 089-871287. www.miramalfi.it. 49 units. 270€–300€ ($378–$420/£189–£210) double; 400€ ($560–£280) suite. Rates include breakfast. Children 2 and under stay free in parent's room. AE, DC, MC, V. Parking 15€ ($21/£11). Closed Nov–Dec 20. **Amenities:** Beach; babysitting; concierge; dining room; laundry service; lounge; outdoor pool; room service. *In room:* A/C, satellite TV, hair dryer, minibar, safe.

MODERATE
Residenza del Duca ★   This tiny hotel—only five rooms—is housed inside a lovingly restored 16th-century *palazzo* in the medieval part of town. The welcoming management immediately makes you feel at home. Each guest room has its own character, with wooden beams, local replicas of the original ceramic tiles, original architectural details, and period furniture. Each opens onto its own balcony or small terrace with views either over the sea or of the medieval district.

Via Duca Mastalo II 3, Amalfi. © **089-8736365**. Fax 089-8736365. www.residencedelduca.it. 5 units. 150€–195€ ($210–$273/£105–£137) double. Rates include buffet breakfast. Children 2 and under stay free in parent's room. AE, MC, V. Parking 18€ ($22/£11). **Amenities:** Lounge. *In room:* A/C, satellite TV, hair dryer, minibar, safe.

INEXPENSIVE

Hotel Amalfi *Finds*   This quiet hotel with a nice citrus garden is hidden away in the medieval part of town, right by the Duomo. It offers comfortable accommodations at moderate prices and with friendly service. The simple guest rooms have modern furnishings chosen with care. Bathrooms, though small, are perfectly adequate.

Via dei Pastai 3, 84011 Amalfi. © **089-872440**. Fax 089-872250. www.hamalfi.it. 40 units. 150€–160€ ($210–$224/ £105–£112) double. Rates include breakfast. Children 1 and under stay free in parent's room. AE, MC, V. Parking 18€ ($25/£13). **Amenities:** Restaurant; bar; garden. *In room:* A/C (only some rooms; extra 10€/$14/£7), satellite TV, hair dryer, minibar, safe.

Hotel La Bussola   It's not only monasteries and villas that have been converted to hotels—La Bussola is housed in the former Pastificio Bergamasco, a historic pasta-making factory. Located right on the seaside promenade, a short walk away from the medieval town, this hotel offers pleasant accommodations and kind, professional service. Guest rooms are bright and comfortable, with functional furnishings, colorful tiled floors, and modern bathrooms. The **restaurant** is very good and offers a menu focused on seafood.

Lungomare dei Cavalieri 16, 84011 Amalfi. © **089-871533**. Fax 089-871369. www.labussolahotel.it. 65 units. 146€–170€ ($204–$238/£102–£119) double. Rates include buffet breakfast. Children 2 and under stay free in parent's room. AE, DC, MC, V. Free parking. **Amenities:** Restaurant; bar. *In room:* A/C (10€/$14/£7), TV.

Hotel Lidomare *Value*   This is a great though small hotel offering friendly service and good accommodations for the money. Family-run, it is housed in a 13th-century building only steps from the beach. The spacious guest rooms have floors brightly patterned with tiles and are decorated with a mix of modern furniture and antiques. Bathrooms are on the small side but are perfectly kept. Some rooms have sea views and Jacuzzis.

Largo Duchi Piccolomini 9, off Piazza Duomo, 84011 Amalfi. © **089-871332**. Fax 089-871394. www.lidomare.it. 15 units. 140€ ($196/£98) double. Rates include breakfast. Children 2 and under stay free in parent's room. AE, MC, V. Parking 15€ ($21/£11). **Amenities:** Lounge. *In room:* A/C, TV, hair dryer, minibar, safe.

WHERE TO DINE
VERY EXPENSIVE

La Caravella ☆☆☆ MODERN AMALFITAN   This is one of the best restaurants in the whole region. Chef Antonio Dipino has succeeded in marrying tradition with creativity, and so the dishes are sometimes elaborate, but simpler fare is also offered—and everything is made with fresh local ingredients. The seaweed fritters are an excellent appetizer, which you can follow with *tubetti di Gragnano al ragù di zuppa di pesce* (short pasta from Gragnano—bronze extruded—with a sauce of stewed seafood) and a superb *pezzogna* (local fish). For those who prefer meat or are tired of seafood, there are choices such as *ziti di Torre Annunziata ripieni di carne alla Genovese* (pasta tubes from Torre Annunziata—also bronze extruded—filled with meat, Genoese style). The desserts and the wine list are on par with the rest of the menu.

Via Matteo Camera 12. © **089-871029**. www.ristorantelacaravella.it. Reservations required. Tasting menu 75€ ($105/£53). Secondi 25€–35€ ($35–$49/£18–£25). AE, DC, MC, V. Wed–Mon noon–2pm and 7:30–10:30pm; daily in Aug. Closed mid-Nov to Dec 25.

Christmas on the Amalfi Coast

Christmas *(Natale)* is always a special time in Italy, when lights and decorations create a suggestive atmosphere in even the smallest of hamlets. Natale on the Amalfi Coast is unique in its own way; the already picturesque villages and towns become truly magical with Christmas illumination, and you will find elaborate *presepi* (manger scenes, or creches) everywhere. However, the unique landscape of this coast plays a part even here; besides the more traditional location inside churches—such as the 10th-century church of **Santa Maria Maggiore**, whose very fine *presepi* dates from its redecoration in the 18th century (Largo S. Maria Maggiore, Amalfi)—*presepi* are placed in fountains and in grottos. Perhaps the most important of these is the one inside **Grotta dello Smeraldo** in Conca dei Marini (see "Conca dei Marini," later in this chapter), which becomes the point of arrival of a procession on December 24, and again on January 6 (Epiphany). Call the visitor center in Amalfi at (© **089-871107** for more information.

MODERATE

Da Gemma *(Kids* AMALFITAN Serving customers for over a century, this venerable restaurant has racked up sheaves of reviews attesting to its quality. The atmosphere is upscale but relaxed enough to be kid-friendly. One of the most famous specialties is *paccheri con gamberetti* (homemade large pasta with shrimp). *Zuppa di pesce per due* (fish stew for two) is another winner. Don't forget to try the typical Amalfian side dish known as *ciambotta* (a mix of sautéed potatoes, peppers, and eggplant). For dessert try the simple homemade *crostata* (a thick crust topped with local citrus-fruit jam). Half-portions are available for children.

Via Frà Gerardo Sasso 9. (© **089-871345**. Reservations required. Secondi 15€–24€ ($21–$34/£11–£17). AE, DC, MC, V. Thurs–Tues 12:30–2:45pm and 7:45–10:30pm; daily in summer. Closed mid-Jan to mid-Feb.

Eolo *⊛* AMALFITAN This is a classic-style restaurant of the no-nonsense kind Italians like—there are simple furnishings, but great attention is paid to the food and service. The seasonal menu focuses on seafood; you will find local traditional dishes such as *scialatielli ai frutti di mare* (homemade pasta with shellfish) and *frittura* (deep-fried medley of seafood).

Via Pantaleone Comite 3. (© **089-871241**. Reservations recommended. Secondi 15€–32€ ($21–$45/£11–£22). AE, DC, MC, V. Wed–Mon 12:30–3pm and 7:30–10:30pm. Closed 2 weeks in Jan–Feb.

INEXPENSIVE

'a Paranza *⊛⊛* AMALFITAN This simple trattoria is popular for its well-prepared seafood at moderate prices. Hidden away off the main street of Atrani—the village adjacent to Amalfi to the east—it offers an ample menu of traditional dishes. The *frittelle di alghe* (seaweed fritters) are a perfect start. Follow them up with *scialatielli alla paranza* (homemade pasta with small fish), finishing with *polipetti in cassuola* (squid stewed in a terra-cotta pot) or a crispy *grigliata* (grilled fish). The wine list is short but includes excellent local wines.

Via dei Dogi, at Traversa Dragone, Atrani. © **089-871840.** Reservations recommended. Secondi 12€–18€ ($15–$23/ £8.40–£13). AE, DC, MC, V. Mid-Sept to May Wed–Mon 12:30–3pm and 7:30–10:30pm; daily in summer. Closed 2 weeks in Nov–Dec.

Lido Azzurro *Kids* AMALFITAN   This simple restaurant enjoys a prime spot on the town's seaside promenade. The menu includes many kinds of pasta with seafood— *tubetti zucchine, vongole e cozze* (short pasta with clams, mussels and zucchini) is quite good. We recommend the day's fresh fish prepared either baked in a potato crust, or *all'acquapazza* (in a light tomato broth). A well-rounded children's menu makes this a good choice for families.

Lungomare dei Cavalieri. © **089-871384.** Reservations recommended on weekends. Secondi 12€–18€ ($17–$25/ £8.40–£13). AE, DC, MC, V. Tues–Sun 12:30–3pm and 7:30–10:30pm. Closed mid-Jan to mid-Mar.

Trattoria San Giuseppe *Finds* AMALFITAN/PIZZA   Hidden away in the medieval part of town, this simple, down-to-earth place is a real local hangout. It's a great alternative to upscale dining, and the traditional food is of high quality. You can get a variety of pasta dishes as well as excellent pizza—probably the best in town.

Salita Ruggiero II 4. © **089-872640.** Reservations recommended on weekends. Pizza 7€–11€ ($9.80–$15/ £4.90–£7.70). Secondi 8€–14€ ($11–$20/£5.60–£9.80). No credit cards. Fri–Wed noon–2:30pm and 7:30–10:30pm.

AMALFI AFTER DARK

Summer is entertainment time in Amalfi, when musical events are held throughout town. Among the most striking are the piano and vocal concerts held in the **Chiostro del Paradiso** (Piazza del Duomo, off the Duomo's atrium) July through September on Friday evenings.

The town's other key entertainment is visiting one of its many pleasant cafes to sip an *aperitivo* or enjoy a *gelato.* On Piazza Duomo, try **Bar Francese** (Piazza Duomo 20; © **089-871049**), with its elegant seating and excellent pastries. Overlooking the sea is **Gran Caffè di Amalfi** (Corso Repubbliche Marinare; © **089-857874**), a standout for *apertivos.* For those with a sweet tooth, **Gelateria Porto Salvo** (Piazza Duomo 22; © **089-871655;** closed Jan–Mar) is very popular—try the *mandorla candita* (candied almond) flavor. For other types of sweets, **Pasticceria Pansa** (Piazza Duomo 40; © **089-871065;** closed Tues) has been creating delicious pastries since 1830.

If instead you'd like to explore the local wines, head to **Cantina San Nicola** (Salita Marino Sebaste 8; © **089-8304559;** closed Sun) for its great atmosphere and wide selection of labels; they hold wine-tastings twice a week during the summer.

6 Ravello

6km (3¾ miles) NE of Amalfi, 29km (18 miles) W of Salerno, 66km (41 miles) SE of Naples

High up in the mountains, Ravello is a terrace over the sea, overlooking the villages of Minori and Maiori. The focal point of the short stretch of coast between Maiori and Amalfi, it has been the refuge of VIPs since Positano lost some of its glamour to the tourist invasion that began in the 1980s. Although tourists invade Ravello, too, during the summer—Gore Vidal's decision to sell his villa here may have been the signal to the jet set that it is no longer cool—the lay of the land is such that the town remains an attractive retreat. Already celebrated by Boccaccio in his *Decameron* and by Turner in his paintings, Ravello is surrounded by luscious fields, vineyards, and citrus groves.

ESSENTIALS

GETTING AROUND   The town is largely **pedestrian,** with steep, narrow lanes and flights of stairs. All cars must stop at the large public parking lot not far from the Duomo. **Taxis** are available at stands on Piazza Duomo, Gradillo, San Giovanni del Toro, and Castiglione, or by calling ℂ **089-857917.**

VISITOR INFORMATION   The **AAST tourist office** (Via Roma 18, 84010 Ravello; ℂ **089-857096;** www.ravellotime.it) is open October to April, Monday to Saturday from 9am to 6pm; May to September 9am to 8pm.

FAST FACTS   You'll find a **pharmacy** on Piazza Duomo (ℂ **089-857189**). You can get **medical attention** at the Guardia Medica Castiglione di Ravello (ℂ **089-877208**). For an **ambulance,** dial ℂ **118.** Call the **police** at ℂ **113** or at ℂ **112.** The **post office** is on Piazza Vescovado and is open Monday to Saturday 8am to 2pm. You'll find **Banca Monte Paschi di Siena** at Piazza Duomo 6 (ℂ **089-857120**), and **Banca della Campania** at Via Roma 15 (ℂ **089-857872**)—both with **ATMs.**

SPECIAL EVENTS   The internationally famous **Festival di Ravello** (Via Roma 10, 84010 Ravello; ℂ **089-857096** or 199-109910 for reservations; fax 089-858422; www.ravellofestival.com) focuses on classical music, but it is also the occasion for other events, including jazz, dance, and visual arts. It is very popular (reserve well in advance) not only for the big names it attracts (among the participants in 2004 were Salvatore Accardo and the St. Petersburg Philharmonic), but also for the magnificent settings. Performances are held at Piazza Duomo, Villa Rufolo, and Villa Cimbrone, among other venues. The festival is organized into several series, including the **Festival Musicale Wagneriano**—classical music concerts held in July in the garden of **Villa Rufolo** ✿— and the unique **Concerti dell'Aurora,** a group of concerts held at dawn (usually starting at 4am), to welcome the day in music. The festival runs July through September; prices depend on the event, and though some events have free admission, tickets for others can cost anywhere between 15€ and 130€ ($21–$182/£11–£91).

Music continues before and after the festival with concerts and events scheduled March through October. You can find information on these other events by contacting **Fondazione Ravello** (ℂ **089-858360;** info@fondazioneravello.it), or the **Ravello Concert Society** (ℂ **089-858149;** www.ravelloarts.org).

EXPLORING THE TOWN

According to local legend, Ravello was founded in the 5th to 6th centuries A.D. by Roman patricians fleeing barbarians who were ransacking Rome. The small town flourished in the Middle Ages, when it became part of the Republic of Amalfi. It was then the elected residence of some of the wealthiest merchant families of the republic, who created the numerous palaces that adorn this small town (many transformed into hotels today) and decorated the churches with works of high art. Often overlooked, the beautiful Romanesque church of **Santa Maria a Gradillo** ✿✿, dating from the 12th century, is the first architecturally noteworthy site you will see upon entering Ravello. Its intertwined arches, tall apses, and airy interior are all characteristic of the Arab-Sicilian style brought to town by the powerful merchant families who made their fortunes trading with Sicily, North Africa, Spain, and Asia. Until the earthquake of 1706 that destroyed it, the atrium in front of the church was used as the meeting hall for the nobles of Ravello.

The heart of town is **Piazza del Vescovado,** a terrace overlooking the valley of the Dragone, and the adjacent Piazza del Duomo. Taking Via Emanuele Filiberto, you

Ravello

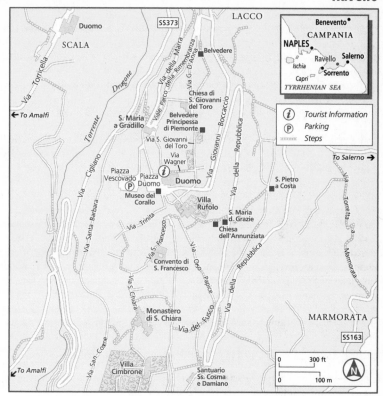

will reach **Via San Giovanni del Toro** ✿✿, which has some of the most beautiful medieval palaces of Ravello, including the 11th-century **Casa Tolla,** today housing the **Municipio.** Crossing the **Belvedere Principessa di Piemonte,** you'll reach **Palazzo Sasso** (today Albergo Palumbo) and **Palazzo d'Afflitto** (now the Albergo Caruso Belvedere). You will arrive at **Piazza Fontana,** with its 13th-century **Convent of Sant'Augostino,** today transformed into the Hotel Parsifal.

Chiesa di San Giovanni del Toro ✿✿   This 12th-century church, restored in 1715 after earthquake damage and again in the 1990s, is one of the most beautiful religious buildings in Ravello. The slender bell tower in Arab-Sicilian style rises beside a facade graced by a triple portal. A steep staircase descends on the right, allowing a view of the three high apses, each crowned by a dome and decorated with intertwined arcs. Inside, the church is divided into three naves by pointed arches supported by eight antique marble columns. The interior is decorated with 13th- and 14th-century frescoes, mosaics, majolica, stucco work, and bas-reliefs. Particularly beautiful is the 12th-century **pergamo** ✿ by Alfano da Termoli, as well as the 14th-century frescoes in the crypt's apse. The church is usually closed, but you can request a visit at Via San Giovanni del Toro 50.

Piazzetta San Giovanni del Toro 3. Donations encouraged. Visit by request (inquire at Via San Giovanni del Toro 50; daily 9:30am to 1 or 2pm and 3–5pm).

Duomo ✦✦✦   Dedicated to San Pantaleone, the patron saint of Ravello, this cathedral is a beautiful example of Romanesque architecture. Built between 1086 or 1087 by the Rufolo family, it was redone in the 12th century and then redecorated in the 18th century. The latest restorations have removed most of the baroque decorations that had affected (some might say afflicted) the interior. The beautiful facade, graced by three marble portals, is famous for the center arch's **bronze door** ✦✦, which was sculpted by Barisano da Trani in 1179 and cast in Constantinople. One of the nicest in Italy, it is decorated with 54 rectangular frames, each with different scenes of carved figures in relief. On the Duomo's right is the 13th-century **bell tower,** showing Arab and Byzantine influences. The Duomo's interior is divided into three naves, each with its own apse; in the central nave to the right is the beautiful **Ambone dell' Epistola** ✦✦✦ from 1130, decorated with precious mosaics representing Jonah. Facing it to the left is the richly carved and decorated **Pergamo** ✦✦✦ from 1272, a splendid work of art by Niccolò di Bartolomeo da Foggia. To the left of the main altar is the **Cappella di San Pantaleone,** built in 1643 for the relic of San Pantaleone. The saint was beheaded in Nicomedia on July 27, 305. On the anniversary of his death, his blood (contained in a vessel) miraculously liquefies. When the vessel is cracked, the second miracle occurs: No blood leaks from the cracked vessel. Beneath the church, the crypt houses a small museum where you can admire the elegant 13th-century **Bust of Sichelgaita della Marra** ✦✦, sculpted by Bartolomeo da Foggia, as well as several precious relic holders, including the **Bust of Santa Barbara** ✦ in silver.

Piazza del Vescovado. ✆ **089-858311** or 089-857122 for the museum. Duomo: free admission. Museum: 2€ ($2.80/£1.40). Duomo daily 9am–1pm and 4–7pm. Museum daily summer 9am–7pm; winter 9am–6pm. Guided tours available.

Museo del Corallo   Created in 1986, this small but extremely interesting museum has a wonderful collection of precious objects made of coral, including cameos, totaling over 600 pieces. Located on the premises of the workshop **Camo,** who specialize in this traditional art (p. 136 for more information), the collection stretches from ancient Roman pieces all the way to the 19th century. Particularly beautiful are the 16th-century **Crucifix** on a crystal cross and a **Madonna** from 1532. Be sure to note the 3rd-century-A.D. Roman amphora with a coral formation inside it, and a beautiful set of 14 cherub heads from the 18th to 19th centuries.

Piazza Duomo 9. ✆ **089-857461.** Free admission. Mon–Sat 9:30am–noon and 3–5:30pm.

Villa Cimbrone ✦   Farther up from the center of town, this 14th- or 15th-century villa belonged to the noble family Acconciagioco, but was largely rebuilt in 1904 by its new owner, an eccentric English lord named William Beckett. The resulting mix of styles is somewhat disharmonious, but the villa and its gardens remain quite lovely. Inside you'll see two towers, the courtyard and, at the end of a delightful alley lined by statues, the famous **Belvedere Cimbrone** ✦✦✦—famed for its awe-inspiring panorama. Between the sculptures which decorate the balustrade, you can look out at a view encompassing Atrani and the whole Gulf of Salerno down to the plain of Paestum and distant Punta Licosa. The villa accepts overnight guests in some of the rooms (see later in this chapter). *Note:* To visit, ring the bell at the entrance. Access to the path to the villa is only by foot and is rather steep.

Via Santa Chiara 26. ✆ **089-858072** or 089-857459 for reservations. Fax 089-857777. www.villacimbrone.it. Admission 5€ ($7/£3.50). Daily summer 9am–sunset.

Villa Rufolo 🖈🖈   In the center of town just to the right of the Duomo, this beautiful villa was built between 1270 and 1280 for the prominent Rufolo family, then passed
on to the Gonfalone e Muscettola family in the 15th century. It was bought in 1851
by the Scotsman Francis Devile Reid, who partially restructured it and thereby affected
its architectural harmony. A public building since 1975, the villa can be visited together
with its beautiful **gardens** 🖈. The original architecture shows much Arab influence,
especially in the detail of intertwined arches, which recurs in the **Entrance Hall** within
the access tower and in the beautiful courtyard. The tower is also decorated with four
statues representing symbols of charity and hospitality. The three-story main building
is at the end of a tree-lined alley and opens over an **Inner Court,** a marvelous cloister
with a double level of loggias over richly decorated and intertwined columns. The **Sala
d'Aspetto (Receiving Hall), Salone (Main Hall),** and **Main Tower** also have interesting details. Across from the entrance is the famous **Terrace** 🖈, which was renamed Terrazza Wagner in memory of the German composer who wrote the Klingsor Garden
scene in the second act of his *Parsifal* here because he was inspired by the terrace's view.
Today, the view—which from 340m (1,115 ft.) above sea level is spectacular—is the
setting for the *Concerti Wagneriani,* a summer festival of classical music.

Piazza Vescovado. 🕐 **089-857657** or 089-857866. Admission 5€ ($7/£3.50). Daily summer 9am–8pm; winter
9am–6pm.

STAYING ACTIVE

Ravello lacks the beaches enjoyed by many of the other villages along this coast, but
in compensation, it offers great opportunities for walks and serious hikes. The walks
we suggest below are quite easy, allowing you to return by bus or taxi, but if you are
more ambitious, you might undertake a complete loop of the two hikes below.

The **Monastero di San Nicola** makes for a pleasant and easy hike, since it only has
a few small stretches of hillside but is very scenic. From the center of Ravello, take the
road for Chiunzi for 1km (½ mile) toward the hamlet of Sambuco, 320m (1,050 ft.)
above sea level (you can also get to this point by car). Descending from here a few
steps to your right, you can reach the trail that climbs to the Monastery of Saint
Nicholas at an altitude of 486m (1,594 ft.). Plan on about 2 hours for the 9km (5¾-
mile) hike. The monastery is currently under restoration, but you can still enjoy the
great views. From the monastery, it is then possible to descend to Minori—or to
Maiori if you prefer—in about a half-hour. Hiking the reverse route (starting from
Minori or Maiori) is more demanding, but you can do it by taking the small road that
connects Maiori with Minori and passes behind the Collegiata to reach the path that
climbs gently toward the monastery. The trail becomes progressively steeper and more
scenic until you reach the top. Figure on spending about 1 hour for the ascent from
Maiori or Minori to the monastery.

Another scenic hike in the area is the one to Minori. From the center of Ravello,
take another footpath—a charming mix of steps and hidden alleys—which descends
all the way to Minori and the sea. Start from the alley to the left of Villa Rufolo,
marked by a small fountain, at an altitude of 350m (1,148 ft.), and begin the descent.
You will pass by the small 13th-century Annunziata church and by San Pietro church.
You will then reach the hamlet of **Torello,** with its church of the Addolorata and
graceful bell tower in Arab-Sicilian style. The picturesque walk will continue among
olive trees all the way down to the sea and the village of **Minori.** The whole hike
should take you only a half-hour; however, allow at least double that for the ascent.

WHERE TO STAY

For a luxury address in town, we also recommend **Villa Cimbrone** (see earlier in this chapter). If you would like more modest accommodations, we recommend the few rooms offered by **Da Salvatore** (see "Where to Dine," below).

VERY EXPENSIVE

Hotel Caruso 🅐   Housed in the splendid Palazzo D'Afflitto, this state-of-the-art hotel has been popular ever since it was a small *pensione* occupying only part of the building. Guest rooms are palatial and welcoming, with Baldaquin beds, heavenly linens, and large bathrooms with separate shower and tub. Most have sea views and open on private balconies, terraces, or small gardens. Pry yourself away to visit the breathtaking outdoor infinity pool or the hotel's tennis courts, a 15-minute walk away.

Piazza San Giovanni del Toro 2, 84010 Ravello. ⓒ **089-858801.** Fax 089-858806. www.hotelcaruso.com. 48 units. 780€–990€ ($1,092–$1,386/£546–£693) double, from 1,300€ ($1,820/£910) suite. Rates include buffet breakfast. Children 11 and under stay free in parent's room. AE, DC, MC, V. Parking 20€ ($28/£14). Closed Nov–Mar. **Amenities:** 2 restaurant; 2 bars; babysitting; concierge; laundry service; lounges; outdoor pool; room service. *In room:* A/C, satellite TV, hair dryer, minibar, safe.

Hotel Palumbo 🅐   This fascinating hotel occupies the 12th-century Palazzo Confalone. The key word here is refinement, with both guest rooms and public areas elegantly decorated and furnished with antiques. Guest rooms are not large, but many have private terraces with gorgeous views. The bathrooms tend to be lavish. The hotel grants access to a nearby swimming pool and to its private beach through free car service. The hotel's restaurant, **Confalone,** offers gourmet dining in its elegant small dining halls and on a splendid panoramic terrace.

Via San Giovanni del Toro 16, 84010 Ravello. ⓒ **089-857244.** Fax 089-858133. www.hotelpalumbo.it. 21 units. 600€ ($840/£420) double, from 800€ ($1,120/£560) suite. Rates include buffet breakfast. Children 2 and under stay free in parent's room. AE, DC, MC, V. Parking 20€ ($28/£14). **Amenities:** Restaurant; bar; babysitting; concierge; garden; laundry service; lounges; outdoor pool; room service; solarium w/Jacuzzi. *In room:* A/C, satellite TV, hair dryer, minibar, safe.

Palazzo Sasso 🅐🅐   This 11th-century palace was transformed into a hotel in 1880, and was the preferred retreat of the rich and famous until the 1960s. It then fell into ruin but was restored and reopened in 1997. Today, it has been transformed into an opulent hotel in a splendid location between plunging cliffs and steep mountainside. Guest rooms are luxuriously appointed with antiques. Some of them afford gorgeous views—the best are from room nos. 1, 201, 204, and 301, and suite 304. Some of the suites are as big as a good-size apartment, and even the lower-priced rooms are spacious (a few at the bottom of the scale have no view). Bathrooms are done up in marble, with large tubs and all the comforts you'd expect. In addition to a very nice garden, solarium, beautiful pool, and spa, the hotel prides itself on its excellent restaurant, **Rossellinis,** where the talented chef Pino Lavarra creates delicious meals from the best local ingredients. *Note:* Wi-Fi service will be introduced shortly.

Via San Giovanni del Toro 28, 84010 Ravello. ⓒ **089-818181.** Fax 089-858900. www.palazzosasso.com. 44 units. 360€–710€ ($504–$994/£252–£497) double; from 930€ ($1,302/£651) suite. Rates include buffet breakfast. Children 2 and under stay free in parent's room. AE, DC, MC, V. Free parking. Closed Nov to mid-Mar. **Amenities:** Restaurant; bar; babysitting; concierge; garden; laundry service; 2 outdoor pools; room service; solarium; spa. *In room:* A/C, satellite TV, hair dryer, Internet access, minibar, safe.

EXPENSIVE

Hotel Rufolo ⚜ In the heart of Ravello, this family-run hotel overlooks the gardens of Villa Rufolo. Housed in a modern building, the interior, with white plaster and columns and arches everywhere, gives off a much older, traditional feeling. The hotel offers comfortable accommodations and friendly service. Guest rooms are different sizes, but all have reproduction and modern furnishings in a restrained decor. While all have varying views, the views from the common sun decks are always superb. The pool is tucked into an attractive garden.

Via San Francesco 1, 84010 Ravello. ☎ **089-857133.** Fax 089-857935. www.hotelrufolo.it. 30 units. 295€–365€ ($148–$183/£158–£183) double. Rates include buffet breakfast. Children 2 and under stay free in parent's room. AE, DC, MC, V. Free parking. Closed Dec 22–28. **Amenities:** Restaurant; bar; babysitting; concierge; laundry service; outdoor pool; room service. *In room:* A/C, TV, hair dryer, iron, minibar.

MODERATE

Hotel Giordano ⚜ This historic family-run hotel is set in a commanding location not far from Villa Rufolo. The entrance and lobby are sparely but handsomely decorated with fine antiques. The comfortable guest rooms are furnished with period or period-style pieces, with colorful tilework on the floors and in the bathrooms (the latter are up-to-date and functional, if a bit small). Public areas include a swimming pool and terraces, as well as some of the facilities of the nearby Villa Maria (below).

Via San Francesco 1, 84010 Ravello. ☎ **089-857170.** Fax 089-857071. www.giordanohotel.it. 30 units. 185€–250€ ($93–$125/£93–£125) double. Rates include breakfast. Children 2 and under stay free in parent's room. AE, DC, MC, V. Free parking in the hotel garage. **Amenities:** Restaurant; bar; babysitting; concierge; laundry service; outdoor heated pool. *In room:* A/C, TV, hair dryer, minibar.

Villa Maria ⚜ This independent hotel is run by the same family that owns the Hotel Giordano (above). Housed in what was once a luxurious private villa, the site has a nice garden with views over the sea. The rooms, especially nice because of their brightness, are spacious and well-appointed, with a few antiques and otherwise quality hardwood furniture. The floors and bathrooms are colorfully tiled. The hotel's **restaurant** features a delightful arbor terrace where you can enjoy wonderful food prepared with organic ingredients from the hotel's own farm. The restaurant also offers weekly cooking classes.

Via Santa Chiara 2, 84010 Ravello. ☎ **089-857255.** Fax 089-857071. www.villamaria.it. 30 units. 230€–290€ ($322–$406/£161–£203) double. Rates include breakfast. Children 1 and under stay free in parent's room. AE, DC, MC, V. Free parking. **Amenities:** Restaurant; bar; babysitting; concierge; garden; laundry service; outdoor pool; room service; solarium. *In room:* A/C, TV, hair dryer, minibar.

INEXPENSIVE

Hotel Graal Enjoying a scenic position, this small hotel offers great accommodations, moderately priced for such a fashionable part of town. The public areas are a bit faded, but guest rooms are bright and decorated in Mediterranean style with modern furnishings. They have good-size bathrooms and balconies with sea views. The restaurant here is very good, with abundant shellfish choices (and a selection of meat dishes for those who've had their fill of seafood). Popular with locals who aren't staying at the hotel, the restaurant is open year-round.

Via della Repubblica 8, 84010 Ravello. ☎ **089-857222.** Fax 089-857551. www.hotelgraal.it. 35 units. 180€–220€ ($252–$308/£126–£154) double. Rates include breakfast. Children 2 and under stay free in parent's room. AE, DC, MC, V. Parking 11€ ($15.40/£7.70). **Amenities:** Restaurant; bar; babysitting; laundry service; outdoor pool; room service; Wi-Fi. *In room:* A/C, satellite TV, minibar.

Palazzo della Marra *Finds*   Housed in the historical 13th-century *palazzo* of the same name, this pleasant B&B offers welcoming accommodations only steps from the Duomo. Guest rooms have wrought-iron beds, some period pieces, tiled floors, and views over the Duomo or the gardens. Before the B&B came the excellent restaurant, now called **Figli di Papà,** serving hearty cuisine with a creative twist (closed on Tues in winter).

Via della Marra 3, 84010 Ravello. © 089-858302. www.palazzodellamarra.com. 10 units. 100€ ($140/£70) double. Rates include breakfast. Children 2 and under stay free in parent's room. AE, DC, MC, V. Parking 18€ ($25/£13). **Amenities:** Restaurant; bar; terrace. *In room:* TV.

WHERE TO DINE
MODERATE
Cumpà Cosimo *Kids* AMALFITAN   Once a simple winery, this place has blossomed into a popular restaurant, favored by locals. Family-run since it opened in 1929—the second generation is still at the helm—it serves generous portions of homemade traditional dishes. The seasonal menu always includes mouthwatering pastas and particularly succulent secondi—you might find *zuppa di pesce* (fish stew) and a fine *fritto misto* (deep-fried medley of seafood), or roasted lamb with herbs. The staff is particularly accommodating to the needs of little ones, and allows half-portions.

Via Roma 44. © 089-857156. Reservations recommended. Secondi 11€–28€ ($14–$35/£). AE, DC, MC, V. Tues–Sun 12:30–3pm and 7:30–11pm; Apr–Oct daily.

INEXPENSIVE
Da Salvatore *Finds* AMALFITAN   This simple restaurant offers local cuisine in a striking setting—the views are superb both from the dining room and the garden terrace, which is open for alfresco dining in warm weather. The style and atmosphere here are relaxed, with simple tables and chairs. You can choose fish or meat from among the traditional dishes, which include *gnoccoloni al pomodoro e basilico* (potato dumplings with fresh tomatoes and basil), grilled fish, and roasted veal. The restaurant has six **guest rooms** for rent.

Via della Repubblica 2. © 089-857227. www.salvatoreravello.com. Reservations recommended. Secondi 12€–18€ ($17–$25/£8.40–£13). AE, V. Tues–Sun 12:30–3pm and 7:30–11pm; Apr–Oct daily.

Ristorante Pizzeria Vittoria AMALFITAN/PIZZA   This family-run restaurant is a good choice for a moderately priced meal. The dining room is welcoming and the service prompt. The wood-oven pizza is top-notch and the menu includes many tasty choices such as the *spaghetti alle vongole* (with clams) to the excellent *pesce alla griglia* (whole grilled fish of your choice).

Via dei Rufolo 3. © 089-857947. Reservations recommended on weekends. Secondi 8€–16€ ($11–$22/£5.60–£11). AE, DC, MC, V. Wed–Mon 12:30–3pm and 7:30–11pm; Apr–Oct daily.

RAVELLO AFTER DARK
Most locals spend their nights sipping an *aperitivo*—or nibbling on sweets—at one of the town's cafes. The activity can take on a theatrical air when the weather is nice and people-watching is at its prime. At the **Bar Calce** (Via Roma 2, next to the Duomo; © 089-857152), people gather for the excellent pastries and homemade ice cream. **Caffè Domingo** (Piazza Duomo; © 089-857142) has been run by the same family since 1929 and is famous for its *babà* (sponge cake) and *dolcezze al limone* (traditional lemon pastries).

7 Scala & Tramonti

Scala is 6km (3½ miles) north of Amalfi. Tramonti is 11km (6½ miles) north of Maiori

Little-known by most tourists, the Ravello environs offer dramatic mountains and sea views as well as peaceful rural retreats. Already established in Roman times, the historic town of Scala rises in a splendid position over the valley of the Dragone, opposite Ravello. It is the gateway to a rocky countryside where little has changed since ancient times. Farther in, the larger village of Tramonti is the heart of an agricultural area famous for its D.O.C. vineyards.

SCALA

Only 6km (3½ miles) north of Amalfi, Scala is the oldest settlement in the area and was, together with Amalfi and Ravello, the center of the Amalfi Maritime Republic. A fortified town, its two castles—one guarding inland approaches, the other overlooking the sea—were connected by walls that enclosed the town completely. Some medieval palaces remain, such as **Palazzo d'Afflitto** with its beautiful **torrione (tower),** where you can see an interesting bath in Arab-Sicilian style, covered by an elegant dome on arches similar to the one inside Palazzo Rufolo in Ravello. You can also visit **Casa Romano,** noted for its imposing entrance. While the first floor has been left as it was in medieval times, the second floor was completely redone and decorated with frescoes during the baroque period. The palace hosts several events, including the summer theater festival and a series of concerts. Contact the **Proloco tourist office,** Piazza Municipio (© **089-858977** or 089-857325) for a schedule of events.

The 12th-century **Duomo** ✦, Piazza Municipio 5 (© **089-857397;** daily 8am–1pm and 6–7pm), dedicated to San Lorenzo Martire, is an impressive church that was redone in 1615 and restored in 1980. A Romanesque portal and medieval sculptures decorate the facade; inside, the majolica floor is still in good condition. From the right nave, a staircase descends to the **crypt** ✦, which boasts a unique, surprisingly bright architecture. Some of the best art pieces are conserved here, including the 14th-century **funerary monument** ✦✦ for Marinella Rufolo, erected by her husband Antonio Coppola and uniquely decorated with colored enamel. Be sure to note the 13th-century **crucifix** over the main altar.

Around Scala you can also visit the several separate bourgs built on the surrounding hills. Each is a smaller replica of Scala's defensive structure—protected by two castles, one facing the sea and one guarding inland. All of these smaller bourgs can be reached by car of course, but also on foot, using the network of footpaths connecting them. These provide an excellent opportunity for short hikes. One of the easiest and most rewarding is the walk to the bourg of **Minuto,** only 1km (½-mile) south of Scala, where you'll find the **Chiesa della Santissima Annunziata** ✦✦, probably Scala's original cathedral. Built between the 11th and 12th centuries, this church is one of the best examples of Romanesque architecture on the whole Amalfi Coast (and the view alone is worth a stop). The handsome covered portico was used in the Middle Ages as the town meeting place; the bell tower is remarkable for its rare octagonal housing. The three portals of the church's facade are decorated with Byzantine frescoes. Inside, the church is divided into three naves by antique columns. If you come here, be sure to visit the **crypt,** where you will find an important cycle of **12th-century frescoes** ✦✦, including a Christ Pantocraor that accurately represents Byzantine style. Note that the church is only opened for mass on Sunday (9:30–10:30am), but it can be visited upon request by asking at the parish house in Via Ficuciello.

STAYING ACTIVE

The mountainous area of Scala is unspoiled and authentic. The best (as well as the most exciting) way to visit it is on horseback. You can sign up for a pleasant **horse ride and guided excursion** in the countryside at local horse farms; the best are **Carmusina**, Via Casa Romana (© **089-857904**), and **La Piccola California**, Via Sento (© **089-858042**). If you prefer to walk, the best **hike** in the area is from **Campidoglio di Scala**—one of the bourgs connected to Scala, at an altitude of 470m (1,542 ft.). The first part is a ridge trail, extremely scenic and not very arduous. You can make the walk more challenging by descending all the way to Amalfi. Along the way you will find, on your left, the ruins of the 12th-century church of Sant'Eustachio. The trail continues through a natural rock formation in the form of an amphitheater, showing the ruins of ancient fortifications, called Castello. It finally reaches the waterfalls at the top of the Vallone delle Ferriere of Amalfi (see later in this chapter); here you are about halfway through the descent. If you wish, you can then walk down along the Vallone and reach Amalfi through the Valle dei Mulini. Figure on spending about 2 hours to get to the waterfall and an additional 2 hours to get to Amalfi.

WHERE TO STAY

Scala provides a good alternative to the more pricey hotels in Ravello, yet it is only a few minutes away by car.

Ristorante Albergo La Margherita Overlooking the valley of the Dragone, this hotel enjoys a delightful position, surrounded by greenery and quiet. The annex nearby—**Villa Giuseppina** (same phone)—offers more rooms, a large garden, and a full-size pool with solarium. Guest rooms are similarly appointed in the two buildings, with simple furnishings, good-size tiled bathrooms, and spacious private terraces affording pretty views over Ravello and the sea. The top-notch on-site **restaurant** (closed Tues and selected evenings in winter) serves well-prepared traditional cuisine on a pleasant terrace and veranda.

Via Torricella 31, 84010 Scala. © **089-857106**. Fax 089-857219. www.lamargheritahotel.it. 30 units. 120€ ($168/ £84) double. Rates include breakfast. Children 2 and under stay free in parent's room. AE, DC, MC, V. Free parking. **Amenities:** Restaurant; bar; outdoor pool. *In room:* TV, minibar.

Zi 'Ntonio Overlooking Ravello from the other side of the valley, this hotel offers comfortable accommodations with good views. A family-run establishment, the hotel basks in a quiet, warm atmosphere, surrounded by chestnut trees. Rooms come simply furnished but with modern bathrooms and amenities; most open onto a private balcony or terrace. The large terrace and nearby pool are added attractions. The **restaurant** prepares dishes made with meat and vegetables from the hotel's own farm. We recommend you call in advance (it's worth it) to request the *pollo alla zi'Ntonio*, chicken prepared with herbs and wine.

Via Torricella 39, 84010 Scala. © **089-857118**. Fax 089-858128. www.zintonio.com. 22 units. 110€ ($154/£77) double. Rates include breakfast. Children 2 and under stay free in parent's room. AE, DC, MC, V. Free parking. **Amenities:** Restaurant; bar; outdoor pool. *In room:* Hair dryer.

WHERE TO DINE

Da Lorenzo ★★ *Finds* AMALFITAN Overlooking the valley, Ravello, and the sea, this restaurant is in Santa Maria, one of the bourgs of Scala. The cuisine is simple and traditional, with homemade dishes focusing on fish in summer and meat in winter. The bread is made in a wood-burning oven that also turns out excellent pizza in the evening. Some of the best dishes here are *scialatielli ai frutti di mare* (fresh pasta with shellfish), *pappardelle con il coccio* (large pasta with a tasty local fish), *grigliata di gamberoni* (perfectly grilled large shrimp) in summer, and *scamorza alla brace* (grilled local cheese) and cured meats in winter.

Via Fra' G. Sasso, Santa Maria, Scala. ℂ 089-857921. Reservations recommended. Secondi 15€–21€ ($21–$29/ £11–£15). AE, DC, MC, V. Winter Sat–Sun noon–2:30pm and 7:30–10:30pm; daily in summer.

TRAMONTI

Up and inland from Maiori by about 11km (6½ miles) is the rural village of Tramonti. Its name comes from the Latin *intra montes* or "between the mountains," and so it is. The 13 historic *casali* (farms) that form the village are far above the sea, and each is graced by its own small church. The **Proloco tourist office** of Tramonti is inside the municipal building in **Polvica** (ℂ **089-856820**).

WHAT TO SEE & DO

The highlight of an excursion to Tramonti is the **Valico di Chiunzi,** high in the mountains, at an altitude of 656m (2,152 ft.), with its spectacular **panorama** ✦✦✦ of the plain of Pompeii and Mount Vesuvius; picturesque ruins remain of its famous castle that protected the coast from inland attacks, now reduced to a single powerful tower.

One thing you must do here is sample the local **wine**—the *Tramonti,* one of the D.O.C. wines of the Amalfi Coast. Another local specialty is *Concierto,* a bitter yet sweet liquor made with nine herbs and spices; it was first concocted in the 17th century in a local convent, the **Regio Conservatorio dei Santi Giuseppe e Teresa,** Località Pucara (ℂ **339-1746893**). The convent is open to visitors, and you can purchase the liquor—which makes an excellent gift or souvenir—at any of the bars and stores in town.

This backcountry farming village has maintained the time-honored craft of chestnut-wood **basket making.** These baskets are very durable as they were traditionally used for carrying fresh lemons from the famed local groves. The wood is steamed into shape and braided into baskets of all shapes and sizes. You'll find them for sale at **Amarante,** Via Corsano 15 (ℂ **089-876715**), the showroom of one of the few remaining craftsmen specializing in this art.

Spilling over from nearby Amalfi, the **Antica Cartiera Amalfitana,** Via Nuova Chiunzi 14 (ℂ **089-855432**) is one of the region's original **paper mills,** and is still operational today. You can tour the mill by appointment and buy the quality filigree paper it produces.

WHERE TO STAY

If you are looking for complete relaxation, the *agriturismo* **Azienda Agrituristica Le Chiancolelle** (Via Valico di Chiunzi, Località Campinola, 84010 Tramonti; ℂ **089-876339;** 5 units) offers a great alternative to regular hotels and restaurants. You'll get a deep immersion in nature while you are enticed by homemade and home-produced foods, including cured meats—from boar to pork—and good jams; much of their production is organic. Another great *agriturismo* nearby is **Azienda Agrituristica Mare e Monti** (Via Trugnano 3, Località Campinola, 84010 Tramonti; ℂ **089-876665;** www. agriturismomaremonti.it; 2 units). There you will be pampered and plied with homemade delicacies ranging from jams made with the farm's organic fruits to sausages and cured meats made on the spot, all accompanied by the farm's own wine.

WHERE TO DINE

Da Nino ⭐ AMALFITAN/PIZZA   Affectionately called "Ninuccio" (little Nino) by the locals, this trattoria offers a warm welcome and delicious specialties, made in large part with ingredients from the owners' farm. For an appetizer, taste the superb salamis and *sottoli* (vegetables preserved in olive oil) with homemade bread and local mozzarella. Follow this with a secondo of pasta or their whole-wheat pizza—the one with veggies *(con le verdure)* is particularly savory.

Via Pucara 39. ⓒ **089-876184.** Reservations recommended on weekends. Secondi 8€–15€ ($11–$21/£5.60–£11). No credit cards. Wed–Mon noon–3pm and 7:30–10pm; daily in summer.

La Violetta *Finds* AMALFITAN   The views are gorgeous and the food is divine at this simple, honest restaurant. The hearty menu includes lots of salamis produced on the farm here, as well as homemade pasta and gnocchi. The *risotto ai chiodini* (risotto with local wild mushrooms) bursts with flavor; and the grilled meats are superb. They also serve a good local red wine.

Via Valico di Chiunzi. ⓒ **089-876384.** Reservations recommended on weekends. Secondi 12€–18€ ($17–$25/ £8.40–£13). No credit cards. Tues–Sun 12:30–3pm and 7:30–11pm; daily in summer.

8 Maiori & Minori

Maiori is 15km (9 miles) west of Vietri and 6km (4 miles) east of Amalfi on SS 163. Minori is 18km (11 miles) west of Vietri sul Mare, and 3km (2 miles) east of Amalfi along SS 163

Back when Amalfi was a powerful maritime republic, one of the few land accesses to its territory was the valley of the large stream, Reginna Maior, which comes into the sea at **Maiori** and lends its name to this village. This was an important little harbor in the Middle Ages and today is a pleasant village with both nice beaches and artistic attractions. At the mouth of a smaller stream—the Reginna Minor—lies **Minori,** a hamlet famous for its beaches. Ravello's notoriety often overshadows the other villages nearby, yet they are well worth your attention (it also secures comparative calm for them). Here you will find a few hidden art treasures, including an 11th-century monastery with beautiful frescoes.

MAIORI

Maiori opens onto one of the largest beaches of the whole Costiera—and, unfortunately, one of the most developed. Maiori, when it was an important town in medieval times, was surrounded by walls and defended by towers and castles, originally built in the 9th century. Today, only ruins remain of these walls and towers. The look of the village was also much changed by the flood of 1954, which destroyed the medieval heart of town. As in Amalfi and other towns along this coast, the Reginna Maior was covered over to gain building space, but the flood blew the lid off, causing the collapse of all the adjacent buildings. The town was rebuilt with a modern look.

ESSENTIALS

The town is small and you'll be able to visit **on foot.** Should you need a **taxi** you can find one at the taxi stand by the harbor or call one at ⓒ **089-877897.** The **tourist office A.A.C.S.T. (Azienda Autonoma di Cura Soggiorno e Turismo)** is at Corso Reginna 73 (ⓒ **089-877452;** www.aziendaturismo-maiori.it).

WHAT TO SEE & DO

Dominating the village from an impressive ramp of 108 steps is a memento of Maiori's glorious past, the **Collegiata di Santa Maria a Mare** (Corso Reginna Maior). Built in the 12th century, this church was redone in later times and is graced by a large majolica cupola. Inside is a precious collection of artwork from the 15th and 16th centuries. The richly carved, wooden ceiling in the main church and the crypt's majolica floor date from the same period. Adjacent to the church is the entrance to the museum, which protects more valuable objects of art from the church's past, dating from the 12th to the 18th centuries.

In the opposite direction of the church is the **beach,** which gets rather crowded in summer. From the beach, if you follow the cliff eastward, you will come to two grottoes. The first is frankly rather smelly, with its sulfur-magnesium mineral spring, but the other—**Grotta Pannone** *&*—is encrusted with stalactites and, particularly in the morning, takes on a color similar to the one of the famous Blue Grotto of Capri.

WHERE TO STAY
Hotel San Francesco   In a quiet position a short distance from the sea, this hotel is surrounded by gardens and has a beautiful private beach. Housed in a modern building, the good-size guest rooms are simply furnished in hardwood and wrought iron, with tiled floors and private balconies affording superior views (the balconies are covered, so you can use them at any time). Though the bathrooms aren't large, they do have quality, contemporary fixtures.

Via Santa Tecla 54, 84010 Maiori. *©*/fax **089-877070.** www.hotel-sanfrancesco.it. 44 units. 140€–170€ ($196–$238/£98–£119) double. Rates include buffet breakfast. Children 2 and under stay free in parent's room. AE, DC, MC, V. Free parking. Closed Nov–Mar. Pets accepted. **Amenities:** Restaurant; bar; babysitting; private beach; laundry service; outdoor pool; room service. *In room:* A/C, satellite TV, hair dryer, minibar, safe.

Reginna Palace Hotel *&*   This elegant hotel sits right in the heart of Maiori, surrounded by a luxurious garden opening onto its private beach. The noteworthy swimming pool is filled with seawater. Guest rooms are spacious and furnished in contemporary style with fine fabrics and artistically tiled floors and bathrooms. A number of the rooms have views over the sea, and some have private balconies. The hotel's private beach is only 50 yards away, and the elegant on-site **restaurant** has a lovely outdoor terrace for dining on fair summer nights.

Via Cristoforo Colombo 1, 84010 Maiori. *©*/fax **089-877183.** Fax 089-851200. www.hotelreginna.it. 67 units. 190€–220€ ($266–$308/£113–£154) double. Minimum 2 weeks' stay around Aug 15. Rates include buffet breakfast. Children 2 and under stay free in parent's room. AE, DC, MC, V. Parking 18€ ($25/£13). Closed Nov–Mar. Internet specials available. **Amenities:** Restaurant; 2 bars; babysitting; private beach; garden; laundry service; outdoor pool; room service. *In room:* A/C, satellite TV, hair dryer, minibar.

WHERE TO DINE
Mammato *(Value* AMALFITAN   Located on the shorefront, this restaurant is popular with locals who come here to eat fish prepared according to the region's traditional recipes. This is a relaxed, local restaurant, decorated sparingly—in other words, it's a classic Italian place. Among the noteworthy classics of that cuisine are *scialatielli ai frutti di mare* (homemade pasta with basil and seafood), and *frittura* (deep-fried calamari and small fish).

Lungomare Amendola. *©* **089-853683.** Reservations recommended. Secondi 12€–18€ ($17–$25/£8.40–£13). AE, DC, MC, V. Wed–Mon 1–3:30pm and 8–11:30pm; daily in summer. Closed 2 weeks in Nov.

MINORI
ESSENTIALS
The **tourist office** is on Piazza Cantilena (*©* **089-877087** or 089-877607; www.proloco. minori.sa.it). You'll find a **pharmacy** on Corso Vittorio Emanuele (*©* **089-877200**).

For an **ambulance,** dial ℂ **118.** The **police** can be reached at ℂ **113** or at ℂ **112.** The **post office** (ℂ **089-853549**) is at Via Pergola. You will find several banks with **ATMs,** including a **Banco di Napoli** (ℂ **089-877150**) at Corso Vittoria Emanuele 29. You can call a **taxi** at ℂ **089-877435,** or flag one from the stand by the harbor. To explore by sea, you can **rent motor- and sailboats** at the **Noleggio,** Via Nazionale 5 (ℂ **0335-5443010;** www.amalficharter.it).

Summer is a special time, with a number of festivals and events—such as the much-acclaimed **summer music festival**—enlivening the town's cultural scene. We particularly recommend **Jazz on the Coast** (Associazione Musical Costiera Amlfitana, ℂ **338-4076618;** www.jazzonthecoast.it), held annually in July. Contact the tourist office, above, for a full schedule of events.

VISITING THE TOWN

Famous for its sandy beach, Minori is a picturesque little town nestled in a glorious setting of blue sea and citrus groves. Appreciated since antiquity, the village, with its small harbor inside a beautiful cove, was the arsenal of the Republic of Amalfi in the Middle Ages. It comes alive in summer with vacationers enjoying its **beaches** and the **music festival** (see above), but the village is worth a visit at any time of year.

Just a few steps from the little harbor you will find the **Basilica of Santa Trofimena.** Built in the 11th century, the cathedral was completely redone in the 19th century; inside are some finely crafted 17th-century marble altars and the original crypt (restored in the 17th century) housing the remains of Saint Trofimena, Amalfi's protector saint. If you walk along the left side of the Basilica and turn right up a ramp of steps, you will reach the wonderful 12th-century **Campanile** ❀❀. The sole remnant of the church of Santa Annunziata, it still shows its original intarsia decorations.

Following the canalized stream—turning right from the beach through the narrow and winding local road—you will reach **Villa Romana,** aka **Villa Marittima** ❀❀ (Via Capo di Piazza 28; ℂ **089-852893;** Mon–Sat 9am to 1 hr. before sunset). One of the many Roman villas that existed in this area, Villa Romana dates from the 1st century A.D. and was discovered in 1932 but was not excavated until the 1950s. The villa was built on two floors around a vast courtyard, graced by a pool and surrounded by a portico. You can admire the hydraulic engineering that brought water to the pool, and the well-conserved rooms decorated with stucco work and remains of frescoes. One side of the portico opens onto the beautiful *ninfeo,* a hall richly decorated with frescoes and stucco work. Also architecturally interesting are the private thermal baths, which have been perfectly preserved. The staircase to the second floor is partially preserved, but you can climb its 29 steps to the **Antiquarium.** It contains a collection of artifacts and frescoes from this and nearby excavations.

WHERE TO STAY

Hotel Caporal   This nice family-run hotel has relatively few units and offers simple and comfortable rooms with access to a private beach—just about everything you could ask for. If you plan to explore the area or spend time sunbathing, the Caporal is a good base (on-site amusements are few). Guest rooms are spacious, bright, and simple but well furnished. They have tiled floors and good-size bathrooms; a number of them have balconies and overlook the ocean.

Via Nuova 20, 84010 Minori. ℂ **089-877408.** Fax 089-877166. 30 units. 130€ ($182/£91) double. Rates include buffet breakfast. Children 2 and under stay free in parent's room. AE, DC, MC, V. Parking 18€ ($25/£13). **Amenities:** Restaurant; bar. *In room:* A/C, satellite TV, hair dryer, minibar, safe.

Hotel Villa Romana 🇸 Last restructured in 2000, this welcoming hotel is Minori's best and holds its own with anyplace on the Costiera. Its swimming pool, private beach, and terraces offer several ways to relax. Bright white walls, woodwork, and tile, as well as wrought iron and glass furniture, are used throughout to create a relaxed but tasteful atmosphere. The covered courtyard dining area is sunny, bright, and warm. The guest rooms are furnished in a similar manner, with some good quality copies of period pieces, but little in terms of wall art and knickknacks—in keeping with the hotel's almost "Mediterranean minimalist" feel.

Corso Vittorio Emanuele 90, 84010 Minori. ✆ 089-877237. Fax 089-877302. www.hotelvillaromana.it. 50 units. 160€ ($224/£112) double. Rates include buffet breakfast. Children 2 and under stay free in parent's room. AE, DC, MC, V. Free parking. **Amenities:** Restaurant; bar; babysitting; business center; concierge; outdoor pool; room service; same-day laundry service; solarium. *In room:* A/C, satellite TV, hair dryer, minibar, safe.

WHERE TO DINE
Proud of its specialties, Minori is a little culinary heaven. *Sarchiapone* is a delicious dish of local squash filled with ground meat and ricotta and cooked in a tomato sauce. Another tasty invention is *'ndunderi,* a pasta that is somewhere between a fat noodle and gnocchi, made with spelt flour and fresh cheese and served with a simple dressing of olive oil, cheese, local herbs, and sometimes chopped walnuts. Some of the local sweets are also noteworthy, particularly the *Sospiri,* aka *Zizz'e monache;* the first name translates as "sighs," and the second as "nuns' breasts;" these are the sacred and profane names for the delicious, pale, dome-shaped small pastries filled with lemon cream.

Moderate
Il Giardiniello 🇸 AMALFITAN/PIZZA Good food and a cozy atmosphere mark this restaurant, which is especially charming in the warm season, when you can dine in the lemon grove. The menu, not surprisingly, focuses on seafood—from a splendid *laganelle alla marinara* (fresh eggless pasta with squid, shrimp, arugula, and cherry tomatoes), a rich *riso al nero di seppia* (rice with squid ink), to satisfying *alici impanate con la provola* (fresh anchovies deep-fried with cheese). In the evening, they make pizza, and very good ones at that.

Corso Vittorio Emanuele 17. ✆ 089-877050. Reservations recommended. Secondi 9.50€–18€ ($13–$25/£6.65–£13). AE, DC, MC, V. Thurs–Tues 12:30–2:30pm and 7:30–10:30pm; daily in summer. Closed Jan.

L'Arsenale 🇸🇸 MODERN AMALFITAN/SEAFOOD Started in 1992 by the three brothers Proto, this small restaurant—it has a few tables under a portico outside—is a moderate, more-than-just-reliable choice on this coast. To the joy of many, the menu includes excellent meat options besides the area's ever-present fish. A large variety of *antipasti* are complemented by tasty and often richly flavored homemade filled pasta, such as *tortelli con crostacei e porcini* (large ravioli with shellfish and porcini mushrooms), and *quadroni di carne con burro e salvia* (square meat ravioli seasoned with sage and butter). For a change of pace when it comes to the *secondi,* you might try the lamb or rabbit.

Via San Giovanni a Mare 20. ✆ 089-851418. Reservations recommended. Secondi 15€–21€ ($21–$29/£11–£15). AE, DC, MC, V. Fri–Wed 12:30–3pm and 7:30–11pm. Closed 3 weeks Jan–Feb.

Inexpensive
La Botte 🇸 *Finds* AMALFITAN/PIZZA Located in a former church near the Villa Romana's archaeological area, the rustic decor of this popular restaurant offers a picturesque setting for a hearty meal and a delightful arbor terrace in the summer. The local cuisine has a creative twist; you will find not only the classic *scialatielli ai frutti*

Limoncello & Other *Rosoli*

The typical liqueur of the region, *limoncello,* is the most famous of the sweet liqueurs made in the area from fruits and herbs—known as *rosoli.* The rarest are *Finocchietto,* made with wild fennel; *Lauro,* made with bay leaves; *Mirto,* made with myrtle; *Nocello,* made with walnuts; the rare *Nanassino,* made with prickly pears; and *Fragolino,* an extremely rare *rosolio* made with *fragoline di bosco,* the wild mini-strawberries from Monti Alburni.

Limoncello is probably the most versatile *rosolio.* You will find local versions—and endless claims of paternity—from Vico Equense on the Sorrento Peninsula all the way to Vietri and beyond, to the islands of Ischia, Capri, and Procida. The liqueur's actual origin is probably the area of Maiori, Amalfi, and Vietri—although Sorrento has good foundations for its claim.

The fact remains that almost every family in Campania has its own recipe, passed on for centuries. The real version is made with Amalfi's special lemon—called *sfusato di Amalfi,* a particular lemon that has obtained the mark D.O.P. (the stamp of controlled origin for produce, similar to D.O.C. for wine). The Amalfi lemon is large, long, and light in color, with a sweet and very flavorful aroma and taste, almost no seeds, and a very thick skin.

Limoncello is sold in pretty, hard-to-resist bottles. If you plan to buy a few bottles as a gift, don't forget to give the recipient tips on how to use it. Always served very cold, the drink can be sipped as a digestive after a meal. It also makes an excellent lemon-flavored long drink—dilute with tonic water or seltzer. Some like it as a champagne cocktail (add a small quantity to a glass of champagne or prosecco). Another great variation is *granita*—dilute the *limoncello* with a light syrup made of sugar and water, and freeze the result, stirring occasionally.

You can buy these liqueurs from various specialty stores, the most reputed of which is **Limunciel,** Corso Vittorio Emanuele 9; Minori (© **089-877393**). This shop was also among the first to commercialize the local *rosolio* and you will find more rare liqueurs such as the exotic *mandarino* (mandarin) and *fragoline di bosco* (wild strawberry), which they prepare in small traditional batches according to their generations-old recipe.

di mare (fresh homemade pasta with shellfish), but such venturesome choices as *ravioli con aragosta e crema d'asparagi* (lobster ravioli with cream of asparagus). Chef Mastro Pantaleone makes his own pasta, such as the delightful pumpkin ravioli served with provola cheese, tomatoes, and porcini mushrooms. In the evening the menu includes a whopping 36 kinds of pizza.

Via S. M. Vetrano 15. © **089-877893.** Reservations recommended on weekends. Secondi 6€–16€ ($8.40–$22/ £4.20–£11). DC, MC, V. Wed–Mon 12:30–3pm and 7:30–11pm; daily in summer. Closed 3 weeks in Jan.

AFTER DARK

The **Summer Music Festival of Minori** (see earlier) is a major attraction on the coast. The evening concerts—held in the open air, and made fragrant by the scent of lemon flowers—are particularly pleasant and well attended.

People also like to meet at the **Pasticceria De Riso,** Via Cantilena 20 (② **089-877396**), to enjoy the best pastries of the whole Costiera, which excels particularly at lemon specialties. Another popular place on the seaside promenade is **Bar Umberto,** Via Roma 58 (② **089-877393**), which makes a rich homemade ice cream.

9 Cetara

Cetara is 6km (3¾ miles) west of Vietri and 15km (9½ miles) east of Amalfi on SS 163

Off the beaten path for most foreign tourists, Cetara is a picturesque village with a still-active fishing tradition. It is a great place for a meal by the sea or for relaxing on the beach.

EXPLORING THE TOWN

Cetara has been an important fishing harbor since Roman times. Its name actually derives from the Latin *cetaria,* a tuna fishery, and the town is still the entire Costiera's main fishing harbor. The town's *tonnare* (tuna-fishing facilities) are big complexes built mostly over the sea. Here, tuna are trapped in huge netting channels out at sea and brought to underwater cages. From there, the fish are pushed into a seawater pool, where they are killed and processed.

This is definitely an industry, not a sport, and we don't necessarily encourage this traditional industry: Recent research has shown that these are actually young tuna that have not yet reached full maturity. Capturing the immature fish before they have had a chance to spawn is contributing to the depletion of tuna from our oceans. Unfortunately, this sad news has not yet been fully accepted by local traditional fishermen, so stay tuned.

If you are not turned off by the above, you might want to at least taste the distinctive local tuna preserved in olive oil inside glass jars. This local industry is celebrated in July with the **Sagra del Tonno (Tuna Festival),** when preserved tuna and other local delicacies are sold in town; the festival also features music and other scheduled events. Contact the **Proloco tourist office,** Piazza San Francesco (② **089-261474**) for more information.

The rest of the year, the key attraction in town is the **San Pietro** church, with its bright majolica cupola and 13th-century bell tower.

The best beach in the area is **Marina di Erchie.** It's located past the next village, only 2km (1¼ miles) west of Cetara. If you don't want to venture that far, there are small beaches by the harbor.

A bit farther west is the promontory of **Capo d'Orso** ⚘⚘. A protected natural area extending all the way west to the eastern edge of Maiori and to the Torrente Bonea at the east, this is perhaps the most scenic stretch of the whole Amalfi Coast. Covering 1,235 acres, the protected area rests on a plateau with an average altitude of 70m (230 ft.) above sea level; the underlying limestone promontory has been eroded by the sea, and stones poke through the blanket of *macchia mediterranea,* creating a unique dolomitic landscape. A scenic trail leads from SS 163 to the **lighthouse** on the cape and the entrance to the protected natural area; it is well worth the hike for its splendid **panorama** ⚘. Past the lighthouse and to the right is the fascinating **Abbazia di Santa Maria de Olearia** ⚘, Via Diego Tajani, Capo d'Orso (② **089-877452;** daily 5–7:30pm), locally known as the Catacombe di Badia. This incredible place was completely carved from the cliff's rocky face. Begun in the 10th century as a shrine dedicated to Santa Maria de Olearia, it was soon surrounded by a few cliff dwellings, which were then transformed into a monastery in the 11th century and frescoed. The main chapel has a vaulted ceiling and an apse, both decorated with 11th-century fresco work; underneath is the crypt, where the best-preserved frescoes depict the Virgin Mary and two saints.

WHERE TO STAY

Hotel Cetus ★ (Value) (Kids)   This is a great hotel (although being the only one in the village gives it a decided advantage). Located in a spectacular panoramic location (hanging from a cliff) just out of town, the Cetus is your best choice if you decide to stay in this off-the-beaten-path village. For the Costiera, the price is a considerable value. Guest rooms are larger than average, comfortable, and bright, and have colorful tiled floors, bathrooms, and scenic views. The Cetus is particularly welcoming to children; it has its own sandy cove with umbrellas and chairs for its guests, along with a playground. Of the on-site restaurants—both upscale—Il Gabbiano offers excellent, traditional food (below); and Falalella serves up gourmet international cuisine.

Corso Umberto I 1, 84010 Cetara. ©/fax 089-261388. 43 units. 260€ ($364/£182) double; low season 130€ ($182/£91) double. Rates include breakfast. Children 2 and under stay free in parent's room. AE, MC, V. Free parking. **Amenities:** Restaurant; bar; babysitting; concierge; laundry service; playground; room service. *In room:* A/C, TV, hair dryer, minibar, safe.

WHERE TO DINE

Anchovies are the specialty here—be they roasted, grilled, deep-fried, or dressed with local herbs. In addition to fresh fish, you can buy locally prepared preserved anchovies at **Pescheria Battista Delfino** (Via Umberto I 78; © **089-261069**) or at **Pescheria San Pietro** (Via Umberto I 72; © **089-261147**).

EXPENSIVE

Faro di Capo d'Orso ★★ MODERN AMALFITAN   This is a special place, one where you'll want to come again and again, both for the haute cuisine and the magical atmosphere—the restaurant is set in an elegant glassed-in dining room with spectacular views over Capri and Ravello. The young chef, Rocco Iannone, loves the fruits of his region and takes the utmost care in combining them, with absolutely wonderful results. The menu changes with the seasons, the market, and his inspiration, with lots of raw or barely cooked fresh seafood. Among the innovative offerings you might find are *totanetti di paranza farciti di gamberetti bianchi* (local squid stuffed with white shrimp), or *linguine con ragù di calamaretti, pomodorini, prezzemolo e ricci di mare* (pasta with squid, cherry tomatoes, and sea urchins). The desserts are equally elaborate, and the wine list includes the very best from the local vineyards.

Via Diego Tajani 48, off Capo d'Orso. © **089-877022.** www.capodorso.org. Reservations recommended. Secondi 28€–32€ ($39–$45/£39–£22). AE, DC, MC, V. Thurs–Mon 12:30–3pm and 7:30–11pm; in summer also Wed. Closed 2 weeks in Jan.

MODERATE

Acquapazza ★★ AMALFITAN   This small and elegant restaurant is a good place to taste the local fish and experience high cuisine without spending a fortune. They prepare a wonderful array of *antipasti,* including *tortino di melanzane e alici* (fresh anchovy and eggplant torte), marinated tuna, and *carpaccio di pesce* (raw fish in a citrus sauce); and a number of tasty pasta dishes, such as *tubetti al ragù di pesce* (short pasta with a seafood and tomato sauce). For a secondo, you can pick your fish from the daily catch display, and have it prepared as you choose.

Corso Garibaldi 36. ℂ **089-261606.** Reservations recommended on weekends. Secondi 16€–21€ ($22–$29/ £11–£15). MC, V. Tues–Sun 12:30–3pm and 7:30–11pm.

San Pietro 𝄂𝄂 AMALFITAN   This down-to-earth trattoria has a small dining room and just a few tables under an arbor, where you can have a satisfying meal for very little money. The dishes of choice are grilled fish, seafood risotto, or *frittura* (deep-fried seafood), all extremely fresh and dependent on the offerings of the local market. They also prepare good pasta with sautéed shellfish.

Piazza San Francesco 2. ℂ **089-261091.** Reservations recommended. Secondi 15€–19€ ($21–$27/£). AE, MC, V. Wed–Mon noon–2:30pm and 7–10:30pm; daily in summer. Closed 2 weeks in Jan.

10 Vietri sul Mare: Gateway to the Costiera

Vietri is 5km (3 miles) west of Salerno and 20km (12 miles) east of Amalfi on SS 163

The gateway to the Amalfi Coast from the north, Vietri is a small working town with a well-established traditional craft industry. Vietri's main street, with its famous ceramic shops, gets a lot of tourist attention; but it usually makes for a hit-and-run shopping excursion, which leaves the area otherwise undisturbed. Vietri is also well worth a visit for its scenic seashore. The **Proloco tourist office** is inside the Municipal Building (Piazza Matteotti; ℂ **089-211285**).

EXPLORING THE TOWN

The heart of town is Via Madonna degli Angeli, closed to car traffic and lined with ceramics shops. The first is the most famous—**Ceramiche Artistiche Solimene** 𝄂 (Via Madonna degli Angeli 7; ℂ **089-212539** or 089-210048), one of Vietri's historical workshops. Besides visiting their showroom and buying ceramics, you can admire the building itself—a beautiful example of organic architecture from the 1930s by the Italian Paolo Soleri, who went on to work in the U.S. with Frank Lloyd Wright. Inside you can visit a rich collection of ceramics by various contemporary artists. You can see more ceramics—these from the 17th century—in the **San Giovanni Battista** church, where the outside cupola and the interior are decorated in painted majolica. The **panorama** 𝄂𝄂 from the square in front of the church is one of the prettiest of the coastal towns.

From Piazza Matteotti in the center of town, you can descend Via Costabile about a half-mile and arrive at the popular beach of **Marina di Vietri,** dominated by a watchtower which was transformed into a villa; if you cross its surrounding park you'll reach a small and more secluded beach. You can swim and sunbathe here at your leisure, although it tends to be crowded at the height of summer.

If you follow the road that heads out of town toward the southwest, after 2km (1 ¼ miles) you will get to **Raito** 𝄂, a picturesque little village of white-washed houses and gardens. Here is the **Museo della Ceramica** (Via Nuova Raito; ℂ **089-211835;** admission 2€/$2.50/£1.20; Mon–Sat 9am–1pm; in summer also Thurs and Sat 5–7pm). Created in 1981, the ceramics museum is housed in the scenic Torretta Belvedere of historic **Villa Guariglia,** surrounded by a park. The museum's collection includes some masterworks and is organized into three sections: religious art; items of daily use; and the "German Period," with works created or inspired by the wave of foreign (mainly German) artists who came to work in Vietri between 1929 and 1947. Only 1km (½-mile) farther on is the little hamlet of **Albori** 𝄂, with its 16th-century church of **Santa Margherita ad Albori,** and prime sea views.

WHERE TO STAY

Hotel La Lucertola *Kids*   This family-run hotel offers pleasant accommodations and cheerful service, just steps from the hotel's private beach. Moderate-size guest rooms are simply furnished but decorated with care, and have tiled bathrooms. The hotel also offers a solarium and a children's playground with slides and swings, making this a good choice for families.

Via Cristoforo Colombo 29, Località Marina di Vietri, 84019 Vietri sul Mare. ℂ **089-210255.** Fax 089-210223. www.hotellalucertola.it. 32 units. 120€ ($168/£84) double. Rates include buffet breakfast. Children 2 and under stay free in parent's room. AE, DC, MC, V. Free parking. **Amenities:** Restaurant; bar; babysitting; business center; laundry service; room service. *In room:* A/C, satellite TV, Wi-Fi.

Hotel Raito *★*   Last renovated in 2004, this is the best hotel in this section of the Amalfi Coast. A modern luxury hotel, it enjoys a superior position high on the cliffs in the village of Raito, 3km (2 miles) south of Vietri. The spacious guest rooms are comfortable, with modern, stylish furnishings; most offer breathtaking views and balconies. All units have good-size (and new) bathrooms. Guests can ride the free hotel shuttle bus down to its private beach. The hotel's **restaurant** is quite good and serves traditional local cuisine.

Via Nuova Raito 9, Frazione Raito, 84010 Vietri sul Mare. ℂ **089-210033.** Fax 089-211434. 52 units. 250€ ($350/ £175) double. Rates include buffet breakfast. AE, DC, MC, V. Free parking. **Amenities:** Restaurant; bar; babysitting; concierge; laundry service; room service. *In room:* A/C, TV, hair dryer, minibar, safe.

WHERE TO DINE
MODERATE

La Sosta *★* AMALFITAN   Housed in a 19th-century relay station for carriage horses, this restaurant has charm to spare, as well as a traditional and well-prepared cuisine that's based on a seasonal menu. The offerings depend on the market, but you might find excellent *linguine con gli scampi* (linguine with prawns). The traditional desserts include a delicious *babà* (a rum-soaked cake filled with cream). The wine list is well rounded with both regional and national labels.

Via Costiera 6. ℂ **089-211790.** Reservations recommended on weekends. Secondi 15€–18€ ($21–$25/£11–£13). AE, MC, V. Thurs–Tues 12:30–3pm and 7:30–11pm. Closed Nov.

Sapore di Mare *★* AMALFITAN/SEAFOOD   At this pleasant, upscale restaurant, you'll find imaginative variations on the seafood theme, made by using local ingredients. The menu is seasonal but you might find *fusilli ai gamberi e peperoni* (short pasta with shrimp and sweet peppers) or *pesce agli agrumi e mandorle* (fish baked with citrus and almonds). The menu always offers fresh seafood from the nearby sea, served grilled or baked.

Via G. Pellegrino 104. ℂ **089-210041.** Reservations recommended. Secondi 18€–25€ ($25–$35/£13–£18). AE, DC, MC, V. Fri–Wed 12:30–3pm; Mon–Wed and Fri–Sat 7:30–11pm; daily in summer. Closed Dec.

Taverna Paradiso *★★* AMALFITAN   If you are looking for a traditional trattoria with reasonable prices, this is the place for you. The Paradiso offers a warm atmosphere and traditional cuisine turned out by the Somma family. They excel at the homemade comfort food of this region. Start with *vermicelli avverniciati,* a sort of carbonara, and follow it with *salsicce e fagioli* (local sausages stewed with beans) or *costatelle di maiale con le pupacchielle all'agro* (pork ribs with a local vegetable). No matter what you choose to eat, wash down your meal with some of the menu's good local and regional wines.

Via Diego Taiani. ✆ **089-212509**. Reservations recommended on weekends. Secondi 10€–18€ ($14–$25/£6–£13). AE, V. Tues–Sun 12:30–3pm and 7:30–11pm. Closed Aug 15.

INEXPENSIVE

La Playa AMALFITAN   A good, inexpensive choice, this plain, modern restaurant offers simple local cuisine focusing on fish. We recommend the excellent homemade pasta, including tasty *scialatielli ai frutti di mare* (pasta with shellfish) as well as deliciously crisp *frittura* (deep-fried seafood) and the *grigliate* (grilled fish).

Via Costiera Amalfitana 24. ✆ **089-761696**. Reservations recommended on weekends. Secondi 9€–15€ ($13–$21/£6.30–£11). AE, DC, MC, V. Wed–Mon 12:30–3pm and 7:30–11pm.

SHOPPING

Ceramics are very much a part of this little town's economy; if you are looking for a unique gift for yourself or for someone at home, chances are that you'll find it here. Enter Vietri's main street; the town will feel like an open-air showroom instead of a historic village or a laid-back resort. The display of color is incredible—the walls along the main streets are literally lined with beautiful tableware, ceramics of all kinds, and shelves burgeoning with variously shaped bowls and vases. After an initial pass-through, you should begin to see stylistic differences and be able to spot individual artists' showrooms–each characterized by a proprietary pattern and color palette. (We are very fond of the little goats that are the trademark of **D'Amore**—they have been imitated by many, so look for his signature on each piece.)

Recommended artists of long standing include **Ceramiche Artistiche Pinto** (Corso Umberto I 27; ✆ **089-210271**); **Ceramiche Artistiche Solimene** (Via Madonna degli Angeli 7; ✆ **089-212539**); and **Tortora & Giordano** (Via Travertino 17; ✆ **089-211894**). Shops generally sell products from a variety of artists and most will ship your things home for you, but ask before buying.

VIETRI AFTER DARK

On most evenings during the summer season, **Villa Guariglia** (Via Nuova Raito; ✆ **089-211835**) becomes the enchanting setting for classical music concerts; call the tourist information office (above) for information on the program.

8

The Jewels of the Gulf of Naples: the Islands of Capri, Ischia & Procida

Campania's coast takes much of its splendor from the islands that define the Gulf of Naples: Procida, Ischia, and Capri. Each with its own character, these three islands have enjoyed completely different fortunes as far as tourism is concerned. Capri, the most well known, has been a lively resort since antiquity, famous for the debauches of Tiberius. Ischia, also known to the ancient world, was noted for its spas, and has traditionally remained a place for relaxation. Procida was and still is a small fisherman's haunt, where locals continue to make their living from the sea and tourists are comparatively rare.

Of the three, Capri is the most sought after (its particularly famous for its Blue Grotto), but it remains a must-see even if you have to brave huge crowds.

Because of their proximity to the mainland, each of these islands makes a good day trip. Even Ischia, the largest of the three, can be enjoyed in a day: You can arrive early in the morning, check in at one of the spas—we love the ones with scenic outdoor facilities—and leave after a gourmet dinner. Of course, after darkness falls and the last ferryboat has gone, the islands become that much more romantic, and we encourage you to stay for the night.

1 Ischia: Isola Verde & Island of Eternal Youth ★★★

42km (26 miles) NW of Naples and 20km (13 miles) W of Pozzuoli

When the Greeks arrived on this coast more than 2,500 years ago, they first landed in Ischia. They felt that Ischia was a perfect base from which to dominate the mainland. Yet, they quickly changed their minds and moved to nearby Cuma, by modern Pozzuoli (see chapter 4) because of Ischia's very active volcano—788m-high (2,585-ft.) Monte Epomeo—which erupted repeatedly until the 14th century. Only then did the island's population start growing, laying the base for the development of the spa industry we see today. The first thermal establishment opened in Casamicciola Terme in 1604, destination of the upper crust of society. The island itself, however, went relatively undiscovered by tourists until the 1950s, when well-to-do Italians came here in the hopes of finding an alternative to overcrowded Capri. Although Ischia is more popular now than it was then, the atmosphere remains quieter than on Capri, partly because of the island's larger size, but certainly also because of its calm and bucolic character.

ESSENTIALS

GETTING THERE Ischia's three main harbors—Ischia Porto (the largest), Forio, and Casamicciola—are very well connected to the mainland through frequent ferry

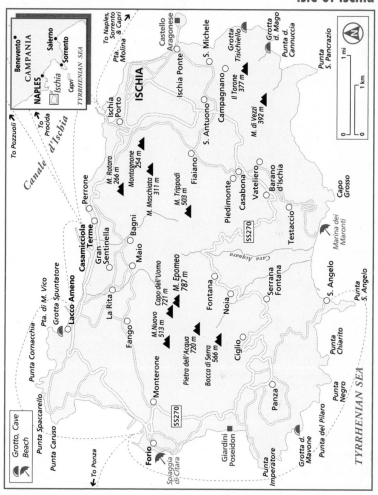

and hydrofoil service. **Medmar** (ℰ **081-5513352;** www.medmargroup.it) offers ferries from Napoli to Ischia Porto and from Pozzuoli to both Ischia Porto and Casamicciola. **Caremar** (ℰ **081-0171998** from abroad or ℰ **892123** from anywhere in Italy; www. caremar.it) runs ferries to Ischia Porto and Casamicciola from Pozzuoli, Procida, and Naples (Molo Beverello). **Alilauro** (ℰ **199-600202** from within Italy or 081-4972222; www.alilauro.it) runs hydrofoils from Mergellina to Ischia Porto and Forio and from Naples (Molo Beverello) to Ischia Porto and to Forio. **SNAV** (ℰ **081-4285555** or 081-4285500; www.snav.it) runs hydrofoils and catamarans from Mergellina, Naples (Molo Beverello), and Procida to Ischia Porto and Casamicciola. **Navigazione Libera del Golfo** (ℰ **081-5520763;** www.navlib.it) operates from Salerno to Ischia. **Alicoast** (ℰ **089-234892** in Salerno; 089-871483 in Amalfi; and 089-811986 in Positano; www. amalficoastlines.com) offers connections from Salerno, Capri, Amalfi, and Positano to

Ischia Porto. Some of the hydrofoil lines are suspended during the winter because of rough seas. Most of the ferries are equipped for car transport but very few of the faster hydrofoils are: If you want to bring your car, make sure you reserve well in advance because space is at a premium. Also, always check with the transport company as local authorities sometimes restrict the number of cars allowed on the islands during the height of the summer, allowing only residents to bring their cars.

GETTING AROUND   Although larger than the other islands, Ischia can easily be toured via public transportation. SEPSA's public **bus** system (© **081-991808** or 081-991828) is very well run and organized: One of its lines tours the island toward the right (*circolare destra* marked CD), and one circles toward the left (*circolare sinistra* marked CS); other lines crisscross the island between its major destinations. Tickets are 1.20€ ($1.70/85p) and are valid for 90 minutes; a daily pass costs 4€ ($5.60/£2.80). You can get a printout of the bus schedule from the tourist office (below).

You can find **taxis** at the stands strategically located around the island, including all harbors and main destinations, or call © **081-984998,** 081-992550, or 081-993720. Some of the taxis are picturesque three-wheelers—*motorette*—but they are rapidly disappearing. A 10€ ($14/£7) minimum charge applies inside the town of Ischia (it's pretty much a flat rate), but drivers use the meter for trips outside town.

You can also rent scooters and small cars on the island directly from **Fratelli del Franco,** Via A. de Luca, Ischia Porto (© **081-991334**), which also rents bicycles, and at **euroscootercar,** Via Iasolino, Ischia Porto (© **081-982722**).

VISITOR INFORMATION   The **AACST tourist office** of Ischia is at Corso Vittoria Colonna 116, 80077 Ischia (© **081-5074231;** fax 081-5074230; www.infoischia procida.it). They also maintain **information booths** on Via Sogliuzzo 72 in the center of Ischia Porto and by the harbor (© **081-5074211;** Mon–Sat 9am–noon and 2–5pm). There you'll find free maps of the island as well as information and brochures.

SPECIAL EVENTS   In May, the island hosts **Ipomea,** an international exposition of rare temperate-zone plants that is held in the exclusive grounds of the **Parco Termale del Negombo** (© **081-986152;** www.negombo.it).

The **Festival of Sant'Anna** on July 26 is celebrated with evocative displays by the Aragonese Castle. The festival originated from the adoration of Saint Ann, the mother of Mary, who is believed to protect pregnant women. Originally, locals would sail to the small bay of Cartaromana with candles on their bows to honor the saint. Slowly, this tradition developed into the spectacular **Festa del Mare,** in which a procession of boats and floats crosses the water, and the castle and harbor are illuminated. If you are in the area around this time, be sure not to miss this memorable sight.

Summer is also the height of the musical season at **La Mortella** (© **081-986220;** www.lamortella.it), the seat of the William Walton Foundation. Besides the concerts, the foundation also hosts a yearly music and opera workshop. An additional musical event is the **Ischia Jazz Festival** (**www.ischiajazzfestival.com** or www.circuitojazz.it/ischia.htm), which usually takes place over 5 days in the beginning of September.

EXPLORING THE ISLAND

Ischia is the largest of Campania's islands, covering about 46 sq. km (18 sq. miles). Its velvety slopes green with pine woods and vineyards have earned it the nickname **Isola Verde (Emerald Isle),** while its fame as a healthy retreat has earned it another nickname, **Island of Eternal Youth,** for its peaceful atmosphere and its spas. These are fueled by the widespread volcanic activity still occurring on the island, although its

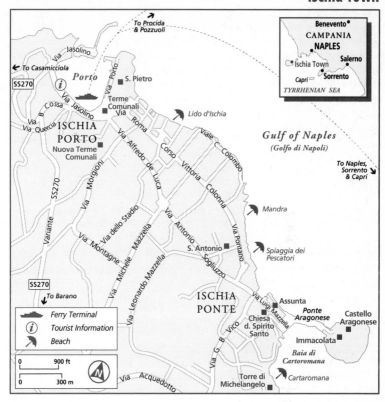

volcano, Mount Epomeo, has long been dormant. Hot springs, mineral-water springs, and steam- and hot mud–holes dot the island's slopes (see later in this chapter).

The largest town on the island is **Ischia** ✦✦, on the island's northeastern corner. The majority of activity is concentrated in **Ischia Porto,** around the main harbor (*porto* means harbor), and **Ischia Ponte** (*ponte* means bridge), by the bridge to the island promontory that flanks a small natural harbor. In between runs the pleasant promenade of Via Roma and Corso Vittoria Colonna—*il corso* in local parlance—stretching about 2km (1¼ miles). The promontory with its small natural harbor was the site of the original settlement, fortified by a castle as far back as the 5th century B.C. The **castle,** Piazzale Aragonese, Ischia Ponte (✆ **081-992834;** www.castellod ischia.it; 10€/$14/£7 adults, 6€/$8.40/£4.20 youth ages 9–19; children 8 and under free; winter 10am–4:30pm, summer 9am–7pm) on the promontory today was built by the **Aragonese** over the ruins of the earlier fortifications. We encourage you to climb up for a visit (though you can take an elevator), as it is quite scenic and picturesque. The last eruption of Mount Epomeo in 1301 destroyed most of the village that had grown around the small natural harbor. The population resettled, but closer to the castle and bridge.

Ischia Porto, the other, now larger, part of town was founded by the Bourbons on a whim. When they took over the island in the 18th century, all that was there was a scenic volcanic lake (originally a volcano crater) and a few villas. The new kings fell in love with a villa-cum-spa built by a doctor, Francesco Buonocore, and decided to establish their residence there. They transformed the villa overlooking the lake into a small palace—what happened to the doctor is unknown; maybe he graciously donated his home to their majesties—the **Casina Reale Borbonica,** which today houses a military spa (not open to the public). They also cut a channel into the outer shore of the lake, transforming it into a large harbor. Inaugurated in 1854, it has been the island's major port ever since, and a lively town has developed around it, with many nice bars and a few restaurants.

A short distance away from Ischia (6.5km/4 miles) on the north shore, you'll find the small village of **Casamicciola Terme** ✦, with its scenic harbor and **marina** (although, being right on the main road, its charm is a bit spoiled by the traffic) and **Villa Ibsen,** where the famous Norwegian writer wrote *Peer Gynt.* Founded in the 16th century to take advantage of the area's thermo-mineral springs, Casamicciola Terme is where the first modern spa was opened on the island in 1604. The village, though, suffered a reversal of fortunes when it was destroyed by the earthquake of 1883. It was immediately rebuilt, but closer to the shore, in its current position by the marina. The remains of the original town are in the inland hamlet of **Bagni,** with the island's oldest spas opening onto its main square, and the village of **Majo,** farther up the slope.

Adjacent to Casamicciola, 8km (5 miles) west of Ischia Porto, is the picturesque **Lacco Ameno** ✦✦, famous for its mushroom-shaped rock a few yards from the sandy shore. The ancient Greeks established their first settlement on this coast; although, daunted by the frequent—at that time—earthquakes and eruptions, they never developed a colony. An unassuming fishing harbor until the 1950s, it was then shaken out of its sleep by Italian publisher Angelo Rizzoli. He built his villa on the promontory of Monte Vico, overlooking the village to the west, and decided to invest in the area and transform it into an exclusive resort. His plan was successful and the promontory has become the most exclusive spa destination in Italy, offering many luxurious hotels and villas. **Villa Arbusto,** Angelo Rizzoli's own summer home, is today a museum— **Museo Civico Archeologico di Pithecusae** ✦ (© **081-900356;** 3€/$4.20/£2.10; Tues–Sun 9:30am–1pm and 4–8pm)—displaying the findings of local archaeological excavation. It is worth a visit, if only to admire the famous **Coppa di Nestore:** Dating from 725 B.C., it bears one of the oldest known Greek inscriptions, which, appropriately, celebrates the wine of Ischia. Nearby is an important Catholic pilgrimage site, the **Sanctuary of Santa Restituta** (© **081-980706** or 081-980538; daily 10am–1pm and 4–7pm), with its attached **archaeological excavations** and **museum.** The original church was created in the 4th or 5th century A.D. by adapting an ancient Roman water cistern, and later restructured.

On the west side of the Monte Vico promontory are the lovely **gardens of Villa La Mortella** ✦✦, Via F. Calise 39, 80075 Forio (© **081-986220;** www.lamortella.it). Covering 2 hectares (5 acres), the gardens were created by the Argentinean wife of William Walton who collected many rare botanical species. Admission is 10€ ($14/£7) adults, 8€ ($11/£5.60) children ages 8 to 12, 6€ ($8.40/£4.20) children ages 5 to 7, and children 4 and under are admitted free (Apr 1–Nov 15 Tues, Thurs, Sat, and Sun 9am–7pm; ticket booth closes 30 min. earlier).

On the western coast of the island, 13km (8 miles) west of Ischia Porto, is the lively town of **Forío,** with its wealth of bars and beaches. Popular among Naples residents, it is usually bypassed by foreign tourists. A favorite retreat of writers and musicians for

---

Fun Fact Flower Power

Ischia's unusual volcanic characteristics have produced more than spa-perfect conditions. The fertile soil and unique subtropical climate have been so favorable to flowering plants and shrubs that you can find on the island 50% of the entire European patrimony of flower species, a number of them indigenous to Ischia.

---

centuries, Forío is also appreciated by those who come to enjoy the locally produced wine and the views of its **watchtower.** The tower was built in the 16th century to defend the town from the Saracens attacks, was once a prison, and now houses a small **museum** (② **081-3332934**) of the work of local poet and sculptor Giovanni Maltese.

The southern half of Ischia is more agricultural, with only one town on the southern shore: the tiny fishing harbor of **Sant'Angelo** 𝄞𝄞, 11km (7 miles) south of Ischia Porto. Shaded by a tall promontory jutting into the sea and connected to the shore by a sandy isthmus (100m/300 ft. long) that is closed to vehicles, it is one of Ischia's most picturesque sights. Far from the hype of the high-priced spa resorts, it is quite exclusive and secluded. The other villages on this part of the island are nested on the steep slopes of the mountain, overlooking the sea. **Serrara Fontana** 𝄞𝄞 (9.5km/6 miles southwest of Ischia Porto) is a tiny hamlet centered around a lookout terrace affording spectacular views.

STAYING ACTIVE

Ischia's shore alternates between rugged cliffs and sandy stretches, to the delight of sunbathers and swimmers. The island's beautiful **beaches** are all the more special because they are a commodity almost completely lacking in the bay of Naples and the Amalfi Coast. The town of Ischia has a beach—or rather several small ones, with the best being the **Spiaggia dei Pescatori,** where local fishermen beach their boats, a short distance west of the Aragonese Castle. You can do way better, though. The island's most beautiful beach is **Spiaggia dei Maronti** 𝄞𝄞𝄞, stretching for about 2km (1¼ miles) east of the village of Sant'Angelo, straight down the cliff from **Barano d'Ischia** (4km/2½ miles south of Ischia Porto). These long stretches of sand are scenic but crowded in the summer. The **Spiaggia di Cartaromana** 𝄞𝄞, down from the village of San Michele on the east coast of the island, is on a slightly more secluded cove. North of Forio is the **Spiaggia di San Francesco** 𝄞, overlooked by the promontory of Monte Vico (p. 232), while south of Forío is the scenic **Spiaggia di Citara** 𝄞𝄞, which used to be the island's largest and most beautiful sandy beach. Though much diminished by erosion, it is still nice and is quite popular for the hot mineral springs that flow out to sea at its southern edge; these springs are the same ones that are used by the spa Giardini Poseidon (below). We also highly recommend **renting a boat** from one of the harbors and visiting those coves that are accessible only by sea.

If you are not into swimming or relaxation, you can visit the countryside, which is dotted with **vineyards** producing well-known—and excellent—D.O.C. wines. You could combine the sampling with some interesting **hikes** up the slopes of Mount Epomeo. We recommend you procure the diminutive brochure from the tourist office in Ischia, entitled *Lizard Trails,* which has descriptions and maps of the island's best trails.

SPAS & THERMO-MINERAL TREATMENTS

What attracts most visitors to Ischia are the island's many **spas,** offering a variety of **thermo-mineral health and beauty treatments.** With over 56 different mineral springs on the island—not to mention the hot mud, hot sands, and numerous steam holes—Ischia is spa paradise. These natural resources, scattered across the island's slopes and beaches, have been harnessed by over 150 spa operators. The spas are perfect for day trips, as a number of the island's modern facilities operate as day parks, but most hotels have their own spas and will offer package stays including meals and basic spa services, such as the use of the thermo-mineral pools. Other establishments specialize in medical treatments, beauty care, and treatments to relieve stress. Even if you are not particularly interested in spa treatments, we highly recommend a visit to the outdoor spa parks, which afford a unique and relaxing experience.

Located between Ischia Porto and Casamicciola, **Parco Termale Castiglione** 🎇 is a state-of-the-art facility offering thermo-mineral waters and mud treatments in a mix of indoor and open-air facilities. The scenic outdoor pools range in temperature from 82°F to 104°F (28°C–40°C). On the promontory of Monte Vico near Lacco Ameno, you'll find **Parco Termale Negombo** 🎇 (© 081-986152; www.negombo.it), nestled on the island's most picturesque cove, **Lido di San Montano.** Here you can enjoy magnificent gardens, a secluded beach, and elegant thermal pools. South of Forío, on the pretty bay of Citara, is **Parco Termale Giardini Poseidon** 🎇🎇, Via Giovanni Mazzella Citara, Forío d'Ischia (© 081-907122 or 081-907420), an open-air facility with 22 pools (both relaxing and curative), a large private beach, and several restaurants. Finally, to the east of Sant'Angelo, you'll find the **Parco Termale Giardini Aphrodite-Apollon** (© 081-999219), an indoor-outdoor facility with lovely grounds and pools that is part of the Park Hotel Miramare (below).

For a more traditional spa experience, we recommend the state-of-the-art **Ischia Thermal Center** 🎇, Via delle Terme 15, Ischia (© 081-984376; www.ischiathermal center.it), offering a wide range of health and beauty treatments. We also recommend the four historical spas of **Casamicciola Terme**—Terme Manzi, Belliazzi, Elisabetta, and Lucibello—opening onto the famous **Piazza Bagni** in the hamlet of Bagni. For an even more exclusive experience, head to the **Terme della Regina Isabella** 🎇 (below), a hotel and thermal resort in **Lacco Ameno.** This is one of the most elegant spas on the island.

WHERE TO STAY

VERY EXPENSIVE

Hotel Regina Isabella 🎇🎇 *Kids*   Set in a beautiful location, with views over the village and harbor, this prestigious historical hotel offers fine accommodations, a state-of-the-art thermal spa (above), and a private cove. The public spaces are palatial, with many original furnishings, and the extra amenities will make your stay idyllic. The large guest rooms are decorated with a mix of contemporary and antique, with handpainted ceramic floors and luxurious bathrooms. Many rooms have private balconies, opening onto views of the sea or the gardens. The hotel's private cove is equipped with floating chairs, suitable for lounging.

Piazza Santa Restituta 1, 80076 Lacco Ameno d'Ischia. © 081-994322. Fax 081-990190. www.reginaisabella.it. 132 units 540€–740€ ($756–$1,036/£378–£518) double; from 950€ ($1,330/£665) suite. Rates include buffet breakfast. 3-day minimum stay. Children 2 and under stay free in parent's room. AE, DC, MC, V. Free parking. **Amenities:** 2 restaurants; 2 bars; babysitting; beach; children's programs during school holidays; concierge; laundry service; Ping-Pong; 2 outdoor pools; indoor thermal pool; room service; solarium; spa; tennis. *In room:* A/C, satellite TV, hair dryer, minibar, safe.

The D.O.C. Wines of Ischia

Ischia's vineyards produce wines that have been increasingly appreciated by connoisseurs; three even earned the D.O.C. label—a government recognition reserved only for those superior wines from specific areas that answer to severe requirements of consistently good quality and characteristics. The winning wines are the red Monte Epomeo, the Ischia (red and white), and the white Biancolella. Wine enthusiasts around the world have to thank the Greeks for this bounty, for it was they who recognized the local potential and planted the varieties of grape still used today to produce the area's wines.

Mezzatorre Resort & Spa ☆☆   Located on the promontory of Monte Vico near Lacco Ameno, this may be the best hotel on the island. Set on its own rocky point looking straight down to the sea and surrounded by a 3-hectare (7-acre) wooded complex, the hotel shares its grounds with a 15th-century watchtower. The elegant public spaces include outdoor tennis courts and an infinity pool on a cliffside terrace. Spacious guest rooms are individually decorated in a tasteful mix of Mediterranean and contemporary style, with geometric-design tiled floors, quality furnishings, and warm-colored fabrics. All are equipped with state-of-the-art bathrooms, many with Jacuzzi tubs. Many rooms enjoy private terraces or gardens, and a number of them have splendid sea views.

Via Mezzatorre, 80075 Forio d'Ischia. © **081-986111.** Fax 081-986015. www.mezzatorre.it. 60 units. 420€–560€ ($588–$784/£294–£392) double; from 760€ ($1,064/£532) suite. Rates include buffet breakfast. Children 3 and under stay free in parent's room. AE, DC, MC, V. Free parking. Closed Nov–Apr. **Amenities:** 2 restaurants; bar; babysitting; concierge; health club; laundry service; outdoor pool; outdoor tennis courts; room service; spa. *In room:* A/C, TV, hair dryer, minibar, safe.

EXPENSIVE

Grand Hotel Excelsior ☆☆   With a perfect location in the town of Ischia—convenient to both Ischia Ponte and Ischia Porto and enjoying a great panoramic view—this hotel offers top-notch service and amenities, like its own private beach. Posh public spaces—a pool with a view, elegant lounges, a spa with a beauty center—are complemented by beautiful guest rooms. The commodious rooms are furnished with great taste and attention to detail and are decorated with wrought-iron bedsteads, handpainted-tile floors, and designer-tiled bathrooms; each room has a private patio-terrace. *Note:* The hotel only offers half-board, which means that breakfast and dinner are included in your nightly rate.

Via E. Gianturco 19, 80077 Ischia. © **081-991522.** Fax 081-984100. www.excelsiorischia.it. 76 units. 330€–450€ ($462–$630/£231–£315) double, from 530€ ($742/£371) suite. Rates include buffet breakfast and dinner. Children 1 and under stay free in parent's room. AE, DC, MC, V. Closed mid-Oct to mid-Apr. **Amenities:** Restaurant; piano bar; babysitting; concierge; health club; laundry service; minigolf course; indoor thermal pool; outdoor pool; room service; spa; Wi-Fi in public spaces. *In room:* A/C, satellite TV, hair dryer, minibar, safe.

Miramare e Castello ☆☆   Located only steps from the Aragonese castle (p. 231), this elegant hotel offers refined accommodations and excellent service. Amenities include a full thermal spa with several pools and treatments. The bright, spacious guest rooms are tastefully furnished and include tiled floors. Some have sea views—even from the bathroom—and a few have private terraces overlooking the sea and the hotel's private beach.

Via Pontano 5, 80070 Ischia. ℂ 081-991333. Fax 081-984572. www.miramareecastello.it. 50 units. 290€–410€ ($406–$574/£203–£287) double, 530€ ($742/£371) suite. Mid-Aug 7-day minimum stay and half-board. Rates include buffet breakfast. Children 4 and under stay free in parent's room. AE, DC, MC, V. Closed mid-Oct to mid-Apr. **Amenities:** Restaurant; bar; babysitting; beach; concierge; laundry service; outdoor pool; thermal outdoor pool; thermal indoor pool; roof garden w/Jacuzzi pools; room service; spa. *In room:* A/C, TV, hair dryer, minibar, safe.

Park Hotel Miramare 🎿 *Kids*   Old-fashioned in style but not in spirit, this hotel is the most elegant in Sant'Angelo. It is also reserves a portion of its beach only for nudists, one of the only such beach areas on the island. Opened in 1923 and run by the same family ever since, the Miramare offers comfortable rooms furnished in a 1920s seaside style, with wicker and wrought-iron furniture as well as some antiques and quality reproductions. Whether in the main building or in one of the two additions, Casa Apollon or Casa del Sole, all guest rooms are bright, with modern bathrooms and private balconies or terraces opening onto the sea. The hotel's spa includes 12 different pools, and extensive treatments and fitness programs. They are very welcoming of families and have devised many special attractions for their younger guests.

Via Comandante Magdalena 29, 80070 Sant'Angelo d'Ischia. ℂ 081-999219. Fax 081-999325. www.hotelmiramare. it. 50 units. 192€–428€ ($269–$599/£134–£300) double; from 520€ ($728/£364) suite. Rates include buffet breakfast. Children 15 and under stay free in parent's room. AE, DC, MC, V. Closed Nov 11–Apr 6. **Amenities:** 2 restaurants; bar; babysitting; children's program; concierge; laundry service; private beach; solarium; spa; Wi-Fi. *In room:* A/C, satellite TV, hair dryer, minibar, safe.

MODERATE

Floridiana Terme *Finds*   This centrally located yet quiet hotel is in the pedestrian area near the harbor. Housed in an elegant former villa surrounded by greenery, it is only a short walk from the sea. Guest units are large, bright, and nicely appointed, with quality furnishings, colorful tiled floors, and good-size bathrooms. All the rooms open onto their own private balcony or terrace, and some have sea views.

Corso Vittoria Colonna 153, 80070 Ischia (NA). ℂ 081-991014. Fax 081-981014. www.hotelfloridianaischia.com. 64 units. 236€–256€ ($330–$358/£165–£179) double. Rates include buffet breakfast and dinner. Children 1 and under stay free in parent's room. AE, DC, MC, V. Closed Nov–Mar. **Amenities:** Restaurant; bar; babysitting; concierge; garden; health club; laundry service; indoor thermal pool; outdoor pool; room service; spa. *In room:* A/C, TV, hair dryer, minibar, safe.

Hotel Casa Celestino *Value*   We like this unassuming hotel that is built vertically, hugging the cliff above the pedestrian promenade and overlooking the pretty harbor. Guest rooms are large and bright, decorated in modern Mediterranean style, with simple furnishings, colorful ceramic-tiled floors, and coordinated fabrics in bold, tasteful colors. Guests appreciate the tiled bathrooms and private terraces (complete with table and chairs), as well as the superb sea views.

Via Chiaia di Rose, 80070 Sant'Angelo d'Ischia. ℂ 081-999213. Fax 081-999805. www.casacelestino.it. 20 units. 200€ ($280/£140) double; 240€ ($336/£168) junior suite; 260€ ($364/£182) suite. Rates include buffet breakfast. Extra bed 30€ ($42/£21). Children 4 and under stay free in parent's room. Mid-Aug 7-day minimum stay. AE, DC, MC, V. Closed Nov–Dec. **Amenities:** Restaurant; bar; Internet point; room service; solarium; access to spa of Hotel Terme San Michele. *In room:* A/C, satellite TV, hair dryer, minibar, safe.

Hotel Terme La Bagattella 🎿 *Finds*   Housed in an elaborate villa with Moorish details and surrounded by a beautiful garden, this hotel has an excellent spa for both thermal and beauty treatments. Guest-room decor is nautical in some and Moorish in others. The junior suites are particularly luxurious—with exposed beams on the whitewashed ceilings, rich fabrics, and private terraces—but the regular rooms are very nice, too, either with private balconies or direct garden access.

Via Tommaso Cigliano 8, 80075 Forío d'Ischia. ℂ 081-986072. Fax 081-989637. www.labagattella.it. 40 units. 154€–198€ ($216–$277/£108–£139) double. Rates include buffet breakfast. Children 1 and under stay free in parent's room. AE, DC, MC, V. Closed Nov–Mar. **Amenities:** Restaurant; bar; babysitting; bike rentals; health club; laundry service; 2 outdoor pools; room service; spa. *In room:* A/C, TV, hair dryer, minibar, safe (8€ [$11/£5.50] per stay).

INEXPENSIVE

Albergo Il Monastero 🏵 *(Finds)* Housed in a former monastery inside Ischia's Aragonese castle (p. 231), this is the island's most picturesque hotel. The atmosphere is unique, the reception warm and welcoming, and the views are quiet are superb. Guest rooms are spacious—especially considering they were monk cells—and are decorated with stylish sobriety, from the whitewashed walls and tiled floors to the solid dark wood or wicker furniture. The bathrooms are small but fully tiled with tasteful design (some are downright tiny with space for only showerheads and a drain in the tile directly below). A few rooms boast small but delightful private terraces, while others open onto a common terrace.

Castello Aragonese, ℂ 081-992435. Fax 081-991849. www.albergoilmonastero.it. 13 units. 120€–150€ ($168–$210/ £84–£105) double. AE, DC, MC, V. Closed Nov–Jan. **Amenities:** Concierge; laundry service; terrace. *In room:* A/C, hair dryer.

Albergo Villa Angelica *(Value)* This small, family-run hotel is an excellent, moderately priced choice. Housed in a whitewashed Mediterranean building with arched doorways and passages, it has a welcoming atmosphere which extends from the public spaces to the guest rooms. These are quiet and cozy, with tiled floors and wrought-iron beds. Most have private terraces. The hotel offers a beautiful thermal swimming pool with a Jacuzzi in the garden.

Via IV Novembre 28, 80076 Lacco Ameno. ℂ 081-994524. Fax 081-980184. www.villaangelica.it. 20 units. 130€ ($182/£91) double. Minimum stay 3 days. Rates include buffet breakfast. Children 1 and under stay free in parent's room. AE, DC, MC, V. Closed mid-Nov to mid-Mar. **Amenities:** Restaurant; bar; babysitting; concierge; laundry service; outdoor pool; room service; spa. *In room:* A/C, TV, hair dryer, minibar.

WHERE TO DINE

Ischia offers a lively dining scene, especially in the neighborhood of **Ischia Ponte** with its many restaurants and bars, and the exclusive **Via Porto**—called Rive Droite by the locals—lined with elegant nightclubs and restaurants.

EXPENSIVE

Melograno 🏵🏵 *(Finds)* NOUVEAU ISCHITAN/SEAFOOD We love this restaurant, tucked away from the main streets of Forío. Elegant and welcoming, it offers delightful outdoor dining in a pleasant garden, and truly interesting and delicious cuisine. Two tasting menus are available, and an a la carte menu—centered on seafood— changes with the market and the whims of the talented chef Libera Iovine. We highly recommend the *mezzi paccheri al ragù bianco di scoglio* (local pasta with a seafood sauce and shrimp and squid) and the *guazzetto di scorfano di fondale con crema di patate* (a moist fish with black olives, capers, and a potato puree). Do not miss the local cheese selection and the creatively delicious desserts.

Via G. Mazzella 110, Forío. ℂ 081-998450. www.ilmelogranoischia.it. Reservations recommended. Prix-fixe menus 50€ ($70/£35) and 58€ ($81/£41). Secondi 18€–30€ ($25–$42/£13–£21). AE, DC, MC, V. Daily noon–3:30pm and 7:30–11pm. Closed Jan 7–Mar 15.

Umberto a Mare 🏵🏵 CAMPANIAN/SEAFOOD This historic restaurant that has been drawing diners for decades is still going strong. The beautiful terrace—which affords a matchless panorama and is so romantic at sunset—combines with the gour-met cuisine for a perfect dinner. The menu is large and changes daily with the market offerings, with a strong focus on seafood. From the copious choices of antipasti we loved the *insalatina di mare* (seafood salad) and the *tartare di palamito al profumo d'arancia* (tartar of local fish with citrus). We recommend you follow it with the deli-cious *pennette all'aragosta e agli asparagi* (short penne with lobster and asparagus) or with the catch of the day, which varies in preparation from classic grilled or *all'acqua pazza* (in a light herb broth), to the more imaginative.

Via Soccorso 2. Forio ⓒ 081-997171. www.umbertoamare.it. Reservations recommended. Prix-fixe menus 55€ ($77/£39) and 65€ ($91/£46). Secondi 18€–32€ ($25–$45/£13–£22). AE, DC, MC, V. Fri–Sun noon–3:30pm and daily 7:30–11pm. Closed Nov–Mar.

MODERATE

Alberto 🏵 ISCHITANO/SEAFOOD   This traditional restaurant, with a veranda right on the beach promenade between the harbor and the Aragonese castle (p. 231), is an excellent spot for sampling this coast's freshest seafood. The menu is small and focuses on local specialties as interpreted by the chef. We highly recommend the *mari-nata mista* for appetizer, a medley of fish marinated in a tangy and delicate citrus sauce, to be followed by the superb linguine *alle vongole* (with clams) and the delicious *pesce all'Alberto,* oven-baked fish with potatoes, olives, and capers. The wine list offers an ample choice of local wines.

Via Cristoforo Colombo, Ischia Porto. ⓒ 081-981259. www.albertoischia.it. Reservations recommended. Secondi 15€–23€ ($21–$32/£11–£16). AE, DC, MC, V. Daily noon–3pm and 7–11pm. Closed Nov–Feb.

Damiano 🏵 ISCHITANO/SEAFOOD   A favorite among locals and visitors who love to come for a romantic dinner, this restaurant is in the outskirts of town, on the steep slope of the mountain. It offers equally tantalizing views and food, with a menu centered on seafood. The dishes change with the market, but we recommend the lin-guine *con le cozze* (with mussels) and the superb grilled catch of the day. Do absolutely leave room for the fantastic homemade desserts.

Via delle Vigne 30, in the upper part of town, Ischia Porto. ⓒ 081-983032. Reservations recommended. Secondi 12€–22€ ($17–$31/£8.40–£15). DC, MC, V. Daily 8–11pm. Apr–June and Sept–Oct, also Sat–Sun 1–3pm. Closed Nov–Mar.

Montecorvo 🏵 *Finds* CAMPANIAN   If you're in the mood for more than fish, this is the place for you. Popular with locals in the off season, it's also a good choice for traditional Ischitan food. The seafood is uniformly good, but you can also choose meat dishes, from a very good *coniglio all'Ischitana* (rabbit cooked with tomatoes and herbs in a terra-cotta casserole) to excellent roasted chicken with herbs.

Via Montecorvo 33, Forío ⓒ 081-998029. Reservations required. Secondi 11€–20€ ($15–$28/£7.70–£14). AE, MC, V. Fri–Sun noon–3:30pm and 7pm–midnight.

INEXPENSIVE

Pirozzi 🏵 *Kids* ISCHITAN/SEAFOOD/PIZZA   Conveniently located on the main promenade to the Aragonese castle (p. 231), this pleasant restaurant offers a nice veranda with sea views and no-nonsense local cuisine at moderate prices. The excel-lent pizza, offered only in the evening, is popular with children (but is so good you might want it too). Among the more elaborate offerings on the menu, the *risotto alla pescatora* (seafood risotto) and the tasty grilled fish are top notch.

Via Seminario 51, Ischia Ponte. ✆ 081-983217. Reservations recommended in the evening and on weekends. Secondi 6€–14€ ($8.40–$20/£4.20–£9.80). AE, DC, MC, V. Daily noon–3pm and 7pm–midnight. Closed Wed Nov–Mar.

Trattoria il Focolare 🕸 *Finds* CAMPANIAN This restaurant offers a welcome break from the fare at other restaurants along this coast, with a focus on the turf rather than surf. The hearty seasonal menu offers masterfully prepared dishes from the local tradition, such as the excellent *tagliata* (steak) or the *tagliatelle al ragu di cinghiale* (fresh ribbon-shaped pasta with wild boar ragout). We highly recommend the *coniglio all'Ischitana* (a local rabbit dish), which is a specialty of the chef. The desserts are also good, including Neapolitan favorites such as *pastiera* (pie filled with ricotta and orange peels).

Via Cretajo al Crocefisso 3, Barano d'Ischia. ✆ 081-902944. www.trattoriailfocolare.it. Reservations recommended. Secondi 8€–15€ ($11–$21/£5.60–£11). AE, MC, V. Thurs–Tues 7:30–11:30pm; Fri–Sun also 12:30–3pm.

Zelluso 🕸 *Finds* *Kids* ISCHITAN/SEAFOOD/PIZZA Hidden away from the marina on a back street, this is a good place to partake of some local culture. Popular with locals and tourist alike, it is often crowded, and you'll have to factor in a wait, even if you have made reservations. The pizza, offered only in the evening, is one of the best you'll ever have and is a great favorite among children. Of the traditional seafood offerings, we recommend the well-prepared *sautee di cozze* (sautéed mussels) followed by the linguine *alle vongole* (with clams), and *fritto misto* (medley of deep fried squid and small fish).

Via Parodi 41, Casamicciola Terme. ✆ 081-994423. Reservations recommended in the evening and on weekends. Secondi 10€–14€ ($14–$20/£7–£9.80). AE, DC, MC, V. Summer daily noon–3pm and 7pm–midnight; winter closed 1 day per week (day varies, so call ahead).

ISCHIA AFTER DARK

The sweet Ischitan nights are best spent outdoors, enjoying a bit of people watching from the terraces of the many cafes strategically located on the most picturesque seaside promenades and panoramic outlooks. The elegant cafes around the harbor in Ischia are perfect for *aperitivo,* but we also like the unassuming **Da Lilly,** a shack on the rocks with a simple terrace overlooking the **Spiaggia dei Pescatori** (p. 233) in Ischia Ponte. **La Floreana** (✆ 081-999570), at the *belvedere* of Serrara Fontana, is perfect for a sunset *aperitivo* (they also have a simple restaurant). Other pleasant cafes line the seaside promenade of Forío and Lacco Ameno; we enjoy **Bar Franco,** Via Roma 94, Lacco Ameno (✆ 081-980880), where you can sit at the pleasant outdoor terrace facing the beach or simply sample their excellent ice cream. We are rather partial to ice cream and highly recommend those made at **De Maio,** Piazza Antica Reggia 9; Ischia Porto (✆ 081-991870), the best ice-cream parlor on the island; claiming 80 years of experience, the shop makes wonderful creamy flavors. A few doors away is **Da Ciccio,** Via Porto 1, Ischia Porto (no phone), which makes more creative flavors by adding in nuts, chocolate bits, and so on.

We recommend the **concerts**—including classical and jazz—organized by the William Walton Foundation in the lovely gardens of **Villa La Mortella,** Via F. Calise no 35, 80075 Forío Isola d'Ischia (✆ 081-986220; www.lamortella.it). The season runs from April to November; concert tickets include admission to the garden and are 15€ ($21/£10) adults and 12€ ($17/£8.40) children ages 8 to 12. If you are lucky enough to be on the island for the **Ischia Jazz Festival** (www.ischiajazzfestival.com) in September, make advance reservations for the scheduled concerts, which usually include some famous international names.

2 Romantic & Unspoiled Procida ⍟⍟

32km (20 miles) NW of Naples; 12km (8 miles) W of Pozzuoli; 7.8km (5 miles) W of Ischia

Not well known among foreign tourists, Procida is an exclusive resort, popular with the rich and famous who have villas here, but also with local tourists, who often come just for the day or for dinner. We think both are excellent ideas.

Procida's landscape is dotted with pretty houses in tones of pink and yellow, contrasting with the green of citrus groves and gardens. Beyond the private residences you'll find beaches and restaurants catering to various levels of taste and budget. And you won't find yourself competing with the kinds of crowds that can envelop Capri.

ESSENTIALS

GETTING THERE & AROUND   Caremar (☏ **081-0171998** from abroad, or ☏ 892123 from anywhere in Italy; www.caremar.it) runs ferries to Procida from Pozzuoli and from Naples. **SNAV** (☏ **081-4285555** or 081-4285500; www.snav.it) runs hydrofoils and catamarans to Procida from Mergellina, Naples (Molo Beverello), Ischia Porto, and Casamicciola.

Given Procida's diminutive size (below), the best way to see the island is definitely **on foot.** You can also take one of the four **public bus** lines run by **SEPSA** (☏ **081-5429965**). All of the buses start from Marina Grande; tickets are 1€ ($1.40/70p) per ride. Or you can use an open **minitaxi**—you'll find stands at each of the three marinas and at the ferry terminal. Unfortunately, the island's short distances have not discouraged the use of cars by locals, so there are regular traffic jams, especially in the summer months.

VISITOR INFORMATION   The AAST maintains a small **tourist office** in Marina Grande near the ferry dock (☏ **081-8101968;** www.infoischiaprocida.it or www.procida.net), open May to September, Monday to Saturday from 9:30am to 1pm and 3:30 to 6pm; the rest of the year it's only open mornings. The nearby travel agency **Graziella** (Via Roma 117; ☏ **081-8969191;** www.isoladiprocida.it) is another good resource for help with hotel reservations and boat rentals.

EXPLORING PROCIDA

The island is basically one whole village, interspersed with citrus groves and gardens and the occasional vineyard, developing northeast-southwest along one main street. The distance from Marina Grande—with the ferry terminal—on the northeastern tip of the island to Marina di Chiaiolella, all the way to the opposite end, is only about 3km (1¾ miles). Several side streets radiate from this main artery. Jutting from the southwestern tip, a bridge connects Procida to the little island of Vivara.

Marina Grande, or Marina di Sancio Cattolico, is the major harbor of the island, and the location of the ferry terminal. A few steps away, along the main street, **Via Principe Umberto,** is **Piazza dei Martiri,** the village's main square. From it you can climb to **Torre Murata,** the highest point of the island, fortified by 16th-century walls. This is where Procida's rulers had their residences, and where you can enjoy some of the most magnificent views of the island and its surroundings. As you climb, you will find a **belvedere** ⍟ affording good views of the Marina di Corricella (below); farther up beyond the Piazza d'Armi, you enter the **medieval citadel** of **Terra Casata** ⍟⍟ and its belvedere with a magnificent view over the Gulf of Naples. On the square is the island's main church, **San Michele Arcangelo,** originally from the 11th century but redone in later times.

From Piazza dei Martiri, it is a short walk to **Marina della Corricella** 🏵🏵, a picturesque and charming fishing harbor originally established in the 17th century. Its colorful houses and narrow streets surround the small port.

If you continue towards the southwestern tip of the island, you should not miss the detour to the left for **Punta Pizzaco** 🏵🏵🏵, from where you can enjoy one of the best views on the whole island.

Farther on, you'll finally reach **Marina di Chiaiolella** 🏵🏵 at the southwestern tip of the island. This crescent-shaped harbor was once the crater of a volcano and now is a pleasant marina, lined with little restaurants and bars. The harbor is dominated by the mountainous, tiny island of **Vivara,** attached to Procida by a bridge, and today a wildlife refuge run by the World Wildlife Federation. *Note:* The bridge has been under restoration since 1999 and still was at presstime, but in 2001 Vivara was connected to Procida by the world's longest Tibetan-style foot bridge, measuring 362m (1,188 ft.). Check with the tourist office when you arrive for guided tours.

We also highly recommend signing up for a **boat excursion** 🏵🏵 around the island. You can rent a boat, with or without driver, from any of the three harbors on the island: Marina Grande, Marina della Corricella, and Marina di Chiaiolella. You'll spend about 25€ ($35/£18) for a 2-hour trip with a boat and driver.

WHERE TO STAY

In addition to the hotels reviewed below we also recommend staying at **Crescenzo** (see "Where to Dine," later in this chapter).

MODERATE

Casa sul Mare *(Finds*   Housed in a typical 18th-century building at the foot of Terra Murata (the historic *borgo* or village of Procida), this little-known, small hotel offers high-quality accommodations with beautiful views over the Marina di Corricella. The elegant guest rooms are furnished with taste, with beautiful tiled floors, wrought-iron bed frames, and good-size bathrooms. Each opens onto its own private terrace enjoying a beautiful view over the sea.

Salita Castello 13. 🕐/fax 081-8968799. www.lacasasulmare.it. 10 units. 170€ ($238/£119) double. Rates include buffet breakfast. Children 1 and under stay free in parent's room. AE, DC, MC, V. **Amenities:** Bar; babysitting; bicycle rental; concierge; garden; Internet point; laundry service. *In room:* A/C, satellite TV, hair dryer, minibar, safe.

INEXPENSIVE

Hotel Celeste   This pleasant, family-run hotel near the Marina di Chiaiolella is a traditional structure where guest rooms open onto the outdoors. Some have private terraces, but others open onto the veranda, the inner courtyard, or the terrace/garden. All are simply furnished with tiled floors and small outdoor spaces with a table and chairs. The service is warm and welcoming; Signora Concetta and her family give you individual attention. The view from the terraces and the solarium is nice.

Via Rivoli 6, 80079 Procida. 🕐 081-8967488. Fax 081-8967670. www.hotelceleste.it. 35 units. 110€–144€ ($154–$202/£77–£101) double. Rates include buffet breakfast. AE, DC, MC, V. Closed Oct–Mar. **Amenities:** Restaurant; bar; babysitting; laundry service; room service. *In room:* A/C, TV, hair dryer.

WHERE TO DINE
MODERATE

Conchiglia 🏵 ISCHITANO   Somewhat more formal in atmosphere and elegant in decor than Caracalè, below, this is a good restaurant in the classic mold, serving dishes prepared according to tradition and seasonal seafood choices. Our favorites are the linguine *all'aragosta* (with local lobster) and the *spiedini di mazzancolle* (prawn skewers), but we also recommend the grilled catches of the day.

Via Pizzaco, Discesa Graziella. (○) 081-8967602. Reservations recommended. Secondi 12€–23€ ($17–$32/£8.40–£16). AE, DC, MC, V. Daily 12:30–3pm and 7:30–11pm. Closed Nov–Mar.

INEXPENSIVE

Caracalè ✿ ISCHITANO   This picturesque restaurant offers traditional cuisine and a lively atmosphere. The delicious food includes many local specialties, most focusing on seafood, but vegetarian and meat choices are also available. We loved the *risotto ai frutti di mare* (seafood risotto) and the catch of the day *all'acqua pazza*.

Via Marina Corricella 62. (○) 081-8969191. Reservations necessary. Secondi 7€–12€ ($9.80–$17/£4.90–£8.40). AE, DC, MC, V. Daily noon–3pm and 7–11pm.

Hotel Ristorante Crescenzo ✿✿ ISCHITANO   This popular restaurant is one of the best on the island. Overlooking the romantic bay of Chiaiolella, right on the marina, it is moderate in price yet offers a well-rounded menu of traditional dishes, including both meat and seafood. The large array of *antipasti* includes such delicacies as *tortino di pesce spada* (swordfish cake) and *schiacciatine pesce spada e melanzane* (swordfish and eggplant fritters). You'll have a hard time choosing among the many pasta dishes, but we recommend *spaghetti cozze e broccoletti* (spaghetti with broccoli-rabe and mussels) and *spaghetti granchio e zucchine* (spaghetti with crab and zucchini). Above the restaurant is a hotel with 10 simply furnished rooms, with plain but scrupulously clean bathrooms. Some of the rooms have balconies, and some enjoy sea views. The nightly rate is 120€ ($168/£84) for a double, including breakfast.

Via Marina di Chiaiolella 33. (○) 081-8967255. Fax 081-8101260. www.hotelcrescenzo.it. Reservations required. Secondi 6€–15€ ($8.40–$21/£4.20–£11). AE, MC, V. Daily 12:30–2:30pm and 7:30–10:30pm.

3. Capri, the Faraglioni & the Blue Grotto ✿✿✿

33km (21 miles) SW of Naples

Italy's most famous island, Capri (pronounced *cap*-ry, not ca-*pree*) is a dramatic rugged mountain soaring out of the sea at the tip of the Sorrento peninsula. A haunt for eccentric characters since antiquity (Roman Emperor Tiberius had his villa of pleasures, the Villa Jovis, here), Capri has been a favorite retreat of artists, movie stars, and other VIPs in modern times. Scottish writer Norman Douglas's novel *South Wind* (1917) is part homage to the island and part satire on its eclectic (and even mad) inhabitants. In recent years, though, the island is completely overrun with tourists May through October. Nights tend to be quieter, since many of the tourists come only for the day. You can come in the off season—Christmastime is popular with Italians—but you will find many businesses shuttered.

ESSENTIALS

GETTING THERE   Just as all roads lead to Rome, ferries leave for Capri from almost every harbor in Campania. **Caremar** ((○) **081-0171998** from abroad or (○) 892123 from anywhere in Italy; www.caremar.it) runs ferries to Capri from Naples and from Sorrento. **Navigazione Libera del Golfo** ((○) **081-5520763;** www.navlib.it) runs to Capri from Naples, Sorrento, Castellammare di Stabia. **Alicost** ((○) **089-234892** in Salerno; 089-871483 in Amalfi; and 089-875032 in Positano; www.lauroweb.com/alicost.htm) links Capri to Salerno, Positano, and Amalfi. **Alilauro**

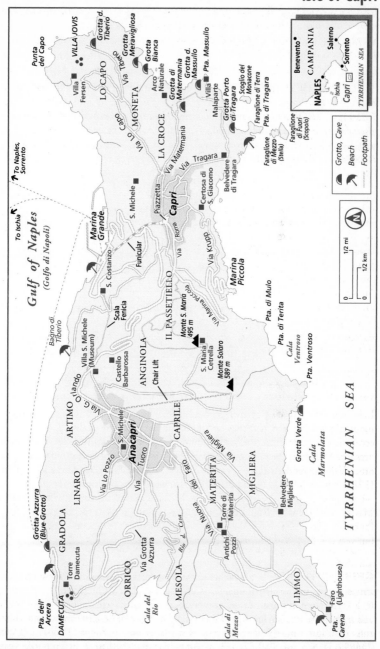

(ⓒ **199-600202** from within Italy or 081-4972222; www.alilauro.it) runs hydrofoils from Ischia Porto to Capri. **SNAV** (ⓒ **081-4285555** or 081-4285500; www.snav. it) runs hydrofoils and catamarans to Capri from Mergellina and Naples (Molo Beverello). **Amalficoastlines** (ⓒ **089-871483;** www.amalficoastlines.com) offers connections to Capri from Salerno, Amalfi, and Positano. **Metrò del Mare** (ⓒ **199-446644;** www.metrodelmare.com) also makes daily runs to Capri. *Note:* Hydrofoil service and the Metrò del Mare are suspended during winter because of bad weather.

GETTING AROUND   Capri gets its name from the ancient Greek *kapriae*, meaning "island of the wild goats." Indeed, only goats can tread these steep slopes and cliffs with ease. There is much that you can do here **on foot**—provided that you are as fit as a goat—otherwise you'll have to rely on public transportation. The **funicolare (funicular)** run by **SIPPIC** (ⓒ **081-8370420**) is the picturesque means of transportation between the harbor of Marina Grande—where the ferry and hydrofoil landing are—and the town of Capri, where it arrives in the heart of town, off Piazza Umberto I. Funiculars leave about every 15 minutes for the 5-minute ride, and you need to purchase tickets in advance at the ticket booth by the ferry landing. **Taxi stands** are at Marina Grande, Marina Piccola, off the Piazzetta in Capri, Anacapri; or you can call one at ⓒ **081-8370543** in Capri and ⓒ 081-8371175 in Anacapri. The well-run public **bus** system is great but quite crowded in the summer, and destines you for a hair-raising ride along the narrow cliff roads that crisscross the island. **ATC** (part of SIPPIC, above) offers service between Marina Grande, Capri, Marina Piccola, and Anacapri, while **Staiano Autotrasporti** (ⓒ **081-8371544** or ⓒ 081-8372422; www.staianogroup.it) offers service between Anacapri, Faro (Lighthouse), and Grotta Azzurra. Tickets cost 1.30€ ($1.80/90p) for either the bus or funicular. You can also get a 60-minute ticket for 2.10€ ($2.95/£1.50) valid for one funicular run and unlimited bus runs during the time limit, or a day pass for 6.70€ ($9.40/£4.70), valid for two funicular rides and unlimited bus service. You can also rent scooters: We recommend **Rent an electric scooter** (ⓒ **081-8375863**) with two locations in Capri: Via Provinciale Marina Grande 210 and Via Roma 68.

Note: We recommend you pack light or be prepared to hire a porter for the climb between the ferry landing and the taxi stand or the funicular station. In general, you'll want to wear comfortable shoes—stiletto heels are definitely not recommended.

VISITOR INFORMATION   The **ACST** of Capri is at Piazzetta I Cerio 11 (ⓒ **081-8375308** or 081-8370424; fax 081-8370918; www.capritourism.com).

EXPLORING THE ISLAND
Your boat will land in **Marina Grande,** the largest harbor on the island. Usually bypassed by tourists, this unassuming hamlet hides the island's oldest church, **San Costanzo** ✸. Dating back to the 5th century, it was enlarged in the 14th century, when its orientation was turned 90 degrees so that the original apse can still be discerned in the right nave. A bit farther to the west are the ruins of the **Palazzo a Mare,** one of the several ancient Roman palaces scattered around the island. Up the steep slope is the town of **Capri** ✸✸✸. This is the island's heart, with its picturesque streets hiding shops, hotels—many of them among the coast's most glamorous—and a wide variety of restaurants and clubs. Social life radiates from the famous **Piazzetta** (Piazza Umberto I), a favorite spot for seeing and being seen. We highly recommend a walk through the narrow streets of the old town. Start from the Piazzetta, graced by the 14th-century **Palazzo Cerio,** the best medieval building remaining on the island. It

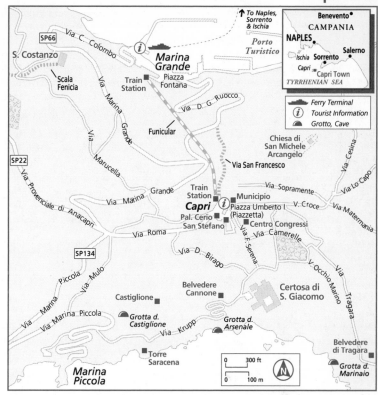

houses the **Museo Ignazio Cerio** (© **081-8376681;** 2.60€/$3.65/£1.80), which has exhibits depicting the island's natural history. Take Via Vittorio Emanuele, the town's main street, past the famous **Grand Hotel Quisisana** (p. 248), which was built in the 19th century as a sanatorium. Make a right on Via Ignazio Cerio, which leads to the **Certosa di San Giacomo** ⚔ (© **081-8376218;** free admission; Tues–Sun 9am–2pm), a religious complex—built in the 14th century and later enlarged—that includes a church, a cloister, and a garden with a belvedere affording great views. Nearby are the **Giardini di Augusto** ⚔⚔, the terraced public gardens affording some of the best **scenic vistas** in Capri.

From the town of Capri you can walk (or take a taxi) to the ruins of **Villa Jovis** ⚔⚔ (Viale Amedeo Maiuri), about 2.4km (1½ miles) from the center of Capri on the northeastern tip of the island. Admission is 2€ ($2.80/£1.40; daily 9am–sunset; ticket booth closes 1 hr. early). This is the best preserved of the 12 villas built on the island by various ancient Roman emperors. Augustus laid claim to a few of them, but the depraved Tiberius had one built for each of the most important gods of the Roman pantheon. Villa Jovis is the one dedicated to Jupiter and, here, as in his other abodes on the island, Tiberius pursued illicit pleasures away from the prying eyes of the Roman Senate. This was his main residence on the island and covered over 5,853 sq. m (63,000 sq. ft.). Its architectural marvels include the **Loggia Imperiale,** a covered promenade on the edge of the cliff. The views from the villa are, to put it mildly, fit for an emperor of even the most jaded tastes.

From Capri, you can also walk (or take a bus or taxi) to the small harbor of **Marina Piccola** 𝄞𝄞 on the southern shore. This is especially popular for its vantage point from which you can admire the famous **Faraglioni** 𝄞𝄞𝄞, a collection of spiky, rocky structures that jut out of the sea a short distance from the coast. Gracing most of Capri's picturesque views, they are indeed very impressive.

Linked to Capri through the famous **Scala Fenicia** (later in this chapter), the other town on the island is **Anacapri** 𝄞𝄞, perched on the higher part of the island, and set among hills and vineyards. The **Church of San Michele** is worth a visit for its beautiful **majolica floor** 𝄞. A short distance out of town is **Villa San Michele** 𝄞 (© **081-8371401;** www.sanmichele.org). The Swedish doctor and writer Axel Munthe had this built as his home in the 19th century, adapting the ruins of an ancient Roman villa. The gardens are also well worth the visit, if anything just to enjoy the matchless views from the terrace (admission 5€/$7/£3.50; Mar 9:30am–4:30pm, Apr 9:30am–5pm, May–Sept 9am–6pm, Oct 9:30am–5:30pm, Nov–Dec 10:30am–3:30pm).

From Anacapri catch the **chairlift,** Via Caposcuro 10 (© **081-8371428;** 5.50€/$7.70/£3.85 one-way, 7€/$9.80/£4.90 round-trip, children 8 and under free; Mar–Oct 9:30am–sunset; Nov–Feb 10:30am–3pm) to **Monte Solaro** 𝄞𝄞𝄞, Capri's highest peak, rising to an altitude of 589m (1,932 ft.). The trip takes only 12 minutes, but the panorama from the top is worth hours of travel. On a clear day, the matchless views encompass the whole stretch of coast and sea, including Mount Vesuvius and the gulfs of Naples and Salerno.

South of Anacapri (a 50-min. walk or a short ride away) is the island's most famous attraction, the **Grotta Azzurra (Blue Grotto)** 𝄞𝄞. The magical colors of the water and walls of this huge grotto are indeed extraordinary, and writers have rhapsodized about it at length since its so-called "discovery" by foreign tourists in the 19th century. In fact, the grotto has been charted since antiquity: On its southwestern corner, the Galleria dei Pilastri displays the remains of a small, ancient Roman dock. The grotto is part of what appears to be a vast system of caverns that is only partially explored. Unfortunately, you'll have no chance to explore on your own, especially if you come at the height of the season. During this period, motorboats line up outside the grotto, waiting for the small rowboats—the only vessels allowed inside—to squeeze a few passengers at a time under the grotto's narrow opening (because of raising sea levels the aperture now extends only about .9m/3 ft. above sea level, and you'll have to lie back in the boat). Because of the long lines, you'll be allowed inside the grotto only for a few minutes. Kids will love the adventure, which conjures up visions of secret expeditions, but adults might find the whole experience wearisome.

The grotto is open daily 9am to 1 hour before sunset; admission is 4€ ($5.60/£2.80). The rowboats that take you inside—unless you want to swim in, which technically is allowed but certainly not recommended given the traffic—charge 5€ ($7/£3.50). We don't particularly recommend signing up for a visit by motorboat, as you'll have to factor in even longer waits and negotiate the tricky switch from the large motorboat to the rowboat that will take you inside. Also, you'll pay about 10€ ($14/£7) more for the privilege. *Note:* As their wages have not risen with inflation, the rowboat operators welcome tips.

Impressions

. . . the creaking and puffing little boat, which had conveyed me only from Sorrento, drew closer beneath the prodigious island—beautiful, horrible and haunted—that does most, of all the happy elements and accidents, towards making the Bay of Naples, for the study of composition, a lesson in the grand style.

—Henry James, *Italian Hours*, 1909

STAYING ACTIVE

Capri's marvelous waters afford great swimming, which you can easily do from one of the small but picturesque local **beaches.** Most are organized by paying beach clubs *(stabilimenti balneari),* which will provide you with a changing cabin, towels, and a deck chair for about 15€ ($21/£11) per day; they are usually open mid-Mar to mid-Nov, 9am to sunset. **Bagni di Tiberio** ⚓ is a nice, sandy beach on the north side of the island, near the ruins of a Roman villa. The beach is only about 1km (½-mile) from Marina Grande, but getting there involves a steep and rocky descent that can be arduous on the return leg. We recommend going by boat instead—you can get a passage there and back for 6€ ($8.40/£4.20) from Marina Grande.

You'll find two more nice beaches in Marina Piccola, on the southern side of the island. To the east of the village is **Marina di Pennaulo,** and to the west is **Marina di Mulo;** both were a favorite haunt of the 1950s and 1960s jet-set. The only **other beaches** on the island are the small one by the Blue Grotto (Via Grotta Azzurra), the one by the Faro (lighthouse), and the one by the Faraglioni (Via Tragara).

We also recommend a **boat tour of the island** ⚓⚓⚓. You can hire a boat with or without a mariner from both Marina Grande and Marina Piccola. **Gruppo Moto-scafisti** (www.motoscafisticapri.com) charges 13€ ($18/£9.10) while **Laser Capri** (www.lasercaprisrl.com) is a bit cheaper: 10€ ($14/£7).

Even if you are only moderately fit, do not miss the opportunity to **hike** Capri's cliffs and soak in the beauty of its trails. Before setting out, stop at the tourist office (see "Visitor Information," above), which can provide you with a map of the paths. One of the easiest hikes is the short trail from **Capri to Marina Piccola** ⚓. From Via Roma in town, turn left onto Via Mulo; a series of steps and a dirt path will lead you down to the harbor through cultivated fields and gardens.

A more demanding hike is the **Scala Fenicia (Fenician Staircase)** ⚓⚓, which descends—or climbs, for the most intrepid—from **Anacapri to Capri.** Built by the Greeks in the 8th century B.C., it was the only access to the sea or to the village of Anacapri until 1877, when the current road was built. The steep path—basically a long staircase with 881 steps—rewards the daring with superb views. Another hike we recommend is the descent from **Mount Solaro** ⚓⚓ (p. 246) on a clearly marked dirt path (after taking the chairlift to the top).

WHERE TO STAY

Capri offers a large number of accommodations in a wide range of styles and prices. As a rule of thumb, accommodations in Anacapri tend to be cheaper but also quieter than those in glitzier Capri town.

VERY EXPENSIVE

Capri Palace ★★★   This is the best hotel in Capri, affording breathtaking views over the island and the gulfs, and absolutely perfect service. Richly decorated with artwork and antiques, it merges classical elegance with modern style and is surrounded by a lovely landscaped garden. The elegant guest rooms are large and furnished in colonial style, with bed canopies, hand-painted ceramic floors, and luxurious marble bathrooms. Many of the rooms open onto a private terrace or garden, and the best have heated private pools. The hotel's restaurant **Olivo** not only enjoys an unmatched setting but also is the best restaurant on the island—and one of the best in the whole region—thanks to the creative cuisine of chef Oliver Glowig. (The restaurant closes simultaneously with the hotel except for 10 days during the Christmas to New Year period).

Via Capodimonte 2b, 80071 Capri. ℂ **081-9780111.** Fax 081-8373191. www.capri-palace.com. 85 units. 420€–850€ ($588–$1,190/£294–£595) double; from 870€ ($1,218/£609) suite. Rates include buffet breakfast. Children 11 and under stay free in parent's room. June–Aug children 9 and under not accepted. AE, DC, MC, V. Closed Nov–Mar. **Amenities:** 2 restaurants; 2 bars; babysitting; concierge; laundry service; lounge; outdoor pool; room service; spa. *In room:* A/C, satellite TV, hair dryer, minibar, safe.

Grand Hotel Quisisana ★★★   This luxurious hotel offers positively splendid accommodations and top-notch service. Built in the 19th century as a sanatorium (the name *qui si sana* means "here we heal"), it quickly changed into a hotel catering to those in need of pampering. Guest rooms are large and bright, opening onto wide arcades with superb views, and decorated with stylish period furniture. The large bathrooms are outfitted in marble or with designer tiles. Even if you don't stay here, come for an after-dinner drink at one of the elegant bars on the premises. We recommend both of the hotel's restaurants, the elegant **Quisi,** perfect for a gourmet candlelight dinner (closed Sun) and the more casual **La Colombaia,** by the outdoor pool.

Via Camerelle 2, 80073 Capri. ℂ **081-8370788.** Fax 081-8376080. www.quisi.com. 150 units. 350€–670€ ($490–$938/£245–£469) double; from 800€ ($1,120/£560) suite. Rates include buffet breakfast. AE, DC, MC, V. Closed Nov–Easter. **Amenities:** 2 restaurants; 3 bars; babysitting; concierge; health club; laundry service; indoor pool; outdoor pool; room service; spa; outdoor tennis courts. *In room:* A/C, TV, hair dryer, minibar, safe.

EXPENSIVE

Hotel Punta Tragara ★★   Standing high on a cliff overlooking one of the best panoramas in Capri, this hotel is in a quiet location slightly away from the heart of things in Capri. Originally a luxurious private villa, it was designed by one of the greatest architects of the 20th century, Le Corbusier. Guest rooms have large windows and open onto private terraces or balconies. They feature modern furnishings, spacious bathrooms, and a restful ambience.

Via Tragara 57, 80073 Capri. ℂ **081-8370844.** Fax 081-8377790. www.hoteltragara.com. 45 units. 520€–780€ ($728–$1,092/£364–£546) double; from 920€ ($1,288/£644) suite. Rates include buffet breakfast. Children 2 and under stay free in parent's room. AE, DC, MC, V. Closed Nov–Easter. **Amenities:** 2 restaurants; babysitting; concierge; health club; laundry service; lounge; nightclub; 2 outdoor pools; room service; salon. *In room:* A/C, TV, minibar, hair dryer, iron, safe.

Hotel Scalinatella ★★   This sophisticated hotel enjoys a unique setting overlooking Capri's Faraglioni (p. 246) and offers a pleasant atmosphere and luxury accommodations. Guest rooms are elegant, with pretty tiled floors, high-quality furnishings, and comfortable bathrooms. Most rooms open onto private terraces and enjoy pretty views.

Via Tragara 8, 80073 Capri. ℂ **081-8370633.** Fax 081-8378291. www.scalinatella.com. 45 units. 540€ ($756/£378) double; from 670€ ($938/£469) suite. Rates include buffet breakfast. Children 2 and under stay free in parent's room.

AE, DC, MC, V. Closed Nov–Mar. **Amenities:** Restaurant; babysitting; concierge; health club; laundry service; lounge; outdoor pool; room service; outdoor tennis court. *In room:* A/C, TV, hair dryer, iron, minibar, safe.

MODERATE

Luna Hotel ⋆ This upscale and modern hotel enjoys a choice cliff-top location and offers luxurious accommodations and attentive service. Guest rooms are quiet and elegantly furnished with a mixture of pieces and styles. Bathrooms are spacious and tiled. Most rooms have private terraces overlooking the cliffs or the hotel's beautiful gardens.

Viale Matteotti 3, 80073 Capri. © **081-8370433.** Fax 081-8377459. www.lunahotel.com. 54 units. 275€–440€ ($385–$616/£193–£308) double; 530€ ($742/£371) suite. Rates include breakfast. Children 2 and under stay free in parent's room. AE, DC, MC, V. Closed mid-Oct to Easter. **Amenities:** Restaurant; babysitting; concierge; health club; laundry service; lounge; outdoor pool; room service; spa. *In room:* A/C, TV, minibar, hair dryer, safe.

Villa Brunella *(Finds)* Set in a panoramic position, this was a private villa until 1963, when it was transformed into its current incarnation as a pleasant family-run hotel. Guest rooms have a welcoming atmosphere and each double has its own flowered terrace or balcony with a sea view. Bathrooms are modest in size but come decorated with modern fixtures and designer tiles. The hotel's restaurant **Terrazza Brunella** is excellent.

Via Tragara 24, 80073 Capri. © **081-8370122.** Fax 081-8370430. www.villabrunella.it. 20 units. 350€ ($490/£245) double; 450€ ($630/£315) junior suite. Rates include buffet breakfast. AE, DC, MC, V. Closed Nov–Apr. **Amenities:** Restaurant; bar; laundry service; outdoor pool; room service. *In room:* A/C, TV, hair dryer, minibar, safe.

INEXPENSIVE

Villa Carmencita *(Finds)* This carefully kept, small modern hotel opens onto its private garden and is located in the modern part of Anacapri. It boasts comfortable and quiet accommodations at moderate rates. The spacious guest rooms are nicely—if simply—furnished, and come with tiled floors and private balconies. Ask about the interesting boating excursions organized by the hotel.

Viale T. De Tommaso 4, 80071 Capri. © **081-8371360.** Fax 081-8373009. carmencita@capri.it. 20 units. 158€ ($221/£111) double. Children 2 and under stay free in parent's room. AE, DC, MC, V. Closed Nov–Mar. **Amenities:** Babysitting. *In room:* A/C, TV.

Villa Sarah ⋆ Located near Capri's orchards and vineyards, this family-run hotel is quiet, friendly, and affordable. Some guest rooms are a bit small, but a number of them have private terraces. Only rooms on the upper floor have sea views, but the others overlook the pretty garden. Organic food is offered at breakfast. Book early, because the hotel is often full.

Via Tiberio 3/a, 80073 Capri. © **081-8377817.** Fax 081-8377215. www.villasarah.it. 20 units. 165€–200€ ($231–$280/£116–£140) double. Rates include buffet breakfast. Children 2 and under stay free in parent's room. AE, DC, MC, V. Closed Nov–Mar. **Amenities:** Bar; babysitting; concierge; laundry service. *In room:* A/C, TV, hair dryer, iron, minibar, safe.

WHERE TO DINE

In addition to the restaurants we recommend in this section, consider dining at the hotel restaurants mentioned above.

EXPENSIVE

La Cantinella ⋆ NEAPOLITAN Near the Giardini di Augusto, this restaurant, housed in a beautiful 18th-century villa with scenic views, combines delectable cuisine with warm, professional service. Its menu changes daily but always includes seafood, meat, and vegetarian choices. You might find excellent *paccheri con frutti di mare e* *rucola* (fresh homemade largish pasta with shellfish and arugula) or superb *pezzogna al sale* (local fish baked in a salt crust). Desserts are always homemade and delicious.

Viale Matteotti 8, Capri. © **081-8370616**. Reservations required for dinner. Secondi 21€–35€ ($29–$49/£15–£25). AE, DC, MC, V. Wed–Mon 12:30–3pm and 7:30pm–12:30am.

MODERATE
Al Grottino ✦ CAPRESE/NEAPOLITAN   Serving seafood and other Neapolitan specialties since 1937, this restaurant was a preferred hangout for VIPs in the 1950s. The food is still good, and you can choose from a variety of traditional Neapolitan comfort food, such as *frittura* (medley of deep-fried seafood) and *mozzarella in carrozza* (deep-fried mozzarella)—prepared in four different ways Excellent Caprese specialties are *zuppa di cozze* (a bean-and-mussel soup) and *ravioli alla caprese* (with fresh mozzarella and basil).

Via Longano 27, Capri. © **081-8370584**. Reservations required for dinner. Secondi 12€–20€ ($17–$28/£8.40–£14). AE, MC, V. Daily noon–3pm and 7pm–midnight. Closed Nov–Mar.

La Pergola CAPRESE/SEAFOOD   This pleasant and welcoming restaurant offers delightful alfresco dining in its private garden. The menu offers traditional dishes that highlight local seafood. We highly recommend the spaghetti *alle vongole e pomodorini* (with fresh clams and cherry tomatoes), as well as the *pezzogna all'acqua pazza* (local fish in a light tomato sauce) and the charbroiled catch of the day.

Via Traversa Lo Palazzo 2. © **081-8377414**. Reservations recommended. Secondi 14€–18€ ($20–$25/£9.80–£13). AE, DC, MC, V. Thurs–Tues 12:30–3pm and 7:30–11pm; daily in summer. Closed mid-Nov to Dec 25.

La Savardina ✦ CAPRESE   This historical address continues to lure locals and visitors to its excellent traditional food and hospitable service. We love it for the variety of its menu, including many vegetarian and meat-based dishes in addition to the typical seafood favorites. We recommend you start with a simple antipasto of grilled vegetables and local cured meat, followed by the very well prepared ravioli *alla caprese* (filled with mozzarella), or with the linguine seasoned with capers, cherry tomatoes, and fresh herbs. For secondi, the *coniglio* (rabbit) is excellent, or try the excellent fish *all'acqua pazza*. The *torta caprese* (traditional chocolate and nut torte) is quite good.

Via Lo Capo 8, Capri. © **081-8376300**. www.caprilasavardina.com. Reservations recommended. Secondi 14€–18€ ($20–$25/£9.80–£13). AE, DC, MC, V. Daily 12:30–3pm and 7:30–11pm in summer (dates vary); Wed–Mon 12:30–3pm and 7:30–11pm in shoulder seasons. Closed Nov–Mar.

INEXPENSIVE
Grottelle ✦ *Finds* CAPRESE   This small restaurant off the beaten path is a great place for sampling the local cuisine. The outdoor terrace is very pleasant during fair weather. The menu is centered on traditional Caprisian cuisine, and we highly recommend the *zuppa di fagioli* (bean soup) as well as the simple but delectable spaghetti *con pomodoro e basilica* (with fresh tomatoes and basil), followed by the perfect *frittura di paranza* (deep-fried seafood). The homemade desserts are very good.

Via Arco Naturale, 13, Arco Naturale. © **0818375719**. Fax 081-8389234 Reservations required for dinner. Secondi 11€–15€ ($15–$21/£7.70–£11). AE, DC, MC, V. Fri–Wed noon–3pm and 7–11pm. Closed Nov–Mar.

La Cisterna *Value* CAPRESE/PIZZA   This small, unpretentious restaurant serves well-prepared pizza and traditional dishes at very low prices. The menu varies but portions are always generous; you might find *lasagne verdi* (green lasagna), *zuppa di pesce* (seafood stew), *frittura* (deep-fried seafood), and the market choice of seafood served charbroiled or *all'acqua pazza* (poached in a light herb broth).

Via Madre Serafina 5. ℂ **081-8375620.** Reservations required. Pizza 5€–9€ ($7–$13/£3.50–£6.30). Secondi 8€–14€ ($11–$20/£5.60–£9.80). AE, DC, MC, V. Daily noon–3:30pm and 7pm–midnight; 11:30am–2pm and 6:30–11pm in winter.

La Rondinella ⭐ CAPRESE/PIZZA   This family-run restaurant is a good choice if you're after relaxation and quiet. They prepare many varieties of brick-oven pizza. Otherwise, the regular menu is traditional and you will find an excellent rendition of *ravioli alla caprese* (mozzarella, fresh tomatoes, and basil); *pezzogna all'acqua pazza* (local fish in a light tomato sauce); and *frittura* (deep-fried seafood medley), which they prepare particularly well. For dessert, local specialties such as *torta caprese* (almond cake) are excellent.

Via G. Orlandi 245, Anacapri. ℂ **081-8371223.** Reservations required for dinner. Pizza 6€–10€ ($8.40–$14/ £4.20–£7). Secondi 11€–16€ ($15–$22/£7.70–£11). AE, DC, MC, V. Daily noon–3pm and 7–11pm. Closed 2 weeks in Feb.

SHOPPING FOR LOCAL CRAFTS ⭐⭐

Dedicated shoppers will lose themselves in Capri's little shops. Many of the island's visitors return just to buy more of the locally made goods, especially the sandals and the jewelry. One of the most famous shopping stops is **Carthusia,** a perfume maker that counts many stars among its customers. Its **laboratory** (Viale Parco Augusto; ℂ **081-8370368;** daily 9:30am–6pm) has been concocting unique perfumes from local herbs and flowers since 1948. There are two outlets on the island, one in Capri (Via Camerelle 10; ℂ **081-8370368**), and one in Anacapri (Via Capodimonte 26; ℂ **081-8373668**). Both are closed from November to March.

Stylish sandals (handmade, of course) can be found at **Canfora** (Via Camerelle 3; ℂ **081-8370487**) in Capri, and at **L'Arte del Sandalo Caprese** (Via Orlando 75; ℂ **081-8373583**) in Anacapri. Finally, the island has an old jewelry-making tradition. You can admire—and purchase—fine examples at **La Perla Gioielli** (Piazza Umberto I 21; ℂ **081-8370641**).

9

Salerno, Paestum, Padula & the Cilento

Salerno is the last (or the first, depending on your approach) stop on the Amalfi Coast, and the largest town in southern Campania. The refuge of artists for centuries, it remains mostly undiscovered by modern-day tourists. Yet its wealth of artistic and historic offerings makes it a worthy destination.

Salerno is the gateway to the Cilento, one of Italy's best-guarded secrets. Covering a large section of the southern part of Campania, this national park—the second largest in Italy—offers unique sights and attractions, including a truly beautiful coastline. Cilento was where the ancient Greeks built some of their most important colonies, whose grandeur is still visible in the unique ruins of Paestum. Cilento's shore is relatively popular with Italians during the summer, but you'll be far away from the swarms of foreign tourists. Most visitors usually see the temples of Paestum and move on, completely missing out on the Cilento's wild interior, scenic shores, and wonderful cuisine.

1 Salerno

55km (34 miles) SE of Naples

With 150,000 inhabitants, Salerno is a lively modern town with a lovely medieval center, which the lack of crowds makes all the more enjoyable. Its *lungomare* (seafront promenade) is the most beautiful on this coast. The most important harbor of Campania after Naples, Salerno used to be the capital of the Southern kingdom. An Etruscan and Campanian town founded around the 6th century B.C., Salerno was absorbed into Magna Grecia, the conglomerate of Greek colonies in southern Italy, during the 5th century B.C. After becoming a Roman colony in 194 B.C., it acquired greater importance as Paestum (located farther south) declined in prestige, and it eventually became an independent principality under the Longobards in the 9th century A.D. Its growth continued in medieval and Renaissance times, when it became an important cultural center thanks to its renowned Scuola Medica Salernitana, one of the first medical schools in the western world. The principality was then ruled by Normans, Swabians, Angevins, and, finally, the Bourbons. Its political and cultural importance declined when Naples became the capital of the new kingdom. Salerno sank back into the quiet life of a smallish provincial town.

ESSENTIALS

GETTING THERE   The nearest **airport** is Naples' Capodichino (p. 70); direct shuttle-bus **service** connects the airport with Salerno. Salerno is a major **train** stop and

Salerno

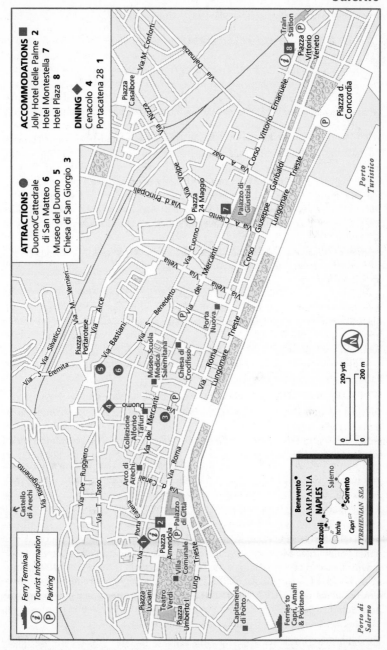

ACCOMMODATIONS ■
Jolly Hotel delle Palme **2**
Hotel Montestella **7**
Hotel Plaza **8**

DINING ◆
Cenacolo **4**
Portacatena 28 **1**

ATTRACTIONS ●
Duomo/Cattedrale
di San Matteo **6**
Museo del Duomo **5**
Chiesa di San Giorgio **3**

Ferry Terminal
ⓘ Tourist Information
Ⓟ Parking

0   200 yds
0   200 m

CAMPANIA
Benevento
NAPLES
Pozzuoli
Ischia
Capri
Sorrento
Salerno
TYRRHENIAN SEA

Porto di
Salerno

Porto
Turistico

is well connected by railroad to all major cities in Italy and abroad, with frequent service from Naples (every 10–30 min.); the 35-minute ride to Salerno costs 5.40€ ($7.60/£3.80). Contact **Trenitalia** (© **892021** from anywhere in Italy; www.trenitalia. it) for fares and information. Trains arrive at the **Stazione** on Piazza Vittorio Veneto.

Slower but far more scenic, the **ferry** is our favorite means of transportation on this coast, especially in the summer, when roads tend to be crowded. Salerno is a major harbor, and ferries arrive here from ports along the Italian shore and the Mediterranean. **Alicost** (© **089-234892** in Salerno; 089-871483 in Amalfi; and 089-811986 in Positano; www.amalficoastlines.com) connects Salerno to Capri, Amalfi, Positano, and Ischia. **Metrò del Mare** (© **199-600700;** www.metrodelmare.com) connects Salerno with all the harbors along this stretch of coast, from Pozzuoli south, including Naples, Sorrento, Positano, and Amalfi. The service runs April through September. Purchase of a **Terra&Mare ticket** entitles you to the ferry ride plus ground transportation for the 45 minutes before and 45 minutes after the ferry link (8.50€/ $12/£5.95). **DiMaio Lines** (© **848-151818** from anywhere in Italy, or 081-8822220; www.dimaiolines.it) connects Salerno with Olbia in Sardinia; **Caronte & Tourist** (© **800-627414;** toll-free within Italy or 089-2582528; www.carontetourist.it) links Salerno with Catania and Messina, while **Grimaldi Ferries** (© **081-496444;** www. grimaldi-ferries.com) connects Salerno with Malta (La Valletta), Tunis, Valencia in Spain, and Palermo in Sicily.

Salerno is also well connected by **bus: SITA** (© **089-226604** or 089-405145; www.sitabus.it) maintains regular runs to Salerno from Naples as well as from the various villages of the Amalfi Coast and the Sorrento peninsula. **CSTP** (© **800-016659;** toll-free within Italy, or 089-487001; www.cstp.it) services Salerno, Pompeii, Paestum, and the Cilento.

You can also reach Salerno by **car.** Off the *autostrada* A3, take the exit marked SALERNO and follow signs for the city center.

GETTING AROUND Although large compared to the compact towns of the Amalfi Coast, Salerno is actually a moderately sized town stretching along its waterfront and can be explored **on foot.** The town's historic district is a pedestrian area that stretches from the train station on **Piazza Vittorio Veneto,** to Piazza Amendola at the western edge of the medieval center. **Taxis** are your best bet for destinations outside the historic district; you'll find taxi stands at Piazza Vittorio Veneto in front of the railway station (© **089-229947**); Piazza Amendola (© **089-229963**); and Piazza XXIV Maggio (© **089-229171**); or call **Radiotaxi** directly at © **089-757575.** The town has a good **public bus** system run by **CSTP** (above); the bus hub is Piazza Vittorio Veneto, across from the rail station.

VISITOR INFORMATION The **AACST tourist office** for Salerno is at Via Roma 258 (© **089-224744;** www.aziendaturismo.sa.it). The tourist office for the whole province, including the Cilento, is the **EPT** of Salerno (Via Velia 15, 84100 Salerno; © **089-230401;** www.eptsalerno.it). They also maintain an office in Piazza Vittorio Veneto, at the train station (© **089-614259**), which is open Monday to Saturday from 9am to 2pm and 3 to 8pm (until 7pm in winter). In advance of your visit, you can check out what's going on in Salerno at www.salernocity.com.

FAST FACTS You'll find several pharmacies in town, including one at Corso Vittorio Emanuele 223 (© **089-231439**), not far from the train station, and one at Via Mercanti 62 (© **089-225142**), in the medieval district. The **hospital Ruggiero**

d'Aragona is on Via San Leonardo (© **089-67111**). For an **ambulance,** dial © **118.** Dial © **113** or **112** for the police, © **115** for the fire department, and © **116** for ACI road assistance. You will find several banks and **ATMs** in Salerno along Corso Vittorio Emanuele, not far from the train station; a convenient one is the **Banca Nazionale del Lavoro** inside the train station. The main **post office**—housed in a majestic build-ing—is at Corso Garibaldi 203 and is open Monday to Saturday from 8am to 2pm.

SPECIAL EVENTS   The Salerno Film Festival Linea d'ombra (Salerno Film Fes-tival of the Shadow Line) ✪ is a major international event, dedicated to new talents in Europe and focusing on the theme of the passage from adolescence to adulthood—the "shadow line" of maturation, a term coined by Joseph Conrad and taken as the fesitval's motto. The festival (Piazza Sant'Agostino 13, 84121 Salerno; © **089-2753673;** fax 089-2571125; www.shadowline.it) is now an annual weeklong event that takes place in April; it celebrated its 10th year in April 2005. Besides films, it includes a number of interesting musical events.

Another important festival is **Salerno Etnica (Ethnical Salerno),** a music festival focusing on music as an expression of culture and tradition. It is held in September during the celebration for Salerno's patron saint, San Matteo (in Piazza Alfano I, in front of the cathedral; and in Piazza Amendola); admission is free. Contact the tourist office for a schedule of events.

During the Ravello Music Festival (chapter 7), concerts are also held in the monastery of Santa Maria della Mercede in Salerno; contact the Festival office for a schedule of events.

EXPLORING SALERNO

During World War II, Salerno was designated the capital of Allied Italy, and much of the town was destroyed by severe bombing. Only the medieval center and part of the 19th-century waterfront were miraculously spared. The reconstruction and expansion that followed, especially to the southeast and northeast of the seafront, gave the town a more modern look. However, in the 1990s, a renovation campaign brought the old sections of Salerno back to their original splendor, particularly its seafront promenade.

Lined with palm trees and opening onto the seascape of the Costiera Amalfitana and Cilentana, **Lungomare Trieste** ✪✪ is the most beautiful seafront promenade in the whole region—and one of the best in Italy. At the western end you'll find the **Villa Comunale** (Piazza Amendola), a pleasant and orderly public garden, adjacent to the **Teatro Verdi** ✪ (Piazza Luciani; © **089-662141;** daily 8am–2pm and 4–8pm). This historic theater was inaugurated on April 15, 1872, with *Rigoletto* by Giuseppe Verdi. A recent face-lift has brought the beautiful baroque and neoclassical decorations back to life, including the magnificent hall with its frescoed ceiling by Domenico Morelli. The theater hosts many important concerts and performances (later in this chapter). The town is dominated by the **Castello di Arechi,** Via Benedetto Croce (© **089-233900;** www.castellodiarechi.it; free admission; daily 7am–noon and 4–7:30pm); originally built by the Byzantines, probably over older fortifications, the castle took on its current mantle under Spanish rule in the 16th century. It now hosts special events, but it's worth a visit just for its view. It can be reached by car, taxi, or on foot—a steep 40-minute climb along a pedestrian ramp.

The medieval heart of Salerno—where most of the town's attractions are concen-trated—is a picturesque place for a stroll. From Piazza Amendola you can take the exclusive shopping street **Via di Porta Catena,** and follow it to charming **Piazza Sedile**

del Campo, the medieval market square, graced by the beautiful **Fontana dei Delfini (Fountain of the Dolfins)** ⍟ and the **Palazzo dei Genovesi** (at no. 3)—today a school—with its grand **portal** ⍟. Off the piazza, in Via Roteprandi, you'll find the church of **Sant'Andrea de Lama,** one of the oldest medieval buildings in Salerno—note its pretty 12th-century bell tower—and, a few steps farther, the even older church of **Sant'Alfonso,** dating from the 10th century. Inside, admire some recently restored frescoes dating from the Longobard era. Return to **Piazza Sedile del Campo** to access **Via dei Mercanti** ⍟, Salerno's major shopping street, which dates from medieval times. This is where you'll find some of the best boutiques and most elegant stores in town. Off to the left is the **Vicolo dei Sartori** with the **Palazzo Fruscione** ⍟, notable for its medieval decorations, including a pretty loggia and intertwined arches. Not far off, on Vicolo Adalberga, is the ancient **Palatine San Pietro a Corte** church ⍟. Its 11th-century frescoes have survived, and excavations of its layered strata have revealed the structure of an ancient Roman thermal bathhouse. Farther along Via dei Mercanti is the 10th-century **Chiesa del Crocifisso** ⍟⍟, Piazza Matteotti 1 (ⓒ **089-233716;** daily 9am–noon and 4–7pm), famous for its beautiful 13th-century **frescoes** in the main and right apses of the crypt. One depicts the Crucifixion and the other three saints; this fresco is reproduced in mosaics over the main altar of the church above.

Chiesa di San Giorgio ⍟   Built in 1647 over an 8th-century church, this is the most beautiful baroque church in Salerno. An atrium with a carved portal stands in front of the imposing facade, and the interior is typically baroque, with ornate gilded stucco and numerous frescoes and paintings. The fresco cycle depicting the *Passion of Christ* in the cantoria, as well as the *Crucifixion* and *San Benedetto* in the transept, are all by Angelo Solimena. *San Michele* (over the 4th altar to the right) and the frescoes of the large chapel are by Franceso Solimena, and other paintings are by Andrea da Salerno. A beautiful carved wooden pulpit is supported by four lions.
Via Duomo 19. ⓒ **089-228918.** Daily 9:30am–12:30pm.

Duomo/Cattedrale di San Matteo ⍟⍟⍟   Arguably Italy's most beautiful medieval church, the Duomo was built in 1076 and consecrated in 1085 to house the relics of Saint Matthew the Evangelist. The front portion of the church is the **Sala San Lazzaro,** which is believed to have been the Main Hall of the **Scuola Medica Salernitana (Salerno Medical School).** A 17th-century staircase leads to the 11th-century Romanesque portal known as **Porta dei Leoni,** with its finely carved architrave; it leads to the church's elegant **Atrium** ⍟. This is surrounded by a portico decorated with stone and tufa intarsia and is dominated by a splendid Romanesque **bell tower** ⍟⍟ (you'll get a better view of the bell tower from Via Roberto il Giscardo, to the right of the Duomo.) From here you can admire the facade of the Duomo, with its beautifully carved **central portal** closed by two **bronze doors** ⍟⍟, which were cast in Constantinople in 1099. In spite of the grave damages caused by the earthquake in 1688, and of the intense 18th-century restoration, the Duomo's interior still holds an amazing quantity of impressive artwork, starting with the two magnificent **ambones** ⍟⍟⍟ in the central nave. The smaller is from the 12th century, while the larger dates from the 1400s and is composed of 12 red and gray granite columns blossoming with birds, figures, and vegetation. On the ambone's facade, note the remarkable mosaic showing a sinner with a snake biting him in the breast, and an eagle digging his talons into the unfortunate sinner's head. The monumental **candle holder** ⍟ in front of the ambone is also impressive. Adjacent to the ambones is the choir, whose sides and floor are embedded with mosaics from the 12th century. The **Cappella delle Crociate (Chapel of the Crusades)** ✶✶ in the right apse is where the Crusaders had their weapons blessed before sailing for the Holy Land. Fine 13th-century mosaics and later frescoes cover the walls and ceiling. Conserved under the altar are the remains of Pope Gregorio VII, who died in exile in Salerno in 1085.

Piazza Alfano I. ✆ **089-231387.** Daily 10am–6pm. Free admission.

Museo del Duomo ✶✶   Adjacent to the Duomo is the museum, which contains a large art collection dating to Roman times. One of the most impressive rooms in our opinion is the one that holds the ivory collection, including some amazing carvings. The best is a 12th-century *paliotto* **(altar front)** ✶✶✶, composed of 54 carved scenes by different artists. Note that four frames are missing; you'll find one in the Louvre in Paris, one in Berlin, one in Budapest, and the last in the Met in New York. In the other rooms are several other important pieces, including paintings and bas-reliefs from the 16th century, and paintings by such artists as Andrea Vaccaro, Luca Giordano, Jusepe de Ribera, and Francesco Solimena. The museum also has a collection of illuminated manuscripts from the 13th and 14th centuries.

Via Monsignor Monterisi. ✆ **089-239126.** Free admission. Daily 9am–6pm.

WHERE TO STAY

Yet undiscovered by international tourists, Salerno offers very advantageous hotel rates, making it a good starting point for exploration of the region.

MODERATE

Jolly Hotel delle Palme ✶✶   Its location at the beginning of the beautiful seaside promenade, within walking distance of both the medieval center and the harbor, makes this the best hotel in town. It's also a very comfortable hotel, with a chain's uniformly polite service and consistent styling. Guest room decor is sober and functional; bathrooms are good size and modern. The hotel's restaurant is not bad—the food is good enough, but the atmosphere and ambience are rather bland.

Lungomare Trieste 1, 84121 Salerno. ✆ **089-225222.** Fax 089-237571. www.jollyhotels.it. 104 units. 173€ ($242/£121) double; 240€ ($336/£168) junior suite. Rates include buffet breakfast. Children 5 and under stay free in parent's room. AE, DC, MC, V. Free parking. **Amenities:** Restaurant; bar; babysitting; business center; concierge; laundry service; room service. *In room:* A/C, satellite TV, hair dryer, minibar, safe.

INEXPENSIVE

Hotel K ✶   South of the center of town, in the modern part of Salerno, this recently renovated (in 2004) and welcoming hotel has been proudly run by the Bartoli family since 1964. Housed in a modern building, it overlooks the sea and offers nicely appointed accommodations and good service. The spacious units have contemporary modern furniture and good-size, tiled bathrooms. Each room has a private balcony overlooking the sea or the hotel's garden-courtyard; some have Jacuzzis and safes. Guests have free access to the hotel's Internet point in the lobby.

Via D. Somma 47, off the Lungomare, 84129 Salerno. ✆ **089-752720.** Fax 089-725516. www.hotelk.it. 53 units. 85€–95€ ($119–$133/£60–£67) double. Rates include breakfast. Children 2 and under stay free in parent's room. AE, DC, MC, V. Free parking. **Amenities:** Snack bar; bar; business center; concierge; Internet point; laundry service; room service. *In room:* A/C, TV, minibar.

Hotel Montestella ✶   This family-run hotel, last renovated in 2000, has a very central location in the pedestrian area between the train station and the medieval center.

The good-size guest rooms come with comfortable, modern furnishings. The bathrooms are medium size, with new fixtures.

Corso Vittorio Emanuele 156, 84122 Salerno. © 089-225122. Fax 089-229167. www.hotelmontestella.it. 46 units. 110€ ($154/£77) double. Rates include breakfast. Specials available. Children 2 and under stay free in parent's room. AE, DC, MC, V. Parking 15€ ($21/£11). **Amenities:** Bar; concierge; laundry service; room service. *In room:* A/C, TV, minibar, safe.

Hotel Plaza This hotel is housed in a large neoclassical building across from the railway station. Inside, it has been completely modernized, and the decor is modern throughout. The guest rooms are not large; but they are certainly adequate, with simple furnishings, carpeting, and either tubs or showers in the bathrooms.

Piazza Vittorio Veneto 42, 84123 Salerno. © 089-224477. Fax 089-237311. www.plazasalerno.it. 42 units. 100€ ($140/£70) double. Rates include buffet breakfast. Children 2 and under stay free in parent's room. AE, DC, MC, V. Parking 15€ ($21/£11). **Amenities:** Bar; babysitting; concierge; laundry service; room service. *In room:* A/C, satellite TV, hair dryer, minibar, safe.

WHERE TO DINE

In addition to the restaurants below, we recommend the literally dozens of moderately priced *pizzerie* catering to the students of the lively local university and the mariners from the nearby commercial port. They are hardly elegant, but often provide surprisingly good pizza.

MODERATE

Cenacolo 🍴🍴 SALERNITAN Located across from the Duomo, this is the best restaurant in Salerno—which might not seem a great achievement in a town that favors cheap eateries, but the food is indeed very good. Owner and chef Pietro Rispoli brings together the best flavors of the region—fresh herbs and vegetables, seafood, local meats, and cheeses—sometimes in new combinations. The menu varies regularly, but you might find *mousse di tonno con composta di pomodori* (tuna mousse with tomato jam), *cavatelli con salsa di zucchine* (a delicious creation of homemade pasta with a sauce of zucchini, lemon peel, anchovies, and local provolone cheese), or *mazzancolle con verdurine grigliate e capperi fritti* (local prawns with grilled garden vegetables and fried capers). The breads and the pastas are exclusively homemade; the wines and cheeses are superb.

Piazza Alfano I 4. © 089-238818. Reservations recommended. Secondi 15€–22€ ($21–$31/£11–£16). AE, DC, MC, V. Tues–Sun 12:30–3pm; Tues–Sat 7:30–11pm. Closed 3 weeks in Aug.

Portacatena 28 *Finds* SALERNITAN This tiny restaurant in the medieval center of Salerno was recently opened with the ambition of bringing creative cuisine to Salerno's depressed—according to gourmets—culinary scene, and as such it succeeds very well. The seasonal menu focuses on meat—an unusual and welcome choice; if it's offered, try the complex and subtle risotto *con porcini, quaglia e tartufo nero* (with porcini mushrooms, quail, and truffle). They also offer a first-rate tasting menu. The wine list focuses on local varieties unlikely to be found elsewhere.

Via Portacatena 28. © 089-235659. Reservations recommended. Prix-fixe tasting menu 45€ ($63/£32). Secondi 14€–18€ ($20–$25/£10–£13). AE, DC, MC, V. Daily 12:30–3pm and 7:30–10pm.

SALERNO AFTER DARK

As a university town and a major harbor, Salerno has a lively nightlife and cultural scene, with a large number of clubs, discos, and cafes. Among the places to hang out, we recommend the **Bogart Cafe** (Via Rafastia 9; © 089-252288), which turns into a disco on weekends, and **Fabula** (Via Porto 1, © **340-1403144**), a popular club that also has live music. Among the Italian pubs, **Galleon** (Via Roma 254-56; © **089-250938**) is a cozy place whose walls are decorated with nautical art and curios.

For more upscale nightlife, heading the top of the list is the above-mentioned **Teatro Verdi,** Piazza Luciani (© **089-662141;** daily 8am–2pm and 4–8pm) which, true to its namesake, is sometimes the venue for Italian opera, but also presents classic or contemporary plays as well as concerts and dance performances. Check with the **tourist office** for the program.

2 The Magic Ruins of Paestum ✦

35km (22 miles) S of Salerno, 100km (62 miles) SE of Naples

A short distance south of Salerno, the fabled ruins of Paestum are everything they are reported to be: Enormously evocative, the three Greek temples (in an excellent state of conservation) occupy a grassy plain that really gives off the sense of a vanished, ancient city. Most of the town walls are intact as well. The temples are a unique sight, especially at sunset, and in spring and fall when Paestum's roses—praised since antiquity—are in bloom. The archaeological area can be reached as a day trip from anywhere in Campania; plan on spending a couple of hours exploring the temples and an hour for the museum, but count on a whole day for a more in depth exploration.

ESSENTIALS

GETTING THERE   Paestum is well connected by public transportation from Salerno, with several **trains** a day making the 30-minute trip. Contact **Trenitalia** (© **892021** from anywhere in Italy; www.trenitalia.it) for fares and information. Trains stop at **Paestum,** about a half-mile from the archaeological area. Paestum is also an easy **bus** connection from Salerno; buses leave from Piazza della Concordia in Salerno, near the train station. **SCAT** (© **0974-838415**) offers five daily runs from Salerno and Agropoli.

By car, take *autostrada* A3 to BATTIPAGLIA and follow the brown signs for Paestum.

GETTING AROUND   If you are just visiting the temples, you will be able to do so **on foot.** Should you want to explore further afield, you can rent a **car** from **Travelcar** on Via Magna Grecia (© **0828-811034;** www.travelcar.it), or from one of the following companies who also offer **car service** with a driver: **Leonardo D'Onofrio,** Via Cesare Pavese 27, Paestum (© **0828-721107** or 339-3201101); **Autonoleggi Meridionali Di Filippo,** Via Fratelli Arenella 3, Capaccio (© **0828-821045** or 0828-821452); and **Fratelli Di Filippo,** Capaccio Scalo (© **0828-724707**).

VISITOR INFORMATION   **AACST,** Via Magna Grecia 887, 84063 Paestum (© **0828-811016;** fax 0828-722322; www.infopaestum.it) maintains an information point at Via Magna Grecia 151, by the Archeological Museum, not far from the main entrance to the temples (Mon–Sat 9am–3pm, Sun 9am–1pm; in July and Aug, Mon–Sat 9am–7pm, Sun 9am–1pm).

FAST FACTS   You'll find a pharmacy in Via Licinella, in Capaccio (© **0828-721190**). For an **ambulance,** dial © **118.** Dial © **113** or 112 for the police, © **115** for the fire department, and © **116** for ACI road assistance. A **bank** (© **0828-811141**) is at Via Licinella 1, in Capaccio, where you'll also find the **post office** (© **0828-811029**).

EXPLORING THE ARCHAEOLOGICAL AREA

The Greeks established the colony of Poseidonia—the name Paestum is ancient Roman—in the 7th century B.C., around the same time that the nearby temple of Hera Argiva (p. 262) was built. The town flourished for almost 3 centuries but dramatically declined after it was overtaken by the Lucanians, a local mountain people, in the 4th century B.C. Only when the Romans established the colony of Paestum in 273 B.C. did the city revive, quickly growing wealthy from its agricultural and commercial activity. The city lost its supremacy during the Middle Ages, when its inhabitants were forced into the hills by the repeated Saracen attacks and the spread of malaria (caused by the fertile plain's transformation into marshland). The Normans arrived in the 11th century, plundering the temples and other buildings for their statuary. The ruins remained known but undisturbed for centuries until the state road was developed in the 18th century and the first archaeological studies were performed.

The **archaeological area and museum** (© **0828 811023;** www.infopaestum.it) are at Via Magna Grecia 917. Magna Grecia cuts through the middle of the archaeological site and leads right to the Roman amphitheater. Up the street from the main gate and the museum is a **tourist information office.** The archaeological area has two more gates—one on Via Magna Grecia by the Temple of Neptune, and the third through the ancient southern gate in the town walls, **Porta della Giustizia (Justice Gate)**—only if you already have a ticket in hand. Admission to the archaeological area and museum is 4€ ($5.60/£2.80) each, but you can purchase a cumulative ticket for both for 6.50€ ($9.10/£4.55). The archaeological area is open daily 9am to sunset (last admission 60 min. earlier), and the museum is open daily 8:45am to 7:45pm (last admission 45 min. earlier) and closed the first and third Monday of each month; both are closed January 1, May 1, and December 25.

Paestum's temples are ranked among the best-preserved Greek temples in the world, second only to the Theseion in Athens. Based on the rich trove of findings in and around the temples, most experts now believe that two structures were actually part of a huge complex dedicated to Hera, the goddess of fertility and maternity (the same goddess honored in the sanctuary near the mouth of the Sele River, p. 262). Indeed, several other smaller religious buildings, all dedicated to Hera, have been discovered nearby. The **Basilica** ✴✴✴ is the oldest of the three largest structures, built in 550 B.C. in Doric Archaic style. The 50 columns of its monumental portico still stand, showing the pot-bellied profile typical of archaic temples, but the roof and the pediment have long ago fallen down. In front is a partially ruined sacrificial altar and, on its side, the square *bothros*—the sacrificial well where the remains were thrown. To the right of the Basilica is the so-called **Temple of Neptune** ✴✴✴, restoration of which was completed in 2004. This grandiose building, dating from around 450 B.C., is lined in travertine stone and glows a magical gold color when hit by the sun's rays. It is considered the best Doric temple in the world, with its perfect proportions and a number of architectural tricks—the columns at the corners have an elliptical section instead of round, and the horizontal lines are slightly convex instead of perfectly straight—giving it slender elegance and power at the same time. It is also the best preserved of Paestum's temples, with its roof and pediments mostly intact. At the temple's front are two sacrificial altars; the smaller was added by the Romans in the 3rd century B.C.

The third temple—the so-called **Temple of Ceres** ✴✴ although it now seems it was dedicated to Athena—is on the opposite side of the ancient town. To reach it, pass through the **Roman Forum,** which may be the oldest known rectangular Roman

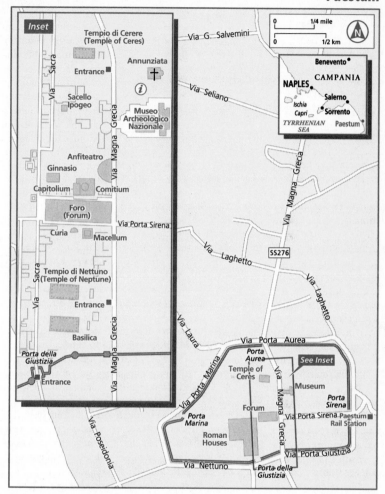

Paestum

forum, lined with Doric porticos—all that is left of the ceremonial and public buildings that surrounded it originally. Walk down the **Via Sacra (Sacred Street),** with its Roman pavement laid over the Greek road. About 12km (7½ miles) long, it originally connected the Greek town of Poseidonia to the ancient temple of Hera and, in Roman times, led to the Roman amphitheater and the Forum. The Via Sacra climbs the plateau where the temple stands. Built at the end of the 6th century B.C., it was transformed into a church in medieval times; that is why, inside its portico, you will see three Christian tombs.

The **National Archeological Museum** ✿✿ houses the finds from the excavations. The 6th-century-B.C. **Statue of Zeus** ✿✿ is well worth seeing as is the rich collection of 6th-century-B.C. **vases** with red or black figures. You'll also see objects from the nearby necropolis, including the famous **Diver's Tomb** ✿ from the 5th century B.C.,

Impressions

And I myself, were I not even now
Furling my sails, and, nigh the journey's end,
Eager to turn my vessel's prow to shore,
Perchance would sing what careful husbandry
Makes the trim garden smile; of Paestum too,
Whose roses bloom and fade and bloom again.

—Virgil, *Georgics*

decorated with beautiful frescoes; and the very interesting paintings and objects found in the **Lucanian Tombs** and dating from the 6th to the 3rd centuries B.C. One whole area of the museum is dedicated to the architectural remains from the **Heraion,** the **Sanctuary dedicated to Hera Argiva** (later in this chapter), including the complete **frieze** ✦ of metopes and triglyphs; a number of the metopes are unfinished, which helps shed light on the carving techniques.

Usually bypassed by harried tourists, a walk along Paestum's defensive **walls** ✦ is quite peaceful and affords nice views. The powerful walls completely surrounded the town, and are one of the very few complete sets of walls left from antiquity. Originally built by the Greeks, they were restored by the Lucanians and then the Romans. Measuring 5m (18 ft.) thick on average, with several square and round towers, they mark a pentagonal perimeter of 4,750m (15,580 ft.), with four main gates at the four cardinal directions. You can walk the whole perimeter or focus on the western side, which is the best preserved. It includes the **Porta Marina;** there you can climb the walls and walk on the patrol paths, enjoying the great views over coast and ruins.

Should you have time for more, pay a visit to the interesting ruins of the **Heraion,** the sanctuary built on the river Sele about 11 kilometers (6¾ miles) north of Paestum and dedicated to Hera Argiva. This was one of the most famous temples of Magna Grecia (the conglomerate of Greek colonies in the Mediterranean) and was hunted by archaeologists since the 18th century. Little more than the foundation of the main temple remains, together with parts of the smaller *thesaurus* (storehouse), and a portico with attached buildings. All the decorations—metopes and votive statuettes—are conserved in the National Archeological Museum of Paestum (above).

More interesting still is the **Museo Narrante del Santuario di Hera Argiva** ✦, Masseria Procuriali (✆ **0828 811016;** www.infopaestum.it; Tues–Sat 9am–4pm), located in a restored farm 9km (5½ miles) from Paestum, a short distance from Heraion. Termed a "narrating museum," it houses an excellent multimedia installation describing the chance discovery of the sanctuary by two young archaeologists—Paola Zancani Montuoro and Umberto Zanotti Bianco—in the 20th century. This is where you'll learn that the cult of Hera (Juno in Latin), which was very powerful in antiquity, did not disappear with the advent of Christianity but was absorbed into Christians's devotion to the Virgin Mary. In the nearby 11th-century sanctuary of the **Madonna del Granato** (road to Capaccio Vecchia; Aug 15 only), the Madonna is depicted holding a pomegranate, the symbol for Hera/Juno.

Though famous for its archaeological area, Paestum is also a great seaside destination. If basking in the sun is your thing, **Marina di Paestum** ✦ is the place to do it, with miles of sandy **beaches;** the sea is warm and great for swimming, too.

WHERE TO STAY

In addition to the following hotels, we also recommend staying at **Il Granaio dei Casabella,** reviewed among the restaurants later in this chapter.

MODERATE

Mec Paestum 🏵🏵   This family-run luxury hotel, just steps from the beach and within walking distance of the archaeological area, is our preferred hotel in the area. Housed in a modern building, guest rooms are comfortable, large, and furnished with good taste, in a modern style. The new, spacious bathrooms all come with Jacuzzi tubs. Each room has a private small terrace with a view—often over the hotel's own private beach.

Via Tiziano 23, Località Sterpinia, 84063 Capaccio. ✆ **0828-722444.** Fax 0828-722305. www.mechotel.com. 52 units. 180€–200€ ($252–$280/£126–£140) double, from 260€ ($364/£182) suite. Rates include buffet breakfast. Children 1 and under stay free in parent's room. AE, DC, MC, V. Free parking. **Amenities:** Restaurant; bar; babysitting; business center; concierge; laundry service; outdoor pool; room service. *In room:* A/C, satellite TV, hair dryer, minibar.

Strand Hotel Schuhmann 🏵   This pleasant hotel offers beachside accommodations not far from the archaeological area. Guest rooms are quiet and well appointed, each with a balcony or a small private terrace with a view. Bathrooms are good size. Guests have access to the private beach and use of beach equipment (chairs, umbrellas, and showers). The hotel building's terrace offers wonderful views over the Gulf of Salerno and Capri.

Via Marittima, Località Laura, 84063 Capaccio. ✆ **0828-851151.** Fax 0828-851183. www.hotelschuhmann.com. 53 units. 160€ ($224/£112) double. Rates include half-board. AE, DC, MC, V. Free parking. **Amenities:** Restaurant; babysitting; beach; concierge; laundry service; lounge; room service. *In room:* A/C, TV, hair dryer, minibar.

INEXPENSIVE

Hotel Ariston 🏵   This luxury hotel is located a couple of miles from the archaeological area, in the little town of Laura. Surrounded by a garden complete with sports equipment and swimming pool, the hotel is not far from its private beach—10 minutes away on foot—but the hotel offers complimentary shuttle service and a beach bar. Guest rooms are quite spacious and come furnished with good-quality modern furniture; bathrooms are substantial and new. The hotel's **Grill Restaurant** is quite good.

Via Lauran 13, Località Laura, 84040 Capaccio. ✆ **0828-851333.** Fax 0828-851596. www.hotelariston.com. 110 units. 130€ ($182/£91) double. AE, DC, MC, V. Free parking. **Amenities:** Restaurant; bar; babysitting; basketball; billiards room; business center; concierge; health club; laundry service; outdoor pool; room service; state-of-the-art spa; soccer field; outdoor tennis court. *In room:* A/C, satellite TV, hair dryer, minibar.

Tenuta Seliano 🏵🏵   This pleasant *agriturismo* is perfect for those who like being pampered in a countryside surrounding. Set in a 19th-century hamlet, the picturesque buildings have been turned into lodgings with large, comfortable guest rooms and a decor with country-style elegance and good taste. A well-groomed garden with swimming pool and some 91 hectares (200 acres) of land complete the property, part of which is dedicated to raising buffalos (for mozzarella, of course). The excellent cuisine prepared by Mrs. Bellelli—who also offers classes—completes the service. You can choose to have all your meals at the farm, or only breakfast.

Via Seliano, in Borgo Antico (Capaccio Scalo), 84063 Paestum. ✆ **0828-723634.** Fax 0828-724544. www.agriturismo seliano.it. 14 units. 120€ ($168/£84) double. Rates include full breakfast. Children 1 and under stay free in parent's room. AE, DC, MC, V. Free parking. Closed Nov–Dec 27 and Jan 7–Feb 28. **Amenities:** Babysitting; dining room; laundry service; lounge; outdoor pool. *In room:* A/C (5€/$7/£3.50 per day), TV.

WHERE TO DINE
EXPENSIVE

Nonna Sceppa ★★ SALERNITAN   This welcoming restaurant has been growing in popularity and is now one of the best in the whole region. The menu changes seasonally but always includes well-prepared traditional dishes. Everything is homemade, from the bread and delicious pasta to the delectable local mozzarella and the desserts. The summer menu focuses on seafood and may include *rombo al forno con patate* (turbot baked over a bed of potatoes), while the winter menu highlights meat dishes, such as the traditional *tiano di carne* (ragout of sausages, pork ribs, and pork rind). We highly recommend the spaghetti *con l' aragosta* (with local lobster) and the classic and masterfully grilled catch of the day. The outdoor terrace is a pleasant incentive during fair weather.

Via Laura 53, Capaccio Scalo. ℂ **0828-851064.** www.nonnasceppa.com. Reservations recommended. Secondi 15€–22€ ($21–$31/£11–£16). AE, DC, MC, V. Fri–Wed 12:30–3pm and 7:30–10pm. Closed 3 weeks in Oct.

Ristorante Nettuno SALERNITAN   This picturesque restaurant is literally inside the ruins of Paestum, housed in a 2nd-century-B.C. tower opening onto a charming garden. Appropriate for the surroundings, the cuisine is traditional, and the menu includes both meat and fish choices. You'll find *crespoline* (savory crepe stuffed with mozzarella and ham), and excellent pasta dishes, as well as a variety of secondi.

Via Nettuno, Paestum. ℂ **0828-811028.** Reservations recommended. Secondi 15€–23€ ($21–$32/£11–£16). AE, DC, MC, V. July–Aug daily noon–3:30pm and 8–11:30pm; Sept–June Tues–Sun noon–3:30pm.

MODERATE

Il Granaio dei Casabella ★ SALERNITAN   Not far from the walls of ancient Paestum, this countryside *residenza* offers refined dining and a delightful veranda overlooking an internal garden. You may be surprised by the delicious *granatine di lardo ai frutti di mare* (little rolls of lard filled with shellfish); *gnocchi con zucca e gamberi in zimino* (potato dumplings with shrimp, pumpkin, and a spinach-and-herb sauce), or *risotto carciofi e aragosta* (rice with lobster and artichokes). For something simpler, try the grilled fish. You can also spend the night here in one of the 14 spacious and nicely appointed rooms (80€/$96/£48 double, including breakfast) located above the restaurant.

Va Tavernelle 4, across from Porta Aurea in the north wall of ancient Paestum, Marina, 84063 Paestum. ℂ **0828-721014.** Fax 0828-811893. www.ilgranaiodeicasabella.com. Reservations recommended. Secondi 12€–18€ ($17–$25/£8.40–£13). AE, DC, MC, V. Daily 12:30–3pm and 7:30–10pm.

Le Trabe ★ SALERNITAN   This is a beautiful restaurant, located in a lovely setting of gardens and streams inside a romantic old mill. The menu is seasonal and changes often, with dishes reminiscent of the local multicultural tradition (Greek, Roman, French, and so on). You may find *taccozzette gamberi e porcini mantecati al provolone* (homemade pasta with shrimp and porcini mushrooms baked with provolone cheese) or *filetto di cernia all'uva* (grouper filet with grapes), or an excellent ragout. The restaurant also has a few rooms (90€/$126/£63 double, including breakfast) to let for the night.

Via Capo di Fiume, Capaccio Scalo. ℂ **0828-724165.** www.ristoranteletrabe.com. Reservations recommended. Secondi 12€–18€ ($17–$25/£8.50–£13). AE, DC, MC, V. Daily 12:30–3pm and 7:30–10pm.

3 Padula & Certosa di San Lorenzo ★★★

98km (59 miles) SE of Salerno

Little-known to foreign tourists, the Carthusian Monastery of St. Lorenzo—one of the largest in the world—is prized for its architectural splendor and rich collection of artistic treasures. Off the beaten path in Salerno's hinterlands, this grandiose 16th-century monastery nestles in the slopes of the hill near the little town of Padula. It is an easy day trip from Salerno, Naples, or Paestum.

ESSENTIALS

GETTING THERE & AROUND   Trenitalia (② 892021 from anywhere in Italy; www.trenitalia.it) offers direct connections from Naples and Salerno to Battipaglia, where you will need to switch to a shuttle (run on schedule with the trains) to Padula and the monastery. You can also take the **bus:** From Salerno, **Lamanna** (② 0975-520426) and **Curcio Viaggi** (② 089-254080; www.curcioviaggi.it) both make runs to Padula from Piazza della Concordia near the train station. Curcio Viaggi also offers direct connection to Padula from Firenze and Siena. From Naples, **Autolinee SLA** (② 0973-21016; www.slasrl.it) offers direct service to Padula; **Simet** (② 0983-520315; www.simetspa.it) has a daily bus that leaves Piazza Garibaldi (across from Stazione Centrale) at 10am. By **car,** take the exit marked PADULA-BUONABITACOLO off the A3 to SS 19, and follow the signs for PADULA.

Padula is small and can be visited on **foot;** the monastery is at the base of the hill on the edge of town.

VISITOR INFORMATION   The local tourist office is **Associazione Pro Loco Padula,** Via Italo Balbo 45, Padula (② 0975-778611; www.prolocopadula.com). The nearest **hospital** (② 0975-312111) is in the town of Marsicovetere, a few miles east. For an **ambulance,** dial ② 118. Dial ② 113 or 112 for the **police,** ② 115 for the **fire department,** and ② 116 for **ACI road assistance.** You will find several banks in town, including a **Banco di Napoli,** Piazza Umberto I 15 (② 0975-778593).

EXPLORING PADULA & THE MONASTERY

Padula is a picturesque hill town, with interesting churches and *palazzi* lining its historic streets. The big attraction here, though, is the huge Carthusian Monastery.

Established in 1306, the monastery was enlarged over the centuries, with the last additions dating from the early 19th century. Once an extremely rich monastery, the **Certosa di San Lorenzo,** Viale Certosa 1 (② 0975-77745; Wed–Mon 9am–8pm, last admission 1 hour earlier; closed Jan 1, Aug 15, and Dec 25; 4€/$5.60/£2.80; www.magnifico.beniculturali.it/certosa.html) is a 51,500 sq. m (554,341 sq. ft.) complex of buildings and courtyards. It has 320 halls, 52 staircases, 100 fireplaces, 13 courtyards, and 41 fountains. Abandoned as a monastery in 1866, the Certosa was only recently been reopened to the public after extensive restorations, including repair from the earthquake of 1980. It is now the setting for important cultural events and international exhibits, not the least of which is the Ravello Music Festival (see chapter 7), which schedules a number of concerts on the grounds every year.

Many of the original medieval structures were redecorated in baroque style, making it one of the most important baroque works of art in Italy. The first **cloister** ★★, near the entrance to the monastery, dates from 1561 and is graced by an elegant portico and fountain. The richly decorated church boasts two magnificent wooden **choirs** ★★★

inlaid with intarsia artwork; one, created for the monks, dates from 1503, while the other, designed by Giovanni del Gallo in 1507, was meant for the lay brothers. Near the church is the original cemetery from 1552, now a **cloister.** The later, larger cemetery is in the splendid 17th-century **main cloister** ✦✦✦. The huge space focuses upon a central fountain surrounded by two levels of porticos decorated with beautiful carvings. Along the portico are the monks' secluded **"cells"**—mini-apartments of three to four rooms with private porticos, small gardens, and even a workshop/studio for some. Note the small opening for delivering food and the aperture that allowed in light, both by the entrance to the cell. You can climb to the upper floor via a beautiful **staircase** in an octagonal tower, where you'll see the **Monk's Promenade** ✦ around the cloister and the **Apartments of the Prior** ✦✦.

The **library** and **reception halls** of the monastery house an **Archeological Museum,** which holds a collection of ancient artifacts from the necropolis found nearby.

WHERE TO STAY & DINE

If you want to stay for the night, the best hotels in town are the atmospheric **Villa Cosilinum,** Corso Garibaldi, Località Sant'Eligio, 84034 Padula (© **0975-778615;** www.villacosilinum.it; 140€/$196/£98 double, including buffet breakfast), which offers elegant accommodations and an excellent **restaurant,** and the **Grand Hotel Certosa,** Viale Certosa 41; 84034 Padula (© **0975-77126;** www.certosa.it; 90€/ $126/£63 double, including breakfast), with warm hospitality, swimming pool, and a good **restaurant-pizzeria.** Two more addresses for an excellent meal are the trendier **Taverna Il Lupo,** Via Municipio (© **0975-778376;** www.tavernaillupo.it; closed Sun dinner and all day Mon) and the more traditional **do' Giulino,** Viale Certosa (© **0975-77335;** closed Wed), both serving local fare.

4 The National Park of the Cilento

110km (68 miles) S of Naples

The Cilento is Campania's loneliest wilderness, well off the beaten track and one of the least inhabited areas in Italy. The population is concentrated on the dramatically beautiful coast, while the comparatively abandoned inland area is crossed by only a few roads. Established as a national park in 1991, this is the second-largest national park in Italy, offering a variety of land- and seascapes, from the mountains of the Alburni—where you'll find some of the most interesting caves in the world—and Monte Cervati, the highest mountain in Campania, to the splendid promontory of Cape Palinuro, so justly praised by Virgil.

The Cilento is also rich in archaeological and architectural mementoes of the various civilizations that inhabited the area since prehistoric times, from the Villanovians to the Lucanians, Greeks, Romans, Byzantines, Longobards, and Normans.

ESSENTIALS

GETTING THERE   During the summer, we recommend using the **boat service** provided by **Metrò del Mare** (© **199-600700;** www.metrodelmare.com; Apr–Sept), which connects Agropoli, Acciaroli, Palinuro, and Camerota with Pozzuoli, Naples, Sorrento, Positano, Amalfi, and Salerno.

Direct **trains** link Naples and Salerno to Agropoli/Castellabate, Pisciotta/Palinuro, and Vallo della Lucania. Contact **Trenitalia** (© **892021** from anywhere in Italy; www. trenitalia.it) for fares and information.

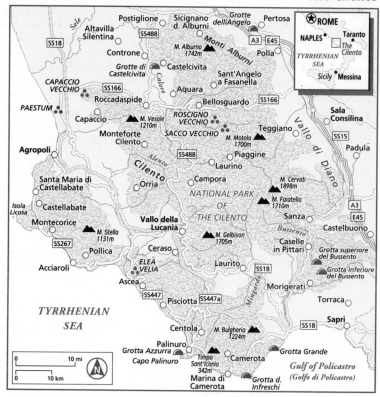

Each of the towns and villages in the park are also served by **bus** from Naples, Pompeii, Salerno, and Paestum: **CSTP,** Piazza Matteo Luciani 33, Salerno (© **800-016659** toll-free within Italy, or 089-487001; www.cstp.it), runs several lines from Napoli, Pompeii, Paestum, and Salerno to Vallo della Lucania, Agropoli, Santa Maria di Castellabate, Acciaroli, and Pollica. **Curcio Viaggi** (© **089-254080;** www.curcio viaggi.it) offers lines from Rome and Salerno to Sicignano degli Alburni, Scario, and Polla. **SCAT** (© **0974-838415**) connects Salerno and Paestum with Agropoli, Santa Maria di Castellabate, and villages along the coast in between. **Lamanna** (© **0975-520426**) offers service from Salerno to Polla. **Giuliano** (© **0974-836185**) buses cover Naples and Salerno to Roccadaspide, Agropoli, Vallo della Lucania, and Pioppi. Finally, **SITA** (© **089-226604;** www.sitabus.it) has lines from Salerno to Pertosa and Polla.

By **car,** take *autostrada* A3 to the exit marked SERRE, turning onto SS 19 toward Serre. Turn right on SS 488 following signs for ROCCA D'ASPIDE to arrive in the heart of the park.

GETTING AROUND Although frequent boat service connects the coastal villages during the summer, and frequent bus service links the various villages inside the park (above), only a **car** will provide the necessary flexibility for extensive exploration of the interior. In addition to the companies we list in chapter 2 (p. 26) and the local companies for each destination, you can rent a car through **Alba Rent Car,** Via Alcide de Gasperi; Agropoli (© **0974-828099**), **Smec,** Peppino Manente Comunale 35, Castellabate (© **0974-961565**), or our favorite, **L.T.Trasporti,** Via Colombo 11, Castellabate (© **0974-961366;** www.ltgroup.it) who also provides taxi and limo service with drivers. For **radio taxi** service call © **339-4820303.**

VISITOR INFORMATION   You'll find the **Visitor Center,** Palazzo Mainenti, Via F. Palombo 16, 84078 (© **0974-719911;** www.pncvd.it) in **Vallo della Lucania,** where the **hospital** (© **0974-711111**) is on Via Cammarota. For an **ambulance,** dial © **118.** Dial © **113** or **112** for the **police,** © **115** in case of **fire,** and © **116** for **ACI road assistance.**

AN ITINERARY IN BRIEF   If you have time for just a quick visit, we suggest a drive south along the scenic SS 18 that crosses through the park and the town of **Vallo della Lucania.** Continue down to the pretty seaside village of **Scario** (about 62km/38 miles), where you will turn back north along the coastal road to make a loop. Be sure to stay on the local road, because for the first half of the way, a newer—and much less scenic—section of SS 18 was built west of the old one.

EXPLORING THE PARK

The park covers an area of almost 180,000 hectares (450,000 acres) extending from the *autostrada* A3 to the east, the Tyrrhenian sea to the west, and encompassing the Alburni mountains to the north and Monte Cervati to the south. The park was declared part of the Biosphere Preservation program of UNESCO in 1997 for its unique natural environment, rich in rare plant species, such as the primula of Palinuro—the flower that is the symbol of the park—and the wild orchid of San Giovanni a Piro.

Entering the town of **Agropoli** (about 49km/30 miles south of Salerno), a belt of uninteresting modern construction greets you on the way to the ramp that climbs up the promontory overlooking the harbor; through the original **gate** is the **fortified medieval *borgo*** ★★ dominated by a powerful **castle** and opening onto a beautiful bay. Below are the picturesque small fishing **harbor** ★★ and a **seafront promenade** ★★. Probably founded by the Byzantines in the 5th century A.D., Agropoli was taken over by the Saracens in 882, who used it as their base until 1028, when they were chased out by the allied forces of Salerno and Capua. You can visit the partially ruined castle originally built by the Byzantines, and walk along the walls that enclose the three towers; from there you can enjoy a fantastic **view** ★★★ over the coast, stretching all the way to Punta Campanella and Capri.

Inland but nearby, some 20km (13 miles) south of Paestum, is the hill town of **Castellabate** ★, with its delightful medieval *borgo* built around a 12th-century castle. South of Castellabate, along the most scenic stretch of the local coastal road (here SS 267), you'll find charming **Acciaroli** with the adjacent medieval hamlet of **Pioppi.** Eighty kilometers (50 miles) southeast of Salerno, the fishing harbor and seaside resort of Acciaroli was the preferred hideaway of Ernest Hemingway, who stayed here several times. Built on a promontory, the village is dominated by a square defense **tower** overlooking the harbor and the pretty 12th-century **church of the Annunziata.**

A little farther south on SS 447 is **Velia** ★★, Marina di Ascea, near the Angevin Tower (© **0974-971409;** daily 9am–sunset; 2€/\$2.80/£1.40), whose archaeological ruins are far lesser known than Paestum. Excavated starting in the 1920s, **Elea** was a Greek colony created around 540 B.C. (it started out as an Italic settlement called

Caselle in Pittari

Rivers sculpted the limestone mountains of the Cilento into scenic narrow valleys. The partially soluble composition of this rock is also at the origin of geological **sinkholes**. This curious phenomenon occurs when a river suddenly descends underground, only to reemerge several miles farther. The most spectacular of all is the sinkhole created by the Bussento River, one of the largest known. The river disappears near the little town of **Caselle in Pittari** into a huge hole in the ground. The Bussento remains underground for about 6km (3¾ miles) until it surfaces a few miles south in the pretty medieval village of **Morigerati** ⚔ to resume its overland course.

Yele). The seat of the famed **Eleatic School of Philosophy,** Elea had grown into such a beacon of Greek culture by Roman times that it was allowed the privilege of maintaining Greek as its official language even after it fell under the rule of the empire and its name was changed to Velia. The Eleatic school was created by the Ionic poet and philosopher Xenophanes of Colofon, together with his pupil, the great philosopher **Parmenides,** who was the founder of metaphysics based on logic. Parmenides, who believed that the earth was a sphere at the center of the universe, passed his studies off to his disciple **Zeno of Elea** (active between 450 and 430 B.C.).

The **lower town** features portions of the walls from the 5th and 4th centuries B.C., as well as, around the south gate, houses originally from the same period but modified in Roman times. Also of note are the Roman thermal baths, with beautiful mosaics in the *Frigidarium.* From there you can climb to the famous **Porta Rosa** ⚔⚔ on a stretch of the original Greek pavement. In the **Acropolis** (the upper town), you'll find ruins of a theater, of an Ionic temple that was partially covered by a Norman castle, and of a sanctuary to Poseidon. From the Acropolis you can walk along the city walls, the northern section of which is still well preserved.

STAYING ACTIVE

GROTTOES   The **Grottoes of Castelcivita** ⚔⚔⚔ ((© 0828-975524; www.grottedi castelcivita.it) are an astounding succession of large galleries and natural halls extending for 4.8km (almost 3 miles) under the Alburni mountains. Inhabited since Paleolithic times and up until the Bronze Age, the grottoes are composed of a central section of galleries and halls, which have been fully studied and are electrically illuminated. Lateral chambers that depart from the main core have been only partially explored. Each hall is very different, some with beautiful stalactite and stalagmite formations, others with multicolored concretions, such as the so-called *Tempio* (Temple). The most spectacular are the grottoes in the farthest section, which are striking both for the beauty of the crystals and the variety of their colors. Remember to bring a jacket: Temperatures remain chilly down here, even in the summer. To reach the grottoes, follow SS 488 toward the small town of Controne; the grottoes are a few miles down the road.

Though perhaps even more magnificent than those of Castelcivita, the **Grottoes of Pertosa,** also called **Grotta dell'Angelo** ⚔⚔⚔ (© 0975-397037; www.grottedi pertosa.it; Tues–Sun 9am–5:30pm) are a bit less accessible. The grotto was inhabited in prehistoric times, with pile-dwellings during the Neolithic period, when the water level was higher, and more traditional dwellings during the Bronze and early Iron

The Cyclops

You may think that here in this paradise of hiking, spelunking, and swimming, you are far from the nightlife of the city. In fact, the legendary **Ciclope** (SS 562, Località Mingardo, Marina di Camerota; ℂ **0974-930318**; www.ilciclope.com) is a club like no other. It occupies four limestone caves of the kind that are found throughout the Cilento. Open only during the summer months, Ciclope features live music on some nights and a DJ on others. "Atmospheric" doesn't begin to cover this weird mixture of the natural and the hip. It's also not the easiest place to find, so take a cab from Marina di Camerota (below), or download directions from the club's website in advance.

Ages. The caves were kept in use during Lucanian and ancient Roman times and, again, during the Christian era, when they were consecrated in the name of Saint Michael the archangel in the 11th century.

A visit here is an adventure, starting with a ride on a raft guided by a metal wire that crosses the first cave. As the stream reaches a waterfall, you need to disembark and proceed on foot. The visit continues along the left branch of the grotto—of the two that open on your right, the first is completely submerged by the subterranean stream, and the other—the central one—is rather plain. Each subsequent hall contains marvelous formations of shapely stalactites and stalagmites, and some pure crystal accretions. To reach these grottoes, follow the signs for PERTOSA on SS 19; the parking area is a short distance off the road to the left.

HIKING   The best of the many hiking trails in the park ascend Monte Cervati (1,898m/6,225 ft.), and Monte Alburno (1,742m/5,714 ft.). **Monte Alburno** ★★★ is nicknamed Mount Panorama for the sweeping views you can enjoy from the top. Climb up one of two trails from **Sicignano degli Alburni,** a town off SS 19 not far from Serre. The first trail climbs directly up to the western peak; the second leads to a fork at 1,400m (4,600 ft.), where one branch heads east and the other west. Allow at least 4 hours for either climb.

The region's highest mountain is **Monte Cervati** ★★★. Cervati is a dramatic sight, especially in the summer, when its extensive lavender fields are in bloom. You can make the ascent via two different trails, both starting from the town of **Sanza,** on SS 517. Allow about 6 hours for either.

BEACHES   The National Park extends all the way to the shore, where the mountains drop into the sea—creating a dramatic coastline of high cliffs and small coves interspersed by lovely beaches. Popular with Italians in the summer, the Cilento offers many opportunities for seaside activities. **Santa Maria di Castellabate** ★★, about 19km (12 miles) south of Paestum, is blessed with two beautiful beaches. The one to the north—the largest—has unusually fine sand, while the smaller one to the south enjoys the proximity of a shady pine grove. The whole stretch of sea here is a **Biological Protected Area and Marine Park** which affords some interesting **snorkeling** and **scuba diving.** We recommend you head for the **Centro Subaqueo,** Via Marina Castellabate (ℂ **0974-961060**), the best operator on the whole coast, for guides and equipment.

A bit farther south is **Palinuro** ★★★, a fishing and resort harbor set among olive groves in a picturesque bay protected by a promontory. Take a walk to the lighthouse, where you can enjoy a sweeping panorama, or, even better, sign up for a **boat tour** of the point. From the water, you can see several grottoes in the cliffs, and even visit the most beautiful of them, the **Grotta Azzurra** 🏵🏵. This blue grotto is far less mobbed than its more famous cousin in Capri, yet it also takes on a wonderful coloration, especially around noon and sunset. You'll find boats with or without crew for rent in the harbor; we recommend **Cooperativa dei Pescatori** (℃ **0974-931233**). The little fishing harbor and seaside town of **Marina di Camerota** 🏵🏵 can be reached by sea in about 1½ hours. This resort is beloved by locals for its pristine coastline and variety of sandy or rocky beaches—such as **Baia della Calanca** 🏵—as well as its coves, grottoes, towers, and great scuba-diving. Located about 10km (6 miles) south of Palinuro, it is also accessible by road, along the scenic SS 562.

WHERE TO STAY

In addition to the hotels reviewed below and the rooms recommended in the next section, we highly recommend staying—and eating—at an ecofriendly *agriturismo*. Serving organic food from their own farm, **Al Castello** 🏵, Piazzetta XI Novembre 3, Morigerati (℃ **0974-982085**; 75€/$105/£53 double), is in the ancient *borgo* of Morigerati. At **Agriturismo Zito–Acqua della Battaglia,** Contrada Acqua della Battaglia, 84029 Sicignano degli Alburni (℃ **0828-973790**; agriturismozito@tiscalinet. it; 70€/$98/£49 double), you can take riding lessons or arrange tours. **Azienda Agrituristica Sicinius,** Contrada Piedi la Serra 22, Frazione Scorzo, 84029 Sicignano degli Alburni (℃/fax **0828-973763**; www.sicinius.com; 52€/$73/£36 double), offers hiking tours and organic produce. **La Bussentina,** Contrada Agno, 84030 Sanza (℃ **0975-322527**; fax 0975-322250; 50€/$70/£35 double), is located in a particularly panoramic location. We also suggest **La Sontina,** Contrada Verlingieri, 84030 Sanza (℃ **0975-322346**; 55€/$77/£39 double), and **Il Giardino dei Ciliegi,** Località Vesolo Contrada Matina, 84030 Sanza (℃ **0975-322344**; 50€/$70/£35 double).

MODERATE

Hotel America 🏵 *Kids*   This pleasant family-run hotel is located in a nice spot surrounded by olive trees and offers good amenities. Public spaces are large and welcoming, and amenities include a garden, a playground for children, and a swimming pool. Guest rooms are spacious and bright, with colorful tiled floors, simple quality furnishings, and large and modern bathrooms. Most have sea views and open onto private small terraces.

Via Bolivar 45, 848–4059 Marina di Camerota. ℃ **0974-932131.** Fax 0974-932177. www.americahotel.it. 54 units. 190€–200€ ($266–$280/£133–£140) double. AE, DC, MC, V. Free parking. Closed Oct–Mar. **Amenities:** Restaurant; bar; beach w/shuttle service (12€/$17/£8.50 per day); concierge; garden; outdoor pool; terrace. *In room:* A/C, satellite TV, hair dryer, minibar.

Il Faro *Kids*   Right by a large white-sand beach, this modern hotel has vowed to redeem its own construction with a proactive ecological policy that includes solar panels, water- and energy-saving bulbs and appliances, as well as routine recycling and choice of low-impact building materials and furnishings. Guest rooms are spacious, warm, and bright, with modern furnishings in light-colored wood and tiled floors. Most open onto their private balcony or small terrace; bathrooms are modern and good size. Hotel services are geared toward families, with children's activities, a playground, and access to a fully equipped kitchen that is equipped for making food for baby.

Via Nicotera 151, Pollica, 84041 Acciaroli. Summer ℃ **097-4904389.** Fax 0974-904709. Winter ℃/fax 089-220431. www.hotelilfaro.it. 59 units. 156€–172€ ($218–$241/£109–£121) double. Special discounts for families. AE, DC,

MC, V. Free parking. **Amenities:** Restaurant; bar; beach (8€–13€/$11–$18/£5.50–£9 per day for umbrella and chairs); children's activities July–Aug; concierge; garden; playground. *In room:* A/C (7€/$9.80/£4.90 per day), satellite TV, hair dryer, minibar, safe.

Villa Sirio ✦ In an elegant atmosphere matched by punctilious service, this historic residence is by the sea yet right in the heart of town. Guest rooms are lovely, large, and bright, and decorated with colorful tiled floors, wrought-iron beds, and period furnishings. Most have their own private balconies overlooking the sea. Bathrooms are nicely tiled and modern.

Via Lungomare De Simone 15, 84072 Santa Maria di Castellabate. © 0974-961099. Fax 0974-960507. www.villasirio.it. 15 units. 240€–280€ ($336–$392/£168–£196) double, including buffet breakfast; half-board 290€–330€ ($406–$462/£203–£230) double required for 10 days in Aug. AE, DC, MC, V. Parking 8€ ($11/£5.50). **Amenities:** Restaurant; piano bar; beach; concierge; solarium. *In room:* A/C, satellite TV, minibar, safe.

INEXPENSIVE

Albergo Santa Caterina ✦ The best hotel in Palinuro, this welcoming hotel is located right in the heart of town. Housed in an elegant building, it offers pleasant public spaces and nicely appointed pastel-colored guest rooms, decorated with hand-painted Vietri tiles. The rooms are not large, but most open onto pleasant balconies and small terraces, and the smallish bathroom are scrupulously clean. The hotel requires half-board from the end of July to the end of August.

Via Indipendenza 53, 84064 Palinuro. © 0974-931019. Fax 0974-938325. www.albergosantacaterina.com. 20 units. 115€–147€ ($161–$206/£81–£103) double; half-board 200€–240€ ($280–$336/£140–£168) required in Aug. AE, DC, MC, V. Free parking. **Amenities:** Restaurant; bar; concierge; room service; panoramic terrace. *In room:* A/C, satellite TV, hair dryer, minibar.

La Colombaia ✦✦ This charming building—formerly a private villa—is surrounded by olive groves and overlooks the sea from its perch atop a cliff. The elegant family-run small hotel offers quiet and well appointed accommodations, all with sea views. Guest rooms, with pastel-colored walls and tiled floors, are tastefully furnished with antiques and period furniture. Bathrooms are small but well kept. There is a 2-day minimum stay requirement.

Via La Vecchia 2, Piano delle Pere, 84043 Agropoli. ©/fax 0974-821800. www.lacolombaiahotel.it. 10 units. 100€ ($140/£70) double. Rates include breakfast. MC, V. Free parking. Closed Nov–Mar. **Amenities:** Restaurant; bar; concierge; gardens; Internet point; outdoor pool; Wi-Fi. *In room:* A/C, hair dryer, minibar, safe, satellite TV, Wi-Fi.

La Mola ✦ Housed in a villa enjoying a commanding position over the sea, this elegant B&B offers quiet and romantic accommodations. Guest rooms are tasteful, with terra-cotta floors, wrought-iron beds, and antique or period furnishings. Bathrooms are modern and relatively large. Each room opens onto a private balcony with a view.

Via A. Cilento 2, 84048 Castellabate. © 0974-967053. Fax 0974-967714; www.lamola-it.com. 5 units. 114€ ($160/£80) double; 124€ ($174/£87) suite. Rates include breakfast. AE, DC, MC, V. Free parking. **Amenities:** Restaurant (dinner for guests by reservation); bar; Internet point. *In room:* TV, minibar, safe.

La Playa ✦ This is one of our favorite hotels in the area, with a beautiful location by the sea, a welcoming atmosphere, and tasteful decor. Amenities include a private beach with umbrellas and chairs, an organic restaurant, and a free shuttle to the hotel's saltwater farm and nature preserve, Tenuta degli Eremi, where you can hike or take a donkey excursion to the national preserve. The hotel is made up of two buildings flanking an interior garden: The one overlooking the sea offers the best rooms, with A/C but no elevator, while the other offers garden views and an elevator, but only fans in the rooms. Bedrooms are large and bright, all with private terraces equipped with table and chairs. Bathrooms are spacious and modern.

Via Nicotera 135, 84041 Acciaroli. © 097-4904002. Fax 0974-904225. www.hotellaplaya.it. 83 units. 110€ ($154/£77) double including breakfast; full board 208€ ($291/£146) double and 1 week minimum stay required for 2 weeks in Aug (dates vary). AE, DC, MC, V. Free parking. **Amenities:** Restaurant; bar; beach; children's activities; concierge; garden w/playground; gym; shuttle to organic farm. *In room:* A/C or fan, satellite TV, hair dryer, minibar.

WHERE TO DINE

In addition to the following dining opportunities, we suggest eating at the restaurants mentioned in "Where to Stay," above.

MODERATE

Da Carmine ✿ CILENTAN/SEAFOOD   Located right on the beach near Castellabate, Da Carmine prepares its excellent dishes according to "the Mediterranean diet": with unsaturated fats (olive oil), seafood, and plenty of fresh seasonal vegetables. The establishment also has a few tastefully appointed guest rooms, most of them with sea views (100€/$140/£70 double with breakfast; 160€/$224/£112 double with half-board, required in Aug).

Via Ogliastro Marina, Ogliastro Marina, 84060 Castellabate. © **0974-963023.** Fax 0974-963900. www.albergoda carmine.it. Reservations recommended on weekends. Secondi 10€–18€ ($14–$25/£7–£13). AE, DC, MC, V. Wed–Mon 12:30–3pm and 7:30–10:30pm.

Il Ceppo CILENTAN/SEAFOOD   This local favorite has been a reliable choice for decades. The pleasant atmosphere and friendly professional service matches the quality of the food. The menu focuses on traditional dishes, such as the delicious *tagliolini con gamberi, fiori di zucca e vongole* (fresh pasta with clams, shrimp, and zucchini flowers) and the excellent catch of the day cooked in a salt crust until perfectly moist and savory. Attached to the restaurant is a small modern hotel offering 20 well-furnished, comfortable rooms, a pretty garden, and a shuttle to the beach (85€–95€/$119–$133/£60–£67 double, including breakfast).

Via Madonna del Carmine 31, 84043 Agropoli. © **0974-843036.** Fax 0974-843234. www.hotelristoranteilceppo. com. Reservations recommended on weekends. Secondi 10€–21€ ($14–$29/£7–£15). AE, DC, MC, V. Wed–Mon 12:30–3pm and 7:30–10:30pm; daily in Aug.

INEXPENSIVE

La Chioccia d'Oro ✿ CILENTAN   This is the place to come for a hearty and well prepared meal. The warm welcome and the enticing menu combine for a perfect—if unsophisticated—dining experience. We highly recommend the wonderful fresh pasta, which is strictly homemade. We loved the lasagna, which was rich and perfectly baked, and the excellent grilled meats. The homemade desserts are good, and so is the local house wine.

Via Biblio di Novi Velia, Vallo della Lucania. © **0974-70004.** Reservations recommended. Secondi 8€–16€ ($11–$22/£5.50–£11). MC, V. Tues–Sun 12:30–3pm and 7:30–10pm. Closed 2 weeks in Sept.

La Taverna del Pescatore CILENTAN/SEAFOOD   This popular tavern is where locals come for very well-prepared seafood. The menu includes local specialties as well as a choice of daily dishes depending on market offerings. If it is available, we highly recommend the splendid *zuppa di pesce* (fish stew); rich with local fresh seafood, it is a meal on its own. The risotto *alla pescatora* (with seafood) is another winner.

Via Lamia, 84062 Castellabate. © **0974-968293.** Reservations recommended. Secondi 11€–18€ ($15–$25/ £7.70–£13). MC, V. Tues–Sun noon–3pm and 7–11pm; closed Nov–Mar.

La Taverna do' Scuorzo CILENTAN   Popular among locals on weekends, this restaurant offers a traditional menu in a pleasant atmosphere. We recommend the fresh pasta—the lasagna is excellent—followed by some of the grilled specialties: from savory caciocavallo and porcini mushrooms (in season), to juicy local meats and splendid sausages. The homemade desserts are also quite good.

Via Nazionale 139, 84029 Sicignano degli Alburni. ℂ **082-8978050.** Reservations recommended on weekends. Secondi 8€–16€ ($11–$22/£5.50–£11). AE, DC, MC, V. Wed–Mon 12:30–3pm and 7:30–10pm.

Ristorante Hotel Grotte Cafaro ⊕ CILENTAN   Not far from the entrance to the Grottoes of Pertosa, this welcoming family restaurant is a local favorite for the superiority of its cuisine and its genuine ingredients. The menu is seasonal, and the chef prides himself on his knowledge of the local culinary tradition. We particularly love the homemade cavatelli *con asparagi* (with wild asparagus) and the *porcini e caciocavallo alla griglia* (charbroiled porcini mushrooms and local cheese). The bread and desserts are always fresh and homemade. The restaurant also offers 18 simply appointed but pleasant guest rooms, and organizes fresh pasta–making classes on request. If you stay at the hotel or eat at the restaurant, you get a discount (up to 2€ off) on your ticket for the grottoes.

Via Muraglione 33, 84030 Pertosa. ℂ **0975-397045.** Fax 0975-397043. www.hotelgrotte.it. Reservations recommended. Secondi 8€–16€ ($11–$22/£5.50–£11). MC, V. Fri–Wed 12:30–3pm and 7:30–10pm.

Taverna Degli Antichi Sapori ⊕ CILENTAN   Priding itself on the quality of its natural—and strictly local—ingredients, and on their family recipes, this local favorite offers a sound seasonal menu. We highly recommend Controne beans, a sort of particularly flavorful pinto bean that is a local staple. They are served in a variety of traditional ways—with porcini mushrooms, with homemade pasta, and simply stewed. If beans are not your thing, try the savory fresh pasta (the ravioli are excellent) or the grilled meat.

Via Nazionale 27, Controne. ℂ **0828-772500.** Reservations recommended on weekends. Secondi 9€–16€ ($13–$22/£6.50–£11). AE, DC, MC, V. Wed–Mon noon–3pm and 8–11pm.

Zi' Filomena ⊕ CILENTAN/PIZZA   We like this welcoming family-run restaurant for its down-to-earth atmosphere and good food. The ample menu includes many local favorites and traditional dishes. We recommend the fresh cavatelli, the roasted lamb, and the excellent pizza (served only in the evening). Do not skip dessert, or the local house wine.

Via Roma, Caselle in Pittari. ℂ **097-4988024.** Reservations recommended on weekends. Secondi 8€–18€ ($11–$25/£5.50–£13). AE, DC, MC, V. Tues–Sun 12:30–3pm and 7:30–10:30pm.

10

Campania's Well-Kept Secrets: Caserta, Benevento & Avellino

Many of Campania's best spots remain mysteriously unknown to most foreign tourists and even to many Italian ones; the tranquil, yet lively, towns of Caserta, Benevento, and Avellino are at the top of that list. Yet, Caserta's Royal Palace (the *Reggia,* as it is called locally) matches its more famous cousin in Versailles for beauty and grandeur, and Benevento's ancient Roman arch happens to be the most well-preserved on earth.

These attractions probably owe their semi-forgotten state to their location away from the main train lines and highways. They are also close enough to Naples and the Amalfi Coast that they're easily sidestepped. As a result, they remain quiet, little visited towns, although they are worth a trip all by themselves.

1 Caserta

17km (11 miles) NW of Naples

The busy town of Caserta lies only a few miles north of Naples. Of uncertain origin—Sannite, Roman, or even Longobard, who would have moved here from Capua in the 13th century—it was only a small, provincial town in medieval times. Everything changed with the arrival of the Bourbons in the 18th century. The new king decided to move his capital here from Naples, and Caserta suddenly appeared on international maps. The palace he built was explicitly meant to rival Versailles. The actual town of Caserta (today Caserta Vecchia) was nearly abandoned, and a new town developed around the *Reggia* to serve the needs of the court. The king also gave new breath to the local economy, creating a small silk industry in nearby San Leucio. Today, Caserta is an important agro-industrial center, serving its fertile environs. The modern town has enlarged to merge with two much older settlements, Capua and the small town known as Santa Maria Capua Vetere. The latter was the former Roman Capua, a glorious major city that was second only to Rome. What is called Capua today, instead, is the Roman harbor on the Volturno River, known in Roman times as Casilinium.

ESSENTIALS

GETTING THERE   Caserta is easily reached by train from Naples. Trains leave Napoli Stazione Centrale every 10 to 20 minutes for the 30-minute trip to Caserta. Contact **Trenitalia** (© **892021** from anywhere in Italy; www.trenitalia.it) for fares and information. Trains arrive at Caserta's **railway station** in Piazza Giuseppe Garibaldi 1 (© **0823-325479**), only a few steps from the Reggia, on the other side of Piazza Carlo III.

Caserta is also easily reached **by car,** from either Rome or Naples; from autostrada A1 take the exit marked CASERTA NORD, and follow the signs for CASERTA CENTRO. Coming into town, you will see signs for SAN LEUCIO, CASERTA VECCHIA, and REGGIA.

GETTING AROUND   The Reggia is too distant from Caserta's other attractions to reach them on foot, but they can be easily reached by taxi. You can walk to one of the two taxi stands in town, one on Piazza Garibaldi across from the train station (© **0823-322400**), and one on Via Ferrara (© **0823-326919**) or call them by phone.

The Reggia is in the center of the new town, near the train station, while the medieval town is about 10km (6 miles) up the hill that overlooks the new town to the east, and is easily reached by **car** via the road that starts off Via Medaglie d'Oro: Follow the signs reading CASERTAVECCHIA. San Leucio is on top of a smaller hill at the northern outskirts of town, off the Via Provinciale (from Piazza Vanvitelli, proceed north following the signs for San Leucio). Santa Maria Capua Vetere and Capua are respectively 6.5km (4 miles) and 11km (6½ miles) west of the Reggia.

VISITOR INFORMATION   The **EPT information office** is on Piazza Dante at the corner with Via Douhet (© **0823-321137;** www.casertaturismo.it). It is open Monday to Saturday from 9am to 7pm.

FAST FACTS   You'll find a **pharmacy,** Corso Trieste 47 (© **0823-326147**), not far from the entrance to the Reggia. The **hospital** *(ospedale civile)* is nearby, at Via Tescione Gennaro 1 (© **0823-304964**); dial © **118** or © **0823-321000** for an **ambulance.** You can call the **police** at © **113** or **112,** and the **fire department** at © **115.** The **post office** on Via del Redentore 27, off Via Giuseppe Mazzini (© **0823-550634**), is open Monday to Saturday from 8am to 2pm.

EXPLORING THE TOWN

The Reggia di Caserta ✦✦✦   One of the most beautiful royal palaces in the world, the Reggia is a masterpiece of harmonious architecture and decorative arts. (If you experience déjà vu during your visit, it may be because the Reggia was used as a location for *Star Wars: Episode I—The Phantom Menace*).

When King Carlo III Bourbon decided to leave Naples which he considered too open to attacks from the sea, he asked his architect Luigi Vanvitelli to build him a palace that could rival the courts of Paris, London, and Madrid. Vanvitelli dedicated the last 20 years of his life to the construction, for which he used the best materials and workmanship available in the country. The Reggia was finally finished 1 year after the architect's death in 1774, but its interior was not fully completed until 1847. The palace is grandiose, measuring over 45,000 sq. m (484,376 sq. ft.), and divided into four wings, each surrounding a separate courtyard.

A visit starts in the very scenic main gallery, where the view stretches all the way to the end of the park and the majestic waterfall (below). You then climb the splendid main **staircase** ✦✦ to a magnificent **octagonal vestibule,** all decorated with precious marble in various colors. The scale of it is almost stupefying: There are 116 stairs, flanked by niches containing sculptures that allude to the grandeur of the kingdom. We love the two sculpted lions by Pietro Solari and Paolo Persico, which are among the most familiar symbols of the Reggia.

The **Palatine Chapel** ✦ opens onto the vestibule. Like everything else at the Reggia, it has imposing dimensions (37m/120 ft. long). Inside, over the entrance, you will

Caserta

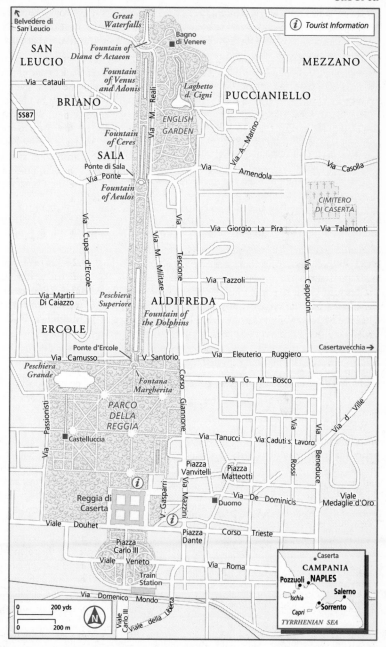

Belvedere di
San Leucio

Great
Waterfalls

Bagno
di Venere

(i) Tourist Information

SAN
LEUCIO

Fountain of
Diana & Actaeon

MEZZANO

Via Catauli

Fountain
of Venus
and Adonis

BRIANO

Laghetto
d. Cigni

PUCCIANIELLO

SS87

ENGLISH
GARDEN

Fountain
of Ceres

SALA

Via A. Marino

Via Casolla

Ponte di Sala

Via
Amendola

Via Ponte

Via M. Reali

Fountain
of Aeulos

CIMITERO
DI CASERTA

Via Cupa d'Ercole

Via Giorgio La Pira

Via Talamonti

Via M. Militare

Via Tescione

Via Tazzoli

Via Martiri
Di Caiazzo

Peschiera
Superiore

ALDIFREDA

Via Cappucini

ERCOLE

Fountain of
the Dolphins

Ponte d'Ercole

Via Camusso

V. Santorio

Via Eleuterio Ruggiero

Casertavecchia →

Peschiera
Grande

Fontana
Margherita

Via G. M. Bosco

Corso Giannone

Via d. Ville

Via Passionisti

PARCO
DELLA
REGGIA

Via Tanucci

Via Caduti s. Lavoro

Via Rossi

Via Beneduce

Castelluccia

Piazza
Vanvitelli

Piazza
Matteotti

(i)

Via Gasparri

Via De Dominicis

Viale
Medaglie d'Oro

Reggia di
Caserta

V. Gasparri

Via Mazzini

Duomo

Viale Douhet

(i)

Piazza
Dante

Corso Trieste

Piazza
Carlo III

Via Roma

Viale Veneto

Train
Station

Viale
Carlo III

Via Domenico Mondo

Viale della Libertà

Caserta

CAMPANIA

Pozzuoli NAPLES

Salerno

Ischia

Capri Sorrento

TYRRHENIAN SEA

0 200 yds
0 200 m

N

277

see the royal box from which the king and queen observed services, while on the main altar you can see the wood model of the ciborium that was never built. Some of the 13 columns defining the gallery still show the damage from the 1943 bombings. (*Note:* The chapel was closed for restoration at presstime.) Also opening onto the vestibule, to the left of the main staircase, are the **Royal Apartments** ★★. The decorations in the *appartamento nuovo* ("new" apartment) date from the early 19th century, with stuccoes, bas-reliefs, and frescoes. Of the several halls, we like the **Sala di Marte** ★, celebrating military virtues through nine bas-reliefs by Valerio Villareale and a large ceiling fresco by Antonio Galliano depicting mythological scenes from Virgil's *Iliad*. Nearby is the **Throne Room,** which was inaugurated in 1845; it dazzles with gild stucco and 46 medallions depicting all the kings of Naples, from the Norman Roger I to Ferdinand II.

The visit continues through the so-called *appartamento vecchio* ("old" apartment), inaugurated by Ferdinando IV and his wife Maria Carolina of Austria in 1780. Beautifully furnished and decorated with frescoes, these were the private rooms of the queen and king. First come the "conversation rooms," decorated according to seasonal themes by Antonio Dominici (*Primavera* and *Autunno,* or spring and fall) and Fedele Fischetti (*Estate* and *Inverno*—summer and winter). Spring and summer make up the receiving room and sitting room, respectively, while fall is the dining room, and winter is the smoking room. After these come the bedroom, the king's study, and the queen's parlor. Our favorite furnishings here are the magnificent **Murano glass chandeliers** ★★ and the **carved chairs and sofas** ★, masterpieces of neoclassical Italian furniture by Nicola and Pietro Di Fiore. The **paintings** are by **Jacob Philipp Hackert** ★, a court painter who was kept very busy by the Bourbons. Goethe called him an "inveterate hard worker," who not only painted prolifically but gave drawing lessons to the royal children and delivered lectures. We particularly like his scenes of the kingdom's harbors in the receiving room, as well as the depictions of royal sites in the king's study. Finally, you'll come to the three rooms of the **library**—notice the frescoes in the third room by Friederich Heinrich Függer, said to contain hidden Masonic meanings, a subject which deeply interested the queen—and to an oval hall which contains the magnificent *presepe reale* (**royal manger scene**) ★★.

Through a side door from the octagonal vestibule near the main staircase, you can access the permanent exhibit **Terrae Motus** ★, composed of over 70 pieces by Italian and foreign contemporary artists—there is even a piece by Andy Warhol and one by Keith Haring—in reaction to the terrible earthquake that shook Campania in 1980.

Back on the ground floor at the end of the main gallery, you come out onto the Reggia's magnificent **park** ★★★. Covering about 120 hectares (296 acres), it is not only enormous, but simply the most celebrated of Italian gardens in the world. The park stretches from the palace to the nearby hills along a central path 3.2km (2 miles) long, graced by a number of fountains, pools, and gardens. A majestic waterfall created by Luigi Vanvitelli cascades from the hills at the end of the park. To fulfill the needs of the palace, he designed an aqueduct to carry water all the way from Monte Taburno, 40km (25 miles) away. The waterfall was the point of arrival of the aqueduct—which he named Caroline Acqueduct after the queen. Today, the water for the fountains is recirculated thanks to pumps, while the aqueduct feeds the town's supply.

Among the fountains depicting mythical events, the most spectacular is the **Fountain of Eolus** ★★, a large construction of grottoes and figures representing the palace of the wind god. Above it and up the hill is a system of **three fountains** ★ feeding into each other, Fountain of Ceres, Fountain of Venus and Adonis, and Fountain of Diana and Atteon. This last is the highest, and we recommend climbing up to it for the superb **view** ★. To the right of this last fountain is the entrance to the **English Garden,** created for Queen Maria Carolina di Borbone by the son of the architect, Carlo Vanvitelli. The Italian architect designed the garden while English botanist and landscape artist Andrea Graefer, created the plant arrangements. Covering over 30 hectares (74 acres), it is a perfect romantic realization, with a lake, a spring, and a small temple, all decorated with ancient Roman statues taken from the ruins of Pompeii. The queen also indulged her infatuation with the Masons here, and the garden is full of hidden symbols and esoteric references. It is accessible only by guided tour.

We recommend taking the horse-carriage tour, which is relatively short, but very romantic. Don't expect it to take you all the way to the top, as the climb is too steep for the horses; the carriages U-turn by the Fountain of Eolus. Another interesting tour is offered on weekend nights June through October. Called **Percorsi di Luce nella Reggia (Paths of Light in the Reggia)** ★ (✆ **0823-4480840** or 0823-462078; www. percorsidiluce.it), it uses music, visual, and performing arts to help the visitor discover the Reggia, the famous gardens, and the kings that inhabited it. The tours are narrated by art historians and accompanied by light effects, 18th-century music, short performances, and multimedia presentations. Started in 2003, this event is scheduled only a year at a time, and cancellation is always threatened due to lack of funds. Make reservations well in advance (admission is 18€/$25/£13; children 5 and under free). Regular guided tours with professional art historians are offered daily during opening hours by **Arethusa** (✆ **0823-448084;** www.arethusa.net); tours are 3.60€ ($5/£2.50) for the 1½-hour visit.

Note: A visit to the palace (and even more so the park) involves extensive walking. The palace is wheelchair accessible through a private elevator in back of the ticket booth; calling in advance is best, but you can also inquire upon arrival. A shuttle bus is provided between the palace to the Fountain of Diane and the entrance of the English Gardens; pay and sign up for the bus at the ticket booth.

You will find a cafeteria inside the Reggia, at the end of the main gallery just before the exit to the gardens; it is open nonstop during visiting hours. In summer, you'll find a temporary snack bar at the entrance to the English Gardens. However, it is a good idea to carry your own water if you are planning a lengthy exploration of the park.

Viale Douhet. (✆ **0823-277430** or 0823-277111. www.reggiadicaserta.org. Admission to apts 4.50€ ($6.30/£3.15); gardens 2.50€ ($3.50/£1.75); both 6€ ($8.40/£4.20). Audioguides 3.50€ ($4.90/£2.45). Guided tours 3.60€ ($5/£2.50). Bus shuttle to Diana Fountain 1€ ($1.40/70p) round-trip. Horse carriage to Eolus's Fountain 10€ ($12/£6) per person round-trip. Royal Apartments: Wed–Mon 8:30am–7:30pm; last admission 30 min. earlier. Park: Wed–Mon 8:30am–sunset; last admission 2 hr. earlier. English Gardens: Guided tours every hour 9:30am to 3 hr. before sunset.

Casertavecchia ★★
This medieval *borgo* is one of the better-preserved in all Italy. When the king built his palace in the valley below he required a large part of the population to move there as well, abandoning the town. Dominated by a castle that is today in ruins, the village is built around the **cathedral** ★★, a fine example of Norman-Arab architectural style. Dedicated to St. Michael, it was built by the Normans in the 12th century, using paleochristian elements as well as material from a nearby temple to Jupiter. The church is built of tufa stone—like the rest of the town—with delicate highlights in white marble: the three portals, the window frames, the decorative columns, and a number of zoomorphic sculptures. The dome is covered by a beautiful *tiburio*—roofed tower—where the Arab influence is readily visible. The

octagonal structure has geometric designs in alternate yellow and gray tufa stone, with an ornate intertwining of arches supported by little white columns. Inside you can admire the altar encrusted in mosaic, and the baptismal font from the 4th century. The handsome facade is completed by a 13th-century bell tower, under which passes the main street of the town; it is topped by an octagonal roof and decorated in similar fashion to the cathedral.

Behind the Duomo, on the main street, is the **Chiesetta dell'Annunziata,** a Gothic church built at the end of the 13th century; the portico was added in the 18th century, but behind it you can admire the original facade with the beautiful marble portal. Farther on is the 11th-century **Norman Castle;** most of its original structure—a central core with six towers—is in ruins, but the powerful main tower remains.

Do take the time to stroll through the *borgo*'s narrow medieval streets, admiring their original paving and the well-preserved medieval decorative details of the buildings and stone archways. Not surprisingly, the town is a favorite dinner destination for locals, who come to enjoy the food, the view, and the atmosphere, especially during warm weather and on weekends. Between the last Monday of August and September 15, Casertavecchia hosts a well-established music and art festival, **Settembre al Borgo** (www.casertamusica.com), and the *borgo* comes alive with concerts, theater, and dance.

Strada Provinciale per Casertavecchia. Duomo: Piazza Vescovado. ✆ 0823-371318. Duomo and Chiesetta: Free admission. Daily 9am–1pm and 3:30–6pm; till 7:30pm in summer.

San Leucio 🏵 To make the colony economically independent, the king promoted the production and manufacture of silk, establishing a silkworm farm and a weaving factory. Following principles that are quite radical even by today's standards (p. 281), the king endowed the colony—with the help of his liberal minister Bernardo Tanucci—with completely innovative laws and organization. Education was obligatory and free from the age of 6 up, and only those skilled in their jobs were allowed to marry and have children. There was no distinction between sexes, and every manufacturer had to contribute a portion of its gains to the common fund for those who became invalids from poor health or old age. The factory became famous for its precious fabrics, exporting its products far and wide. The farm has disappeared today, but the weaving factory is still operating (privately, under the Stabilimento Serico De Negri) and the craft is still alive, with expert artisans weaving damasks, brocades, and other fabrics of international reputation.

Opening onto **Piazza della Seta,** the original colony is very scenic, with ordered rows of houses offering beautiful views over the Reggia and the surroundings. The small **church** preexisted the hamlet and is probably of Longobard origin. Following a small road to the right past the building that housed the silk factory, you will find the **Casino Reale di Belvedere,** a small (compared to the Reggia) palace in the delightful green surroundings of a park. This was the king's hunting lodge, beyond which starts the royal hunting preserve that is connected to the park of the Reggia. In the casino are the **Royal Apartments** 🏵🏵, richly frescoed with **allegoric scenes** on the ceilings painted by Fedele Fischetti; those in the queen's bathroom are by Philipp Hackert. The view from the **Belvedere** 🏵🏵 is superb. The casino contains original weaving machinery that is still in working order—you can ask to see one functioning—as part of the **Museo della Seta (Silk Museum),** which also displays many examples of the wonderful original fabrics that were produced.

The Radical Philosophy of Gaetano Filangeri

Gaetano Filangeri, the mind behind the inventive Bourbon King Ferdinando IV, was an important 18th-century Neapolitan jurist and philosopher. Little-known to most, he was in frequent correspondence with Benjamin Franklin during the years of the American Revolution and the elaboration of the American Constitution. Franklin obtained several copies of Filangeri's main work, the six-volume *The Science of Legislation,* and tried to include some of the principles in the U.S. Constitution.

Born near Naples in 1752 as Prince of Arianello, Filangeri was an encyclopedist and a reformer; his work was central to the birth of a liberal movement in southern Italy, and some of his ideas continue to be rediscovered to our own day. He was particularly strong on public education, which he believed to be the foundation of everything, leading to happy, healthy, satisfied citizens. Hence he considered that public education was also the foundation of public tranquillity. Among his other ideas, he believed that honesty was the primary social virtue, and that merit should be the only distinction among individuals . . . ideas as much in need today as in his own time.

Filangeri's work was cut short by his early death in 1788, and the sixth volume is only an outline. However, the other volumes have been translated into English, French, German, and Spanish.

The road that leads toward the left from below the steps of the original silk factory on Piazza della Seta climbs to the **Hunting Lodge** of the Aquaviva princes, the original owners of the estate; nearby is the **Vaccheria,** the stables where Ferdinand established the colony's first weaving activity before he built the village.

Piazza della Seta, off Strada Statale SS87. ℂ **800-411515** or 0823-301817. 6€ ($8.40/£4.20). Wed–Mon winter 9:30am–6pm, summer 9:30am–6:30pm. Closed Jan 1, Easter, Aug 15, and Dec 24–25.

2 Santa Maria Capua Vetere & the Anfiteatro Campano

6.5km (4 miles) W of Caserta and 24km (15 miles) NW of Naples

Capua is a bit like the mythical phoenix, cyclically achieving greatness and splendor, only to be destroyed down to the ground. Starting as a small Oscan (one of the local Italic populations) village, Capua was transformed into a town by the Etruscans in 589 B.C., and then taken over by the Sannites (the Italic population of the Benevento region) in 438 B.C. Located in a fertile area, Capua grew rapidly to become—in the words of Roman historian Livy—the richest and largest town in Italy outside of Rome. The city, though, committed the mistake of trying to go its own way, and Rome punished it with complete political annihilation in 211 B.C. Only in 89 B.C. did the Romans decide to rebuild a colony here, and the town rapidly grew to become the second-most significant city in the empire once more. The Via Appia, *regina viarum* (queen of all roads) of the ancient Romans, was created to unite Rome and Capua; it was the first large road the Romans built (the 1st "consular" road, as they are still locally called) and was later extended all the way to Brindisi, the harbor on the eastern Apulian coast. This was the highway for transporting precious goods from Asia, and Capua was a major stop.

Capua prospered even through the barbarian invasions after the end of the empire, but finally met its match in the Saracens, who in A.D. 840 destroyed the city, leaving only the Duomo standing. Slowly, a new village developed from the ruins around the church, and once again Capua prospered. It had lost its name though, taken by the fleeing population who had established the new Capua on the Volturno River, over the ruins of the Roman hamlet of Casilinum. So the town was renamed Santa Maria Capua Vetere (*vetere* means "old" in Latin). Its modern-day population is now double that of nearby Capua.

ESSENTIALS

GETTING THERE & AROUND You can get to Santa Maria Capua Vetere by **train** from Caserta and Naples. Check with **Trenitalia** (© 892021 from anywhere in Italy; www.trenitalia.it) for fares and schedules. By **car,** follow autostrada A1 to the exit marked CASERTA NORD and look for signs to SANTA MARIA CAPUA VETERE and Via Appia. From Caserta, take Viale Douhet past the Reggia and follow it westward out of town; it will become Via Appia. Two parking lots are located off the main road, one behind Piazza San Pietro, and another off Via F. Pezzella, which you can reach from Corso Garibaldi.

Santa Maria Capua Vetere is small enough to be toured **on foot;** it spans either side of the ancient Appian Way, which is called Corso Aldo Moro since the new stretch of the Appia was built to bypass the modern town.

EXPLORING THE TOWN

As you walk along ancient Via Appia, keep an eye out for archaeological remains which are everywhere: pieces of column, sculpted busts of gods and goddesses, and capitals, all incorporated into more modern buildings over the centuries. After your visit to the main attractions below, you can visit the **Museo Archeologico dell'Antica Capua,** Via Roberto D'Angiò 48, off Corso Aldo Moro (© 0823-844206; admission 2.50€/$3.50/£1.75 includes access to Anfiteatro Campano and Mitreo; Tues–Sun 9am–6pm). Housed in the Torre di Sant'Erasmo—a tower originating before the Longobards—this museum displays a large collection of local archaeological findings ranging from the 10th century B.C. to the 1st century A.D. Behind the museum is the **Mitreo** ⋆, Vicolo Mitreo (visit by guided tour only; sign up at the ticket booth of the Anfiteatro Campano), one of the few existing temples dedicated to the god Mithras (worshipped by a Persian cult that diffused in Rome during the 1st century A.D.). Discovered by chance in 1922, the temple was built between the 2nd and 3rd centuries A.D., and is very well-preserved. Its vaulted ceiling is decorated with a large fresco of Mithras sacrificing a white bull. Above the stalls are remains of frescoes depicting the seven stages of initiation into the cult of Mithras.

Anfiteatro Campano ⋆⋆ Second in size only to the Colosseum in Rome, this Roman amphitheater was probably built around A.D. 3, enlarged in 119 by the Emperor Hadrian, and further embellished by Emperor Antoninus Pius. It remains majestic in spite of having been used—like so many Roman buildings in Italy—as a quarry for quality marble and construction materials over the centuries. It was also picked apart in the 9th century onwards during searches for bronze and lead (the

building's large stone components were broken apart to get at the heavy metal clamps that held them together). Some of its columns and stones were even used to rebuild the town and the Duomo (below). This practice—common throughout the Roman world in the centuries after the fall of the empire—could be called an early version of recycling.

Judging from what remains, though, the amphitheater must have been quite a sight back in those days. Four stories tall, it was completely covered in travertine stone, with marble busts of gods serving as keystones for each of the 240 arches on the lower floors, and full-length statues under the arches of the second and third floors. You can still see the carved keystones over the main entrance (busts of Ceres and Juno). The giant arena has a maximum length of about 170m (557 ft.) and can seat over 60,000 people. The corridors below the arena are relatively well conserved and still show traces of stuccoes and frescoes. This is where the gladiators waited between combats, and where all the scene props were kept. The bestiary—home of the fighting animals—was also here. You can also see the remains of a paleochristian altar and paintings inside one of the small rooms here, which was transformed into a Christian oratory in the 9th century.

The garden in front of the amphitheater has been turned into an open-air museum where you can admire many of the fragments of the original decorations of the amphitheater as well as from other buildings in town. Among the objects on display is the beautiful 2nd-century **mosaic** ✹ depicting Nereides and Tritons.

A permanent exhibit dedicated to gladiatorial fights is housed in the **Museo dei Gladiatori (Gladiators' Museum)** ✹, also in the garden. On display are four complete suits of gladiator armor, and a model reconstruction of the amphitheater. You can also watch a good animation of a gladiator fight. Spartacus, the slave made famous by the 1960 Stanley Kubrick film, was a graduate of the gladiator school located near this amphitheater.

Piazza Ottobre, off Piazza Adriano. ✆ 0823-798864. Admission 2.50€ ($3.50/£1.75) cumulative ticket including Museo Archeologico dell'Antica Capua and Mitreo. Tues–Sun 9am–5:30pm.

Duomo ✹✹ Dedicated to Santa Maria Maggiore, the core of this church was built in A.D. 432 by Capua's bishop Saint Simmaco over the town's catacombs by the Grotto of Saint Prisco; Arechi II added the two external naves in A.D. 787. When it was restored in 1666, the apse was completely rebuilt. The interior is quite suggestive, with five naves supported by columns topped with Corinthian capitals taken from the nearby amphitheater and Roman temples. It is richly decorated with Renaissance artwork, including a carved **cyborium** ✹ located in the chapel at the end of the right-hand nave, and a **wooden choir** ✹ in the apse. Our favorite chapels are the ones opening off the left-hand nave—gated **Cappella del Conforto** ✹✹, with a beautiful altar in colored marble inlay, and **Cappella della Morte** ✹, featuring more notable inlay work at the end of the nave.

Via Sirtori 3, off Piazza Matteotti. ✆ 0823-846640. Free admission. Daily 9am–12:30pm and 4:30–6pm.

3 Capua

11km (6½ miles) W of Caserta and 28km (17 miles) NW of Naples

Located at a bend in the Volturno River, this village is built over the ruins of Casilinum, the fluvial harbor serving ancient Roman Capua (today's Santa Maria Capua Vetere; above). The village guarded the important bridge of the Appian Way over the river, but lost importance as the Roman Empire gained stability and the need for the bridge's defense disappeared. It was brought back to life when Capua's inhabitants took refuge here after their town was destroyed by the Saracens in A.D. 840. They came with all they could save from their old town, even the town's name, so that Casilinum was renamed Capua. Its strategic position made it into an independent principality, though it was repeatedly besieged by various powers until the unification of Italy in 1860. As the seat of a bishopric, it played an important religious role throughout the centuries, which is still visible in its many churches.

ESSENTIALS

GETTING THERE & AROUND Capua is well connected by **Trenitalia** (✆ 892021 from anywhere in Italy; www.trenitalia.it) train service from Caserta and Naples. By **car**, take autostrada A1 to the exit marked CAPUA, which leads to Via Appia. Follow the signs for CAPUA; the town is to your left after you cross the bridge over the Volturno River. From Caserta, take Viale Douhet past the Reggia and follow it westward out of town; it will become Via Appia and pass through Santa Maria

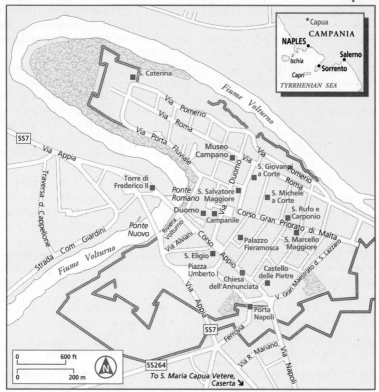

Capua Vetere before reaching Capua. You will find a parking lot off Via Appia at Piazza Umberto I, near the center of town.

Capua can be easily visited **on foot** or by **taxi** ✆ **0823-963142** or 0823-963521.

SPECIAL EVENTS During Carnival, Capua is the seat of an important festival including a grand parade, farcical theater performances, often reflecting on recent political events, and cabaret shows. Always featured is the famous character **Pulcinella** (p. 300), whom Capuans claim as one of their own. (Check with the tourist office in Caserta for a schedule of events).

EXPLORING THE TOWN

Capua maintains the feeling of an ancient town, thanks to the fact that most of its fortifications are intact, including parts of its two castles. The old Appian Way traverses the center of town (today named Corso Appio), crossing over the bridge that was built after the perfectly functional ancient Roman one was destroyed by bombing in 1943. A stroll along it will take you past most of Capua's historic buildings and many churches, which feature ancient Roman artifacts. The facade of 16th-century **Palazzo del Municipio** (Piazza dei Giudici, off Corso Appio), for instance, is graced by six marble **busts** ✿ representing Jupiter, Neptune, Mercury, Juno, Ceres, and Mars, which were taken from the Anfiteatro Campano of Santa Maria Capua Vetere (see earlier in this chapter). Toward the eastern end of town, the 11th-century Norman **Castello delle Pietre** (Via Andreozzi, by the 15th-century eastern gate, Porta Napoli) still boasts one of its four original crenellated towers.

Duomo, aka Cattedrale di Santo Stefano e Sant'Agata 🏛🏛 After the original building was severely damaged by bombing in 1943, an immense restoration campaign faithfully re-created it according to the original plan. The church dated from A.D. 856, with additions from 1120. The 11th-century atrium, built with columns and Corinthian capitals from the 3rd century A.D., and the Duomo's 9th-century bell tower, supported at its base by four ancient Corinthian columns, is still original. Among the medieval sculptures decorating the bell tower, you can admire three Roman bas-reliefs from the amphitheater in Santa Maria Capua Vetere (earlier in this chapter).

Inside the church, a large range of artwork dates from the 12th century to the present. We love the splendid, lavishly decorated 13th-century **ceremonial candle holder** and the two columns supported by carved lions on the modern pulpit—all that remain of the original 13th-century **ambo.** Other parts of the original ambo, including some mosaics, were used to decorate the small chapel in the **crypt** under the presbytery. In the **Cappella del Sacramento** at the end of the right-hand-side nave is a beautiful **altar** made of marble and precious stones, while in the presbytery behind the altar, you'll find the *Assunta* painted by Francesco Solimena. We also recommend a visit to the **Museo Diocesano** (ⓒ **0823-961081;** admission 3€/$4.20/£2.10; daily 9:30am–1pm and 3:30–7pm), housing the church's **treasure** inside the **Cappella del Corpo di Cristo,** adjacent to the cathedral. Among the objects on exhibit is a collection of Islamic carved crystal dating from the 11th and 12th centuries.

Piazza Landolfo, off Via Duomo. ⓒ **0823-961081.** Free admission. Daily 8–11am and 5:30–7:30pm.

Museo Campano 🏛🏛 Housed in the Palazzo Antignano (graced by an unusual 15th-century **portal** 🏛 in Catalán-Moorish style at no. 76 of Via Roma), the museum, established in 1874, is dedicated to the art, religion, and history of Campania. Its wealth of holdings is divided into two sections: Archaeological finds are on the first floor, while medieval displays, including the parchment collection, and the picture gallery are on the second.

The archaeology section includes Oscan (the Osci were the local Italic population), Etruscan, and Roman artifacts from a number of sites in the area. Among the Etruscan-Oscan pottery, we liked the beautiful black dishes decorated with fish and dating from the 4th century B.C. The most poignant artifacts, however, are **Le Madri (The Mothers)** 🏛🏛, in room nos. V through IX. This is a whole group of statues and architectural structures with Oscan inscriptions which were found in a field near Santa Maria Capua Vetere. They pertain to an Oscan sanctuary that was active between the 6th and 1st centuries B.C. and was dedicated to the Italic goddess of fertility and maternity, Matuta. Several of these figures, carved in tufa stone, show mothers offering their children to view and (probably) thanking the goddess for the gift of maternity. The **Roman mosaic** on the second floor in room no. X was found in the temple of Diana Tifatina near Sant'Angelo in Formis (later in this chapter).

Among the holdings in the medieval section, the most famous is the collection of **Federician Sculptures** 🏛 in room no. XXVI. Among this group of marble sculptures from the castle built by Federico II in 1239 in Capua are a few portraits of Federico himself. One of the greatest of medieval rulers, he was crowned king of Sicily at the age of 4 and became Holy Roman Emperor in 1220. He participated in the Sixth Crusade, and crowned himself king of Jerusalem in 1229. Called **Stupor Mundi** ("wonder of the world") by his contemporaries, he was also much distrusted by the papacy and was excommunicated twice.

Via Roma 68, off Via Duomo. ℭ 0823-961402. www.museocampano.it. Free admission. Tues–Sat 9am–1:30pm and Sun 9am–1pm.

Sant'Angelo in Formis ✿✿✿   Maybe the most fascinating medieval church in Italy, this little-visited artistic treasure is located a short distance from Capua, on the slopes of Mount Tifata.

Sant'Angelo is easily reached via the bus across from Capua's train station. You can also get here by a short **taxi** ride from Capua (earlier in this chapter). By **car**, take Via Roma from Capua's town center, and continue out of town following signs for S. ANGELO IN FORMIS. You'll come first to the village and then, higher up along the road, to a church standing alone in the square.

Enjoying an ideal position up the mountain overlooking Capua and affording, on clear days, a **view** ✿✿ that stretches all the way to Ischia, this basilica was built over the ruins of the **Temple of Diana Tifatina,** the most important pre-Christian sanctuary in this region. Turned into a church sometime before the 10th century, it was then bequeathed to the nearby monastery of Montecassino. Its abbot, Desiderio of Montecassino, decided to establish the sanctuary as an important religious site, and had the basilica completely redone in 1073. Note how the lateral arches in the portico in front of the church are pointed arches typical of Islamic architecture. Under the portico you will see the first series of frescoes, with a wonderful **Saint Michael** ✿✿ from the 11th century, and others from the 12th and 13th centuries.

Inside, the basilica is divided into three naves by 14 columns topped with beautiful antique Corinthian capitals. The greatest attraction is really the **frescoes** ✿✿✿ that were painted by local art students. Along the sides of the central nave is the cycle depicting scenes from the Old and New Testaments, and on the inner facade is the Last Judgment. Little remains of the 11th-century mosaic floor—you'll see some at the end of the right nave—and parts of the marble floor are original to the temple of Diana (dated by an inscription from 74 B.C.).

Piazza della Basilica di Sant'Angelo in Formis. ℭ 0823-960492. Free admission. Sun and holidays 10am–4pm yearround; summer Mon–Sat 9:30am–noon and 3–7pm; winter Mon–Sat 9:30am–12:30pm and 3–6pm.

WHERE TO STAY IN THE AREA
MODERATE

Hotel Europa   This is considered (together with the Jolly below) the best hotel in Caseta, with large, comfortable rooms, only a few steps from the Reggia and the railway station. Although it has good amenities—including a fitness room, billiards room, and modern bathrooms—the hotel's furnishings are unimaginative and the decoration is minimal. Suites sleep four and include small kitchens.

Via Roma 19, 81100 Caserta. ℭ 0823-325400. Fax 0823-325400. www.hoteleuropacaserta.it. 57 units. 160€ ($224/£112) double; 235€ ($329/£165) suite. Rates include buffet breakfast. Children 2 and under stay free in parent's room. AE, DC, MC, V. Parking 18€ ($25/£13). Closed Dec 31–Jan 1. **Amenities:** Bar; business center; concierge; health club; laundry service. *In room:* A/C, TV, hair dryer, minibar.

Hotel Jolly Caserta   Housed in a large pink building, the Jolly offers over a hundred rooms with the standards and uniformity you would expect from a chain hotel;

it may not be charming and quirky, but it is clean and comfortable. The medium-size guest rooms have large beds; decor and furnishings are modern.

Viale Vittorio Veneto 9, 81100 Caserta. ✆ 0823-325222. Fax 0823-354522. www.jollyhotels.it. 107 units. 185€ ($259/£130) double. Rates include buffet breakfast. Children 15 and under stay free in parent's room. AE, DC, MC, V. Free parking. **Amenities:** Restaurant; bar; concierge; conference room. *In room:* A/C, satellite TV, hair dryer, minibar, safe.

INEXPENSIVE
Hotel Belvedere   Located in San Leucio, this hotel offers good value for the amenities. The spacious modern rooms have wood floors and functional furniture, including comfortable beds. Some have balconies or small terraces, and all have good-size bathrooms. The **restaurant** is quite good and enjoys a pleasant outdoor terrace in the summer season.

Via Nazionale Sannitica km 31. Localitá Vaccheria, San Leucio, 81100 Caserta. ✆ 0823-304925. Fax 0823-485914. www.hotelbelvederesanleucio.it. 35 units. 100€ ($140/£70). Rates include buffet breakfast. Children 1 and under stay free in parent's room. AE, DC, MC, V. Free parking. Small pets allowed. **Amenities:** Restaurant; bar; business center; concierge; disco; gym; laundry service; room service. *In room:* A/C, TV, hair dryer, safe.

Hotel Caserta Antica   Located near the old *borgo*, this hotel has comfort to spare and features an on-site restaurant, bar, terrace, and, best of all, a 14m×8m (45 ft.×26 ft.) swimming pool. The rooms are simply—sometimes spartanly—decorated, but are cozy enough, with doubles, triples, and quads available; most units have balconies.

Via Tiglio 41, Casertavecchia, 81100 Caserta. ✆ 0823-371158. Fax 0823-371333. www.hotelcaserta-antica.it. 25 units. 85€ ($119/£60) double. Rates include breakfast. Children 1 and under stay free in parent's room. AE, DC, MC, V. Free parking. **Amenities:** Restaurant; bar; concierge; outdoor pool. *In room:* A/C, TV, safe.

WHERE TO DINE
EXPENSIVE
Le Colonne ✦ MODERN CASERTAN   This elegant restaurant located right across from the Reggia is a welcome addition to Caserta's dining scene. The menu showcases hearty offerings made from the area's best local products. The house specialty is buffalo meat (from the same animal whose milk makes the famed mozzarella), and we highly recommend trying the smoked version, served as an appetizer as well as a main course. We also recommend the fresh tasty *alici* (anchovies); served in a variety of ways, we recommend the classic *tortino di alici* (layered and oven roasted with potatoes).

Via Nazionale Appia, 7, Caserta. ✆ 0823-467494. Fax 0823-467988. www.lecolonnemarziale.it. Reservations recommended for dinner. Secondi 18€–25€ ($25–$35/£13–£18). AE, DC, MC, V. Wed–Mon 12:30–3pm. Closed 2 weeks in Aug.

MODERATE
Antica Hostaria Massa ✦ CAMPANIAN/CASERTAN   This simple restaurant favored by locals, especially for the midday meal, prepares and serves good food in a pleasant atmosphere. They always have a variety of seafood dishes—pasta *alle cozze e vongole* (with mussels and clams) is excellent—and a number of meat choices, including very tasty local sausages.

Via Mazzini 55, Caserta. ✆ 0823-456527. Fax 0823-214641. Reservations recommended. Secondi 10€–16€ ($14–$22/£7–£11). AE, DC, MC, V. Daily 12:30–3pm and 7–10:30pm.

Antica Locanda CAMPANIAN/CASERTAN   This atmospheric restaurant right in the heart of San Leucio's picturesque piazza offers well-prepared local dishes as well as a number of regional favorites. The menu changes often, but you should always find the excellent *scialatielli ai frutti di mare* (homemade eggless pasta with seafood) and grilled baby pig.

Piazza della Seta 8, San Leucio. ℂ 0823-305444. Reservations recommended on weekends. Secondi 10€–16€ ($14–$22/£7–£11). AE, DC, MC, V. Daily 12:30–3pm and 7–10:30pm.

Da Teresa ✸ CASERTAN/PIZZA   This restaurant enjoys the best location in Casertavecchia, with a beautiful terrace and a garden offering great views over Caserta and—on clear days—all the way to the sea beyond. The restaurant is large and includes a regular dining room and a picturesque inner courtyard. In addition to good-quality pizza, they have an extensive menu of local specialties, such as *misto alla brace* (charbroiled mixed platter with local vegetables, meats, and sausages). The dishes vary daily, but the always-available *menu del ghiottone* (gourmet menu) offers such choices such as *cinghiale alla brace* (charbroiled wild boar). They also offer four prix-fixe menus (including a primo, a secondo, a side dish, and a dessert), which can be a good choice for between 15€ and 25€ ($21–$35/£11–£18).

Via Torre 6, Casertavecchia 81020. ℂ 0823-371270. Reservations recommended for dinner. Secondi 8€–16€ ($11–$22/£5.60–£11). AE, DC, MC, V. Thurs–Tues 11:30–3pm and 7pm–midnight.

Via Roma ✸ CAMPANIAN/CASERTAN   This is the best restaurant in town, so don't be put off by the formal atmosphere and the elegant decor: The service is very welcoming and accommodating, and the food's excellent. You'll find a seasonal menu offering traditional specialties as well as more sophisticated innovations based on local ingredients, such as homemade pappardelle *con mazzancolle e porcini* (with local shrimp and porcini mushrooms) and the roasted pork.

Via Roma 21. ℂ 0823-443629. Reservations recommended for dinner. Secondi 9€–14€ ($13–$20/£6.30–£9.80). AE, DC, MC, V. Daily 12:30–3pm and 7–10:30pm.

INEXPENSIVE

Mastrangelo CAMPANIAN/CASERTAN   Similar in clientele to Antica Hostaria Massa above, this is also a good local restaurant, with an ample choice of dishes. The menu varies, but it always includes both surf and turf, true to the Casertan tradition. The homemade *cannelloni di pesce* (tubes of pasta filled with seafood) is very good, as is the daily catch *all'acqua pazza* (cooked in a light tomato-and-herb broth).

Piazza Duomo 5. ℂ 0823-371410. Reservations recommended for dinner. Secondi 8€–14€ ($11–$20/£5.60–£9.80). AE, DC, MC, V. Daily 12:30–3pm and 7–10:30pm.

Ristorante Pizzeria L'Oasi PIZZA   You can't beat this simple restaurant for convenience—it's right on Piazza Duomo. The food is good and the "no-frills" atmosphere youthful. Pizza, the house specialty, is available with a variety of toppings. The regular restaurant menu offers a good choice of dishes; while the pasta is good, expect it to be simple, not gourmet.

Piazza Duomo 6. ℂ 0823-622755. Reservations recommended in the evening. Secondi 7€–14€ ($9.80–$20/£4.90–£9.80). AE, DC, MC, V. Daily noon–3pm and 7–11pm.

Ristorante Romano CAPUAN   Very central, this restaurant is a bit more formal than the Oasi (below) and is favored by locals, especially for midday meals. The menu varies but always includes a variety of very well-prepared primi—the *rigatoni cacio e pepe* (short pasta with cheese and black pepper) was very good, as was the *panzotti* (a sort of ravioli) served with local *mozzarella di bufala* and fresh tomatoes. Afterwards, you can enjoy classic secondi, often seafood offerings that change daily according to the market.

Corso Appio 34, Capua. ℂ 0823-961726. Reservations recommended in the evening. Secondi 9€–16€ ($13–$22/£6.30–£11). AE, DC, MC, V. Daily 12:30–3pm and 7:30–11pm.

4 Bewitching Benevento

51km (31 miles) E of Caserta and 86km (53 miles) NE of Naples

With its heritage of mysterious witchcraft and Roman art, this unique inland town holds many interesting sights, yet it is rarely visited by foreign tourists. A powerful Sannite town inhabited since around the 7th century B.C., it was soundly defeated by the Romans in 275 B.C., after fierce opposition. The empire established a colony there and changed the town's name from the original Malies, or Maloenton—which in Latin sounded like a bad omen—to Beneventum. Taken by the Goths at the end of the Western Roman Empire, it was rescued by the Byzantines, who then relinquished it in turn to the Longobards. The latter established the town as a principality and was very influential in the local culture until Benevento was absorbed into the state of the Church of Rome. Relatively peaceful from the 16th century onward, it was almost completely destroyed by the earthquake of 1688. The city's archbishop—who, in later years, was to become Pope Benedetto XIII—rebuilt the city and supported its cultural and spiritual development. The reborn Benevento enjoyed a new period of prosperity until World War II, when the town was heavily bombarded in 1943—65% of it, including important monuments, was destroyed, and 2,000 people died. The town has recovered since and has become a lively and pleasant provincial town with an interesting hinterland.

ESSENTIALS

GETTING THERE   Benevento is well connected by **train,** with frequent service from Naples, Caserta, Avellino, and Rome. Contact **Trenitalia** (② **892021** from anywhere in Italy; www.trenitalia.it) for fares and information. Trains arrive at Benevento's **Stazione** (② **0824-50159**) located in Piazza Colonna 2, to the north of town.

By **car,** take autostrada A16 to the exit signed BENEVENTO and continue on the short stretch of highway to the town.

GETTING AROUND   The center of Benevento is small and accessible **on foot;** however, it extends uphill, so you might want to use public transportation as well. The town's **bus** system maintains a number of lines that crisscross the area; most leave from the hub across from the train station. Lines 1 and 7 both pass by Trajan's Arch, going up to the Rocca dei Priori in the heart of the historic district. You'll need to buy bus tickets at a tobacconist or a newsstand before boarding; tickets cost .65€ (90¢/45p) and are valid for 90 minutes. You'll find a **taxi stand** in Piazza Colonna, across from the railway station; you can also call one at (② **0824-50341**).

Although most of the villages are served by **SITA bus service** (② **0892-26604;** www.sitabus.it), a **car** is the best way to explore Benevento's surroundings. You can rent a car in town with **Cardillo,** Via dei Mulini 91 (② **0824-359775**).

VISITOR INFORMATION   The excellent local **tourist office EPT,** Via Nicola Sala 31, 82100 Benevento (② **0824-319911;** www.eptbenevento.it) maintains an **information office** in Piazza Roma 11 (② **0824-319938**).

FAST FACTS   You'll find a **pharmacy** in Piazza Orsini 13 (② **0824-21590**). The hospital is **Ospedale Fatebenefratelli** at Viale Principe di Napoli 14–16 (② **0824-50374**). For an **ambulance,** dial ② **118** or the **Croce Rossa Italiana** (② **0824-315000**). You can call the **police** at ② **112.** There is a **post office** (② **0824-24074**) in Piazza Colonna Vittoria, where the railway station is located. It's open Monday to Saturday from 8am to 2pm.

Benevento

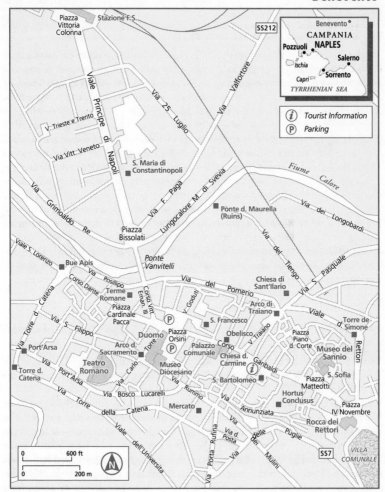

EXPLORING THE TOWN

Enjoying a great location on a hill at the heart of a hilly green valley, Benevento is a very pleasant town. Once completely enclosed by defensive walls, only fragments of them are still visible today, together with the fortress—**Rocca dei Rettori** (Piazza IV Novembre)—located in the highest part of town. Built by the Pope in 1321 over the preexisting Longobard and ancient Roman defensive structures, the fortress was recently restored, but only some of it can be visited through the Museo del Sannio (below), as it houses the provincial government. Across from it are the delightful public gardens of the **Villa Comunale** ✿. Designed in the late 19th century and graced by elegant Liberty-style fixtures such as lamps and benches, it was recently restored to the tune of about $7 million.

The Witches of Benevento

Legend has it that Benevento is a land of witches, and has been for thousands of years. The origins of the legend lie with the Egyptian cult of Isis—goddess of magic and mystery among other things—which found fertile ground in Benevento during the Roman era. The cult remained an important force here even after the cult was replaced by Christianity in other parts of Italy. When the Longobards from Central Europe took the town in A.D. 571, they imported their own religion, a nature cult based on the adoration of the god Wothan and his sacred walnut tree. They elected an old walnut near the **Ponte Leproso** as the town's sacred tree. (The Ponte Leproso was a bridge built by the Romans over the Sabato River at the Via Appia's entrance to Benevento. The bridge is still in use today; you can see it by taking a short walk west of the Teatro Romano). Around this walnut tree—known as the Noce di Benevento—the Longobards held their nocturnal open-air rituals which, combined with knowledge of the cult of Isis and the vivid imagination of the locals, gave rise to the witchcraft legend.

The Longobards were converted to the Catholic religion by Saint Barbato, the town's bishop, in the 7th century A.D., and the bishop had the tree cut down. The dances stopped; yet, some say, the witches remained, and can still be seen dancing by the site on certain nights.

Arco di Traiano (Trajan's Arch) ✸✸✸   This is quite simply the best conserved—it's practically pristine considering its 2,000 years of age—ancient Roman triumphal arch in the world. The lengthy restoration—mainly a careful cleaning that took 14 years—was completed recently (2001) and the arch is again visible in all its glory. Built between A.D. 114 and 117 by Rome to honor the Emperor Trajan, it was located at the beginning of the Via Traiana, what was then a new—and shorter—route that led from Benevento to Brindisi, the harbor that was Rome's gateway to the eastern Mediterranean. The arch's reliefs celebrate the deeds of this illuminated leader, who enlarged and strengthened the Empire while implementing a generous social policy and numerous public works. During the Middle Ages, this superb work of art was enclosed in the city walls and used as the main gate into town (hence the local name for the arch: Port'Aurea), which contributed to its conservation. The nearby church, **Sant'Ilario a Port'Aurea** ✸ (Via San Pasquale, off the Arco di Traiano; ✆ **0824-21818**), a Longobard church from the 10th century, houses a permanent exhibit on the arch and on life in Rome under the Emperor Trajan.
Via Traiano, off Corso Garibaldi.

Duomo ✸   The first version of this church goes back to the 7th century A.D., when it had only a central nave. After consecration in A.D. 780, during Longobard domination, two naves were added in the 9th century and two others in the 12th century. The structure was then restored and redecorated in the 18th century, at which point it became known as one of the most beautiful Romanesque churches in Italy. However, the bombing of 1943 destroyed almost the entire ancient church, except for the bell tower and the elegant Romanesque facade, a 13th-century Pisan-style marvel of striped marble and rich carvings. The richly carved jambs of the central portal date from the 12th century; they once bracketed 13th-century sculpted bronze doors which were considered rivals of the famous ones of Florence's baptistery. They were blown to pieces by the bombing, and what was saved was painstakingly restored; you can now see the 72 frames that composed the doors displayed inside the church. The top 43 are decorated with scenes from the life of Christ, from the Annunciation to the Ascension, while the bottom 29 depict local religious personalities. The **Museo Diocesano**—housed partly in the crypt and partly in the adjacent Palazzo Arcivescovile (Piazza Orsini 27; © **0824-54717**)—holds remains from the destroyed Duomo, including what was left of the extremely rich treasure.

Piazza Duomo. © **0824-47591**. Free admission. Daily 9am–12:30pm and 5–7pm.

Museo del Sannio ✯

Housed in the former monastery of Santa Sofia (below), this museum holds a picture gallery and a good collection of archaeological and medieval artifacts. Among the most interesting items on display is the collection of Egyptian art coming from the local temple of Isis (built by the notoriously cruel Emperor Domitian in A.D. 88). It was decorated both with statues imported from Egypt and others produced locally in the Egyptian style—including a portrait of Domitian in Egyptian attire. The picture gallery holds a collection stretching from the 15th to the 20th centuries, including major names such as Francesco Solimena *(Madonna col Bambino e i Santi)* and Carlo Maratta *(Sacra Famiglia)*. Part of the collection is displayed in the elegant **cloister** ✯, an interesting architectural merger of Moorish arches and Romanesque columns, carved with strange, fantastic, or everyday scenes, such as boar hunts and pilgrimages.

The museum's historical section (documents and signatures of famous historical figures) is housed in the scenic Rocca dei Rettori (access with the same ticket) on Piazza IV Novembre.

Piazza Matteotti. © **0824-21818** or 0824-28831. Admission 3€ ($4.20/£2.10). Tues–Sun 9am–1pm.

Santa Sofia ✯

This medieval church is one of our favorites in Italy. Its unique design singles it out as an architectural marvel and shows the intermingling of Longobard and Christian cultures. Begun in 762 by the Longobard Arechi II when he became Duke of Benevento, the church's star-shaped structure is composed of a central hexagon, covered by a dome, and supported by six powerful columns; around this are eight square pillars and two columns topped by Corinthian capitals. The pillars are aligned with the surrounding walls, which are part circle and part star, creating a strange perspective. In the apse you will see fragments of a great cycle of frescoes from the 8th century, representing, among other things, scenes of the life of Saint Zaccaria; the surrounding walls, however, are decorated with representations of nature and symbols derived from the Longobard religion. The bell tower stands alone, isolated from the church; it was redone in 1703. Attached to the church is the monastery, now housing the **Museo del Sannio** (above). It was actually a convent of the order of Benedictine nuns founded at the same time as the church. It became one of the most powerful monasteries in Italy during the 12th century, famous for its type of writing, which became known as *"scriptorium Beneventanum." Note:* The church was under restoration at presstime, and no date was announced for the reopening.

Piazza Matteotti. © **0824-21206**. Free admission. Daily 10am–noon and 4:30–7pm.

Strega—the Brew of Benevento

In addition to the preparation of *torroncini* (Italian bite-size nougat)—which Beneventians created in the 17th century—the town has reached national fame for a brew called *Strega,* or witch. Made from a secret mixture of 17 herbs and spices, the liqueur has a strong bittersweet flavor that complements the likes of coffee, fruit salad, and ice cream. The liqueur also comes in a "cream" variety (similar to Bailey's), which is quite good. You'll find both at **Alberico Ambrosino,** Corso Garibaldi 111 (℃ **0824-28546**); **Umberto Russo,** Via Gaetano Rumno 17 (℃ **0824-24472**); and **Fabbriche Riunite Torrone di Benevento,** Viale Principe di Napoli 113 (℃ **0824-21624**). We also recommend the *caramelle Strega,* hard candy with a soft, creamy Strega-flavored center.

Teatro Romano ⭐   Theater performances, including drama, comedy, and poetry as well as music, were very important to Roman culture and a matter of everyday life. Theaters (the classic hemicycle) were ubiquitous, to the extent that even little towns often had more than one. But while grandiose ruins remain of the great amphitheaters dedicated to contests and spectacles—such as Rome's Colosseum and the Anfiteatro Campano in Santa Maria Capua Vetere (earlier in this chapter)—most ancient Roman theaters have been integrated into later constructions. This makes Benevento's Roman theater an important exception. Built in the 2nd century A.D., it had a diameter of 90m (295 ft.) and could contain up to 20,000 spectators. Most of the original structure is still visible, and only the third floor was completely lost. The path that leads from the ticket booth to the theater takes you past assorted sculptures, capitals, and massive hunks of marble that once graced the structure. A portion of the second level also still stands, with corridors leading to the mostly intact seating area, still used during the summer for opera performances and classical dramas (contact the tourist office for a schedule of events).

Via Port'Arsa. ℃ **0824-29970.** Admission 2€ ($2.80/£1.40). Wed–Mon 10am–5pm.

WHERE TO STAY

MODERATE

Cristina Park Hotel   This pleasant hotel is surrounded by a beautiful park, and public spaces are large and comfortable. The spacious guestrooms are nicely appointed, with wooden furniture, and bathrooms are good size and modern. The **restaurant** is quite good.

Via Benevento 102, 82016 Montesarchio. ℃/fax **0824-835888.** www.cristinaparkhotel.it. 30 units. 120€ ($168/£84) double. Rates include buffet breakfast. Children 2 and under stay free in parent's room. AE, DC, MC, V. Free parking. **Amenities:** Restaurant; bar; business center; concierge; laundry service; room service. *In room:* A/C, TV, minibar.

Grand Hotel Telese ⭐   The best hotel in Telese is also conveniently located nearby the town's main thermal facilities. It offers elegant accommodations as well as its own small spa. Built at the end of the 19th century, it offers grand public spaces. Guest rooms are elegantly appointed, with plush period furniture, carpeting, and modern bathrooms.

Via Cerreto 1, 82037 Telese. ℃ **0824-940500.** Fax 0824-940504. www.grandhoteltelese.it. 180€ ($252/£126) double. Rates include buffet breakfast. Children 2 and under stay free in parent's room. AE, DC, MC, V. Free parking. **Amenities:** Restaurant; concierge; laundry service; park; soccer field; spa w/indoor pool; outdoor tennis court. *In room:* A/C, TV, hair dryer.

President Hotel   In the center of town, this modern service-oriented hotel caters to a business and tourist clientele alike. The rooms are airy and open, with hardwood floors and furniture. Decor is simple, functional, and tasteful, the beds large and comfortable. The hotel's public areas are also roomy, with plenty of space to relax.

Via Perasso 1, 82100 Benevento. ℰ 0824-316716. Fax 0824-316764. www.hotelpresidentbenevento.it. 69 units. 115€ ($161/£81) double. Rates include buffet breakfast. Children 2 and under stay free in parent's room. AE, DC, MC, V. Free parking. **Amenities:** Restaurant; bar; business center; concierge; laundry service; room service. *In room:* A/C, TV, hair dryer, Internet, minibar.

INEXPENSIVE

Agriturismo Mustilli ⟡⟡   The welcoming and spacious guest rooms at this unusual *agriturismo* are in the 18th-century **Palazzo Rainone,** in the historic center of Sant' Agata; they are furnished with a mix of period furniture, modern pieces, and assorted antiques. The **restaurant** (Vico dei Fiori 20) serves superb meals prepared with the farm's produce.

Palazzo Rainone, Piazza Trento 4, 82019 Sant'Agata dei Goti. ℰ 0823-718142. Fax 0823-717619. www.mustilli. com. 6 units. 90€ ($126/£63) double. Rates include buffet breakfast. Children 2 and under stay free in parent's room. AE, DC, MC, V. Free parking. **Amenities:** Restaurant. *In room:* A/C, TV, hair dryer.

Grand Hotel Italiano ⟡   Offering hospitality since 1920, this family-run hotel has been updated many times but retains its old-fashioned hospitality. It is conveniently located not far from the train station, in a pleasant residential part of town with lots of shops; the center of town is a 15-minute walk or a short bus ride away. The large guest rooms are well-thought-out, comfortable, and modern, and all have good-size bathrooms. In summer, the hotel offers discounted access to a nearby swimming pool and gym. The **restaurant** on the premises is very good and quite popular with locals.

Viale Principe di Napoli 137, 82100 Benevento. ℰ 0824-24111. Fax 0824-21758. www.hotel-italiano.it. 71 units. 88€ ($123/£62). Rates include buffet breakfast. Children 2 and under stay free in parent's room. AE, DC, MC, V. Limited free parking. **Amenities:** Restaurant; bar; babysitting; business center; concierge; laundry service; room service. *In room:* A/C, TV, hair dryer, minibar.

WHERE TO DINE

If you enjoy wine, don't miss the local D.O.C. varieties: Aglianico del Taburno, Solopaca, Guardiolo, Sannio, Sant'Agata dei Goti, and Taburno. Another famous wine from the region is the refreshing Falanghina, a white wine with an aromatic bouquet and a dry flavor. We also recommend a stop in Sant'Agata dei Goti for a gelato at **Bar Gelateria Normanno,** Via Roma 65 (ℰ 0823-953042), which makes its own delicious gelati: We love the *bacio Normanno,* and the proprietary *spumone all'Annurca* (a sort of shake made with the renowned local apple).

MODERATE

Antica Trattoria Pascalucci ⟡⟡ *Finds* SEAFOOD/SANNITE   Located on the Appian Way between Benevento and San Giorgio del Sannio, this restaurant is famous for its attentive service and large menu of tasty local peasant cuisine—this is the kind of place where Italians like to go on a family outing on weekends (Read: It is often packed) or for a special dinner with friends. Erminia De Cicco is faithful to the Sannite tradition and prepares top-notch fish dishes and grilled meats. Start with the *antipasti* for a taste of local cured meats and *sottoli* (delicious vegetables prepared and kept in olive oil).Continue with *tubetti alle cozze* (short pasta with mussels) or *fusilli ai funghi porcini* (fresh pasta with porcini mushrooms). You can then attack the secondi, choosing between perfectly grilled meats or *pesce al forno in umido* (fish baked with tomatoes)—the type of fish depends on the market. Simply wonderful.

Via Lanassi 2, Localitá Piano di Cappelle. (✆ 0824-778400. Reservations recommended. Secondi 10€–22€ ($14–$31/ £7–£15). AE, DC, MC, V. Daily noon–3pm and 7:30–11:30pm.

Gino e Pina 🏵🏵 SANNITE/ENOTECA/PIZZA   The meeting place of young locals, this excellent restaurant and *enoteca* serves well-prepared traditional dishes along with D.O.C. wines. Among the seafood, meat, and truly excellent pizza, standouts are the *impepata di cozze* (mussels cooked in a peppery broth), as well as the *cavatelli con vongole e zucchini* (with clams and zucchini), and the delicious *agnello al forno* (roasted lamb).

Viale delle Università, Benevento. (✆ 0824-24947. Reservations recommended. Pizza 7€–10€ ($9.80–$14/£4.90–£7). Secondi 11€–22€ ($15–$31/£7.70–£15). MC, V. Mon–Sat 12:30–3pm and 7:30–11pm. Closed 2 weeks in Aug.

INEXPENSIVE

Il Cervillo 🏵 SANNITE   You can eat very well at this welcoming restaurant specializing in traditional local cuisine. The menu is seasonal, with the likes of fresh pasta served with a tasty meat *ragu*, followed by savory roasted lamb or a *grigliata maista* (medley of charbroiled meat and sausages). Above the restaurant are 11 simply but nicely appointed **guest rooms** (65€/$91/£46 double, including breakfast).

Strada Provinciale Guardia-Cerreto, Via Cervillo, Guardia Sanframondi. (✆ 0824-861047. www.ilcervillo.it. Reservations recommended on weekends. Secondi 9€–16€ ($13–$22/£6.30–£11). AE, DC, MC, V. Thurs–Mon noon–3pm and 7:30–11:30pm.

Nunzia 🏵 BENEVENTAN   This is a welcoming, family-run restaurant where you'll enjoy the local cuisine and feel as if you were invited into the home of a Beneventan host. You'll also spend very little, so it's not surprising that this place is very popular with locals. Be sure to come early, or make a reservation. The highlights are the *primi* and the soups, which might include tasty *spaghetti e piselli* (pasta with peas) and delicious *pasta e ceci*. If they have it, do not miss their specialty, *baccalá con capperi e olive* (salt cod in an olive-and-capers sauce).

Via Annunziata 152. (✆ 0824-29431. Reservations recommended for dinner. Secondi 6€–12€ ($8.40–$17/ £4.20–£8.40). MC, V. Mon–Sat noon–3pm and 7–11pm.

Ristorante Pizzeria Traiano 🏵 BENEVENTAN/PIZZA   Excellent local cuisine and great pizza (available only in evening) make this a popular place. Open the almost unnoticeable entrance door and you'll find yourself in a crammed little restaurant with two small dining rooms, usually filled with people happily downing large dishes of food. This place is particularly famous for its variety of *antipasti* that come either as appetizers or as side dishes—try *involtini di melanzane* (eggplant rolls) if they have them. The restaurant is also famous for its homemade desserts. Both antipasti and desserts are on display near the entrance. Pasta dishes—such as *spaghetti alle cozze e vongole* (with mussels and clams)—are also excellent.

Via Manciotti 48. (✆ 0824-25013. Reservations recommended for dinner. Secondi 6€–11€ ($8.40–$15/£4.20–£7.70). MC, V. Wed–Mon noon–2:30pm and 7:30–11pm.

AROUND BENEVENTO
VALLE CAUDINA 🏵🏵
This beautiful valley, dominated by the Monte Taburno, is where the SS 7 (the Appian Way) passes between Capua and Benevento. If you take it out of Benevento, going

toward Capua (earlier in this chapter), you'll first come to the village of **Montesarchio,** picturesque with its imposing 15th-century **fortress,** but surrounded by modern sprawl. Just outside of town is the national park of **Monte Taburno** (1,394m/4,572-ft.; www.parcotaburno.it), which is a good place for a **hike.** Incidentally, this is the origin of the aqueduct that feeds the fountains of Caserta's Reggia (earlier in this chapter). To reach the trail head, take the scenic local road marked VITULANO at the eastern edge of Montesarchio, skirting the fortress and climbing the mountain; after 14km (8½ miles) you will reach a fork in the road (at Piano Caudio), where you need to bear left toward the **Rifugio-Albergo Taburno,** a bar/restaurant, at an altitude of 1,050m (3,444 ft.). The trail starts from the rifugio; it's a fairly easy climb that will take about an hour. From the top you can enjoy a splendid **panorama** ✸✸. Continuing on road SS 7, you'll reach **Sant'Agata dei Goti** ✸✸, a scenic medieval town built on a high tufa-stone cliff. Despite having been severely damaged by the earthquake of 1980, the town—which is built along an unusual semi-circular urban plan—is graced by many churches. The most attractive is the **Duomo** (originally from the 10th century but redone in the 12th), which retains some of its beautiful mosaic floor and, in the crypt, the original frescoes from the 10th century. Other noteworthy churches are the 13th-century **Chiesa dell'Annunziata** and 11th-century **Chiesa di San Menna.**

VALLE TELESINA ✸

Along route SS 372 and beyond is the valley of **Solopaca,** producer of the best D.O.C. wines in the region. Among the small medieval towns high up on the vine-yard-covered hills, the most attractive are **Torrecuso** ✸, **Guardia Sanframondi** ✸, and **Cusano Mutri** ✸✸, each complete with medieval *borgo* and castle. The most popular destination in this valley, though, is **Telese Terme,** a green and pleasant little town, famous for its spa. The town's sulfuric thermal springs—good for the skin and beneficial to ear ailments as well as respiratory illness—suddenly appeared after the earthquake of 1349. The spa, called **Terme di Telese** ✸ (✆ **0824-976888;** www.termeditelese.it), is in a beautiful park where pavilions and pools have been built over the natural springs, offering baths, mud applications, and a number of other therapies. Within walking distance (1km/½ mile southeast) is the pretty **lake of Telese** ✸; a couple of miles out of town to the west are the ruins of **Telesia** ✸, a Sannite and then Roman town, whose walls and many ruins can be admired.

Farther along you'll come to **Cerreto Sannita** ✸✸, a harmonious late baroque town that was completely rebuilt after the earthquake of 1688. Many of its churches are worth a visit, including the **Cathedral, San Martino,** and **San Gennaro.** Today, local artists in Cerreto and in the nearby village of **San Lorenzello** continue the tradition of crafting 18th-century Capodimonte porcelains. You can admire the local craft at the **Mostra Permanente della Ceramica Antica e Moderna,** Piazza L. Sodo, off Corso Umberto I (✆ **0824-861337** or 0824-861700), and the **Museo Civico e della Ceramica,** Corso Umberto I, inside the church of San Gennaro and the Convent of Sant'Antonio (✆ **0824-815211**). To purchase some of the craftwork, head for **Keramos,** Via Nicotera 84 (✆ **0824-861463**), one of the best showrooms in town.

Farther north in **Pietraroja** ✸ is the **Geo-Paleontological Park** (✆ **0824-868000;** www.geologi.it/pietraroja), which displays many fossils, including a complete baby dinosaur—officially called Scipionyx Samniticus, but nicknamed Ciro by locals.

VAL FORTORE ⋆

This area is the home of the famous Padre Pio (Father Pius), who died in 1968 and was canonized by Pope John Paul II in 2002. He was born in **Pietrelcina** and became an important figure for his work with kids and teenagers; his town has now become a pilgrimage site. The excursion is well worth it, if only for the ride alone—the meandering road takes you through scenic green mountains that afford great views. From Benevento take SS 212; Pietrelcina is only about 12km (7½ miles) away.

We also recommend a visit to the medieval *borgo* of **San Marco dei Cavoti** ⋆, the hometown of *torroncini,* a delicious bite-size nougat candy, made with honey and nuts, and often dipped in dark chocolate. Among the best are the *baci* (kisses) from **Premiata Fabbrica Cavalier Innocenzo Borrillo,** Via Roma 66 (© **0824-984060**). Other fine torroncini artisans are **Anna Maria Borrillo,** Via Martiri di Bologna 18 (© **0824-984939**), **Dolciaria Borrillo,** Contrada Catapano 22 (© **0824-995099**), and **Antonina Petrillo,** Vico San Vincenzo 2 (© **0824-969266**), in Montefalcone di Val Fortore, a picturesque village nearby.

5 Avellino & the Hill Towns of Irpinia

35km (22 miles) S of Benevento and 54km (34 miles) E of Naples

On the outskirts of Naples, Irpinia is a mountainous region of hilltop medieval villages and green hills. It is renowned among connoisseurs for its food and wine, considered the best in Campania and among the best in Italy.

AVELLINO

The capital of Irpinia, Avellino grew out of the fortified village built by the Longobards near the site of Roman Abellinum (3km/2 miles to the west); the older city was abandoned because it was too difficult to defend. The population moved up to the new Avellino, which became an important town because of its strategic position dominating the road between Benevento and Salerno. The numerous earthquakes that have hit the area—last and not least the one in 1980, whose terrible economic repercussions are still felt here—have left little standing, yet there is still much that is well worth a visit.

GETTING THERE & AROUND   Avellino is easily reached by **train** from Benevento, Naples, and Salerno. Contact **Trenitalia** (© **892021** from anywhere in Italy; www.trenitalia.it) for fares and information. Trains arrive at Avellino's train **station,** on Via Francesco Tedesco.

If you are arriving by **car** (which we highly recommend for this area), take the AVELLINO exit off autostrada A16. You'll find a covered garage in Via Terminio 20 (© **0825-23574**).

You can easily get around Avellino **on foot,** although **SITA buses** (© **089-226604;** www.sitabus.it) serve most villages. To visit the rest of the area, we recommend renting a **car** through **Win Rent,** Corso Umberto I 89, Avellino (© 0825-756237), or **Hertz,** Via Tagliamento 337 (© **0825/39227;** www.hertz.com) and **Sixt,** Corso Umberto 87 (© **0825/756237;** www.e-sixt.com), both of which have an agency in town.

TOURIST INFO   The local tourist office is at Piazza della Libertà 50 (© **0825-74732**) and is open Monday through Friday 8am to 2pm and 2:30 to 4:40pm;

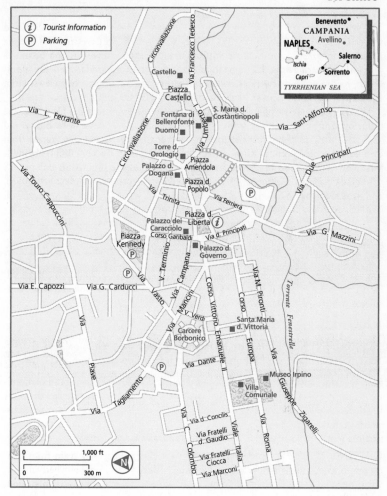

Map labels:

(i) Tourist Information
(P) Parking

Benevento
CAMPANIA
NAPLES   Avellino
Ischia
Capri
Salerno
Sorrento
TYRRHENIAN SEA

Castello
Piazza Castello
Via L. Ferrante
Via Francesco Tedesco
Circonvallazione
Fontana di Bellerofonte
Duomo
S. Maria d. Costàntinopoli
Via Sant'Alfonso
Torre d. Orologio
Palazzo d. Dogana
Piazza Amendola
Piazza d. Popolo
Via Ferriera
Via Due Principati
Circonvallazione
Via Touro Cappuccini
Via Trinità
Via d. Principati
Piazza d. Libertà
Palazzo dei Caracciolo
Corso Garibaldi
Via G. Mazzini
Piazza Kennedy
Palazzo d. Governo
Via E. Capozzi
Via G. Carducci
V. Terminio
Via Vasto
Via Marconi
Via Campana
Corso Vittorio Emanuele II
Via M. Pironti
Corso Europa
Torrente Fenestrelle
v. Verdi
Santa Maria d. Vittoria
Carcere Borbonico
Via Piave
Via Dante
Museo Irpino
Villa Comunale
Via Giuseppe Zigarelli
Via Roma
Via Tagliamento
Via C. Colombo
Via d. Concilis
Viale Italia
Via Fratelli d. Gaudio
Via Fratelli Ciocca
Via Marconi

0   1,000 ft
0   300 m
N

Saturday 9am to 1pm. The **EPT** office for the province is at Via Due Principati 5 (© **0825-74731** or 0825-74695; fax 0825-74757; www.eptavellino.it).

FAST FACTS   You'll find a **pharmacy** in Corso Vittorio Emanuele 11 (© **0825-35097**). You will find a number of banks and **ATMs** along Corso Vittorio Emanuele II, such as the **Banca di Roma,** Corso Vittorio Emanuele II 35 (© **0825-24737**). The **hospital San Giuseppe Moscati** is at Via Cristoforo Colombo 20 (© **0825-23343** or 0825-36891). For an **ambulance,** dial © **118.** You can call the **police** at © **113** or at © **112.** The **post office** is at Via Francesco De Sanctis 3, off Corso Europa (© **0825-781209**).

Pulcinella

Pulcinella, the famous white-dressed, black-masked, pizza- and spaghetti-eating character, is the Campanian counterpart to the Venetian masks of the *Commedia dell'Arte*. His familiar figure has become a sort of local hero, and plays an important role in celebrations, especially during **Carnival.** Many towns in Campania have claims for the paternity of this character—Capua for one—but the truth is more complicated. In Acerra (a little town just north of Naples), a tailor named Andrea Calcese "Ciuccio" is supposed to have invented Pulcinella sometime before his death around 1656 (you can still see his house in town at Via Suessola 6). Ciuccio did not actually invent Pulcinella; he popularized him after a farmer from Giffoni created him.

According to historians, though, the Pulcinella character already existed in the *Atellane* (traditional theatrical farces with typical characters, similar to the *Commedia dell'Arte*, which were common in Campania during the late Roman Empire), and that his name was derived from *pullicenus*, late Latin for "chick."

Whatever its origins, you will probably encounter Pulcinella at various turns if you travel through this region.

SPECIAL EVENTS   The town is famous for **Carnevale Irpino,** the festival organized for the celebration of Carnival. Included are traditional performances, the most famous of which is **Zeza.** Taking its name from the wife of Pulcinella, this musical farce narrates the adventures of the family when their daughter Porzia decides to get married to Don Zenobio. Contact the **EPT** (above) for a schedule of events.

EXPLORING THE TOWN

The little that remains of old Avellino centers around **Corso Umberto I,** crossing the medieval town toward the **Castello.** This was ruined not by earthquakes, as was most of the town, but during the Spanish wars at the beginning of the 18th century.

Duomo, aka Cattedrale dell'Assunta ✦   This 12th-century church was redone and added to in following centuries. The elegant facade is neoclassical, as are the decorations inside. The cathedral holds many masterpieces, including a beautiful **tabernacle** by Giovanni da Nola that you can admire in the chapel to the right of the main one. Also take note of the 16th-century carved **choir** at the back of the church, in the apse. Under the Duomo, you'll find the Cripta dell'Addolorata, or Church of Santa Maria dei Sette Dolori. It was created in the 17th century by adding a nave to the original Romanesque crypt and is decorated with **frescoes** and with Roman and medieval capitals. From the presbytery you can access the courtyard, where you can see remains of the original Longobard church and the partially restored Romanesque bell tower, decorated with Roman marble inscriptions from Abellinum.

Piazza Duomo. Free admission. Daily 9–11am and 5–7pm.

Museo Irpino 🌟🌟   Across from the public park of Villa Comunale, this modern museum houses an important collection of fascinating artifacts dating as far back as 4000 B.C. The extensive archaeological collection is in the main building, together with the grandiose 18th-century artistic *presepio* and a rich collection of **porcelain** from the late-18th to the early-19th century. The **picture gallery,** with an ensemble of 17th-, 18th-, and 19th-century Neapolitan masters, has been moved to the **Carcere Borbonico** (Piazza d'Armi, off Via Mancini, same hours as the museum), an interesting hexagonal building that once housed the prisons of the Bourbon kings. In rooms no. II and III are the artifacts excavated from the aeneolithic necropolis of Madonna delle Grazie (near Mirabella Eclano), including the reconstruction of a complete tomb of a tribal chief, buried with his dog. (By the way, "aeneolithic" means the transitional period between the neolithic and the Bronze Age; we looked it up.) A number of findings document life in the old Abellinum, including a great **mosaic** 🌟 from the 1st century (in the entrance hall), ceramics, fragments of frescoes, and the funerary collection from the 2nd-century **tomb of a young woman** 🌟, all in rooms no. VIII and IX. A new hall displays the recent findings from the Sanctuary of the Goddess Mefite, a cult going back to the 6th century B.C. that persisted through the Roman era. These were found in a site near the Passo di Mirabella.

Corso Europa. ⓒ 0825-38582. Free admission. Sun–Fri 8:30am–2pm.

WHERE TO STAY IN THE AREA
MODERATE
Hotel De La Ville 🌟   With its central location, luxury service, and elegant romantic vibe, this glitzy modern hotel wins the prize for best in town. Comfortable guest rooms are large and well-appointed, and bathrooms are good size. Public spaces are spacious and furnished with elegance—down to a garden complete with swimming pool (heart-shaped, no less). The hotel's restaurant **Il Cavallino** is excellent, serving traditional and historical Neapolitan and Irpinian dishes.

Via Palatucci 20, 83100 Avellino. ⓒ 0825-780911. Fax 0825-780921. www.hdv.av.it. 69 units. 210€ ($294/£147) double; from 360€ ($504/£252) suite. Rates include buffet breakfast. Children 2 and under stay free in parent's room. AE, DC, MC, V. Parking 10€ ($14/£7). **Amenities:** Restaurant; bar; billiards room; business center; concierge; disco; laundry service; outdoor pool; room service. *In room:* A/C, satellite TV w/pay movies, hair dryer, Internet, minibar, safe.

INEXPENSIVE
Agriturismo Pericle 🌟 *Kids*   This pleasant countryside villa offers elegant country-style accommodations on an organic farm. It is conveniently located for hiking and exploring the area, and offers good family-oriented amenities such as horseback and bicycle riding. They raise organic pigs (think sausages, salami, and wonderful roast pork) and other animals, and produce their own wine, an excellent Aglianico. The **restaurant** creates scrumptious meals of the farm's delicious offerings. If you like the cooking, you might want to take a cooking class with the chef, Mamma Rina.

Via Sottomonticchio, Montella. ⓒ 0827-609161. www.agriturismopericle.it. 10 units. 60€ ($84/£42) double. Rates include buffet breakfast. AE, DC, MC, V. Free parking. **Amenities:** Restaurant; bicycle rental; playground; 2 outdoor pools. *In room:* TV, minibar.

Hotel Serino 🌟🌟   This modern hotel graciously blends into the natural surroundings of the slopes of Monte Terminio (above), affording breathtaking views from its gardens and terraces. Guest rooms are comfortable and large, and a panoramic swimming plus and a good restaurant complete the offerings.

Via Terminio 119, 83028 Serino. ✆ **0825-594901**. Fax 0825-594166. www.hotelserino.it. 50 units. 100€ ($140/£70) double. Rates include buffet breakfast. AE, DC, MC, V. Free parking. **Amenities:** Restaurant; bar; business center; concierge; disco; laundry service; outdoor pool; soccer field; room service. *In room:* A/C, satellite TV, minibar.

WHERE TO DINE
MODERATE
Antica Trattoria Martella ✸✸✸ IRPINIAN   This historic restaurant is the best in Avellino, serving difficult-to-find specialties in an elegant yet unsophisticated style. The vaulted ceilings, wooden chairs with straw seats, white tablecloths, and attentive service create an old-fashioned atmosphere, which is perfect for experiencing the seasonal local menu. If they have it, try the unusual *fusilli affumicati con ricotta e pancetta* (lightly smoked homemade pasta with ricotta and pork belly) or the *tagliatelle al tartufo nero*, seasoned with the famous local black truffles. We also recommend the *coniglio ripieno con patate* (stuffed rabbit with potatoes).

Via Chiesa Conservatorio 10, Avellino. ✆ **0825-32123**. www.ristorantemartella.it. Reservations recommended. Secondi 12€–16€ ($17–$22/£8.40–£11). AE, DC, MC, V. Tues–Sun 1–3pm and Tues–Sat 8–11pm.

Gastronomo ✸ IRPINIAN/PIZZA   Simplicity, a welcoming atmosphere, and excellent food and wine combine to make this local favorite a great place for a meal. The pizza is very good, but we also recommend the *antipasto della casa*, the best way to sample a variety of local cheese and cured meats. The homemade ravioli is delicious and the lamb stew superb.

Via Nazionale 39, 83050 Montemarano. ✆ **0827-67009**. Reservations recommended. Secondi 11€–18€ ($15–$25/£7.70–£13). AE, DC, MC, V. Thurs–Tues noon–3pm; Thurs–Sat and Mon–Tues 7:30–11pm.

INEXPENSIVE
Da Mario ✸ IRPINIAN   This down-to-earth trattoria prepares hearty, home-style dishes, from *cavatelli* and *ravioli*, to *brasato* (beef in wine sauce), *agnello* (lamb), and *coniglio arrosto* (roasted rabbit). Do not expect elegance—this is a traditional local restaurant where you will get good food and service. The local wine is excellent.

Via Laura Beatrice Oliva Mancini 15. ✆ **0825-26499**. Reservations recommended for dinner. Secondi 8€–12€ ($11–$17/£5.60–£8.40). AE, DC, MC, V. Mon–Sat noon–3pm and 7:30–11pm.

Valleverde-Zi Pasqualina ✸ IRPINIAN/ENOTECA   This homey trattoria-cum-enoteca serves excellent, always-fresh food. The *antipasto della casa* is a medley of cheese, cured meats, and other local specialties, and their homemade fusilli and ravioli are superb. For secondi, the *pollo alla cacciatora* (chicken stew) is flavorful, or just jump directly to the simple but rich desserts (homemade, of course).

Via Pianodardine 112, Atripalda. ✆ **0825-626115**. www.ziapasqualina.it. Reservations recommended. Secondi 8€–12€ ($11–$17/£5.60–£8.40). AE, DC, MC, V. Mon–Sat noon–3pm and 7:30–11pm. Closed Aug, Easter, Christmas period.

BEYOND AVELLINO
SANTUARIO DI MONTEVERGINE ✸✸✸
Very close to Avellino, **Sanctuario di Montevergine** ✸ (✆ **0825-72924**; www.santuario dimontevergine.it) is famous for its art and for the splendid view, encompassing the whole valley down to Mount Vesuvius and the Gulf of Naples. On a sunny day, the

panorama is beautiful enough—some say—to justify your whole trip to Campania; in really bad weather, we wouldn't even attempt the drive up.

Located almost at the top of Mount Montevergine, at an altitude of 1,270m (4,166 ft.)—the summit rises 1,493m (4,897 ft.)—the sanctuary is a popular pilgrimage destination which attracts over a million people every year, especially between May and September. Founded by Guglielmo da Vercelli in 1119 for his order of the Verginiani—San Guglielmo Day is June 25, an occasion for important celebrations—the sanctuary is composed of a hostel, the monastery, a museum and gallery, and **two churches.** The smaller, original church was probably consecrated in 1124; the huge new basilica, finished in 1961, is nestled into the older one at a right angle, over the original church's left nave.

In the presbytery of the **New Church,** rich in marble decorations, you can admire the so-called *Throne of the Madonna,* the great 13th-century painting of the **Madonna di Montevergine** ✸. On each side of the new presbytery, small doors lead to the **Old Church.** Built in the 12th century, the Old Church was completely redecorated in the 17th century but still shows its Gothic structure. In the presbytery, you will see the splendid 17th-century **main altar** ✸, a masterpiece of intarsia in marble and precious stones. In the apse is a beautiful carved choir from the 16th century. At the end of the right nave is the Gothic **Cappella del Sacramento,** holding a magnificent 13th-century **baldaquin** ✸ in mosaic, and the ornate 15th-century marble **cyborium** ✸. The church is rich in funerary monuments with amazing stone inlay work, such as the grandiose **Monument to Caterina Filangeri** from the 15th century, located at the end of the right nave to the left, before the Cappella del Sacramento. The Gothic portal of the original church is also very beautiful, and warmer than the rather austere modern style of the new construction.

To reach the monastery from Avellino (21km/13 miles away), take SS 7bis and then switch to SS 374 following signs for MERCOGLIANO; here you take the winding mountain road to MONTEVERGINE. Continuing up the road past the monastery, you'll reach after 1.5km (1 mile) the head of the trail to the mountaintop. The short walk takes only about 15 minutes, and from the summit you can enjoy an even better panorama than from the sanctuary.

EN ROUTE TO MIRABELLA ECLANO

Leaving Avellino in an easterly direction, you will come to a fork in the road. Bear left, and follow the signs for PRATA DI PRINCIPATO ULTRA. This village is only about 11km (6½ miles) north of Avellino and is famous for its **Basilica dell'Annunziata** ✸✸✸, located 1.3km (¾ mile) north of the village. The church (✆ **0825-961019**), which was recently restored, is considered one of Irpinia's most important monuments. Built by the Longobards, it still shows remains of a paleochristian catacomb and a 6th-century basilica. From the modern little church you will access an elliptical **apse,** carved of tufa stone. This is believed to be from the 7th century and at its end has a fresco of *Madonna and Saints* dating to the 8th century. At the end of a courtyard to the left of the church is the entrance to the grotto, a Christian catacomb from the 3rd and 4th centuries and decorated with frescoes, altars, and sarcophagi.

Retracing your steps to the main road, take the scenic local route following signs for PRATO LA SERRA and SERRA. Continue in the direction of the sign for PIETRA DE FUSI, passing over the highway, and switch to the SS 90 at the sign for PASSO DI MIRABELLA.

This will eventually take you to the lively little town of **Mirabella Eclano,** at 47km (29 miles) northeast of Avellino. Mirabella grew over the ruins of Acquaputida, the town founded in the 11th century after Aeclanum (below) was abandoned due to Saracen attacks. Acquaputida, though, didn't have a long life: It was partially destroyed by natural catastrophes and civil wars in the 14th century. If you take a stroll in the streets, you will see many marble carvings and inscriptions from Roman and medieval times built into the walls of the houses. In the main square of the upper town is **Santa Maria Maggiore** church, with its beautifully carved and painted *Crocefisso* 🏛 from the 12th century, a Romanesque masterpiece by a Campanian artist.

Only 3.5km (2 miles) to the southwest (follow the signs for TAURASI) is the important **Eneolithical Necropolis of Madonna delle Grazie** 🏛. Dating back to 2000 B.C., these tombs were excavated in the tufa stone and have given up a rich collection of artifacts; most are on display in the Museo Irpino of Avellino (earlier in this chapter).

Back on SS 90, just before you reach **Passo di Mirabella,** are the ruins of **Aeclanum** (✆ **0825-449175**). One of the most important Sannite centers, the Aeclanum was taken by the Romans in 89 B.C. and became an important stop on the Via Appia. Aeclanum was destroyed in A.D. 662 during the wars against the Longobards, and the town of Quintodecimo was built on its ruins—which survived until the 11th century when it, too, was destroyed in the wars between Byzantines and Saracens. In the archaeological area you can see many remains of the Roman town, including segments of the walls, the theater, and the market square, as well as portions of houses and shops. The most important findings are conserved in Avellino's Museo Irpino (earlier in this chapter).

ON THE WAY TO SANT'ANGELO DEI LOMBARDI

Going east out of Avellino, bear right at the fork in the road with the sign for ATRIPALDA. Only 3.5km (2¼ miles) east of Avellino, **Atripalda** is a smallish agricultural town founded in the 11th century by the Longobards near the ruins of Roman **Abellinum** 🏛🏛. Although the large archaeological area has been used as a marble and construction-material "quarry" for centuries, you can see the ancient walls with semicircular towers and, inside the walls, the ruins of a large Roman house. In the center of Atripalda you can visit the **Collegiata di Sant'Ippolisto** 🏛 and its **crypt,** which was part of the **Specus Martyrum,** the subterranean structure where Saint Ippolisto and the other martyrs of Abellinum, killed by the notoriously cruel Emperor Domitian, are buried. The crypt is decorated with a beautiful fresco of a Christ Pantocrator from the 14th century.

Continuing east, you will come to **Montemarano** 🏛 19km (12 miles) east of Atripalda. Built on the top of a hill, it has a well-preserved **castle.** Another interesting attraction is the **Chiesa dell'Assunta,** where you can admire the nicely carved 16th-century portal and, inside, a unique 15th-century **folding chair,** decorated with delicate carvings and a *Sacra Famiglia* by Andrea Vaccaro; the seat was used by the bishop until recent times. This ancient little town is also famous for its **Carnival** celebrations. Festivities start on January 17—the feast of Sant'Antonio Abate—and continue until Mardi Gras. During the first weeks of Mardi Gras, groups of dancers and musicians, guided by a Pulcinella, tour the little town asking for offerings, but as Carnival ripens, the events multiply, including the now rare ritual of the *Tarantella,* that famous frenzied dance. Among the lighter events are farcical performances and the traditional

Parade of the Pulcinella, in which the entire town's Pulcinella characters participate. Contact **UNPLI Provinciale,** Via Derna 7 (© **082-524013**), for a schedule of events.

A few miles east of Montemarano, you can follow the signs for MONTELLA and then for PIANO DI VERTEGLIA, which will take you on a scenic road (SS 574) along the slopes of **Mount Terminio** ✶✶. This is an area of great natural beauty and is considered part of the Regional Park of the Monti Picentini. The little town of **Montella** is famous for its chestnuts.

Appendix A: Campania & the Amalfi Coast in Depth

A land of ancient civilizations, Campania has been inhabited since at least 4000 B.C., as shown by the many excavated necropolises here. A wonderful and fertile land, it attracted many people, who frequently fought for possession of it over the past 3,000 years. Its three main sections each had slightly different historical fates: the plains in the region's northern part and the hinterland of Naples—the *Campania Felix* of the Romans; the mountainous Sannio dominated by Benevento; and, to the south, the Amalfi Coast and the Cilento.

1 A Look at the Past

This brief survey of Campania's long and complex history is oriented toward the Amalfi Coast, but the rest of Campania is covered as well. Once we hit the Renaissance, the focus shifts primarily to Naples and its surroundings, which became the center of power in the region.

THE GREEKS

After a short stop on the island of Ischia, Calcidians founded the city of Cuma in 750 B.C., the first Greek city of Magna Grecia—the Greek cities outside the mainland. Cuma became a beacon of Greek civilization in Italy. Their expansion into the region, though, was contested by the Etruscans (below). In spite of this, they established other important colonies in the current area of Naples: first Partenope around 680 B.C., then Dicearchia (Pozzuoli) in 531 B.C., and then Neapolis in 470 B.C. In the meantime, Greeks from Sibari founded Posidonia (Paestum) in 600 B.C. and Elea (Velia) in 540 B.C.

Greeks won two major battles in Cuma against the Etruscans, one in 524 B.C. and the final in 474 B.C. Nevertheless, weakened by their fights with the Etruscans,

they could not resist the Sannite invasion in the 5th century B.C.

THE ETRUSCANS

While the Greeks colonized Campania's coast, the Etruscans colonized the inner plains, the rich agricultural areas around Capua, which they founded in the 9th century B.C., and south all the way down to the hinterland of Paestum. They, too, were weakened by their fights for supremacy in the region against the Greeks (above), so that when the Sannites began their expansion, Etruscan power in the area came to an end.

THE SANNITES

This mountain people, originally from nearby Abbruzzo, had been expanding south in the Appennines, with an economy based on sheep husbandry. Also a warrior culture, they established a flourishing civilization in Benevento and then moved toward the coast in the 5th century B.C., causing conflict with both Greeks and Etruscans.

Sannite attacks were successful; they took over Capua in 424 B.C. and then took Cuma 3 years later in 421 B.C. Their influence quickly expanded to other cities such as Neapolis, Pompeii, and Herculaneum and gave birth to a new civilization, the Oscans (below).

The inland Sannites of Beneventum, in the meantime, came into opposition with the Romans who, by the 4th century B.C., had started their expansion southward. This led to the three famous Sannite wars. It took Rome from 343 B.C. to 290 B.C. to overcome the Sannites. The strongly independent Sannites, however, kept creating problems for the Romans. Finally, Beneventum was destroyed and later rebuilt as a Roman colony.

THE LUCANIANS

Another Italic mountain population, the Lucanians came from the nearby region of Basilicata. Slightly less belligerent than their Sannite cousins, they also started a migration toward the coast. They took over Posidonia (Paestum) in 400 B.C., but failed to overcome Elea (Velia). Like the Sannites farther north, they merged with the existing Greek population into the cultural melting pot that became the Oscans (below).

THE OSCANS

After their victories over the Greeks and Etruscans, the Sannites in the plains merged culturally with Etruscans and Greeks, giving birth to the Oscan civilization. This original population had strong Sannite roots, blending important cultural elements of the other two civilizations in a way that created a unique individual character with its own language. They made their capital in Capua.

Over time, the Oscans became so distinct from the original Sannites, however, that they actually shifted their support to Rome during its conquest of Campania.

THE ROMANS

The Romans took advantage of the opposition between the Oscans and the Sannites to extend their influence in the region. In exchange for allegiance to the Republic, Rome bestowed Roman citizenship, with the right to vote and decide on public affairs (but with the obligation of military service). Citizen colonies were set up as settlements of Roman farmers after the original people had given allegiance (voluntarily, or by sheer force). This worked better with the Oscans than with the Sannites, who continued to oppose Rome even after they lost the war (above). The Romans founded Paestum in 273 B.C., Beneventum in 268 B.C., then Salernum and Puteoli (modern Pozzuoli) in 194 B.C. These cities were fortified and linked to Rome by the famous Roman roads, such as the Appian Way, which led to Capua, then Beneventum,

Dateline

- 4000 B.C. Local people are already organized in villages and active in commercial exchange with other Mediterranean groups.
- 800 B.C. The first Greek settlements appear along the southern coast. Cuma and Ischia are founded.
- 600 B.C. Parthenope is founded over Monte Echia (behind Piazza del Plebiscito

in modern Naples) by Greek colonists. In the meantime, the Etruscans have been establishing colonies in the interior of Campania, as far down as the Sele River, inland of Paestum.

- 524 B.C. The first battle of Cuma between Etruscans and Greeks is won by the Greeks.
- 474 B.C. The second battle of Cuma occurs, when allied

Cumans and Syracusans defeat the Etruscans.

- 400 B.C. The Sannites descend from their inland towns on the hills toward the plains and the sea. They occupy Capua in 424 B.C. and Cuma in 421 B.C.
- 343–290 B.C. The three Sannite wars between Romans and Sannite end with a Roman victory, but the Sannites continue to rebel.

continues

and then all the way to Brindisi, on the Ionian Sea on Italy's eastern coast.

In this way, a stern Roman culture was added to the pre-existing local mixture. The social war from 91 B.C. to 88 B.C.—and, even more so, the civil war instigated by the dictator Sulla from 82 B.C to 81 B.C.—caused great destruction in Campania, especially to the rebellious Sannio region, which was almost completely wiped out. Peace came again with the advent of Rome's first emperor, Gaius Octavius Augustus.

Under the Empire, Campania was completely Romanized, but its agricultural strength was slowly supplanted by the production of Africa and Spain, leading to a strong local recession.

When the Empire ended in A.D. 395, the richest plains of Capua and Paestum had been abandoned and were in the throes of a malaria epidemic; the population was forced to found new villages up in the mountains, a situation that would not improve dramatically until the 20th century.

THE BYZANTINE & THE LONGOBARDS

With the end of the Roman Empire, barbarian invasions began. The Goths from the north invaded the region in 410, while the Vandals from Africa sacked and destroyed Capua in 456; the Byzantines counterattacked against the Goths and finally drove them out in 555; but (only a few years later, in 570), the Longobards arrived from the Appennines and took over the interior. The Byzantines struggled to maintain power but eventually lost, keeping only the harbors of Naples, Sorrento, and Amalfi; even Salerno was occupied by the Longobards in 630.

The Longobards' aristocracy oppressed Latin populations, but the yoke was lifted a bit when the Longobards converted to Catholicism thanks to the bishop of Benevento, Barbato; the conversion allowed the monasteries to begin operating again, and their role in preserving classical culture was immense. Later (in the 13th century), the Abbey of Monte Cassino, in northern Campania, would be, for a time, the home of the greatest philosopher-theologian in Europe, St. Thomas Aquinas.

In the second half of the 8th century, the Longobard prince Arechi II moved his court from Benevento to Salerno, causing an increasing tension between the two towns, which resulted in civil war and the splitting of the Longobard realm into two independent principalities in 849. This marked the beginning of the end for the Longobards; in the 10th century, Capua also became an independent

- 275 B.C. Rome defeats the rebellious Sannites of Maluentum and changes the name of the town to Beneventum, turning it into a Roman colony in 268 B.C.
- 273 B.C. Rome establishes a colony in Paestum.
- 211 B.C. Rome completely defeats the Sannites of Capua and turns that town into a Roman colony as well.

- 194 B.C. The Romans refound Pozzuoli with the name of *Puteoli,* as well as Salerno.
- A.D. 79 On August 24, Mount Vesuvius erupts, burying the prosperous towns of Pompeii, Herculaneum, and Stabiae.
- 476 Romolo Augustolo, the last Roman emperor, dies inside the *castrum lucullanum*—today's Castel dell'Ovo.

- 5th century Campania is divided among Goths, Longobards, and Byzantines.
- 553 The Byzantines chase the Goths from Naples and establish a duchy.
- 570 The Longobards descend from the Appennines and eventually take Benevento.
- 839 Amalfi chases out the Longobards who had occupied the city 3 years before.
- 9th century Naples and Amalfi, allied with Gaeta,

principality, after having been destroyed by the Saracens in 841 and refounded on more secure grounds.

In the meantime, Amalfi became independent from the Byzantine Duchy of Naples and started gaining strength and power as a maritime commercial republic, maintaining strong contact with both the Byzantine and the Muslims in the East.

THE SARACENS

The Arab period in Sicily began in 827. Taking advantage of the Longobards' civil war, the Saracens—Arabs who had started out in the region as mercenaries—took over a few small harbor towns (particularly Agropoli in 882), and started attacking and sacking the other towns along the coast.

Under these repeated assaults, the once-prosperous coastal towns of Campania became deserted, as the people sought refuge in the hills and the countryside. Some of the towns were then reborn, often in more defensive locations and surrounded by heavy fortifications.

THE NORMANS, SWABIANS & ANGEVINS

Things changed with the arrival of the Normans, who reintroduced the concept of central government and unity in southern Italy. Their first base was Aversa, near Naples, established in 1029, and from there they rapidly expanded their conquest to Capua in 1062, Amalfi in 1073, and Salerno in 1076, where they established their capital until Naples was also annexed to the kingdom in 1139. The Normans then proceeded south and won over Sicily, displacing the Arabs who had ruled the island for 2 centuries.

Salerno became a splendid town and a beacon of culture and learning, thanks to the development of its medical school, the first and most important medical center of the whole Western world. Benevento, on the other hand, had passed appraisal by the power of the Popes in 1051 and stayed so until the unification of Italy in 1860.

The Normans introduced feudalism, a repressive social system that discouraged individual economic initiative, and which undermined the very base of the kingdom. When the dynasty became weaker, it passed to the Swebians and then to the Angevins. The feudal chiefs in Sicily revolted and attacked the central monarchy in the famous "Sicilian Vespers" of 1282. Led by Aragonese elements, the Angevins resisted and succeeded in retaining their power in Campania, but the Cilento—right at the border of the reduced kingdom, and the coastal towns suffered immense casualties and depopulation.

---

defeat the Saracens and the Muslim Turks (who had established themselves in Licosa in 845), in Agropoli in 882, and at the mouth of the Garigliano River in 883.

- **915** The Arab colony at the mouth of the Garigliano River is defeated and the Arabs are forced out.
- **10th & 11th centuries** Amalfi's Maritime Republic reaches its apogee.

- **1030** The Norman Rainolfo Drengot obtains the county of Aversa, opening the way to the establishment of Norman rule in Campania.
- **1139** Naples surrenders to Ruggero II, and becomes part of the Norman kingdom of Sicily.
- **1194** The Swabian dynasty replaces the Norman one in the southern kingdom.

- **1225** Birth of St. Thomas Aquinas at Rocca Secca.
- **1266** The Angevins defeat the Swabians in the battle of Benevento, taking over the kingdom. Carlo I transfers the capital from Palermo to Naples.
- **1442** The kingdom passes to the Aragonese dynasty. It changes hands several times during the rest of the century.

continues

In the mid-13th century, the Angevins had established the capital in Naples, which flourished, but the kingdom's interior was abandoned to heavy feudal rule, which smothered commerce and economic activity and led to extreme poverty, which in turn fostered the growth of groups of bandits in the hills who made all road communication unsafe. The legacy of these centuries of stagnation and misrule persists to this day. The situation worsened still when the rule of the kingdom shifted to Spain.

SPANISH RULE

Spanish rule was seemingly so backward that even many histories of Naples contain a large blank spot for this 2-century-long period. The main events of Spanish rule were revolts against it—in 1547, 1599, 1647, and 1674, to name the major ones. The former kingdom of Naples was ruled by a Spanish viceroy, and the resulting extraction of taxes and the imposition of authoritarian rule were onerous. Philip IV called Naples "a gold mine which furnished armies for our wars and treasure for their protection." The Spanish did build some great palaces and churches, though it is perhaps symbolic that Naples's Palazzo Reale was built for King Philip III, who never lived here. The great plague also occurred during this period, and wiped out half the population.

THE BOURBONS

During the tangled period of the War of Spanish succession in the early 18th century, Naples was ruled by Austrians for 27 years. Naples regained its independence in 1734, with Carlo di Borbone. The independence of the kingdom of Naples was at last recognized by Spain and the Papacy. Carlo revitalized the kingdom, improving the roads, draining the marshes in the area of Caserta, and creating new industries—such as the silk manufacturers in San Leucio, the ceramic artistry in Capodimonte, and the cameo and coral industries in Torre del Greco. The improvements continued during the 10 years of Napoleonic power, when the feudal system was completely dismantled and land was redistributed, creating new administrative and judicial structures. This gave new life to the provinces but, once the Bourbons returned, they were unable to strike a balance with the developing bourgeoisie. The region was thus poised for rebellion when Garibaldi arrived and brought about the unification of Italy in 1861.

A UNITED ITALY

Thanks to the brilliant efforts of Camillo Cavour (1810–61) and Giuseppe Garibaldi (1807–82), the kingdom of Italy was proclaimed in 1861. Victor Emmanuel

---

- **1503** The French are finally driven from Naples, and the kingdom falls under Spanish rule.
- **1509** Naples refuses the establishment of the Inquisition. The attempt to establish the "Santo Oficio" fails again in 1547: Naples will be the only town in the Catholic world to successfully stave it off.
- **1528** Naples almost falls to the French, but Admiral

Andrea Doria sides with the Spaniards and secures a victory.
- **1558** The Saracens—in this case, the Barbary pirates—sack Sorrento.
- **1631** On December 16, Mount Vesuvius erupts again, killing over 3,000.
- **1647** Masaniello's Rebellion, a revolt against Spanish taxes and oppression, is led by a fish peddler in Naples.

- **1656** The plague seizes Naples for 6 months. Half of the population—over 200,000 people—is killed.
- **1707** The Austrian Habsburgs obtain Naples as a result of the Spanish succession wars.
- **1734** The kingdom of Naples recovers its independence with the Bourbon dynasty.
- **1799** In Naples, insurrection leads to the establishment of

(Vittorio Emanuele) II of the House of Savoy, king of Sardinia, became the head of the new monarchy.

Unfortunately, if the new kingdom was politically good for Campania, it was disastrous for Campania's economy: The northern government imposed heavy taxes, and the centralized administration paid little attention to local differences and needs. This killed the burgeoning industry that had been developing thanks to the Bourbons' paternalism and protection. Despite these setbacks, though, toward the end of the 19th century the coastal area started to develop the agricultural specialties that still exist today.

FASCISM & WORLD WAR II

Fascism achieved little success outside the urban area of Naples and was mostly embraced by prefects and notables in the rest of Campania. The region paid a heavy toll during World War II, when it was heavily bombarded in preparation for the Allied landing on September 8, 1943, when 55,000 Allied troops stormed ashore. Known as the "Salerno Invasion," it actually involved landings in a long arc from Sorrento and Amalfi to as far south as the area of Paestum. The Nazis occupied the region and set up a desperate resistance, retreating slowly for long months just north of Caserta along the Garigliano River. This involved one of the war's most notorious battles, the several-months siege of Monte Cassino, which left the ancient monastery a heap of rubble. The Nazis destroyed as much as they could during their retreat, sacking and vandalizing everything—even the most important section of the Naples State Archives was burned.

In September 1943, Naples revolted and managed to chase out the occupiers, only days before the Allied forces arrived in the city. Other towns' insurrections resulted in horrible massacres; men and women organized guerrilla groups against the Nazis, hiding out in the mountains and hills and striking mostly at night, while the Allies bombarded their towns and cities. After many hard months of fighting, Campania was finally freed in June 1944.

THE POSTWAR YEARS

In 1946, Campania became part of the newly established Italian Republic—although Naples had given its preference to the monarchy in the referendum—and reconstruction began. Even though the war had left Italy ravaged, the country succeeded in rebuilding its economy. By the 1960s, as a member of the European Community (founded in Rome in 1957), Italy had become one of the world's leading industrialized nations, prominent in the manufacture of automobiles and

---

the short-lived Parthenopean Republic.

- **1806** After several battles, the kingdom of Naples is taken over by the French.
- **1816** The Bourbons take back the kingdom.
- **1840** The road SS 163—the famous Amalfi Drive—is opened to traffic.
- **1860** On September 7, Garibaldi enters Naples; Campania becomes part of the new kingdom of Italy.

- **1940** On September 9, "Operation Avalanche," the Allied landings around Salerno, begins. On November 1, Allied planes bomb Naples. It is the first of 105 attacks that will cause over 22,000 deaths.
- **1943** On October 1, Allied troops are welcomed into a Nazi-free Naples.
- **1946** The Italian Republic is officially established in

Naples, although the city had given its preference to the Monarchy in the referendum.
- **1950s** Naples grows explosively, with 80,000 dwellings built within a decade.
- **1980** On November 23, a violent earthquake (10 on the MCS scale) produces great destruction, especially in the provinces of Avellino and Salerno, causing over 3,000 deaths.

continues

office equipment. Campania was slow to recover; the terrible destruction that it suffered, the plague of corruption, plus the rising development of the Camorra, Campania's Mafia-like organization, hindered the region's development more than others.

The great earthquake (10 on the MCS scale) that hit the region on November 23 gave it another push back, causing great destruction and economic hardship—over 3,000 people died, especially in the provinces of Avellino and Salerno, at the heart of the quake.

In the 1990s, a new Naples mayor and new regional government began investing more time and money in the restoration of Campania's artistic treasures, the reorganization of old museums, and the creation of new museums throughout the region. Just as important, the new government declared war on corruption and criminality. The millennium celebrations and the Papal Jubilee of 2000 brought about further renovations. Results have been spectacular; the center of Naples has been transformed from a depressed state into a sort of open-air museum with tons of artistic and historical attractions.

At the same time, the escalating war against the Camorra in Naples has attracted much press attention over the past year or so, casting doubt on the city's safety. In our opinion, however, the accounts are sensationalized. Life in the historical part of the city has remained virtually untouched by Camorra violence, and improvements continue to be made, to the extent that Naples's artistic treasures, as well as the attractions of the whole Campania region, become more and more accessible to visitors every day.

2 Art & Architecture in Campania

Campania's fertile and rich lands have attracted various peoples since prehistoric times, so it's not surprising that the territory bears the marks of the many civilizations. Campania boasts Italy's richest trove of monuments from antiquity, with superb Greek ruins and unique Roman remains. You'll also find medieval castles and towns, Longobard, Norman, and Norman-Sicilian (or Arabo-Norman) architecture, and some of the richest collections of Renaissance and baroque monuments in Italy. However, art here didn't die with modern times—Naples continues to be a lively center of artistic life, especially in music and the figurative arts.

- **1993** Antonio Bassolino is elected mayor of Naples. A major cleanup, restoration, and anti-crime campaign begins.
- **1994** The G7 meeting is held in Naples, attended by the heads of state of the seven leading industrialized countries.
- **1995** The historic center of Naples is included in the UNESCO list of World Heritage. The archaeological areas of Pompeii, Herculaneum, and Torre Annunziata, as well as the Reggia of Caserta and the Amalfi Coast, are added in 1997.
- **2005** In the early part of the year, a crime war between rival Camorra factions gets international press, but historic Naples is unaffected.

PREHISTORY

The islands and mountains of Campania are home to a huge trove of prehistoric art, from the grottoes of Palinuro and Marina di Camerota, to the necropolis of Mirabella Eclano, to the beautiful painted terra cottas of the Grotta delle Felci in Capri, to the rich Grotta di Pertosa near Salerno. Prehistoric Italy is probably the least appreciated aspect of Italian history, but it's fascinating.

THE LEGACY OF THE ETRUSCANS & THE GREEKS ON LOCAL ITALIC ART

The Greeks and the Etruscans started to introduce their artistic styles to Campania in the 9th century B.C. From the ruins of **Cuma**—the first Greek colony in Italy—to the wonderful temples of **Paestum,** to the acropolis of **Velia,** Campania is rich with examples of Greek architecture, and the region's jewelry and metal work bear the mark of Etruscan influence. Etruscan and Greek styles were deeply embedded in the art of the local Italic populations when the Sannites took over the region in the 5th century B.C. The best examples of Italic art are the marvelous statues from the Sanctuary of the Goddess Matuta in **Santa Maria Capua Vetere;** and in particular the superb wall paintings from the tombs of **Cuma, Capua,** and **Paestum,** in the archaeological museums of Naples, Capua, and Paestum.

THE ROMANS

With its harbors, fertile plains, and thermal waters, Campania was a key region for the Romans when it came to local artistic development. To the great private homes built along the coasts and on the islands—especially in **Herculaneum, Pompeii, Oplontis,** and **Boscoreale**—Rome added many grand public buildings, such as the amphitheater in **Capua Vetere;** the triumphal arch in **Benevento;** the villas of **Minori, Pozzuoli, Baia;** and the rich collections now in the museums of Naples, Capua, and Salerno.

THE BYZANTINES, THE NORMANS & THE LONGOBARDS

Most of the early examples of art and architecture of the Middle Ages suffered from extensive damage, particularly by the Longobards. Only with the citizens' conversion to Catholicism and then with the arrival of the Normans did Byzantine art have a rebirth. The cathedrals of **Capua, Salerno,** and **Amalfi** are the richest examples of medieval art in the area, together with the **Basilica of Sant'Angelo in Formis,** the cathedral of **Sant'Agata dei Goti,** and the cathedral of **Casertavecchia,** as well as the Sanctuary of **Montevergine** and the cloister of Sant'Antonio in **Ravello.**

Campania also boasts several examples of magnificent medieval bronze doors, such as the ones in the cathedrals of Amalfi, Atrani, and Salerno. Classic Romanesque and Arab and Sicilian architecture intersect in these cathedrals. So do many of Campania's local cloisters, such as Amalfi's cathedral and the ex-convent of the Capuchins, Ravello's Palazzo Rufolo, and Sorrento's cloister of Saint Francis.

RENAISSANCE & BAROQUE

When the Angevins moved the capital of their kingdom to Naples, the enormous artistic development that was the Renaissance exploded in Campania. Famous artists came here from Tuscany—Lello da Orvieto, Giotto, Tino da Camaino, and Donatello—while local artists emerged on the scene: Roberto d'Oderisio, Niccolò di Bartolomeo da Foggia, and Colantonio, the teacher of Antonello da Messina. The results are visible in the many churches of Naples and in the Castel Nuovo.

In Salerno, the local painter Antonio Sabatini da Salerno gained renown in the early 16th century. Some of the most powerful examples of Campanian High Renaissance style are in Naples, where many Italian artists were active, including Rossellino, Benedetto and Giuliano da Maiano, fra' Giocondo, and Giovanni da Verona; Pietro Bernini, Giorgio Vasari, Polidoro da Caravaggio, and Antonio Solaro. The chapels of Monteoliveto and the Duomo in Naples are some of the best from this period.

In the 17th century, Caravaggio visited Naples and gave birth to the "Neapolitan School" of painting, which flourished in the 17th and 18th centuries under such names as Battistello Caracciolo, Andrea Vaccaro, Francesco Guarini, and Luca Giordano. Other Italian artists active in Naples during that period were Artemisia Gentileschi and Domenichino.

As with the rest of Italy, baroque art eventually gained dominance in Naples. The painter Francesco Solimena, together with the sculptors Domenico Antonio Vaccaro (son of Lorenzo) and Giuseppe Sanmartino, were among its most famous practitioners. Among the many area architects, Luigi Vanvitelli, with his work on the Reggia di Caserta, emerged as the preeminent figure. Music by such important artists as G. B. Pergolesi and Domenico Cimarosa was also produced during this period.

CONTEMPORARY ART

The 19th and 20th centuries saw the continuation of Campania's artistic potential, with the School of Posillipo (Anton Pitloo, Salvatore Fergola) and later the Scuola di Resina in the 19th century, the Gruppo Sud, and the Gruppo 1858 in the 20th century. Modern painters such as Domenico Morelli and Francesco Paolo Michetti, along with sculptors such as Francesco Jerace, gained fame in the early 20th century, while one of the more contemporary artists to emerge is the painter Gianni Pisani. While the most famous composers of Italian opera generally hailed from other cities, the region did produce probably the most famous operatic performer of all time: Enrico Caruso, who was born in Naples in 1873.

3 Gastronomia Campania & Its Wines (A Taste of Campania)

Food has always been one of life's great pleasures for the Italians. This has been true even from the earliest days: To judge from the lifelike banquet scenes found in Etruscan tombs, the Etruscans loved food and took delight in enjoying it. The Romans became famous for their never-ending banquets and for their love of exotic and even decadent treats, such as flamingo tongues.

Much of the Naples's cookery of **Naples** (spaghetti with clam sauce, or with ragù [meat sauce], meatballs, pizzas, fried calamari, and so forth) is already familiar to North Americans because so many Neapolitans moved to the New World and opened restaurants. However, Campanian cuisine has an enormous list of specialties that are much lesser known, especially those from the region's other provinces. **Avellino,** for example, shares many specialties with Naples, but also has a number of unique typical dishes which come from the mountain tradition, such as dishes flavored with **truffles,** and the delicious cakes made with **chestnuts,** both typical local products. **Benevento,** instead, has a completely different cuisine, reflecting its distinct history—it was part of the church's kingdom from the Renaissance onwards—and because of its strong Sannite heritage. Beneventan cuisine favors meat over fish and includes a large number of specialties made with pork and wild boar.

PASTA, MOZZARELLA & PIZZA

The stars of Campanian cuisine are so well known, they have become epicurean symbols of the nation: Italian cuisine as a whole is associated with pasta, pizza, and mozzarella. Yet these three creations were a direct consequence of the fertility and characteristics of Campania, defined by the Romans as *"Campania Felix,"* or the happiest and most perfect of countrysides. To this day, Campania is considered one of the most important and even ideal agricultural provinces around.

Famous for the quality of their **pasta** since the 16th century, the many mills of the Monti Lattari, at the beginning of the Sorrento peninsula, are counted among the best producers of pasta in the world (the ones in Gragnano are particularly renowned). The pasta here is still *trafilata a bronzo* (extruded through bronze forms), a procedure that leaves the pasta slightly porous, allowing for a better penetration of the sauce for tastier results (as opposed to steel forms, which makes the pasta perfectly smooth).

This region created the kinds of pasta that we eat today—*penne, fusilli, rigatoni,* and so on, each type strictly defined: *Spaghetti* is thicker than *vermicelli,* and both are thicker than *capellini.*

The warm plains of Campania are also home to the rare native buffalo, which is still raised in the provinces of Caserta and Salerno. Campanians have made **mozzarella** with delicious buffalo milk for centuries and look with disdain on what we all know as mozzarella—the similar cheese made with cow's milk—to which they refer a different name, *fiordilatte* (literally, "flower of milk"). Indeed, once you've tasted the real **mozzarella di bufala,** with its unique delicate flavor and

lighter texture, you'll surely be converted too, and will look down on regular mozzarella as an inferior kind of cheese. It's delicious as is, or try it in the *caprese,* a simple salad of sliced mozzarella, fresh tomatoes, and basil seasoned with extra-virgin olive oil.

Putting together the wheat, the mozzarella, and the third famous produce of this region, the tomato, Neapolitans one day invented **pizza.** The unique local tomatoes—especially those produced on the slopes of Mount Vesuvius—have basically no seeds: Imagine a tomato with no central cavity (no spongy, white stuff, either), but filled just with fruit meat, both flavorful and juicy. These are the *pomodoretti,* or small tomatoes of Mount Vesuvius. Obviously the result couldn't be anything but a bestseller, and pizza quickly spread from Naples throughout the world.

Be forewarned that many tourists, however, are disappointed by Neapolitan pizza. Here the dough and the tomatoes are the key ingredients—together with the olive oil, of course—and cheese is an option. The traditional "Neapolitan pizza" is actually called "marinara," with a thick crust that is crunchy on the outside and covered with fresh tomatoes, olive oil, and oregano. Funny enough, what Romans and the rest of Italy call Neapolitan pizza (pizza Napoletana, with tomatoes, cheese, and anchovies) is referred to here in Naples as "Roman pizza" (alla Romana). Therefore, cheese lovers beware! If you ask for a Neapolitan pizza in Naples, you'll be offered a marinara, with no cheese at all.

The Passeggiata

This time-honored tradition takes place nightly in every town in Italy. Shortly after 6pm, men and women, young and old alike, stroll before dinner in the town center, usually through the main piazza and surrounding streets. Often members of the same sex link arms or kiss each other in greeting. There's no easier way to feel a part of everyday life in Italy than to make the *passeggiata* part of your evening routine.

The second traditional pizza in Naples is the *margherita.* Named after Margherita di Savoia, queen of Italy, who asked to taste pizza during her residence in the Royal Palace of Naples before the capital was moved to Rome, the pizza bears the colors of the Italian flag: basil for the green, mozzarella for the white, and red for the tomatoes. The new pizza met with immediate favor, eventually surpassing the popularity of its older counterpart. Pizza evolved with the addition of a large variety of other toppings, but purist pizzerias in Naples (such as Da Michele in Naples—see chapter 3) that serve only these two types. In Naples, you can also taste another wonderful type of pizza: **pizza fritta.** This wonderful creation is served only in truly old-fashioned places where a double round of pizza dough is filled with ricotta, mozzarella, and ham, and deep-fried in a copper cauldron of scalding olive oil. It arrives as puffy as a ball, but as you poke into it, the pizza flattens out, allowing you to delve into the delicious (though not exactly cholesterol-free) dish.

ANTIPASTI E CONTORNI
Italian delight in food has remained strong in Campania throughout the centuries, seemingly in spite of the region's poverty. In fact, the region's poverty prompted the development of an important local characteristic when it comes to food: expediency. Ease and quickness, and making something out of almost nothing, were the driving forces behind Campanians coming up with some of the most delicious, yet simplest, concoctions in the history of cuisine. Check out the *antipasti* buffet of any good restaurant, and you'll be certain to find variety, from scrumptious vegetable dishes to seafood preparations like *sauté of shellfish,* delicious mussels and clams sautéed in a pan with garlic and olive oil. Alternatively, go for *polipetti in cassuola* or *affogati* (squid

cooked with a savory tomato-and-olive sauce inside a terra-cotta small casserole). Among the vegetables, do not miss the typical *zucchine a scapece,* a round of zucchini fried in olive oil and seasoned with tangy vinegar and fresh mint dressing (the same preparation is sometimes used for eggplant); or *involtini di melanzane* (a roll of deep-fried eggplant slices, filled with pine nuts and raisins, and warmed up in a tomato sauce) and, when in season, the *friarelli,* a local vegetable that is a cousin to broccoli but much thinner; it's often sautéed with garlic and red pepper, and is at its best paired with local sausages.

SOUPS & PRIMI
One of the most surprising and delicious associations you'll come across here is the delicious *zuppa di fagioli e cozze* (beans and mussels soup), which is common south of Naples and on Capri; another good and unique soup is the *minestra maritata,* a thick concoction of pork meat and a variety of fresh vegetables. The simple comfort food *pasta e patate* (pasta and potatoes smothered with cheese) will surprise you by how tasty it is. At the other end of the spectrum, the elaborated *sartù* (a typical Neapolitan baked dish made with seasoned rice filled with baby meatballs, sausages, chicken liver, mozzarella, and mushrooms) matches the difficulty of its preparation with the satisfaction of eating it.

Our preferred dish is the local pasta, including *scialatielli* (a fresh, homemade, eggless kind of noodles), served with sautéed seafood *(ai frutti di mare).* Another delicious, but more difficult-to-find pasta, is homemade *fusilli.* They can be served with all the traditional sauces: *con le vongole* (with clams), *zucchine e gamberi* (shrimp and zucchini), or *al ragù* (a meat sauce, where many kinds of meat can be cooked with tomatoes, including *braciole,* a meat *involtino* with pine nuts and raisins).

Listen Up: Restaurant Lingo

**Sezione fumatori o
  non fumatori?**
*seh-TSYOH-neh foo-mah-TOH-
ree oh nohn foo-mah-TOH-ree*

Smoking or
  nonsmoking?

È necessaria la giacca.
*EH neh-chehs-SAH-ryah lah
JAHK-kah*

You'll need a jacket.

**Mi dispiace, non sono
  permessi i pantaloni corti.**
*mee dee-SPYAH-cheh nohn
SOH-noh pehr-MEHS-see ee
pahn-tah-loh-nee KOHR-tee*

I'm sorry, no shorts are
  allowed.

**Posso portarle qualcosa
  da bere?**
*POHS-soh pohr-TAHR-leh
kwahl-KOH-zah dah BEH-reh*

May I bring you something
  to drink?

**Gradisce la carta
  dei vini?**
*grah-DEESH-eh lah KAHR-tah
day VEE-nee*

Would you like to see a
  wine list?

**Vuol sentire le nostre
  specialità?**
*vwol sehn-TEE-reh leh NOHS-
treh speh-chah-lee-TAH*

Would you like to hear
  our specials?

È pronto -a per ordinare?
*EH PROHN-toh -ah pehr
ohr-dee-NAH-reh*

Are you ready to order?

**Mi dispiace signore / signora,
  ma la suacarta di credito è
  stata rifiutata.**
*mee dee-SPYAH-cheh seen-NYOH-
reh / seen-NYOH-rah mah lah
SOO-ah KAHR-tah dee KREH-dee
-toh EH STAH-tah ree-few-TAH-tah*

I'm sorry sir / madame,
  your credit card was
  declined.

SECONDI

The cuisine of Naples—shared by most of Campania's coast—focuses on seafood, and some of the best main courses are made with fish. The *frittura* (*fritto misto* elsewhere in Italy) of shrimp and calamari is always a great pleasure, and here you will also find other kinds, such as the *fragaglie* (very small fish). The local version of *zuppa di pesce* is not often offered, but it is a delicious fish stew. Much more common and equally delicious are the *polpi affogati* or *in cassuola,* squid or octopus slowly stewed with tomatoes and parsley. Large fish is served grilled, with a tasty dressing of herbs and olive oil; *all'acqua pazza,* poached in a light broth made of a few tomatoes and herbs; or *alle patate* (baked over a bed of thinly sliced potatoes, and absolutely delicious). You might also find it *al sale* (cooked inside a crust of salt) to keep retain its moisture and flavors. Finally, if you have a taste for lobster, you should not miss out on the rare and expensive local clawless variety—*astice.*

For the turf, you might try *coniglio alla cacciatora* (rabbit with wine and black olives), a very tasty creation typical of Ischia; *brasato,* beef slowly stewed with wine and vegetables; *braciola di maiale*—a pork cutlet rolled and filled with prosciutto, pine nuts, and raisins cooked in a tomato sauce; or the simpler meat *alla pizzaiola,* a beef cutlet sautéed in olive oil and cooked with fresh tomatoes and oregano.

SWEETS

If Sicilians are famous for having a sweet tooth, Neapolitans come in a close second, with many delicious specialties on offer. Naples is famous for its *pastiera,* a cake traditionally prepared for Easter but so good that it is now offered year-round in most restaurants. Whole-grain wheat is soaked, boiled, and then used to prepare a delicious creamy filling with ricotta and orange peel in a thick pastry shell.

Another famous dessert is *babà,* a soft, puffy cake soaked in sweet syrup with rum and served with pastry cream. The famous *sfogliatelle* (flaky pastry pockets filled with a sweet ricotta cream) are so good with typical Neapolitan coffee that you shouldn't leave without tasting them; a special kind from Conca dei Marini on the Amalfi Coast is the *sfogliatella Santa Rosa,* filled with pastry cream and *amarene* (candied sour cherries in syrup) instead of ricotta, which was invented in the 14th-century Convento di Santa Rosa.

Each town in Campania, including the smaller villages, has some kind of sweet specialty, such as the *biscotti di Castellammare,* shaped like thick fingers in several flavors, and the several lemon-based pastries from the Sorrento and Amalfi regions: *ravioli al limone* (filled with a lemon-flavored ricotta mixture) from Positano; the *Sospiri* ("Sighs")—also called *Zizz'e Nonache* ("Nuns' Breasts") depending on which aspect you focus, the taste or the look. The dome-shaped small, pale pastries filled with lemon cream come from Maiori and Minori; and *dolcezze al limone,* the typical lemon pastries of Sorrento, are small puff pastries filled with lemon-flavored cream.

AND SOME VINO TO WASH IT ALL DOWN

Italy is the largest wine-producing country in the world (more than 1.6 million hectares/4 million acres of soil are cultivated as vineyards). Grapes were cultivated as far back as 800 B.C., probably introduced by the Greeks, and wine has been produced ever since. However, it wasn't until 1965 that laws were enacted to guarantee consistency in winemaking and to defend specific labels. Winemakers have to apply to have the right to add "D.O.C." *(Denominazione di Origine Controllata)* on their labels, and only consistently good wines from specific areas receive this right. The "D.O.C.G." on a label (the "G" means *garantita*) applies to even better wines from even more strictly defined producing areas. Vintners who are presently limited to marketing their products as unpretentious table wines—*vino da tavola*—often expend great efforts lobbying for an elevated status as a D.O.C.

Of Campania's five provinces, Benevento is the one with the largest number of D.O.C. wines, including the ***Aglianico del Taburno, Solopaca, Guardiolo, Sannio, Sant'Agata dei Goti,*** and ***Taburno,*** but Avellino is the only one with three D.O.C.G. wines: the wonderful *Taurasi,* considered to be one of the best Italian red wines, up there with Brunello and Barolo; the *Greco di Tufo,* straw-yellow and dry, with a delicate peach-almond flavor; and the *Fiano di Avellino,* a dry and refreshing white wine which received its D.O.C.G. label only in 1993.

From the volcanic soil of Vesuvius comes the amber-colored *Lacrima Christi* ("Tears of Christ"), and from the area of Pozzuoli, the D.O.C. *Campi Flegrei.* With meat dishes, try the dark mulberry-colored *Gragnano,* in the Sorrento peninsula, which has a faint bouquet of faded violets, and *Penisola Sorrentina.* From the islands come the *Ischia* red and white, and the *Capri.*

The Amalfi Coast also has its share of D.O.C. wines. the *Costa d'Amalfi* includes the *Furore*—white, red, and dry rosé—the red *Tramonti,* and the *Ravello*—white and dry with an idea of gentian, the rosé dry with a delicate violet and raspberry bouquet and with a slightly fuller body, and a red with the most body.

Produced in the Salerno area, the *Castel San Lorenzo* red and rosé are D.O.C., but there is also a *barbera* (fizzy red), a white, and a *moscato* (sweet). Farther south is the *Cilento,* another excellent D.O.C. wine.

From Caserta come the *Falerno,* the D.O.C. *Galluccio,* and the D.O.C. *Asprino d'Aversa,* which is light and slightly fizzy.

OTHER DRINKS

Italians drink other libations as well. The most famous Italian drink is **Campari,** bright red in color and flavored with herbs; it has a quinine bitterness to it. It's customary to serve it with ice cubes and soda.

Campania also excels at the preparation of *Rosolio,* sweet liquor usually herb- or fruit flavored, prepared according to recipes passed down by families for generations. The most famous is **limoncello,** a bright yellow drink made by infusing pure alcohol with the famous lemons from the Amalfi Coast, but others deserve similar fame, like the rare *nanassino,* made with prickly pears; and the *finocchietto,* made with wild fennel. Limoncello has become Italy's second-most popular drink (above). It has long been a staple in the lemon-producing region of Capri and Sorrento, and recipes for the sweetly potent concoction have been passed down by families there for generations. About a decade ago, restaurants in Sorrento, Naples, and Rome started making their own versions. Visitors to those restaurants as well as the Sorrento peninsula began singing limoncello's praises and requesting bottles to go. Now it's one of the most up-and-coming liqueurs in the world, thanks to heavy advertising promotions.

Beer, once treated as a libation of little interest, is still far inferior to wines produced domestically, but foreign beers, especially those of Ireland and England, are gaining great popularity with Italian youth, especially in Rome. This popularity is mainly because of atmospheric pubs, which now number more than 300 in Rome alone, where young people linger over a pint and a conversation. Most pubs are in the Roman center, and many are licensed by Guinness and its Guinness Italia operations. In a city with 5,000 watering holes, 300 pubs might seem like a drop, but because the clientele is young, the wine industry is trying to devise a plan to keep that drop from becoming a steady stream of Italians who prefer grain to grapes.

High-proof **grappa** is made from the "leftovers" after the grapes have been pressed. Many Italians drink this before or after dinner (some put it into their coffee). It's an acquired taste—to an untrained foreign palate, it often seems rough and harsh.

Appendix B:
Molto Italiano

Classified as a Romance language, Italian is closely related to Latin, French, Spanish, Portuguese, and Romanian. It arose from the Vulgar Latin of the late Roman Empire. The Italian alphabet has 21 letters. The letters **h**, **j**, **k**, **w**, **x**, and **y** are used only in words taken from other languages (such as jazz). Certain combinations of letters have special sounds in Italian, just as **ch**, **sh**, **th**, and **ng** have special sounds in English.

Italian has few pitfalls like silent letters; a word's sound closely resembles its written form. Such straightforward pronunciation makes this melodious language accessible and appealing to even the most casual student. Often **c** and **g** are stumbling blocks for beginners. Both have a soft sound before **e** or **i**, a hard sound before **a**, **o**, and **u**. Think **cubo** *KOO-boh* (cube) versus **arrivederci** *ahr-ree-veh-DEHR-chee* (bye) and **gala** *GAH-lah* versus **Luigi** *loo-EE-jee*. Double consonants should be pronounced twice— or lengthened and intensified. English speakers are already familiar with this from phrases such as gra**b b**ag, bla**ck c**at, goo**d d**ay, hal**f f**ull, goo**d j**ob, ho**t t**ea and ki**ds z**one. Enjoy the language's drama and richness, but don't slip into an operatic parody. Italians often accuse foreigners of doubling all consonants. Yet no native, when listening to an aria, would ever confuse **m'ama** (she loves me) with **mamma** (mom)!

1 Basic Vocabulary

English	Italian	Pronunciation
Thank you	**Grazie**	*graht*-tzee-yey
You're welcome	**Prego**	*prey*-go
Please	**Per favore**	*pehr* fah-*vohr*-eh
Yes	**Si**	see
No	**No**	noh
Good morning or Good day	**Buongiorno**	bwohn-*djor*-noh
Good evening	**Buona sera**	*bwohn*-ah *say*-rah
Good night	**Buona notte**	*bwohn*-ah *noht*-tay
How are you?	**Come sta?**	*koh*-may *stah*
Very well	**Molto bene**	*mohl*-toh *behn*-ney
Goodbye	**Arrivederci**	ahr-ree-vah-*dehr*-chee
Excuse me (to get attention)	**Scusi**	*skoo*-zee
Excuse me (to get past someone)	**Permesso**	pehr-*mehs*-soh

Where is . . . ?	Dovè . . . ?	doh-*vey*
the station	la stazione	lah stat-tzee-*oh*-neh
a hotel	un albergo	oon ahl-*behr*-goh
a restaurant	un ristorante	oon reest-ohr-*ahnt*-eh
the bathroom	il bagno	eel *bahn*-nyoh
To the right	A destra	ah *dehy*-stra
To the left	A sinistra	ah see-*nees*-tra
Straight ahead	Avanti (*or*	ahv-*vahn*-tee
	sempre dritto)	(*sehm*-pray d*reet*-toh)
How much is it?	Quanto costa?	*kwan*-toh *coh*-sta
The check, please.	Il conto, per favore	eel kon-toh *pehr* fah-*vohr*-eh
When?	Quando?	*kwan*-doh
Yesterday	Ieri	ee-*yehr*-ree
Today	Oggi	*oh*-jee
Tomorrow	Domani	doh-*mah*-nee
Breakfast	Prima colazione	*pree*-mah coh-laht-tzee-*ohn*-ay
Lunch	Pranzo	*prahn*-zoh
Dinner	Cena	*chay*-nah
What time is it?	Che ore sono?	kay *or*-ay *soh*-noh
Monday	Lunedì	loo-nay-*dee*
Tuesday	Martedì	mart-ay-*dee*
Wednesday	Mercoledì	mehr-cohl-ay-*dee*
Thursday	Giovedì	joh-vay-*dee*
Friday	Venerdì	ven-nehr-*dee*
Saturday	Sabato	*sah*-bah-toh
Sunday	Domenica	doh-*mehn*-nee-kah
January	Gennaio	*jehn-NAH-yoh*
February	Febbraio	*fehb-BRAH-yoh*
March	Marzo	*MAHR-tso*
April	Aprile	*ah-PREE-leh*
May	Maggio	*MAHD-joh*
June	Giugno	*JEWN-nyo*
July	Luglio	*LOOL-lyo*
August	Agosto	*ah-GOHS-toh*
September	Settembre	*seht-TEHM-breh*
October	Ottobre	*oht-TOH-breh*
November	Novembre	*noh-VEHM-breh*
December	Dicembre	*dee-CHEHM-breh*

A Little Tip

By adding a diminutive suffix, **-ino -a**, or **-etto -a**, or a combination of the two, you can make anything smaller or shorter. These endings replace the original -o and -a, respectively:

a really little bit   **pochino -a** (*poh-KEE-noh -nah*)

a really teeny tiny bit   **pochettino -a** (*poh-keht-TEEnoh-nah*)

NUMBERS

1	**uno** (*oo*-noh)	30	**trenta** (*trayn*-tah)
2	**due** (*doo*-ay)	40	**quaranta** (kwah-*rahn*-tah)
3	**tre** (tray)	50	**cinquanta** (cheen-*kwan*-tah)
4	**quattro** (*kwah*-troh)	60	**sessanta** (sehs-*sahn*-tah)
5	**cinque** (*cheen*-kway)	70	**settanta** (seht-*tahn*-tah)
6	**sei** (say)	80	**ottanta** (oht-*tahn*-tah)
7	**sette** (*set*-tay)	90	**novanta** (noh-*vahnt*-tah)
8	**otto** (*oh*-toh)	100	**cento** (*chen*-toh)
9	**nove** (*noh*-vay)	1,000	**mille** (*mee*-lay)
10	**dieci** (dee-*ay*-chee)	5,000	**cinque milla** (*cheen*-kway *mee*-lah)
11	**undici** (*oon*-dee-chee)		
20	**venti** (*vehn*-tee)	10,000	**dieci milla** (dee-ay-chee mee-lah)
21	**ventuno** (vehn-*toon*-oh)		
22	**venti due** (*vehn*-tee *doo*-ay)		

2 A Glossary of Italian Architectural Terms

Abside (Apse)   Half-rounded extension behind the main altar of a church. Christian tradition dictates that it be placed at the eastern end of an Italian church, the side closest to Jerusalem.

Ambo or **Ambones**   Pulpit, either serpentine or simple in form, erected in an Italian church.

Atrio (Atrium)   Courtyard, open to the sky, in an ancient Roman house; the term also applies to the courtyard nearest the entrance of an early Christian church.

Baldacchino or **Ciborio (Baldachin, Baldaquin,** or **Ciborium)**   Columned stone canopy, usually placed above the altar of a church; spelled in English.

Basilica   Any rectangular public building, usually divided into three aisles by rows of columns. In ancient Rome, this architectural form was frequently used for places of public assembly and law courts; later, Roman Christians adapted the form for many of their early churches.

Battistero (Baptistery)   Separate building or a church area where the rite of baptism is held.

Calidarium   Steam room of a Roman bath.

Campanile   Church's bell tower, often detached.

Capitello (Capital)   Four-sided stone at the top of a column, often decoratively carved. The Greek classic architectural styles included three orders: Doric, Ionic, and Corinthian.

Cariatide (Caryatid)   Column carved into a standing female figure.

Cattedrale (Cathedral)   The church where a bishop has his chair.

Cavea   The curved row of seats in a classical theater; the most prevalent shape was that of a semicircle.

Cella   The sanctuary, or most sacred interior section, of a Roman pagan temple.

Chiostro (Cloister)   Courtyard ringed with a gallery of arches or lintels set atop columns.

Chiesa   Church.

Cornice   The horizontal flange defining the uppermost part of a building, especially in classical or neoclassical facades.

Cortile   Courtyard or backyard.

Cripta (Crypt)   Church's underground chapel, mostly used as a burial place, usually below the choir.

Cupola   Dome.

Duomo   A town's most important church, usually also a Cathedral.

Foro (Forum)   The main square and principal gathering place of any Roman town, usually adorned with the city's most important temples and civic buildings.

Ipogeo (Hypogeum & Hypogee)   Adjective describing any subterranean structure, a temple, a chamber, or a chapel. Often used as a tomb.

Loggia   Roofed balcony or gallery.

Navata (Nave)   Each of the longitudinal sections of a church or basilica, divided by walls, pillars, or columns.

Palazzo   Palace or other large building, usually of majestic architecture.

Pergamo   Pulpit.

Piano Nobile   The floor of a palazzo reserved for the owner's use (usually the second floor), as opposed to the floors used by the house staff and for other services.

Pietra Dura   Semiprecious stone, such as amethyst and lapis lazuli.

Portico   A porch with columns on at least one side, usually for decorative purposes.

Presbiterio   Area around the main altar of a church, elevated and separated by columns or, in the oldest churches, by a screen (transenna), which was traditionally reserved for the bishop and the officiating clergy.

Pulvino (Pulvin)   A typical structure of Byzantine architecture consisting of a four-sided stone, often in the shape of a truncated pyramid and often decorated with carvings of plants and animals, which connected the capital to the above structure.

Putto   Artistic representation of a naked small child, especially common in the Renaissance.

Stucco   A building compound composed of sand, powdered marble, lime, and water. Stucco is applied to a surface to make it smooth, or used to create decorative reliefs.

Dos & Don'ts

Italians measure foodstuffs by the kilogram or smaller 100g unit (**etto-grammo** abbreviated to *etto*: equivalent to just under 4oz). **Pizzerie al taglio** (pizza slice shops) generally run on this system, but hand gestures can suffice. A good server poises the knife, then asks for approval before cutting. **Più** (PYOO) is "more," **meno** (MEH-noh) "less." **Basta** (BAHS-tah) means "enough." To express "half" of something, do say **mezzo** (MEHD-zoh).

Telamone or **Atlante**   Statue of a male figure used as structural support.

Terme   Thermal baths or spa, such as the ancient Roman ones.

Timpano (Tympanum)   The triangular wall—sometimes decorated with reliefs—between the cornice and the roof.

Transenna   Screen (usually in carved marble) separating the presbytery from the rest of an early Christian church.

Travertino (Travertine)   Type of porous limestone—white, pale yellow, or pale reddish in color—commonly found in central Italy.

3 Campanian Menu Terms

Acqua pazza   Light herbed broth used to poach fish.

Agnello   Lamb, usually grilled or baked.

Antipasti   Succulent tidbits served at the beginning of a meal (before the pasta). The choices might be sliced cured meats, seafood (especially shellfish), and cooked and seasoned vegetables.

Aragosta   Lobster.

Babà   Puffy soft cake soaked in rum and served with pastry cream.

Baccalà   Dried and salted codfish usually prepared as a stew.

Braciola   In the rest of Italy this means chop, usually lamb or pork; here it refers to an *involtino* filled with raisins and pine nuts and cooked in *ragù* sauce, a meat-based tomato sauce.

Brasato   Beef braised in white wine with vegetables.

Bruschetta   Toasted peasant-style bread, heavily slathered with olive oil and garlic and often topped with tomatoes.

Bucatini   Thick hollow spaghetti.

Calzone   Filled pocket of pizza dough, usually stuffed with ham and cheese, and sometimes other ingredients. It can be baked or fried.

Cannelloni   Tubes of fresh pasta dough stuffed with meat, fish, or vegetables and then baked with cheese, tomato sauce, and sometimes béchamel (creamy white sauce).

Caprese   Salad of fresh tomatoes and fresh mozzarella, seasoned with fresh basil and olive oil.

Carciofi   Artichokes.

Carpaccio   Thin slices of raw beef, seasoned with olive oil, lemon, pepper, and slivers of Parmesan. Sometimes raw fish is served in the same style but without the cheese.

Cassuola   Small terra-cotta casserole; also the process of cooking something in terra cotta—usually squid or octopus.

Coniglio alla Cacciatora   Rabbit cooked in wine with olives and herbs.

Cozze   Mussels.

Fagioli   Beans.

Fiordilatte   Type of *mozzarella* made with cow's milk.

Fragaglie   Very small fish, usually served deep-fried.

Fresella   Whole-wheat rustic bread served as a salad with fresh tomatoes, fresh basil, salt, and olive oil. The special bread is sold in the shape of flat rounds.

Friarelli   Local type of thin broccoli sautéed with olive oil, garlic, and red pepper and often served with sausages.

Frittata   Italian omelet.

Frittura   Deep-fried medley of seafood, usually calamari and shrimp.

Frutti di Mare   Translated "fruits of the sea," it refers to all shellfish.

Fusilli   Spiral-shaped pasta; the traditional one is fresh and homemade.

Gelato (Produzione Propria)   Ice cream (homemade).

Gnocchi   Dumplings usually made from potatoes *(gnocchi alla patate)* or from semolina *(gnocchi alla romana)* and often served with a tomato sauce.

Granita   Flavored ice, usually with lemon or coffee.

Insalata di Mare   Seafood salad (usually including octopus or squid) seasoned with olive oil, lemon, sometimes vinegar, and whatever the chef fancies—usually parsley and other herbs and spices.

Involtini   Thinly sliced beef, veal, pork, eggplant, or zucchini rolled, stuffed, and sautéed, often served in a tomato sauce.

Melanzane   Eggplant.

Minestra Maritata   Thick soup of pork meat and vegetables.

Minestrone   Rich and savory vegetable soup usually sprinkled with grated *parmigiano*.

Mozzarella di Bufala   Typical Campania cheese, this is an unfermented cheese, made exclusively from fresh buffalo milk, boiled, and then kneaded into a rounded ball, and served fresh. What is called *mozzarella* in the rest of Italy and abroad is mere *fiordilatte,* a similar kind of cheese made with cow's milk.

Panna   Heavy cream.

Panzerotti   Reminiscent of ravioli, panzerotti is half-round in shape and deep fried. They can be savory—filled with ricotta, ham, and mozzarella—or sweet, in which case they are filled with jam.

Parmigiano   Parmesan is a hard and salty yellow cheese usually grated over pastas and soups but also eaten by itself; the best is *parmigiano-reggiano.* A pale imitation is *grana padano.*

Pastiera   Sort of a thick pie filled with a creamy mixture of wheat grains, ricotta, and candied orange peels. Traditionally prepared for Easter but sold all the time now.

Peperoni   Green, yellow, or red sweet peppers (not to be confused with pepperoni, which doesn't exist in Italy).

Pesce al Cartoccio   Fish baked in a parchment envelope and seasoned with whatever the chef fancies.

Pesce Spada   Swordfish.

Pesto   Fresh basil, garlic, and olive oil, finely chopped into a paste.

Pizza   Among the varieties is *margherita* (with tomato sauce, cheese, fresh basil, and memories of the first queen of Italy, Marguerite di Savoia, in whose honor it was first made by a Neapolitan chef); *marinara* (with tomatoes and oregano); and *romana* (tomatoes, cheese, and anchovies). Quite hilariously, these are the same toppings that in Rome make the pizza *napoletana*.

Pizzaiola   Process in which something (usually a slice of beef or a filet of fish) is cooked in a tomato-garlic-oregano sauce.

Polipetti   Squid.

Polpo or **Polipo**   Octopus.

Ragù   Meat-based tomato sauce, where the chef's imagination rules.

Ricotta   Soft, bland cheese served very fresh and made from sheep's milk or, in lesser-quality versions, from cow's milk.

Risotto   Italian rice, cooked with wine and other ingredients to a creamy consistency.

Risotto alla Pescatora   Rice cooked with wine, a little tomato, and lots of fresh seafood.

Sartù   Delicious baked rice dish in which a crown of rice is filled with baby meatballs, mozzarella, sausages, and other ingredients.

Scapece   For this special preparation for zucchini and eggplants, the vegetables are fried, then seasoned with vinegar and fresh mint.

Semifreddo   Frozen dessert; usually ice cream with sponge cake.

Seppia   Cuttlefish (a kind of squid); its black ink is used for flavoring certain sauces for pasta and risotto dishes.

Sfogliatella   Flaky pastry filled with a sweet ricotta mixture.

Sogliola   Sole.

Soffritto   Typical Neapolitan sauce made with pork tidbits cooked at length in a tomato sauce with olive oil and red pepper.

Spaghetti   Long, round, thin pasta, served different ways: *al ragù* (meat sauce), *al soffritto* (see above), *al pomodoro* (with fresh tomatoes), *ai frutti di mare* (with a medley of sautéed seafood), and *alle vongole* (with clam sauce) are some of the most common.

Spiedini   Pieces of meat grilled on a skewer over an open flame.

Tagliatelle   Flat egg noodles.

Tonno   Tuna.

Torta Caprese   Rich cake made with chocolate and almonds.

Tortelli   Pasta dumplings stuffed with ricotta and greens.

Vermicelli   Very thin spaghetti.

Zabaglione or **Zabaione**   Egg yolks whipped into the consistency of a custard, flavored with Marsala, and served warm as a dessert.

Zuccotto   Liqueur-soaked sponge cake, molded into a dome and layered with chocolate, nuts, and whipped cream.

Zuppa Inglese   Sponge cake soaked in custard.

Index

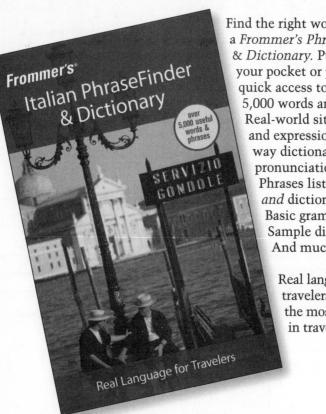

FROMMER'S® COMPLETE TRAVEL GUIDES

Alaska
Amalfi Coast
American Southwest
Amsterdam
Argentina
Arizona
Atlanta
Australia
Austria
Bahamas
Barcelona
Beijing
Belgium, Holland & Luxembourg
Belize
Bermuda
Boston
Brazil
British Columbia & the Canadian
  Rockies
Brussels & Bruges
Budapest & the Best of Hungary
Buenos Aires
Calgary
California
Canada
Cancún, Cozumel & the Yucatán
Cape Cod, Nantucket & Martha's
  Vineyard
Caribbean
Caribbean Ports of Call
Carolinas & Georgia
Chicago
Chile & Easter Island
China
Colorado
Costa Rica
Croatia
Cuba
Denmark
Denver, Boulder & Colorado Springs
Eastern Europe
Ecuador & the Galapagos Islands
Edinburgh & Glasgow
England
Europe
Europe by Rail

Florence, Tuscany & Umbria
Florida
France
Germany
Greece
Greek Islands
Guatemala
Hawaii
Hong Kong
Honolulu, Waikiki & Oahu
India
Ireland
Israel
Italy
Jamaica
Japan
Kauai
Las Vegas
London
Los Angeles
Los Cabos & Baja
Madrid
Maine Coast
Maryland & Delaware
Maui
Mexico
Montana & Wyoming
Montréal & Québec City
Morocco
Moscow & St. Petersburg
Munich & the Bavarian Alps
Nashville & Memphis
New England
Newfoundland & Labrador
New Mexico
New Orleans
New York City
New York State
New Zealand
Northern Italy
Norway
Nova Scotia, New Brunswick &
  Prince Edward Island
Oregon
Paris
Peru

Philadelphia & the Amish Country
Portugal
Prague & the Best of the Czech
  Republic
Provence & the Riviera
Puerto Rico
Rome
San Antonio & Austin
San Diego
San Francisco
Santa Fe, Taos & Albuquerque
Scandinavia
Scotland
Seattle
Seville, Granada & the Best of
  Andalusia
Shanghai
Sicily
Singapore & Malaysia
South Africa
South America
South Florida
South Korea
South Pacific
Southeast Asia
Spain
Sweden
Switzerland
Tahiti & French Polynesia
Texas
Thailand
Tokyo
Toronto
Turkey
USA
Utah
Vancouver & Victoria
Vermont, New Hampshire & Maine
Vienna & the Danube Valley
Vietnam
Virgin Islands
Virginia
Walt Disney World® & Orlando
Washington, D.C.
Washington State

FROMMER'S® DAY BY DAY GUIDES

Amsterdam
Barcelona
Beijing
Boston
Cancun & the Yucatan
Chicago
Florence & Tuscany

Hong Kong
Honolulu & Oahu
London
Maui
Montréal
Napa & Sonoma
New York City

Paris
Provence & the Riviera
Rome
San Francisco
Venice
Washington D.C.

PAULINE FROMMER'S GUIDES: SEE MORE. SPEND LESS.

Alaska
Hawaii
Italy

Las Vegas
London
New York City

Paris
Walt Disney World®
Washington D.C.

FROMMER'S® PORTABLE GUIDES

Acapulco, Ixtapa & Zihuatanejo
Amsterdam
Aruba, Bonaire & Curacao
Australia's Great Barrier Reef
Bahamas
Big Island of Hawaii
Boston
California Wine Country
Cancún
Cayman Islands
Charleston
Chicago
Dominican Republic

Florence
Las Vegas
Las Vegas for Non-Gamblers
London
Maui
Nantucket & Martha's Vineyard
New Orleans
New York City
Paris
Portland
Puerto Rico
Puerto Vallarta, Manzanillo & Guadalajara

Rio de Janeiro
San Diego
San Francisco
Savannah
St. Martin, Sint Maarten, Anguila & St. Bart's
Turks & Caicos
Vancouver
Venice
Virgin Islands
Washington, D.C.
Whistler

FROMMER'S® CRUISE GUIDES

Alaska Cruises & Ports of Call

Cruises & Ports of Call

European Cruises & Ports of Call

FROMMER'S® NATIONAL PARK GUIDES

Algonquin Provincial Park
Banff & Jasper
Grand Canyon

National Parks of the American West
Rocky Mountain
Yellowstone & Grand Teton

Yosemite and Sequoia & Kings Canyon
Zion & Bryce Canyon

FROMMER'S® WITH KIDS GUIDES

Chicago
Hawaii
Las Vegas
London

National Parks
New York City
San Francisco

Toronto
Walt Disney World® & Orlando
Washington, D.C.

FROMMER'S® PHRASEFINDER DICTIONARY GUIDES

Chinese
French

German
Italian

Japanese
Spanish

SUZY GERSHMAN'S BORN TO SHOP GUIDES

France
Hong Kong, Shanghai & Beijing
Italy

London
New York
Paris

San Francisco
Where to Buy the Best of Everything.

FROMMER'S® BEST-LOVED DRIVING TOURS

Britain
California
France
Germany

Ireland
Italy
New England
Northern Italy

Scotland
Spain
Tuscany & Umbria

THE UNOFFICIAL GUIDES®

Adventure Travel in Alaska
Beyond Disney
California with Kids
Central Italy
Chicago
Cruises
Disneyland®
England
Hawaii

Ireland
Las Vegas
London
Maui
Mexico's Best Beach Resorts
Mini Mickey
New Orleans
New York City
Paris

San Francisco
South Florida including Miami & the Keys
Walt Disney World®
Walt Disney World® for Grown-ups
Walt Disney World® with Kids
Washington, D.C.

SPECIAL-INTEREST TITLES

Athens Past & Present
Best Places to Raise Your Family
Cities Ranked & Rated
500 Places to Take Your Kids Before They Grow Up
Frommer's Best Day Trips from London
Frommer's Best RV & Tent Campgrounds in the U.S.A.

Frommer's Exploring America by RV
Frommer's NYC Free & Dirt Cheap
Frommer's Road Atlas Europe
Frommer's Road Atlas Ireland
Retirement Places Rated

CLOSED
due to
accidental demolition

WEGEN BISSIGEN
EICHHÖRNCHEN GESCHLOSSEN

CERRADO
CABRAS

Κλειστό
Μετεωρίτες

プールも

POOL CLOSED

閉鎖中

ELECTRIC EELS

Hotel
closed for
facelifting

FERMÉ POUR
RAISON
DE GRÈVE
DES BONNES

FECHADO!
POR CAUSA DE
ATAQUES DOS CROCODILOS

— *I don't speak
sign language.*

A hotel can close for all kinds of reasons.
Our Guarantee ensures that if your hotel's undergoing construction, we'll
let you know in advance. In fact, we cover your entire travel experience.
See www.travelocity.com/guarantee for details.

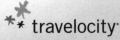

travelocity®
You'll never roam alone.

There's a parking lot where my ocean view should be.

 À la place de la vue sur l'océan, me voilà avec une vue sur un parking.

 Anstatt Meerblick habe ich Sicht auf einen Parkplatz.

 Al posto della vista sull'oceano c'è un parcheggio.

 No tengo vista al mar porque hay un parque de estacionamiento.

 Há um parque de estacionamento onde deveria estar a minha vista do oceano

 Ett parkeringsområde har byggts på den plats där min utsikt över oceanen borde vara.

 Er ligt een parkeerterrein waar mijn zee-uitzicht zou moeten zijn.

 هنالك موقف للسيارات مكان ما وجب ان يكون المنظر الخلاب المطل على المحيط .

 眼前に広がる紺碧の海・・・じゃない。窓の外は駐車場！

停车场的位置应该是我的海景所在。

— I'm fluent in pig latin.

Hotel mishaps aren't bound by geography.
Neither is our Guarantee. It covers your entire travel experience,
including the price. So if you don't get the ocean view you booked,
we'll work with our travel partners to make it right, right away. See
www.travelocity.com/guarantee for details.

You'll never roam alone.